10.98

THE ECOLOGY OF ROCKY COASTS

essays presented to J. R. Lewis

Edited by
P. G. MOORE and R. SEED

New York   Columbia University Press   1986

Printed in Great Britain

Library of Congress Cataloging in Publication Data

Main entry under title:
The Ecology of rocky coasts.
  Bibliography: p.
  1. Coastal ecology—Addresses, essays, lectures.
2. Intertidal zonation—Addresses, essays, lectures.
I. Lewis, J. R. (John R.), 1930– .
II. Moore, P. G. (P. Geoffrey) III. Seed, Raymond.
QH541.5.C65E27   1985   574.5′2638   85-11038
ISBN 0-231-06274-5

Opp. Mid-littoral populations of mussels (*Mytilus edulis*), barnacles (*Semibalanus balanoides*) and
      dogwhelks (*Nucella lapillus*) on low-lying, rocky scars at Robin Hood's Bay, Yorkshire
      (Photo: A. E. Simpson).

Frontispiece

To
Jack Lewis
from fellow Epimethean
Water Babies

Mid-littoral populations of mussels (*Mytilus edulis*), barnacles (*Semibalanus balanoides*) and dogwhelks (*Nucella lapillus*) on low-lying, rocky scars at Robin Hood's Bay, Yorkshire (Photo: A.E. Simpson).

Frontispiece

'*There is no end to our researches. Our end is in the other world. It is a sign of contraction of the mind when it is content; or of lassitude. No noble spirit stays within itself; it ever aspires and rises above its strength. It soars beyond its deeds; if it does not advance and does not press forward, and does not back and does not clash with itself, it is only half alive. Its pursuits are boundless and formless, its food is wonder, the chase, ambiguity.*'

> Montaigne, *Essays*,
> translated by E.J. Trenchman,
> Oxford University Press, 1927

'*There is no getting away from the fact that good ecological work cannot be done in an atmosphere of cloistered calm, of smooth concentrated focussing upon clean, rounded, and elegant problems. Any ecological problem which is really worth working upon at all, is constantly leading the worker on to neighbouring subjects, and is constantly enlarging his view of the extent and variety of animal life, and of the numerous ways in which one problem in the field interacts with another.*'

> C.S. Elton, *Animal Ecology*,
> Sidgwick & Jackson, 1927

'. . . *the naturalist is well aware that almost any one species of animal, however numerically common, would take a man his whole lifetime thoroughly to examine and explain in all the points of its development, habits, and structure. Also, for any attempt at a full investigation there is scarcely anything more advantageous than that an animal should be common.*'

> T.R.R. Stebbing, *The Naturalist of Cumbrae*,
> Kegan, Paul, Trench, Trübner Ltd., 1891

CONTENTS

LIST OF CONTRIBUTORS

Dr John M. BAXTER — Department of Biological Sciences, University of Dundee, Dundee, DD1 4HN, Scotland

Ms Rosemary S. BOWMAN — N.E.R.C. Rocky Shore Surveillance Group, University of Newcastle-upon-Tyne, Dove Marine Laboratory, Cullercoats, Tyne and Wear, NE30 4PZ, England

Dr George M. BRANCH — Department of Zoology, University of Cape Town, Rondebosch 7700, South Africa

Professor Joseph H. CONNELL — Department of Biological Sciences, University of California, Santa Barbara, Calif. 93106, U.S.A.

Dr Roland H. EMSON — Department of Zoology, King's College, Strand, London, WC2R 2LS

Dr Robert J. FALLER-FRITSCH — c/o Department of Zoology, King's College, Strand, London, WC2R 2LS

Dr Christopher J. FEARE — Ministry of Agriculture, Fisheries and Food, Worplesdon, Guildford, Surrey, GU3 3LQ, England

Dr John D. FISH — Department of Zoology, University College Aberystwyth, Aberystwyth, SY23 3DA, Wales

Dr John W. GRAHAME — Department of Pure and Applied Zoology, The University of Leeds, Leeds, LS2 9JT, England

Dr Geoffrey R.F. HICKS — National Museum of New Zealand, Private Bag, Wellington, New Zealand

Dr Keith HISCOCK — Oil Pollution Research Unit, Orielton Field Studies Centre, Pembroke, Dyfed, SA71 5EZ, Wales

Dr Roger N. HUGHES — School of Animal Biology, University College of North Wales, Bangor, Gwynedd, LL57 2UW, Wales

Dr Ian W. JARDINE — 18, Kirkhill Road, Edinburgh, EH16 5DD, Scotland

Dr Allan M. JONES — Department of Biological Sciences, University of Dundee, Dundee, DD1 4HN, Scotland

Professor Jack A. KITCHING, F.R.S. — School of Biological Sciences, University of East Anglia, Norwich, NR4 7TJ, England

Dr Tomas LUNDÄLV — Kristinebergs Marinbiologiska Station, Kristineberg 2130, S-450 34 Fiskebackskil, Sweden

LIST OF CONTRIBUTORS

Dr P. Geoffrey MOORE	University Marine Biological Station Millport, Isle of Cumbrae, KA28 OEG, Scotland
Professor Trevor A. NORTON	Department of Marine Biology, University of Liverpool, Port Erin, Isle of Man, U.K.
Harry T. POWELL, Esq.	Scottish Marine Biological Association, Dunstaffnage Marine Research Laboratory, P.O. Box 3, Oban, Argyll, PA34 4AD, Scotland
Dr Kenneth P. SEBENS	Biological Laboratories, Harvard University, 16 Divinity Ave., Cambridge, Mass. 02138, U.S.A. now Director, Marine Science and Maritime Studies Centre, Northeastern University, Nahant, Mass. 01908, U.S.A.
Dr Raymond SEED	School of Animal Biology, University College of North Wales, Bangor, Gwynedd, LL57 2UW, Wales
Ms Lynne SHARP	Department of Zoology, University College Aberystwyth, Aberystwyth, SY23 3DA, Wales
Dr Alan J. SOUTHWARD	Marine Biological Association of the United Kingdom, The Laboratory, Citadel Hill, Plymouth, PL1 2PB, England
Dr Thomas H. SUCHANEK	Division of Environmental Studies, University of California, Davis, Calif. 95616, and Bodega Marine Laboratory, Bodega Bay, Calif. 94923, U.S.A.
Dr Ronald W. SUMMERS	Ministry of Agriculture, Fisheries and Food, Coypu Research Laboratory, Jupiter Road, Norwich, N0R 9ON, England
Dr Christopher D. TODD	Gatty Marine Laboratory, Department of Zoology and Marine Biology, University of St Andrews, St Andrews, KY16 8LB, Scotland
Dr Anthony J. UNDERWOOD	School of Biological Sciences, University of Sydney, Sydney, N.S.W. 2006, Australia
Dr David S. WETHEY	Department of Biology and Marine Science Program, University of South Carolina, Columbia, SC 29208, U.S.A.

FOREWORD

A.J. Southward

Littoral ecology has flourished mightily since its revival by the first batch of post-1945 graduates, which included Jack Lewis and myself. It is true that during the war much effort was directed into studying the autecology of several species of brown seaweeds and to studies of fouling organisms. Such projects were conducted for urgent economic reasons, although the presence of leading research workers in the study groups did mean that important basic advances were made (e.g. Parke, 1948). It was the freeing of the mind from cramping restraints after the war that produced the first new wave of broadly-based ecological studies. Though the mind was freed, the purse strings were scarcely loosened, and graduates of the past ten years may find the number of stations we worked and the amount of data we gathered hard to believe, in those days when every penny (old) and shilling (5p) had to be accounted for in detail in the back of the field notebooks, and when even the purchase of the then cheap Ordnance Survey maps (13p) could cause a deficit in accounts heavily weighted down by petrol at 23p a gallon and overnight accommodation at 38p! Yet, as Jack Lewis has argued (Lewis, 1975), the right-minded naturalist thirsting for knowledge, and armed only with notebook and pencil, can still overcome lack of research finance and make fundamental contributions to ecology. Many of today's biologists, orientated towards expensive equipment and computer modelling, seem to have lost sight of the animals and plants they are supposed to be studying, and number-crunching appears to have become an end in itself. Perhaps the present precarious financial position of scientific research will lead to a new appraisal of the simple approach, and it is one of the purposes of this book to stress the need for realistic organismic ecology.

The post-war batch of ecologists were able to show wide adaptive radiation. In my own case, under the tutelage of J.H. Orton (who had catholic tastes himself) I ventured to study, all at once and suitably quantified, both rocky shores and the infauna of sediments, with subsidiary work on geographical distribution, year-to-year changes, and the effects of environmental factors, with it has to be confessed, only partial success. Under a different mentor, the late Alan Stephenson (Stephenson and Stephenson, 1972), Jack Lewis concentrated on rocky shore ecosystems, and made the first detailed studies of how rocky shore zonation varies on local and wider scales, applying and modifying for use on British shores the Stephensonian technique devised for the South African surveys (Stephenson, 1939). The photographs in his book (Lewis, 1964) show that Jack has a remarkable eye for zonation patterns. Other people, seeing his illustrations, will wonder how they could have failed to spot something so obvious, yet fail they did: the old adage about the wood and the trees is as applicable on the seashore as in the arboretum. As Geoff Moore and Harry Powell explain in their introductory chapter, these detailed studies by Jack Lewis developed into an investigation of the causes of zonation and of anomalies in distribution, at first by descriptive and deductive methods. Later, with the permanent establishment by Leeds University of the laboratory at Robin Hood's Bay, it was possible for Jack to adopt what we would now call an experimental monitoring approach; to follow the evolution of zonation patterns and populations on specific stretches of shore, and to see how important were biotic factors such as competition and predation when viewed in the cold light of harsh and fluctuating abiotic factors such as temperature, winds and currents.

In this volume there is gathered together a number of papers by former students or old colleagues of Jack Lewis. Each author has determined the scope of his/her treatment of the subject. Whether directly inspired by Jack's pioneering studies, or contributing to aspects of shore ecology in which Jack is interested, or extending his methods to other habitats, all have their origins underpinned by Jack's influence. The contributions fall into three groups: major 'background' reviews; critical reviews of certain aspects of zonation or littoral ecology; and original research papers dealing with the biology of certain species which contribute significantly to the overall community structure of rocky shores. They are arranged in a sequence that mirrors the evolution of Jack's own contributions to the subject, starting with descriptive surveys and zonation patterns, and leading on to the dynamics of key species, local heterogeneity and the problems this poses for monitoring and surveillance programmes.

As always, the hottest controversies rage over how stable are the communities with time, and what is the extent of the variation in their zonation pattern? These topics are reviewed by Joe Connell in his usual incisive style. No doubt all ecologists have their own ideas of what constitutes stability, but it will do them no harm to consider the views of one of the experts in this line, especially those ecologists who are involved in monitoring programmes or environmental impact studies. My own view of stability is no doubt as idiosyncratic as the rest, but I feel that we must not ignore geographical factors, particularly oceanic influences *vis-à-vis* embayed influences, especially the contrast between blue-water systems and those subject to turbidity and scour. Fjord conditions are different again, perhaps dominated to a greater degree than hitherto anticipated by biological interactions. Where Joe Connell stops – at the base of the eulittoral – Keith Hiscock takes over and reviews the sublittoral communities to which he has applied Jack's methods. The debate on stability is extended for sublittoral communities by Ken Sebens, who gives the results of six years' studies in Massachusetts. A more specialized aspect of sublittoral monitoring is discussed by Tom Lundälv, whose detailed photographic technique has attracted much attention.

The remaining general reviews deal with major features of rocky shore zonation, each stressing one particular dominant. The algal zones described by Trevor Norton, lest it be forgotten by the zoologists, are the primary producers, and source of much of the energy for the rest of rocky shore life. They are also structurally important, and in concert with interacting species control zonation patterns. On most rocky shores of the world the algae are in continuous antagonism with grazing limpets, and their mutual equilibrium can determine the extent of the development of other species. This aspect is reviewed by George Branch, illustrated with examples from South African shores, where the importance of limpets was recognized early on in the Stephenson surveys (Stephenson, 1936), and is now properly determined and quantified. To achieve the same realization of the importance of limpets in North-West Europe we had to pass through the trauma of several major oil-spills, though there had been some pioneering 'experimental' studies conducted with hammers – not quite the same thing! (e.g. Lodge, 1948; Southward, 1956). The review of the rôle of mussels in the littoral zone, by Tom Suchanek, fills a real need for critical appreciation of their effects on community structure and zonation in relation to local environmental factors. It has long puzzled shore ecologists why some reefs always seem to carry mussels, while others are dominated by limpets and barnacles (cf. Stephenson, 1943). No doubt another comprehensive review of the rôle of barnacles could have been included in this volume, since the barnacle zone is an important feature of the Stephensonian/Lewisian zonation scheme, but the editors decided to avoid the risk of unnecessary duplication of material appearing in a book of reviews on the biology of barnacles, which I am editing, dedicated to Dennis Crisp.

Turning to the critical reviews of species or specialized features of the shore, there are several on aspects central to the hypotheses constructed by Jack Lewis. Rosemary Bowman gives an account of many years spent following the reproduction and recruitment around Britain of *Patella vulgata*, a key species in the structure and zonation of littoral communities, and discusses how its success in breeding could cause fluctuations in associated organisms. A more specialized aspect of the biology of *Patella vulgata* – its value as a monitoring organism to detect pollution – is dealt with by Allan Jones and John Baxter based on their experiences in Orkney.

As a contrast to these 'native' studies there is a critical review by Tony Underwood on the influence of physical factors in controlling the grazing, competition, and distribution of rocky shore gastropods. This review is based on work in New South Wales, where a new school of experimental ecology has developed, and it is refreshing to see attention focussed once more on physical factors. Nevertheless, we cannot ignore biological interaction, especially predation, as the critical review by Roger Hughes shows. More specialized aspects of predation are dealt with by Chris Feare and Ron Summers, who discuss the effects of birds, and by Jack Kitching, who describes variation in shell shape of the dogwhelks. Birds are not often included in structural analyses of littoral communities, perhaps because most littoral ecologists who specialize on sedentary invertebrates keep their eyes firmly fixed on the ground or else create too much noise by their hammering and scraping! Dogwhelk shell variation has been studied – on and off – since 1934, and a review of the subject and its ecological importance is timely. John Colman may be said to have begun the careful study of animals living on or in seaweeds with his intensive sampling at Wembury in Devon. In this volume we have a review of the littoral epifaunal communities of algal fronds by Ray Seed, another on the meiofauna of seaweeds by Geoff Hicks, and another on the amphipod fauna of kelp holdfasts by Geoff Moore. The latter is an extension of the author's previous studies of the epibionts of *Laminaria* forests. The remaining critical reviews deal with ecological aspects of organisms that are presently in the limelight; their reproductive 'strategies' and life histories. The more general review by Chris Todd tells us how much or how little the different life forms are adapted to their niches on rocky shores, and may engender some surprise to those whose diet is confined to the textbooks. Ro Emson deals briefly with the more specialized topic of adaptation to life in rock pools, thus returning to one of the facets of marine biology that excited naturalists of the last century, and which is now being revived by our popular educators, who will persist, however, in seeding high-shore pools with patently sublittoral life forms to enhance televisual effects!

The specialized research contributions in the volume deal with aspects of the biology of barnacles and gastropods, organisms of importance to Jack Lewis's ideas. David Wethey has extended his earlier studies of the detailed settlement of *Semibalanus balanoides* in Maine to Jack's homeground in Yorkshire, where conditions are different from those in New England. The very small littorinids are discussed by John Fish and Lynne Sharp, who have studied the very well-named *Littorina neglecta*, so often overlooked in its dry weather refuge inside dead barnacle shells, yet probably an important element supporting maintenance of the barnacle zone. Bob Faller-Fritsch and Ro Emson return to the more-studied winkle, *Littorina 'rudis'*, and note the causes of its mortality, including predation and parasites. The demography of the near-relatives of the littorinids, the chink-shells (*Lacuna*) is described by John Grahame for the Robin Hood's Bay area, filling another gap in our knowledge of the smaller inhabitants of rocky shores. Another little-studied, but more striking inhabitant of the lower shore, the smallest British top-shell, *Gibbula cineraria*, is discussed by Ian Jardine, who shows how growth is limited by factors connected with emersion.

The reviews and scientific contributions included in this volume show how much progress has been made in studies of life on rocky shores and the immediate sublittoral since 1952, and how much of this work has been influenced by Alan Stephenson and then by Jack Lewis. Among his many major contributions to littoral ecology Jack has shown (Lewis, 1955) how varied the pattern of zonation can be within the confines of the Universal System of Stephenson and Stephenson (1949), and the extent of fluctuations in settlement and recruitment that can occur on shores with relatively high levels of physical stress (Lewis and Bowman, 1975). It is important to continue this work and to determine the rôle of abiotic factors versus biotic factors in controlling the apparent stability and/or the successional sequence in both highly stressed and more benign environments. As an outstanding educator of shore ecologists during the past thirty years, Jack can gain comfort from the fact that his retirement will not necessarily mean the end of his style of work.

Jack Lewis

PREFACE

The British can usually be relied upon to deliver of themselves a vigorous verdict on another's achievements when that person has safely departed this world. In the belief, however, that a grain of encouragement *ante mortem* is worth a bushel of appreciation *post mortem*, we present this Festschrift as a small tribute to someone from whom we have derived much and for whom we have a deep affection and lasting respect, Jack Lewis.

In the tradition of his mentor, T.A. Stephenson, Jack brings to shore ecology more than just a scientific mind; his assessment of a shorescape has much in common with an artist's appreciation of a beautiful woman, whose capture in all her subtleties is an act of love. That his warmth, sparkle and natural teaching ability have inspired generations of undergraduates, many present contributors can testify; his early retirement will dilute the pleasures of learning for present and future marine biological acolytes at Leeds University.

Never a man to be distracted from his own map-reading simply by visions of others stampeding in different directions, he has often been discomfited by that intellectual isolation which all crusaders trail in their wake – a special burden for someone like Jack, of such a garrulous nature – and one exacerbated and made more tangible in his mind by the geographical isolation and small size of 'his' laboratory at Robin Hood's Bay (now sadly closed as one result of Government spending cuts). It is characteristic of the man though, that where others might have responded by cutting corners as a means to personal advancement, Jack won the respect of his postgraduates by unselfishly allowing them liberty to publish alone. Even without an inflated publication list, his influence is unquestionable and the contributions made by this tiny laboratory over only a meagre span of years are an enduring testament to his leadership. The scope of his influence can be judged from the breadth and depth of contributions to this volume and from the realization that everyone who has studied rocky shores in Britain during the last two decades will have derived enlightenment at some point from his classic work, *The Ecology of Rocky Shores*.

Guaranteed to be in the thick of any controversy to do with shore ecology and always ready to respect in his protégés that free spirit which is one of his own endearing qualities, Jack can never be accused of having opted for 'the quiet life' – even in the Yorkshire outback! Those who passed through this invigorating experience recall the intellectual generosity and strength of character of one human enough sometimes to be wrong but big enough always to admit it. Maybe that accounts for the remarkable ease with which we, as editors, have been able to entice busy people to produce these contributions and pragmatic industrialists to help finance the venture. Jack may not agree with all the science herein, but he can rest assured that the intention was immaculate. We hope that he will accept these salutations and continue to enlighten us on the ecology of rocky shores for many years to come.

Millport & Bangor
July 1985

P.G. Moore
R. Seed

ACKNOWLEDGEMENTS

The editors would like to record their gratitude to all contributors for responding so positively and enthusiastically, both to the initial invitation to participate and to the barrage of editorial queries which was the inevitable result of acceptance. (This latter also applies to the many taxonomists whose views on species' authorities have been sought mercilessly.) Many biologists, well qualified to contribute to this volume, have not had the opportunity to do so simply because of the constraints of space and cost. We hope that all such people will find their own contributions to the field recognized in the literature quoted by others and will not read any ulterior motive into their omission. We owe our sponsors a lasting debt for backing the project so readily from the word go. It is a pleasure also to acknowledge the patient and sympathetic way in which our publishers, Hodder and Stoughton Educational, have acceded to the editors' every suggestion and request, even up to and including the eleventh hour. In particular we record our indebtedness to Susan Devlin, Philip Walters and Alison Fisher for their help and support.

We thank Jacquie Weir and Gordon Gale for computational assistance in organizing the reference list and Alan Simpson (ex-Chief Technician, Wellcome Marine Laboratory) for his photographic skills in producing the Frontispiece and portrait of the Laboratory. Dr R. Wynne Owen kindly provided biographical information. Dr Moore wishes to record his indebtedness to the staff at Millport, and in particular to Dr Jim Atkinson and Dr Phil Rainbow, for their consideration in shouldering burdens on his behalf so that editorial duties could continue alongside other commitments. Both editors wish to thank their wives and families for the good-natured way in which they accepted the inevitability of neglect during the gestation period of this volume.

Copyright material has been used with permission as follows. For the quotations used as epigraphs we thank Kegan, Paul, Trench, Trübner & Co. (*The Naturalist of Cumbrae*), Mr Charles S. Elton, F.R.S. and Sidgwick & Jackson Ltd. (*Animal Ecology*) and Oxford University Press (*The Essays of Montaigne*). The vignettes of sea nymphs, which have been reproduced with permission of the Ray Society from T.A. Stephenson's *British Sea Anemones*, forge an artistic link between three academic generations which seems to us most appropriate. We thank Mrs. Stephanie Walmsley and Wm. Collins & Sons for permission to quote from Leo Walmsley's *So Many Loves* (see Retrospect). The illustration by Linley Sambourne featured on the dedication page is taken with permission of Macmillan, London and Basingstoke, from the 4th edition of *The Water Babies* by Charles Kingsley. Elsevier Biomedical Press B.V. and the Conchological Society of London are thanked for permission to use material incorporated in Fig. 17.6. The *Journal of Animal Ecology* granted permission to use material incorporated in Fig. 17.5. Elsevier Biomedical Press B.V. is thanked for permission to reproduce and simplify Figs. 2.1 (thanks also to Dr W.E. Jones) and 2.5, as are Aberdeen University Press and Dr R.G. Hartnoll for use of Fig. 2.6. The Systematics Association and Professor A.D. Boney gave permission to use Fig. 2.3. The *Journal of Ecology* is thanked for permission to use Fig. 2.4. Permission to reproduce Table 2.1 from *Estuarine Coastal and Marine Science* (1979, 8/3, Table 3) copyright 1979 was given by Academic Press Inc. (London) Limited.

P.G.M.
R.S.

CHAPTER I

J.R. LEWIS AND THE ECOLOGY OF ROCKY SHORES

P.G. Moore and H.T. Powell

With a birth date of the 19th of January (1924), few astrologers would be surprised that John Robert Lewis was destined to come as close as possible to the water without actually getting wet, that date coming as it does immediately before Aquarius and Pisces! Although Jack's early education at Older-shaw Grammar School, Wallasey, was within sight of the sea, he never studied biology there, gaining University entrance qualifications in Arts subjects. He served with the Fleet Air Arm during the War (1942–45), latterly contracting T.B. for which he was medically discharged. This setback, however, brought him one enduring joy – he met his future wife Betty in the same hospital. Zoology was also to benefit, for after the War he enrolled at University College of Wales, Aberystwyth, determined to follow a course leading eventually to outdoor employment. His initial bent, however, was towards plant breeding and other agricultural sciences, subjects well served at Aberystwyth, but for which intending students, not surprisingly, were required to assimilate some biology! At the beginning of his Finals year he had a recurrence of lung trouble, and seeing that the Botany Department was four floors up (with no lift) and Zoology was on the ground floor, Jack finally opted for the latter. Although Zoology was headed by T.A. Stephenson, Jack's early enthusiasm for marine organisms was chiefly fostered by others. He remembers with what rapturous enthusiasm the Aberystwyth amphipod specialist Emrys Watkin ('. . . the best lecturer I ever met . . .') was able to fire students during weekly practical sessions on the Cardigan Bay beaches, and how Ron Evans, then a littoral postgraduate of Stephenson introduced him to the ecology of red algae. His initial leanings towards plant biology were also encouraged by the phycologist Lily Newton, then heading the Aberystwyth Botany Department, from which Harry Powell, his earliest collaborator, was also emerging. When circumstances kept him in Zoology though, and it became clear to all that he would acquit himself well in his Honours year (he took a First in 1949), Stephenson offered him the chance of postgraduate research under his tutelage.

Stephenson, a talented artist (see Stephenson, 1947) with a passion for sea anemones, having journeyed far and wide since his pioneering work on South African shores (summarized in Stephenson and Stephenson, 1972), had come to Aberystwyth with relatively little experience of the detail of British shores. Having set Ron Evans the task of investigating the ecology of the common animals on Welsh and southwestern shores (Evans, 1947a,b,c, 1949, 1953, 1957) he devoted himself to writing a compendious work on the theme of 'A scientist looks at Art', a project which occupied years of his time during Jack Lewis's period under him.

Jack, in a fashion which those who know him well will recognize immediately, determined to go and see the shore biology of the rest of Britain for himself! So for five years between 1949 and 1954 he and Betty (or he and H.T.P.) were most likely to be found coaxing an old, converted ambulance around the then debatable roads of North and West Scotland and the South and West of Ireland, exploring as many types of shore as possible. For his initial findings, Jack was awarded a Ph.D. in 1952 and after a two-year postdoctoral fellowship he followed his Aberystwyth compatriot and lifelong friend, the parasitologist Wynne Owen, to Leeds University in 1954. There he remained all his working life, rising from Assistant Lecturer to Senior Lecturer in 1964.

In research terms, Jack spent the fifteen years between 1949 and 1964 describing the littoral flora and fauna of the British Isles and attempting to explain most patterns of distribution in terms of major environmental gradients. Prior to his work, there existed only a few intensive surveys of limited areas done by other pioneers like A.D. Cotton, Jack Kitching and John Colman, or confined to single species or taxonomic groups (e.g. Hilary Moore's work). Surprisingly little was then appreciated about how such parochial information fitted into the broader ecological picture of British and northwestern European coasts, and only rarely had plants and animals been studied together as parts of the same system. Support for this extensive fieldwork came through grants from the former D.S.I.R. and the Royal Society and through collaboration with the Scottish Marine Biological Association (S.M.B.A.) at Millport in the person of Harry Powell.

Initially the principal results were published as descriptive accounts of the shore populations from different regions, mostly in Scotland (Powell and Lewis, 1952; Lewis, 1954b, 1957a,b; Lewis and Powell, 1960a,b, 1963), but also in Wales (Lewis, 1953) and in near tide-less conditions in parts of Scandinavia (Lewis and Tambs-Lyche, 1962; Brattegard and Lewis, 1964; Lewis, 1965). This wealth of field experience led to important theoretical advances in our understanding of the factors responsible for zonation (Lewis, 1955), with a clear separation for the first time of the concepts of 'intertidal' (a physical entity) and 'littoral' (a biological entity) (Lewis, 1961). Jack's independent line on the issue of the 'Universal System of Zonation', however, brought him into conflict with the Stephensons (T.A. and Anne) and there can be few but Jack who have agreed to append another's rebuttal to their own ideas as an appendix to their paper expressing them (Lewis, 1955)! The subsequent relationship between Alan Stephenson and Jack was never able to bridge this schism, although after Stephenson's death (1961) and despite a major change in his research interests by 1972 (see below), Jack agreed to contribute a chapter (Lewis, 1972b) on the British Isles to Anne Stephenson's final project, the long-intended book summarizing the Stephenson's world-wide view of shore ecology which eventually appeared in 1972 under the dated title *Life between Tidemarks on Rocky Shores*.

Jack had, however, received strong encouragement from Alan Stephenson to summarize his findings in a book of his own (with the strategic paternal advice that one book is worth a dozen.papers!) and he abandoned his early policy of separate regional descriptions in favour of a single comprehensive, comparative account of the British Isles (including Ireland). This *magnum opus* appeared in 1964 as *The Ecology of Rocky Shores*, a volume of lasting significance in the history of the subject. In this classic work, Jack now placed emphasis upon the species composition of the major types of shore communities and their local or wider geographical variations, and upon general themes such as zonation and the factors influencing local and geographical distribution. Although drawing on the work of others, particularly zoologists like Alan Southward, Dennis Crisp and Harold Barnes and botanists like Kenneth Rees, Dorothy Gibb and Harry Powell (to name only a few), the book was essentially a research monograph and it has remained the definitive account of the fauna and flora of British rocky shores to this date. Largely on account of this achievement, Jack Lewis was awarded his D.Sc. by the University of Wales in 1970.

Since the days of Walter Garstang's tenure as Professor of Zoology, Leeds University had had an interest in an old Coastguard Station (see Retrospect, p. 393) as a base for summer fieldwork at Robin Hood's Bay on the Yorkshire coast (in those early days shared with Sheffield University). Sheffield's interest, however, had lapsed long before the time that J.M. Dodd succeeded Eric Spaul to the Leeds Zoology Chair. Jimmy Dodd's own interest in elasmobranch endocrinology provided the basis for an approach for financial support to the Wellcome Trust which resulted in a permanent laboratory at Robin Hood's Bay – the Wellcome Marine Laboratory – being opened in 1965 (ironically, see Retrospect, p. 393, a move opposed by the then successful novelist Leo Walmsley) as an outstation of the Zoology Department. Jack Lewis moved to the coast as Senior Lecturer-in-Charge, assuming the title of Director in 1972 when the Laboratory became an establishment of the University independent of the Zoology Department.

Jack's pre-1965 survey work had revealed many apparent anomalies of local distribution which suggested the existence of cycles or irregular fluctuations with timescales out of phase from one locality to another. Speculations had been offered along these lines in Ch. XVIII (and perhaps the most important chapter) of his book and the 'dynamic phase' of research which has so preoccupied himself and other researchers in the last two decades grew as a natural consequence out of the 'descriptive phase' and subsequently clothed these speculations with hard, supportive fact.

The permanent Laboratory at Robin Hood's Bay (see Retrospect), sited by some of the most extensive, platform-type rocky shores in Britain (see Frontispiece) gave Jack, together with a succession of research students and research assistants (e.g. Ray Seed, Chris Feare, Rosemary Bowman, Chris Todd, Mike Kendall, Phil Williamson, Ian Jardine), the opportunity to make intensive and continuous studies of life cycles, biological interactions and temporal and spatial variations in abundance of several of the most common species of wave-exposed rocky shores. Jack's initial work on limpets (Lewis, 1954a), barnacles (Lewis and Powell, 1960b) and mussels (Lewis and Powell, 1961) had highlighted the degree of our ignorance concerning common, conspicuous elements of the shore fauna, whose potential influence had been demonstrated graphically at Port Erin by smashing limpets (see Foreword) (Jones, 1948b; Lodge, 1948; Southward, 1956). Later characterized as 'keystone' species by Bob Paine, such organisms as mussels, barnacles and limpets were to engage Jack's attention in detailed studies spanning decades (Lewis and Seed, 1969; Lewis and Bowman, 1975; Bowman and Lewis, 1977; Lewis, 1977a,b; Lewis, Bowman, Kendall and Williamson, 1982; Kendall, Bowman, Williamson and Lewis, 1982; Todd and Lewis, 1984; Sebens and Lewis, 1985; Kendall, Bowman, Williamson and Lewis, in review).

The outcome of all this work has been the demonstration of natural fluctuations which vary greatly in spatial and temporal scales. Some have obvious local causes (predation, competition, etc.) but the intensity and scale of such biological interactions frequently have their origins in prior substantial fluctuations of annual recruitment, these again being influenced by little-known climatic events. Lacking adequate laboratory facilities at 'the Bay' to try to simulate the effects of climatic change (and indeed lacking the white-coated experimentalist's faith where simulations of littoral conditions are concerned – see Lewis, 1975), Jack waited for natural experiments to take place in the real world or specifically sought comparisons between geographical areas with different climatic regimes.

This development of awareness about natural fluctuations in shore populations and of our frequent ignorance of their timescales and causes, coincided in the late 60s and 70s with increasing concern about pollution of the seas. Industrialists and environmental consultants were anxious to generate quick 'baseline' studies against which to assess man-made impacts. Jack Lewis mounted what seemed at some times to be a one-man Canute act (Lewis, 1970, 1971, 1972a, 1976, 1977b, 1978a,b, 1979, 1980a,b, 1982) to stem the tide of often meaningless trivia which resulted. Most of his arguments were based on the rapidly increasing data from natural, unpolluted habitats. Under Jack's supervision, however, Geoff Moore surveyed the 'dying', polluted coastline of Northeast England and convincingly demonstrated that even there the distribution of kelp fauna was primarily determined by the previously ignored natural factor of turbidity. Geoff Hicks was later to extend these ideas to littoral, phytal meiofauna as Garstang Research Fellow at Robin Hood's Bay.

As a result of his tireless campaigning, Jack Lewis has been in great demand as an industrial adviser since the late 60s, being involved in a long string of consultations in Britain and abroad (Ireland, Hong Kong, Kuwait, Cayman Islands). He has also brought his expertise to bear on a number of N.E.R.C. committees and working parties (Marine Wildlife Conservation (1971–72); Marine Surveillance (1973–74); Nature Conservation in the Marine Environment (with N.C.C., 1975–78); Aquatic Life Sciences Committee) and has been widely in demand as a Visiting Professor abroad, especially in the U.S.A., Canada and Scandinavia (Woods Hole; University of Miami; Nanaimo, University of Newfoundland; Catalina Marine Laboratory; Friday Harbor; Fiskebackskil and the Universities of Oslo, Bergen, Trondheim, Tromsö and Stockholm). In 1976 he initiated an annual short course at University College, Galway, and he has continued ever since to share his expertise and a glass of porter with Irish students enthusiastic for both!

That the case for a deeper understanding of the natural system in a marine context has now been widely accepted, both on its own merits and as an aid to pollution assessment, is attributable in no small measure to Jack's tireless campaigning. For him, it resulted in 1978 in a much expanded programme of research, funded by N.E.R.C. and involving permanent personnel, into the natural recruitment variability of selected common species around the British Isles. Gradually, this intensive and geographically extensive approach began to unravel long-standing enigmas, demonstrating that (depending on frequency and severity) the same factor can both cause recruitment fluctuations and set geographical limits of distribution (Kendall *et al.*, 1982). In 1979, after two years of preliminary discussions, eleven European countries agreed to collaborate in a series of projects in marine benthic ecology, based on Jack's British programme and under his chairmanship. This project, COST 47 of the E.E.C. Environment Programme (see Lewis, 1984), aims to place the inevitably local data and outlook of most benthic studies in a much wider spatial and temporal context, thereby allowing distinctions to be drawn between the effects of local factors and those of broadscale climatic significance.

Despite Jack's personal achievements and the high reputation of the Robin Hood's Bay Laboratory in terms of the quality and quantity of its research output, Leeds University saw fit to terminate its existence (in December, 1982) as part of its response to the general policy of retrenchment forced upon British Universities by the Thatcher Government in the early 80s. Jack therefore opted for early retirement after seeing 'his' N.E.R.C. Unit personnel ensconced at Newcastle University's Dove Marine Laboratory, along the coast at Cullercoats, where he retains an advisory rôle over their work. He is using his new-found 'leisure' to explore tropical shores (Kenya, Goa) and to work on a sequel to *The Ecology of Rocky Shores* (for which the present volume is no substitute) summarizing his views on the 'dynamic phase' of littoral ecology, so beloved of American authors.

He has witnessed the early 'physical control' concepts of shore ecology being eroded, and largely replaced in many younger minds by 'biological control' schemes and he is able now to preside as the wheel, to some extent, turns full circle and physical explanations for biological 'dynamic' events and irregularities begin to accumulate (Bowman and Lewis, 1977; Kendall *et al.*, 1982; Todd and Lewis, 1984; Sebens and Lewis, 1985; Norton, this volume; Underwood, this volume). The truth, of course, lies in their mixture.

His students, first to last, together with colleagues worldwide who value his contributions to date, leave this volume to take up the tale from here. (*For references to Lewis's papers see following list, for other authors see main Reference list.*)

J.R. Lewis's Publications

Powell, H.T. and Lewis, J.R. (1952) Occurrence of *Fucus inflatus* L. forma *distichus* (L.) Börgesen on the North coast of Scotland. *Nature, Lond.*, **169**, p. 508 only.

Lewis, J.R. (1953) The ecology of rocky shores around Anglesey. *Proc. Zool. Soc. Lond.*, **123**, 481–549.

Lewis, J.R. (1954a) Observations on a high-level population of limpets. *J. Anim. Ecol.*, **23**, 85–100.

Lewis, J.R. (1954b) The ecology of exposed rocky shores of Caithness. *Trans. R. Soc. Edinb.*, **62**, 695–723.

Lewis, J.R. (1955) The mode of occurrence of the universal intertidal zones in Great Britain: with a comment by T.A. and Anne Stephenson. *J. Ecol.*, **43**, 270–290.

Lewis, J.R. (1957a) Intertidal communities of the northern and western coasts of Scotland. *Trans. R. Soc. Edinb.*, **63**, 185–220.

Lewis, J.R. (1957b) An introduction to the intertidal ecology of the rocky shores of a Hebridean island. *Oikos*, **8**, 130–160.

Lewis, J.R. and Powell, H.T. (1960a) Aspects of the intertidal ecology of rocky shores in Argyll, Scotland: I. General description of the area. *Trans. R. Soc. Edinb.*, **64**, 45–74.

Lewis, J.R. and Powell, H.T. (1960b) Aspects of the intertidal ecology of rocky shores in Argyll, Scotland: II. The distribution of *Chthamalus stellatus* and *Balanus balanoides* in Kintyre. *Trans. R. Soc. Edinb.*, **64**, 75–100.

Lewis, J.R. and Powell, H.T. (1961) The occurrence of curved and ungulate forms of the mussel *Mytilus edulis* L. in the British Isles and their relationship to *M. galloprovincialis* Lamarck. *Proc. Zool. Soc. Lond.*, **137**, 583–598.

Lewis, J.R. (1961) The littoral zone on rocky shores – a biological or physical entity? *Oikos*, **12**, 280–301.

Lewis, J.R. and Tambs-Lyche, H. (1962) *Littorina neritoides* in Scandinavia. *Sarsia*, **7**, 7–10.

Lewis, J.R. and Powell, H.T. (1963) Further observations on the distribution of *Chthamalus stellatus* and *Balanus balanoides* in Argyll, Scotland. *Rep. Challenger Soc.*, **3** (15), p. 27 only.

Brattegard, T. and Lewis, J.R. (1964) Actual and predicted tide levels at the Biological Station, Espegrend, Blomsterdalen. *Sarsia*, **17**, 7–14.

Lewis, J.R. (1964) *The Ecology of Rocky Shores*. English Universities Press, London, 323 pp.

Lewis, J.R. (1965) The littoral fringe on rocky shores of southern Norway and western Sweden. Proc. 5th Mar. Biol. Symp., *Botanica Gothoburg.*, **3**, 129–143.

Lewis, J.R. (1968) Water movements and their role in rocky shore ecology. Proc. 2nd Europ. Symp. Mar. Biol., *Sarsia*, **34**, 13–36.

Lewis, J.R. and Seed, R. (1969) Morphological variations in *Mytilus* from South-West England in relation to the occurrence of *M. galloprovincialis* Lamarck. *Cah. Biol. Mar.*, **10**, 231–253.

Lewis, J.R. (1970) Pollution studies at Robin Hood's Bay. *Mar. Poll. Bull.*, **1**, 53–55.

Lewis, J.R. (1971) Reflections on a ministerial judgement. *Mar. Poll. Bull.*, **2**, 85–87.

Lewis, J.R. and Quayle, D.B. (1971) Aspects of the littoral ecology of British Columbia. *Fish. Res. Bd Can., Rep.* 1213, 23 pp.

Lewis, J.R. (1972a) Problems and approaches to baseline studies in coastal communities. In, *Marine Pollution and Sea Life*, ed. M. Ruivo, Fishing News (Books) Ltd., London, pp. 401–404.

Lewis, J.R. (1972b) Ch. 12. The British Isles. In, *Life Between Tidemarks on Rocky Shores*, by T.A. Stephenson and Anne Stephenson, W.H. Freeman & Co., San Francisco, pp. 351–384.

Lewis, J.R. (1975) Laboratory charges. *Nature, Lond.*, **257**, p. 640 only.

Lewis, J.R. and Bowman, R.S. (1975) Local habitat-induced variations in the population dynamics of *Patella vulgata* L. *J. Exp. Mar. Biol. Ecol.*, **17**, 165–203.

Lewis, J.R. (1976) Long-term ecological surveillance: practical realities in the rocky littoral. *Oceanogr. Mar. Biol. Ann. Rev.*, **14**, 371–390.

Bowman, R.S. and Lewis, J.R. (1977) Annual fluctuations in the recruitment of *Patella vulgata* L. *J. Mar. Biol. Ass. U.K.*, **57**, 793–815.

Lewis, J.R. (1977a) Ch. 8. Rocky foreshores. In, *The Coastline*, ed. R.S.K. Barnes, John Wiley & Sons, London, pp. 147–158.

Lewis, J.R. (1977b) The role of physical and biological factors in the distribution and stability of rocky shore communities. In, *Biology of Benthic Organisms*, 11th Europ. Symp. Mar. Biol., ed. B.F. Keegan, P. Ó Céidigh and P.J.S. Boaden, Pergamon Press, Oxford, pp. 417–424.

Lewis, J.R. (1978a) The implications of community structure for benthic monitoring studies. *Mar. Poll. Bull.*, **9**, 64–67.

Lewis, J.R. (1978b) Benthic baselines – a case for international collaboration. *Mar. Poll. Bull.*, **9**, 317–320.

Lewis, J.R. (1979) Oil pollution – how much misplaced effort? *Mar. Poll. Bull.*, **10**, 94–95.

Lewis, J.R. (1980a) Ch. 1. Objectives in littoral ecology – a personal viewpoint. In, *The Shore Environment*, Vol. 1: *Methods*, ed. J.H. Price, D.E.G. Irvine and W.F. Farnham (Syst. Ass. Spec. Vol. 17a), Academic Press, London, pp. 1–18.

Lewis, J.R. (1980b) Options and problems in environmental management and evaluation. *Helgoländer Wiss. Meeresunters.*, **33**, 452–466.

Lewis, J.R. (1982) The composition and functioning of benthic ecosystems in relation to the assessment of long-term effects of oil pollution. *Phil. Trans. R. Soc. Lond.* B, **297**, 257–267.

Lewis, J.R., Bowman, R.S., Kendall, M.A. and Williamson, P. (1982) Some geographical components in population dynamics: possibilities and realities in some littoral species. Proc. 16th Europ. Mar. Biol. Symp., *Neth. J. Sea Res.*, **16**, 18–28.

Kendall, M.A., Bowman, R.S., Williamson, P. and Lewis, J.R. (1982) Settlement patterns, density and stability in the barnacle *Balanus balanoides*. Proc. 16th Europ. Mar. Biol. Symp., *Neth. J. Sea Res.*, **16**, 119–126.

Todd, C.D. and Lewis, J.R. (1984) Effects of low air temperature on *Laminaria digitata* in Southwestern Scotland. *Mar. Ecol. Prog. Ser.*, **16**, 199–201.

Lewis, J.R. (1984) Temporal and spatial changes in benthic communities: COST 47 approach. *Mar. Poll. Bull.*, **15**, 397–402.

Sebens, K.P. and Lewis, J.R. (1985) Rare events and population structure of the barnacle *Semibalanus cariosus* (Pallas, 1788). *J. Exp. Mar. Biol. Ecol.*, (in press).

Kendall, M.A., Bowman, R.S., Williamson, P. and Lewis, J.R. (in review) Annual recruitment of *Semibalanus balanoides* on the North Yorkshire coast 1969–1981. *J. Mar. Biol. Ass. U.K.*

CHAPTER II

THE ZONATION OF SEAWEEDS ON ROCKY SHORES

T.A. Norton

2.1 Patterns of Seaweed Distribution

In spite of the limitations imposed by excessive wave action and voracious grazers and the insecure attachment provided by friable rock, most temperate shores support algal vegetation. Indeed, seaweeds are often so abundant and the individual plants so large, that they are by far the most conspicuous organisms in the littoral zone. The presence of dense beds of seaweed provides not only an enormous surface for the attachment of epiphytic organisms, it also determines the nature of the habitat occupied by creatures dwelling on the rock beneath. The plants provide food for herbivores, a sheltering breakwater when the tide is in, and a moist protective blanket when the tide is out. The ecological importance of seaweed beds is therefore immense.

The distribution patterns of seaweeds in the littoral are so striking that they have received considerable attention. This is particularly true in northern Europe where seaweed beds are well developed. Most seaweeds thrive best on sheltered or semi-sheltered shores (Fig. 2.1). It is here that luxuriant stands of *Fucus* spp. and *Ascophyllum nodosum* (L.) Le Jol. thrive, and individual plants are often large, reaching, in the case of *Ascophyllum*, a length of several metres. With increasing wave exposure these fucoid algae become progressively sparser and the plants stunted. The fucoids of the littoral zone are usually replaced by red algae and *Alaria esculenta* (L.) Grev. appears (Fig. 2.1). On the most exposed shores few if any seaweeds persist.

Why some species are confined to relatively sheltered shores is not certain. Some seaweeds may lack the tenacity of adhesion or the mechanical strength to survive persistent buffeting by waves. However, among the most wave-tolerant species are *Alaria esculenta* and *Porphyra umbilicalis* (L.) J. Ag. (Fig. 2.1), two species with thalli that seem more flimsy than average, rather than the reverse. Clearly, immense mechanical strength is not a prerequisite for plant survival in the sea. No 'underwater oak tree', however mighty, could stand against storm waves. Seaweeds do not confront the waves, they yield to them. Pliability and elasticity are more important assets than simple strength. By conforming to the water flow and minimizing their drag profile, seaweeds reduce the danger of being damaged or uprooted (Norton *et al.*, 1982). Probably abrasion is a greater enemy, whether caused by sand-laden waves or by the plant being rasped against the rock beneath.

We have a great deal to learn about the wave tolerances of seaweeds. There is as yet no explanation of why a species such as *Ascophyllum nodosum*, that is virtually confined to sheltered coasts in Britain, is found over a much wider range of exposure in both Norway and New England. We also have very little evidence to explain the absence of some species from sheltered shores. It is tacitly assumed that they are excluded by biotic factors.

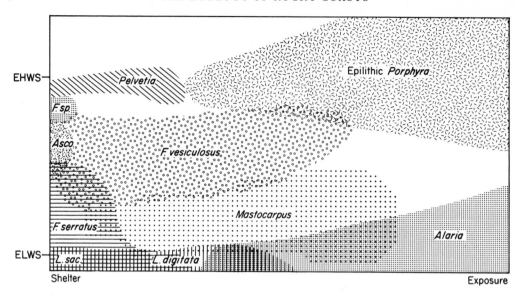

FIG. 2.1. The distribution of littoral seaweeds in relation to wave exposure in North Wales. *F.sp.* = *Fucus spiralis*; *Asco* = *Ascophyllum nodosum*; *L.sac* = *Laminaria saccharina*; EHWS = Extreme High Water of Spring Tides; ELWS = Extreme Low Water of Spring Tides; *Mastocarpus* = *Gigartina stellata* (modified from Jones and Demetropoulos, 1968).

The most striking distribution pattern exhibited by littoral seaweeds is their vertical zonation. The most intensively studied of the zones are those of the fucoid algae found on many rocky shores in northern Europe, overlying and often obscuring the 'universal' zones described by Lewis (1964). The vertical sequence is predictable and usually approximates to that displayed in Fig. 2.2, with *Pelvetia canaliculata* (L.) Dcne. et Thur. at the very top of the shore followed by *Fucus spiralis* L., *F. vesiculosus* L. and/or *Ascophyllum nodosum* with *F. serratus* L. at the lowest levels. All five species share a similar anatomy and a similar mode of reproduction.

Why such zones should exist has been one of the longest standing and most debated enigmas of marine ecology. Only in recent years have we been able to state with any confidence the extent to which they are a reflection of the differing physiological tolerance ranges of organisms to shore conditions and of biotic interactions between species.

2.2 Dispersal and Colonization

How do seaweeds initially colonize the shore and establish the patterns of zonation? The main mode of dissemination for virtually all seaweeds is by means of tiny propagules that are liberated into the sea. They are usually asexually produced spores, or zygotes resulting from gametic fusion. They are invariably tiny, mostly between $10\mu m$ and $150\mu m$ in diameter. The largest algal egg is about the same size as the tiniest seed produced by flowering plants.

Unlike seeds, seaweed propagules are not equipped for dormancy. Under suitable conditions they germinate and develop immediately after (or sometimes even before) liberation from the parent plant. In unfavourable conditions, development may be arrested, but during this time the propagule is not protected from stressful conditions, nor is it furnished with immense food reserves to sustain it until suitable conditions arise. In short, survival depends on settling in an appropriate place. Since the plant is then fixed to the spot, there is no mechanism by which its position can be adjusted later should

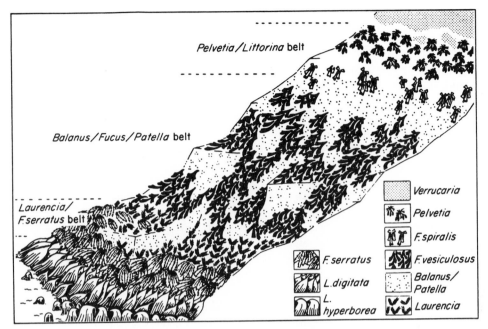

FIG. 2.2. Pictorial representation of the seaweed zonation, on an intermediately exposed rocky shore (from Lewis, 1964). NB. *Balanus* has now changed to *Semibalanus*.

conditions prove unfavourable. A seaweed is condemned to inhabit the site initially colonized by the propagule.

Propagules are released from the plant in a single large batch (as in many green seaweeds), or in a succession of discrete batches (as in *Sargassum muticum* (Yendo) Fensholt), or as a chronic dribble, sustained over an extended fertile period (as in *Fucus* spp.). Clouds of suspended propagules wash over the shore, at the mercy of tides and waves. Their discontinuous distribution in the water may be partially responsible for the patchy distribution that many species exhibit later on the shore (Hruby and Norton, 1979).

In some species, the majority of the propagules may settle within a few metres of the parent plant (see Deysher and Norton, 1982) thus helping to keep the plants close to the appropriate zone. The spread of propagules from large beds of fertile plants is much wider than from isolated individuals, and Burrows and Lodge (1950) found *Fucus* plants arising more than 60m along the shore from the nearest stand of parent plants.

Although the propagules of many green and brown algae are motile, their powers of locomotion are puny in comparison with the water motion into which they are liberated. Their dispersal is therefore passive, and probably all seaweed propagules rely on being swept downwards onto the substratum by water turbulence and being caught in the tiny depressions and concavities of the rock surface (Norton and Fetter, 1981).

Unlike many invertebrate larvae, algal propagules are, as far as we know, unable to select an appropriate substratum. Except in exceptionally calm conditions, their motility seems of little use. Of far greater value is the stickiness of their outer coat, which allows them to adhere immediately on contact with a substratum.

Successful colonization can take place only where suitable space is available. Established stands of seaweeds represent a barrier between settling propagules and the rock beneath (Hruby and Norton,

1979; Clokie and Boney, 1980b; Deysher and Norton, 1982; Chapman, 1984). Dense turfs of green or red seaweeds form particularly effective barriers. Large fucoids are less effective, for although they can blanket the shore, settlement takes place when the tide is in and the fucoid cover is being continually parted and lifted by water motion.

Clearance of established vegetation by storms, grazers or experimentalists opens 'windows' for settlement. Such 'windows' can be rapidly closed by the growth of ephemeral algae that reinstate a barrier (Deysher and Norton, 1982). Colonization is therefore the result of the coincidence of the seasonal availability of propagules and the intermittent availability of space.

It is often claimed that colonization of bare rock occurs in a set sequence, first bacteria, then microalgae, green seaweeds and eventually the re-establishment of the former dominant. This frequently seen pattern is not, however, a sequence of colonization, but largely a reflection of the relative growth rates and longevity of the participants. *Fucus* often colonizes newly exposed rock immediately, only to be swamped by faster-growing ephemeral green algae that settled later. Only when the greens die down can the *Fucus* germlings surviving beneath grow away and become apparent (Hruby and Norton, unpubl.). The rate of succession can be accelerated by grazers preferentially removing ephemeral competitors (Lubchenco, 1983).

There is a great deal of evidence that the presence of one species can prevent colonization by, or retard the growth of another, but few indications that the pioneer species actually facilitate the successful establishment of later colonizers. One example of the latter is where barnacles provide spatial refugia for *F. vesiculosus* plants allowing them to colonize smooth rock in the otherwise limiting presence of grazing *Littorina littorea* (L.) (Lubchenco, 1983). Another, somewhat special case of facilitation involves a marine angiosperm (Turner, 1983).

Once settled, the propagules are stranded on the shore. When the tide retreats they are exposed to the vagaries of aerial conditions. Clearly such tiny objects must gain some protection from the microtopography of the rock, and the film of water that clings to the surface. Some mutual protection may also be afforded by the close proximity of adjacent germlings. There is experimental evidence that dense crowds of germlings can survive longer periods of aerial exposure than can sparser stands (Hruby and Norton, 1979). There are also data to indicate that the advantage so gained is much more marked for a lower shore dweller such as *Fucus serratus* than an inhabitant of the high shore such as *F. spiralis* (Bray and Norton, unpubl.).

Of course, close proximity of neighbouring plantlets also leads to intraspecific competition. Laboratory experiments with *Fucus* spp. have clearly shown that self-thinning can occur and that the greater the initial settlement density, the smaller the average size of the resultant juvenile plants (Bray and Norton, unpubl.). This may place the plants at a disadvantage in competition with those of other species, although it seems that in spite of the reduction in *average* size, some plants break through and grow rapidly. Therefore, if only the largest plants are measured, no effects of crowding are evident (Vadas, 1972; Hruby and Norton, unpubl.). Dense stands may also be better suited to survive grazing, both when the plants are germlings (Lubchenco, 1983; Bray and Norton, unpubl.), and when they are adult (Hay, 1981).

Seaweeds have high fecundity that compensates for the heavy mortality that befalls their early stages. For *Laminaria digitata* (Huds.) Lamour. for example, the sporophytes inhabiting a single square metre of rock can produce 20.2×10^9 spores, but only 0.98×10^6 spores colonize the rock surface beneath, and of these, only two grow into adult plants (Chapman, 1984). Even if they colonize the appropriate zone, as many as 90 – 100% of the propagules of *Fucus vesiculosus* may die within 17 days of settlement (Bray and Norton, unpubl.), and for *Ascophyllum nodosum*, the mean life expectancy of unprotected, newly-settled zygotes is only 10 days (Miller and Vadas, 1984).

Dissemination by water motion, combined with an inability to select suitable settlement sites results in many algal propagules being deposited 'out of zone' in positions where survival to adulthood is extremely unlikely. Moreover, the bulk of the resulting mortality occurs whilst the juvenile plants are still microscopic. In other words, considerable truncation of the species' vertical distribution may take place *before* new plants are visible on the shore. Further restriction takes place subsequently, often over a period of several years (Fig. 2.3). It is largely this later 'sharpening' of the zones that is studied by marine biologists.

2.3 Factors Controlling the Upper Limits of Littoral Seaweeds

As seaweeds are marine plants they might be expected to grow best when submerged. This has been confirmed by culture experiments (McLachlan *et al.*, 1971; Edwards, 1977; Hruby and Norton, 1978; Schonbeck and Norton, 1979a). Several workers have tried to investigate whether fucoid algae can photosynthesize and respire whilst exposed to air, with conflicting results, but Schonbeck and Norton (1979a) clearly demonstrated that even the upper shore dwellers, *Fucus spiralis* and *Pelvetia canaliculata*, grow rapidly only if illuminated whilst submerged. Those illuminated only whilst subjected to humid air and presumably therefore under no drought stress, grew little if at all in 42 days.

It follows that for seaweeds aerial emersion should constitute an adverse stress, and prolonged emersion high on the shore might prove fatal. This is confirmed by the observation that protection from the worst effects of aerial emersion seems to allow many species to survive higher up on the shore than would otherwise be possible. Many species that are confined to lower levels on an open sunny stretch of shore often venture much higher in shaded situations, or beneath an overlying canopy of other seaweeds or on north-facing surfaces where the effects of insolation and therefore desiccation are less. Rock pools allow some species to extend higher up the shore than they do on the open rock surface. The same phenomenon has been observed experimentally by Frank (1965b) who allowed seawater to trickle out of a large container placed high on the shore and also by Dayton (1971) who constructed an artificial rock pool that leaked. In both instances seaweeds grew to a higher level in the path of the run-off than on the adjacent drier rock.

Although high irradiances that have little effect on high-shore fucoids can inhibit the growth of

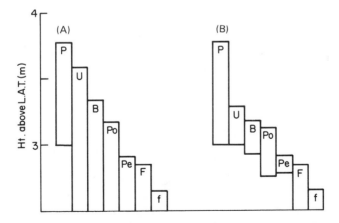

FIG. 2.3. Zone sharpening in the littoral fringe at Hunterston, Ayrshire, Scotland. A, Vertical distribution of settled propagules, from summer, 1975, until winter, 1978–9. B, Vertical distribution of macroscopic plants, February, 1979. P = *Prasiola stipitata*; U = *Urospora bangioides*; B = *Blidingia minima*; Po = *Porphyra umbilicalis*; Pe = *Pelvetia canaliculata*; F = *Fucus spiralis*; f = *Fucus* plants of indeterminate species. L.A.T. = Lowest Astronomical Tide (modified from Clokie and Boney, 1980b).

lower shore species (Strömgren, 1977), the bulk of observations indicate that desiccation and over-heating may be more critical components of aerial emersion than high irradiation, rainfall or frost. This was confirmed by Schonbeck and Norton (1978) who studied the zonation of littoral fucoids on a shore on the West coast of Scotland where there were five species of fucoid algae each forming a fairly well-marked zone.

Firstly, they correlated the condition of the seaweeds on the shore with changes in climatic conditions over a period of two and a half years. They found that the upper limits of the zones highest on the shore, those dominated by *Pelvetia canaliculata*, *Fucus spiralis* and *Ascophyllum nodosum*, were periodically 'pruned back' during the summer. The uppermost plants of each species predictably showed signs of tissue damage about four weeks after a period of drying conditions had coincided with neap tides thus subjecting the plants to the atmosphere for days on end. High air temperature aggravated the damage, which could be so severe that all the uppermost plants of each species were killed. On spring tides or in rough weather the plants were wetted every day and little damage accrued, irrespective of climatic conditions. Nor was damage ever observed during cool, dull weather in summer, or in winter, even after rain fell every day for two months or when the plants were frozen solid for four consecutive days (Schonbeck and Norton, 1978). Indeed, both *Ascophyllum* and *Fucus vesiculosus* can withstand freezing at $-20°C$ without suffering tissue damage (MacDonald *et al.*, 1974).

The picture that emerged was of plants that could survive for long periods at the upper margin of their zone, but a few critical days in summer were sufficient to damage or even kill those individuals which had settled just a little too far upshore. If, as in *F. spiralis*, the young plants grew fairly rapidly, damaged plants were quickly replaced so that the upper edge of the zone could be killed off and recolonized during a single summer. If the slower growing *Pelvetia* plants were killed, it might take a year for them to recolonize the area.

These two species and also *Ascophyllum* were clearly growing close to their physiological limits for certain conditions. Only the top-most plants in each zone were adversely affected. On several occasions Schonbeck and Norton (1978) observed a fairly extensive belt of *Pelvetia* living at a higher level than the brown and dying uppermost plants of *Fucus spiralis*. Below these stretched healthy plants of *F. spiralis* which in turn contrasted with the damaged plants of *Ascophyllum* living lower down. Clearly the differing upper limits of these species on this shore were a reflection of their differential tolerances to aerial conditions. Certainly *Ascophyllum* dies if transplanted into the *F. spiralis* zone and *F. spiralis* cannot survive in the *Pelvetia* zone (Hatton, 1938; Schonbeck and Norton, 1978).

The latter authors also demonstrated that the tolerance of different species of fucoids to drying conditions in the laboratory was related logically to their respective positions on the shore. Under similar conditions, the upper shore species *Pelvetia* and *Fucus spiralis* survived about four times longer than the mid-shore species *F. vesiculosus* and *Ascophyllum*. Severe drying conditions which killed the lower shore dweller *F. serratus* outright, caused only sub-lethal damage to *F. spiralis*, whilst *Pelvetia* suffered no visible damage and on resubmergence suffered little depression of photosynthesis and subsequently grew well.

Several workers have shown that the ability to tolerate desiccation and then resume photosynthesis is greatest in seaweeds inhabiting the upper shore. Stocker and Holdheide (1937) found that slight drying had virtually no effect on the rate of photosynthesis of *F. spiralis* on resubmergence, but halved that of *F. serratus*. Montfort (1937) found that after severe drying, *F. spiralis* resumed photosynthesis more promptly and more completely on resubmergence than did mid-shore species of *Fucus*. F.A. Brown (in Dring, 1982), using five littoral species, confirmed that if drying was severe, the extent of photosynthetic recovery was related to the plants' natural position on the shore, being greatest in *Pelvetia* and least in *Laminaria digitata*. Seaweeds other than fucoids also seem to exhibit drought tolerances related to their distribution on the shore.

One might expect that upper shore seaweeds, like xerophytic land plants, would possess mechanisms for retarding water loss. Several workers have attempted to measure the rate of water loss in littoral seaweeds. The conflicting results obtained by Zaneveld (1937) and Kristensen (1968) probably stem from their tiny sample sizes and failure to pay sufficient attention to the exact size of the plants used or their surface area to mass ratios. In the most recent and detailed studies, Jones and Norton (1979, 1981) used a porometer to measure the resistance to water loss offered by the outer layers of the thallus, and Schonbeck and Norton (1979b) measured the weight loss of plants dried under controlled conditions. They found that the species of fucoid algae inhabiting the upper shore possessed no more effective means of curbing water loss than did lower shore species. The tissues of *Pelvetia* and *Fucus spiralis* dried out just as quickly as those of *F. serratus*. The epidermis of both lost water at about 85% of the rate of evaporation from a free water surface (Schonbeck and Norton, 1979b), although the speed of desiccation influences the tissues' resistance to water loss (Jones and Norton, 1979, 1981). When air-dry, all the species tested retained some water bound in the cells, but adult plants of upper shore species did not retain more water than those inhabiting the lower shore. The mucilage production that is a feature of many seaweeds seems to play no rôle in water conservation (Jones and Norton, 1979).

Another possible method of drought avoidance is to possess a shape with a low surface area to mass ratio, like a cactus. In young fucoids, the thalli of upper shore species do seem to have a lower surface area to mass ratio than those of the lower shore and this may be beneficial, but in adult plants the trend is reversed. Clearly they do not adopt the 'cactus strategy', although, as the drying plant shrinks, the reduced size of its evaporating surface undoubtedly helps to conserve water (Jones and Norton, 1979).

The shape of the plant affects the surrounding boundary layers and therefore the rate of evaporation. In the fucoids, the nearly cylindrical thallus of *Ascophyllum* encourages a faster rate of water loss than the flattened lamina of *Fucus*. Contrary perhaps to expectations, the thallus of *Pelvetia* which has a deep, gutter-like channel on one side, does not discourage water loss. Whatever retardation is caused by the channel is counteracted by the convex surface on the other side of the plant (Schonbeck and Norton, 1979b). Since, when the tide is out, the plant usually flops channelled-side-downwards, it is the evaporation-enhancing convex surface which governs the rate of water loss. The usefulness of the channel may be that it forms a humid microclimate in which developing zygotes of *Pelvetia* can lodge during the vulnerable early stages of growth; later to fall out and possibly attach to the rock (Moss, 1974).

Perhaps the most important factor influencing the rate at which seaweeds lose water in nature is the degree to which the thallus is overlain by its own branches or by those of adjacent plants. Schonbeck and Norton (1979b) found that the overlapping in natural stands of upper shore fucoids reduced the exposed evaporating plant surface to only 20% of that of isolated plants. This should drastically reduce the rate at which the plants dry out. However, *Fucus spiralis* benefited at least as much from mutual protection as did *Pelvetia*, and what is more, it achieved this protection earlier in life, for its young stages grow much faster than those of *Pelvetia* and form dense stands earlier.

In spite of mutual protection, plants of both *Pelvetia* and *F. spiralis* often become air-dry in nature. However, both can also recover with only slight damage after losing 95% of their water content whilst exposed on the shore (Schonbeck and Norton, 1979b). Fucoid algae clearly do not seem to *avoid* drought, they merely tolerate it. The real advantage of upper shore species rests not so much on their ability to withstand tougher conditions, but in their ability to tolerate being air-dried for longer periods. This is in keeping with the situation in nature, for the stresses to which plants on the upper shore are subjected are not intrinsically more severe than those found lower down, they are merely more prolonged.

Some aerial conditions are obviously more critical than others. Schonbeck and Norton (1980a) found that both *Pelvetia* and *F. spiralis*, dried under various conditions in the laboratory, suffered more damage at an air temperature of 25°C than at 9°C and at the higher temperature the damage was aggravated by a high relative humidity, not, as might be expected, by low humidity. Since in nature, upper shore fucoids are most severely affected by high air temperatures, it is advantageous to them to become air-dry rapidly in hot weather. Hence it is not surprising that they have developed no really effective mechanisms to impede water loss. Their most important adaptation seems to be their ability to become air-dry under natural conditions without suffering serious damage.

Complete dehydration in the laboratory was fatal, but drying to a low relative humidity of 35 to 40% seemed to forestall metabolic injury. In nature, the relative humidity probably rarely falls below this level and the algae are able to retain the small amount of residual moisture necessary for survival. The experiments indicated that partial desiccation was only disadvantageous if there was a sudden shower. 48 hours of simulated rain had no adverse effects on turgid plants other than a superficial blistering which is also seen in nature, but if the plants were partly dried, the osmotic shock of a sudden downpour of fresh water was much more damaging (Schonbeck and Norton, 1980a). Sublethal desiccation stress resulted in a loss of cell contents, and incomplete re-imbibition of water, both symptomatic of damage to cell membranes. The time-dependent and temperature-dependent nature of some aspects of injury were more indicative of metabolic disturbance (Schonbeck and Norton, 1979b).

Drought tolerance is not a fixed property of a seaweed, it varies as a result of the previous experience of the plant. Repeated exposure to sub-critical desiccation drought-hardens the plants. In consequence, plants from the top of their zone are more drought tolerant than those from mid-zone.

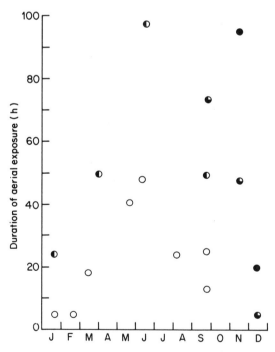

FIG. 2.4. Drought tolerance of *Fucus spiralis* collected at different times of year. Each symbol represents single tests on 5–15 plants dried at 26°C and 53% relative humidity and denotes the plants' response thus: open circle = no observable adverse effects; half circle = growth somewhat retarded and/or slight visible damage; three-quarters circle = moderate to severe damage, but plant survived; closed circle = killed (from Schonbeck and Norton, 1979c).

Tolerance also varies seasonally, increasing in spring, becoming maximal in summer and declining in winter (Fig. 2.4). Drought-hardening of *F. spiralis* could be induced experimentally in response to sub-critical drying. De-hardening also took place in plants transferred to physiologically less stressful conditions, as when moved to below their normal zone on the shore, or kept permanently submerged in culture (Schonbeck and Norton, 1979c).

The stresses accompanying prolonged aerial exposure are obvious, but it follows that the longer a seaweed spends in air, the shorter the duration of its submergence in the sea. There is evidence to suggest that *Pelvetia* can thrive high on the shore because it is adept at utilizing a nutrient supply that is only available during brief and intermittent periods of submergence (Table 2.1). Whether this ability results from a rapid uptake of nutrients or from low nutrient requirements is yet to be investigated.

Some of the red seaweeds inhabiting the lower shore can be damaged or even killed when low spring tides coincide with hot weather (Hawkins and Hartnoll, in press), but neither these authors nor Schonbeck and Norton (1978) ever observed a periodic pruning-back of the upper limits of either *Fucus vesiculosus* or *F. serratus*. Moreover, both these species can survive when transplanted to slightly above their natural zone on the shore (Schonbeck and Norton, 1978). Neither species therefore, can be living up to the limits of its physiological tolerances, but must be restricted by biotic facors. Certainly, their upper limits are often depressed by a luxuriant growth of the species above (Lewis, 1964, p. 216). Furthermore, many seaweeds which characteristically inhabit the lower shore will encroach higher if a competitor or a grazer in the zone above is depleted naturally, or removed experimentally (Lodge, 1948; Knight and Parke, 1950; Burrows and Lodge, 1951; Lewis, 1964, p. 216; Southward and Southward, 1978; Hawkins, 1981a; Hawkins and Hartnoll, in press). Even relatively inedible plants may benefit from grazer removal. For example, calcareous encrusting 'lithothamnia' may ascend the shore after the removal of grazers allows the development of an algal canopy beneath which it is protected from desiccation (Southward and Southward, 1978; Lubchenco, 1980; Hawkins, 1981a).

2.31 Rock pools

The foregoing discussion has dealt exclusively with plants attached to the open rock surface, but many shores are pitted with basins and gulleys which retain reservoirs of seawater when the tide retreats. Since protection from desiccation by wave splash enables many littoral species to inhabit higher levels on the shore, rock pools might be expected to have a similar effect. To some extent they do. Pools on the lower shore often represent aquaria of sublittoral species on the shore, and deep mid-shore pools

TABLE 2.1

Linear growth (mm·month^{-1}) of two species of fucoid algae cultured for 6–8 weeks in two simulated tidal regimes and in sea water with different concentrations of added nutrients
(from Schonbeck & Norton, 1979a).

| | Pelvetia canaliculata | | Fucus spiralis | |
| | Tidal regime (h emersion per 12h cycle) | | | |
Nutrient enrichment	10 h	2 h	10 h	2 h
Full concentration	5.6$_a$	7.8$_a$	15.1$_a$	12.2$_b$
1/5 concentration	4.9$_a$	5.1$_b$	4.5$_b$	20.7$_a$
1/20 concentration	2.8$_b$	7.2$_a$	4.5$_b$	21.6$_a$
Unenriched	1.7$_b$	5.3$_b$	1.5$_c$	10.9$_b$

In each column, values with different subscripts are significantly different at P = 0.05.

occasionally contain some species such as *F. serratus*, which on the open rock are confined to lower levels. However, pools higher on the shore are usually inhabited by specialist pool-dwellers, and the fucoids that dominate the adjacent open rock are conspicuously absent. Undoubtedly the conditions in many rock pools are not comparable with submergence by the sea (see Goss-Custard *et al.*, 1979) and may not favour the growth of fucoids. Nonetheless, at least in the case of *F. vesiculosus*, colonization of eulittoral pools can be encouraged by the removal from the pool of both herbivores and algal competitors (Lubchenco, 1982).

2.4 Factors Excluding Sublittoral Seaweeds from the Eulittoral Zone

The sublittoral fringe is inhabited by seaweeds tolerant of the severe mechanical stresses imposed by the excessive turbulence often found in shallow water, as well as occasional brief exposures to air. Often a supple thallus will serve both needs as in *Alaria esculenta* and *Laminaria digitata*. These plants flop when exposed to air so that their fronds remain prostrate, slopping about in the water even when the tide has dropped lower than their holdfasts. This is in stark contrast to *Laminaria hyperborea* (Gunn.) Fosl. a truly sublittoral plant with such a rigid stipe that if emersed by the tide, it sticks up out of water, erect like a tree, exposing to the elements the sensitive meristem at the base of its lamina.

Undoubtedly, their sensitivity to the vagaries of aerial conditions excludes many sublittoral algae from the shore. When intact sublittoral communities were uplifted 12cm into the littoral zone by a movement of the rock caused by an underground nuclear explosion, the sublittoral plants were soon replaced by a littoral species, *Fucus distichus* L. (Lebednik, 1973). Even in undisturbed situations, it is not uncommon to see the thalli of sublittoral plants that have ventured too high bleached green or white after aerial emersion. I have seen a forest of *Saccorhiza polyschides* (Lightf.) Batt. plants destroyed by a single exceptionally low tide on a sunny day. The same fate can befall *Laminaria digitata* if it is emersed on either very hot or very cold days (Todd and Lewis, 1984; Hawkins and Hartnoll, 1985).

The tissues of *L. digitata* offer even less resistance to water loss than those of littoral fucoids (Jones and Norton, 1981) and evaporation must be rapid from such a broad flat lamina. Sublittoral algae are also far less tolerant than littoral plants to desiccation. Sublittoral kelps were killed by only one hour in adverse conditions that had little effect on littoral algae even after one or two days (Muenscher, 1915). Biebl (1938) also demonstrated that a variety of red algae could only survive aerial emersion if the air was close to being 100% saturated, whereas littoral red algae could survive for the same length of time at relative humidities of ~86%. Also in contrast to littoral seaweeds, not a single sublittoral species out of 43 tested withstood freezing for 12 hours, whereas all the littoral species did. The littoral species also survived 12 hours at temperatures of 30°C or even 35°C whereas many sublittoral species succumbed at a temperature of only 27°C and all died at 35°C (Biebl, 1938, 1958). Even if the plants were not killed they suffered severe physiological setbacks from the effects of temperature shock resulting from emersion and resubmergence.

Sublittoral species are mostly shade plants and their photosynthetic pigments can be damaged by bright light (Jones and Dent, 1971). Simply clearing an area of *Laminaria* forest results in some usually shaded red algae in the understorey flora turning a fluorescent orange colour indicative of pigment denaturation. In contrast, littoral algae require far more light than sublittoral species for maximal photosynthesis and are much more resistant to high irradiances. Biebl (1952, 1956) showed that only one or two hours' exposure to strong sunlight killed a variety of sublittoral algae, but had no effect on littoral species, which could survive at least 5 hours exposure to the same irradiance.

In some areas grazing seems to prevent the upward extension of *Palmaria palmata* (L.) O. Kuntze onto the shore (Hawkins and Hartnoll, 1983a), and *Laminaria digitata* advanced upshore after pollution had killed off a limpet population (Southward and Southward, 1978). Although there is little evidence for the competitive exclusion of sublittoral species from the shore, *Fucus serratus* is such a doughty competitor, so well suited to dominating the lower eulittoral zone, that its presence must discourage the shoreward advance of at least some species.

2.5 Factors Controlling the Lower Limits of Littoral Seaweeds

Since they are essentially marine organisms, even littoral fringe dwellers ought to thrive on the lower shore. Indeed, in culture, several inhabitants of the upper shore exhibit their most rapid growth if kept permanently submerged rather than repeatedly subjected to air (see p. 11). There is very little evidence that littoral seaweeds *need* to be periodically emersed. Rusanowski and Vadas (1973) claimed that germlings of *F. vesiculosus* and *F. distichus* subs. *edentatus* (Pyl.) Powell only grew when emersed for four to six hours daily, but the growth rates were in any case so low that one can only conclude that their culture conditions were unsuitable. Similar claims by Fischer (1929) and Fulcher and McCully (1968) are not supported by convincing evidence.

The only seaweed that may require periodic emersion is *Pelvetia canaliculata*. When transplanted to the mid-shore it thrived throughout the summer, but during the winter declined and eventually decayed (Schonbeck and Norton, 1980b). Possibly light limitation contributed to its failure. Certainly on the mid-shore, tidal submersion can reduce light to well below the saturation level for photosynthesis, and growth slows markedly in the short dull winter days. However, in culture, even under bright irradiance, *Pelvetia* soon decays if kept permanently submerged, although it can be grown for long periods if frequently taken out of water (Schonbeck and Norton, 1980b). No satisfactory explanation for this decay has yet been put forward. Nothing like it is exhibited by other upper shore fucoid algae. *Pelvetia* does not seem to require aerial conditions for its photosynthesis, indeed it only grows well if illuminated while submerged. Plants illuminated while out of the water grew little even when protected from desiccation stress (Schonbeck and Norton, 1979a). It is possible that this species is peculiarly susceptible to pathogenic micro-organisms that are killed off by periodic desiccation, but there is as yet no evidence to support this theory.

Whatever the cause of the susceptibility of *Pelvetia*, it is not shared by other littoral algae. Some species have their downshore distribution curtailed by physical conditions. In turbid waters for example, the lower limits of some low-shore fucoids may be controlled by insufficient irradiance (Dring, 1984). Also, seaweeds such as *Ascophyllum* that have gas bladders, may be restricted by pressure effects on the lower reaches of shores where there is a large tidal range (Damant, 1937). Most littoral seaweeds can, however, thrive at lower levels on the shore than those they normally inhabit. Many species can be found sporadically below their usual zone, *F. vesiculosus* even making occasional incursions into the sublittoral zone. Indeed, both *Pelvetia* and *F. spiralis* actually grow more rapidly when transplanted to below their normal limits than within their own zone (Schonbeck and Norton, 1979b, 1980b).

There is little doubt that the downward distribution of most species on most shores is restricted by the presence of other organisms. For example, following the removal of limpet grazers, plants of *F. vesiculosus* and *F. spiralis* were found at all levels on the shore down to ELWS (Burrows and Lodge, 1951). Interspecific competition is also influential. Removal of plants of one species usually allows other species to extend their ranges. For example, the removal of *Chondrus crispus* Stackh. allowed *Fucus* to colonize the *Chondrus* zone (Menge, 1975), and *Fucus serratus* occasionally appeared in cleared areas in the sublittoral *Laminaria* forest (Kain, 1975a). Clearing *Ascophyllum* allowed the ingress of *F. spiralis* from above (Burrows and Lodge, 1951). Some of these plants persisted until the following year and became fertile.

Systematic weeding experiments are also very instructive. In a series of such experiments Schonbeck and Norton (1980b) denuded areas of shore in the *Pelvetia* and *F. spiralis* zones when both species were fertile. They allowed the areas to become colonized by both species and then repeatedly weeded out

F. spiralis plants from parts of the cleared areas. In the unweeded sectors *Pelvetia* came to dominate only within its usual zone, but where *F. spiralis* was removed, *Pelvetia* ranged well down into the *Fucus* zone (Fig. 2.5).

What enables *F. spiralis* to out-compete *Pelvetia* is primarily its vastly greater growth rate. I have observed areas colonized by both these species in summer. By the following spring *F. spiralis* had established its dominance, but in a warm dry summer every single *Fucus* plant was killed leaving the tougher, unaffected plants of *Pelvetia* to grow on unmolested. However, a new generation of *F. spiralis* plants arose that summer and rapidly overtook the *Pelvetia* plants to dominate the area by the following year. In other words, even if *Pelvetia* is given a year's start, it grows so slowly that it is easily supplanted by *F. spiralis*. This type of relationship may explain much of the zonation on the shore. On a gradient of environmental conditions, competition between species can result in zone formation as demonstrated by Pielou's (1974) model. Certainly, if cultured under identical conditions, the rate of growth is slowest in *Pelvetia* and progressively faster in those fucoid species inhabiting successively lower levels on the shore. The more tolerant species above can only take over at a level where the growth advantages of the species below are counteracted by environmental stress. In nature both Hatton (1938) and Schonbeck and Norton (1979a) have demonstrated that several species of littoral

FIG. 2.5. The effects of experimental weeding on the Isle of Cumbrae, Scotland. A, The experimental site, 12 September, 1975, showing a mixed stand of young *Pelvetia canaliculata* and *Fucus spiralis*. On transects 1 and 3 (from the left) all *F. spiralis* plants were removed on 26 September, 1975 and periodically thereafter. Transects 2 and 4 were left undisturbed. B, the same site on 19 July, 1976, showing a sharp zonal boundary between *Pelvetia* and *F. spiralis* in the undisturbed transects, but a dense cover of *Pelvetia* along the entire length of the weeded transects. No *Pelvetia* survived beneath the *F. spiralis* (from Schonbeck and Norton, 1980).

fucoids grow more slowly towards their upper limits than they do lower down in mid-zone. Indeed Knight (1947) observed that the growth of tiny juvenile plants of *F. vesiculosus* and *F. serratus* near to the upper margin of their zones could be arrested almost completely for very long periods, although growth rapidly resumed if the plants were transferred downshore. Such growth inhibition is partially because the plants grow faster when submerged for longer, but also because sublethal aerial emersion causes intermittent hiatuses in growth, the effects of which persist after re-submergence. As a result, the uppermost plants in a zone may be stunted, fail to form a substantial canopy and exhibit reduced fertility (Norton *et al.*, 1981). Clearly this would diminish any advantage in growth that a species might have over the species inhabiting the zone immediately above it, for the latter, although intrinsically slower growing, would be less affected by drought.

Occasionally, a slower growing competitor can succeed. *Ascophyllum* for instance is relatively slow growing in its early stages, but persists for many years, and in suitable conditions its longevity ensures its ultimate dominance over faster growing rivals. *Chondrus crispus* can exclude faster growing *Fucus* species because its holdfasts fuse, forming a continuous crust which the spores of *Fucus* apparently cannot colonize (Lubchenco, 1982). There is evidence that secretions from various algal crusts can inhibit the settlement of animal larvae and the growth of adjacent algae (Conover and Sieburth, 1966; Fletcher, 1975; Khafaji and Boney, 1979). However, many of the species that dominate the lower levels of the shore do not actually occupy much of the available rock surface. Holdfasts of adjacent *Fucus* plants may be well spaced out, with stretches of unoccupied rock between them. However, the fast-growing fronds form a dense canopy which can blanket the shore, shading the potential competitors beneath and suppressing their growth.

Various factors may contribute to the removal of unsuccessful competitors. Dayton (1975) showed that rivals were physically dislodged by the continual sweeping movements of the dominant plant *Lessoniopsis littoralis* (Farl. et Setch.) Reinke, which acted liked a large windscreen wiper driven by the surf. It is not unusual to see halos of rock cleared in this manner around *Fucus* plants on exposed shores. However, as the limits of the zones are often more clearly defined on sheltered shores than on exposed ones, this cannot be the major factor involved. A very dense canopy could perhaps shade the underlying plants so efficiently that they might remain beneath the compensation point almost continuously. Eventually, their reserves depleted, the plants would die off. At best, shading would drastically reduce the growth rate of the unsuccessful competitors beneath the canopy. Grazing animals may also contribute to their eventual demise, for it seems that many littoral algae are most vulnerable to grazing when still tiny. By rapid development they find refuge in size (Knight and Parke, 1950; Lubchenco, 1983) and are also better able to replace tissue damaged by grazers. Thus plants in the dense shade of an overlying canopy may have their growth arrested whilst still juvenile and they would therefore remain susceptible to grazing for an intolerably long period. This factor alone might explain the absence of *Pelvetia* from the mid-shore wherever grazers are present, for even under ideal conditions its germlings can remain vulnerable to grazing for almost 18 months (Schonbeck and Norton, 1980b). In any case, grazing pressure increases downshore: there are more grazers and, because of longer periods of submergence, they graze for longer each tide.

Germlings of some species might also avoid excessive grazing pressure by passing through their most vulnerable phase during the winter, when littorinid snails are much less active. *F. serratus* releases spores in the winter, and its sporelings grow rapidly so that their chances of survival on the lower shore are maximized. In contrast *Pelvetia* and *F. spiralis* both release their spores in summer when the snails are most active and would probably consume the majority of the sporelings before they become macroscopic.

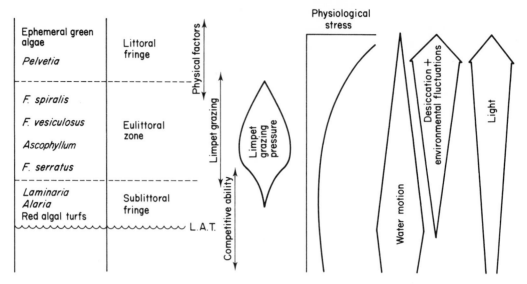

FIG. 2.6. A diagram of algal zonation summarizing the main factors influencing distribution. It displays, from left to right: the distribution of seaweeds in relation to Lewis' scheme of zonation; the dominant structuring agencies, with overlap indicating a balance between factors; a generalized physiological stress gradient for seaweeds; and the main physical factors causing stress to seaweeds. L.A.T. = Lowest Astronomical Tide (modified from Hawkins and Hartnoll, 1983a).

2.6 Conclusions

In summary therefore (Fig. 2.6), the zonation of seaweeds is determined by events after the settlement of their propagules. The physiological tolerance of the plants to aerial conditions is least in sublittoral species and greatest in littoral fringe dwellers. For inhabitants of the upper shore the most critical factor influencing their upper limits on the shore is aerial emersion at neap tides during warm, dry summer weather. Similar conditions at spring tides can trim back the upper limits of sublittoral species. Seaweeds inhabiting the mid- and lower shore are subjected to critical physical conditions only rarely. Their upper limits are determined by their ability to compete with other species and to survive the attentions of grazers. Similarly, the lower limits of almost all shore-dwelling seaweeds are usually controlled by biotic interactions.

The discussion has centred largely around the fucoid algae of northern Atlantic shores simply because they are the most intensively studied species and they occupy the region that most interested Jack Lewis. Nonetheless, many of the generalizations made apply equally to other species in other parts of the world. For example, the periodic destruction of plants that have ventured too high upshore is just as obvious on the coasts of Chile (Santelices *et al.*, 1981) or Australia (Fuhrer *et al.*, 1981, plate 139) as it is in Scotland (Schonbeck and Norton, 1978). The results of Schonbeck and Norton (1979b) on water loss from littoral algae are paralleled in the experiments of Bérard-Therriault and Cardinal (1973) in Canada and by Chapman (1966) and Dromgoole (1980) in New Zealand. A rapidly growing literature demonstrates that biotic factors are also of prime importance in delimiting seaweed distribution on shores world-wide (see for example Hawkins and Hartnoll, 1983 and Underwood, this volume).

Since the publication of *The Ecology of Rocky Shores* by Lewis in 1964, the application of phytosociological and statistical methods has enabled littoral communities to be described much more objectively than before (Russell and Fielding, 1981). Increasingly refined and complex models of the structure and dynamics of shore communities have also been developed (Seip, 1983). However, we still remain woefully ignorant of the ecology of many common eulittoral seaweeds such as *Laurencia pinnatifida* (Huds.) Lamour. and *Lomentaria articulata* (Huds.) Lyngb. Even for the well-studied fucoids we can only guess at their fecundity and the ecology of their propagules.

Undoubtedly, the most striking change that has taken place in recent years is the development of a consuming interest in biotic factors. Inevitably, the fascinating and often dramatic results obtained by manipulating natural populations has led to a neglect of other factors. The once firmly held dogma that littoral zonation was simply a reflection of tidal phenomena, has been replaced by an equally erroneous belief that all can be explained by biotic factors. That this is not so has been cogently argued by Lewis (1977b). Indeed, the existence or otherwise of 'critical tidal levels' (Colman, 1933) is still hotly debated (Lewis, 1961, 1964; Underwood, 1978a; Swinbanks, 1982).

Even within the realm of biotic interactions several fundamental phenomena remain largely uninvestigated. For example, the majority of grazers feed on a film of microalgae and tiny juvenile seaweeds rather than on macroalgae (Underwood, 1984b). What is more, the herbivorous snail *Littorina littorea* feeds selectively on seaweed germlings in the film, consuming some species, shunning others (Watson and Norton, in press). This may be of immense importance on the shore, for preferential grazing on the juvenile seaweeds may influence community structure and algal distribution in a way that selectivity for the adult phases cannot do unless the grazing pressure is abnormally severe. Unfortunately, the microalgal film is virtually invisible and even its species composition is rarely investigated. However, the difficulties of working with the microalgal layer must not lead us to overlook its ecological importance.

With regard to interspecific competition, what becomes of the defeated competitors? Often they do not merely do badly, they vanish altogether (Fig. 2.5). Is their demise slow or sudden? Is it a direct result of being overgrown and overshadowed, or do such unsuccessful plants fall prey to grazers? We rarely know with any degree of certainty. A great deal has been learned of the ecological assets possessed by successful competitors from the study of invasive introduced species such as *Sargassum muticum* (Norton, 1976). The biological interest generated by such plants should not blind us to the dangers inherent in casual introductions. Until a species invades a new region, its potential effects are unpredictable. *S. muticum*, an unremarkable, 'well-behaved' plant in its native Japan, has proved to be the epitome of an aggressive weed in Britain. Accidental invasions may be regrettable, deliberate introductions are unforgivable. It was only in the face of vociferous opposition from phycologists that the scheme to cultivate the giant kelp *Macrocystis* off the Atlantic coast of France was shelved. The ecological repercussions of the presence of such enormous plants were likely to be immense and once the plants had reproduced in the sea, the experiment would have been completely out of control.

Some native species are also exploited commercially. One such is *Ascophyllum nodosum*, widely harvested for the alginate industry. If too severely cropped however, it appears to die back rather than regenerate. It also recolonizes the shore only with great difficulty (see Schonbeck and Norton, 1980b). Under normal circumstances the extreme longevity of the plants enables populations to persist in spite of a very low rate of recruitment. Therefore removal or destruction of the adult plants could jeopardize the existence of huge beds of *Ascophyllum* whose presence imposes long-term community stability on many sheltered shores.

Clearly, the future of our shore biota must not be dictated solely by commercial criteria. If, however, the ecologist's voice is to be heard, his opinions must be based on a profound understanding of shore ecology, an understanding that will be built on the foundations laid by J.R. Lewis.

CHAPTER III

ECOLOGICAL PATTERN IN THE EPIFAUNAL COMMUNITIES OF COASTAL MACROALGAE

R. Seed

3.1 Introduction

Rocky coasts in cool temperate waters, especially those at least partially sheltered from the direct impact of wave action, are frequently festooned with various species of large brown algae. Typically fucoids (Fucales) predominate in the littoral zone but at or around low water mark these generally give way to kelps (Laminariales) which extend sublittorally as far as light and suitable substratum allow. Such macroalgae, which include some of the fastest growing and most productive plants anywhere in the world (see Mann, 1982) provide a favourable and extensive habitat for a wide variety of epifaunal invertebrates.

The epifaunal communities associated with low littoral or shallow sublittoral macroalgae are dominated by numerous sessile suspension feeding groups such as bryozoans, hydroids, spirorbids, sponges and tunicates (e.g. Kitching and Ebling, 1967; Stebbing, 1973a; Boaden *et al.*, 1975; Seed and Harris, 1980; Seed and O'Connor, 1981a; Fletcher and Day, 1983). The relatively impoverished fauna associated with algae in the physically more rigorous conditions of the higher littoral zone, on the other hand, typically consists of mobile species that can migrate into the more humid recesses of the weed beds during periods of aerial emersion (e.g. Hazlett and Seed, 1976; Moore, 1977c; Dunstone *et al.*, 1979).

However, despite their widespread distribution and their obvious suitability for the study of spatial competition within a predominantly sessile community, algal epifaunas have been surprisingly neglected (see Hayward, 1980; Seed and O'Connor, 1981b for reviews). Their value is especially great as a contrast to the well-studied rock surface communities, firstly because different processes of patch creation and disturbance operate to provide different suites of constraints for competing organisms, secondly because predation – a major organizing force in rocky shore communities – is here generally less important, and thirdly because individual algae can be readily manipulated and transplanted thereby allowing experimental investigations of environmental perturbations on communities at or near equilibrium.

This Chapter provides an overview of our current understanding of how algal epifaunas are organized. Particular attention is focused on the importance of resource generation (through plant growth) as an alternative to the 'disturbance' and 'competitive network' paradigms of community structuring (e.g. Dayton, 1971; Buss and Jackson, 1979). The review is restricted primarily to the sessile macrofauna associated with the two-dimensional surfaces of algal fronds and does not treat of the extensive vagile faunas (see Hicks, this volume) or of the diverse infaunal communities that characterize certain algal holdfasts (see Moore, this volume).

3.2 Major Determinants of Ecological Pattern

3.2.1 Environmental factors

a) *Choice of physical environment.* In Strangford Lough, Northern Ireland, eight of the eleven most common species associated with the low littoral fucoid, *Fucus serratus* L., were most abundant at sites experiencing a high degree of water flow and turbulence but a low silt loading (Boaden *et al.*, 1975, 1976a; O'Connor *et al.*, 1979; Seed *et al.*, 1983). Fig. 3.1 shows the effects on three of the dominant members of this epifauna when *Fucus* plants were transferred from a relatively clean, fast-current area to one of sluggish water movement and high silt load. The two bryozoans *Flustrellidra hispida* (Fabricius) and *Alcyonidium hirsutum* (Fleming) increased in abundance on both the transferred and the control plants but this increase, especially in the case of *Flustrellidra*, was considerably greater at the cleaner more turbulent site. The hydroid *Dynamena pumila* (L.) flourished in its 'preferred' habitat but regressed rapidly (by almost 50%) on plants transferred to quiet silt-laden water. Similar

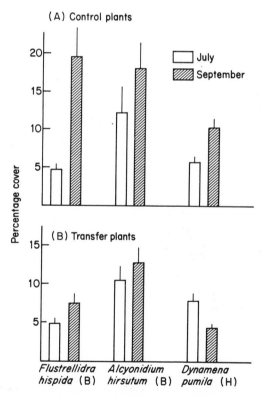

FIG. 3.1. The effects on three of the dominant members of the *Fucus serratus* epifauna when plants were transferred from a relatively clean fast current area to one of sluggish water movement and high silt load within Strangford Lough, Northern Ireland. Each point is based on 60 selected frond segments which were photographed at the beginning (July, 1979) and end (September, 1979) of the experimental period. B = bryozoan, H = hydroid. Vertical bars indicate ± 1 S.E. (after Elliott, 1982).

results have been obtained for *Sertularia operculata* (L.) in Lough Ine in southwest Ireland by Round *et al.* (1961) who concluded that the accumulation of sediment was probably responsible for the regression of this hydroid in more protected habitats within the lough. Fletcher and Day (1983) found that increased amounts of lashing by other plants and abrasion by sand particles were detrimental to the hydroids present on the fronds of the kelp *Ecklonia radiata* (C. Agardh) J. Agardh at Portsea in Australia.

Water movement and sedimentation are also clearly important factors with regard to larval dispersal and recruitment. Certain sessile invertebrates settle only within restricted current velocity gradients. In Strangford Lough relatively few *Spirorbis spirorbis* (= *borealis*) L. settled on *Fucus serratus* exposed to excessively turbulent conditions (Seed *et al.*, 1981) despite their prevalence on plants nearby. Marked reductions in the density of *Spirorbis*, especially amongst juveniles and recently settled spat, occurred on plants transferred from an area of sluggish water movement to an area of fast water flow and high turbulence; on control plants, however, the density of adults and spat actually increased over the experimental period (Fig. 3.2). Whether strong currents prevent settlement or dislodge recruits immediately following their attachment is not certain, though Doyle (1975) has demonstrated that turbulence can be a major source of post-settlement mortality in spirorbids. The susceptibility of larvae to clogging by silt appears to be important in limiting the spread of certain bryozoans. This could also explain the failure of *Flustrellidra* larvae to settle on silt-laden *Fucus serratus* (Seed *et al.*, 1981). On the other hand, certain species such as the bryozoans *Celleporella* (= *Hippothoa*) *hyalina* (L.) and *Tubulipora plumosa* Harmer (Kitching and Ebling, 1967), the tubeworm *Spirorbis spirorbis*

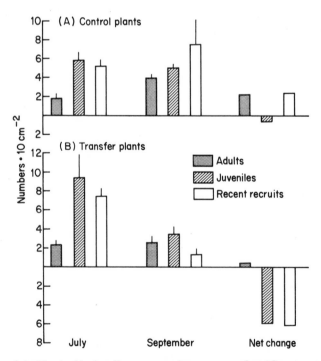

FIG. 3.2. The effects on *Spirorbis spirorbis* when *Fucus serratus* plants were transferred from an area of sluggish water movement to an area of fast current flow and high turbulence within Strangford Lough, Northern Ireland. Each point is based on 60 selected frond segments which were photographed at the beginning (July, 1979) and end (September, 1979) of the experimental period. Vertical bars indicate ± 1 S.E. (after Elliott, 1982).

(O'Connor and Lamont, 1978) and the tunicate *Didemnum maculosum* (Milne Edwards) (Boaden *et al.*, 1976a) are evidently more tolerant of sediment and are maximally abundant in quieter, more turbid conditions. These species include the relatively well-calcified members of the epifauna, sharing this with other bryozoans also regularly present in silt-laden habitats, notably *Electra pilosa* (L.), *Membranipora membranacea* (L.) and *Schizoporella unicornis* (Johnston). Such calcification could provide substantial protection against the abrasive and scouring effects of sediment particles. However, special adaptations are also required to withstand algal flexure caused by wave action. The tightly coiled shell structure of *Spirorbis* is such an adaptation (Daly, 1978), so too are the flexible zoecia of *Membranipora*. Other more rigidly calcified forms, e.g. *Schizoporella unicornis* (Hayward, 1980), will fracture or detach under wave surge. Consequently such species are normally confined to hard substrata and colonize only algal beds in the quietest waters.

Variations in the age-structure of algal populations from one physical environment to another may also be expected to play a significant rôle in determining the overall structure of epifaunal communities; longer-lived plants more typical of shores protected from wave surge may permit denser epifaunal assemblages.

b) *Choice of algal species.* Not all species of macroalgae are equally attractive to epifauna, owing largely to choice of substrata by larvae at the time of their settlement (see reviews by Scheltema, 1974; Crisp, 1976a; Ryland, 1976). Some species are relatively eurytopic, others highly specific in their choice of algae, though the precise choice may vary geographically. Interpopulation differences in substratum preferences have been reported for *Spirorbis*, with larvae exhibiting a marked preference for algal species supporting their parents (Knight-Jones *et al.*, 1975; MacKay and Doyle, 1978). In laboratory experiments the larvae of certain littoral bryozoans settled preferentially on precisely those algae on which they normally occurred on the shore (Ryland, 1959, 1962 and pers. obs.).

Habitat selection appears to be related to the chemical nature of the settlement surface since inert surfaces become more attractive to bryozoans, spirorbids and hydroids when filmed with specific algal extracts (Crisp and Williams, 1960; Williams, 1964; Nishihira, 1968). This ability of larvae to recognize different substrata could be important in speciation since it will effectively maintain species in reproductive isolation. Habitat selection is also modified by population pressure. In at least two species – *Spirorbis spirorbis* (O'Connor and Lamont, 1978) and *Alcyonidium hirsutum* (Wood, 1983) – growth and survival are negatively density-dependent. Consequently, the advantages of being in an optimal habitat may be offset by the greater crowding experienced there. This is true of within-plant distributions (O'Connor *et al.*, 1975) and also occurs in especially favourable habitats where certain epifaunal species will then colonize less-preferred algal species.

c) *Choice within plants.* Individual plants of *Fucus serratus* vary in length and the extent to which they branch. O'Connor *et al.* (1979) have shown that when the combination of these two factors is taken into account the major bryozoan species (except for *Membranipora*) are largely segregated (Fig. 3.3). Similarly the major epifaunas of the gulfweed *Sargassum natans* (L.) Meyen are effectively isolated from each other by their differential use of bladders, leaflets and stem regions of the plants they colonize (Ryland, 1974a).

Many epifaunal species settle preferentially in surface concavities such as those provided by midline grooves (Wisely, 1960), by depressions in crinkly fronded weeds (Eggleston, 1972) and by the channeled sides of algae such as *Pelvetia canaliculata* (L.) and *Mastocarpus* (= *Gigartina*) *stellatus* (Stackh.) Guiry (Ryland, 1976) where they presumably obtain some local protection against physical abrasion. The hydroid, *Clava squamata* (O.F. Müller), occurs mainly around the margins of air vesicles and in the axils of lateral branches of *Ascophyllum nodosum* (L.) and *Fucus vesiculosus* L. Settlement in the troughs that run along the blades of *Macrocystis pyrifera* (L.) Ag. effectively separates *Spirorbis spirillum* (L.) and *Lichenopora buskiana* Canu and Bassler from *Celleporella hyalina* which

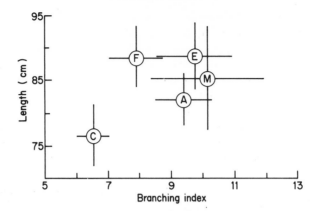

FIG. 3.3. Niche segregation of Bryozoa in relation to the length and branching index of *Fucus serratus* plants. Branching index measured as volume (ml) to length (cm) ratio. Vertical bars indicate ± 1 S.E. A = *Alcyonidium*; F = *Flustrellidra*; E = *Electra*; M = *Membranipora*; C = *Celleporella* (after O'Connor *et al.*, 1979).

occurs principally on the ridges (Bernstein and Jung, 1979). Species diversity was significantly greater on crinkled than on smooth plants of *Ecklonia* (Fletcher and Day, 1983).

The fronds of *Fucus serratus* are partially folded, giving recognizable concave and convex surfaces. Most species tend to occur on the concave surfaces, though some appear to favour the obverse surface (Boaden *et al.*, 1975). Some species are not only commoner on the concave surface but also achieve greater size there (Boaden *et al.*, 1976b; Wood and Seed, 1980; Seed and O'Connor, 1981b). While this apparent preference for concave surfaces partially reflects larval preferences at settlement, the possibility that established colonies may obtain some degree of local protection from the current or from the abrasive effects of adjacent fronds, or may benefit from local food-bearing eddies cannot be entirely dismissed. It is perhaps significant, therefore, that this effect is often most marked in taxa with erect growth habits – i.e. hydroids and sponges.

Organisms are not distributed at random along algal fronds but rather occur in relatively distinct zones. Thus on heavily encrusted *Fucus serratus* fronds tunicates and sponges are largely basally located, most bryozoans, hydroids and spirorbids occur further out on the central parts of the plants whilst *Electra* is predominantly distal in situation (Fig. 3.4). Similar zonation patterns among the epifaunas of *Sargassum* spp. and *Ecklonia* are described by Kato *et al.* (1961) and Fletcher and Day (1983) respectively. Such zones can be the outcome of responses to micro-environmental gradients along the plants, competitive interactions between the component species within the community or interactions between the epifauna and the host plant.

For an attached alga, the frond surface from holdfast to tip constitutes a micro-environmental gradient. Given specific gross environmental preferences the different members of the community must have different position optima on the plant. O'Connor *et al.* (1979) have reported a downward shift in the position of peak *Alcyonidium* abundance on *Fucus serratus* as site turbulence increases, presumably because the optimal turbulence regime was then lower down the plant. Similar physical gradients are also evidently important in the zoning of epifaunas along certain hydroids (Hughes, 1975) and foliose bryozoans (Stebbing, 1971). Desiccation risk during low tide emersion also varies with position within the plant. The zonation patterns of several species show corresponding variation when comparison is made between peripheral and central fronds of any one plant (O'Connor and Lamont, 1978) or between plants from different points on the littoral exposure gradient (Wood and Seed, 1980).

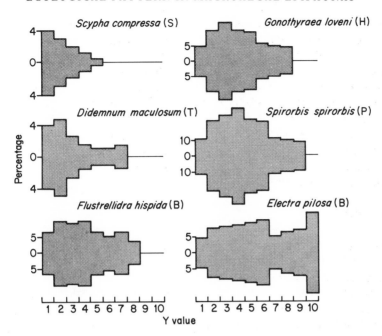

FIG. 3.4. Distribution of selected epifaunal species, measured as the percentage of available frond faces colonized, along the longest fronds of *Fucus serratus* from Strangford Lough, Northern Ireland. Y value is a measure of position along the fronds; Y_1 is the basal dichotomy of the plant and thus includes the holdfast. S = sponge; T = tunicate; B = bryozoan; H = hydroid; P = polychaete (after Seed and Boaden, 1977).

A number of bryozoans display marked orientation of growth, usually in the direction of the growing edge of the frond (Ryland, 1979). Such directional growth is of adaptive value especially for competitively weak species in that it maximizes their growth onto areas least likely to bear a superior competitor. It appears to result from a rheotropic response (Norton, 1973; Ryland, 1974b). Sensitivity to current flow, however, is probably not the universal basis of such oriented growth since *Membranipora* achieves settlement orientation on pelagic *Sargassum* fronds in the probable absence of consistent water flow over the fronds (Ryland, 1974a).

3.2.2 Reproductive factors

The sessile fauna associated with algal fronds may have solitary or colonial form. Colonial organisms occur in a variety of body forms but Jackson (1979) has shown that several basic morphologies tend to recur even amongst taxonomically unrelated groups. In algal epifaunas three colonial growth forms – sheets, runners and arborescent forms – are especially well represented. The limiting resource in epifaunal communities is usually two-dimensional living space and colonial forms are, on the whole, better able to utilize this resource than are solitary forms, partly because of their capacity for indeterminate growth and partly because of their capacity to resist overgrowth by competing species. Colonial species do resort to sexual reproduction to meet their needs for dispersal stages and for the maintenance of genetic variability but it is their asexual proliferation ability that largely underlies their great success in epifaunal communities.

Most sessile epibenthic invertebrates have a free-living larval stage at some time during their life cycles. Dispersal capacity is especially important for fugitive species dependent on reaching isolated and/or temporary habitat patches. The bryozoans *Electra* and *Membranipora* for example produce planktotrophic cyphonautes larvae. The general pattern for epifauna, however, is of relatively short-lived lecithotrophic larvae. The limited dispersal capabilities of these offspring, aided to some extent by the combination of well-developed larval selectivity and patchy environmental conditions, can lead to locally dense aggregations (e.g. Seed and O'Connor, in press).

Several of the commoner epifaunal groups must aggregate for successful breeding since self-fertilized embryos are generally non-viable or totally sterile. At the same time, however, the animals require room to grow and reach reproductive size. Spacing out has been adequately demonstrated in *Spirorbis* (Wisely, 1960; Harvey *et al.*, 1976). In this case spacing out behaviour is independent of habitat selection discussed earlier (see section on choice of plant species) but certain bryozoans have been shown to aggregate on algal fronds only in response to microhabitat features and not through spacing and gregarious behaviour (Ryland, 1976).

3.2.3 Interspecific factors

a) *Plant-animal interactions.* Epifaunal loads can potentially impose a selective cost on the host algae. Oswald *et al.* (1984) have recently shown that photosynthesis is significantly depressed in *Fucus serratus* fronds heavily fouled by fleshy encrusting bryozoans. Since this could influence plant growth and possibly also plant structure, and since photosynthesis is reduced differentially by different bryozoan species, it is perhaps worth recalling that the major bryozoans associated with *F. serratus* in Strangford Lough were largely segregated from each other when the combination of plant size and branching ratios were taken into account (Fig. 3.3). Fouling impairs growth rate and causes stunting in *Macrocystis pyrifera* (Woollacott and North, 1971). Fouled *Macrocystis* plants also suffer greater blade loss than clean plants (Dixon *et al.*, 1981) and are also more readily damaged by carnivorous fish which forage on the attached invertebrate fauna (Bernstein and Jung, 1979). *Membranipora* is known to inhibit sporulation in *Laminaria hyperborea* (Gunn) Foslie (Kain, 1975b).

Many algae, especially the large brown seaweeds, are known to release tannin-like substances which are both anti-bacterial and toxic, even at very low concentration, to the growth of certain components of the epifauna (Sieburth and Conover, 1965; Al-Ogily *et al.*, 1977). Hornsey and Hide (1976) showed that production of antibiotics is not uniform along the fronds; the precise pattern varies from one alga to another. Many algae also release large amounts of dissolved organic material and there is growing evidence that some sessile animals may benefit nutritionally by assimilating such exudates (de Burgh and Fankboner, 1979; Oswald, pers. comm.).

Many organisms settle onto or orientate their growth towards the younger regions of the algal fronds (e.g. Kato *et al.*, 1961; Stebbing, 1972; Ryland, 1979), a feature of obvious adaptive advantage in a space-limited system. The location of new plant tissue varies. In fucoids and other algae with apical meristems it develops distally. In laminarians, development is from an intercalary meristem between the stipe and the frond, and new tissue is added basally; on such algae, larval settlement is correspondingly basal (Fig. 3.5). Whilst the precise mechanism by which larvae identify the age gradients involved is uncertain, bacterial films (Cundell *et al.*, 1977; Mihn *et al.*, 1981; Brancato and Woollacott, 1982), physiological gradients (Kain, 1979; Dieckman, 1980; Oswald *et al.*, 1984) or gradients in anti-microbial compounds (Hornsey and Hide, 1976; Al-Ogily *et al.*, 1977) could all provide the necessary cues. Moreover, for some species orientation of growth is rheotropic (Norton, 1973) and thus not determined by reference to the age gradient at all.

As stated earlier, not all macroalgae are equally attractive to epifauna. Whilst this may largely be due to larval selectivity, Filion-Myklebust and Norton (1981) have recently suggested that regular shedding of the epidermis in some algae may serve as an effective antifouling mechanism.

b) *Predation.* Surprisingly little quantitative information is available as to the significance of

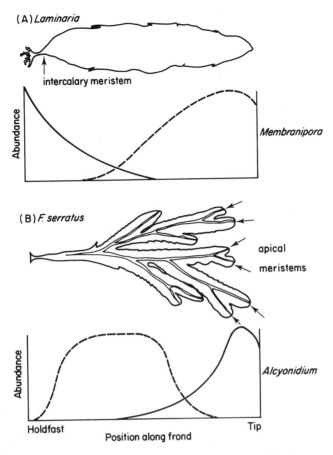

FIG. 3.5. The relative distribution of adult colonies (dashed lines) and recently established ancestrulae (solid lines) of two bryozoans. A, *Membranipora membranacea* on *Laminaria saccharina* and B, *Alcyonidium hirsutum* along the longest fronds of *Fucus serratus*.

predators in structuring algal epifaunas. In rocky littoral (Dayton, 1971; Connell, 1972; Paine, 1974; Menge and Sutherland, 1976) and in various sublittoral communities (Porter, 1974; Sutherland, 1974; Karlson, 1978; Russ, 1980) moderate levels of selective predation enhance species richness by reducing the abundance of competitively superior species. On macroalgae dominant species are extensively consumed by a variety of invertebrate predators and by fish. Fish are important predators of tunicates, sponges and bryozoans; eolid nudibranchs of hydroids and dorid nudibranchs and pycnogonids of bryozoans. Many of these predators are polyphagic but a few are closely associated with particular prey.

Structural diversity can reduce the impact of predation by refuge provision and/or reducing the foraging efficiency of predators (Rosenzweig and MacArthur, 1963) so it is perhaps of interest that the only recorded instances of major predatory impact within algal epifaunas have been on structurally simple kelps (e.g. Seed, 1976a; Bernstein and Jung, 1979; Yoshioka, 1982).

It was noted earlier that epifaunal communities tend to be dominated by colonial organisms. Amongst such forms predation is often restricted to parts of the colony, but rapid recovery through asexual proliferation from the survivors occurs. In addition, specialist defenses are commoner in colonial forms. Sutherland (1980) found that fish predation was of minor importance in community development on tropical mangrove roots where the community was dominated by sponges of high toxicity. Yoshioka (1982) notes that *Membranipora* colonies exposed to nudibranch predation develop spine-bearing zooids in defense. What the costs of developing such defenses may be is unknown but as the diversion of zooids from feeding or brooding functions to defense must reduce reproductive output of the short-lived (< 8 wk) colonies, they represent a hidden cost of predation.

c) *Competition*. Space is often the most important limiting resource in marine hard substratum environments and dominant space-holding species are potentially capable of monopolizing the entire resource. Several authors (see, for example, Paine, 1977) have emphasized that such dominance by one or relatively few species is generally prohibited either by physical disturbance or by selective predation yielding disproportionate mortality among the dominant competitors at the top of the hierarchy. On macroalgae a further process, plant growth, provides a third channel of escape from competitive dominance. Such growth is frequently exceedingly rapid and allows limited success to fugitive species within the algal epifauna, even where physical disturbance and predation may be negligible.

Segregation of habitat – achieved in response to the environmental factors already considered – can provide for the avoidance of competition. Moreover, recent evidence suggests that larvae of some marine invertebrates are able to detect members of competitively dominant species and avoid settling near them (e.g. Grosberg, 1981). Encrusting species differing in site or type of plant colonized clearly do not compete for the same space. However, isolating mechanisms are not infallible and species do come into direct competition in at least part of their range.

(i) *Overgrowth*. Interference competition between sessile marine invertebrates often takes the form of overgrowth or of suppression of one species by another, but pre-emption of settlement space also occurs. The use of allelochemicals in suppressing competition has been established for sponges (Green, 1977) and ascidians (Stoecker, 1980) and is a primary component in competitive network maintenance in cryptic reef systems (Jackson and Buss, 1975). In algal epifaunas, chemical defenses seem less important than overgrowth. On *Fucus serratus*, overgrowth is most intense in the crowded central zone of the fronds (e.g. O'Connor *et al.*, 1980; Wood and Seed, 1980). Several growth responses are possible when encrusting species meet. These include the redirection of growth, the formation of a new growing edge by frontal budding (such that the colony effectively overgrows itself), overgrowth of one colony by another (usually the thicker and fleshier of the two species), and the formation of special defensive barriers. Of the common epifaunal bryozoans in Britain, *Electra pilosa* is frequently overgrown by other species despite the presence of protective spines which are therefore often regarded as defenses against physical abrasion or buffeting by adjacent fronds. But, as noted by Stebbing (1973a), these spines are often localized in parts of the colony immediately threatened by overgrowth. O'Connor *et al.* (1980) found that overgrowth of *Electra* by other bryozoans was halted or reversed in 61% of the interactions examined. The ability to extend laterally is particularly valuable in inter-bryozoan competition and is the most frequent outcome. However, in competition with sponges and compound ascidians producing toxic allelochemicals, the group fares badly and generally succumbs to them (e.g. Green, 1977; Jackson, 1977; Stoecker, 1980).

Non-encrusting species have fewer options in meeting overgrowth competitors. Spirorbids have, however, been found to alter their growth plane in these circumstances, from the normal spiral track to one aligned away from the frond surface. In this way the animal can continue to feed successfully from an unobstructed tube opening. Hydroids may also alter their growth form when overgrown by encrusting species. In stoloniferous species, overgrown stolons appear to function but not to proliferate; further development occurs by vertical growth from the feeding zooids. Kato *et al.* (1967) showed that intraspecific overgrowth amongst hydroids could occur without any mutual disruption whereas interspecies contacts frequently suppress growth. The feeding behaviour of a canopy of arborescent hydroids may effectively reduce the intensification of competition by filtering out larvae that would otherwise attach to the surface below (Standing, 1976).

Amongst encrusting bryozoans the angle at which competing colonies are encountered has a significant influence on the outcome (Jackson, 1979). In addition, any deterioration in the surface condition of a colony – due, for instance, to prior fouling by other organisms – may greatly reduce competitive ability. The relative growth rates of competing species can also be expected to prove important. Overgrowth ability amongst the epifauna of *Fucus serratus* varies seasonally and with position along the fronds. For example, the relative competitive abilities of *Flustrellidra* and *Alcyonidium* are reversed as interactions further from the holdfast are considered, a reversal associated with the ability of *Alcyonidium* to adjust its distribution along the plant to the prevailing turbulence (O'Connor *et al.*, 1979).

Studies on temperate shores indicate that physical factors are more frequently limiting to hard substratum communities at high littoral levels whilst biological factors (competition and predation) are more important in the low littoral and shallow sublittoral zones (e.g. Seed, 1969b; Dayton, 1971; Connell, 1972; Paine, 1974). Similar variations exist within algal epifaunas. In the Menai Strait (Wales), *Fucus serratus* occupies a particularly wide range of shore levels corresponding to springtide emersions of from 2.7–7.2 hrs. Over this range the number of sessile taxa dropped from ten to three (Wood and Seed, 1980). In addition, most of these species decreased in abundance shorewards with consequential implications for competitive interactions. Desiccation and reduced feeding times are the obvious correlates of the trends reported, and these may have limited the shorewards expansion of species adapted primarily for sublittoral rather than littoral life.

(ii) *Spatial and temporal heterogeneity*. Structural heterogeneity on hard substrata significantly influences community composition (Menge and Sutherland, 1976), largely through effects on predation and competition. MacArthur and Wilson (1967) consider that structure principally mediates competitive coexistence via habitat specialization. In macroalgae this occurs in two ways. First, as already discussed, the floating (and/or collapsed) frond provides a micro-environmental gradient with respect to local turbulence or exposure, along which the various species perform differentially. Second, in a structure with multiple dichotomies such as a *Fucus serratus* plant, patch renewal by annual frond growth is related to the size and structure of the plant. According to Horn and MacArthur (1972) competitively inferior fugitive species can more easily persist as regular members of a community in conditions of high patch regeneration. In keeping with this expectation, *Membranipora* – competitively the least successful of the *Fucus serratus* bryozoans – occupies progressively larger and more branched plants in sites of higher bryozoan abundance. *Electra*, also competitively weak, similarly occupies more branched plants within the plant size class it shares with the dominant *Flustrellidra* (O'Connor *et al.*, 1979).

Temporal heterogeneity provides alternative channels of escape for competitively inferior species and, in the case of *Fucus serratus* epifaunas, combines with spatial patterning in allowing competitive coexistence of the two dominant bryozoans *Flustrellidra* and *Alcyonidium*. The crucial feature of the system is the annual growth of the plant. Plants grow rapidly from about March through October, thus generating pristine settlement space throughout the summer. *Flustrellidra* ancestrulae appear thereon in the spring and settle sequentially on the extending distal growth until late summer (Fig. 3.6). Commencement of plant growth results immediately in a broad band of developing *Flustrellidra* colonies. Larvae also settle freely elsewhere on the fronds, but the main pulse of recruitment is distal. Plants continue to grow rapidly for some time after *Flustrellidra* settlement has ceased. These areas of new and uncolonized fronds are heavily colonized by *Alcyonidium* larvae on their release in mid-winter (Fig. 3.6). This settlement, however, remains in a narrow non-growing band until spring when growth resumes. Further annual cycles of *Flustrellidra* and *Alcyonidium* recruitment thus result in alternating bands of these two bryozoans across the fronds. As *Alcyonidium* colonies develop each spring and

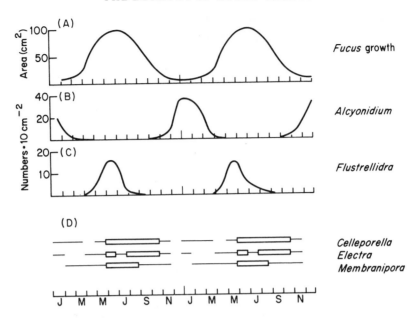

FIG. 3.6. A, Seasonal growth of *Fucus serratus* measured as net monthly addition of new distal frond tissue in 30–40cm long plants. Recruitment of the two dominant bryozoans, B, *Alcyonidium* and C, *Flustrellidra* on distal *Fucus* dichotomies. D, The extended recruitment of three opportunistic bryozoans on *F. serratus* (after Seed and O'Connor, 1981b).

summer, many come into mutual contact and develop vertical protrusions. Many of these subsequently become unstable and detach from the fronds generating patches of open space available for colonization by *Flustrellidra* (but not by *Alcyonidium* which only recruits onto distal, newly created frond tissue). Such sloughing-off has been recorded previously of carpets of solitary organisms in rocky shore communities (e.g. Seed, 1969b) and in fouling communities (e.g. Sutherland, 1978) and identified as an important source of patch renewal. Although undoubtedly a contributory factor in altering local community structure, such space creation in *Fucus serratus* is an order of magnitude less than that originating through plant growth.

Another component in the maintenance of bryozoan diversity in these communities is the time independence of *Electra*, *Membranipora* and *Celleporella* recruitment (Fig. 3.6). These species are competitively inferior to *Flustrellidra* and *Alcyonidium* (O'Connor *et al.*, 1980) and have refuges in sites unused by them (O'Connor *et al.*, 1979). They show low rates of settlement throughout the year and on *Fucus serratus* have wide zones of settlement. This allows them to settle into patches newly freed by *Alcyonidium* loss in winter. In addition, these calcareous species are generally more tolerant of environmental conditions, in particular of silt loading, than is *Flustrellidra* and in the more turbid waters of winter *Electra* wins more overgrowth contests with *Flustrellidra* that it does in summer. *Spirorbis* populations also benefit seasonally in this way and establish themselves successfully in these temporary patches of clear frond. Replacement of *Alcyonidium* is thus not inevitably by the dominant *Flustrellidra* and fugitive species can persist by virtue of their early arrival on unpredictably freed patches.

3.3 Community Organization – a Synthesis

Two major factors are important for community organization in algal epifaunas, (i) seasonal increase in the frond surface available for colonization, particularly the effects in relieving inter- and intraspecific competition, and (ii) larval selectivity in respect of acceptable environments.

Sessile marine benthic communities are broadly organized in one of three distinct manners, pertaining respectively to rocky littoral and shallow sublittoral communities (e.g. Dayton, 1971; Sebens, this volume), cryptic reef communities (e.g. Buss and Jackson, 1979), and macroalgal epifaunas (Seed and O'Connor, 1981b). On temperate rocky shores, community structure is largely determined by the interaction of both physical (e.g. desiccation, log damage) and biological (e.g. predation, herbivory) disturbance within the competitive repertoire of monopolist species. Diversity is enhanced because the tendency for any one dominant competitor to monopolize the available surface is repeatedly checked by moderate levels of disturbance, the patches thus created being exploited by competitively inferior species that might not otherwise persist in the system (see Paine and Levin, 1981, for patch dynamics). Several striking differences in community structure between temperate and tropical rocky shores have recently been documented by Menge and Lubchenco (1981). In Panama, for example, holes and crevices in the rock surface appeared to provide the only effective refuge from continuously high levels of predation and herbivory and were thus identified as being especially important in maintaining species diversity within these tropical communities. In cryptic reef communities, rather stable environments and minimal predation have resulted in intensely competitive situations organized as networks rather than hierarchies, introducing a degree of stabilizing negative feedback as the population of any one species waxes and wanes (Buss and Jackson, 1979). A diverse community therefore persists, despite the absence of space-creating disturbance. Although the prevalence of competitive networks within coral head communities has recently been disputed (e.g. Quinn, 1982; Russ, 1982), the intransitive pattern of interspecific overgrowth probably does enhance the ability of competitors to coexist. In algal epifaunas, diversity is kept high because algal growth constantly renews the limiting resource of frond surface, and competitively inferior species can repeatedly renew their populations as the older populations are lost in competition with more dominant species. Most algae with diverse epifaunas live in rather benign environments. Their faunas vary seasonally (e.g. Seed *et al.*, 1981) and with gross environment (see section on environmental factors, above). Moreover, at no time has it been necessary to postulate the existence of one or more 'keystone' species (*sensu* Paine, 1969a) whose presence or absence alters the community structure. Disturbance (in a broad sense) is undoubtedly present, as established dominants are lost by sloughing-off or through winter mortality, and the patches thus created are indeed exploited by opportunistic species; but such patches are an order of magnitude smaller than those originating in plant growth.

These three channels of organization – disturbance, competitive networks, and resource generation – are not peculiar to the paradigms above; Woodin and Jackson (1979), for example, have analysed soft sediment communities as parallels to cryptic reef systems. Each basis for community organization is distinctive, though certain features are held in common. Specific differences in the timing of settlement on frond surfaces in relation both to frond growth and to smaller scale disturbance patches were important in algal epifaunas and are also recognized as significant for rock community development (e.g. Osman, 1977). Disturbance is dominant in most rocky shore systems but appears to be only of minor importance in cryptic reef systems and in algal epifaunas (but see Fletcher and Day, 1983). Competitive chains are unidirectional and open – as linear hierarchies – in rocky shore systems and unidirectional and closed – as competitive networks – in cryptic reef systems, but in algal epifaunas directional strengths vary and create features of both hierarchies and networks (Fig. 3.7). Finally, while space creation in cryptic reef systems is on a small scale and unpredictable, it occurs on a large but unpredictable scale on rocky shores and on a large and predictable scale (through seasonal plant growth) in algal epifaunas.

The large scale provision of space through plant growth enables an unusually large number of fugitive species to become established in algal epifaunas despite the potentially high levels of spatial

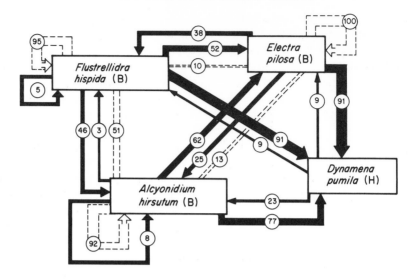

FIG. 3.7. Dominant trends in inter- and intra-specific competition among a subset of the major epifaunal species associated with *Fucus serratus* in the Menai Strait, North Wales. Each value represents the percentage of the total number of interactions involving the species connected by the lines. Dashed lines: colonies met with no overgrowth; solid lines: overgrowth occurred in the direction indicated. B = bryozoan; H = hydroid (after Wood and Seed, 1980).

competition present within these communities. This is emphasized by the abundance of such species on kelps. Whilst *Ascophyllum* plants may live for 12–15 years and *Fucus* spp. and *Pelvetia* for 3–5 years (Chapman, 1974), kelps regenerate their blades as often as five times each year (Mann, 1973). The short life span of kelp blades restricts the range of species able to colonize them successfully; species must have short life cycles and high growth rates in order to establish breeding populations – they must thus be opportunistic and/or have specialized life cycles closely synchronized with that of their host (e.g. Eggleston, 1972; Bernstein and Jung, 1979; Cancino, 1983). By contrast, the perennial fronds of fucoids (also kelp holdfasts and stipes) are available for colonization by longer-lived species with annual life cycles and no specialized integration of the life cycle with that of the host plant is required.

The relationship between macroalgae and their epifaunas is clearly very intimate: epifaunas are adapted in order to exploit the alga as a substratum but there are also effects and responses by the algae themselves. It seems likely, therefore, that over evolutionary time such relationships will have become increasingly complex and that varying degrees of inter-dependence will almost inevitably have occurred. Only recently have we begun to understand these complex interrelationships between epifaunas and their living hosts and much work still remains, therefore, to be undertaken in this fascinating field of coastal ecology.

ACKNOWLEDGEMENTS

This Chapter is largely the outcome of a research project which was initiated by Dr P.J.S. Boaden, Dr R.J. O'Connor and myself whilst we were all staff members at The Queen's University, Belfast. Much of that research project is already published under joint authorship (see References). Valuable contributions by Victoria Wood and Robert C. Oswald (postgraduate students), Michael N. Elliott (research assistant) and a host of undergraduate students both at The Queen's University, Belfast, and at the University College of North Wales, Bangor, are gratefully acknowledged. This research has been partially supported by a grant from the Natural Environment Research Council.

CHAPTER IV

MEIOFAUNA ASSOCIATED WITH ROCKY SHORE ALGAE

G.R.F. Hicks

4.1 Introduction

Macroalgae are not only conspicuous elements of rocky shore communities, but they also provide an important habitat for assemblages of small invertebrates. Many of these organisms, particularly macrofaunal taxa such as peracarid crustaceans, polychaete worms and gastropod molluscs, are well known and frequently studied because of their abundance and 'convenient' size. Yet of more importance in terms of both abundance and diversity are the smaller representatives of this assemblage, the *meiofauna* (= meiobenthos). They are loosely defined as those small, mobile benthic metazoans capable of passing through a 2mm mesh sieve but which are retained on a sieve with a mesh smaller than 0.1mm. This size designation separates them from the larger macrofauna and the smaller microbiotic organisms such as bacteria, microalgae and Protozoa. Larval and juvenile macrofauna often fall within this size category and are termed 'temporary' meiofauna, but for the purposes of this Chapter only the 'permanent' members will be considered. Almost all the known metazoan groups are represented in the permanent meiobenthos and they have attracted considerable attention particularly as part of investigations of sedimentary habitats. Perhaps surprisingly though, less is known of those associated with rocky shore seaweeds, a realm frequently referred to as the *phytal*. Depending upon locality, permanent members of the phytal meiobenthos include representatives from the Nematoda, Copepoda, Ostracoda, Acarina, Turbellaria, Oligochaeta, Rotifera, Tardigrada, Archiannelida, Kinorhyncha and Gnathostomulida. Of these, the first four taxa together constitute nearly the entire assemblage (commonly > 98%). As such, these groups have been the most seriously investigated ones from rocky shore macroalgal environments. Less frequently encountered taxa (e.g. Kinorhyncha, Moore, 1973d; Gnathostomulida, R.A. Farris, unpubl.) are little known ecologically.

Research on phytal meiofauna had its roots primarily in taxonomic studies in the Bay of Kiel by the now generally acclaimed pioneer of meiobenthic research, Adolf Remane (see Remane, 1933, 1940), and his associates (e.g. Schulz, Gerlach, Klie, Schäfer, Noodt, etc.). Two of the earliest independent reports were by Fraser (1936) on copepods 'which lurked amongst the weeds' of Manx rockpools, and by Otto (1936) whose qualitative account of the meiofauna associated with *Enteromorpha* in the Bay of Kiel set the scene for the broadly descriptive ecological investigations which gained periodic impetus over the following two decades (e.g. Colman, 1940; Dahl, 1948; Wieser *inter alia*, 1951a, 1952; Chapman, 1955). Much the same approach has continued to date, although with increasing degrees of theoretical, experimental and analytical sophistication (e.g. Hagerman, 1966; Jansson, 1967; Ganning, 1971a; Moore, 1971, 1973b, 1974; Pallares and Hall, 1974a,b; Bartsch, 1979; Beckley and McLachlan, 1980). Today, the phytal meiofauna is being used to test a number of ecologically relevant hypotheses utilizing both correlative and *in situ* manipulative techniques (Hicks, 1980, 1982; Choat and Kingett, 1982; Gunnill, 1982a,b, 1983; Coull and Wells, 1983). Because of their diversity, abundance and accessibility for study, phytal invertebrates – and the meiofauna in particular – continue to offer unparalleled opportunities for the examination and appraisal of many of the concepts current in functional morphology and ecology. For this reason it is appropriate to survey the status of phytal meiofaunal research.

This contribution does not pretend to be exhaustive; rather the intention is to highlight areas of phytal meiofaunal ecology which are seminal in their own right or which have contributed significantly to trends in research direction. The scope of this Chapter is largely restricted to the rocky shore marine environment and coverage does not include literature on the seagrasses typical of estuarine environments. Where relevant, however, literature dealing with meiofauna associated with brackish water macroalgae (usually in the Baltic Sea) has been included.

4.2 Community Structure, Adaptations and Dynamics

4.2.1 Abundance compared to level-bottom sediments

Meiofauna represent the most abundant metazoans in marine sediments, extending from the high littoral zone to abyssal depths. World-wide average meiofaunal densities are in the order of 10^6 individuals$\cdot$m^{-2} with the highest known densities of $25 \times 10^6\cdot$m^{-2} on muddy bottoms (Vernberg and Coull, 1981). On rocky shores, meiofaunal animals occur predominantly as associates of marine algae, but they are also conspicuous members of other rocky shore micro-environments where sediment may accumulate e.g. mussel clumps, crevices, beneath boulders and inside vacant barnacle tests. They are sometimes found as facultative associates of littoral macrofauna including bryozoan and hydroid mats and polychaete reefs and have even been recorded inside the mantle cavity of grazing gastropods (Branch, 1974c).

On macroalgae, meiofauna characteristically occupy three primary sub-habitats: (i) within the interstices of complex ramifying holdfasts (e.g. Moore, 1971, 1973b); (ii) associated with inorganic sediment and detritus accumulated at the bases of fronds (e.g. Hicks, 1977b); (iii) on the surfaces of the fronds themselves (e.g. Hagerman, 1966; Pallares and Hall, 1974a,b). Each of these spatially discrete sub-habitats may be occupied by a different suite of species (Ott, 1967; Hicks, 1977c). Moreover, any one of these zones may be further subdivided by differently aged components of the population (Ott, 1967). Meiofaunal abundance partitioned within each of these sub-habitats has never been assessed in detail, but total densities (usually covering all 3 of these zones) are equivalent to those found on particulate shores, especially sandy substrata (see Tables 1 and 2 in McIntyre, 1969; Table 6 in Hicks, 1977b). Abundance estimates vary with different sampling and analytical techniques, but in those studies where numbers of animals are expressed per m^{-2} of algal-covered rock surface, total invertebrate densities associated with rocky shore algae may reach 4×10^6 (Wieser, 1959), of which about 85% is contributed by typically meiofaunal taxa (e.g. Beckley, 1982). Certain dominant meiofaunal groups may alone, however, contribute very high values. Jensen (1984) reported up to 5×10^6 nematodes$\cdot$m^{-2} associated with the *Cladophora – Pilayella* belt in the outer archipelago of Finland, equivalent to a biomass of 1.2g org.C$\cdot$m^{-2} (based on an organic carbon estimate of 12% of wet weight – see Jensen, 1984). Such impressive abundance is not generally found in fully marine situations where total meiofaunal densities on algae, although highly variable, range typically from 1.0×10^4 to $3.1 \times 10^6\cdot$m^{-2} (Colman, 1940; Chapman, 1955; Sarma and Ganapati, 1972; Kito, 1975, 1982; Hicks, 1977b,c). Highest densities are usually attained on algae with a complex surface morphology amongst which is also deposited medium grade sediment and detritus. Conversely, lowest densities tend to be found on exposed shore algae of reduced physiognomic structure, though deviations from such a direct algal morphology–individual species abundance relationship are common (Hicks, 1980). Lack of any strong correlation between these two variables is often the result of a single species attaining high relative densities on simple, flattened algal blades to which they may be particularly well adapted.

Phytal meiofaunal biomass varies greatly, but one study (Beckley and McLachlan, 1980) puts it at less than 10% of phytal macrofaunal biomass, a value somewhat lower than the 30–50% range considered as general for sediment meiobenthos (Platt and Warwick, 1980).

4.2.2 Species composition

Species composition of meiofauna associated with algae containing low levels of deposited sediments is usually quite distinct from often closely adjacent sedimentary habitats. As such, phytal assemblages constitute a discrete biocoenosis commonly with a specific faunal composition and regularly predictable dominant forms. The dominant and most ubiquitous meiofaunal taxa on algae, as in sediments, are harpacticoid copepods and nematodes (e.g. Colman, 1940; Dahl, 1948; Wieser, 1952; Kito,

TABLE 4.1

Dominant phytal meiofaunal taxa in relation to the accumulation of fine deposits
(modified from Hicks and Coull, 1983).

Location	Alga	Silt/clay or detrital load	Dominant taxa	Reference
U.K.	Various littoral algae	Low High	Copepods, ostracods Amphipods, nematodes	Colman, 1940
U.K.	Various algae	Low High	Crustaceans Nematodes	Wieser, 1952
Germany	*Fucus*, by dredging	?	Nematodes in summer, copepods in winter	Ohm, 1964
Denmark	*Fucus*	Low	Ostracods, copepods	Hagerman, 1966
Japan	*Sargassum*	Low	Copepods	Mukai, 1971
Japan	*Sargassum*	Low	Copepods	Kito, 1975
U.K.	Kelp holdfasts	High	Nematodes	Moore, 1973b
Sweden (Baltic)	*Cladophora*	?	Rotifers	Jansson, 1974
Sweden (Baltic)	Red algae (3 spp.)	Low	Ostracods, copepods	Kautsky, 1974
New Zealand	*Corallina*	Low	Copepods	Hicks, 1977b
Sweden (Baltic)	Macrophytic epiphytes on *Fucus*	High	Nematodes	Kangas, 1978
South Africa	Algae (9 spp.)	Low?	Copepods	Beckley and McLachlan, 1980
New Zealand	*Corallina, Champia*	Low	Copepods	Coull and Wells, 1983
South Carolina (U.S.A.)	Algae (4 spp.)	Low	Copepods	Coull et al., 1983

1975; Beckley and McLachlan, 1980; Coull *et al.*, 1983). Occasionally, however, ostracods and halacarid mites may predominate (Ohm, 1964; Hagerman, 1966; Mukai, 1971; Bartsch, 1979), in contrast to their generally low representation on inorganic substrata. Under reduced silt-clay or detrital loads, harpacticoids usually dominate algal meiofaunas. Should deposited material increase, either in more sheltered conditions or in species of algae whose morphology enhances silt accumulation, then nematodes dominate the assemblage (Table 4.1).

It is now well established that certain families and genera of meiofaunal organisms occur both frequently and in high enough numbers to constitute 'typical' phytal assemblages. The most characteristic of these are presented in Table 4.2, which shows that the same genera repeatedly dominate algae from widely separated coastlines in both northern and southern hemispheres. Typical nematode genera from fully marine algal frond systems are *Enoplus*, *Oncholaimus*, *Anticoma*, *Chromadora*, with the genus *Thoracostoma* more abundant in kelp holdfasts (Moore, 1971). In low salinity waters Jensen (1984) selected 11 genera as distinctive of a nematode community in the brackish waters of the Baltic and N. Europe. Representative harpacticoid copepod genera from fully marine algal fronds are *Harpacticus*, *Tisbe*, *Dactylopodia*, *Parathalestris*, *Porcellidium* and *Scutellidium* with genera in the Laophontidae assuming greater importance in holdfasts (Dahl, 1948; Moore, 1973b). In northern cool temperate regions the Harpacticidae is clearly the distinguishing family of copepods on thalloid straps of brown algae (e.g. Colman, 1940; Noodt, 1957; Hicks, 1980), while in southern cool temperate seas the Porcellidiidae (*Porcellidium*) and Tisbidae (*Scutellidium*) displace harpacticids as more familiar forms (Pallares and Hall, 1974a,b; Hicks, 1977c). In the tropics, *Porcellidium* regularly dominates on green algae (Sarma, 1974; Sarma and Ganapati, 1975). Rhombognathine mites and the ostracod genera *Xestoleberis* and *Loxoconcha* (Athersuch, 1979; Bartsch, 1979 – see Table 4.2) complete this inventory of generalized components of a typical phytal meiobenthic assemblage. Within this hypothetical grouping, however, dominant species are determined not only by the seaweed species occupied, but also by the influence of a number of spatio-temporally fluctuating variables including degree of wave exposure, structure and biochemical composition of the algal surface, growth and decay cycles of the plant, and sediment load. Despite the imposition of such variability, one feature is prominent – the frequency with which certain genera occupy certain habitat types and the globally repetitive nature of this phenomenon (Table 4.2).

TABLE 4.2

Most abundant phytal meiofaunal genera and, where data are available, the total number of species represented on specified algae. Note that sample number for species counts is not constant.

Genus	Alga	Location	Total number of species	Reference
COPEPODA				
Tisbe, Harpacticus, Dactylopodia, Paradactylopodia	Various	Isle of Man, U.K.		Fraser, 1936
Nitocra	*Enteromorpha*	Kiel Bay, Germany	8	Otto, 1936
Tisbe, Nitocra, Parathalestris, Diarthrodes	*Fucus*	Plymouth, England	20	Colman, 1940

TABLE 4.2 *Cont'd*

Genus	Alga	Location	Total number of species	Reference
Diarthrodes, Tisbe	*Ascophyllum*	Plymouth, England	28	Colman, 1940
Parastenhelia	Various	Gullmar Fjord, Sweden		Dahl, 1948
Dactylopodia, Tisbe, Parathalestris, Ameira	*Mastocarpus* (= *Gigartina*)	Plymouth, England	16	Wieser, 1952
Parastenhelia, Harpacticus	*Corallina*	Azores		Chapman, 1955
Harpacticus, Mesochra, Nitocra	Various	Denmark, Germany		Noodt, 1957
Tisbe, Scutellidium, Eupelte, Porcellidium, Harpacticus, Diarthrodes, Dactylopodia	Various	Aegean area, Mediterranean		Wieser, 1959
Harpacticus	*Fucus*	Kiel Bay, Germany	21	Ohm, 1964
Zaus	*Fucus*	Øresund, Denmark	19	Hagerman, 1966
Nitocra, Mesochra	*Fucus*	Tvärminne, Finland	7	Noodt, 1970
Nitocra	*Enteromorpha*	Askö, Sweden		Ganning, 1971a
Ameira, Dactylopodia, Heterolaophonte, Mesochra	Various	Black Sea Coast, Rumania		Marcus, 1973
Dactylopodia, Tisbe	*Laminaria* holdfasts	Beadnell, England	49	Moore, 1973b
Porcellidium, Scutellidium, Tisbe, Parathalestris, Harpacticus	*Macrocystis*	Ria Deseado, Argentina	61	Pallares and Hall, 1974a,b
Porcellidium, Harpacticus, Parastenhelia, Diosaccus, Amphiascopsis, Longipedia	*Caulerpa*	Visakhapatnam, India	21	Sarma, 1974
Dactylopodia, Harpacticus	*Sargassum*	Hokkaido, Japan	50	Kito, 1975, 1977
Porcellidium, Laophonte	*Ulva*	Visakhapatnam, India		Sarma and Ganapati, 1975
Tisbe, Paralaophonte, Porcellidium, Scutellidium, Neopeltopsis	Various	Cook St, New Zealand	22–59	Hicks, 1977c
Nitocra, Mesochra	Various	Rockall, N. Atlantic		Moore, 1977b

TABLE 4.2 *Cont'd*

Genus	Alga	Location	Total number of species	Reference
Zaus, Harpacticus, Dactylopodia, Parathalestris	Various	N.E. Coast, England and Scotland	6–39	Hicks, 1980
Orthopsyllus, Parastenhelia, Phyllopodopsyllus	Gelidium	Algoa Bay, S. Africa		Beckley, 1982
Scutellidium, Harpacticus, Porcellidium	Pelvetia	California, U.S.A.		Gunnill, 1982b
Harpacticus	Various	S. Carolina, U.S.A.	3–9	Coull et al., 1983
NEMATODA Monhystera, Chromadora, Chromadorita, Enoplus, Oncholaimus	Enteromorpha	Kiel Bay, Germany	37	Otto, 1936
Anticoma, Oncholaimus, Enoplus	Ascophyllum	Plymouth, England		Colman, 1940
Enoplus	Various	Plymouth, England		Wieser, 1952
Chromadora, Chromadorina, Enoplus, Monoposthia, Syringolaimus	Various	Rovinj, Yugoslavia		Wieser, 1959
Chromadora, Cyatholaimus, Monhystera, Chromadorella	Various	Piraeus, Greece		Wieser, 1959
Monhystera, Prochromadorella, Enoplus	Fucus	Kiel Bay, Germany	31	Ohm, 1964
Enoplus, Euchromadora, Chromadorina	Cystoseira	Rovinj, Yugoslavia	32	Ott, 1967
Enoplus, Anticoma	Laminaria holdfasts	N.E. Coast, England and Scotland	23	Moore, 1971, 1973b
Chromadorina, Monhystera, Araeolaimus	Various	Rockall, N. Atlantic		Moore, 1977b
Oncholaimus, Enoplus	Various	Scilly Is.		Warwick, 1977
Monhystera, Chromadora	Sargassum	Hokkaido, Japan	49	Kito, 1982
Monhystera, Prochromadorella	Macrocystis	Vancouver Island, Canada	9	Trotter and Webster, 1983

TABLE 4.2   *Cont'd*

Genus	Alga	Location	Total number of species	Reference
Chromadora, Oncholaimus, Enoplus	Various	S. Carolina, U.S.A.	1–16	Coull *et al.*, 1983
Chromadorita, Monhystera	Various	Tvärminne, Finland		Jensen, 1984
OSTRACODA				
Loxoconcha, Xestoleberis, Cytherura, Cytheromorpha	*Enteromorpha*	Kiel Bay, Germany	5	Otto, 1936
Xestoleberis	*Ascophyllum*	Plymouth, England		Colman, 1940
Cythere, Cytherura	*Fucus*	Kiel Bay, Germany	8	Ohm, 1964
Cytherura	*Fucus*	Øresund, Denmark	17	Hagerman, 1966
Paradoxostoma, Xestoleberis, Semicytherura, Elofsonella	*Corallina*	Fanafjord, Norway	14	Hagerman, 1968
Heterocypris	*Enteromorpha*	Askö, Sweden		Ganning, 1971a
Loxoconcha, Quadracythere	*Corallina*	Cook St, New Zealand		Hicks, 1971
Cythere	*Laminaria* holdfasts	Spittal, England	8	Moore, 1973b
Paradoxostoma, Xestoleberis, Semicytherura, Elofsonella	Various	Cardigan Bay, Wales	6–12	Whatley and Wall, 1975
Xestoleberis, Loxoconcha, Paradoxostoma, Aurila	*Cystoseira, Jania* and encrusting spp.	Cyprus		Athersuch, 1979
Loxoconcha, Xestoleberis	*Corallina*	Northland, New Zealand	9	Hayward, 1981
Cytheridea, Xestoleberis	*Gelidium*	Algoa Bay, S. Africa		Beckley, 1982
HALACARIDA				
Hyadesia, Rhombognathus	*Enteromorpha*	Kiel Bay, Germany	8	Otto, 1936
Rhombognathus	*Lichina* (lichen)	Plymouth, England	3	Colman, 1940
Rhombognathides, Halacarellus	*Fucus*	Kiel Bay, Germany	8	Ohm, 1964
Rhombognathus	*Fucus*	Øresund, Denmark	5	Hagerman, 1966
Hyadesia, Rhombognathides	*Enteromorpha*	Askö, Sweden		Ganning, 1971a
Rhombognathus	*Laminaria* holdfasts	Spittal, England	5	Moore, 1973b

TABLE 4.2 *Cont'd*

Genus	Alga	Location	Total number of species	Reference
Rhombognathides, Halacarellus	*Cladophora*	Askö, Sweden		Jansson, 1974
Rhombognathus, Hyadesia	Various	Rockall, N. Atlantic		Moore, 1977b
Isobactrus, Rhombognathus	*Enteromorpha*	Brittany, France	10	Bartsch, 1979
Rhombognathides, Metarhombognathus, Halacarellus	*Fucus, Pelvetia, Catenella*	Brittany, France	1–5	Bartsch, 1979
Metarhombognathus	*Enteromorpha*	Various, U.S.A.	7	Bartsch, 1982
Metarhombognathus, Isobactrus	*Fucus*	Various, U.S.A.	9	Bartsch, 1982
Rhombognathides	*Ascophyllum*	Various, U.S.A.	8	Bartsch, 1982
Hyadesia	*Gelidium*	Algoa Bay, S. Africa		Beckley, 1982

The concept of parallelism or 'isocommunities' (*sensu* Thorson, 1957) wherein often widely separated yet similar substrata are inhabited by the same dominant genera, but with species changing from place to place, is supported by studies on phytal meiofauna. Comparing kelp holdfast nematode species composition from the sublittoral North Sea coast of Britain (*Laminaria hyperborea* (Gunn.) Fosl.), and the littoral of Chile (mostly *Durvillea*), Moore (1971) found that the Enoploidea contributed about 80% of the fauna in both systems. *Enoplus communis* Bastian dominated in the North Sea (43.9%), while in Chile *E. michaelseni* Linstow was most abundant (20.2%). The genera *Anticoma*, *Thoracostoma*, *Phanoderma* and *Camacolaimus* all had representative species in both localities. There is also a high taxo-ecologic similarity between harpacticoid copepods inhabiting brown algae in Cook Strait, New Zealand and the Ria Deseado, Argentina (Hicks, 1977c); the significant pan-Atlantic representation of halacarid mite genera from comparable biotopes (Bartsch, 1982) is similarly in agreement with the concept of parallelism.

Apart from being amongst the most abundant meiofaunal organisms, harpacticoid copepods are also the most speciose. In southern cool temperate regions, up to about 60 species have been recorded during annual sampling regimes from a single algal species (Table 4.2), while nearly 50 species of nematode have been found on attached *Sargassum confusum* Agardh from Japan (Kito, 1982); ostracods and mites on the other hand are represented by fewer species in phytal habitats (Table 4.2). Factors which influence the species richness and relative abundance of phytal meiofauna are considered in the following sections and relate principally to the morphological structure or architecture of the alga itself.

4.2.3 Morphological specializations

Some of the morphological specializations enabling phytal meiofauna to occupy algae successfully and attain considerable densities, often in very turbulent regions, have evolved in response to the physiognomic structure of their habitat. Any apparent substratum 'preference' of phytal meiofauna can be viewed as the outcome of a reinforcement of optimal feeding requirements and morphological adaptation to that particular algal substratum. Body size, setation, cuticular structures and visual function are related to substratum in nematodes (Wieser, 1953b, 1959; Ott, 1967; Moore, 1971; Warwick, 1977; Kito, 1982), and harpacticoids also show special mechanisms facilitating purchase on algae. These can be broadly divided into three categories: (i) suction mechanisms, (ii) clinging appendages, (iii) mucus adhesion.

The families Tisbidae, Porcellidiidae, Peltidiidae and certain genera in the Harpacticidae (e.g. *Zaus*, *Zausopsis*) and Thalestridae (*Idomene*, *Amenophia*) are variously dorso-ventrally flattened as an adaptation to strong water flow over flat thalloid algal surfaces: their characteristic habitat (Dahl, 1948; Noodt, 1971). An extreme example is seen in *Porcellidium* (Fig. 4.1A). Moreover, adhesion to flat algal surfaces is maintained by a 'suction cup' disposition of various mouthpart appendages. This suction apparatus incorporates mandibular palps, maxillules, maxillae, maxillipeds and the first pair of thoracic legs (Fig. 4.1B). By contraction of strong dorso-ventral body muscles (see Tiemann, 1975), the oral assembly is flattened ventro-laterally, functioning in a somewhat analogous way to the tentacle suckers of cephalopod molluscs. Nauplius larvae of *Scutellidium* (Tisbidae) also possess a discrete ventral sucker which may be used for substratum attachment (see Branch, 1974c).

Different morphological structures have evolved in copepods inhabiting shrubbier, more divaricated algae. Usually, these involve modifications of the maxillipeds and first pair of legs, and are best seen in the Harpacticidae, Thalestridae, Diosaccidae, Laophontidae, Tegastidae, Peltidiidae and

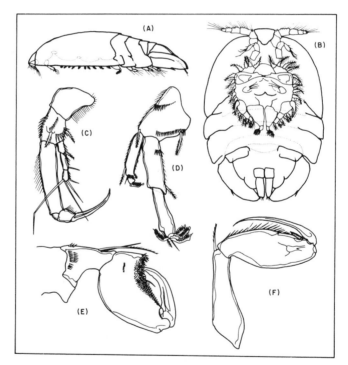

Fig. 4.1. Some morphological specializations in harpacticoid copepods enabling secure contact with seaweeds; A, lateral view of a species of *Porcellidium* showing streamlined body condition (× 50); B, Ventral view of *Porcellidium* showing 'suction disc' arrangement of mouthparts, posterior swimming legs omitted (× 50); C, Right side first swimming leg of *Heterolaophonte longisetigera* Klie, showing pronounced claw on terminal segment of endopod (× 275); D, Right side first swimming leg of *Zaus spinatus spinatus* Goodsir, showing claws and development of exopod (× 210); E, Right side maxilliped of *Thalestris longimana* Claus, showing apposition of strong claw and spinulose palm (× 210); F, Right side maxilliped of *Parategastes sphaericus* (Claus), showing lanceolate condition of claw (× 450).

Parastenheliidae. Powerful excavate and strongly prehensile maxillipeds (Fig. 4.1E) are commonly used to seize algal filaments and other fine micro-habitat structures (Hicks, 1980). In other instances (e.g. some tegastids and peltidiids) lanceolate prehensile maxillipeds (Fig. 4.1F) are used not only to straddle clusters of attached colonial diatoms, but also to grasp surface-borne sheets and strands of algal derived mucilage (pers. obs.). Strong claws which often oppose stout spines or cushions of spinules on the proximo-lateral edge of the palm (Fig. 4.1E) ensure a very secure grasp. The first pair of swimming legs are often used efficiently as grappling hooks to maintain contact with seaweeds. The endopods of the first pair of legs in laophontids are often massively built with a single, large curved terminal claw (Fig. 4.1C) used to embrace foliose vegetation and skeletal elements of sessile inverte- brate associates (e.g. Bryozoa and hydroids). In some families (e.g. Harpacticidae), the exopod of the first leg is more developed than the endopod (Fig. 4.1D), bearing an effective set of claws and spines, but in others (e.g. Thalestridae), the exopods and endopods are often equally well developed and prehensile.

Currently two families are suspected of using self-elaborated mucopolysaccharides to 'glue' them- selves to algae. The thalestrid genus *Diarthrodes* contains species capable of secreting large amounts of encapsulating mucus with which they may attach themselves to algae (Fahrenbach, 1962; Hicks and Grahame, 1979). Although a chiefly trophic rôle was ascribed to this behaviour by these latter authors, the use of mucus as a substratum anchoring device was not precluded. *Ectinosoma melaniceps* Boeck and *E. californicum* Lang can frequently be seen trailing mucous threads immediately after their removal from seaweed (pers. obs.). Whether or not these are accumulations of algal-derived mucilage or self-produced is unknown. However, 'spinule-like chitinous stripes' (Lang, 1965) on the trailing edges of the cephalosome in these species (and in other ectinosomatids) pay more than a passing resem- blance to cuticular mucous pores or vents (see Figs. 2 and 3 in Hicks and Grahame, 1979). Should this be confirmed it may well be that mucus production, similar to that described for *Diarthrodes*, may assist in substratum anchorage and other biological functions in the phytal ectinosomatids. Indeed such a behaviour might be much more widespread amongst the Harpacticoida than previously thought.

4.2.4 Seasonal variations

Studies of seasonal phenomena in phytal meiofaunal populations are few, but suggest that seasonal fluctuations in species composition and abundance result from changes in both availability of food and periodicity of reproductive activity. Furthermore, since algae undergo cycles of growth and decay, variability in populations associated with them would be expected to be influenced accordingly. Mukai (1971) and Kito (1975) for example, reported how the fluctuations in density of organisms inhabiting two species of *Sargassum* in Japan were generally allied to the standing crop of the plant. The total number of individuals increased gradually toward winter coincident with *Sargassum* growth and reached a maximum in spring when the standing crop of the seaweed was highest. Changes in meiofaunal composition also occurred during this period. When new *Sargassum* fronds were growing, harpacticoids dominated nematodes, but when fronds began to divaricate and increase in complexity later in the season, copepods decreased relative to nematodes (cf. Ohm, 1964). It is probable that as complexity increases suspended sediments and organic matter are more readily trapped amongst the weed, thus favouring the expansion of nematode populations (see below). As the fronds wither and fragment, nematodes maintain their dominance (Mukai, 1971; Trotter and Webster, 1984); most individuals being associated with bacterial populations that are contributing to the breakdown of algal tissue and mucilage exudates (see *inter alia* Linley and Newell, 1981; Stuart *et al.*, 1981). Mukai and others (e.g. Lepez, 1974; Sarma, 1974; Kito, 1975, 1977, 1982) have concluded that the seasonal increase (growth) and decrease (senescence, defoliation) of algal biomass directly influences the abundance dynamics of the surface-grazing meiofauna. Indeed, organisms feeding directly on macrophytic tissue, such as the mite *Hyadesia fusca* (Lohmann), have their abundance closely linked to the abundance of the alga (Ganning, 1970). The species-abundance-area concept is implicit in this relationship (see Connor and McCoy, 1979, for review), viz. as habitable space with its attendant resources increases, so does the species diversity and carrying capacity of that environment. However, in species of algae inhabiting more equable environments which do not undergo drastic seasonal defoliation, e.g. representatives of the Cook Strait flora in New Zealand (Hicks, 1976, 1977b,c), the seasonal periodicity of resident meiofauna tends to occur independently of gross substratum-related events.

Spatial and temporal variations in abundance of epiphytic food resources, particularly as they are related to the state of the algal substratum, are suspected as being fundamental factors influencing the reproductive dynamics of the grazing meiofauna, and hence their seasonal cycles of abundance. Warwick (1977) linked abundance oscillations of phytal nematodes in the Scilly Isles with differences in seasonally available food and demonstrated a succession of species adapted to different feeding 'strategies'. Trotter and Webster (1983, 1984) have indicated that the epiphytic diatom *Cocconeis scutellum* Ehr. occurs in great abundance on Canadian Pacific coast *Macrocystis integrifolia* Bory in April–July and decreases in August. The epigrowth feeding nematode *Prochromadorella neapolitana* Micoletsky had abundance cycles covarying with those of the diatom which suggested a trophic interaction controlling the abundance dynamics of this apparently food-specific nematode. Such an interaction was, moreover, confirmed in laboratory food selection experiments (Trotter and Webster, 1984). Similar coupling between the bactivorous species *Monhystera disjuncta* Bastian and epiphytic bacterial populations is also indicated by these authors.

Harpacticoid copepods exhibit pronounced seasonal changes in population density with maxima occurring at different times (e.g. Kito, 1977) – events which are claimed to be the result of differential reproductive activities of the constituent species (Hagerman, 1966; Hicks, 1977c,d). Some species attain maximum densities in late winter, spring and summer, subsequent to peaks of ovigerous females, while others peak in autumn. Such pronounced variability in harpacticoid reproductive patterns led Hicks (1979) to hypothesize that ambient seawater temperature was not the factor which directly controlled breeding, but that energy limitations associated with food availability were ultimately of more importance (see also Hicks and Coull, 1983). Fava and Volkmann (1975), on the other hand, suggested that competitive factors may also control the cycling of congeneric species on algae. Three of the four most abundant nematodes investigated by Kito (1982) (*Monhystera refringens* Bresslau and Stekhoven, *Chromadora nudicapitata* Bastian, *Araeolaimus elegans* de Man) were found to reproduce throughout the year irrespective of temperature, a characteristic suggested as contributing to their numerical superiority in phytal systems. Continuous reproduction in phytal harpacticoids has also been argued by Hicks (1979) and Gunnill (1983) to have the same consequence.

Whatever the direct cause, the precise way in which temperature and/or food supply conspire to influence *in situ* reproductive periodicity, with (via recruitment) its attendant effects on species abundance, remains to be fully and critically investigated.

4.2.5 Feeding relations

The vast majority of phytal meiofauna graze epiphytic microbiota which they scrape, lick, suck and sweep from algal surfaces. Food items consist of bacteria, diatoms, phytoflagellates, Fungi, blue-green algae, yeasts and ciliates, all characteristic microbial components of the *aufwuchs* (surface film) community of algae. Many of these organisms are non-motile and are bound with mucilaginous exudates not only of their own making, but from the macrophyte itself.

Predatory, herbivorous and bactivorous nematodes can be distinguished on the basis of buccal cavity morphology. Species with large buccal cavities and no teeth are generally regarded as non-selective deposit feeders; those with small buccal cavities and no teeth as selective deposit feeders; those with teeth and small buccal cavities as epigrowth feeders; and those with large buccal cavities and teeth as omnivores and/or predators (Wieser, 1953a). Selection of food within these categories appears to be primarily a function of food cell size and shape in relation to the buccal morphology, and biochemical differences of the foods themselves. The two chromadorids *Chromadora macrolaimoides* Steiner and *Chromadorina germanica* (Bütschli) are equipped with small teeth in the buccal cavity, and Tietjen and Lee (1977) have shown that diatoms (*Nitzschia, Achnanthes, Cylindrotheca* and *Fragillaria*) form a significantly greater fraction of their diet than do bacteria (see also Jensen, 1982, for *Chromadorita tenuis* (G. Schneider)). However, in nematodes without buccal armature (e.g. *Monhystera denticulata* Timm, *Rhabditis marina* Bastian), bacteria constitute the organisms most heavily grazed. Nematodes inhabiting exposed coast kelp (*Laminaria*) holdfasts have been similarly appraised with 52% of the species being regarded as omnivores and predators, 24% as epigrowth feeders, 18% as selective deposit feeders and 6% as unselective deposit feeders (Moore, 1971). Moore claimed that such a distribution of feeding types indicated that the epiflora and epifauna of the holdfast constituted the most important source of food and that the sparse occurrence of deposit feeders reflected a paucity of suitable deposits within the particular holdfasts examined. Similarly, nematodes on kelp (*Macrocystis*) blades, also exhibit distinct food preferences. *Prochromadorella neapolitana* showed a particular preference for diatoms, *Monhystera disjuncta* a preference for bacteria, while *M. refringens* exhibited no preference for either (Kito, 1982; Trotter and Webster, 1984). Kito moreover, showed that epigrowth feeding species dominated *Sargassum* in Japan, and he generalized that epigrowth feeders were, by and large, the characteristic feeding type amongst phytal nematodes (see also Ott, 1967). Species with a broader feeding niche such as *M. refringens* are capable of dominating through competitive displacement of others.

Because of the significance of specific feeding behaviour with selective ingestion and digestion (Tietjen and Lee, 1977), spatial and seasonal variations in abundance of food types on algae may account for distinctive patterns of abundance and distribution of phytal meiofauna in general and nematodes in particular. Amongst the nematode associations of the Scilly Isles, Warwick (1977) found that in spring and early summer carnivore-omnivores or deposit feeders without discrete visual organs or any preference for frond tips of algae, dominated the fauna. Later in the year, apparently responding to a change in available food, epigrowth feeders, which possessed light detecting ocelli or visual pigments, were dominant. Visual function may be necessary to maintain the worms' position near frond tips, where light intensity is higher and the epiflora upon which they feed consequently richer. Kito (1982) has essentially corroborated these patterns in the nematode fauna associated with *Sargassum* in Japan. A close relationship between preferred food and the grazing population can therefore be expected to influence seasonal meiofaunal dynamics and species composition. High relative abundance of *Monhystera disjuncta* during most of the year has been linked to the corresponding year-round population of bacteria on kelp blades (Trotter and Webster, 1984), while seasonal pulsing of diatoms carried with it species feeding predominantly on them. Hicks and Coull (1983) have presented an equivalent trophic model for harpacticoid copepods. High bacterial densities at frond tips or at regions of active fragmentation and decay of algal tissue with its consequent release of dissolved organic material (DOM) (see *inter alia* Newell and Lucas, 1981), act as a focus for a high abundance of bactivorous nematodes (Kito, 1982; Trotter and Webster, 1984) or those possibly capable of direct uptake of DOM (Chia and Warwick, 1969; Lopez *et al.*, 1979). Furthermore through their own secretion of mucopolysaccharides, some phytal meiofauna may attract, sustain and indeed 'garden' their own microbial populations upon which they subsequently graze (see Hicks and Grahame, 1979).

Other meiofaunal taxa generally graze the same microbial components of the *aufwuchs* as nematodes and as such are in potential competition with them. Feeding in marine harpacticoids, including phytal species, has been treated elsewhere (Hicks and Coull, 1983), but many ostracods and some mites also feed on bacteria and diatom populations (Hagerman, 1966). Ganning (1971b) reported that up to 90% of the summertime stomach contents of the *Enteromorpha*-associated ostracod *Heterocypris salinus* (Brady) consisted of unicellular algae (*Scenedesmus, Pediastrum, Chlorella*). Although a number of ostracods, particularly paradoxostomine forms are said to feed on cellular material of the macrophyte by piercing cell walls with their styliform mandibles (Elofson, 1941), Whatley and Wall (1975) argued that the frequent association of these species with hard impenetrable algae (*Corallina, Laminaria* holdfasts) is evidence that their principal food is epiphytic diatoms and bacteria. Perhaps the most characteristic plant 'suckers' amongst the meiofauna are mites of the subfamily Rhombognathinae, feeding directly on cellular fluids of the macrophyte (Otto, 1936; Wieser, 1959; Ganning, 1970; Bartsch, 1979). Direct consumption of macroalgal tissue such as epidermal cell walls and cell contents is predominantly the reserve of a single family of harpacticoids. The Thalestridae contains three genera of algal frond-mining and gall-producing species (*Thalestris rhodymeniae* (Brady) – see Harding, 1954; *Dactylopusioides macrolabris* (Claus) – see Green, 1958; *Diarthrodes feldmanni* Bocquet – see Bocquet, 1953 and *D. cystoecus* Fahrenbach – see Fahrenbach, 1962). In all cases there is a direct trophic dependence of the naupliar stages on the medullary tissue of macroalgae, especially members of the Rhodymeniales. Nauplii burrow through tissues ingesting as they go and form ramifying tunnels, while the adults occupy pronounced galls which are used mainly as a place to copulate and hatch the young.

Meiofaunal predators include certain turbellarians, nematodes and mites of the subfamily Halacarinae. These prey particularly on other meiofaunal organisms such as oligochaetes, nematodes, mites and harpacticoid copepods, especially juveniles (e.g. Wieser, 1953a, 1959; Hagerman, 1966; Bartsch, 1979; Jensen, 1984).

4.2.6 Phytochemical attraction

The apparent specificity of a number of meiofaunal taxa to particular algal substrata may reflect several often interrelated factors. Specific substratum selection for its own sake must be weighed against interactions with other taxa resulting in, for example, competitive constraints or predator avoidance, which might predispose species to occupy one algal habitat or another. Jensen (1984), for instance, maintained that the preference of the nematode *Enoplus brevis* Bastian for the algae *Furcellaria lumbricalis* (Huds.) Lamour. and *Rhodomela confervoides* (Huds.) Silva is because this predatory nematode feeds specifically on naidid oligochaetes which themselves have a restricted distribution on these algae. Complex trophic inter-relationships such as these may therefore be involved in what appear to be 'preferred' distributions on particular seaweeds. Despite these interpretative difficulties, experimental evidence is available to suggest that meiofaunal species are capable of finely-tuned, active substratum selective behaviour.

In laboratory experiments, Jensen (1981) demonstrated that the itinerant phytobenthic nematode *Chromadorita tenuis* was capable of active swimming from sediment to containers filled with *Cladophora glomerata* (L.) Kutz., the alga from which the nematodes were originally extracted in the field. Hitherto, *C. tenuis* had been regarded as a typical member of the soft-sediment benthos. In field observations in southern Finland, however, Jensen found it to be a permanent member of the phytal, where it feeds and reproduces while the submerged macrophytes are attached. During the winter the nematode lives on the sea bottom in detritus originating from decaying macrophytes. In localities where macrophytes are present throughout the year, the nematode restricts itself to algae, preferring a phytal habitat to a benthic one. Unlike Jensen's observations, which indicated that *C. tenuis* normally inhabits several different macrophytes existing under various environmental conditions, the harpacticoid *Porcellidium dilatatum* Hicks has been shown in Y-maze experiments, to be capable of an active response toward the specific alga upon which it is characteristically found in nature (Hicks, 1977a). When isolated from tactile and visual contact with weeds and offered a range of waters tainted with different, commonly coexisting algae, *P. dilatatum* consistently chose water delivered from reservoirs containing *Zonaria turneriana* J.Ag. On the shore in Cook Strait (New Zealand) this copepod contributed 71% of the total annual harpacticoid fauna on *Zonaria*, the highest relative percentage abundance of any species investigated (Hicks, 1977c). Conversely, *Scutellidium armatum* (Wiborg) showed no clear preference for any algae presented to it in the laboratory (Hicks, 1976). Such a lack of response is consistent with its eurytopy in the field, where it occurred in moderate densities across a wide range of algae. Localized high densities of *P. dilatatum* specifically on *Zonaria*, and *C. tenuis* generally on a range of algae, are believed, therefore, to be due to active substratum preferences, rather than the product of other biological interactions.

Both Jensen and Hicks have suggested that meiofaunal organisms are attracted by properties relating directly to the macrophyte, and/or to the attached surface microbial film (= *aufwuchs* community). Hicks (1977a) found that the chemo-attractive properties of *Zonaria* to *P. dilatatum* could be destroyed or reduced by simple physico-chemical treatments of the seaweed prior to testing (boiling, rinsing in distilled water or dilute formalin). It is well known that macroalgae release a range of chemical compounds as by-products of cell metabolism. Some of these exudates, e.g. tannins, terpenes and phenols, have considerable antibiotic and antifungal properties which greatly influence the growth, survival and composition of surface dwelling microbial populations (e.g. Sieburth, 1968; Ragan and Jensen, 1977). Presence or absence of such activity and the variable effect on the microbial population (components of which are ultimately the primary food of most phytal meiofauna) may, along with other variables outlined in this Chapter, dictate different interalgal distribution patterns in nature. Indeed in some meiofaunal species, the composition of the microbial film may contribute to algal-specific attraction of those organisms with specific feeding requirements.

4.3 Relations with Macrophytic Structure

4.3.1 Habitat complexity and heterogeneity

Probably the most powerful correlative aspect of macrophyte-meiofauna relations yet examined is the impact of spatial heterogeneity, or habitat structural complexity, and its influence upon species composition and diversity. While some authors use 'heterogeneity' and 'complexity' interchangeably, the former term really implies horizontal variation or patchiness within a larger scale environment. Complexity, on the other hand, relates to smaller scale attributes of habitat physiognomy such as, in the phytal, the shape, texture, architecture or surface structure of the plant. The approach is couched in the species–area concept whereby both increasing complexity and increasing heterogeneity of the habitat can be predicted to increase organismic diversity and abundance (see Menge and Sutherland, 1976; Connor and McCoy, 1979, for reviews).

Techniques with which to measure structural complexity in phytal habitats are variable and largely independent. Some authors have simply weighed the amount of algae in a sample, relating this to animal densities or diversities (Colman, 1940; Ohm, 1964; Hagerman, 1966; Mukai, 1971; Kautsky, 1974; Sarma and Ganapati, 1972, 1975; Whatley and Wall, 1975; Kangas, 1978; Beckley and McLachlan, 1980; Kito, 1982; Coull *et al.*, 1983), while others have equated abundance with algal volume (e.g. Dommasnes, 1969). However, simple weighing or volumetric measuring techniques fail to account for differences in mass of particular algal species. For example, some corallines and kelps are heavier per unit (Hicks, 1977b; Beckley and McLachlan, 1980) than delicate ephemeral species (e.g. *Enteromorpha*), yet may not necessarily offer greater living space to associated meiofauna. More appropriately, since it is the surface of algae that is exploited by meiofauna, direct estimates of the degree of branching or surface area of algae as indices of habitable space have been made (Wieser, 1951b; Moore, 1973a; Hicks, 1977b, 1980; Warwick, 1977; Edgar, 1983a; Coull and Wells, 1983). The 'best' measure of complexity for meiofauna is claimed by Coull and Wells (1983) to be one incorporating both surface area and volume into a ratio. Caution should be exercised in adopting one measure over another, however, without at first defining what such measurements are required to show, and their applicability within different phytal systems or between different species of algae.

The practical operation of habitat complexity gradients can be seen in the provision of an increased number of exploitable resources, whether they be surfaces on which to live and/or feed or refuges from predators. Flattened, thalloid algal fronds and compact, disc-like holdfasts offer only planar surfaces from which to feed, and give little protection from turbulence, desiccation or predation. In general, meiofaunal assemblages occupying such algal physiognomies are reduced in both their species richness (Table 4.3) and individual species abundance. Conversely, fine densely-tufted and branched

TABLE 4.3

Number of species of phytal harpacticoid copepods from mid-littoral and shallow sub-littoral sites ranked against surface area (cm^2) of 1g of algae, and quantities of deposited sediments (g dry weight/total algal sample – see Hicks, 1977b, 1980). Algae with asterisks are from St Abbs, Scotland, others from Cook St, New Zealand; data are from mid-summer samples only. Correlation coefficients derived from untransformed values.

Alga	Surface area	Sediment	Number of species
*Laminaria**	7	0.08	6
Ecklonia	7	0.09	9
Xiphophora	10	0.04	11
*Fucus**	12	1.2	17
*Mastocarpus (= Gigartina)**	38	5.3	22
*Palmaria**	43	4.9	16
*Ceramium**	80	9.6	18
Zonaria	80	0.3	19
*Ulva**	110	4.1	13
Pterocladia	113	5.4	21
*Corallina**	120	29.9	39
Corallina	135	47.3	42
*Cladophora**	216	12.7	32

$$r = 0.56 \qquad r = 0.89$$
$$P < 0.05 \qquad P < 0.001$$

$$r = 0.73$$
$$P < 0.005$$

shrub-like fronds and tangled, divaricated holdfasts afford greater living space which can allow more species to coexist (Table 4.3). Such complex algal growth forms offer shelter and refuge, consequently dictating patterns of feeding and locomotion. There is thus an interaction between body size of an organism and its adaptability to a particular growth form of weed. For example, large nematodes (e.g. *Enoplus communis*, *Thoracostoma coronatum* (Eberth) and *Anticoma eberthi* Bastian) are much more abundant in coarser algae whilst smaller species (*Chromadora nudicapitata*, *Chromadorella filiformis* (Bastian) and *Monhystera refringens*) are more widespread across different algal growth forms (Warwick, 1977). An ability to navigate through foliage of different texture and composition is therefore an important determinant of species composition (Moore, 1971, this volume). Indeed the question of scale and of how organisms perceive and react to their environment must be addressed in studies such as these. Such has been demonstrated by Edgar (1983c) who found little association between his measure of algal complexity (surface area) and diversity of amphipods, contrary to Hicks' findings (1977c, 1980, 1982). Macrofaunal amphipods possibly treat complex filamentous algae as a single habitat but partition the wider thalloid algae into several habitats of differing scale. On the other hand harpacticoid copepods are assumed to respond to surface area of thalloid algae as a unit but subdivide the filamentous habitat to allow in more species. Support for this interpretation comes from McKenzie and Moore (1981) who concluded that more complexly branched *Laminaria hyperborea* holdfasts facilitated better conditions for the smaller meiofauna than the bulbous haptera of *Saccorhiza polyschides* (Lightf.) Batt. which alternatively favoured macrofauna. Organism size–habitat scale relationships need therefore to be appreciated.

The interaction of an increasingly complex algal structure together with possibly more diverse food resources increases the potential of the habitat to attract and maintain more species, some of which even move in from surrounding sedimentary biotopes (Hicks, 1979; Jensen, 1981; Kito, 1982). Seasonal changes in growth form of the alga (see p. 45) together with changes in the trophic structure that this might engender can be responsible for variations in meiofaunal species composition. Kito (1982) considered standing crop of the plant as a measure of structural complexity of *Sargassum confusum* in the Japan Sea and showed an increase in the number of nematode species between May and September when the plant developed a more complex growth form prior to defoliation. The increase was due mostly to rare species which were only recorded intermittently at other times of the year. It is still unresolved whether these species were responding directly to habitat expansion, or to variable trophic resources becoming available during the associated withering and defoliation phase of the plant (and hence possible reduction in competition with dominant species) (see also Trotter and Webster, 1983). However, the increased relative abundance of bactivorous epigrowth feeders at this time (e.g. *Chromadora nudicapitata*, *Euchromadora ezoensis* Kito, *Acanthonchus tridentatus* Kito) implies the latter. Since substratum complexity and increased trophic diversification are in this case interdependent variables, it is unprofitable to search for a proximate and ultimate cause to the pattern observed.

Increased complexity of the macrophytic substratum also provides increased surface for attachment of other multicellular epiphytes (e.g. *Polysiphonia*, *Ceramium*, *Sphacelaria*), further contributing to larger scale spatial heterogeneity with its attendant effect on meiofauna abundance and diversity (Colman, 1940; Wieser, 1952, 1959; Hagerman, 1966; Ott, 1967; Moore, 1971; Sarma and Ganapati, 1972; Sarma, 1974; Whatley and Wall, 1975; Kangas, 1978; Athersuch, 1979; Gunnill, 1982b; Edgar, 1983a,b). The response of various meiofaunal taxa to habitat expansion presented by epiphytation is variable. For instance, certain algae such as *Fucus*, which alone yields few ostracods (Whatley and Wall, 1975), have an abundant ostracod fauna when supporting filamentous epiphytes (Elofson, 1941; Hagerman, 1966; Williams, 1969; Kangas, 1978). However, Hagerman (1966) and Bartsch (1979) noted that mites tend to favour flatter, leaf-like fronds without epiphytes, and Jensen (1984) concluded that the species composition of phytal nematodes in the Baltic was not influenced by algal architecture or their silt retaining capabilities, but by salinity and food availability. In general, though, mixed stands of algae and particularly those including large amounts of filamentous epiphytic species provide a greater heterogeneity of utilizable habitat over their more homogeneous monospecific counterparts (Gunnill, 1982b). Moreover, the accumulation of medium- or even coarse-grained deposits (Hicks, 1977b) and encrusting sessile invertebrates such as Bryozoa and hydroids may also provide an additional habitat dimension exploited by specialized meiofauna, e.g. predaceous nematodes and mites (Ott, 1967; Bartsch, 1979) and certain laophontid harpacticoids (Hicks, 1980).

Another important component of spatial heterogeneity in macroalgal environments is large scale patchiness within an algal stand or zone. Many algal zones (*sensu* Lewis, 1964) are not uniform in appearance due to physical and biological disturbances such as storm and wave action, grazing effects and disease, and seasonal events such as senescence and defoliation of epiphytic and ephemeral species. Since algal stands are continually subjected to disturbances which vary both spatially and temporally, mosaics of different age and species composition occur which add to the overall heterogeneity of the shore. Within-habitat diversity and pattern diversity are thus increased which may lead to elevated species richness and abundance of meiofaunal colonists (Gunnill, 1982a,b, 1983). Overall size of algal stands and distance from large stands of smaller isolated units (Gunnill, 1982a,b) are now known to be powerful contributors to within-habitat diversity and abundance of meiofaunal taxa.

4.3.2 Impact of particulate matter

As the foliage complexity of algae increases, so too does its propensity for accumulating particulate matter (Table 4.3). Fine sediments such as silt-clays and coarser material like sand particles, shell fragments and detritus are effectively screened out of the overlying water and trapped amongst fronds and holdfasts. In more sheltered environments levels of deposition are predictably higher. While sediment accretion might be regarded as a master factor controlling species composition and abundance (Dahl, 1948; Wieser, 1951a, 1954, 1959), the amount of sediment trapped and retained amongst algal foliage and holdfasts is invariably a function of algal complexity (Moore, 1972, 1973a,b; Hicks, 1977b,c, 1980 – see Table 4.3). Because of its stiff, erect and greatly tangled growth form, and its common occurrence in relatively sheltered tidal pools, *Corallina officinalis* L. consistently collects sediment in excess of any other algae hitherto investigated (Fretter and Manly, 1977; Hicks, 1977b, 1980 – see Table 4.3). Clearly there is a causal interaction between physiognomic structure and the levels of material accumulated amongst algal surfaces and holdfasts.

The importance of the 'detritus' factor to the composition of algal microarthropods was extensively appraised by Dahl (1948). It should be stated that Dahl's 'detritus' was an encompassing term for deposits of both an organic and inorganic nature and not biogenic material *sensu stricto* referred to as detritus (Darnell, 1967). Dahl allocated *inter alia* various harpacticoid copepod and halacarid mite species to categories within a 'detritus' gradient of levels 0 (low) to 3 (high). Although the copepod *Parastenhelia spinosa* (Fischer) was selected by Dahl as a principal indicator of high levels of deposits in the Gullmar Fjord, Moore (1973b) classified the species as indicative of clear water in North Sea kelp holdfasts. Comparison of complete harpacticoid faunal lists in Colman (1940), Dahl (1948), Moore (1973b) and Hicks (1980) from both Britain and Scandinavia reveals further anomalies of this kind, and emphasizes the shortcomings of labelling species on arbitrary scales from different localities. There is no doubt, however, that increased levels of sediment and detritus on algae can encourage the establishment of species more commonly located on level-bottom sediments. For instance, Wieser (1954, 1959) suggested that monhysterid nematodes, characteristic on fine and muddy sand substrata (Heip *et al.*, 1982), increased their dominance ranking on fronds and in holdfasts as a response to increasing deposition of fine sediment. In more sheltered conditions an increasing proportion of true deposit feeding species would be expected at the expense of epigrowth feeders and omnivores (see also Ott, 1967; Moore, 1971; Warwick, 1977; Kito, 1982). Hicks (1977c) found that the thick layer of detrital sandy sediment trapped at the bases of *Corallina* in New Zealand supported a distinct fauna of epistratum and burrowing harpacticoids (e.g. tetragonicipitids, cletodids, ancorabolids), differing from those more typical phytal forms (e.g. tisbids, thalestrids, peltidiids) occupying the fronds. In Cyprus, algae contaminated with sandy sediments contained ostracods (e.g. *Hiltermannicythere rubra* (Müller) and *Urocythereis distinguenda* (Neviani)) normally found on adjacent sandy substrata (Athersuch, 1979). Sedimentation can thus allow a degree of habitat expansion into the phytal for species normally restricted to level-bottom deposits. Furthermore, from the point of view of species diversity and individual species abundance, the granulometric properties of the deposited material are of great significance. Particle size analysis of accumulated sediments largely reflects surrounding geology and levels of turbulence. In exposed Cook Strait, New Zealand and St Abbs, Scotland, hard local lithologies mean that while large amounts of fine particles are collected by *Corallina*, so too are substantial quantities of larger particulate material. This results in a granulometry equivalent to a poorly sorted, medium sand (see Fig. 5 in Hicks, 1977b). As this is a heterogeneous mixture of fine and coarse particles, species richness (see Table 4.3) and abundance of associated harpacticoids is significantly enhanced, in line with theoretical expectations outlined in the previous section. Conversely, at Robin Hood's Bay, N. Yorkshire, where local geology consists of soft erodable boulder clays, the deposit – even on the same alga – is much finer (silt-clay) and more homogeneous; the effect is to lower both species richness and the total number of individuals (Hicks, 1980). Hence the specific properties of the entrapped sediments are important to the outcome of species relative abundance patterns, a distinction recently overlooked by Bell and Coen (1982).

While from a trophic point of view very fine deposits on algal fronds and holdfasts encourage certain deposit-feeding nematodes, it is not known precisely how these small contaminating particles influence harpacticoids. A number of potentially detrimental effects have been proposed (Dahl, 1948; Moore, 1977a; Hicks, 1980), including clogging of feeding structures, interference with feeding behaviour, depression of reproductive and growth rates and interruption of the moulting process. Excessive turbidity and siltation may also infill microhabitat spaces on seaweeds and reduce copepod motility, therefore impairing the capacity to avoid predators. Turbidity and deposited fine sediments may also reduce light penetration which would inhibit growth of some algal (diatom) food items. Siltation therefore may well set distributional limits and contribute to faunal discontinuities between continually clear water and intermittently turbid localities (Moore, 1973b, 1974). Consequently, whilst coarser, heterogeneous deposits are likely to enhance diversity and abundance of some meiofaunal taxa (copepods, ostracods), very fine deposits prove to be detrimental – except, that is, to those favouring it as a source of abundant food (some nematodes). This may be regarded as a causal explanation for why nematodes tend to dominate in algal substrata heavily laden with fine deposits (see Table 4.1).

4.3.3 Refuge from predation

The theoretical prediction that more structurally complex habitats afford prey a greater degree of protection from roving predators by the provision of spatial refuges, is now being tested empirically with phytal meiobenthos. Most small littoral fishes (e.g. blennies, gobies, clingfish) or juveniles of larger inshore fish are well known predators of phytal meiofauna, particularly harpacticoid copepods (Zander and Heymer, 1977; Roland, 1978). It has been hypothesized that predation of phytal harpacticoids inhabiting complex algae should be reduced compared with those inhabiting structurally simple algae, because of impenetrability of the predator into refuge centres (Hicks, 1980).

The first definitive test of this notion using meiofauna has recently appeared (Coull and Wells,

1983) and concludes that substratum complexity of algae is indeed a powerful factor in reducing predation by offering increased refuges to prey. In a series of laboratory and field experiments in Cook Strait, New Zealand, these authors presented the predatory littoral blennioid fish *Helcogramma medium* (Günther) with a selection of rocky shore algae and other artificial structures of various shape. For total meiofauna and for harpacticoids, *Corallina officinalis* was the only alga of sufficiently complex structure to offer refuge from predation. Irrespective of whether or not the prey was originally collected from *Corallina* or some other alga tested, the result was the same; *Corallina* was the only substratum having a significant effect on prey survivorship. Moreover, of the 31 species of harpacticoid identified from *Corallina*, only *Amphiascus lobatus* Hicks was significantly less abundant after predation, indicating that it was selectively preyed upon by the fish. *Helcogramma* does not penetrate the clumps of *Corallina* in search of food but lies in wait outside, whereupon prey that move to the periphery are captured. The high incidence of *A. lobatus* in the fishes' guts may suggest merely that this species is more readily accessible by virtue of occupying the outer parts of fronds. Nevertheless, these results, supported by parallel field trials, are consistent with the hypothesis that increased complexity of the algal surface reduces predation on abundant prey items by reducing foraging efficiency.

Coull and Wells' experiments (1983) highlighted earlier work on phytal macrofauna which claimed that predation does not act in a simple linear way, but resembles a step function wherein algal surfaces of low or intermediate complexity offer no refuge, unlike surfaces of very high complexity. This implies a threshold level of complexity above which predatory success is greatly diminished. Since *Corallina* was the only alga to mediate the predation effect significantly, it would be instructive to see if *Cladophora rupestris* (L.) Kutz., which Hicks (1980) notes as having an even higher surface area (= complexity) than *Corallina*, does indeed 'protect' its residents in the way that Coull and Wells claim.

Meiofauna without access to algogenic refuges should theoretically exist in an environment imposing periodic or continuous predatory removal. How this removal affects the population dynamics of the prey is only now beginning to be appraised. Choat and Kingett (1982) recorded high densities of the mullid fish *Upeneichthys porosus* (Cuvier and Valenciennes) over *Corallina* turf in north-eastern New Zealand, coinciding with periods of lowest total invertebrate abundance. These observations indicated that the fish might have a key rôle in determining the seasonal patterns of invertebrate abundance. Fish exclusion cages were used to test for causal events between predator presence and density of prey. While the predominant meiofaunal prey was ostracods, these authors failed to demonstrate significant differences between treatments, suggesting that the temporal dynamics of ostracod prey occurred independently of the predator. Therefore, although Coull and Wells (1983) demonstrated significant differences in meiofaunal prey abundance in relation to habitat structure at one instant, the impact of predatory removal appears minimal over a longer period (Choat and Kingett, 1982). Since both investigations involved the complex habitat of *Corallina officinalis*, Choat and Kingett's results can be further interpreted in two ways: (i) *Corallina* offers a similar refuge to ostracods as it does to harpacticoids, but that despite a certain level of predatory removal this is never significant enough to alter population levels greatly, or (ii) there is no refuge effect and those ostracods removed represent a significant proportion of the population at any one time, but because of high population resilience, predation is relatively unimportant in the temporal sequence of prey abundance. It is not possible to unravel these effects presently, but results supporting the latter idea are available from studies on sediment-dwelling harpacticoids where no apparent refuges were available. In these, while large numbers of harpacticoids have been shown to be consumed, the overall impact on the harpacticoid population in terms of drastic reductions in abundance has been shown to be slight (see Berge and Hesthagen, 1981; Alheit and Scheibel, 1982; Evans, 1983; Hicks, 1984). There is, however, considerable evidence supporting an alternative view (e.g. Warwick, 1981), whereby predators do regulate prey abundance.

4.3.4 Algal patchiness and colonization

Phytal habitats are often patchy in their distribution (habitat 'islands') and locally transient. Blooms of ephemeral algae and cycles of growth, erosion and decay of perennial algae frequently generate distinct spatio-temporal mosaics which are periodically accessible to invasion by meiofauna.

Despite the fact that practically all meiofaunal animals lack planktonically dispersed larval stages, many – particularly phytal harpacticoid copepods – are capable of active swimming (Dahl, 1948; Wieser, 1952; Hauspie and Polk, 1973; pers. obs.), which is therefore a primary mechanism for colonization. Following defaunation and transplantation of the alga *Pelvetia fastigiata* (J. Ag.) De Toni in California, Gunnill (1982a) provided evidence that equilibrium abundances of the harpacticoid *Scutellidium lamellipes* Monk on individual plants resulted from both immigration and emigration together with *in situ* reproduction. In accordance with the theoretical predictions of island biogeography (MacArthur and Wilson, 1967), immigration rates of *S. lamellipes* to transplanted *Pelvetia* decreased significantly, not only with increasing distance (up to 30m) from large stands of unmanipulated *Pelvetia*, but also with decreasing plant size. On plants close to a pool of residents in untouched *Pelvetia*, early colonization was facilitated predominantly by nauplii and adults, but as the distance away from the pool increased, nauplii were eliminated as effective colonists. This suggests that while individuals dispersed freely and maintained high densities within large aggregations of *Pelvetia*, they did not migrate as readily between isolated plants, even as close as 30cm. Tidally induced patterns of invasion have also been suggested. Wieser (1952) divided copepods into groups inhabiting *Mastocarpus* (= *Gigartina*) during high water and low water, finding them (particularly *Dactylopodia vulgaris* (Sars) and *Tisbe minor* (T. & A. Scott)) to leave their seaweed cover with the receding tide and occupy algae lower on the shore, only to reinvade high shore weeds again on the flood. This may reflect either a physiological response to reduced oxygen levels amongst weeds at low tide (Wieser and Kanwisher, 1959), or direct tidally-induced behavioural rhythms. In any case this emphasizes the importance of between-plant movements, in addition to any *in situ* reproductive recruitment that may occur.

Gunnill (1982b) further demonstrated that immigration and colonization can maintain relatively constant numbers of species on *Pelvetia*, but that such equilibria frequently differ over small spatial scales on the shore. Harpacticoid populations associated with persistent algae such as *Corallina* and *Cladophora* in Britain have also been regarded as approaching equilibria of species immigration and local extinction (Hicks, 1980). Deviations from such island predictions may result, however, from the transience of either the animal population (Gunnill, 1982a,b), or the habitat patch (alga) itself (Hicks, 1980, 1982). On some unpredictable or ephemeral substrata rates of colonization may not be rapid enough to allow species equilibria to develop. Colonization of the short-lived red alga *Ceramium rubrum* (Huds.) C.Ag. by harpacticoids proceeds as an invasion from other nearby algae and sediments. However, before an equilibrium state is established, the alga defoliates and declines. Conversely, some other ephemeral algae (e.g. *Ulva*) may be characterized by rapid turnover of opportunistic species, wherein some level of equilibrium may be attained, despite the short-term persistence of the substratum.

Evidence to date, therefore, tends to support some of the theoretical tenets of insular biogeography. Algae of different growth form, extent and distribution on the shore may dictate not only the covariance of local faunal abundance and diversity, but also the rates of immigration and emigration, and the way in which these interact to generate states of dynamic equilibrium. It remains that harpacticoid assemblages on algae with a greater surface area (= complexity) more closely approximate states of species equilibrium than those on structurally simple algae (Hicks, 1982).

4.4 Perspectives

Our knowledge of the relationships between marine macroalgae and meiofauna is far from complete despite the considerable data base available. From the descriptive point of view we know the levels of abundance and number of species likely to be attained and we are also able to recognize characteristic species and genera on certain algal types or within holdfasts. The recognition of like species within common genera whose incidence is repeated world-wide, has enabled the prediction of a typical 'assemblage of phytal meiofaunal taxa. What is not known is how this taxo-ecologic repeatability is maintained, although the interaction of feeding specializations and substratum-oriented morphological adaptations would seem to be fundamental to such a phenomenon. A considerable amount is known about the broad feeding tactics of phytal meiofauna but there is no clear understanding of the basis for food preferences and how these interact to control reproductive and abundance dynamics or how they affect interalgal distribution patterns. The structural complexity of the algal surface is identified as the most significant ecological factor influencing the species composition, species richness and abundance of resident meiofauna. Algal growth form influences the number of exploitable resources such as surfaces from which to feed or places to avoid predators. Nevertheless, we need to define more clearly what contributes most to increased meiofaunal abundance and diversity, the provision of more refuges from higher level predators, or habitable area which can in its own right be partitioned to allow more species and individuals to coexist. The relation between algal complexity and its propensity for trapping particulate matter has also been recognized. However, information on precisely how accumulated deposits detrimentally affect sensitive species is inadequate. The accessibility of the rocky littoral zone is beginning to foster progressive work such as that on predator–prey interactions and colonization and abundance relations in patchy algal environments. These studies have emphasized how *in situ* experimental and manipulative techniques using meiofauna may be used to test the universality of hypotheses generated by terrestrial ecologists.

Some additional questions can be directly addressed using phytal meiofauna. For example: (i) within the context of ecological biogeography, how general is the species-area relationship between meiofauna and algae? (ii) on the basis that plant–insect interactions have shown how the local distribution of the host plant influences local species richness, do common species of algae, for instance, support more species of meiofauna than rare algae, and do algae with broad geographic ranges support more species than those with restricted distributions? (iii) does predation greatly influence meiofaunal community organization, or are the effects merely identifiable in certain vulnerable species? (iv) from the competitive point of view, how are individual algal plants partitioned, and how specific are particular meiofauna to particular sections of the thallus? (v) although the effects of macrofaunal grazers on rocky shore algae are well known, what are the effects of meiofaunal grazers on the community dynamics of the surface *aufwuchs* (microbial) community? (vi) how does the age of the host alga influence meiofaunal populations? In what way might the latter be controlled by the release of secondary compounds (allelopathy), and how do these relate to discrimination or attraction to host plants?

Finally, we need to understand much more about the interaction between the living algal substratum – its own biological cycles and processes – and the *aufwuchs*, ultimately the primary food source for most phytal meiofauna.

ACKNOWLEDGEMENTS

I am grateful to Susan S. Bell and Graham S. Hardy for their deliberations on earlier drafts of this Chapter.

CHAPTER V

VARIATION AND PERSISTENCE OF ROCKY SHORE POPULATIONS

J.H. Connell

5.1 Introduction

Naturalists have been impressed alternately with the constancy and variability of natural assemblages on seashores. The ubiquity of the 'barnacle zone' or the 'infralittoral fringe' of algae is a reminder of the seemingly unchanging nature of shore communities. Since populations have been seen to persist in certain sites for long periods, it is natural to conjecture that some sort of stabilizing forces operate; 'the balance of nature has been a background assumption in natural history since antiquity' (Egerton, 1973, p. 322). Yet many have also been impressed with the devastation of shore populations by extreme storms or oil spills (and the 'clean-ups' thereafter), by shifts in species composition after extreme winters (Crisp (ed.), 1964), or by invasions of predators. In this Chapter I will discuss the nature and evidence for numerical constancy and persistence of populations on rocky shores; sublittoral species will not be discussed.

As far as possible, I have avoided using the term 'stability' in this paper. In much of ecological usage stability implies that an equilibrium state exists and that an ecosystem is capable either of resisting disturbing forces that might shift it away from that state, or if so perturbed, is capable of adjusting back to it. Connell and Sousa (1983) concluded that it was difficult to apply these theoretical concepts to actual populations or communities. Abundances are continually fluctuating so that it is seldom, if ever, possible to designate an equilibrium level to which actual populations recover after disturbances. Therefore I will limit my discussion to fluctuations in abundance, particularly to population extinction or persistence.

5.2 The Importance of Scale

In deciding whether a given population is persistent, one needs to consider certain scales in time and space. With regard to time, Frank (1968) pointed out the tautology in reasoning that communities are stable when in fact they have remained constant simply because the same long-lived individuals have survived there. That a mussel or algal bed occupies the same site for several years may only reflect the long life of the occupants and says nothing about its stability. To avoid this tautology, Connell and Sousa (1983) suggested that numbers be compared over an interval in which a complete turnover of all individuals has occurred. By observing the patterns of change over at least one complete turnover, the degree of variability is scaled to the life history of that population, thus allowing comparison between populations with different life histories.

In some species most individuals die at an early age, with a few surviving much longer. To require a complete turnover in analysing variability would rule out most of these species because few long records exist. Yet to use a shorter interval, such as mean generation time, would run the risk of including the same long-lived individuals in both censuses, Frank's (1968) tautology. As an alternative one could compare the numbers at the start and end of an interval during which a large majority have died, while excluding all survivors from both numbers to avoid the tautology. Counts at intermediate times are valuable in detecting more rapid changes (e.g. local extinctions and recolonizations) which would be missed with widely-spaced censuses.

The spatial scale of the population also affects judgements of persistence. The area of study should include enough sites suitable for the establishment of juveniles and their growth to maturity, to allow complete replacement. Consider, for example, a species that requires bare patches of a certain minimal size for establishment of juveniles and their survival to maturity. To analyse persistence, a study of this species needs to encompass an area in which enough such sites exist or are created within the period of a complete turnover of the population, to ensure replacement of all adults.

Compared to those in large areas, populations in small areas are less likely to be found to be either constant or persistent. They could often become extinct by chance, or be destroyed by single disturbances. Over a wider area, the regional population would be more likely to be persistent, providing that local populations become extinct asynchronously, and are subsequently recolonized by dispersal from extant ones (Andrewartha and Birch, 1954). A statistical procedure for deciding whether real populations are 'narrowly bounded' has been proposed by Keough and Butler (1983). Murdoch (1979) has pointed out the desirability of demonstrating the existence of density-dependent mechanisms that tend to prevent the population from exceeding the bounds.

5.3 Evidence of Persistence in Rocky Shore Populations

5.3.1 Persistence and quantitative variation on larger scales of space and time

Changes in distribution or abundance over large temporal and spatial scales are of great interest and importance. For rocky shore populations one of the best documented examples is that of Southward and Crisp (1954). In 1949–52 they made a survey of two barnacle 'species' around the British Isles and compared it to an earlier survey made in the 1930s by Moore and Kitching (1939). There had been a general expansion of the boundary of distribution and an increase in relative abundance of two species of *Chthamalus*, as compared to these characteristics in *Semibalanus balanoides* L. The general climate was warming during the period, apparently making conditions more favourable for the southern *Chthamalus* and less so for the northern *Semibalanus*. The climate began to cool after 1950 (Mitchell, 1977; Davis, 1984) and at one site in southern England where *Semibalanus* had disappeared by 1951, it had recolonized by 1975 (Southward, 1976). In this case, persistence was in part determined by long-term trends in climate. Other examples of large-scale changes are introductions of species into a different geographical region. These have often spread widely, but little is known of their effects on the persistence of the native species.

Evidence of variation or persistence over longer periods is rare for rocky shore species. Some records are available from archaeological studies of middens containing shells of shore species eaten by people who lived on sea coasts. For example, in middens on the Channel Islands, California, the red abalone (*Haliotis rufescens* Swainson) was very common in deposits older than 5000 years before present (B.P.). Since then, it has only been found rarely, being replaced by the black abalone, *Haliotis cracherodii* Leach (Hubbs, 1955; Glassow, in prep.). Since these people did not dive for shellfish, this record suggests a shift in distribution of the red abalone about 5000 B.P., from the shore to the immediately offshore zone where it lives at present.

5.3.2 Persistence and quantitative variation on smaller scales

Most studies have been limited to one or a few sites in a local area. Qualitative observations of populations that have existed at a particular site over periods encompassing at least one turnover constitute evidence of persistence even if the degree of fluctuation in abundance has not been measured quantitatively. For example, the study site on Waadah Island used by Dayton (1973) to study *Postelsia palmaeformis* Ruprecht populations had been called 'Postelsia Point' by Rigg and Miller (1949), indicating that this annual plant had probably persisted there for many generations. Likewise, Paine (1979) noted that *Postelsia* was present for 11 years in 7 sites on Tatoosh Island.

In quantitatively estimating persistence within bounds, Keough and Butler (1983) have proposed a method to determine whether populations are 'narrowly bounded.' For statistical reasons this requires at least six censuses, which could be accomplished in six years for an annual species. However, it apparently cannot yet be applied to shore species, since the only available data are for long-lived species, none of which have more than three observations separated by complete turnovers (see Table 5.1).

Connell and Sousa (1983) have summarized the variability of all cases found in a literature survey of natural populations with records spanning a period of at least one turnover. Variability was measured as the standard deviation of the logarithms of census values spaced at least one complete turnover apart. This index of variation is sensitive to low values (because logarithms are used). Another common index is the coefficient of variation, which is sensitive to high values. Since we were particularly interested in variation at low numbers, the former index seemed more appropriate.

Table 5.1 lists the records available for shore species. These data were gathered by making censuses at intervals at four locations, near Plymouth, England, the Isle of Cumbrae, Scotland, San Juan Island, Washington, and Santa Catalina Island, California. The time of one complete turnover was estimated as the maximum length of life of the individuals during the period of observation. Some individuals may have exceeded this maximum, but it is highly probable that after 10 to 12 years for small barnacles and snails, or 20 years for large barnacles and starfish, the turnover was complete. The data were either numbers at a particular age, or all individuals on a site at the same season. Because of the longevity of these species, counts spaced one turnover apart were available for only two or three censuses.

The index of variation for these rocky shore species ranged from 0.03 to 1.34. The complete survey in Connell and Sousa (1983) included 45 studies of 94 non-shore species of plants, parasitic microorganisms, and animals from terrestrial, freshwater and marine habitats. The index of variation for all these ranged from 0 to 1.79, so shore species from only four locations spanned a great part of the range found in all other organisms surveyed by Connell and Sousa (1983). In this same survey, 16 of the 97 non-shore populations disappeared locally; 4 of the 29 populations of shore species in Table 1 became extinct, and 2 were recolonized.

It is probably appropriate to compare in detail only similar organisms of about the same body size, sampled at a similar spatial scale. Some of the data of this sort in Table 5.1 show interesting patterns of variation. For example, *Semibalanus balanoides* is much more variable in all four sites in southern England (Table 5.1, species 2), which is at the edge of its geographical range, then at the single Scottish site (species 4) further within its boundary. The same is true of *Chthamalus*, the Scottish site (species 3) being nearer its range boundary, although the overall variation may have been reduced at the English sites (species 1) by the fact that two species were combined there.

Among the predatory snails of the genus *Nucella*, the species in Scotland (Table 5.1, species 5) showed less variation than any of the three in Washington (species 9, 10, 11). This may have been due to the fact that the former was living on a continuous rocky shore, whereas in Washington they were living on a large concrete piling located a short distance from shore. Among the latter, *Nucella lamellosa* (species 11) showed the least variation; it lives on the low shore and in the sublittoral, and so

TABLE 5.1

Variability of rocky shore populations studied for at least one complete turnover of all individuals.
(See footnotes for details of sites, units and sources.)

Species	Location, Age (yr) or shore level (see notes)	Assumed turnover time (yr)	Abundance at each census						Statistics on log(x + 1) of abundance values	
			Year	Abundance	Year	Abundance	Year	Abundance	Mean	S.D.
1. Chthamalus stellatus and C. montagui	a	20	1934	42.5	1951	49.2	1975	15.1	1.76	0.04
	b	"	"	18.9	"	31.1			1.40	0.15
	c	"	"	9.9	"	9.6			1.08	0.09
	d	"	"	0	"	0.4			0.07	0.10
2. Semibalanus balanoides	a	20	1934	25.9	1951	0	1975	7.9	0.71	1.01
	b	"	"	57.6	"	0			0.88	1.25
	c	"	"	30.7	"	0			0.82	0.76
	d	"	"	9.6	"	0.2			0.55	0.67
3. Chthamalus montagui	0.1 yr	20	1954	93.5	1977	0.2			1.03	1.34
	0.6 yr	"	1957	16.2	1979	5.3			1.02	0.31
	1.1 yr	"	1953	19.1	1976	0.2			0.69	0.87
4. Semibalanus balanoides	0.1 yr	20	1953	348.0	1977	459.2			2.60	0.08
	0.6 yr	"	1954	95.6	1982	121.5			2.04	0.07
	1.1 yr	"	1952	22.0	1981	3.8			1.02	0.48
5. Nucella lapillus	middle & lower	10	1953	86.8	1970	51	1982	66.1	1.83	0.11
6. Patella vulgata	a. middle	10	1953	62.9	1970	20.7	1982	20.5	1.49	0.27
	b. lower	"	"	90.0	"	20.0	"	33.3	1.61	0.32
7. Balanus glandula	upper	10	1959	4.0	1969	46.0	1980	23.2	1.25	0.50
	middle	"	"	3.5	"	20.0	"	18.0	1.08	0.37
	lower	"	"	4.5	"	2.0	"	0.8	0.49	0.24
8. Semibalanus cariosus	middle	20	1959	21.0	1980	4.0			1.02	0.45
	lower	"	"	27.0	"	12.0			1.28	0.24

TABLE 5.1 Cont'd

Species	Location, Age (yr) or shore level (see notes)	Assumed turnover time (yr)	Abundance at each census						Statistics on log(x + 1) of abundance values	
			Year	Abundance	Year	Abundance	Year	Abundance	Mean	S.D.
9. Nucella emarginata	all levels	10	1959	99	1969	34	1980	0	1.18	1.05
10. Nucella canaliculata	all levels	10	1959	16	1969	0	1980	0	0.41	0.71
11. Nucella lamellosa	all levels	10	1959	1329	1969	355	1980	244	2.69	0.39
12. Pisaster ochraceus	a. low	20	1960	14.2	1983	16.0			1.21	0.03
	b. low	"	1966	16.7	"	39.7			1.41	0.27
13. Eisenia arborea	a. low	5	1979	144	1984	49			1.93	0.33
	b. low	"	"	162	"	61			2.00	0.30

Notes on sources of data: Spp. 1 & 2, no. per 10sq.cm. For 1934, data from Moore (1936a), for 1951 from Southward and Crisp (1954), and for 1975 from Southward (1976), averaged over all tide levels that had some barnacles in any year; no intermediate observations. a) Amory Bight, b) Misery Pt., c) Tinside, d) Hen Pt. *Spp. 3 to 6:* data from Connell (1956, 1961a, 1961b, unpubl.), at Farland Pt., Is. of Cumbrae, Scotland; longest period without observations was 12 years. Sp. 3, no. per 10sq.cm. in and just below the high adult zone. Sp. 4, no. per 10sq.cm. at levels spanning the entire shore. *Spp. 5 & 6,* no. per sq.m. from counts in July, Aug. or Sept. a) mean tide level, b) 0.3m below mean tide level. *Spp. 7 to 12,* data from Connell (1970, unpubl.); longest period without observation was 4 years. All censuses made during the summer on and near a large concrete piling at Cantilever Pier, except for sp. 12b where censuses were done on rocky shore at Pile Pt., all on San Juan Is., Wash., USA. Spp. 7 & 8, percentage cover; spp. 9, 10, 11, total no. on the piling; sp. 12a, no. along 20m of rocky shoreline; sp. 12b, no. per 20m along 150m of rocky shoreline. *Sp. 13,* unpubl. data collected by J. Kastendiek at Big Fisherman's Cove, Santa Catalina Is., Ca., USA. No. of plants per 40 sq.m., 0.5m above to 2.0 m below mean low tide level. In 1980, between the 2 censuses, a storm destroyed 94% of plants on site a, 4% on site b. All plants tagged in 1979 were gone by 1984 (see Kastendiek, 1982). Of the first 12 species, all but nos. 5, 9, 10, and 11 have planktonic larvae.

can move freely between the piling and the shoreline. Both of the other two (species 9 and 10) had small populations and became extinct; they live at higher zones and so may seldom move between the piling and shore. Since neither has a planktonic stage, recolonization of the piling may take some time.

I have been unable to find other quantitative records of persistence of rocky shore populations that span a period of a complete turnover. Such records should be relatively easy to obtain for short-lived species, particularly annuals. For longer-lived species, a single re-census after a long interval is sufficient, although intermediate censuses at shorter intervals would allow detection of local extinctions and recolonizations that would be missed with longer intervals. Although many population counts have been made on rocky shores, apparently few investigators have returned after a passage of years to make a second census of the same species. May I suggest, as a holiday activity for shore ecologists, a return pilgrimage to the site(s) they studied as postgraduate students?

5.3.3 Persistence of rarer species

All of the species discussed so far are common ones, abundant enough to have been chosen for quantitative study. However, in any assemblage there are rare species which are not usually chosen for detailed study, simply because of the difficulty of obtaining data. Thus the existing evidence for variability and persistence applies almost solely to common species.

When lists of species are gathered for a site in taxonomic surveys, all species, rare and common, are usually noted. A second census of the site, if done with the same degree of effort and taxonomic skill, will yield data on local extinctions and recolonizations of all the species. There may be a bias, in that rare species are more likely to be missed because of their scarcity. However this is balanced to some degree by the fact that in taxonomic surveys there is usually more interest in finding rare species than common ones, so rarities may be searched for harder.

Taxonomic surveys of the same sites, spaced at intervals long enough to ensure a complete turnover, and done with the same effort, are rare. I will discuss one that seems to meet most of these criteria. It is the survey of rocky shore algae by Dawson (1959) and repeated by Thom and Widdowson (1978) 15 to 16 years later. The same or nearby transects at 42 sites in southern California were censused in both surveys, and the presence or absence of species was noted. Using the data in Table 1 in Thom and Widdowson (1978) together with their equation for similarity, it is possible to calculate the percentage of the original number of species that were still present at a site in the later survey. This estimate of taxonomic persistence at a site ranged from 30% to 83%, with a median of 64%. The percentage of species in the second survey that were new at a site since the first survey is an estimate of colonization rate; it ranged from 19% to 69%, with a median of 46%. Thom and Widdowson (1978, p. 4) state that none of the commoner species became extinct, and the new colonists were 'either inconspicuous (due to small size) or of rare occurrence'. Thus about one-third of the species, the rarer ones, did not persist over the 15 year period.

R. Doyle (pers. comm.) resurveyed 13 of Dawson's original sites in 1982–83, 25 years later. He searched for only ten of the larger conspicuous species, and did not restrict his efforts to the narrow transects used by Dawson, thus reducing the chance of not recording a species if it was present. Dawson listed 15 records of these species among these sites. In Doyle's survey, 10 of these records were unchanged and 5 had disappeared. Thus of the 15 original records, 10 had persisted. This 67% rate of persistence over 25 years of a sample of the larger species is about the same as the 64% persistence of species of all sizes over 15 years described above.

These qualitative long-term surveys give a perspective different from the detailed studies of common species. The latter tend to exhibit a high degree of persistence, in part because the investigators had chosen to study them in sites where they were among the commoner organisms. In contrast, the extensive qualitative surveys reveal a great deal of local extinction and recolonization in rarer or smaller species over short intervals and in larger species over longer periods. Only once the population dynamics of a group of rare species have been studied over a series of sites will we know whether their ecology is similar to or different from that of common species.

5.4 Mechanisms Promoting Persistence in Rocky Shore Populations

5.4.1 The planktonic stages

In species with planktonic stages, population losses on the shore are replaced by immigration, either by settlement of juveniles from the plankton or movement of older individuals from nearby populations. The latter occurs in mobile species (Branch, 1975a) and in some sessile species such as mussels (Bayne, 1964) and sea anemones (Sebens, 1981a). I will not consider such secondary immigration here and will concentrate on the original settlement from the plankton.

Planktonic larvae are sometimes regarded as passive particles, completely at the mercy of currents and predators. In these circumstances, shore populations would persist only in places where currents brought larvae to the site at rates sufficient to balance shore mortality. However, there is abundant evidence that planktonic larvae do not behave as passive particles, but instead use clues to select certain habitats over others in ways that increase their chances of eventually reaching favourable shore habitats. For example, Bousfield (1955) found that in an estuarine barnacle, *Balanus improvisus* Darwin, early stage larvae released from adults in the upper estuary were first carried seaward in the surface flow, then later stages swam down or sank and so were carried back up the estuary in the subsurface flow. About 90% mortality occurred between spawning and the cyprid stage. Persistence of the adult population was in part dependent upon the 'larval navigation' displayed by the successive larval stages (nauplii and cyprids) of *B. improvisus*. This early study remains one of the most complete and detailed yet done on this difficult subject.

Another detailed study of both larval dispersal and recruitment in an estuarine barnacle, *Balanus pallidus* Darwin, was made by Sandison (1966) in Lagos Harbour, Nigeria. The distribution of adults shifted seasonally with the dry and wet seasons, because the adults were killed at either high or low salinities. Larvae were abundant in the plankton when and where intermediate salinities occurred, and scarce at high or low salinities. New recruitment occurred at intermediate salinities, either in the lower harbour when freshwater discharge was great in the rainy season, or in the upper harbour when discharge lessened in the dry season. This species is therefore a fugitive from the seasonally varying harsh physical conditions. It persisted by rapid maturation and larval dispersal when conditions deteriorated. Adult populations persisted all year in a refuge, a backwater tidal creek where the salinity never reached the extremes found in the main harbour.

The only study of both settled populations and planktonic larval abundance in the immediate proximity of intertidal surfaces is that of Grosberg (1982). In a study of vertical distribution of planktonic larvae beneath a pier, he found that cyprids of the shore species, *Balanus glandula* Darwin, occurred near the water surface, whereas those of the immediately offshore *B. crenatus* Brug. were several metres below it. The vertical limits of the planktonic larvae were closely correlated with those of both settled juveniles and adults. Other plankton studies have been done for offshore barnacle species settling on panels suspended from rafts (deWolfe, 1973; Geraci and Romairone, 1982).

Some other studies show positive correlations between the spatial distributions of planktonic larvae and settled adults of shore barnacles. Crisp and Southward (1958) found such correlations between horizontal distributions of nauplius larvae and adults of three barnacle species in Cornwall, as did Wilson (1982) for the same three species in Northumberland. Larvae of the shore species *Semibalanus balanoides* were the most concentrated toward the coast. Of the two low-shore to shallow sublittoral barnacles, larvae of *B. crenatus* were slightly less concentrated toward the shoreline, whereas those of

Verruca stroemia (O.F. Müller) extended furthest offshore.

Even if larval behaviour increases the chance of their reaching favourable shore habitats, mortality in the plankton may so reduce numbers that the settlement rate may be below that necessary to replace losses on the shore. A study has been made of the variations over several years in the abundance of both planktonic larvae and recruits to the shore, at the Isle of Cumbrae, Scotland by Pyefinch (1948), Barnes and Powell (1950), Barnes (1956), and Connell (1961a). Data on variations in planktonic larvae are available for nine years; five were termed 'normal' years by Barnes (1956) since there was a steady sequence of planktonic larval stages in March. The other four were termed 'failure' years since the March larval development failed completely. In two of the failure years a later release of larvae developed normally a month later than usual. The most likely cause of the failure of planktonic development was food shortage, due to adverse winds which disrupted the normal development of the spring diatom bloom (Barnes, 1956). This happened in three of the four failure years; in the two failure years when the barnacle larvae developed late, a later diatom bloom also took place. Data on shore recruitment are available for seven years, four being normal years, three failure years. In each of the four normal years, a good recruitment on the shore occurred in early April. In the two failure years when the normal March planktonic development failed, a late larval development occurred in April, followed by good recruitments in May (Connell, 1961a). Thus, there was a complete failure of recruitment due to lack of larval development in the plankton in only one of the seven years on record. Since this species survives for several years in upper shore refuges (Connell, 1961a), such occasional failures of recruitment are probably not crucial to its persistence at this site.

Some authors have used theoretical demographic models to calculate the likelihood that individual adults will produce enough offspring to replace themselves within their life-span. Connell (1970) and Hines (1979b) used the net reproductive rate, R_0 (Leslie, 1966), while Wethey (1985) used matrix techniques (Leslie, 1945). All these models assume a closed population with fixed age-specific schedules of fecundity and survival. The population is considered to encompass all the adults in a region that contribute larvae to the planktonic pool from which local settlement comes. The empirical demographic data taken from the study site are assumed to be representative of this regional population.

For the case of *Balanus glandula* in Connell (1970), Dayton and Oliver (1980) have questioned this last assumption. They suggest that the fecundity schedule used by Connell (1970), based upon the observations of Barnes and Barnes (1956) from a site on Vancouver Island, is likely to be higher than that of the adults on the study site on San Juan Island. If so, the net reproductive rate calculated for the latter would be too high. In contrast, a recent survey of the fecundity of *B. glandula* in the region around San Juan Island supports the assumption (Strathmann *et al.*, 1981). Among several sites similar to that of Connell (1970) on continuous rocky shores on San Juan Island and at the nearest site on Vancouver Island, the age-specific fecundity schedule was judged to be the same by Strathmann *et al.* (1981). Since the production of larvae per unit area was also estimated to be similar among the same sites, the combination of adult densities and/or age structures must also have been similar. Other sites, either the few in the region near mud or sand, or those at greater distances, had higher larval production per unit area. Thus it is probable that the adult populations that contribute most of the larvae to the plankton in the region are similar.

Connell (1970) doubled the age-specific fecundity schedule on the assumption that *Balanus glandula* releases two broods of embryos per year. This assumption is supported by observations of newly settled individuals in both late spring and early autumn as well as observations of individual adults containing both well-developed larvae and unfertilized eggs (Connell, 1970). It is also supported by observations by Johnson and Miller (1935), Barnes and Barnes (1956) and Strathmann *et al.* (1981). Dayton and Oliver (1980) have questioned this procedure, suggesting that doubling the fecundity would thereby increase the net reproductive rate. However, this is erroneous: multiplication of the entire fecundity schedule by a fixed amount will not affect the net reproductive rate as calculated by Connell (1970). This follows because the survivorship of a year class (Connell, 1970, Table 14B) was calculated beginning with the larval production over an entire year, calculated from the numbers and fecundity of adults of the previous generations (Connell, 1970, Table 14A). Using this method, Connell (1970) concluded that, since the net reproduction rate was near 1.0 for two different year-classes, the adult population of *Balanus glandula* at high-shore levels in this region was capable of replacing itself. Hines (1979b) calculated a net reproductive rate of 1.35 for a population of *B. glandula* at Morro Bay, California; here the species released six broods per year. Similar calculations for *Chthamalus fissus* Darwin gave a rate of 1.22, and for *Tetraclita squamosa* Darwin it was 1.19.

While the application of this demographic model suggests that all the populations studied by Connell (1970) and Hines (1979b) were capable of self-replacement, these results should be regarded as tentative, since all the assumptions have not been rigorously tested. For example, Wethey (1985) has recently shown that fecundity varies annually to a marked degree. He used simulation models to predict persistence or extinction of *Semibalanus balanoides* in New England. He used different constant schedules of fecundity and survival in the simulations, based upon empirical measurements that showed annual differences in both these variables. Ice scour of mid- and low-shore levels destroys many barnacles in hard winters in New England; the high-shore is a refuge from ice. He suggests that species that live only in mid-shore zones or lower, particularly if they do not reproduce in the first year, would not persist in this region, due to the high frequency of winters in which sea ice occurs.

5.4.2 The rôle of initial settlement

Most of the evidence on variations in settlement of shore species with planktonic stages consists of counts made some time after initial settlement has occurred. Since newly settled juveniles are very delicate, early mortality on the shore is usually heavy. For example, Connell (1961a, Table 6, Fig. 5) found that 20% of attached barnacle cyprid larvae died before metamorphosis; mortality of newly metamorphosed barnacles was also high, and gradually declined with age. Thus counts made a few days (Denley and Underwood, 1979), a month (Caffey, 1982), or several months (Bowman and Lewis, 1977) after initial settlement may include a significant amount of post-settlement mortality. I will refer to such data as recruitment and will reserve the term settlement for counts made almost immediately after initial attachment; for shore species, counts every day at low tide are at present the best evidence available.

To persist, populations with planktonic stages must have some settlement within the lifetime of the adults. The question is, do local populations become extinct because of lack of initial settlement within the lifetime of the residents? While this is certainly possible, there are, to my knowledge, no published examples of it. There is at least one example in which observations of both initial settlement (from daily counts on sites either cleared daily or allowed to accumulate) and of mortality through the adult stage have been made for a shore species. In *Semibalanus balanoides* at Millport, Scotland, the settlement densities were not limited by planktonic larval supply; heavy settlement occurred every year, and the population persisted for the 3 years of study (Connell, 1961a). This study was made in the large enclosed Sea Area where Barnes (1956) studied the planktonic larvae of this species, as described earlier. In such areas, larvae are less likely to become dispersed and lost offshore than on open coasts where great variation in recruitment has been observed (Caffey, 1982, in press).

While there are examples of local rocky shore populations becoming extinct, in none of them, to my knowledge, has it been shown that the extinction was caused by lack of initial settlement, rather than mortality after settlement. For example, in the disappearance and recolonization of *Semibalanus balanoides* at locations near Plymouth, England (Southward and Crisp, 1954), there were no data on settlement or on post-settlement mortality. Populations of *Donax gouldi* Dall on sandy beaches in southern California appear at high densities and then disappear at intervals, but the relative importance of initial settlement vs. mortality thereafter is unknown (Coe, 1957). Thus the question of whether local extinction could be the result of absence of settlement remains unanswered for lack of evidence. The rôle of planktonic larval supply or of initial settlement behaviour, in the persistence of shore species, remains an important unsolved problem at this time (Connell, in prep.).

5.4.3 Persistence after settlement

There are several mechanisms that promote the persistence of populations after settlement on the shore. In the following discussion I will devote most attention to attached species that require space on hard substrata, e.g. plants, anemones, tube-building worms, barnacles, mussels, oysters, and tunicates. They can be classed into three groups with different mechanisms promoting persistence: (i) those possessing superior ability in interspecific competition and in resisting impacts of physical extremes, predation, etc., (ii) those that are inferior in interspecific competition, or in resisting the impacts cited, but have a refuge from them either in space or (iii) in time. Various terms have been applied to populations with these traits; I will refer to them here as (i) dominants, (ii) refugees, and (iii) fugitives, respectively. A single species may qualify for all three categories under different environmental circumstances.

Dominants are species which can competitively eliminate or exclude all others from a particular region or zone and in addition have traits that resist extremes of physical factors, predators, grazers, etc. The most important such trait is large body size which makes individuals invulnerable to predators (Connell, 1975; Paine, 1976a) or to grazers (Underwood and Jernakoff, 1981). Some rocky shore examples are the mussel *Mytilus californianus* Conrad (Paine, 1966, 1974; Dayton, 1971; Harger, 1972b), the barnacle *Semibalanus cariosus* Pallas (Connell, 1972, 1975), the algae *Lessoniopsis littoralis* (Tild.) and *Hedophyllum sessile* (C. Ag.) (Dayton, 1975), and *Gigartina canaliculata* Harv. (Sousa, 1979b). Such species dominate by maintaining dense populations; rates of larval or spore recruitment and their survival to maturity are usually sufficient to maintain a population within the zone occupied by adults. Clonal species such as some algae or anemones may supplement this by vegetative propagation. Since these are all long-lived species, it is difficult to obtain data on rates of replacement. Some direct evidence for persistence beyond one turnover comes from *Semibalanus cariosus* in Washington (Table 5.1; see also Connell, 1972, 1975; Murdoch and Oaten, 1975).

Refugees are species with breeding populations in spatial refuges that protect them from elimination. Examples are species with spatial refuges from predators and/or competitors in the upper shore zone, e.g. *Semibalanus balanoides* (Connell, 1961a), *Chthamalus montagui* Southward (Connell, 1961b), *C. fragilis* Darwin (Wethey, 1983), *Balanus glandula* (Connell, 1970), *Mytilus edulis* L. (Seed, 1969b; Suchanek, 1978). Larval settlement also occurs below the refuge, but such individuals seldom survive to maturity. Cracks and crevices offer spatial refuges from crushing by wave-borne objects and from desiccation (Dayton, 1971).

Lastly, *fugitives* are species that have a temporal refuge from competition with dominants. They invade newly opened patches, created either within existing assemblages of dominant mussels, barnacles, algae, etc., or as discrete patches isolated from existing assemblages, e.g. recently overturned boulders (Sousa, 1979b). Having colonized the new patch they grow to maturity quickly but are doomed to eventual local extinction by direct or indirect interactions with dominants. Examples are early succession algae, e.g. *Ulva* (Sousa, 1979b), *Postelsia palmaeformis* (Dayton, 1973; Paine, 1979), and some of the animals referred to above (Paine and Levin, 1981). Persistence in a particular region is possible only if a sufficient number of suitable open patches are created within it during the lifetime of the adults and within the distance of larval dispersal from them. All patches may not be equally suitable; their size, type of substratum, density of grazers or predators, etc., are characteristics for which particular species may have special requirements. Patches are created by disturbances of physical or biotic origin. If the rate of disturbance is low, patches will be scattered in a matrix of dominants. If the disturbance rate is high, open patches of various ages may occupy most of the surface, with the dominant being rare (see reviews by Sousa (1985) and Connell and Keough (1985)).

A single species may fall into all three classes in sites with different environments. *Semibalanus cariosus* in Washington is vulnerable to predation by small predators (mainly snails) but once every few years reaches a size large enough to become invulnerable (Connell, 1972, 1975). It never becomes invulnerable to very large predators (e.g. the starfish *Pisaster ochraceus* Brandt), and has a spatial refuge from them in the upper shore zone. Here cracks and crevices provide refuges from physical damage, and in such spatial refuges it is apparently the dominant. Young barnacles also settle in open patches in mussel beds lower on the shore where they are fugitives, eventually being eliminated by direct or indirect interactions with the mussel *Mytilus californianus* (Paine and Levin, 1981). In summary, *Semibalanus cariosus* populations persist because individuals survive to reproductive age in various refuges. They have a refuge from small predators in large body size, from large predators and physical damage in spatial refuges, and from superior competitors in a temporal refuge, patches created by disturbances. Suchanek (1978) gives evidence that *Mytilus edulis* L. has the same ecology in Washington.

Refugees and fugitives persist because of environmental heterogeneity. The intertidal gradient of increasing physical stress towards higher-shore levels can create refuges from predators and competitors at these upper levels. Predators have less submerged time in which to handle their prey in higher zones (Connell, 1961a, 1970, 1975). Growth rates, particularly of suspension feeders, are reduced at higher-shore levels (Barnes and Powell, 1953), and both increasing desiccation (Hatton, 1938; Connell, 1961a; Foster, 1971) and less time for planktonic settlement (Strathmann and Branscombe, 1979) may reduce population density there. All these factors result in a lessening of competition for space at high-shore levels. Temporal variation in activity or density of predators allows occasional year-classes of prey to reach invulnerable sizes, e.g. *S. cariosus* (Connell, 1975), *Mytilus californianus* (Paine, 1976a). Open patches are created by variations in weather, log damage and predation (Dayton, 1971; Sousa, 1979b; Paine, 1979; Paine and Levin, 1981). Thus persistence in refuges of various sorts is ultimately a consequence of environmental heterogeneity in time and space.

There have also been some studies of persistence of mobile species on rocky shores. The predatory snail *Nucella lapillus* (L.) is found in the quiet waters of Lough Ine, with a robust shell morphology that protects it from crab predators; on the nearby wave-beaten shore it has an entirely different morphology (Kitching and Ebling, 1967). In Washington, *Nucella emarginata* (Deshayes) occurs on the high shore, which is probably a spatial refuge from crab and starfish predators (Connell, 1970). Likewise, the grazing snail *Tegula funebralis* (A. Adams) survives only at upper shore levels in locations where its predators (*Octopus bimaculatus* (Verrill) and *Pisaster ochraceus*) are common, but extends its range downshore where they are rare (Fawcett, 1984).

Some studies of the rôle of interspecific competition in the persistence of mobile species have been made. Stimson (1970) showed that adults of the limpet *Lottia gigantia* (Gray) were the dominant in spatial competition with smaller acmaeid limpets. *Lottia* probably persisted by excluding all potential competitors from individual territories which provided a relatively constant supply of food. Black (1979) found that the pulmonate limpet *Siphonaria kurracheensis* (Reeve) lived at higher densities both high and low on the shore, probably being reduced in density at intermediate shore levels by the acmaeid limpet *Notoacmea onychitis* (Menke). Bertness (1981) found that the hermit crab *Clibanarius albidigitus* (Nabili) lives in a refuge higher on the shore or at the edges of pools, whereas a superior competitor *Calcinus obscurus* (Stimpson) occupied a lower zone and the centres of pools. A similar situation was demonstrated experimentally between two species of sea urchins in pools. *Strongylocentrotus purpuratus* (Stimpson), the inferior competitor, was restricted to the tops of boulders by the aggressive behaviour of *S. franciscanus* (A. Agassiz) on Santa Cruz Island, California (Schroeter, 1978).

To discover the precise mechanisms by which a population is eliminated outside a refuge requires very detailed observations. The effects of predators or the physical environment were revealed by field experiments in most of the above examples. The mechanisms of competitive elimination have been directly observed in some sessile species. Direct observations showed that *Semibalanus balanoides* gradually overgrew, undercut or crushed laterally many of the slower-growing *Chthamalus* below the upper shore refuge of *Chthamalus* (*C. montagui*, Connell, 1961b, in Scotland; *C. fragilis*, Wethey, 1983, in Connecticut). *Chthamalus anisopoma* Pilsbry have been observed to overgrow many *Tetraclita squamosa stalactifera*, forma *confinis* Pilsbry in Mexico (Dungan, 1984). The mechanisms underlying other competitive interactions have been inferred rather than observed directly. Short-term antagonistic behavioural interactions probably explain the rapid shifts in distribution in the hermit crabs studied by Bertness (1981). Smothering of other sessile species after overgrowth by mussels is inferred, although the precise mechanism is unknown. Either direct smothering by the mussels, or predation or grazing by animals associated with them, may be involved (Suchanek, 1978).

Indirect interactions may also be responsible for non-persistence. Disturbances, either physical or biotic, may reduce predators and grazers, with a consequent increase in their prey. The latter may then exclude others by pre-emption of space, or eliminate them by direct interference or more efficient exploitation of resources. Such indirect interactions have been indicated by field experiments in several rocky shore communities (Paine, 1966, 1974; Paine and Vadas, 1969; Menge, 1976; Lubchenco, 1978). However, there is little evidence of the extent to which these events occur naturally. Such evidence would require long-term observations of population variations in predators, grazers and their prey, coupled with experimental manipulations of them. For example, in the Gulf of California, the starfish, *Heliaster kubiniji* Xantus, was the commonest large predator on rocky shores before 1978. Then it suddenly declined almost to zero over a large region, possibly as a result of a disease. There is apparently little indication of change in populations of its former prey species (Dungan *et al.*, 1982).

Predators can allow persistence of two prey populations if they switch their attacks among them in a particular way. If the number of attacks on a species is disproportionately large when it is abundant relative to other prey, and disproportionately small when it is relatively rare, such 'switching' behaviour potentially can reduce fluctuations in the numbers of the prey populations. Such behaviour has been demonstrated by Murdoch (1969) for a system of three shore species, the predatory snail *Acanthina spirata* (Blainville) feeding on *Mytilus edulis* and *Balanus glandula* in the laboratory. Switching occurred when the predator showed only a weak preference for one prey over the other and after it had been trained by feeding on only one prey species for awhile. No switching occurred if there was strong preference for one prey species (i.e. between two mussel species) or if no training had taken place. Thus switching might be expected in nature if the more abundant prey occurred in single-species patches so that the predator could become trained to it.

All local populations, whether of dominants or fugitives, run some risk of extinction through chance destruction, particularly when numbers are low. Regional persistence depends upon the asynchrony of such local extinctions, together with their recolonization by dispersal of juveniles or older individuals from extant populations within the region. In addition to those cited earlier, the long-term study by Spight (1974) of 39 local populations of the littoral snail, *Nucella lamellosa* (Gmelin) is a noteworthy example of such asynchrony and interchange between populations.

5.5 Discussion

Judgements of the persistence of a population depend upon the temporal and spatial scales on which it is sampled. For example, a population of fugitives may persist on a local patch for only one generation before being replaced there by a different species. However, over a larger region with many patches, the larger population of fugitives persists by invading patches that are newly opened asynchronously. In rocky shore species with planktonic stages, persistence on a site is possible only because of immigration of larvae produced by the population over a much larger region. In habitats such as estuaries, replacement and persistence of species with planktonic stages is facilitated by 'larval navigation' behaviour (Bousfield, 1955). There may be similar larval behaviour in open coast species that would tend to keep them within a small region, but there is no evidence for this other than the observations discussed earlier that planktonic larvae of shore species tend to be closer to the coastline than those of sublittoral offshore species.

For species with non-planktonic stages, juveniles come from a much smaller region and the mechanisms that ensure persistence probably operate over a smaller spatial scale than in those with planktonic stages. Overall, the spatial and temporal scales on which the mechanisms operate depend upon the life histories of the species of interest.

Most evidence about persistence comes from studies of common species over short periods. However, some surveys over long periods have shown that local extinctions are quite frequent among small or rare species, and over even longer periods, among larger species. Little is known for most rare species, because their population dynamics have never been studied in detail. Records of abundance of rocky shore species available at present cover periods of less than half a century. Studies of coastal middens may extend the records back to almost 10,000 years.

The relative importance to persistence of the supply of planktonic propagules, rate of initial settlement and post-settlement events has not been studied for any single shore species. Most attention has been directed at the latter up to now. While planktonic supply or initial settlement may determine persistence in some localities such as open coastlines, this hypothesis has yet to be tested rigorously.

ACKNOWLEDGEMENTS

I would like to thank P. Dayton, J. Dixon, S. Holbrook, T. Hughes, D. Lohse, R. Paine, P. Raimondi, R. Schmitt, S. Schroeter, W. Sousa, and S. Swarbrick for helpful comments, and R. Doyle and J. Kastendiek for both comments and unpublished data.

CHAPTER VI

MUSSELS AND THEIR RÔLE IN STRUCTURING ROCKY SHORE COMMUNITIES

T.H. Suchanek

6.1 Introduction

Molluscs represent the second most diverse group of animals and marine bivalves are the most abundant molluscs (Russell-Hunter, 1983). Of these, mussels (family Mytilidae) have achieved an impressive ability to dominate rocky shores on all continents. Their world-wide success as dominant space occupiers is most pronounced at exposed or semi-exposed sites in temperate habitats, especially on horizontal or gently sloping rocky substrata. The development of byssal attachment threads by adult bivalves, as in the extant genus *Mytilus*, has allowed them to exploit hard substrata and dominate rocky habitats. Associated with the evolution of the byssal apparatus is a typical reduction of the anterior end of the body and the enlargement of the posterior region, producing a triangular shape and heteromyarian condition (the 'typical' mussel form). Evolutionarily the use of byssal threads by adults may have been a neotenous retention of byssus by byssate post-larval stages of some burrowing taxa (Yonge, 1962). In the Ordovician *c.* 40% of marine bivalves were endobyssate (i.e. they attached byssal threads to the inside of a partial or complete burrow), and their success was attributed to the use of byssal threads that allowed them to maintain a stable position at the sediment–water interface (Stanley, 1972). Stanley (1972) also suggested that from the Devonian to the Jurassic the Mytilidae evolved from largely endobyssate forms such as *Modiolus*, through an intermediate stage (the extinct genus *Promytilus*) to a greater diversity of epibyssate forms such as *Mytilus* spp. (that attach byssus directly to exposed hard substrata such as rock or wood). However, Yonge (1976) questioned this progression, suggesting instead that endobyssate species evolved from epibyssate forms and that the 'typical' mussel form is what has made the Mytilidae so successful. Initially mytilid mussels may have competed with brachiopods in offshore habitats since their early radiation occurred near-shore. Regardless of the cause of the great Permo-Triassic brachiopod extinction (Bretsky, 1969; Stanley, 1968, 1972; Suchanek and Levinton, 1974), the Mytilidae then became more numerous, subsequently radiating to offshore environments (Stanley, 1972), the deep-sea (Allen, 1983) and even into the Galapagos Rift communities as evidenced by the relatively recently discovered mytilid *Bathymodiolus thermophilus* Kenk and Wilson from *c.* 2500m depth (Corliss *et al.*, 1979; Rau and Hedges, 1979; Kenk and Wilson, 1985).

Mussels, especially those that live in exposed habitats, represent some of the most productive species on earth, rivalling the productivity of tropical rain forests and kelp beds (Whittaker, 1975), with a standing crop of up to 6.5 kg·m^{-2} and a productivity of *c.* 2.0 kg·m^{-2}·y^{-1} for low littoral *Mytilus californianus* Conrad beds at Tatoosh Island, Washington State, U.S.A. (Leigh *et al.*, in prep.). Because of their productivity and predictability mussels have been and still are being utilized heavily as a human food resource, having a history of harvest and cultivation for over 700 years in Europe (Mason, 1976). *Mytilus* spp. were also used for food and tools in prehistoric and historic times by native American Indians and by the Pilgrim settlers in 1622 (Miller, 1980). Because of their strength and size, *M. californianus* shells were used as tools (specifically whaling harpoon tips) by Makah Indians in Washington State.

With few exceptions, in most exposed or moderately exposed locations in temperate zone habitats, mytilid mussels form the foundation for complex rocky littoral communities. Here I shall discuss the distribution, structure, and dynamics of dominant littoral mussel beds (with additional reference to some important sublittoral mussel beds) and the communities of associated organisms which they support.

6.2 Geographical and Zonational Distributions of the Dominant Mytilidae

Although most mytilid mussel populations are found in littoral habitats, all of the Mytilidae appear to have the ability to live sublittorally. In fact, the occasional sublittoral individuals of typically littoral species (e.g. *Mytilus edulis* L. and *M. californianus*) are invariably more robust (Paine, 1976b; Suchanek, 1978). Recently several naturally occurring sublittoral mussel populations have received considerable attention (e.g. *Aulacomya ater* (Molina) and *Choromytilus meridionalis* (Krauss) in South Africa and *Modiolus modiolus* (L.) in New England, U.S.A.). Although this Chapter deals primarily with littoral mussels, I have included relevant information on these sublittoral forms as well. It appears that competition and especially predation are the factors that prevent most mytilid mussels from developing sublittoral populations (see below).

Mytilus edulis and its species complex is the most widely distributed mytilid entity, having a circumpolar distribution in temperate habitats of both the northern and southern hemispheres (Soot-Ryen, 1955; Seed, 1976b). Until recently, on Pacific coasts, *M. edulis* (the 'bay mussel') had been considered an inhabitant of more protected embayments (Ricketts and Calvin, 1939; Harger, 1970a,b, 1972a,b). However, it has now been shown to occur abundantly and persistently in some of the most exposed rocky shore sites known, such as Tatoosh Island, Washington and Torch Bay, Alaska (Suchanek, 1978). These findings are consistent with the generally eurytopic nature of *M. edulis* in habitats worldwide, especially with respect to temperature, salinity, and siltation. However, more work is needed to explain why it does not occur abundantly in exposed habitats elsewhere, such as in Oregon and California.

Few other mussel species are widely distributed; however, four deserve mention. *Aulacomya ater* occurs littorally and sublittorally in Chile, South Africa and the Kerguelen Archipelago (sublittoral forms not reported here). *Modiolus modiolus* is found in typically dense beds sublittorally on the East coast (New England) and West coast (San Juan Archipelago, Washington) of the U.S.A. and in Europe. On the shore it is more sporadic, sometimes being found as dense beds in rock pools (Torch Bay, Alaska) or as scattered individuals in dense *Mytilus californianus* beds (Tatoosh Island, Washington). *Perna perna* (L.) typically occupies littoral and sublittoral sites in Venezuela and on the East and West coasts of Africa. Finally, *Septifer bilocularis* L. never forms dense beds, but occurs as scattered individuals littorally in crevices or under stones and/or sublittorally on the East coast of Africa and on the shores of Australia. The remainder of the dominant space-occupying mussels have, for the most part, contiguous geographical distributions. A review of common or dominant world-wide mytilid mussels is given in Table 6.1, with information on geographical and vertical distributions, size and relevant references.

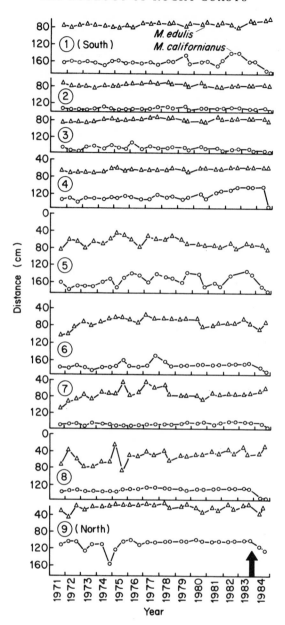

FIG. 6.1. Upper limits for *Mytilus edulis* and *Mytilus californianus* from 1971–84 at Tatoosh Island, Washington. Relative distances were measured from 9 permanent markers fixed to the rock substratum above the mussel beds. Site markers no. 1 and no. 9 at the southern and northern ends (respectively) of the transect line. Heavy arrow on abscissa denotes time of major freeze in December, 1983. Data courtesy of R.T. Paine.

TABLE 6.1

Geographical and vertical distributions of the dominant Mytilidae of the world

('–' indicates no data found).

Mussel species	Geographical range	Vertical range	Maximum known length (mm)	References
North America: Pacific				
Modiolus modiolus (L.)	Arctic Ocean to Monterey, California	littorally and dense beds sublittorally	–	Soot-Ryen (1955) Suchanek (in prep.) Suchanek (pers. obs.)
Mytilus californianus Conrad	Aleutian Islands, Alaska to Isla Socorro, Mexico	mid-littoral and sublittoral (to – 73m)	⩾266	Ricketts and Calvin (1939) Berry (1954) Soot-Ryen (1955) Chan (1973) Paine (1976a,b) Levinton and Suchanek (1978) Suchanek (1978)
Mytilus edulis L.	Arctic Ocean to Cabo San Lucas, Baja California	high- to low-shore and occasionally sublittoral to – 29m (– 220m?)	140	Soot-Ryen (1955) Suchanek (1978) Lutz (1980)
Mytilus edulis diegensis Coe	Northern California to Baja, California	littoral to slightly sublittoral in bays and sloughs	108	Coe (1945, 1946)
North America: Atlantic				
Geukensia demissa (Dillwyn) (= Modiolus (= Brachidontes) demissus) Dillwyn	Gulf of St. Lawrence to northeast Florida	in salt marshes from mid- to low-shore and occasionally on pilings	120	McDougall (1943) Kuenzler (1961a,b) Lent (1967, 1968, 1969) Pierce (1970) Abbott (1974) Lutz and Castagna (1980) Seed (1980a,b) Bertness and Grosholz (in prep.)
Modiolus modiolus (L.)	Arctic Seas to New Jersey	rocky and gravelly substrata generally sublittoral to at least 183m	150	Soot-Ryen (1955) Rowell (1967) Abbott (1974) de Schweinitz and Lutz (1976) Witman (1980, 1983, 1984)

TABLE 6.1 *Cont'd*

Mussel species	Geographical range	Vertical range	Maximum known length (mm)	References
Mytilus edulis L.	Arctic Ocean to South Carolina (and Cuba?)	mid-littoral to sublittoral	107	Scattergood and Taylor (1950) Soot-Ryen (1955) Abbott (1974) Peterson (1979) Lutz (1980) Menge (1983, pers. comm.)
South America: Pacific				
Aulacomya ater (Molina)	Callao, Peru to the Strait of Magellan	low-shore and sublittoral (to at least − 20m)	200	Soot-Ryen (1955) Knox (1960) Tomicic (1966, 1968) Lozada (1968) Marincovich (1973) Lozada et al. (1974) Suchanek (pers. obs.)
Choromytilus chorus (Molina)	Pacasmayo, Peru to Orange Bay, Tierra del Fuego	littoral and sublittoral	300	Soot-Ryen (1955) Stuardo (1960) Lozada et al. (1971) Aracena et al. (1974) Yañez (1974) Walne (1979) Tomicic (pers. comm.) Suchanek (pers. obs.)
Mytilus edulis L. (= M. edulis chilensis Hupe)	Valparaiso, Chile to Beagle Channel, Argentina	mid- to low-littoral	120	Soot-Ryen (1955) Knox (1960) Padilla (1973) Reid (1974) Yañez (1974) Suchanek (1978) Miranda and Acuna (1979) Langley et al. (1980)
Perumytilus (Brachidontes) purpuratus (Lamarck)	Ecuador to the Strait of Magellan	high- to low-littoral	41	Soot-Ryen (1959) Alveal (1970) Marincovich (1973) Viviani (1975) Castilla (1981) Paine et al. (1985) Suchanek (pers. obs.)
Semimytilus algosus (Gould)	Paita, Peru to Valparaiso, Chile	low-littoral and sublittoral (to − 9m)	≥ 21	Soot-Ryen (1955, 1959) Olsson (1961) Marincovich (1973) Paine et al. (1985) Suchanek (pers. obs.)

TABLE 6.1   *Cont'd*

Mussel species	Geographical range	Vertical range	Maximum known length (mm)	References
South America: Atlantic				
Aulacomya ater (Molina)	southern Brazil to Strait of Magellan and Falkland Islands	littoral and sublittoral to at least 15m depth	–	Soot-Ryen (1955) Knox (1960) Lozada *et al.* (1974)
Brachidontes rodriguezi D'Orb. (? = *Perumytilus purpuratus* (Lamarck))	Santa Cruz, Argentina to Strait of Magellan	littoral	30	Penchazadeh (1973)
Mytilus edulis Linne (= *M. edulis platensis* Orbigny)	southern Brazil to Argentina	–	–	Knox (1960) Penchazadeh (1971) Abbott (1974) Seed (1976b)
Perna perna (L.)	Venezuela to the Strait of Magellan	–	–	Soot-Ryen (1955) Davies (1970) see also Seed (1976b)
Europe				
Modiolus modiolus (L.)	Iceland and Barents Sea to northern Britain and sporadically to the Bay of Biscay	low-littoral in pools and sublittoral to – 200m	200	Coleman and Trueman (1971) Coleman (1973) Roberts (1975) Seed and Brown (1975, 1977, 1978) Brown *et al.* (1976) Brown and Seed (1977) Comely (1978, 1981)
Mytilus edulis L.	White Sea to the Mediterranean and in northern Africa	high-littoral to sublittoral	90	Kitching *et al.* (1959) Lewis (1964) Kitching and Ebling (1967) Seed (1969a,b) Stephenson and Stephenson (1972) Kautsky and Wallentinus (1980) Kautsky (1982)
Mytilus galloprovincialis Lamarck	mostly Mediterranean and Ireland to the Black Sea	high-littoral to sublittoral	90	Lewis and Seed (1969) Seed (1971, 1972, 1974, 1978b) Gosling and Wilkins (1981) Skibinski *et al.* (1978, 1980, 1983) Skibinski and Beardmore (1979) Gosling (1984) Lubet *et al.* (1984)

TABLE 6.1 *Cont'd*

Mussel species	Geographical range	Vertical range	Maximum known length (mm)	References
Africa: Atlantic Ocean				
Aulacomya ater (Molina)	at least in South Africa	mid-littoral to sublittoral	95	Velimirov *et al.* (1977) Griffiths (1977, 1980a) Griffiths and King (1979a,b) Pollock (1979) Field *et al.* (1980) Griffiths and Seiderer (1980) Seiderer *et al.* (1982) Stuart, Field and Newell (1982) Stuart, Newell and Lucas (1982) Wickens and Griffiths (in press)
Choromytilus meridionalis (Krauss)	at least in South Africa	mid-littoral and sublittoral (to – 30m)	101	Griffiths (1977, 1980a,b) Griffiths (1981a,b,c,d) Griffiths and Seiderer (1980) Griffiths and Buffenstein (1981) Penney and Griffiths (1984) Wickens and Griffiths (in press)
Perna perna (L.)	sporadically from Mauritania to the Cape of Good Hope	mid-littoral to sublittoral	112	Stephenson and Stephenson (1972) Berry (1978) Griffiths (1981a) Wickens and Griffiths (in press)
Africa: Indian Ocean				
Brachidontes variabilis (Krauss)	northern Mozambique to lower Natal	scattered littoral	–	Stephenson and Stephenson (1972) Jackson (1976)
Perna perna (L.)	Mozambique to the Cape of Good Hope	mid-littoral to sublittoral	–	Stephenson and Stephenson (1972) Jackson (1976)
Septifer bilocularis L.	at least Mozambique to Natal	scattered littoral	–	Stephenson and Stephenson (1972) Jackson (1976)

TABLE 6.1 *Cont'd*

Mussel species	Geographical range	Vertical range	Maximum known length (mm)	References
India and Southeast Asia				
Mytilus smaragdinus Gmelin (? = *Perna (= Mytilus) viridis)* (L.)	South China Sea: Philippines, Thailand and Singapore	littoral to sublittoral	> 300?	Jones and Alagarswami (1968) Davies (1970) Obusan and Urbano (1968) E.L. Tan (1971) W.H. Tan (1975a) Blanco (1973) Ling (1973) Sribhibhadh (1973) Tham *et al.* (1973) Korringa (1976) Parulekar *et al.* (1982)
Kerguelen Archipelago				
Aulacomya ater (Molina)	Kerguelen Islands	high- to low-littoral	–	Arnaud (1974) Bellido (1981) Lawrence and McClintock (in prep.)
Mytilus edulis L. (= *M. desolationis* Lamy) (= *M. kerguelensis* Fletcher)	Kerguelen Islands	high littoral	–	Knox (1960) Arnaud (1974) Bellido (1981) Lawrence and McClintock (in prep.)
Japan				
Mytilus edulis L.	northern Japan	mid-littoral	> 60	Hoshiai (1960, 1961, 1964) Hoshiai *et al.* (1964) Tsuchiya (1979, 1980, 1982, 1983)
Mytilus galloprovincialis Lamarck	southern Japan	mid-littoral to sublittoral	112.5	Hosomi (1977, 1978, 1980)
Septifer virgatus (Wiegmann)	northern Japan	mid-littoral	> 60	Hoshiai (1961, 1964) Hoshiai *et al.* (1964) Tsuchiya (1979, 1983)

TABLE 6.1 *Cont'd*

Mussel species	Geographical range	Vertical range	Maximum known length (mm)	References
U.S.S.R.				
Crenomytilus grayanus Soot-Ryen	Kuril Islands south to the Philippine Islands	mid-littoral to sublittoral	> 128	Saito and Sakamoto (1951) Soot-Ryen (1955) Sadykhova (1967, 1970a,b,c) Levinton (pers. comm.)
Mytilus edulis L.	–	–	–	Kuznetzov and Mateeva (1948) Mateeva (1948) Palichenko (1948) Savilov (1953)
Australia and Tasmania				
Brachidontes rostratus (Dunk.) (? = *Brachidontes variabilis*)	South Australia to New South Wales and Tasmania	sparsely in upper to mid-littoral	–	Guiler (1950, 1951, 1955) Bennett and Pope (1953, 1960) Knox (1960, 1963) Wilson and Hodgkin (1967) Stephenson and Stephenson (1972)
Mytilus edulis L. (= *M. edulis planulatus* Lamarck)	Fremantle, Western Australia to Port Stephens, New South Wales and throughout Tasmania	low-littoral and sublittoral (to – 18m)	–	Guiler (1950, 1951) Bennett and Pope (1953, 1960) Allen (1955) Knox (1960, 1963) Wilson and Hodgkin (1967) Stephenson and Stephenson (1972)
Septifer bilocularis L.	in Western Australia south to Cape Leeuwin	littorally in crevices and under stones and sublittorally (to – 5.5m)	–	Wilson and Hodgkin (1967)

TABLE 6.1 *Cont'd*

Mussel species	Geographical range	Vertical range	Maximum known length (mm)	References
Xenostrobus (Modiolus) pulex (Lamarck)	Victoria and Tasmania	upper littoral	–	Guiler (1950, 1951, 1955) Bennett and Pope (1953, 1960) Knox (1960, 1963) Wilson and Hodgkin (1967) Stephenson and Stephenson (1972)
New Zealand				
Aulacomya maoriana Iredale	North and South Island	scattered widely from high- to low-littoral	–	Knox (1953, 1960) Batham (1958) Stephenson and Stephenson (1972) Kennedy (1976, 1977)
Mytilus edulis L. (= *M. planulatus* Lamarck) (= *M. edulis aoteanus* Powell)	North and South Island and some distant island possessions	mid-littoral to sublittoral	–	Knox (1953, 1960) Batham (1958) Kennedy (1976, 1977)
Perna (Mytilus) canaliculus Gmelin	North and South Island	mid-littoral to sublittoral (to – 18m)	180	Knox (1953, 1960, 1963) Batham (1958) Greenway (1969a,b, 1975) Paine (1971) Stephenson and Stephenson (1972) Kennedy (1976, 1977) Luckens (1976)
Xenostrobus (Modiolus) pulex Lamarck (= *Modiolus neozelanicus* Iredale)	North and South Island	high- to low-littoral	20	Knox (1953, 1960) Batham (1958) Paine (1971) Kennedy (1977)

6.3 Factors Limiting Mussel Zonation

6.3.1 Upper limits

While there may be significant fluctuations in some mussel populations, especially at lower shore levels, upper limits are often very constant over long periods of time (Lewis, 1964, 1977b; Paine, 1974, 1984). Lewis (1977b) has presented 10 years' data showing a consistent percentage cover of high shore *Mytilus edulis* at Robin Hood's Bay, England. At Tatoosh Island, Washington, Paine (1974, 1984) has shown a constancy in the upper limit of the *Mytilus californianus* zone over 12 years (1971–83). Similar trends in the upper limit of the *M. edulis* zone at Tatoosh Island over five years are seen in Suchanek (1978), with moderately predictable seasonal fluctuations caused by summer mortality as a result of desiccation. Evidence of periodic desiccation was clearly visible at Tatoosh Island during August, 1984, when 'windrows' of thousands of empty (non-drilled) *M. edulis* shells (many with viscera remaining) were piled up on high-shore platforms (pers. obs.).

Thirteen years' data on the upper limit of both *M. edulis* and *M. californianus* are presented in Fig. 6.1 (data courtesy of R.T. Paine). These data represent *linear* (not vertical) distances (cm) measured each spring and autumn down from 9 markers permanently fixed into the rock substratum, to the upper limits of both the *M. edulis* and *M. californianus* zones. This transect is positioned along a North (no. 9) to South (no. 1) inclined slope. The rock angle is steepest at the South end, resulting in a shorter linear distance for each unit change of vertical height. These data show moderate stability for the upper limits of both species, especially *M. californianus*, with occasional events disrupting this level. The greatest fluctuations in the *M. californianus* upper limit (e.g. at markers no. 5 and no. 9) are associated with winter disturbance patches which incorporated a portion of the upper edge. Also, a freeze in December, 1983 (at arrow on abscissa), significantly lowered this upper limit at all marker sites (see below). In the field *M. edulis* appears less affected by winter storms, but typically suffers some mortality at the upper edge from desiccation each summer.

While reduced food intake at higher-shore levels may result in slower growth rates and eventually smaller-sized adults (Baird, 1966; Seed, 1976b; Griffiths, 1981b; Griffiths and Buffenstein, 1981), physiological intolerance to desiccation is probably the single most significant factor determining the upper limits of mussel zonation. Several authors have noted casually that mussels can survive above the upper limit of their normal littoral zone when protected in cracks or crevices (Batham, 1958; Griffiths, 1981a; Lawrence and McClintock, in prep.) or have suggested desiccation as an upper limiting factor (Paine, 1974; Hosomi, 1978). Actual mortality from high temperatures and/or desiccation in upper zones has also been well documented (Coe, 1946; Luckens, 1976; Suchanek, 1978; Peterson, 1979; Griffiths, 1981a; Tsuchiya, 1983). In an excellent series of field and laboratory studies Kennedy (1976) determined the influence of desiccation and temperature on three species of rocky shore mussels (*M. edulis aoteanus* Powell, *Perna canaliculus* Gmelin and *Aulacomya maoriana* Iredale) in southern New Zealand. These results indicated strongly that the relative positions of the three mussel species on the shore were consistent with their respective tolerances to temperature and, especially, desiccation. Particularly important findings in this study were the combined and/or synergistic effects of temperature, wind, relative humidity and species-specific or age-specific behavioural differences on desiccation-related mortality. Furthermore, juveniles were more susceptible to desiccation than adults and tended to settle or aggregate into clumps of conspecifics or other mussel species, a result supported by evidence from studies on other mytilids (Lukens, 1976, for *Perna canaliculus* in New Zealand; Suchanek, 1978, 1981, for *M. californianus* in Washington; Bertness and Grosholz, in prep., for *Geukensia demissa* (Dillwyn) in New England).

Contrary to popular belief, it is not only drastic changes in temperature that affect bivalve mortality. Small temperature differences can have dramatic effects on the survival of bivalves and may ultimately determine their local as well as geographical distributions. In laboratory tests it has been shown that an increase of 1.0°C can change mortality rates from low to high levels for some bivalves (Kennedy and Mihursky, 1971), and that differences in thermal tolerance between four species of infaunal bivalves correlated well with their relative latitudinal, tidal and infaunal positions. Dickie (1958) showed that environmental temperature differences as small as 0.3°C can increase mortality by 25% in scallops. Currently we lack comparable data on mussels, but attention is drawn to the works of Henderson (1929), Wells and Gray (1960), Read and Cumming (1967), Lent (1968), Waugh (1972), and Bayne *et al.* (1976) that deal specifically with the effects of small temperature differences on survival and/or distributions for various species of Mytilidae.

The importance of behavioural differences between species should not be underrated as an important factor affecting the littoral distributions of mussels. For example, short periods of gaping by the epibyssate mussel *Modiolus modiolus* when subjected to air contribute significantly to water loss and subsequent mortality and may be closely related to its typical low littoral to sublittoral distribution in England (Coleman and Trueman, 1971; Coleman, 1973). A different view of air-gaping is reported for an endobyssate modiolid, *Geukensia* (= *Modiolus*) *demissa*, which air-gapes both for aerial respiration and for evaporative cooling, allowing this species to penetrate high-shore habitats in salt marshes (Kuenzler, 1961a,b; Lent, 1968, 1969). The significant differences here are that despite water loss, *G. demissa* (i) has a much higher upper thermal tolerance limit (37°C), some 14 degrees higher than that of *M. modiolus*, and (ii) lives in semi-protective burrows in marsh mud (Bertness, 1980; Bertness and Grosholz, in prep.), further reducing the effects of desiccation. In fact, if epibyssate species (such as *Mytilus* spp., *Choromytilus* spp., and *Perna* spp.), did evolve from endobyssate forms (such as the modiolid *Geukensia demissa*) then this radiation (Stanley, 1972), although involving only minor morphological changes, may have necessitated significant behavioural and/or physiological adaptations for survival in intertidal regions where aerial exposure can be dangerous or even fatal.

Freezing can be equally as important as desiccation in determining upper zonational limits for some mussel species. The range of *Mytilus californianus* extends from the Aleutian Islands, Alaska to Baja, California (Soot-Ryen, 1955). Throughout its range *M. californianus* lives in sympatry with *M. edulis*, but is a dominant space occupier in the mid- to low-shore only from Sitka, Alaska southwards (Ricketts and Calvin, 1939). When this occurs, *M. californianus* outcompetes *M. edulis* and relegates it to a high-shore band (Suchanek, 1978, 1981). North of Sitka the smaller *M. edulis* dominates much of the littoral zone, in some places (e.g. Glacier Bay, Alaska) covering over 5.5 vertical metres of space (Suchanek and Duggins, in prep.). *M. edulis* is much more eurythermal and has an exceptional tolerance to winter freezing (Bayne *et al.*, 1976). In fact, in the Hebron Fjord, Labrador, entire beds of *M. edulis* remain alive after spending six to eight months frozen solid in ground ice at – 20°C and below, after which they are chipped out by the Eskimos for food in the spring (Kanwisher, 1955).

In locations such as Torch Bay, Alaska, when littoral *M. californianus* are exposed to freezing, they suffer 100% mortality (Suchanek, 1978); hence their local distribution is restricted to shore pools, extremely low-shore sites or sublittoral habitats (Suchanek and Duggins, in prep.). Occasionally, even in more temperate climates *M. californianus* can be affected by freezing. In December, 1983, a major freeze occurred in Washington State and the upper limit of the Tatoosh Island populations of *M. californianus* was lowered significantly (Fig. 6.1), leaving a gap between the lower limit of *M. edulis* and the upper limit of *M. californianus*. Lag periods exist between the time when mussels die and the time their shells are washed free of the matrix of binding byssal threads; in the case of *M. edulis* and *M. californianus*, dead shells may take as long as six to eight months to wash out of the system completely (Suchanek, 1978 and Fig. 6.1). In addition, the exceptionally hot summer of 1984 could have exacerbated this situation by eliminating even more *M. californianus* at the upper limit. Populations of

M. edulis experienced some fluctuations up or down in the upper limit, but no uni-directional trend was observed in association with this freeze (Fig. 6.1).

6.3.2 Lower limits

Several observational and/or experimental studies have shown how biological factors (i.e. predation and competition) contribute greatly to setting the lower limit at which mussels can survive. Some of the pioneering work in this area was done by Newcombe (1935b) in the Bay of Fundy, who strongly implicated a sea urchin (*Strongylocentrotus*), a dogwhelk (*Purpura* = *Nucella*), and especially two species of sea stars (*Asterias*) as predators on, and determinants of, lower limits for *M. edulis* populations. Paris (1960) also suggested such predator-control of *Mytilus* in the San Juan Islands of Washington State. In Ireland, Kitching *et al.* (1959), Ebling *et al.* (1964) and Kitching and Ebling (1967) have described a suite of predators that feed on *M. edulis* (the crabs *Carcinus* and *Liocarcinus* (= *Portunus*), the whelk *Nucella* and the sea star *Marthasterias*), and suggest strongly that the sea star was the agent controlling the littoral distribution of this mussel. The distribution of littoral *M. edulis* in New England is controlled by a guild (*sensu* Root, 1967) of predators: the whelk *Nucella* (= *Thais*); two sea stars, *Asterias* spp.; and three crabs, *Cancer* spp. and *Carcinus* sp. (Menge, 1976, 1978a,b, 1979, 1983; Lubchenco and Menge, 1978; Menge and Lubchenco, 1981). In the mid-zone of protected shores they claim that *Nucella* is the only important predator, although this has been questioned by Edwards *et al.* (1982) who feel that fish (specifically the cunner *Tautogolabrus*) may play a significant rôle in controlling the vertical distribution of both *Mytilus* and *Modiolus* at these sites (also see reply by Menge, 1982b). In the low littoral at protected sites Menge and Lubchenco felt that the entire guild of predators is at work with the crabs, the sea stars and the whelk (in decreasing order of importance) controlling *M. edulis* as well as barnacles. At low littoral sites exposed to heavy wave action they reported that predators do not control *M. edulis* and, therefore, it achieves long-term spatial dominance, in some places reaching into the sublittoral zone (Menge, pers. comm.). In New Jersey, similar control of *M. edulis* populations on dock pilings and a rocky jetty were noted by Peterson (1979). There the predators are two crabs (*Callinectes* and *Neopanope*) and the sea star *Asterias*.

Predator-controlled lower limits of three other mytilid species have been shown experimentally by R.T. Paine in a series of removals of predatory sea stars: *Pisaster* in Washington (Paine, 1974), *Stichaster* in New Zealand (Paine, 1971) and *Heliaster* in Chile (Paine *et al.*, 1985). In each case the dominant mussels at these sites (*Mytilus californianus*, *Perna canaliculus* and *Perumytilus purpuratus* (Lamarck) respectively) extended their vertical range downward in the littoral zone. When predators were allowed to return to these sites, the *Perumytilus* system returned to the original condition. In some cases, *Perna* and *Mytilus* were able to grow beyond the size capable of being consumed by the sea stars (Paine, 1976a) and thus these manipulations created temporarily altered states which may persist for ten (for *Mytilus*) to thirty years (for *Perna*) (Paine *et al.*, 1985).

Other examples of predation controlling the lower limits of mussel distributions have been implied from laboratory feeding experiments by Seed (1980a) for the crabs *Callinectes* and *Panopeus* on *Geukensia*. Seed felt that this mechanism was especially probable on wharf pilings and sea wall sites, but possibly not as important in salt marshes where the prey are less accessible.

Competition has also been shown to control lower littoral limits for mussels. Experimental manipulations on *Perna* in New Zealand by Paine (1971) have shown that in addition to being controlled at its lower limit by the predatory starfish *Stichaster*, *Perna* can be outcompeted by the giant kelp *Durvillea* which occurs in the lower littoral. When the latter species is removed *Perna* settles and proliferates in the available space. Further evidence for the influence of competition on lower limits was given by Suchanek (1978, 1981) for *Mytilus edulis*. In Washington *M. edulis* occurs in (i) a high littoral band occupying *c*. 0.3m vertically, (ii) in the mid- to low-shore in gaps formed in the dominant *M. californianus* band, and (iii) in holdfasts of the kelp *Lessoniopsis*. Whenever *M. californianus* is removed, either naturally by winter storms or artificially by ecologists, *M. edulis* colonizes these lower littoral sites. In Alaska, where *M. californianus* often freezes on the shore (see above), the more tolerant *M. edulis* occupies a major band in the littoral where *M. californianus* would normally be expected to occur (Suchanek and Duggins, in prep.).

The control of mussel upper limits by physical factors (such as heat and desiccation) and lower limits by biological factors (predation and competition) fully support those findings of Connell (1961a,b) for rocky shore barnacle distributions and his speculations that these factors also control other littoral forms.

6.4 Population Dynamics and Life History Patterns of Mussels

6.4.1 Reproductive cycles and spawning

Reproductive cycles and spawning periods in mytilid mussels are tremendously variable, both with respect to fluctuations between different species at the same location as well as those within a single species at different geographical sites. For example, along the West coast of North America most authors have reported a limited spawning period each year for *Mytilus edulis* in the late autumn or early winter months [October to February] (see Morris *et al.*, 1980 and Suchanek, 1981, for a review). This may be an adaptation for locating available settling sites (i.e. storm-generated patches of bare rock). In the same region, *M. californianus* appears to 'dribble' gametes throughout the year never spawning-out completely (Suchanek, 1981; Edwards, 1984). This may equally be related to its own continuously available settling sites (conspecific byssal threads). Alternatively, spawning periods of *M. edulis* from many different locations show tremendous temporal variability with spawning occurring at virtually any time of the year (Seed, 1976b). However, at each location there is reasonable agreement in spawning dates (see Seed, 1976b and Suchanek, 1981, for reviews).

The proximate cues involved in stimulating an actual spawning event are still not fully understood but may involve a combination of both endogenous and exogenous factors (Seed, 1976b). Temperature appears to be an extremely important cue both for initiating spawning as well as setting upper and lower thermal limits for reproduction. This is clearly evidenced from many species that initiate gametogenesis as sea temperatures are falling and then begin spawning as temperatures rise, or vice versa (see Engle and Loosanoff, 1944; Chipperfield, 1953; Sugiura, 1959; Lozada, 1968; Moore and Reish, 1969; Bayne, 1975; Seed, 1975; Kennedy, 1977). Spawning in *Mytilus californianus* may be influenced by absolute temperatures, whereas *M. edulis* may respond to more rapid changes in temperature (Lubet, 1959). Thermal limits may also be set by long-term average temperatures. Elvin and Gonor (1979) speculated that average temperatures may set threshold levels for nerves responsive to thermal shock and that rapid thermal changes then trigger the release of neurosecretions from cerebral ganglia and associated spawning events. These thermal limits can, in turn, ultimately influence geographical and latitudinal distributions (see especially Allen, 1955; Wells and Gray, 1960; Read and Cumming, 1967; Wilson and Hodgkin, 1967).

Another exogenous factor, often noted but not fully understood, is physical stimulation. For many years it has been known that *Mytilus edulis* will spawn in response to jarring, rattling or scraping the shell and/or pulling or cutting the byssal threads (Field, 1922; Young, 1942, 1945, 1946; Loosanoff and Davis, 1963; Brenko and Calabrese, 1969). These are precisely the same environmental cues as received during a winter storm, which also signal the presence of storm-generated patches of bare rock on which *M. edulis* can settle. This pattern correlates well with spawning and subsequent settlement events for this species observed on the West coast of North America. However, other physical or biological correlates such as light levels (Elvin, 1976) or phytoplankton blooms (Griffiths, 1977) may be equally important. Currently, the relative contribution of each of these factors to spawning is unknown.

Interestingly, height on the shore seems to have little influence on the relative degree of gonad development and gametic production, although more gametes will be produced per individual from lower shore sites because the lower shore population is composed of larger individuals. While increased temperature and desiccation stress in upper shore zones produce higher metabolic costs, energy appears to be shunted away from growth (Baird and Drinnan, 1957; Baird, 1966; Seed, 1976b; Griffiths and Buffenstein, 1981), but not gametic output (see Seed, 1976b, for *Mytilus edulis* in England; Griffiths and Buffenstein, 1981, for *Choromytilus* in South Africa; Suchanek, 1981, for *M. californianus* in Washington, U.S.A.; Jordan and Valiela, 1982, for *Geukensia* in New England).

Seed (1976b) presented an excellent review of literature on spawning periods for *Mytilus edulis* and several other important mytilid species. Here I complement that list with information on works since that time that deal with reproductive cycles, spawning times, larval dispersal periods, settlement/recruitment times and/or growth rates for the common dominant mytilid species of the world (Table 6.2).

6.4.2 Larval dispersal and recruitment

Of all the environmental parameters influencing the abundance and distribution of adult rocky shore mussels we know least about life-spans, dispersal distances, predators or almost any other factors limiting mussel larvae. Because of the tremendous difficulty in following larval cohorts in the field (if such cohorts even remain as discrete entities), most larval life-spans have been determined either directly from laboratory cultures (Field, 1922; Bayne, 1965; de Schweinitz and Lutz, 1976) or inferred from the difference between the spawning date of a local population and subsequent recruitment dates into that same region (Kennedy, 1977; Griffiths, 1981a; Suchanek, 1981). This second approach is dangerous because it ignores the importance of immigration and emigration of larvae. For example, Kuenzler (1961a) found spawning in *Geukensia* during July and August, but significant recruitment only in March to June. It is highly unlikely that such larvae produced in mid-summer would either survive seven to eight months or remain in this localized region if they did survive. Much more likely is that the settling larvae either originated from a sub-population of the one under study, or from a different source entirely.

When the life-spans of mussel larvae have been estimated, they range in the order of two to four weeks (Nelson, 1928b; Bayne, 1964, 1965, 1976; de Schweinitz and Lutz, 1976), a period in which currents could easily wash the larvae into a different region. For what portion of that period a larva is 'competent' to settle (*sensu* Jackson and Strathmann, 1981), over what distances mussel larvae typically disperse, and what factors control immediate post-settlement survival are virtually unknown for nearly all mussel species, although Bayne (1964) and Seed (1969a,b) have presented a nearly complete picture for *M. edulis* in England. Only with concurrent investigations of spawning cycles, larval abundance and distribution patterns, and recruitment events can we make significant contributions to the understanding of complete mussel life history patterns.

Settlement and recruitment patterns for littoral mussels often show predictable annual trends, but occasionally they show massive settlements where the spatfall can vary by as much as one to three orders of magnitude (Suchanek, 1978; Hosomi, 1980; Griffiths, 1981a; Paine, pers. comm.). To my knowledge no long-term ($\geqslant$ 10 yr) studies have been conducted on mytilid recruitment patterns to this end. At Tatoosh Island, 1972 and 1983 were massive recruitment years for *M. edulis* which resulted in the occupation of low littoral patches of cleared space in the *M. californianus* zone with up to 80% cover of *M. edulis*. Alternatively, some studies have even shown no recruitment, e.g. for five

TABLE 6.2

Information and references on reproductive cycles, spawning, recruitment and growth of mytilid mussels ('–' indicates no data found).

Species	References	Size (mm) at first sexual maturity	Comments
Aulacomya ater			
Africa:	Griffiths (1977) Griffiths and King (1979b)	15	Spawning almost anytime of year especially Aug./Sept. to Jan. or March
Chile:	Lozada *et al.* (1974)	–	settlement in Dec./Jan.
Aulacomya maoriana			
New Zealand:	Kennedy (1977)	–	gonads ripe from June to Sept., spawning and redevelopment, Aug. to Nov.
Brachidontes variabilis			
Australia:	Wilson and Hodgkin (1967)	–	ripe in January, brief spawning in late March/early April, settlement in April
Choromytilus chorus			
Chile:	Aracena *et al.* (1974) Yañez (1974)	–	settlement in April and Aug.–Sept.
Choromytilus meridionalis			
Africa:	Griffiths (1977, 1981a,b,d) Griffiths and Buffenstein (1981)	20	spawns most of year, especially July to Feb., greater reproductive output in littoral populations, recruitment all year
Crenomytilus greyanus			
Japan?:	Saito and Sakamoto (1951)	–	males develop in late Dec., females develop in early April, spawning in July and Aug.
U.S.S.R.:	Sadykhova (1970b)	–	spawns year-round with two peaks
Geukensia demissa			
North America (Atlantic):	Kuenzler (1961a,b) Bertness (1980) Jordan and Valiela (1982) Bertness and Grosholz (in prep.)	–	ripe in June/July spawn in July/Aug. or Aug./Sept. highest settlement March–June in the low littoral

TABLE 6.2 *Cont'd*

Species	References	Size (mm) at first sexual maturity	Comments
Modiolus modiolus			
Europe:	Wiborg (1946)		spawning in March/April
	Seed and Brown (1975, 1977, 1978)	30–40	littorally: spawn in autumn
	Brown and Seed (1977)	40–50	and winter
			sublittorally: no annual
			spawning cycle
	Comely (1978)		spawning early spring/late
			summer
New England:	Witman (1984)	–	settlement sublittorally Sept./Oct.
Mytilus californianus			
North America (Pacific):	see Seed (1976b) and Suchanek (1981) for reviews and	15	spawns and settles year-round, sometimes with peaks in spring and autumn
	Nelson (1928b)		larval life span *c.* 3 weeks
	Dehnel (1956)		
	Harger (1970a)		
	Paine (1974, 1976a)		
	Elvin (1975)		
	Jessee (1976)		
	Petraitis (1978)		
	Suchanek (1978)		
	Elvin and Gonor (1979)		
	Hines (1979a)		
	Paine and Levin (1981)		
	Kelley *et al.* (1982)		
	Trevelyan and Chang (1983)		
	Edwards (1984)		
	Petersen (1984a,b)		
Mytilus edulis			
World-wide:	see Seed (1976b) for review	–	variable spawning times dependent on geographic location, larval life span 15–30 days with settlement possible up to 40 days
Europe:	Kautsky (1982)		
	Lowe *et al.* (1982)		
North America:	see Suchanek (1981) for review and	–	
	Suchanek (1978)	–	
	Newell *et al.* (1982)	–	spawning from July
	Edwards (1984)	–	(May?)–Nov. with a peak in Sept. and Oct.

TABLE 6.2 *Cont'd*

Species	References	Size (mm) at first sexual maturity	Comments
Mytilus edulis aoteanus			
New Zealand:	Pike (1971)	–	
	Kennedy (1977)	–	maturation Feb.–July, gonads ripe from Jan.–Sept., spawning from Aug. (July?)–March
Mytilus edulis chilensis			
Chile:	Padilla (1973)	–	settlement in spring and summer
	Yañez (1974)	–	settlement in summer
Mytilus edulis diegensis			
North America (Pacific) (California only):	Coe (1945, 1946)	–	spawns year-round, especially March–June and early winter
Mytilus edulis planulatus			
Australia:	Allen (1955)	–	settlement June/July to Dec.
	Wisely (1964)	–	spawns June to mid-Aug.
	Wilson and Hodgkin (1967)	30	ripe and spawning Apr.–July and Sept., spawning April and July/August and Sept.–Nov., settlement June and Aug.–Nov.
Mytilus edulis platensis			
Argentina:	see Seed (1976b)		
	Moreno *et al.* (1971)	–	spawns in early spring
Mytilus galloprovincialis			
Japan:	Hosomi (1980)	–	recruitment mostly in summer
Europe:	see Seed (1976b) for review and	–	variable spawning times dependent on location
	Seed (1978)	–	spawning Aug.–March/April
Mytilus smaragdinus			
Philippines:	see Seed (1976b)		
	Obusan and Urbano (1968) and	–	spawns year-round with peaks in May and November
	Barkati and Ahmed (1974)		
	Tan (1975b)		
	Nagabhushanam and Mane (1978)		
	Shetty (1981)		

TABLE 6.2 *Cont'd*

Species	References	Size (mm) at first sexual maturity	Comments
Perna canaliculus			
New Zealand:	Havinga (1956) Greenway (1969a,b, 1975)	– 70	– settlement in February and May
	Pike (1971) Luckens (1976)	– 30–40	spawns in summer and August spawns in spring and summer settlement occurs year-round
	Kennedy (1977) Hickman and Illingworth (1980)	–	–
Perna perna			
Venezuela:	Carvajal (1969)	–	spawning and larvae abundant in Dec.–Jan., March, June–July
Brazil:	Lunetta (1969)	–	spawning year-round, especially in April–June and Sept.
	Velez and Epifanio (1981)		
Perumytilus purpuratus			
Argentina:	Penchaszadeh (1973)	–	settlement in late spring/early summer
Chile:	Lozada and Reyes (1981)	8–12	spawns year-round, both sexes develop and spawn simultaneously
Septifer bilocularis			
Australia:	Wilson and Hodgkin (1967)	–	ripe December to April, brief spawning in mid-April
Xenostrobus pulex			
Australia:	Wilson and Hodgkin (1967)	–	spawning Aug./Sept. and Oct./Jan., settlement in Sept.
	Luckens (1976)	8–10	spawns Aug.–Jan., settlement in low littoral–all year, settlement in high littoral– variable

years on littoral (Brown and Seed, 1977) and two years on sublittoral (Comely, 1978) *Modiolus modiolus* beds.

Planktonic mussel larvae may suffer as much as 99% mortality (Bayne, 1976). The most important factors that affect this mortality and, conversely, larval recruitment success are (i) suitable environmental conditions, (ii) adequate food supply, (iii) predation, (iv) accidental ingestion by filter-feeding invertebrates, and (v) location of a suitable settling substratum (Hancock, 1973; Bayne, 1976). To date we have some information on environmental factors critical to mussel larvae, especially temperature (Thorson, 1950 and see Bayne, 1976, for review). Virtually nothing is known about larval mytilid food supplies, although Bayne (1965, 1976) suggested that death due to starvation is highly unlikely. General categories of natural predators on mussel larvae are well known (see Mileikovsky (1974) and Bayne (1976) for reviews), but I know of no detailed works for any species. Accidental ingestion and mortality due to filter-feeding invertebrates has received considerable attention (Thorson, 1946, 1966; Bayne, 1964; Hancock, 1973; Mileikovsky, 1974). These reports show that mussel larvae can be bound in pseudofaeces or ingested and passed, sometimes alive (Mileikovsky, 1974), through the digestive tract of a filter-feeder, even a conspecific.

Information concerning suitable settling substrata, including data from laboratory tests (Trevelyan and Chang, 1983; Petersen, 1984b), indicates that considerable species–substratum specificity exists between different mytilid larvae, although this may be less acute in the field (Thorson, 1966; Petraitis, 1978). *M. edulis* has been shown to settle on a wide variety of filamentous substrata: byssal threads of their own species (Seed, 1969a; Dayton, 1971; Petraitis, 1978), filamentous algae (Colman, 1940; DeBlok and Geelen, 1958; Bayne, 1964; Seed, 1969a; Suchanek, 1978; Petersen, 1984a,b), and on sticks or filamentous ropes used in the mytiliculture industry (Korringa, 1976; Mason, 1976; Lutz, 1977, 1980). *Modiolus modiolus* larvae prefer adult conspecific periostracal 'hairs' (Brown and Seed, 1977; Comely, 1978). In Washington, where *Mytilus edulis* and *M. californianus* co-occur, plantigrades of the latter species are more often attracted to adult conspecific byssal threads (Petraitis, 1978; Suchanek, 1978, 1981), although this specificity was questioned by Petersen (1984a,b). Results of these types, involving two closely related sympatric species producing larvae in the same region at the same time, if they are to be meaningful, depend totally upon the investigators' abilities to identify pediveligers correctly to the species level, or to grow them successfully to an identifiable stage. In these cases the use of electrophoresis could aid in discriminating between closely related pediveligers unidentifiable by morphology alone.

Evidence also suggests that some mussels may rely heavily upon earlier ecological (possibly successional) stages for recruitment. Enhanced mussel settlement has been noted in the presence of the hydroid *Tubularia* (Lambert, 1939) and various species of barnacles (Obusan and Urbano, 1968; Tham *et al.*, 1973; Luckens, 1976; Mason, 1976; Menge, 1976; Suchanek and Duggins, in prep.). The significance of this phenomenon to mussel community development remains unknown.

6.4.3 Growth

For an in-depth discussion of growth in mussel larvae and adults see Bayne (1976) and Seed (1976b), respectively. In addition, attention is drawn especially to the following works on *Aulacomya ater* (Lozada *et al.*, 1974; Griffiths and King, 1979a,b; Griffiths, 1980a), *Choromytilus chorus* (Molina) (Aracena *et al.*, 1974), *Choromytilus meridionalis* (Griffiths, 1980a, 1981a,b,c,d; Griffiths and Buffenstein, 1981), *Geukensia demissa* (Kuenzler, 1961a,b; Lent, 1967; Bertness, 1980; Lutz and Castagna, 1980; Seed, 1980b; Jordan and Valiela, 1982; Bertness and Grosholz, in prep.), *Modiolus modiolus* (Seed and Brown, 1975, 1978; Brown *et al.*, 1976; de Schweinitz and Lutz, 1976; Brown and Seed, 1977; Comely, 1978), *Mytilus californianus* (Paine, 1976a; Elvin and Gonor, 1979; Suchanek, 1981; Trevelyan and Chang, 1983), *Mytilus edulis* (Lutz, 1976; Tsuchiya, 1980, 1982; Suchanek, 1981),

Mytilus galloprovincialis Lamarck (Seed, 1978b; Hosomi, 1980), *Perna canaliculus* (Luckens, 1976), and *Xenostrobus pulex* (Lamarck) (Luckens, 1976).

6.4.4 Physical and biological factors causing mortality in adults

a) Physical factors

In addition to the effects of temperature and desiccation mentioned above, factors associated with harsh winter conditions (i.e. ice, storm-generated waves and wave-driven logs) are the foremost physical factors causing mussel mortality. In salt marshes of New England, ice-rafting can remove large regions of vegetation and attached fauna, including populations of *Geukensia demissa* (Bertness and Grosholz, in prep.), although quantitative data on such mussel mortality have not been published. Ice-crushing or scouring can also cause severe mortality for *Mytilus edulis* populations in Boreal regions such as Baffin Island (Stephenson and Stephenson, 1972) and Glacier Bay, Alaska (pers. obs.).

Storm-generated waves and/or wave-driven logs cause dramatic mortality for rocky shore mussels. At Tatoosh Island, an extremely wave-exposed site, storm-related events caused the disruption of up to 65% of the area of some *Mytilus californianus* beds, leaving patches of bare space as large as 38m^2, with much greater size and frequency of patch initiation occurring during winter months and at sites exposed to more wave action (Levin and Paine, 1974; Paine and Levin, 1981). This disturbance rate varied over six winters of study from 0.4 to 5.4% of the mussels removed per month. Initial patch size may later enlarge from wave shock up to *c.* 5000% (Dayton, 1971), most likely as a result of weaker byssal thread attachments in the interior portions of these mussel beds than at the edges (Witman and Suchanek, 1984). Subsequent processes that are involved in the 'healing' of such patches are described in the following section.

Other studies on this system, where *Mytilus edulis* and *M. californianus* occur sympatrically, have indicated that greater levels of disturbance should occur when more *M. edulis* are present because the former species cannot attach itself effectively at sites with high wave exposure (Harger, 1968, 1970c; Harger and Landenberger, 1971). Harger extended this argument further to explain the absence of *M. edulis* from exposed Californian sites where *M. californianus* is dominant. However, as mentioned previously, *M. edulis* is abundant in some of the most wave-exposed sites known (Tatoosh Island, Washington and Torch Bay, Alaska). Further, Harger also suggested that, although *M. californianus* can attach strongly, it does not crawl as effectively as *M. edulis* and suffers burial and mortality from excessive siltation in protected embayments, eliminating it from those habitats. An alternative explanation was presented by Petraitis (1978) who showed that *M. californianus* larvae were lacking in protected bays where *M. edulis* was dominant.

Other *Mytilus*-dominated systems display similar winter disturbance phenomena. Menge (1976) and Lubchenco and Menge (1978) related wave shock to the organizational states of New England rocky shore communities where *M. edulis* was present, but did not quantify the levels of disturbance on *M. edulis*. In fact, their most exposed sites had the greatest cover of *M. edulis*, a result of the ineffectiveness of predators on *Mytilus* under such conditions.

b) Biological factors

Competition. Because mussels are effective and dominant competitors for space on horizontal or gently sloping substrata, only rarely do we see other species displacing them under these conditions at mid- to low-shore sites. However, occasionally, when two or more mytilid species live sympatrically (as do *Mytilus edulis* and *M. californianus* in Washington), interspecific competition can result in the partial exclusion of one species (in this case *M. edulis*). This competitive superiority results in the sharp lower limit of *M. edulis* beds on the high-shore (see above under *Lower Limits*). Whether this exclusion in Washington is the result of crushing by the larger, thicker-shelled *M. californianus* (proposed by Harger, 1970c, 1972b) or of its superior predator-deterring mechanisms, remains unknown. Another example of mortality from interspecific competition derives from the field manipulations of Paine (1971) where the low-shore kelp *Durvillea* in New Zealand seemed to exclude *Perna canaliculus* from this zone (see above under *Lower Limits*).

On more vertical faces in Washington the gooseneck barnacle *Pollicipes polymerus* Sowerby effectively outcompetes both *Mytilus* species (Paine, 1974). Although the mechanism for this is unknown, it may be related either to the relatively greater attachment strengths of *Pollicipes* on more vertical slopes, or to the inherent behavioural tendency of *M. californianus* to move downward. This lack of competitive superiority by mussels on vertical surfaces is true for *M. edulis* in New England as well (Menge, 1976).

Intraspecific competition can also cause mortality as a result of overcrowding which results in either (i) diminished food intake (Stiven and Kuenzler, 1979; Bertness, 1980), or (ii) subsequent instability of the mussel matrix and detachment by strong wave action (Seed, 1976b; Griffiths, 1981a).

Predation. Predation is undoubtedly one of the most significant and well-known sources of mortality for mussels. Typical predators include gastropods, sea stars, crabs and birds, with sea urchins, lobsters, fish and some mammals being less well-known. Until the last decade, our understanding of how predators affect mussel populations was derived almost entirely from studies on *Mytilus edulis*, with the exception of Paine's work (1966, 1969a) on *M. californianus* in Washington and his later work (1971) on *Perna canaliculus* in New Zealand. Since that time many excellent studies have helped to improve our understanding of world-wide patterns of predation on mytilid populations.

Seed (1976b) reviewed the most significant predators on *M. edulis* and gave some information on other mussel species. Additional works on *M. edulis* include those of Field (1922) who listed several other predators including the naticid gastropods *Lunatia heros* (Say) and *Polinices* (= *Neverita*) *duplicata* (Say), herring gulls, night herons, crows, ducks, killifish, cunners, scaups, tautogs, squeteagues, flounders, cod and eels, as well as the gray rat *Rattus norvegicus norvegicus* (Berkenhaut) and the muskrat *Ondatra zibethica* (L.). More recent studies on the Atlantic coast of North America deal directly with the dog whelk *Nucella* (= *Thais*) *lapillus* (L.) (Menge, 1976, 1978a,b, 1983; Menge and Sutherland, 1976; Lubchenco and Menge, 1978), the oyster drill *Urosalpinx cinerea* (Say) (Peterson, 1979), the sea stars *Asterias forbesi* (Desor) and *A. vulgaris* Verrill (Lubchenco and Menge, 1978; Menge, 1979, 1983; Peterson, 1979), and the crabs *Cancer borealis* Stimpson, *C. irroratus* Say, *Carcinus maenas* (L.) (Menge, 1983) and *Callinectes sapidus* Rathbun and *Neopanope sayi* (Smith) (Peterson, 1979). Further studies on *M. edulis* in Europe include work on predator preference, the mechanics of shell crushing, and energy maximization by the shore crab *Carcinus maenas* (Seed and Brown, 1975; Elner, 1978; Elner and Hughes, 1978). On the Pacific coast of North America similar groups of predators have been identified for *Mytilus edulis*: the gastropods *Nucella canaliculata* (Duclos), *N. emarginata* (Deshayes), *N. lamellosa* (Gmelin), and *N. lima* (Martyn), the sea stars *Evasterias troschelii* (Stimpson), *Leptasterias hexactis* (Stimpson), *Pisaster ochraceus* Brandt and *Pycnopodia helianthoides* (Brandt) (Suchanek, 1978, in prep.; Paine, 1980), and a number of shorebirds (scoters, surfbirds, crows and gulls).

On the East coast of North America, recent studies have shown few predators on adult *Geukensia demissa* living in mid- to high-littoral sites in salt marshes, although small mussels may be especially susceptible to predation by the crab *Callinectes sapidus* (Peterson, 1979; Hughes and Seed, 1981; Bertness and Grosholz, in prep.), and/or *Panopeus herbstii* H. Milne Edwards (Seed, 1980a). Through a series of laboratory feeding experiments on a closely related sublittoral mytilid in Europe (*Modiolus modiolus*) Seed and Brown (1975, 1978) showed similar trends for selection of small mussels by a suite of predators (the sea star *Asterias rubens* L. and the crabs *Cancer pagurus* L., *Carcinus maenas*, *Pagurus* (= *Eupagurus*) sp. and *Liocarcinus* (= *Portunus*) sp.).

In Chile, work by Paine and Palmer (1978) has identified the clingfish *Sicyases sanguineus* Müller and Troschel as a significant rocky shore predator on both *Perumytilus purpuratus* and *Semimytilus algosus* (Gould). Further work in Chile by Paine *et al.* (1985) has shown that the sea star *Heliaster helianthus* (Lamarck) exerts strict control on *P. purpuratus* populations (see above under *Lower Limits*).

A flurry of recent work on sublittoral *Aulacomya ater* and *Choromytilus meridionalis* in South Africa has shown that their major predator, the rock lobster *Jasus lalandii* (H. Milne-Edwards), consumes smaller size-classes and greater numbers of *C. meridionalis*, resulting in domination of kelp bed sites by *A. ater* (Pollock, 1979; Pollock *et al.*, 1979; Griffiths and Seiderer, 1980; Griffiths, 1981a,c; Seiderer *et al.*, 1982). Other predators on these mussels, especially *C. meridionalis*, include the gastropods *Natica tecta* Anton (Griffiths, 1981a,c; Penney and Griffiths, 1984) and *Nucella cingulata* (L.) (Penney and Griffiths, 1984; Wickens and Griffiths, in press), the sea star *Marthasterias glacialis* (L.) (Branch, 1978; Griffiths, 1981a; Penney and Griffiths, 1984), the kelp gull *Larus dominicanus* Lichtenstein, the oystercatcher *Haematopus moquini* Bonaparte and the musselcracker fishes *Cymatoceps nasutus* (Castlenau) and *Sparadon durbanensis* (Castlenau) (Griffiths, 1981a; Penny and Griffiths, 1984).

In New Zealand, Luckens (1976) has identified several predators on the littoral mytilids *Perna canaliculus* and *Xenostrobus pulex*, although no quantitative data were given on their relative importance in controlling the mussel populations. These predators included the gastropods *Thais orbita* (Gmelin) (= *Dicathais scalaris* (Menke)) and *Lepsiella scobina* (Quay and Gaimard) for both mussel species and the rock cod *Acanthoclinus quadridactylus* (Bloch and Schneider) on *X. pulex*.

One of the reasons that certain mussel species can coexist with their predators is that they have 'escaped' to a size too large to be opened or drilled. Dayton (1971) inferred such size-limited predation for *Nucella* and Paine (1976a) demonstrated this clearly for *Pisaster* on *Mytilus californianus* in Washington. Similar results have been shown for crab predation on sublittoral *Modiolus modiolus* in England (Seed and Brown, 1978) and for sublittoral *Aulacomya ater* and *Choromytilus meridionalis* in South Africa for a number of predators (Pollock, 1979; Pollock *et al.*, 1979; Griffiths and Seiderer, 1980; Griffiths, 1981c; Penney and Griffiths, 1984).

Boring and fouling organisms. Seed (1976b) reviewed the literature on boring organisms such as the sponge *Cliona* and other parasites that affect mussels by degrading either the shell or tissues. *Cliona* is found occasionally on *Mytilus californianus* shells in Washington, but none appeared to cause mortality (Suchanek, 1979 and pers. obs.).

Fouling organisms are now being recognized as significant sources of mortality for mussel populations, both littorally and sublittorally. In Washington, the brown alga *Postelsia palmaeformis* Ruprecht can and does overgrow the valves of *Mytilus californianus* and, after the plants grow to 10cm, they are capable of dislodging some of their hosts (Dayton, 1971; Paine, 1979). In fact, over 25 species of algae and over 64 species of invertebrates foul the shells of *M. californianus* and can produce potentially detrimental effects (Suchanek, 1979, in prep.). Mortality from fouling can occur in two ways: (i) overgrowth of the valve openings causing restriction or total blockage of the feeding currents resulting in starvation (e.g. by sponges or barnacles) and (ii) dislodgement as a result of increased weight or shearing stresses encountered during winter storms (e.g. by algae or barnacles). I know of no published works for the first scenario. However, a survey of *M. californianus* shells washed ashore onto Shi Shi Beach, Washington, after winter storms revealed that 79% were either heavily fouled, or inexorably bound by byssus to a mass of mussels that were fouled, by algae or barnacles (Witman and Suchanek, 1984). Further, data from field measurements and laboratory experiments showed that mussels that were overgrown by kelp encountered flow-induced forces 2 to 6 times greater than unfouled mussels (Witman and Suchanek, 1984).

Sublittoral mussel beds provide additional evidence for mortality from kelp fouling. After 11 months of monitoring marked *Modiolus* in New England, Witman (1984) found that 84% of fouled mussels and 0% of unfouled mussels were dislodged, showing that fouling negatively affects mussel survival. Without causing mortality outright, fouling organisms can also simply lower the fitness of mussels by reducing body tissue and/or gametic development. This has been documented for sub-littoral populations of *Mytilus californianus* (Paine, 1976b) as well as for sublittoral *Modiolus modiolus* (Witman, 1984). The mechanism responsible for such lowered fitness is most likely to be related to lowered food intake for the sublittoral *Mytilus californianus* and to the greater expenditure of energy on maintenance and production of more byssal threads for secure attachment instead of gametic output or growth for *Modiolus modiolus*.

6.4.5 Recovery from disturbance

For mussel populations recovering from the disturbance events documented above, both the recovery rates and the types of recovery processes involved can vary considerably. Factors that seem to be especially critical to the rate (and details) of mussel bed recovery are: disturbance patch size, disturbance season, height on the shore, angle of substratum, thickness of mussel bed and larval recruitment. When *Mytilus californianus* populations are artificially or naturally disrupted, a series of moderately predictable events leads to the eventual return of this competitive dominant, beginning with diatoms and filamentous algae (Hewatt, 1935) and a series of macroalgae (Dayton, 1971). Work by R.T. Paine and colleagues (Levin and Paine, 1974, 1975; Suchanek, 1978, 1981, in prep.; Paine and Levin, 1981; Paine, 1984) showed that recovery is deterministic. Certain species which are competitively subordinate to *M. californianus* can colonize initially if the season of disturbance corresponds to their recruitment periods (e.g. in winter the barnacles *Pollicipes polymerus* and *Semibalanus cariosus* Pallas, the brown alga *Hedophyllum sessile* (C. Ag.) and *Mytilus edulis*). These species, however, are eventually outcompeted with the system returning to the competitive dominant within seven to ten years in the mid-shore (Paine and Levin, 1981).

The size of disturbance affecting a *Mytilus californianus* bed is also a critical element in the recolonization process. In small disturbance patches 'healing' may be achieved by mussels leaning over, especially when adjacent mussel beds are thick and disturbance patches are moderately small (Paine and Levin, 1981; Suchanek and Duggins, in prep.). Grazers such as limpets and chitons that live in the interstices of the mussel bed also graze out to a predictable distance from the perimeter of the bed into smaller disturbance patches. Their grazing distances have been measured at *c.* 25–30cm from the perimeter of a bed, and often result in a barren halo or 'browse zone' adjacent to the bed (Dayton, 1971; Suchanek, 1978). When disturbance patches have areas less than a critical size (*c.* 2500cm^2 for circular patches; i.e. < 25–30cm radius) the entire primary substratum of the patch is grazed heavily. Patches larger than this (at least in their central portions) will undergo the predictable sequence of colonization mentioned above, with adult mussels rolling in and re-attaching and larval mussels later recruiting from the plankton at a mean patch age of *c.* 26 months and reclaiming primary substratum at a rate of 2.0–2.5%·mo^{-1} (Paine and Levin, 1981).

Height on the shore also has a dramatic effect on rates of recovery. Recovery ('healing') of artificially induced 0.10m^2 disturbance patches in *Mytilus californianus* beds was very rapid in the low-shore (sometimes within 6–12 months), intermediate in mid-shore (1–2 years) and extremely slow in high-shore patches (some not recovering after 10 years) (Suchanek and Duggins, in prep.). These rates, however, were also highly correlated with the thickness of the mussel beds at these sites. Exposure may also be important as sites more protected from wave action (e.g. Shi Shi) had considerably longer recovery rates than those at more exposed locations (e.g. Tatoosh Island). Similar slow recovery rates have been noted in disturbance patches in *M. edulis* beds in Alaskan rocky shore sites (Suchanek and Duggins, in prep.).

Mussel recovery may also be enhanced by the presence of prior barnacle cover. In one New England site Menge (1976) found that *Mytilus edulis* recolonized 90% of barnacle-covered substrata in seven months, but 0% where no barnacles occurred. Similar trends have been found in Torch Bay, Alaska where recolonization of *M. edulis* on smooth, barnacle-free substrata was supressed for over seven years (Suchanek and Duggins, in prep.).

In sublittoral habitats in New England, Witman (1984) found similarly slow recovery patterns for *Modiolus modiolus*. In a series of artificially cleared 115cm² patches in *M. modiolus* beds, after 24 months none was recolonized by mussels but 47% were recolonized by laminarian kelps (Witman, pers. comm.). However, it is uncertain what longer term patterns may be revealed in this system.

6.5 Mussels as Habitat Structure for Associated Organisms

As structurally complex entities, mussel beds provide refuge and habitat for a wide diversity of associated organisms. Although the diverse nature of some of these associations has been known for many years (Hewatt, 1935), until recently quantification of the member species and development of this community – along with any documentation of their importance to community dynamics – has been non-existent. Such associated communities have been noted for *Aulacomya ater* (Lawrence and McClintock, in prep.), *Brachidontes rodriguezi* D'Orb. (Penchazadeh, 1973), *Brachidontes rostratus* (Dunk.) (Bennett and Pope, 1953; Stephenson and Stephenson, 1972), *Modiolus modiolus* (Brown and Seed, 1977; Comely, 1978; Witman, 1984), *Mytilus californianus* (Hewatt, 1935; Ricketts and Calvin, 1939; Kanter, 1978; Suchanek, 1979, 1980, in prep.; Paine and Suchanek, 1983), *Mytilus edulis* (Nixon *et al.*, 1971; Tsuchiya, 1979; Tsuchiya and Nishihira, in prep.; Suchanek, unpubl. data), *Perumytilus purpuratus* (Ramirez, 1965; Suchanek, unpubl. data), and *Septifer bilocularis* (Jackson, 1976).

A mussel bed community consists of three major components: the mussel matrix, a diverse assemblage of associated organisms, and accumulated detritus at the base of the mussel bed. The mussel matrix is structurally more complex than the surrounding substratum, which, as in many other biological systems (e.g. aquatic, marine and terrestrial; see respectively Allan, 1975; Kohn and Leviten, 1976; MacArthur, 1964), leads to increased species richness. Increasing the thickness of the matrix (i) decreases the influence of wave action, temperature, and sunlight at the base of the bed and (ii) increases relative humidity and sedimentation. For *Mytilus edulis* this matrix can reach a thickness of 10cm (Nixon *et al.*, 1971); for *M. californianus* the matrix is often 5 or 6 mussel layers deep and can reach a thickness of *c.* 35cm (Suchanek, in prep.).

Associated organisms can be classified into three typical categories: epibiota (the fauna and flora that grow on, or bore into, the mussel shells), mobile fauna (those organisms that move freely throughout the mussel matrix), and infauna (those animals that are restricted to, and often dependent upon, the organic detritus and shell debris that accumulates at the base of the mussel bed matrix). There may be some overlap between categories. Together, these organisms comprise a community conveniently defined by the physical limits of the mussel matrix, with all trophic levels represented (except for external sources of zooplankton and phytoplankton). There is, of course, interaction and energy flow between other systems and/or populations of organisms such as fishes, birds, and a certain amount of migration by mobile animals that move out of the mussel matrix, for example, at high tide. Witman (1984) found that 22% of the species in a sublittoral *Modiolus* community were restricted to the mussel matrix.

Accumulated detritus contains faeces and pseudofaeces, other organic detritus, and inorganic components such as shell debris, sea urchin spines and sediment. In 22cm thick *Mytilus californianus* beds in Washington, the dry weight of detritus can reach 65 kg·m^{-2} (Suchanek, in prep.). Comparable values for a 10cm thick *M. edulis* bed in Rhode Island are 14.4 kg·m^{-2}, with an organic content of 3.86% (Nixon *et al.*, 1971).

Species richness of associated organisms has been documented for the *Mytilus californianus* community (over 303 taxa – Suchanek, 1979, 1980, in prep.), the *Modiolus modiolus* community (90 taxa – Brown and Seed, 1977; 23 taxa – Witman, 1984), and the *M. edulis* community (69 taxa – Tsuchiya and Nishihira, in prep.b). Both species richness and diversity indices are correlated with age and structural complexity of the mussel matrix (Suchanek, 1979, in prep.; Tsuchiya and Nishihira, in prep.a,b). Species richness is also correlated with height on the shore. Through a series of field experiments using artificial mussels in varying degrees of structural complexity, Suchanek (1979, in prep.) showed that the physical structure of the matrix was the most important factor promoting species diversity (H' = Shannon-Weiner index), but not necessarily species richness (S = total number of species) at both high- and low-shore sites. Within one year these artificial mussels attracted an associated community equivalent to real mussel beds of comparable structural complexity.

6.6 Mutualism and the Rôle of Associated Grazers

Mytilus edulis has the inherent ability to clean fouling organisms from its shell by use of a prehensile foot (Theisen, 1972). This adaptation has not been shown for any other mytilid. As a result shells of *M. edulis* contrast sharply with other species of mussels from naturally occurring populations by the distinct absence of potentially harmful fouling organisms (Suchanek, in prep.). When barnacles or kelp severely foul mussel shells, mortality is a well documented result (see above). One mechanism that protects mussels from overfouling and subsequent mortality is the constant action of mobile grazers such as limpets, chitons and/or sea urchins within the mussel matrix (Suchanek, 1979, in prep.; Witman, 1984).

The mussel matrix provides increased protection for these mobile grazers from predation and/or desiccation. In the littoral *Mytilus californianus* system birds such as oystercatchers, surfbirds, sandpipers, turnstones, wandering tattlers, crows and gulls forage extensively for limpets and chitons at low tide (Suchanek, in prep.). In the sublittoral *Modiolus modiolus* system, fish (cunners) and invertebrates (crabs and lobsters) are the major predators on grazing sea urchins that seek refuge in these mussel beds (Witman, 1984). Clearly, mussels benefit also from this association because the grazers continually remove potentially harmful fouling organisms (see above). Thus, mutual benefit is derived by increasing the fitness both of mussels and associated grazers when they co-occur.

This grazer-related benefit to mussels has been confirmed experimentally both littorally and sublittorally. By removing associated grazers from isolated littoral *M. californianus* beds, Suchanek (1979, in prep.) documented the disappearance of the grazing halo around such beds and the development of a heavy fouling of barnacles and algae on the mussels. Witman (1984) similarly removed sea urchin grazers from sublittoral *Modiolus modiolus* beds and documented a thirty-fold increase in kelp-induced dislodgement of mussels from urchin-free areas, i.e. without grazers, compared with control sites.

These data strongly indicate that a mutualistic relationship exists between grazers and mussels. Grazers in both systems also occur in habitats other than the mussel beds, making this a facultative, rather than an obligate mutualism (*sensu* Boucher *et al.*, 1982).

6.7 Conclusions

Mytilid mussels seem to outcompete most other rocky shore species in exposed or semi-exposed temperate zone habitats throughout the world. A strong but flexible attachment mechanism (byssal threads) has enabled them to exploit rocky substrata, especially littoral sites where wave action is intense. Littoral mussels usually exist in discrete and predictably stable zones. The upper limits of these zones appear to be controlled by physical factors such as temperature (heat or freezing) and/or desiccation. Lower limits seem to be more under the biological control of intra- or interspecific competition or predation by a wide variety of taxa, both invertebrate and, less commonly, vertebrate.

Reproductive cycles, spawning, and recruitment phenomena for mussels are variable, but are usually consistent for any one species within a particular geographical region. Although we know little about the details of larval life histories, the planktotrophic veliger larvae of some mytilid mussels have life spans of two to four weeks.

Dominant mussel beds are often disrupted during winter storms, more so at increasingly wave-exposed sites. Subsequent recovery to full mussel cover usually proceeds through a predictable sequence of events. Recovery speed is dependent upon many parameters including disturbance season, initial size of disturbance, height on the shore, angle of the substratum, thickness of adjacent mussel bed, and stochastic events of local mussel recruitment (by both larvae and adults).

Mussel beds provide habitat structure for a wide diversity of associated organisms. The species richness of these associates appears to be correlated with both mussel-bed age and especially the stuctural complexity of the physical mussel matrix. In one littoral and one sublittoral mussel system, a facultative mutualism has been shown to exist between some of the associated grazers and the mussels. Grazers benefit by gaining protection from predators within the mussel matrix. Mussels also benefit from the continual grazing activities of the grazers which remove fouling algae and barnacles that could dislodge mussels during periods of increased wave action, causing mortality.

CHAPTER VII

LIMPETS: THEIR RÔLE IN LITTORAL AND SUBLITTORAL COMMUNITY DYNAMICS

G.M. Branch

7.1 Introduction

Limpets are of major importance on most littoral shores and in shallow waters, and their biology (Branch, 1981) and rôle as herbivores (Lubchenco and Gaines, 1981; Hawkins and Hartnoll, 1983a) have recently been reviewed. They were amongst the animals that received particular attention from Jack Lewis, and one of the major contributions that he and his co-workers made was the long-term analysis of limpet populations in relation to physical and biological factors (Lewis and Bowman, 1975; Bowman and Lewis, 1977; Lewis, 1980b; Lewis et al., 1982; Workman, 1983). The focus of this chapter is an analysis of the factors controlling limpet populations, including adaptations to these factors, and the impact that limpets have on community structure. In particular, I emphasize those studies that have led to conceptual advances in our understanding of the dynamics of littoral and shallow-water communities.

7.2 Adaptations to Physical Factors

A plethora of studies has established that the tolerance of limpets to physical factors such as high temperatures, extreme salinities and desiccation is correlated with their zonation (e.g. Davies, 1969b; Wolcott, 1973; Bannister, 1975; Branch, 1975a), and a wide range of adaptations to physical conditions has also been described.

Among these adaptations, the habit most limpets have of homing to a fixed site has long been assumed to be a protection against desiccation. Curiously, this has remained an assumption until very recently, when Verderber et al. (1983) experimentally tested the effect of depriving Siphonaria alternata (Say) of its scar, and found that the osmotic concentration of the body fluids increased 55% more in limpets that were prevented from homing than in control animals which returned to their scars. No mortalities, however, were recorded amongst those limpets which were prevented from homing, so that in this instance homing may not be essential to survival. Garrity (1984) has recorded that three tropical limpets remain on their scars during low tide, and that if they are moved away from their scars they desiccate faster than controls left on scars. Furthermore, one of the species (Scurria stipulata (Reeve)) experienced up to 33% mortality over a single low tide if denied access to scars.

Homing to a fixed site also ensures that the shell fits flush with the substratum (Lindberg and Dwyer, 1983). Limpets can thus clamp down and isolate the body from extreme external salinities (Arnold, 1957; McAlister and Fischer, 1968), a factor of some importance considering the fluctuations of salinity in littoral pools and the inability of limpets to osmoregulate.

Temperatures which approach lethal limits may be countered by lifting the shell, thus cooling the body by evaporation (J.B. Lewis, 1963; Lowell, 1984). Garrity (1984) recorded that during sunny low tides *Scurria stipulata*, *Siphonaria gigas* Sowerby and *S. maura* Sowerby elevated their shells and curled up the edge of the foot. This allowed evaporative cooling and reduces contact with the substratum. While increasing water loss, this behaviour lowers body temperatures as much as 5°C; in the case of *Scurria stipulata*, individuals prevented from elevating their shells suffered 97% mortality, so this response is vital, even if it incurs the risk of desiccation.

The precise orientation of limpets also reduces desiccation. Collins (1976), for instance, showed that *Collisella scabra* (Gould) loses water more slowly as the angle of inclination of its substratum increases (even in desiccators where solar radiation is not an issue), possibly explaining why small *C. scabra* most often occur on vertical or sloped rocks. Several littoral limpets migrate upshore during cooler conditions and then retreat downwards during summer (Lewis, 1954; Breen, 1972; Branch, 1975c). Conversely, the Antarctic limpet *Nacella concinna* (Strebel) migrates downshore into the sublittoral zone in winter, avoiding lethally low air temperatures (Walker, 1972).

Thus there are many behavioural adaptations alleviating physical stress. But morphological features may also be important. Shell shape and texture, in particular, can be correlated with physical conditions. Davies (1969b; see also Seapy and Hoppe, 1973) measured the rate of water loss from *Patella vulgata* L. and *P. aspera* Lamarck and showed that the taller a shell is in relation to its length, the lower the rate of water loss. He was able to quantify this by measuring the exponent (b) which links body mass (M) to rate of water loss (WL): $WL = cM^b$. In theory, if body proportions remain constant (isometry), b will equal -0.33. In fact, b ranged from -0.44, in low-shore individuals of *P. vulgata*, to -0.55, in high-shore representatives of the same species. This could be linked with the fact that *P. vulgata* becomes more domed as it ages, proportionally decreasing the circumference of the shell (from which water loss occurs). This effect was most marked in high-shore limpets – precisely the animals most in need of reducing water loss. Branch (1975a) has confirmed this and shown that $b = -0.33$ only in those species whose growth is isometric. They also remain in the low- to mid-shore throughout their lives and do not migrate upshore. Lowell (1984) has recently challenged some of these results, mainly because they came from laboratory experiments in which the animals would have lost the water that normally lies between the shell and the body. When this water is present, water loss will take place from the circumference of the shell only, since a meniscus will form between the shell and the substratum. In the absence of this extravisceral water, desiccation will occur from the surface area of the mantle cavity. Under field conditions, Lowell could detect no effect of shell-shape on desiccation, and suggested that shell-shape is adapted to factors other than desiccation, including predation, hydrodynamic drag and attachment force (since it influences foot size).

Shell texture may play a rôle in thermoregulation. Vermeij (1973) has noted that, both within and between species, high-shore limpets tend to be relatively tall, decreasing the area exposed to solar radiation. He also remarks that shade-dwelling limpets often have smooth shells while those exposed to direct sunlight are sculptured. He could not, however, detect obvious gradients of sculpture related to the zonation of limpets. Sculpture may increase re-radiation of heat, thereby reducing heat stress. To test whether this effect is biologically meaningful, Johnson (1975) prepared gold-plated silver casts of two species of limpets to measure their convection coefficients. *Collisella scabra*, a ribbed spinose species, had a significantly higher convection coefficient than smooth-shelled *C. digitalis* Eschscholtz, facilitating heat loss by convection.

Antarctic limpets face the opposite problem – having to survive sub-zero temperatures. Hargens and Shabica (1973) have discovered that *Nacella concinna* produces a thick mucous sheath when trapped beneath ice, which increases survival at low temperatures. The secretion of mucus lowers the fluid content of intercellular spaces, hindering the propagation of ice through the limpet tissues down to -10°C.

Shell-shape may also influence hydrodynamics. Some limpets are characteristic of strong wave action, others prevail in calmer waters. Their relative tolerance of wave action will be influenced partly by shell-shape and partly by power of adhesion. Warburton (1976) has studied both factors in *Helcion* (= *Patina*) *pellucidus* (L.) which, being a kelp-dweller, experiences a unidirectional flow of water because the kelp sways with the water movement. *H. pellucidus* has an elongate shell with an apex about one-third from the anterior margin. Both factors increase streamlining provided, of course, that the limpets face directly into the current. *Patella compressa* L., another kelp-dweller, has a similarly streamlined shell (Branch, 1981). Warburton calculated that the drag on an *H. pellucidus* shell aligned transversely to the current is double that of an animal facing directly away from the current which, in turn, has double the drag of a limpet facing into the current.

For rock-dwelling limpets direction of water flow is relatively unpredictable since waves swash back and forth, and their shells are not streamlined. Even so, the shape of their shells profoundly influences drag. Comparing six *Patella* species, Branch and Marsh (1978) demonstrated four-fold differences in drag between tall domed species and those with relatively flat shells. Shell texture is also important, modifying the coefficient of drag. Branch and Marsh found that species occurring in wave-beaten areas had shells which were textured with delicate ribs or nodules. These decrease turbulence behind the shell and become especially important at high current velocities, when a slightly textured shell has a lower coefficient of drag than a completely smooth object of similar proportions. Strongly textured species with large ribs lose this advantage, for what they gain in reducing turbulence is more than offset by increases in frontal drag.

Despite these patterns, Branch and Marsh (1978) could find no correlations between shell-shape and the relative intensity of wave action that each species normally experiences. There was, however, a correlation between wave action and power of attachment, the latter varying enormously between species, from 6990g·cm⁻² in *Patella argenvillei* Krauss down to 484g·cm⁻² in *Acmaea dorsuosa* (Gould) (see Branch, 1981, for a review). In the six species examined by Branch and Marsh, power of tenacity was inversely related (i) to the amount of mucus secreted by the foot, (ii) to the flexibility of the foot, and (iii) to the speed of locomotion. It seems that high tenacity and high mobility are incompatible. Their relative importance may be determined partly by energetic considerations, for species which are fast-growing and have a high reproductive output forage widely and may depend on mobility, while slow-growing species are relatively sedentary and have high powers of tenacity. When Branch and Marsh compared shell drag with tenacity, they found two polarized groups of limpets: those with a high ratio of drag: tenacity (0.80), all of which do not live where wave action is severe; and those with a much lower ratio (0.36) which live at wave-beaten sites.

The attachment of limpets is largely due to pedal mucus, analysed in detail by Grenon and Walker (1978, 1980, 1981). The mucus acts as a tacky adhesive and is viscoelastic and capable of performing both as a liquid and a solid; when stressed it is elastic and acts like a solid, but if the stress is considerable or continued for long enough it becomes liquid. Indeed, during locomotion the limpet itself uses this feature on a micro-scale to detach small portions of the foot and slide them forwards while maintaining contact with the substratum with the rest of the foot.

All of these morphological adaptations are partly constrained by evolutionary history and may be influenced by the energetic costs of adaptations. The shell, for instance, is composed of crystalline calcium carbonate and an organic matrix. The energetic cost of the organic fraction is easy to assess since its energy content can be measured; and in limpets it accounts for less than 7% of energy devoted to production (Branch, 1981; Parry, 1982b). But quantification of the cost of producing calcium carbonate has remained a 'persistent unknown'. Palmer (1983b) had produced indirect evidence that the organic fraction is the metabolically more expensive element. Using 15 species of gastropods, he demonstrated that rate of shell regeneration is inversely proportional to the percentage of organic material in the shell. Palmer recalled the evolutionary loss of shell microstructures which contain high levels of organic matrix – such as the nacre and prismatic layers of gastropod and bivalve shells – and suggested that the seemingly enigmatic loss of these mechanically superior structures can be explained by the high cost of their production.

7.3 Do Physical Factors Control Limpets?

Quite clearly limpets display a wide range of adaptations which seem correlated with physical stresses. But such adaptations do not alone prove that physical factors control either the abundance or distribution of limpets. Additional evidence is needed that physical conditions may at times be lethal. There are many isolated records of deaths due to extreme conditions, for example during extremely cold winters (Crisp, 1964; Walker, 1972), or high temperatures coincident with prolonged low tides (Lewis, 1954). Even in the sub-Antarctic, mass mortalities of *Nacella macquariensis* Finlay and *Kerguelenella lateralis* (Smith) have been recorded and ascribed to heat stress and desiccation respectively (Simpson, 1976). The most detailed and long-term study of physical factors on the distribution of limpets is that of Wolcott (1973), who studied five species of acmaeids over three years. He recorded that field temperatures never became lethal and that extremes of salinity seemed very unlikely to control zonation (except where there was substantial seepage of fresh water). On the other hand, high-shore species were periodically killed by desiccation. Building upon these findings, Wolcott (1973) developed the hypothesis that high-shore species fringe upon a habitat which is physically demanding (and potentially lethal) but which is relatively unexploited. He proposed that it will profit high-shore limpets to expand their range upwards to the limits of their tolerance to benefit from the unexploited food resources, even if this involves risk of death. Presumably there is sufficient gain in the form of increased reproductive output due to the higher food supply to more than offset the losses due to mortality. In contrast, mid- to low-shore limpets have to contend with high-shore competitors in the zone above and do not have access to an unexploited habitat. Because of this, Wolcott suggested that mid-shore species will remain well within their limits of physical tolerance, and that their zonation will never be set by physical conditions but rather by behaviour or by interactions with other organisms.

Wolcott's hypothesis has wide relevance to ecological theory and deserves to be more fully explored in other environments. In part, it has been tested by Choat (1977) who found when he experimentally removed a high-shore limpet (*Collisella digitalis*) that a mid-shore species (*C. strigatella* (Carpenter)) then expanded its range upwards in the absence of competition. It seemed that *C. strigatella* was normally excluded from the high-shore by *C. digitalis*, in conformity to Wolcott's predictions; its zonation being controlled by other species rather than by being set by physical factors.

At the time when Wolcott put forward his ideas they were a departure from earlier thinking, in that the upper limits of zonation were previously considered to be controlled by physical factors, although the lower limits were held to be biologically controlled. This generalization harks back to the idea of 'critical tidal limits' – abrupt changes in the duration of emergence and submergence as one moves from the high-shore to the low-shore. These critical levels were for long held to limit the zonation of species and to be associated with changes in faunal and floral composition, a view criticized by Lewis (1961, 1964). Underwood (1978a) has dealt this idea a further blow by recalculating the emersion curves for the selfsame shores on which the original concept was built, showing that not only were there no abrupt changes in the duration of emersion/submergence, but there were no particular heights on the shore where the upper or lower limits of zonation of different species coincided more often than would be expected on the basis of chance.

Thus, for various reasons, it seems that physical factors are less important in establishing zonation patterns than previously assumed – although the upper limits of some species are fixed this way. It must, however, be remembered that most of the relevant research has been undertaken on temperate species. In the tropics physical stress is more severe and there are fewer algae and sessile organisms to provide shelter. Physical factors may therefore assume greater importance, and may confine limpets and other grazers to certain microhabitats. For example, in Panama *Siphonaria gigas* is most common on vertical surfaces or in crevices, *Scurria stipulata* is confined almost entirely to vertical habitats, and *Siphonaria maura* predominates in crevices or pools. All three forage only when awash, and their foraging excursions are restricted to the vicinity of microhabitats providing refuge from physical stress. Intensity of grazing will therefore vary with distance from such refuges, with obvious implications for algal community structure and heterogeneity (Garrity, 1984).

Another issue is that the rôle of physical factors is intimately linked with body size. Small animals lose water proportionally faster than large individuals. Limpets below a wet flesh weight of 1g are particularly vulnerable, losing up to 15% of their body water per hour (Branch, 1975a). *Patelloida mufria* (Hedley), a small acmaeid which is very susceptible to desiccation, depends largely on its specialist association with other gastropods to avoid lethal desiccation. It occurs predominantly on shells of the winkle *Austrocochlea constricta* (Lamarck), shows a strong preference for winkles in pools and occupies the lower whorl of the shell where shading reduces desiccation. Indirectly, desiccation therefore regulates the distribution of *P. mufria*, and is probably the most important factor maintaining the limpet's association with *A. constricta* (Mapstone *et al.*, 1984).

The juveniles of many limpets are limited to the lower shore while the adults move upshore as they grow, thus establishing size gradients on the shore (Vermeij, 1973). Juveniles of other species are restricted to cryptic habitats until they are large enough to tolerate the stress of the open rock face. *Patella vulgata*, for instance, only survives in 'wet-settlement sites' after recruitment, and desiccation apparently determines the initial zonation of the recruits of this species (Bowman and Lewis, 1977).

More work is needed on the rôle of physical factors in relation to newly settled limpets and, more particularly, on the process of recruitment. Lewis (1980b) has shown that the annual density of *Patella vulgata* at Robin Hood's Bay is closely correlated with recruitment at the beginning of each year (Fig. 7.1A). But if the annual survival of recruits is analysed in more detail, it varies between sites, being much higher (almost 100%) in areas dominated by barnacles than in mussel beds or on bare rocks (where loss is between 30% and 55%). Clearly recruitment, coupled with early mortality, is a major issue in determining population density.

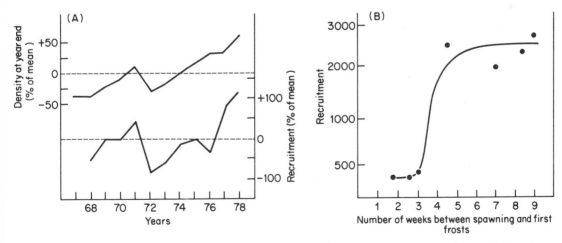

FIG. 7.1. A, The relationship between annual recruitment (lower line) of *Patella vulgata* and the density of the population at the end of each year (after Lewis, 1980b). B, Recruitment of *Patella vulgata* relative to the duration of the frost-free period after spawning (after Bowman and Lewis, 1977).

The probable influence of frost on the recruitment of *P. vulgata* has been analysed by Bowman and Lewis (1977). Figure 7.1B shows that if less than five weeks elapse between spawning and the appearance of frost, recruitment is greatly reduced. But frost is only one of the factors influencing recruitment (and it is not an issue in more clement climates), so the analysis of factors controlling larval recruitment and settlement, and the early survival of juveniles, remains a pressing problem (see Bowman, this volume).

Geographical distribution may also be limited by physical factors. Towards the northern (colder) geographical extremes of some species, recruitment becomes increasingly irregular and several years may pass between successful recruitments (Lewis *et al.*, 1982). The geographical limits of such species, which include *Patella vulgata*, seem set by the ability of larvae to recruit, rather than the survival of adults. Similarly, Branch (1984b) has shown that *Patella* species which are characteristic of the warm temperate South coast of South Africa do penetrate the cold temperate West coast, but their recruitment there is intermittent. During a recent 'warm event' in 1982/1983, spectacular increases in the recruitment of these warm-water species were recorded on the West coast, associated with a failure of the recruitment of cold-water species near their southern (warmer) geographical limits.

Thus the effect of physical conditions on recruitment and early survival have far-reaching implications for the zonation, abundance and geographical distribution of limpets.

7.4 Algal–Limpet Interactions

It has been established repeatedly that limpets may regulate the abundance and distribution of littoral algae. One of the earliest demonstrations of this remains the most spectacular – when Lodge (1948) removed all limpets from a band 10m wide running up the shore on the Isle of Man. A dense settlement of algae was recorded over most of the shore, including areas normally bare of algae. Comparable results have been described by many others (e.g. Hay, 1979; Underwood, 1980; Jernakoff, 1983; Cubit, 1984; Jara and Moreno, 1984; and see reviews by Branch, 1981; Lubchenco and Gaines, 1981; Hawkins and Hartnoll, 1983a). Oil spills have led to a similar outcome – massive deaths of limpets being followed by dense settlements of algae, particularly colonizing types such as *Ulva* (Southward and Southward, 1978). Other authors have described how limpets eliminate or curtail the growth of microflora (Castenholz, 1961; Nicotri, 1977).

The effect that limpets have on algae is linked with their method of feeding. Patellacean limpets, which have radular teeth that are reduced in number but large and strengthened, are capable of excavating the surface of the rock and removing all algal sporelings. Siphonarian limpets have a radula with numerous relatively fragile teeth which can only rasp at the surface: and most siphonarians feed by biting off fragments of macroalgae (Creese and Underwood, 1982). The difference is important, for patellacean limpets have the ability to prevent totally the development of algae while siphonarians can only graze back existing macroalgae and seldom influence their abundance. This generalization does not, however, always hold true. Kitting (1980) described how one particular patellacean limpet, *Acmaea scutum* Eschscholtz, maintained a mixed diet of relatively fixed proportions even in the face of changes in the relative abundance of available algae. Kitting associated this with the fact that, even at abnormally high densities, *A. scutum* fails to change the percentage cover of any of the algae eaten. Kitting suggested that a mixed diet can only be maintained in species which have little effect on their food resources (or are mobile and shift to a new locality when desirable food plants are rare). In a similar vein, Levings and Garrity (1984) have shown that *Siphonaria gigas* can influence the growth of macroalgae. Since *A. scutum* is a relatively small limpet and *S. gigas* unusually large for a siphonariid, size may be an additional factor influencing the impact of limpets on algae.

Wave action may modify the interplay between limpets and algae (e.g. Levings and Garrity, 1984). In Britain *Fucus* spp. prevail in sheltered localities, *Patella vulgata* on moderately exposed shores and *P. aspera* at extremely wave-beaten sites. Under intermediate conditions cyclic changes take place, first *Fucus* being abundant and then limpets (Southward and Southward, 1978; Thompson, 1980).

The regulation of algae by limpets also depends on the rate of algal growth. In the mid- and high-shore where physical stress suppresses algal growth, limpets dominate and visible algal growth may be absent. But lower on the shore growth of algal sporelings may be rapid enough for some plants to escape the attentions of limpets and develop. In an important finding, Underwood and Jernakoff (1981) have shown that, if the limpet *Cellana tramoserica* (Sowerby) is transplanted from the mid-shore into algal beds in the low-shore, it starves to death in the midst of a seeming abundance of food. Because *C. tramoserica* seems incapable of feeding on macroalgae it is excluded from the luxuriant algal beds of the low-shore. Thus the balance between algae and limpets is tipped by the growth rate of the algae, in turn determined by physical conditions.

There are other limpets which evidently cannot feed on macroalgae. For instance, the numbers of sublittoral *Cellana stellifera* (Gmelin) are correlated with those of a sea urchin, apparently because the urchin prevents macroalgae from developing, thus providing *C. stellifera* with 'bare' rock on which it grazes for microalgae (Ayling, 1981). Similarly *Acmaea mitra* Rathke seems to rely on urchins or chitons to curtail the growth of upright frondose macroalgae (Paine, 1980).

In many parts of the world limpets are abundant on the high- and mid-shore but are replaced by algal mats on the low-shore. One clear exception to this pattern is *Patella cochlear* Born. which dominates a narrow band at the level of low-water spring tides on South African shores, reaching densities of up to $1600m^{-2}$ (Branch, 1975b). Algae flourish both above and below the *cochlear* zone, and experimental removal of *P. cochlear* is followed by substantial algal growth. Once foliose macroalgae establish themselves they may prevent further settling of *P. cochlear* for prolonged periods. Perhaps for this reason, the *cochlear* zone is a mosaic, with *P. cochlear* the dominant over most of the zone but with patches of macroalgae interspaced. *P. cochlear* reaches greatest densities under moderate but not severe wave action, being replaced by algae in shelter and by mussels on severely wave-beaten shores. Its unique ability to control algal growth at the low-tide mark seems related to its specialized habit of developing 'gardens' of fine red algae which form a narrow fringe around each limpet. Exceptionally fast-growing, these fine red algae have a high productivity and are apparently essential to sustain the high densities of *P. cochlear* (Branch, 1981). Experimental removal of all *P. cochlear* allows the gardens to flourish initially, but within 10 to 20 weeks they disappear. If isolated limpets are removed, their scars are occupied by juvenile limpets, which abandon their normal position on the shells of larger *P. cochlear* to occupy vacant scars. Thus under natural conditions the gardens are perpetuated after the death of the limpet because they are taken up by a smaller limpet. This is one of the reasons why *P. cochlear* has remarkably stable populations.

It is not always a disadvantage for an alga to be grazed by limpets. For instance, Black (1976) has described how *Acmaea insessa* (Hinds), which lives solely on the kelp *Egregia laevigata* (Setchell), grazes only on a small fraction of its host, although it does form deep scars which weaken the rachis. If as a result the main rachis is broken, the plant can compensate by developing lateral branches on the remaining rachis, and its potential to reproduce remains unchanged. Furthermore, the damage done to the main rachis by the formation of limpet scars may be an advantage, for it ensures that the plant breaks at a weak point rather than being torn free in its entirety during storms.

A much more intimate relationship has been revealed between crustose coralline algae and grazers (Steneck, 1982). For example, *Acmaea tessulata* (Müller) is regularly associated with one particular coralline, *Clathromorphum circumscriptum* (Strømfelt) Fosl., recruiting specifically to it and grazing preferentially on it. *C. circumscriptum* depends on grazing to remove epiphytes which would otherwise smother it, and is morphologically adapted to tolerate grazing, possessing a thick epithallus that protects the meristem. So dependent is *C. circumscriptum* on grazing that if it is not grazed the epithallus thickens and shades the plastids, killing the plant.

Not all encrusting algae are equally adapted to grazing. In tropical Panama, where crusts are the dominant form of algal growth, the abundance of a blue-green algal crust (? *Schizothrix calcicola*) is inversely related to the density of the dominant limpet, *Siphonaria gigas*. Experimental removal of *S. gigas* increased the cover of *Schizothrix* but decreased other encrusting species (e.g. *Ralfsia*) which appeared to be outcompeted by *Schizothrix* in the absence of *S. gigas* (Levings and Garrity, 1984). *Schizothrix* exists in two forms: a fleshy green morph and a white calcified morph. The calcified morph decreases if limpets are removed, and Levings and Garrity suggest that the development of calcification is 'a functional response by healthy (fleshy green) plants to damage by grazers'. This is of extreme interest, for it is one of the first suggestions that algae may develop defences phenotypically in response to grazing – a subject ripe for further research.

Steneck and Watling (1982) have analysed the feeding capabilities of herbivorous molluscs and note that only the limpets and chitons are capable of excavating encrusting corallines because they have hard mineralized teeth, complex robust radular muscles and a reduced number of teeth – this last feature increasing the pressure applied to each of the limited number of teeth. In addition to chitons and limpets, sea urchins and fish are capable of excavating corallines, and Steneck (1983) suggested that their collective appearance after the mid-Mesozoic had a profound influence on encrusting corallines. Corallines probably evolved from the solenopores, but they possess four features that give them a great advantage in a competitive situation or where grazing is intense. First, they have an outer protective epithallus. Secondly, they possess a basal layer of cells (the hypothallus) which increases the thickness of the crust and the rate of lateral growth. Both features increase competitive ability. Thirdly, their reproductive conceptacles are sunken and armoured to protect them from grazing. Finally, the corallines have fusion cells which allow translocation of photosynthates from the surface to the rest of the plant and may be important in sustaining the hypothallus. Steneck (1982) considered these adaptations to be the key features which allowed the encrusting corallines to radiate when herbivory intensified during the Mesozoic and Cenozoic – at a time when their parental solenopores were becoming extinct. Indeed, many of the crustose corallines are like *Clathromorphum circumscriptum* in relying on grazing to prevent smothering by epiphytes or silt (see for example Raffaelli, 1979c; Clokie and Boney, 1980a; Paine, 1980).

Curiously, when comparing different kinds of corallines, Padilla (1984) came to different conclusions. She found coarsely-branched upright corallines (such as *Calliarthron tuberculosum* (Post. and Rupr.)) to be resistant to grazing. When Padilla offered such corallines to limpets and chitons she found that they were never eaten. She concluded that body structure is the key feature protecting *C. tuberculosum*, since it is readily eaten when ground up and placed in agar, and is therefore not unpalatable. Conversely, Padilla recorded that crustose corallines were readily eaten by three out of four grazers. More interestingly, she also recorded that the encrusting forms are better competitors than either the finely- or coarsely-branched upright species, consistently overgrowing their bases and even their erect branches. Thus paradoxically, encrusting corallines are more efficient competitors than their upright counterparts and yet depend on grazing to prevent being smothered by faster-growing epiphytes.

Various authors have suggested that a heteromorphic algal life cycle – the alternation of an encrusting stage with an upright foliose stage – is an adaptation to variations in the intensity of grazing. For example, Slocum (1980) demonstrated that the alga *Gigartina papillata* (C.Ag.) J.Ag. has a flat crustose phase which is dependent on grazers to prevent its overgrowth, and an upright phase which flourishes when grazing is reduced, and is a superior competitor. Dethier (1981a) came to similar conclusions and Lubchenco and Cubit (1980) have linked the two phases with seasonal changes in herbivory, grazing gastropods being less active in winter when the upright phase is prevalent. Jara and Moreno (1984) describe how the canopy-forming stage of *Iridaea boryana* (Setch. et Gardn.) Skottsb. prevails when grazers are reduced in number, while crusts form when limpet numbers are high.

Such adaptations, dependency and specificity between grazers and algae are predicted by a general model put forward by Steneck (1982), which suggests that trophic specialization will be high when the grazer is relatively small, slow-moving and has low energetic requirements; and when the alga is relatively large, long-lived, tolerant of grazing and is of low quality as a food. Limpets cover extremes in terms of this model. Those that graze on microalgae tend to feed in a non-specific manner and to suppress the development of macroalgae by eliminating sporelings. Those that feed on large plants such as kelps or long-lived corallines form very specific associations, often leading to coevolution and interdependency. Fig. 7.2 shows that for 11 southern African *Patella* species there is a correlation between dietary specialization and the ratio of plant to limpet sizes, providing support for part of Steneck's model.

There are of course many other factors affecting algal–herbivore relationships, including the palatability, energetic content, growth rate, size, life-span, abundance and detectability of algae; and the food preferences, mobility, sensory capabilities, energetic requirements, digestive capabilities, ability to detoxify noxious compounds and density of herbivores. All these factors must be set against the backdrop of the particular community in which the organisms interact and against physical conditions which may modify interactions. Lubchenco and Gaines (1981) provide a stimulating summary and a reminder of how many gaps there are in our understanding of these relationships.

Grazers may influence the species composition and diversity of algae and, depending on whether they attack algae which are competitive dominants or subordinates, they may increase or decrease

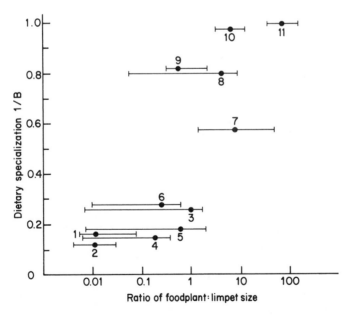

FIG. 7.2. The correlation between dietary specialization of 11 southern African *Patella* species and the ratio of the mean size of the food plants to mean limpet size. Dietary specialization is the inverse of Levins's index of dietary niche breadth, data being taken from Branch (1981, 1984a, 1985c). Horizontal bars indicate ranges.
1 = *Patella concolor* Krauss; 2 = *P. granularis*; 3 = *P. argenvillei*; 4 = *P. granatina*; 5 = *P. oculus*; 6 = *P. barbara* L.; 7 = *P. longicosta*; 8 = *P. miniata* Born.; 9 = *P. cochlear*; 10 = *P. tabularis*; 11 = *P. compressa*.

diversity respectively (see Lubchenco and Gaines, 1981). For instance, Jara and Moreno (1984) have shown that limpets and chitons virtually prevent the growth of the upright foliose form of *Iridaea boryana*. This allows the development of short-lived algae such *Petalonia* and *Scytosiphon* which are normally competitively excluded by *I. boryana*. At the same time, the elimination of a canopy of *I. boryana* results in the disappearance of other algae which only occur in the mid-shore if they can shelter under *I. boryana*. The impact of limpet-grazing may therefore have secondary effects on the algal community.

7.5 Limpet–Barnacle Interactions

Limpets often hinder the establishment of barnacles by grazing on newly settled cyprids or 'bulldozing' juvenile barnacles from the rockface (Branch, 1975b; Dayton, 1975; Denley and Underwood, 1979; Underwood *et al.*, 1983), although it seems that small, solid-shelled barnacles such as chthamaloids are relatively immune since they are flatter and can grow in crevices (Paine, 1981). Barnacles reduce the growth rate and reproductive output of some limpets (Branch, 1976; Choat, 1977; Underwood *et al.*, 1983) and may increase the mortality of pre-reproductive limpets (Choat, 1977). At the same time, the densities of juvenile limpets are often positively correlated with those of barnacles. As an example, Choat (1977) has recorded that recruitment of *Collisella digitalis* is proportional to barnacle density. Barnacles appear to hinder the grazing of at least those limpets which are moderate to large in size (Choat, 1977) and Hawkins and Hartnoll (1982a) record that the timing and duration of activity rhythms of *Patella vulgata* are altered by barnacles. The relationship between limpets and barnacles is further complicated when their interactions with algae are considered. Underwood *et al.* (1983) have shown that at very high densities the limpet *Cellana tramoserica* reduces recruitment and survival of the barnacle *Tesseropora rosea* (Krauss), but in the absence of this limpet, or even when its densities are low, algae develop and smother the barnacles or prevent settlement of further spat. Because of this interplay, highest densities of *T. rosea* are associated with low to intermediate densities of *C. tramoserica*.

In Chile, Jara and Moreno (1984) have shown that the removal of limpets and chitons allows the alga *Iridaea boryana* to form a foliose canopy, largely precluding barnacles. But in the presence of these grazers the growth of *I. boryana* is restricted to a crustose sheet and barnacles become abundant. This interaction is complicated by seasonal effects. Unoccupied rock-space periodically becomes available when rocks are broken or when waves rip away patches of barnacles and algae. If this occurs in autumn, barnacles settle densely, leading to a community dominated by barnacles and encrusting algae. This condition then persists provided grazers are present. If space is freed in spring, there is an initial settlement of ephemeral algae, followed by small numbers of barnacles, and culminating in stands of upright *I. boryana*. The latter flourishes until herbivores immigrate and feed on the fronds, weakening them so that waves tear them free. Thus although seasonal patterns determine which organisms settle, the presence or absence of grazers is the ultimate factor determining the success of foliose algae and thus of barnacles.

Other authors have pointed to cyclic changes that occur in limpet, barnacle and algal abundance on British shores (Burrows and Lodge, 1950; Southward and Southward, 1978; Hartnoll and Hawkins, 1980; Hawkins, 1981a,b, 1983). Large algae such as *Fucus* species reduce settling of barnacles, possibly because of the whiplash action of their fronds (although high on the shore *Fucus* may increase the survival of barnacles by sheltering them from physical stresses). *Patella vulgata* immigrates to stands of *Fucus* and prevents the development of further fucoid sporelings. Eventually the established adult *Fucus* are eliminated by wave action, partly because grazing by limpets weakens their stipes. As the fucoids decline, barnacle settlement increases. Barnacles retard colonization by some algae, such as diatoms and *Enteromorpha*, possibly because they filter spores from the water column, but they seem to enhance the settlement of fucoids because their sporelings settle on or between the barnacles where they are relatively inaccessible to limpets. As a result, these sporelings may escape the attentions of limpets until they are large enough to be comparatively immune to grazing (Hawkins, 1981b).

Creese (1982) has shown that *Patelloida latistrigata* (Angas), a relatively small limpet, is dependent on barnacles. In the absence of barnacles the density of a larger limpet, *Cellana tramoserica*, increases and *P. latistrigata* is outcompeted. This interplay depends partly on the predatory whelk *Morula marginalba* Blainville which preferentially preys on oysters, *P. latistrigata* and adults of the barnacle *Tesseropora rosea*, while largely ignoring *Cellana tramoserica* and a second barnacle, *Chamaesipho columna* Spengler (Fairweather et al., 1984). Thus the whelk can affect the numbers of *P. latistrigata* directly, by preying on the limpet and indirectly, by eliminating *T. rosea* and thus allowing *C. tramoserica* to increase in numbers. The availability of crevices also influences the rate with which *Morula marginalba* eliminates prey species, for the whelk depends on sheltering in crevices between feeding excursions. Physical topography may thus influence the interplay.

Clearly barnacles and limpets may have both positive and negative effects on each other. The balance may change seasonally or may depend on the presence or absence of competitors or predators. The regularity (or irregularity) with which the participating species settle will therefore play an important rôle in the dynamics of rocky shores.

7.6 Competition between Limpets

In almost every case where experimental tests have been undertaken, competitive interactions within and between limpet species have been demonstrable. In different instances intraspecific competition has been shown to influence growth, survival, recruitment, body weight and reproductive output (Branch, 1975b; Creese, 1980; Fletcher, 1984a,b; and see Branch 1981, 1984a, for reviews). Several possible mechanisms exist for reducing intraspecific competition. For instance, MacKay and Underwood (1977) have shown that the incidence with which *Cellana tramoserica* homes to a fixed scar is greatest when food is readily available, so that the limpets move away from areas where food is short, countering the effects of intraspecific competition. Cook and Cook (1980) demonstrated that in *Siphonaria normalis* Gould and *S. alternata* the 'heading choice' (the direction a limpet moves off its scar to feed) is different whenever limpets make two grazing trips on the same tide, so that they avoid covering the same ground. Breen (1972) and Branch (1975c) describe how *Collisella digitalis* and *Patella granularis* L., respectively, migrate upshore as they age, leading to size gradients with the largest limpets highest on the shore. Workman (1983), in an analysis of the energetics of high- and low-shore populations of *Patella vulgata* has shown that although consumption and growth are higher low on the shore, longevity is greater in the high-shore, with the result that lifetime reproductive value is greater in the upper shore. This is an important finding for it puts into new perspective the supposed disadvantages of living in an environment where food is short and growth slow. Both Branch and Breen ascribe upshore movement to an avoidance of competition, although direct proof of this is lacking. In this context, it should be noted that in *Notoacmea petterdi* (Tenison-Woods) size gradients are caused by intraspecific competition rather than being a means of reducing competition. *N. petterdi* settles very high on the shore and, possibly because of this, moves little during its life and is tied to a home scar. The density of new recruits declines upshore and Creese (1980) has shown that growth and body size are greatest high on the shore where density is lowest, in spite of there being less food available there.

These examples are all pointers to the fact that intraspecific competition is a significant factor for most limpets; but of greater interest is the prevalence of interspecific competition and whether it controls the distribution and abundance of limpets. In an early demonstration of competition between limpets, Haven (1973) experimentally removed either *Collisella digitalis* or *C. scabra* from areas where the two species coexisted, and showed that both species grew faster in the absence of the other. Similarly, by manipulating the densities of three gastropods in experimental cages, Underwood (1978b) demonstrated that *Nerita atramentosa* Reeve outcompeted both *Bembicium nanum* (Lamarck) and *Cellana tramoserica*, the survivorship and body weight of these two species decreasing in proportion to the density of *N. atramentosa*. In turn, *C. tramoserica* outcompetes *B. nanum*. Part of the reason for the superiority of *N. atramentosa* is that it moves further and feeds at a faster rate than either of the other two species. *C. tramoserica*, being able to excavate the substratum and remove both superficial and embedded algae, has a competitive advantage over *B. nanum*, which has numerous short teeth and apparently feeds by brushing food from the surface of the rock. For a similar reason, *C. tramoserica* also outcompetes two pulmonate limpets, *Siphonaria denticulata* Reeve and *S. virgulata* Hedley. Both species grow more slowly and experience a higher mortality rate if they are experimentally caged with *C. tramoserica* (Creese and Underwood, 1982). The starfish *Patiriella exigua* (Lamarck), which feeds at least partially on loosely attached superficial microalgae, also suffers from being caged with *C. tramoserica*, its body weight dropping in proportion to the density of *C. tramoserica* (Branch and Branch, 1980).

The zonation of certain limpets may be influenced by competition. Choat's demonstration (1977) that the removal of high-shore *Collisella digitalis* allows *C. strigatella* to move upshore (see above for details) is an important example. Black (1979) has described how *Notoacmea onychitis* (Menke) intrudes upon the zonation of *Siphonaria kurracheensis* (Reeve), which has a bimodal zonation pattern, being most abundant above and below the mid-shore zone dominated by *N. onychitis*. After experimental removal of all limpets, Black recorded that *S. kurracheensis* establishes itself and develops highest densities in the zone normally occupied by *N. onychitis*. Similarly, *Patella cochlear* dominates the low-shore zone on South African coasts and excludes practically all other limpets. One species, *P. longicosta* Lamarck is common above and below the *cochlear* zone, but only occurs in this zone in any numbers after experimental elimination of *P. cochlear* (Branch, 1976 and unpubl.).

While competitive dominance between limpets may be achieved by superior exploitation of a food supply, interference and territoriality play an important rôle. For instance, Connor (1975) describes how the chiton *Mopalia muscosa* (Gould) reacts aggressively to *Collisella pelta* (Rathke), pushing it away upon contact. In the presence of *M. muscosa*, the density of *C. pelta* is lower, its mean body size smaller, and its rate of emigration faster. *M. muscosa* is never aggressive towards another acmaeid limpet, *Collisella limatula* (Carpenter) – which is interesting because *C. limatula* (unlike *C. pelta*) eats different algae from *M. muscosa* and presents no competitive threat to it.

A more dramatic example is the territorial behaviour of *Lottia gigantea* (Gray), a large limpet which occupies patches of an algal film, which it defends by thrusting against intruding limpets. Removal of *L. gigantea* results in an invasion of its territory by numerous smaller acmaeids which eliminate the algal film. Normally resident *Lottia* virtually exclude these acmaeids from the territories. *Lottia gigantea* also ousts other herbivores (including members of its own species) and some space-occupying organisms, and at least retards encroachment by mussels (Stimson, 1970). The growth rate of *L. gigantea* is correlated with the size of its territory, and it expands its territory when algae become scarce, so that its densities are higher in areas where food is abundant. The reason *L. gigantea* does not eliminate the algal film in its territory seems related to its size: the larger the limpet, the greater the amount of alga it leaves behind when grazing (Stimson, 1973).

Territoriality is now well known in a number of limpets. *Patella compressa* occurs singly on the stipes of its kelp host and reacts aggressively to conspecifics that move onto the stipe (Branch, 1975c). *P. cochlear* defends a fringing 'garden' of fine red algae that surrounds each animal, and is spaced out regularly so that contact between individuals is minimized – a feature of some importance considering the unusually high densities achieved in many populations (Branch, 1975b). Perhaps the most specialized territorial limpets are *P. longicosta* and *P. tabularis* Krauss, which maintain monospecific patches of the encrusting alga *Ralfsia expansa* (J.Ag.) J.Ag. Both species react aggressively to intruding limpets and to other herbivores. Removal of *P. longicosta* results in the eventual disappearance of the garden, either because it is overshadowed by encroaching erect algae or because it is grazed away by other herbivores. *P. longicosta* cuts regular paths in the *Ralfsia*. This effectively increases the growing edge of the alga and almost doubles its growth rate in comparison with control patches of *Ralfsia* which are not grazed by the limpet. The productivity of *Ralfsia* declines upshore, and this may determine the upper limits of zonation for *P. longicosta* (Branch 1976, 1981).

The territorial defences of *Lottia gigantea* and the responses of intruding limpets both seem more ritualized than they were portrayed in early descriptions. If *L. gigantea* intrudes onto another limpet's territory it withdraws immediately it comes into contact with a territory-owner. This evasive behaviour avoids the violent thrusting reaction that territorial limpets are capable of and which can dislodge intruders. Such evasive action is only taken by limpets that are on another limpet's territory, irrespective of the size of the resident limpet, and has never been recorded for limpets that are on their own territories (Wright, 1982). Even more striking escape responses are displayed by some of the smaller acmaeids, which flee if they come into contact with any other limpet while on the territory of *L. gigantea* – whether the other limpet is the resident *L. gigantea* or not. *Collisella digitalis* recognizes and avoids *L. gigantea* territories, even in the absence of the territory-owner (Wright, 1977).

Territoriality in limpets may have arisen as an intraspecific device to defend the food resource against members of the same species (Branch, 1984b), but its efficacy against other species is well established, and it appears to have led to the evolution of the evasive responses described above.

7.7 Competition, Community Structure and Evolution

It has become almost a paradigm that on rocky shores predators or physical disturbance are key factors preventing competitive dominants from monopolizing the habitat. Indeed, there are several well documented instances in which organisms such as mussels do dominate much of the shore in the absence of predators (e.g. Paine, 1974). On the other hand, it is clear that competition (by both exploitation and interference) is an important factor in the population dynamics of many limpets and other littoral organisms (Branch, 1984a, 1985c). Its effect on community structure is more difficult to pinpoint. Underwood (1978b) has pointed out that competition between mobile herbivores such as limpets is very different from that in sessile species. The latter most often compete for space, which is an essential requirement, is not self-renewing and, once occupied, remains unavailable to other organisms until the death or displacement of the occupant. Mobile herbivores compete more often for food, which is a relative requirement, for most organisms (and particularly invertebrates) can survive on sub-optimal amounts of food. Food is also self-renewing.

I have recently analysed 192 examples of competition between marine organisms (Branch, 1984a, 1985c). Building on Underwood's ideas, two further relevant points emerge from this review. First, competition for food is usually by means of exploitation (68% of the cases analysed) while competition for space is by interference (82% of cases). Interference is more likely to result in exclusion of one species by another, provided competition is allowed to run its course. By contrast, when exploitation is involved, coexistence is the norm (occurring in 96% of the cases). Secondly, the rôle played by predators differs depending on the nature of the competitors. Sessile species are more vulnerable to predators and, if they are eliminated, have to rely on larval recruitment for replacement; mobile herbivores can hide, escape or even retaliate against predators, and can be rapidly replaced by immigration.

Taken collectively, these points suggest that the rôles played by competition and predation depend on the interacting species. Sessile species, competing for space, have the capacity to monopolize the habitat and to oust other species; predation and disturbance may thus be important in preventing this monopolization. Indeed, in 66% of the cases researched by Branch (1985c), predators (or physical disturbance) achieved this effect, increasing species diversity in the process. Mobile forms competing for food are likely to coexist even in the absence of predators or disturbance, and in 30% of the cases analysed predators had no effect on species diversity, while in 64% they decreased diversity.

The contribution of sessile and mobile species to a community may thus influence how the community functions and the relative importance of competition and predation. In a recent comparison of the biomass on twelve littoral rocky shores around the coast of the Cape Peninsula, South Africa, McQuaid and Branch (1984, in prep.) concluded that wave action was the key factor determining the incidence of sessile and mobile species. In particular, they found that in wave-exposed areas the biomass of sessile filter-feeders increased enormously, to the extent that much of the shore was totally covered by filter-feeders; while on sheltered shores herbivores, particularly limpets, had a proportionately greater biomass than on exposed shores. Amongst other possible explanations, wave action may make filter-feeding more efficient, introduce more particulate food, and reduce the effectiveness of predators.

The long-term evolutionary implications of competition between limpets are more problematic. It is impossible to test directly whether past competitive interactions have shaped the evolution of limpets and, instead, one is forced to search for correlations and patterns which depart sufficiently from random to reasonably expect that they were caused by competition. Even then, competition is only one of several factors that may originally have been responsible for the patterns seen today.

Murphy (1976) has produced compelling electrophoretic evidence of genetic differences between acmaeids which may be due to competition. His analysis of the incidence of eight leucine aminopeptidase (*Lap*) alleles shows that the stenotopic species, which never overlap the habitat of other species, have very similar allele frequencies; while eurytopic species which frequently co-occur all differ in the frequencies of these alleles. More significantly, two of the species display greater differences when they coexist than when they do not. It seems that competition may have caused character displacement of the *Lap* alleles. Although more work is needed, this is a significant example for it is one of the few cases in which 'character displacement' seems almost certainly to be genetically controlled. It is also amenable to further experimentation testing the rôle competition plays in the displacement.

On the other hand, the existence of specialized species does not necessarily indicate that competition caused the specialization. For example, *Patelloida mufria* occurs almost exclusively on the shells of other gastropods, particularly *Astrocochlea constricta* (Mapstone *et al.*, 1984). Predation on this limpet by the whelk *Morula marginalba* virtually never occurs when the limpets are attached to other shells, but the whelk readily eats *P. mufria* living on rocks. Occupation of particular host molluscs also decreases the chances that *P. mufria* will be killed by desiccation. Thus its specialized habitat has survival value in terms of reducing predation and desiccation. Past competition seems highly unlikely as an explanation of its specialization. Specialized segregation of habitats has been described between two coexisting species of *Patelloida*, *P. pygmaea* (Dunker) occurring on stones or dead shells, while *P. lampanicola* Habe lives exclusively on living *Batillaria* species (Morton, 1980); but again there is no evidence that this 'partitioning' is a means of avoiding competition – or even that the two species have competed at any stage.

Similarly, in relation to the occurrence of certain limpets on specific laminarian hosts, Choat and Black (1979) considered that competition was unlikely to have been the cause of such specialization, and that 'using arguments based on interspecific competition to predict patterns of habitat and resource partitioning in phenotypically similar species seems to be unproductive'.

There are, however, some patterns that are difficult to explain if competition does not influence the specialization of species. Branch (1981) has described a close correlation between the number of

Patella species coexisting at various points around the coast of southern Africa and the mean specialization of the diets and habitats of these species. The most interesting feature about this correlation is that it is not due to changes in the specialization of individual species. As the number of coexisting species rises around the coast, mean specialization rises simultaneously simply because the species being added to the faunal list are those that are specialized. Thus in Moçambique and northern Namibia where there are few *Patella* species, all are generalized; but towards the southern coast of South Africa it is the addition of specialized species that raises the average specialization of all the species combined. If the individual species are not responding to the number of coexisting species, what explains the correlation between diversity and specialization? Possibly the character of a new species is moulded by competitors at the time of speciation. The more pre-existing competitors there are, the less likely will be the survival of the new species if it shares limiting resources with these species. Specialization may thus be forced on a species when it first arises, and its character is then relatively fixed from that time on – as I have outlined more fully elsewhere (Branch, 1984a, 1985a,c). This argument does not imply that specialization only originates because of competition, for there are many possible causes of specialization, but rather that the chances of a newly-arising species being specialized will be greatest in the presence of pre-existing established competitors.

Another interesting point about this pattern is that as the number of coexisting *Patella* species rises, so does the incidence of species competing by interference (i.e. territoriality). Improved ability to compete is one possible evolutionary response to threats posed by competitors. Indeed, in reviewing competition in marine organisms, I found that interference was the predominant mode of competition in the sea, occurring in 80% of the examples analysed. Furthermore, in 94% of the cases involving interference, the interaction led to local displacement of one species by another, or at least a significant reduction in the numbers of the subordinate (Branch, 1984a, 1985c). Thus interference is prevalent and potent, and is a far more logical an evolutionary solution to competition than niche apportionment or character displacement.

7.8 Adaptations to Predators

Many animals are important predators of limpets, including whelks (Black, 1978), crabs (Chapin, 1968), starfish (Dayton *et al.*, 1977; Blankley and Branch, 1984), octopus (Wells, 1980), gulls (Blankley, 1981; Lindberg and Chu, 1983), oystercatchers (Feare, 1971b; Frank, 1982; Hockey, 1983a; Hockey and Underhill, 1984) and fish (Paine and Palmer, 1978; Stobbs, 1980; Cook, 1980; Levings and Garrity, 1984).

Quantification of the impact of individual predators is usually difficult. Working on a relatively simple ecosystem at sub-Antarctic Marion Island, Blankley and Branch (1985) have used the densities and feeding rates of a series of predators to estimate their annual depredation of the limpet *Nacella delesserti* (Philippi) – the dominant macroinvertebrate on the shores of the island. The starfish *Anasterias rupicola* (Verrill) accounts for about 40% of the mortality of limpets in the size range 25 to 60mm; in shallow waters the kelpgull *Larus dominicanus* Lichtenstein consumes 20% of the limpets that are over 35mm in length; and the cod *Notothenia coriiceps* Richardson accounts for an estimated 15 to 30% of the limpets.

Parry (1982a) estimated that each year oystercatchers (*Haematopus fuliginosus* Gould) eat 9% of the population of *Cellana tramoserica* at Victoria, Australia; and that wrasses (*Pseudolabrus* spp.) annually remove 52% to 70% of *Patelloida alticostata* (Angas) and almost 100% of *Patella peroni* (Blainville).

Even allowing for the fact that these figures are estimates, they clearly indicate that for at least some limpets predation is a major source of mortality, and it is not surprising that a range of defensive mechanisms has been evolved.

The colour and shape of the shell is likely to be important for limpets that are sought by visual predators. Hockey and Branch (1983) have noted that oystercatchers (*Haematopus moquini* Bonaparte) preferentially prey on those *Patella granularis* that have slightly pear-shaped shells rather than those that are uniformly elliptical; and their rate of predation is sufficient to influence shell-shape in an exploited limpet population compared with areas where there are no oystercatchers or habitats where oystercatchers cannot feed. Camouflage is another obvious adaptation. Hartwick (1981), for instance, has shown that *Collisella digitalis* with dark shells are removed by oystercatchers (*Haematopus bachmani* Audubon) more often than their paler counterparts, and kelpgulls (*Larus dominicanus*) feed most frequently on pale forms of *Nacella delesserti* (Branch, 1985b). Giesel (1970) has suggested that polymorphism in *C. digitalis* is maintained by the differential survival of different morphs on rock surfaces cf. among gooseneck barnacles; and proposed that shore-birds eliminate morphs that are ill-matched against their background. Despite these suggestions, formal proof of the value of visual camouflage to limpets is still lacking.

Far more exciting has been the discovery of chemical camouflage in *Notoacmea paleacea* (Gould) (Fishlyn and Phillips, 1980). *N. paleacea* occurs on the surfgrass *Phyllospadix*, and it incorporates at least one chemical from this food plant into its shell. As a result the predatory starfish *Leptasterias hexactis* (Stimpson) seems unable to detect the limpet against the chemical background of the host plant. Many marine predators hunt by chemical detection of prey and further work on the existence and prevalence of chemical camouflage is much needed.

Limpets may also detect predators at a distance (Phillips, 1975) and have species-specific responses which allow them to escape (Phillips, 1976). In most cases escape involves elevation of the shell and rapid flight away from the predator (Bullock, 1953; Clark, 1958; Feder, 1963; Margolin, 1964a; Branch, 1978); but some species roll the margin of the mantle over the shell, making it more difficult for predators to attach themselves (Margolin, 1964b; Branch and Branch, 1980). Several species of small limpets live on the shells of other gastropods. Such an association provides *Patelloida mufria* with protection from a common predatory whelk, presumably because of the escape responses of its host (Mapstone *et al.*, 1984).

Very large limpets have the option of retaliating against predators. Large individuals of *Patella oculus* Born. and *P. granatina* L. lift the shell and smash it down on predators – a behaviour that is size-specific and predator-specific (Branch, 1979). Sheer size may also be a defence. For instance Stobbs (1980) has shown that there is a linear relationship between the size of the giant clingfish *Chorisochismus dentex* (Pallas) and the maximum size of the limpets it can eat. Similarly, the African black oystercatcher (*Haematopus moquini*) seldom feeds on limpets that exceed 60mm in length, presumably because it cannot prise larger limpets off rocks (Hockey and Underhill, 1984; Hockey and Branch, 1984).

Some limpets may be toxic. *Siphonaria capensis* Quoy and Gaimard has massive mucous glands liberally distributed over its foot and mantle, which release a white viscous mucus seemingly repugnant to a wide range of predators. Eight predators, including two whelks, the oystercatcher *Haematopus moquini*, and five fish, refuse to eat live *S. capensis* although they readily feed on patellid limpets (Branch and Cherry, 1985). In the light of this it is interesting that siphonariids, rather than patellids, predominate in the tropics where predation is more intense. At least some *Siphonaria* species are, however, eaten by tropical predators (Cook, 1980; Levings and Garrity, 1984).

Both the habit of homing to a scar and the timing of activity rhythms may be important in reducing predation. Experiments have shown that it takes an octopus twice as long to consume *Collisella scabra* which are attached to their scars than when they lack scars (Wells, 1980). If *Siphonaria gigas* is prevented from homing to a scar, its mortality rate rises thirteen-fold, probably because it becomes more vulnerable to predatory fish (Garrity and Levings, 1983).

Bertness *et al.* (1981) have compared the relative rates at which littoral gastropods are preyed upon on tropical and temperate shores. Their approach was to glue gastropods to open rock faces and record the rate that they were removed and the incidence with which their shells were crushed by predators. While little predation took place in temperate areas, the rate of predation was impressive in the tropics, more than 6% of the gastropods being crushed each tidal cycle. Bertness *et al.* related this difference in the intensity of predation to a divergence in the activity patterns of gastropods in the two areas. All the temperate gastropods they examined (*Thais* and *Littorina* spp.) were active while submerged during high tide. By contrast the tropical species (a much wider array of species, which included nine limpets) were active only at low tide while the rocks were damp, particularly by night, and the limpets all homed to fixed scars and fed in discrete areas around the home scars. Bertness *et al.* suggested that tropical gastropods cannot leave their shelters or home scars to forage at high tide because of the threat posed by predatory fish.

Activity patterns that minimize predation are not, however, restricted to the tropics. Wells (1980) has shown that two temperate limpets, *Collisella scabra* and *C. limatula* forage only when awash (or during the nocturnal low tide). During high tide *C. limatula* hides in crevices and under boulders while *C. scabra* retires to home scars. Wells considered these activity patterns to be means of reducing the attentions of swift-moving visual predators – the octopus being important in this instance.

7.9 Interaction with Predators: Effects on Community Structure

Predators obviously have a considerable and direct influence on limpet abundance, but they also have an indirect effect by restricting the timing, duration and extent of grazing. Both effects have implications in terms of the influence of limpets on community structure. Their importance must, however, be viewed against the backdrop of physical conditions and the rôle of other organisms. For instance, Levings and Garrity (1984) have shown that the impact *Siphonaria gigas* has on tropical algae and barnacles is modified both by physical factors and by predators. *S. gigas* feeds only when awash, on the one hand because of the risk of predation when it is fully submerged and on the other due to the dangers of physical stresses during the daytime low tide. Such restrictions on grazing may influence algal growth; but the algae themselves are also directly affected by herbivorous fish during high tide and by physical stresses. A further complication is that local topography alters the influence of physical factors. *S. gigas* is more common in areas where the substratum is irregular, and in wave-exposed rather than sheltered sites. These conditions will blunt physical stresses and make it more difficult for predators to feed. Consequent increases in the density of benthic herbivores may influence the settling of barnacles and algae, but the same conditions should enhance barnacle settlement and increase algal productivity because damper cooler conditions will promote survival and photosynthesis. Thus in calmer areas and on homogeneous substrata where grazers are scarce, physical stress may on its own prevent development of dense beds of foliose algae and barnacles; while on wave-beaten shores and on broken substrata, where physical stresses are ameliorated, grazers such as *S. gigas* appear to become increasingly important in controlling the abundance of algae and barnacles. Indeed, Levings and Garrity (1984) record that over a wide range of conditions in tropical Panama barnacles are scarce and crustose algae predominate, while erect algae (which are relatively intolerant of grazing and physical stress) are rare. At sites exposed to extreme wave action the community structure is, however, very different; the density of *S. gigas* decreases abruptly (presumably because of dislodgement), upright macroalgae cover two-thirds of the canopy and barnacles are abundant. Extreme wave action may thus reduce grazing and physical stress simultaneously, permitting erect algae and barnacles to competitively replace crustose algae.

The tolerance of benthic predators to physical factors, their feeding preferences and the relative abundance of prey species are also issues which may alter the effect predators have on limpets. As an example, the predatory whelk *Morula marginalba* has clear preferences for some prey species, including *Patelloida latistrigata*, while largely ignoring others, such as *Cellana tramoserica*. But its preferences are only a guide to the effect it will have on different species, for although it will normally ignore less preferred species, it readily feeds on them when more desirable prey are unavailable (Fairweather *et al.*, 1984).

Thus interactions may be complex, as exemplified by recent work on the influence which sea-birds have on rocky shore communities on the West coast of South Africa (Hockey, 1983a; Hockey and Branch, 1983, 1984; Hockey and Underhill, 1984; unpubl. data from Hockey, Bosman, du Toit, Finlay and Branch). Much of this work is based on observational and experimental comparisons made between mainland sites (which lack large bird populations) and near-shore islands supporting large colonies of roosting and breeding sea-birds.

The African black oystercatcher, *Haematopus moquini*, is more abundant on islands, reaching a density of 75 birds·km^{-1} of shore, than on the mainland where there are about 3 birds·km^{-1}. *Patella granularis*, the dominant limpet in the mid-shore, forms a substantial fraction of the oystercatcher's diet, and its numbers are lower on the islands (averaging 94·m^{-2} in the mid-shore) than on the mainland (164·m^{-2}). On the islands 73% of the limpets are concentrated in habitats inaccessible to oystercatchers, while on the mainland they are randomly distributed (Fig. 7.3A). Their microdistribution and density therefore seem influenced by the oystercatchers. Furthermore, on islands where the level of predation by oystercatchers is high, the size composition of limpets is different in accessible and inaccessible habitats, being depressed over the size range attacked by oystercatchers in accessible habitats (Fig. 7.3A). On the mainland the size structure of the limpet population is similar in accessible and inaccessible habitats.

Another striking difference is that the mid- and upper shore on islands is covered by large beds of macroalgae while mainland sites virtually lack such beds. In part this is due to differences in the intensity of grazing, for in areas on the islands where the limpets are experimentally thinned or their numbers are naturally low due to oystercatcher predation, algal growth increases (Fig. 7.3B), paralleling the finding of Moreno *et al.* (1984) that human predation of limpets enhances algal growth in Chile. Prey selection also plays a rôle in this process, for while oystercatchers feed extensively on *P. granularis* they never eat another abundant limpet, *Siphonaria capensis*, which is apparently noxious. Because *S. capensis* is incapable of controlling algal growth in the manner that *P. granularis* does, its immunity to predation is of little consequence to algal growth.

There is, however, another reason for the differences in algal cover between mainland and island sites, for even when limpets are experimentally excluded, algal productivity (measured on artificial strips glued to intertidal rocks) is substantially higher on the islands than on the mainland (Fig. 7.3C). Hockey and Branch (1984) suggest that this is because sea-bird guano enriches the littoral zone of the islands. Support for this comes from experiments from which seawater drips were arranged in such a manner to supply sections of a mainland rocky shore with either seawater or with seawater enriched with guano (Fig. 7.3D). Settling and early growth of algal sporelings were significantly increased by the enriched seawater (J. du Toit, G.M. Branch, P.A.R. Hockey and A. Bosman, in prep.).

The enhancement of algal productivity on islands due to guano runoff thus complements the effects of reduced limpet densities, leading to higher standing stocks of algae. This has a ripple of effects. First, the higher productivity of sporelings leads to faster growth rates of limpets and to far greater maximum sizes of the limpets (Fig. 7.3A), which attain 95mm on island sites compared with 47mm on the mainland. Since oystercatchers feed most often on limpets between 20 and 43mm (and never on any exceeding 64mm), the enhanced growth of limpets on islands increases the chance that they will reach a size where they escape further depredation by oystercatchers (Fig. 7.3A). Because of their greater size, the biomass of limpets on the islands is 281g·m^{-2} (wet weight) compared with 71g·m^{-2} on

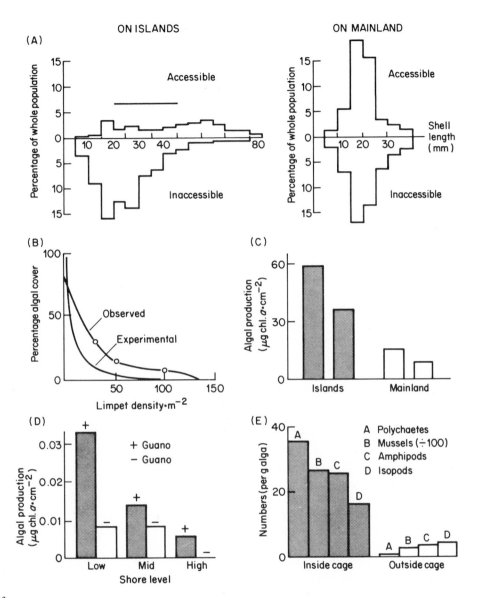

FIG. 7.3.

A. The size composition of *Patella granularis* on island and mainland sites on the west coast of South Africa, in habitats which are respectively accessible and inaccessible to oystercatchers. The horizontal bar shows the size range of limpets attacked by oystercatchers (modified from Hockey and Branch, 1984.)

B. The amount of algal cover on the mid-shore of islands, in relation to limpet density. The two lines are for field observations and for manipulative experiments (Hockey and Branch, 1984; K. Findley, unpubl.).

C. Rate of algal colonization and growth (measured as μg chl a·cm^{-2} month^{-1}) on artificial surfaces placed in the littoral zone of two island and two mainland sites (A. Bosman and P.A.R. Hockey, unpubl.).

D. Settling and growth of algal sporelings in areas treated with seawater drips which had or had not been enriched with guano (J. du Toit *et al.*, unpubl.).

E. The relative abundance of four groups of cryptic organisms in the macroalgal beds of islands, inside or outside cages that prevent predation by waders (P.A.R. Hockey and A. Bosman, unpubl.).

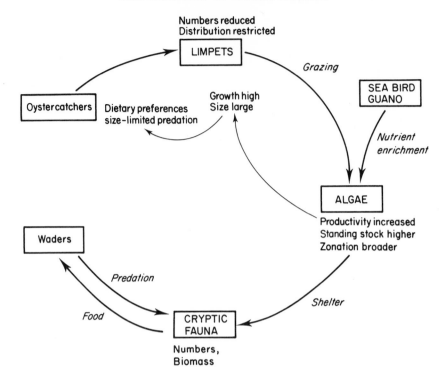

FIG. 7.4. Conceptual model of the interactions between birds, limpets and macroalgae on sea-bird islands off the West coast of South Africa.

the mainland; and their estimated gametic output is $62\text{g}\cdot\text{m}^{-2}$ while on the mainland it is a mere $6\text{g}\cdot\text{m}^{-2}$ (Hockey and Branch, 1984).

The dense algal beds on islands have a second effect in sheltering a cryptic fauna of invertebrates which is rare on the mainland, and this fauna supports smaller waders such as the turnstone (*Arenaria interpres* (L.)) which are four times more common on the islands than on the mainland. Indirectly, the oystercatchers may thus facilitate the feeding of these waders by reducing limpet numbers, thereby increasing the cover of algae and their associated fauna (Fig. 7.4). The waders make substantial inroads into these invertebrate populations, which have densities 3 to 36 times higher inside exclusion cages than in areas where the waders feed (P.A.R. Hockey and A. Bosman, unpubl. data; Fig. 7.3E).

Clearly these cascading interactions have an important influence on the rôle of limpets. If there is a 'take-home message', it is that while limpets indisputably play a significant part in the ecology of rocky shores, their precise effects are species-specific and are modified by a multiplicity of factors, both physical and biological.

CHAPTER VIII

HEIGHT ON THE SHORE AS A FACTOR INFLUENCING GROWTH RATE AND REPRODUCTION OF THE TOP-SHELL *GIBBULA CINERARIA* (L.)

I.W. Jardine

8.1 Introduction

One of the great opportunities for investigation proferred by the littoral marine environment is that considerable environmental changes can occur over a few vertical metres whereas equivalent changes in terrestrial environments may only occur over hundreds of kilometres (Sutherland, 1970). Several studies of molluscan populations have chronicled differences in the dynamics of conspecific populations over relatively short distances on the shore. Such studies have served to improve the understanding of the factors which regulate natural populations.

To date studies of this kind have concentrated largely on bivalves and limpets due no doubt to the relative ease of assessing their densities and of recapturing individuals. Seed (1969b) showed that individuals in higher shore populations of the bivalve *Mytilus edulis* L. had lower growth rates but better survivorship than those in lower shore populations, resulting in very different population size- and age-structures. A similar situation was found in the limpet *Patella vulgata* L. by Lewis and Bowman (1975) although the extent of barnacle cover in any area was also an important determinant of limpet population dynamics. In contrast however Sutherland (1970) found that individuals in higher shore populations of the limpet *Collisella* (= *Acmaea*) *scabra* (Gould) had both better survivorship and faster growth rates than those on the lower shore, although they did have a more restricted breeding season. The lower densities of the higher populations were believed to be responsible for the faster growth rate.

Gibbula cineraria (L.) is the only common trochid gastropod which inhabits rocky shores on all British coasts (Lewis, 1964). In Britain, it is restricted to the lower edges of the littoral zone, normally below the level of mean low water neap tides (M.L.W.N.) (Fretter and Graham, 1962, 1977). On some shores however, particularly on parts of the East coast where gently-shelving shores retain areas of standing water at low tide, this species extends its range further up the shore, as at Robin Hood's Bay, North Yorkshire, where the work described here was carried out. Even at Robin Hood's Bay however the vertical range of this species extends to less than 3m above Chart Datum and it is restricted to pools and permanently damp areas beneath fucoid seaweeds.

This study was begun with the intention of investigating whether over such a short tidal range there was any evidence of changes in survivorship and recruitment patterns. Initial results however resulted in more effort being devoted to comparisons of growth rates between the sites studied.

8.2 Sampling Sites and Sampling Methods

8.2.1 Population structure and growth rates

At Robin Hood's Bay a series of five large shallow pools leads down from the sea water inlet pipe of the former Marine Laboratory (at *c.* M.T.L.) to the lower shore. These pools were surveyed for *G. cineraria* and the lowest three, Pools 3–5, were adopted as sampling sites. A fourth site was chosen in a gulley on the extreme lower edge of the littoral zone, the bottom of which was never uncovered even on the lowest spring tides. The sites and their heights above Chart Datum are therefore as follows: Pool 3 (+ 2.6m), Pool 4 (+ 2.2m), Pool 5 (+ 1.6m) and Low (*c.* 0.0m). The pool sites were visually very similar with little macroalgal biomass, such as there was consisting of *Corallina officinalis* L., *Mastocarpus* (= *Gigartina*) *stellatus* (Stackh.) Guiry and *Fucus serratus* L. The low-shore site however had extensive coverings of *F. serratus*, *Laminaria saccharina* (L.) Lam. and *L. digitata* (Huds.) Lam., especially in the late summer and autumn.

To obtain a sample of snails each site was traversed repeatedly, and animals removed from above and below the stones which covered the floor of these sites, as well as from the surfaces of weeds and occasional large boulders between the stones until eighty stones had been examined. Animals collected in this way were taken back to the laboratory and the maximum basal diameters of the shells were measured to the nearest 0.1mm using a vernier caliper. These measurements were used to construct size–frequency histograms. All animals were returned to their site of origin 24h after the sample was taken.

8.2.2 Reproduction

At approximately monthly intervals samples of 50 adult snails were taken from each of two sites. Site A was a pool adjacent to sample site Pool 3, and Site B was at the level of the Low site. Animals collected from these sites were kept in seawater for 48h to empty their guts before being killed by immersion in magnesium chloride solution isotonic with seawater. They were then preserved in 4% seawater formalin until they could be examined. Subsequently the animals were boiled for 1min in seawater and then extracted from their shells. The gonad was dissected away and the shell, body and gonad dried in a vacuum oven at 50°C for 24h before being weighed separately.

8.3 Population Density

Assessing the density of snails in a three-dimensional habitat such as a rock pool poses problems. The method used was to sample a given number of stones in each pool. Since one is presumably sampling from the same distribution of stone sizes on each occasion then major changes in density within a site should be reflected in changes in sample size obtained. For comparisons between sites to be valid the distribution of stone sizes would need to be the same in all sites.

The bedrock in Robin Hood's Bay is Liassic shale. The stones which covered each site were also predominately shale and were flat and roughly elliptical in shape. Most snails were found beneath these stones. On the first two sampling occasions the maximum and minimum diameters of each stone examined were recorded and the time taken to collect the sample noted. The approximate area of each stone was calculated as $\pi \, d'd''/4$ and the values obtained were plotted in the form of size–frequency histograms (Fig. 8.1). From Fig. 8.1 it can be seen that the distribution of stone sizes in the three pool sites was broadly similar, but that the Low site had a greater proportion of larger stone sizes. Todd (1979a) used a similar method for calculating the areas of stones at Robin Hood's Bay in order to assess the densities of nudibranch molluscs.

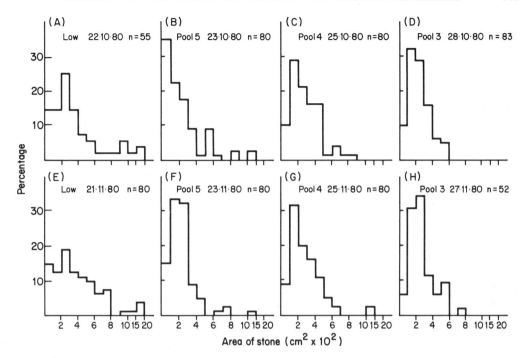

FIG. 8.1. Percentage size–frequency histograms of the areas of stones sampled on the first two sampling occasions. The date of the sample and the sample size (number of stones) is given in each case.

Table 8.1 summarizes the information obtained on the first two sampling occasions, and includes two indicators of species density; the number of individuals $\cdot$ m^{-2} of under stone area and the number of individuals collected $\cdot$ h^{-1}. Both these indicators suggest that there are two higher density sites, Pools 4 and 5, and two lower density sites, Pool 3 and Low. While the sample sizes in all sites declined slightly over the course of the study, samples obtained in Pools 4 and 5 were consistently larger than those obtained in the other sites.

8.4 Population Size Structure

The percentage size–frequency histograms obtained for the three Pool sites were broadly similar and the data for Pool 3 are representative (see Fig. 8.2). The first column of size frequencies shows two clear peaks, between 5mm and 10mm and between 10mm and 15mm. There is also a suggestion of a peak at around 2mm – presumed to represent newly settled individuals – sometimes termed the '0-class'. In the second column are samples taken in the spring and summer of 1981. As growth commenced in the spring the first major peak moves steadily across until it merges with the other peak. By October, 1981 (top of column 3), a new peak has formed at around 5–10mm presumably due to individuals growing to a size where they can be easily sampled. The pattern was repeated in 1982.

From these histograms it was deduced that: (i) growth is seasonal, occurring between April and October, (ii) in winter the characteristic size distribution consists of one major peak at about 7mm composed of one year old animals and a second peak centred around 15mm and composed of more than one older age class, (iii) the 0-class is considerably undersampled by the methods used.

Fig. 8.3 shows the size–frequency histograms of all samples taken in the Low site. The growth pattern is the same as for Pool 3 but the peaks occur at slightly smaller sizes (the first at *c.* 5mm and the

TABLE 8.1

Summary of results obtained on the first two stone sampling occasions

Site	Date	Number of stones	Number of animals under stones	Total calculated area of stones (m²)	Snails·m⁻² under stones	Time taken (hours)	Number of snails collected·h⁻¹
Low	22.10.80	55	208	2.1755	95.6	2:30	115.0
Pool 5	23.10.80	80	309	1.8956	163.0	2:45	168.0
Pool 4	25.10.80	80	303	2.2989	131.8	2:30	133.2
Pool 3	28.10.80	83	212	1.9612	108.1	2:00	119.0
Low	21.11.80	80	319	3.7032	86.1	3:00	120.7
Pool 5	23.11.80	80	279	1.9395	143.9	2:00	194.0
Pool 4	25.11.80	80	391	2.2871	171.0	2:30	192.4
Pool 3	27.11.80	52	131	1.3841	94.9	1:30	117.3

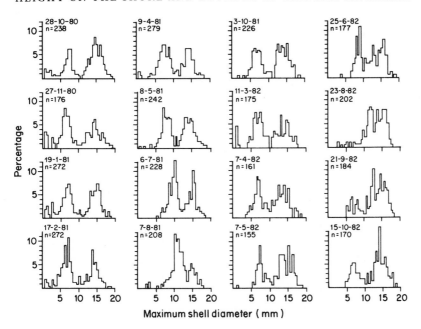

FIG. 8.2. Percentage size–frequencies of all *G. cineraria* samples taken in Pool 3 in the course of this study. Histograms are arranged sequentially within columns and the date of sample and sample size are given for each. A class interval of 0.5mm has been used.

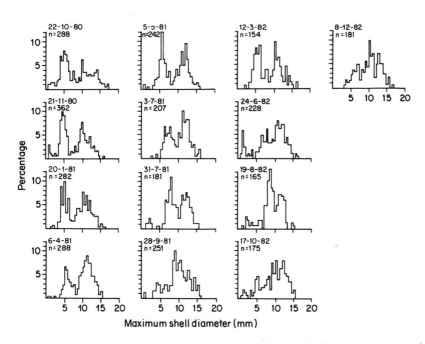

FIG. 8.3. Percentage size–frequencies of all *G. cineraria* samples taken in the Low site. Histograms are arranged sequentially within columns and the date of sample and sample size are given for each.

second from *c.* 9mm to 15mm). This difference could be due to either later settlement or to slower growth rates on the lower shore.

8.5 Growth Checks and Population Age Structure

The shells of many species of mollusc which have seasonal growth patterns show winter growth checks (Haskin, 1954; Wilbur and Owen, 1964). Such checks were first used by Crozier (1918) to analyse the age structure of the polyplacophoran *Chiton tuberculatus* L. Williamson and Kendall (1981) demonstrated the annual nature of visible shell markings in the top-shell *Monodonta lineata* (da Costa) and used these to analyse the population age structure. Similarly growth checks have been used to age individuals of the North American top-shell *Tegula funebralis* (A. Adams) (Darby, 1964).

In *G. cineraria*, new growth was discernible in spring as a darker band at the growing edge of the shell. In most animals this new growth was still identifiable in October when growth ceased. Thus, in the September/October samples, two shell measurements could be obtained for most individuals; the present diameter and the diameter at the last growth check. Just as plotting histograms based on the present diameters allowed the identification of the one year old age class (Figs. 8.2 and 8.3) so plotting histograms based on the last growth check allows the identification of last years one-year-olds, i.e. present two-year-olds. When the data were plotted in the form of last growth check against present diameter these first two year classes separated out as clouds of points (Figs. 8.4 and 8.5).

Some animals in the older age classes showed a distinct sequence of growth checks. Each check usually consisted of a series of lines across the shell parallel to the growing edge, and there was often a 'step' in the shell or a change in colour or pattern at these points. Other animals possessed a few clear checks but other checks, usually the oldest, were not identifiable due to wear. The position of these

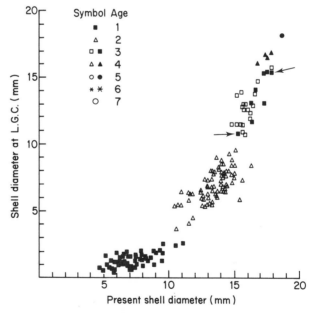

FIG. 8.4. Shell diameter at last growth check (L.G.C.) plotted against present diameter for the Pool 3 *G. cineraria* taken on 15 October, 1982. Each age-class is illustrated by a symbol given in the key. For age groups 3–6 years an open symbol indicates that a clear sequence of growth checks was not visible on the shell while a closed symbol indicates that the animal could be aged from the sequence of checks on the shell. An arrow placed beside a datum point indicates that the animal had been marked in May 1982.

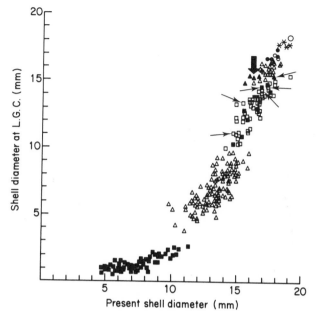

FIG. 8.5. Shell diameter at the last growth check (L.G.C.) plotted against present diameter for the Pool 4 *G. cineraria* sample for 18 October, 1982. The symbols and format used are the same as for Fig. 8.4, except that the solid arrow to a datum point indicates an animal which had been marked in April, 1981, and May, 1982.

checks could be inferred by comparisons with smaller individuals of commensurate size. Animals which could not be aged were allocated to a particular age class on the basis of their proximity to points representing animals of known age. Occasionally animals were assigned to an age class on the basis of appearance and shell wear, although this was only done after extensive comparisons with individuals already allocated to potential peer groups.

In April, 1981, and May, 1982, some animals in the Pool sites were marked by making a groove in the shell next to the growing edge. It is clear from the position of these marked individuals in Figs. 8.4 and 8.5 that the last growth check was being identified correctly.

The samples for Pools 3 and 4 from October, 1982, are shown in Figs. 8.4 and 8.5 as representative (of the eight samples taken in late September or early October, 1981 and 1982, which were analysed in this way) because they illustrate the case with fewest age classes (Fig. 8.4) and with most (Fig. 8.5). In the 1981 Pool 5 sample one individual was assessed as being eight years old. The decomposed size–frequency histograms from September/October for all sites in both years are shown in Figs. 8.6 and 8.7.

χ^2 contingency tables constructed using the number of snails in each age class are given in Tables 8.2 and 8.3. For both years the null hypothesis that there is no difference in the age structure between sites is rejected (1981, $P < 0.001$; 1982, $P < 0.01$). That this is largely due to differences between sites in the proportions of animals in the older year classes can be seen by looking at the component χ^2 values for particular age classes. The pattern is, however, different in the two years involved and the only tentative generalization emerging is that survivorship seems to be poorest in the highest site (Pool 3) and best in Pool 5.

The ability to analyse population age-structure allows the construction of cross-sectional growth curves by plotting the average size of animals in any year class against the age in years. These curves

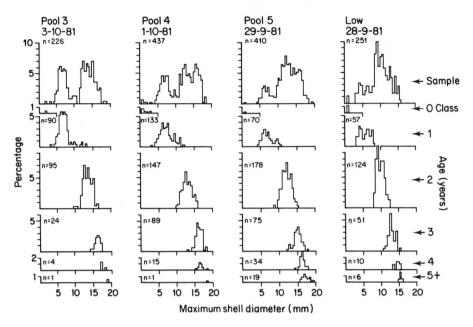

FIG. 8.6. Components of the size–frequency histograms of *G. cineraria* samples taken in late September or early October, 1981. The top row shows the sample size–frequencies and each row below this gives the size–frequencies for a particular age-class within the sample, as indicated by the numbers at the far right hand side (n = sample size).

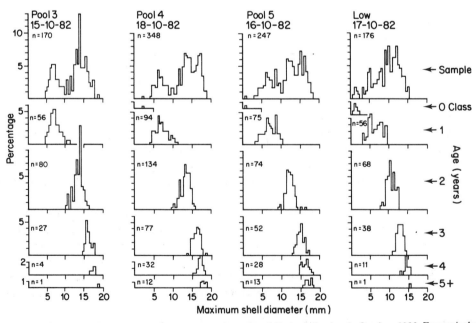

FIG. 8.7. Components of the size–frequency histograms of samples of *G. cineraria* taken in October, 1982. Format is the same as for Fig. 8.6.

TABLE 8.2

χ^2 **contingency table for 1981 population structure.** Expected values are given in parenthesis after the observed values. Overall the null hypothesis that there is no significant difference in the age structure between sites is rejected at the 0.1% level. The null hypotheses that there are no differences in the proportions of particular age classes are rejected in the case of 1 and 4 year olds and those of 5 years or more, ns = not significant, df = degrees of freedom.

Age	Pool 3	Pool 4	Pool 5	Low	Total row	df	χ^2	Probability of χ^2 value
1	45(32.9)	133(103.8)	70(101.4)	57(66.9)	305	3	23.85	<0.001 ***
2	48(53.6)	147(169.2)	178(165.2)	124(109.0)	497	3	6.55	>0.05 ns
3	24(25.8)	89(81.4)	75(79.5)	51(52.4)	239	3	1.13	>0.05 ns
4	4(6.8)	15(21.4)	34(20.9)	10(13.8)	63	3	12.32	<0.01 **
5+	1(2.9)	1(9.2)	19(9.0)	6(5.9)	27	3	19.67	<0.001 ***
Total Column	122	385	376	248	1131	15	63.52	<0.001 ***

TABLE 8.3

χ^2 **contingency table for 1982 population structure.** Format as per Table 8.2. The overall null hypothesis that there is no difference in age structure between sites is rejected at the 1% level. The null hypotheses that there are no differences between the proportions in particular age classes are rejected in the case of 4 year olds and those of 5 years or more.

Age	Pool 3	Pool 4	Pool 5	Low	Total row	df	χ^2	Probability
1	56(51.0)	94(106.0)	75(73.5)	56(50.4)	281	3	2.5	>0.05 ns
2.	80(63.2)	134(131.3)	74(91.0)	60(62.5)	348	3	7.8	>0.05 ns
3	27(35.2)	77(73.2)	52(50.8)	38(34.8)	194	3	2.4	>0.05 ns
4	4(13.6)	32(28.3)	28(19.6)	11(13.5)	75	3	11.32	<0.05 *
5+	1(4.9)	12(10.2)	13(7.1)	1(4.8)	27	3	11.38	<0.01 **
Total Column	168	349	242	166	925	15	35.4	<0.01 **

are shown in Fig. 8.8. From these curves it can be seen that growth rates are highest in the highest sites, Pools 3 and 4, slightly lower in Pool 5 and lowest in the low-shore site.

8.6 Growth Rates and Growth Functions

The growth curves in Fig. 8.8 are cross-sectional, thus the size of animals in any age group is the result of several years growth. Since it was possible at the end of the growing season to measure the present diameter and the diameter at the last growth check it was possible also to evaluate the annual growth rate of individuals solely for the years in question, that is, 1981 and 1982.

Growth rate data in this form can be treated either as individual growth vectors or they can be used to fit a growth function. The advantage of fitting a growth function is that 'information about growth rates and accelerations can be extracted by mathematical rule of thumb rather than by tedious and more or less inaccurate numerical or geometrical approximations' (Medawar, 1945).

Three growth functions have been used extensively to describe the growth of invertebrates: the von Bertalanffy, the logistic and the Gompertz. Several authors, including Medawar (1945), Yamaguchi (1975), Haukioja and Hakala (1979), and Kaufmann (1981) have compared the properties and suitability of these functions. No growth function is universal in its application. The von Bertalanffy or monomolecular growth function has been most widely used, particularly for describing the growth of bivalves (Brousseau, 1979; Bachelet, 1981).

For the von Bertalanffy function to be a good description of the growth of an animal, plots of size increment against initial size should be a straight line (Yamaguchi, 1975). The Pool 3 data for 1981 plotted in this way did not conform to a straight line but showed a maximum at around 5mm (Fig. 8.9). This pattern has been shown by other gastropods in which information from all size classes has been available (Yamaguchi, 1977; Williamson and Kendall, 1981) and suggests that a growth curve with an inflection would be more appropriate. Since the pattern shown in Fig. 8.9 is asymmetric it is likely that the Gompertz function would be a more apt model than the symmetrical logistic function.

With the Gompertz function, plots of specific growth rate (dS/Sdt) against the natural logarithm of

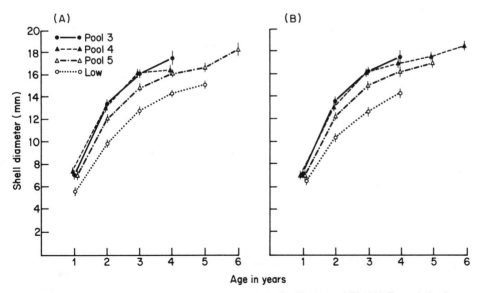

FIG. 8.8. Growth curves for *G. cineraria* based on age structure analysis, for (A) 1981 and (B) 1982. For each site the mean size ± 95% confidence limits of animals in a particular age group is plotted against the age in years.

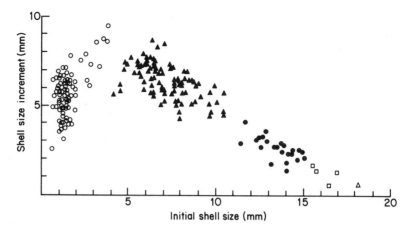

FIG. 8.9. Shell size increment plotted against initial shell size of *G. cineraria* shells where the increment is the difference between the present diameter and the diameter at the last growth check. This last measurement is also taken as the initial size. Measurements are for snails in the Pool 3 sample for October, 1981. Each year class is represented by a different symbol; one year olds = open circles; two year olds = closed triangles; three year olds = closed circles; four year olds = squares; five year olds = open triangles.

size should be a straight line (Kaufmann, 1981). Specific growth rate can be considered as the proportional increase in size per unit time and itself has units of 1/time. Since dS/Sdt = dlnS/dt the value for specific growth rate of *G. cineraria* in the populations studied was calculated as the difference between the natural logarithm of the present diameter (S_{t+1}) and the diameter at the last growth check (S_t). The value against which this should be plotted is the geometric mean of the two values S_t and S_{t+1} (Kaufmann, 1981). The data for Pool 3 from October, 1982, plotted in this way, against a logarithmic x-axis, are shown in Fig. 8.10. These data are well described by a straight line.

Gompertz functions were therefore fitted to the growth rate data evaluated for all four sites in 1981 and 1982 using the method described by Kaufmann (1981), using regression lines such as that shown in Fig. 8.10. By this method the gradient of the line is k in the Gompertz equation:

$$S = S_\infty e^{-e^{-k(t + t_0)}}$$

S_∞ is the theoretical maximum size and is the anti-log of the x-axis intercept in Fig. 8.10, t_0 is the time at which S = 0, and e is the base of natural logarithms. The fitted functions for both years (A: 1981, B: 1982) are shown in Fig. 8.11 and the equations of the curves are given in Table 8.4. For the 1981 data however the one year old animals appeared to be described by a different regression line than the older individuals. The Gompertz functions were therefore fitted using only data from adult specimens for those four samples.

In both years, growth rate and maximum size were greatest in the highest site, Pool 3, and declined downshore.

8.7 Reproduction

For each sample the values for dry gonad weight were regressed on shell weight and the average gonad weight predicted for a standard male and female animal of 1g shell weight. This is similar to the method used by Picken (1980) for the limpet *Nacella (Patinigera) concinna* (Strebel). Shell weight is a better indicator of age than body weight, which may vary seasonally.

The values ($\pm 95\%$ confidence limits) calculated for all samples taken are given in Figs. 8.12 and

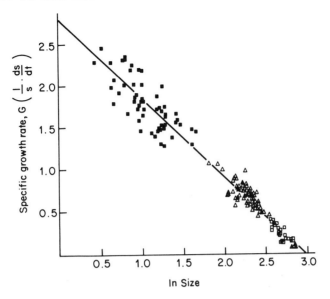

FIG. 8.10. The relationship between specific growth rate, G (mm/mm/year) and the natural logarithm of size, S (maximum diameter in mm) for the Pool 3 sample of *G. cineraria* taken in October, 1982. Regression equation for line of best fit: Y = − 0.9748X + 2.7705.

8.13. For the low shore site data are only available from October, 1980, to October, 1981, (Fig. 8.13). There is a clear annual cycle (Fig. 8.13) with low gonad weights in winter and early spring, rising suddenly in May to *c.* 13mg dry weight in males and 11mg in females. Thereafter gonad weight declines presumably due to spawning.

Fig. 8.12, showing comparable data for the higher shore level from November, 1980, to October, 1982, is rather more dramatic. In winter and spring of 1980–81 the gonads were heavier than in the lower shore animals. In April and May the weights rose to around 30mg for males and 27.5mg for females. Weights then declined rapidly until August when there was apparently a second, lesser ripening and spawning until in October gonad weights were comparable to those in animals from the lower shore. The pattern was similar in 1982. Generally, for a given shell weight, male gonads were heavier than female.

8.8 Discussion

The only previous investigation into the growth rates of *G. cineraria* was by Gaillard (1965) at a site near Dinard in Brittany. While the growing season for this population was very similar to that at Robin Hood's Bay the individuals grew more slowly and reached a smaller maximum size (13mm), although they had greater longevity (10 to 12 years maximum). Gaillard (1965) estimated the age of individuals from growth rate data and did not use growth checks. Neither did he attempt to fit a standard growth equation to his data.

There has been considerable criticism over the use of growth equations, particularly of the von Bertalanffy function (Calow, 1973; Roff, 1980). Such models of growth can only be regarded as 'reasonably good' descriptions of growth in many species. Frank (1965a) commented that the simplicity of the model does not presume the simplicity of growth and Calow (1973) presented evidence that growth does not conform to a pre-set pattern but that homeostatic feedback mechanisms can operate to

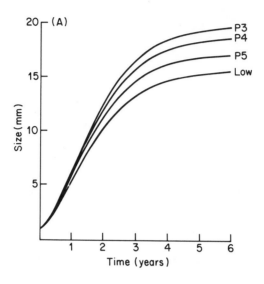

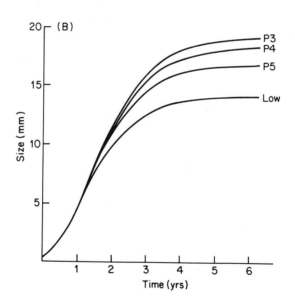

FIG. 8.11. Gompertz growth functions fitted to the growth rate data for *G. cineraria* in all four sites in (A) 1981 and (B) 1982. The equations of these curves are given in Table 8.4.

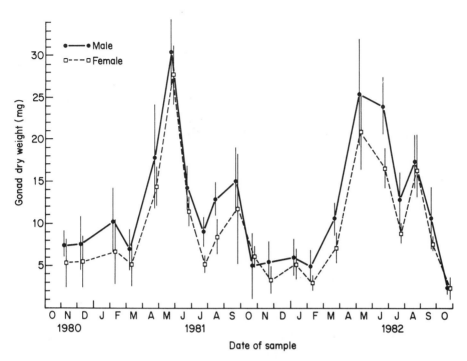

FIG. 8.12. The mean gonad dry weight (± 95% confidence limits) predicted for *G. cineraria* with a shell weight of 1g based on samples taken from site A between November, 1980, and October, 1982. Data for males and females are shown separately.

TABLE 8.4

Equations of Gompertz functions fitted to growth rate data for *G. cineraria* in 1981 and 1982. The curves are shown in Fig. 8.11.

Site	*Fitted equation (1981)*	*Fitted equation (1982)*
Pool 3	$S = 19.816e^{-e^{-.925(t - 1.182)}}$	$S = 19.420e^{-e^{-1.0087(t - 1.078)}}$
Pool 4	$S = 18.732e^{-e^{-.933(t - 1.153)}}$	$S = 18.448e^{-e^{-1.0386(t - 1.030)}}$
Pool 5	$S = 17.161e^{-e^{-.952(t - 1.098)}}$	$S = 16.915e^{-e^{-1.0954(t - 0.949)}}$
Low	$S = 15.682e^{-e^{-.923(t - 1.098)}}$	$S = 14.297e^{-e^{-1.1337(t - 0.863)}}$

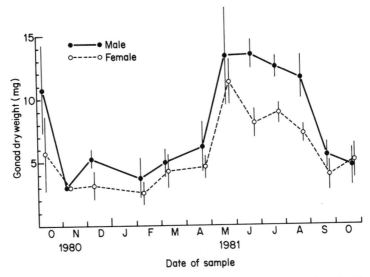

FIG. 8.13. The mean gonad dry weight (± 95% confidence limits) predicted for standard *G. cineraria* with a shell weight of 1g based on samples taken from site B in 1980 and 1981. Males and females are indicated separately as in Fig. 8.12.

compensate for periods of restricted growth caused, for example, by starvation. In the present case the Gompertz function was used simply because it did seem to be a reasonable description of the growth pattern of *G. cineraria*.

The Gompertz function was first used to describe the growth of molluscs by Weymouth *et al.* (1931) in a study of the bivalve *Siliqua patula* (Dixon). Weymouth *et al.* (1931) also provide perhaps the most succinct description of what is implied by the statement that growth follows a Gompertz function: 'That is, growth is an exponential function of time, but the exponent is a changing one, decreasing with time in an exponential fashion . . . . This formula can also be derived from the fact so long insisted on by Minot and since confirmed by others that the relative growth rate declines through most of the life cycle; it is only necessary to postulate that this decline is at a constant percental rate' (Minot, 1908; Weymouth *et al.*, 1931). Here 'relative growth rate' is the same as specific growth rate. A general criticism of asymptotic growth functions has been that they assume a theoretical maximum size at which animals stop growing, whereas most molluscs seem to continue growing, even if very slowly, throughout their lives (Frank, 1965a, 1969). This would also seem to be true in the present case and these functions are of little value in predicting the growth rates of older animals.

Underwood (1972a) investigated the reproductive cycle of *G. cineraria* at Heybrook Bay near Plymouth. During the year of his study he found no evidence of a gonad cycle and concluded that this population failed to breed in that year. On the basis of successful laboratory fertilization of egg samples, however, Underwood (1972a) concluded that this species usually breeds in the spring on the British South coast and he went on to describe the larval development and settlement behaviour of the species for the first time (Underwood, 1972b). The present study showed that a very distinct gonad cycle occurred in Robin Hood's Bay populations, with spawning taking place in summer and autumn. These results agree with those reported by Gersch (1936) for *G. cineraria* populations in the southern North Sea.

The data from growth checks and growth rates presented here indicate that growth rate in the four sites declined with decreasing height on the shore. Furthermore animals in more elevated sites also reached a larger size and produced larger gonads than those lower downshore. Presumably the larger gonad size of animals in the higher site is indicative of greater fecundity. It is also assumed that the populations of *G. cineraria* in the four sites are not genetically distinct. Since the eggs are shed singly into the water, the progeny from all sites will intermingle and will not necessarily settle at the same shore level as their parents. All the phenotypes are therefore drawn from the same gene pool. Differences in growth rate and fecundity are interpreted as being phenotypic responses to environmental heterogeneity.

It is established that molluscs show physiological responses to different shore levels. The heart rate of *Collisella* (= *Acmaea*) *limatula* Carpenter is faster and less temperature-dependent in populations lower on the shore than in higher populations, but the animals acclimatize to the appropriate level if transplanted (Segal *et al.*, 1953; Segal, 1956). The feeding rate of *Gibbula umbilicalis* (da Costa) is also faster in lower shore animals, and the animals can acclimatize to new conditions over short periods (Cornelius, 1972). In general then: 'the relation of invertebrate activity to shore level cannot be as constant as has sometimes been suggested' (Cornelius, 1972). Several studies have demonstrated differences in the growth rates of littoral molluscs at different shore levels. Studies of the littoral bivalves, *Mya arenaria* (L.) (Newcombe, 1935a), *Mytilus californianus* Conrad (Dehnel, 1956), *M. edulis* (Seed, 1969b) and *Scrobicularia plana* da Costa (Hughes, 1970) have indicated that growth rate declines at higher shore levels, possibly due to a reduced time available for feeding. In other species however such as *Tellina tenuis* da Costa (Stephen, 1928) and *Venerupis pullastra* (Montagu) (Quayle, 1951) growth rate was faster in higher shore populations. However, Stephen (1928) considered that the low densities of *T. tenuis* at higher levels led to the higher growth rate. Lewis and Bowman (1975) showed that growth rate of the limpet *Patella vulgata* declined upshore but that biological factors, particularly the proportional cover of the barnacle *Semibalanus balanoides* (L.), were more important in determining observed growth rates. In other cases littoral gastropods have been observed to show faster growth in higher sites: *Littorina 'saxatilis'* (Berry, 1961; Gaillard, 1965), *Collisella* (= *Acmaea*) *scabra* (Sutherland, 1970) and *Haliotis tuberculata* (L.) (Hayashi, 1980). In the case of *C. scabra* upper shore populations were fast growing but existed at much lower densities than the slow-growing lower shore populations (Sutherland, 1970). When the density of the lower populations was reduced to the level of the upper shore populations the situation was reversed. However, algal growth was much greater in the lower site and food was a limiting factor in both sites under natural conditions. Reducing the density of lower shore animals removed the restrictions of food availability. A proper comparison would necessitate upper shore animals growing without feeding constraint as well.

Sutherland (1970) also found that the more elevated of his *Collisella scabra* populations had a more distinct, and restricted, spawning period than the lower one, but no assessments of fecundity were made. Barker and Nichols (1983) showed that sublittoral populations of the starfish *Asterias rubens* L. developed smaller gonads, and had a less clear gonad cycle, than low-littoral populations. Differences in food availability were held to be responsible. It is evident, therefore, that differences in gonad cycles and fecundity can exist over quite short distances in species of littoral invertebrates and it is likely that these are phenotypic responses to environmental restrictions. For the freshwater prosobranch *Viviparus georgianus* (Lea), Browne (1978) found seven-fold differences in fecundity between populations in different lakes in the same geographical locality, and again suggested food availability as the cause.

From the above review then, there are at least two other low-littoral/sublittoral species (besides *G. cineraria*) which appear in some respects to 'do better' in higher than lower sites, namely the ormer, *Haliotis tuberculata*, and the starfish, *Asterias rubens* (Hayashi, 1980; Barker and Nichols, 1983).

In some cases experimental manipulations have demonstrated that high population densities can reduce growth rates in herbivorous littoral gastropods (Underwood, 1976, 1979). In the present case, while the upper Pool 3 was shown to have slightly lower densities than the lower Pools 4 or 5 (which could explain the faster growth rate), the Low site combined lower densities with the lowest growth rates and lower fecundity. A simple relationship between population density and growth rate is thus not supported.

Since low spring tides occur at mid-day in Robin Hood's Bay, pools higher up the shore are likely to heat up more than those lower down. Temperature records for these sites are sporadic, but on a warm April day, temperatures in Pool 3 reached 9°C while the sea temperature at the Low site was 5.6°C. Pools higher on the shore not only heat up more but are subjected for longer to higher light intensity. Temperature could act directly upon the physiological processes determining growth, or, in conjunction with light intensity, could increase food availability by speeding up the growth of microalgae in the pools. Calow (1973) has demonstrated for a species of freshwater snail that increased temperatures will increase both growth rates and the maximum size attained even when food is in excess at all temperatures, and a similar set of circumstances may be operating for G. cineraria.

The questions remain however, that if sites at the elevation of Pool 3 seem so good for growth and gonad development, why is the distribution of the species centred lower on the shore? and why does the abundance of G. cineraria decline rapidly above Pool 3, so that in the next pool up, a vertical height of barely 0.5m above Pool 3, G. cineraria is quite rare? Admittedly it is not known whether animals in Pools 4 and 5 have even greater fecundities than those in Pool 3 but the fact that the abundance of the species is similar in Pool 3 and the Low site is remarkable in view of the vast differences in individual performance between these sites. The apparently small difference in survivorship between these sites seems unlikely to effect the advantages gained by being higher on the shore, unless mortality is in fact much higher in Pool 3 and animals are being replaced by migrants from lower down the shore.

Underwood (1979) presented three major hypotheses to account for the upper distributional limits of littoral gastropods, (i) *that upper limits are set by physiological tolerances*. There is indeed little evidence to support this theory since most species appear to live well within their physiological tolerances (Wolcott, 1973; Underwood, 1979). *G. cineraria* only inhabits pools and permanently damp areas, and there is a plentiful supply of these at all shore levels at Robin Hood's Bay and so desiccation does not limit its distribution. Furthermore the highest temperature recorded in Pool 3 on a sunny August day was 19°C, well below the species upper lethal limit of 33°C (Southward, 1958), (ii) *that competition for food with other species at adjacent shore levels limits species distribution*. G. cineraria feeds on microalgae and detritus (Fretter and Graham, 1977) and has no obvious competitors which appear above the level of Pool 3. The gastropod *Littorina littorea* (L.) is still relatively rare at this level being abundant only in shallow pools much higher upshore, (iii) *that species are confined to particular levels on the shore by behavioural adaptations to avoid sub-optimal areas*. In such cases no competitive or physiological factor would act directly to prevent the upward spread of a species. *G. cineraria* has indeed been shown to exhibit behavioural responses to environmental stimuli which would act to maintain its zonation on the lower fringes of the littoral zone (Micallef, 1969). These responses have presumably evolved over the species' range to cope with all types of rocky shore encountered. They would appear to ensure that individuals avoid mid-shore areas where the risk of desiccation is generally greater, temperatures higher and more variable, and where potential competitors such as the closely related species *G. umbilicalis* and *G. pennanti* (Philippi) occur over a considerable part of its distribution. At Robin Hood's Bay, however, it appears that the mid-shore is not a sub-optimal area for *G. cineraria*, yet the species still avoids it. It is nevertheless possible that if there is strong selection over the species' range for behavioural mechanisms leading to avoidance of mid-shore areas that such behaviour may be too inflexible to accommodate particular local conditions such as those found at Robin Hood's Bay in 1981 and 1982. Such behaviour would therefore be a poor adaptation in the particular local conditions reported here but a vital adaptation for the survival of the species throughout its European range. Vermeij (1982a) has shown that species like *G. cineraria* with pelagic larvae show little or no evidence of local morphological adaptations to shore conditions, and the same may therefore also be true of behavioural adaptations. The observation that *G. cineraria* extends its range up the shore on the British East coast (Fretter and Graham, 1962) though may indicate that some cline in behavioural adaptation does exist. Clearly such a hypothesis as that outlined above will need to be tested by experimental manipulations of animals on the shore.

ACKNOWLEDGEMENTS

I would like to thank my supervisors Drs J.R. Lewis and J.W. Grahame for their help and advice. I am also grateful to Dr Lewis and Professor R. McN. Alexander for the provision of laboratory facilities at Robin Hood's Bay and at the University of Leeds.

This work was financed by a grant from the Natural Environment Research Council.

CHAPTER IX

THE POPULATION BIOLOGY OF TWO SPECIES OF *LACUNA* (CHINK-SHELLS) AT ROBIN HOOD'S BAY

J. Grahame

9.1 Introduction

The ecology of the smaller prosobranchs of British shores has been comparatively neglected. Three species of the genus *Lacuna* (Prosobranchia: Littorinacea) are known from Robin Hood's Bay: *L. pallidula* (da Costa), *L. vincta* (Montagu) and *L. parva* (da Costa). The last species occurs sublittorally on the red alga *Delesseria*, and it has not been studied at Robin Hood's Bay. The other two occur in the littoral zone on *Fucus serratus* L., with *L. vincta* occurring on kelps in the sublittoral as well. *F. serratus* is the most abundant fucoid at Robin Hood's Bay, forming extensive stands on the lower scars (a *scar* or *scaur* is a low reef of rock in the sea, see *Frontispiece*).

L. pallidula and *L. vincta* are strictly annual at Robin Hood's Bay. They have been used in an investigation of the energetics of species with contrasting life histories: *L. pallidula* is an *in situ* breeder with lecithotrophic development, while *L. vincta* has a brief period of benthic development after which the eggs hatch into long-life planktotrophic veligers. That work has been reported by Grahame (1977, 1982).

Observations have also been made on their populations on the shore. D.A.S. Smith (1973) reported a study of the population dynamics of both species at Whitburn, on the coast of County Durham, 57km north of Robin Hood's Bay. Therefore the work on this aspect was seen as being largely corroborative. However it became clear that in one interesting aspect, namely that of the sex ratios of the populations, there were modifications to be made to the conclusions drawn by Smith (1973). He did not investigate the sex ratio of *L. vincta*, but reported that in the case of *L. pallidula* it was biased towards the males, with an average of about 2 males to 1 female. This obtained practically all year except in June when the last adults were disappearing at the end of their lives. Smith (1973) was first able to sex the population in November, using body size as the criterion – mature females being considerably larger than mature males in this species. In the Yorkshire study reported here, sexing of the population was achieved as early as September by the use of internal characters.

9.2 Methods

Populations were sampled at about monthly intervals. A study scar was selected immediately above L.W.S.T., running roughly Northeast to Southwest along the shore for about 200m. A starting point was defined at the southern end of the scar, where the flat *Fucus*-covered rock gave way to boulders. Samples were taken by placing a quadrat of area 0.25m² at intervals paced out along the scar, the intervals being determined using random number tables (one pace ≈ 1m). If insufficient *Fucus* was taken from one quadrat, the adjacent area was also cleared, and so on until about 1 kg of alga had been taken. The usual number of samples on any one occasion was five – a compromise had to be reached between the need for adequate samples and the need to avoid substantial damage to the habitat.

In the laboratory the alga was weighed damp. It was washed in hot water from a domestic-type cylinder supply (≈ 60°C). This treatment was extremely effective in dislodging snails, as was shown by careful search of treated alga. The dead snails were collected on a plankton gauze of mesh 0.41mm and preserved in alcohol for measurement under a binocular dissecting microscope with a measuring eyepiece.

For investigations of sex ratio, samples of snails were sorted into 0.1mm size classes and the shells dissolved using 10% nitric acid. The bodies were examined for the presence of a penis, or alternatively the prominent oviduct of females. When these characteristics could be distinguished in the smallest size category of snail present, the sample could be accurately sexed.

9.3 Results

9.3.1 *Lacuna pallidula*

Data consisting of numbers of snails · 100g⁻¹ of *Fucus* are available from 11 August, 1975, until 1 September, 1977, and for 13 January, 1978 (Fig. 9.1). The population was at peak densities in August and September after hatching of juveniles. Mortality in the period October to December was very high

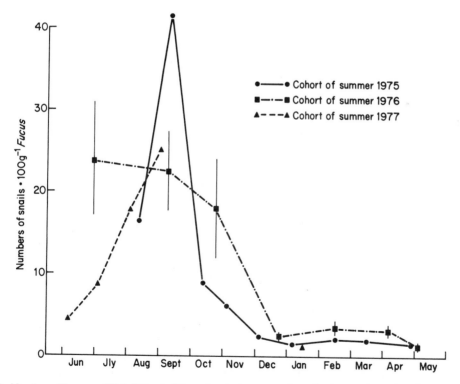

FIG. 9.1. Numbers of *Lacuna pallidula*·100 g⁻¹ of *Fucus*. Standard errors are shown for the 1976 data points; they are typical of the data as a whole.

in 1975 and 1976, resulting in decreases from $\approx 40 \cdot 100g^{-1}$ and $\approx 20 \cdot 100g^{-1}$ to $\approx 2 \cdot 100g^{-1}$ in the two years. In 1977, the numbers increased up to early September when regular samples ceased, nonetheless the following January figure was $\approx 1 \cdot 100g^{-1}$, again indicating heavy autumn mortality. As these data are for snails per unit weight of alga they are compensated for changes in algal cover. The data on the weight of *Fucus* $\cdot$ m^{-2} showed no regular changes during the study period: the average cover was 1.7 kg $\cdot$ m^{-2} varying from 0.5kg (April, 1977) to 2.5 kg $\cdot$ m^{-2} (September, 1976, 1977; January, 1978).

During the spawning season, beginning in January, there is no evidence of mortality until April or May, when numbers began to decline before the juveniles of the next generation appeared. The change from heavy mortality in autumn to apparently zero mortality in winter and early spring is very marked. In both years for which complete winter data are available, the numbers increased very slightly between December/January and February. The reason for this is not known – it must have been due either to immigration or to sampling error. It is unlikely that there was substantial immigration to the site, as the adults were not observed on the kelps below low water – except as very occasional single animals – while at the same time they persisted on *Fucus* above the study site. *L. pallidula* is very sedentary in behaviour.

Size–frequency histograms for the 1975/76 cohort are shown in Fig. 9.2. In August the juvenile population was slightly bimodal; this feature had largely disappeared in September. By October all the snails could be sexed. In the months from October to January there was a gradual separation of the population into two groups. Growth in males slowed and stopped, while the females continued to grow, so that by February the population consisted of two distinct groups: small males and larger females. Growth in the females did not appear to slow until February/March. The early cessation of growth in males gives rise to the well-know sexual dimorphism of *L. pallidula*. The cohort of June, 1976, followed the same pattern, with males ceasing growth in late autumn and females continuing to grow until late winter.

In October, 1975, the ratio of males to females was 1:0.98, which is not different from 1:1 ($\chi^2 = 0.01$). Sex ratios and chi-square values for successive months are: November, 1:0.79, $\chi^2 = 1.44$; December, 1:0.63, $\chi^2 = 5.93\star$; January 1976, 1:0.52, $\chi^2 = 7.91\star$; February, 1:0.73, $\chi^2 = 2.51$; March, 1:0.43, $\chi^2 = 20.16\star$; and April, 1:0.45, $\chi^2 = 13.17\star$. Significant χ^2 values (P $\leq$ 0.05) are shown with an asterisk. In 1976/77 the pattern was the same, with a sex ratio in September of 1:1.07, in December 1:0.55, $\chi^2 = 12.1\star$, reaching 1:0.38, $\chi^2 = 21.74\star$ in April, 1977.

It seems clear that the sex ratio in the Robin Hood's Bay populations of *L. pallidula* is originally 1:1, but this changes in the late autumn so that the population becomes male-dominated. The change in the sex ratio begins just after the females emerge as a separate, larger size group than the males. It appears that at this time they become more vulnerable to some source of mortality. In the two years for which data are available, survivorship of the two sexes between October and December was as follows: 1975, females 15.7%, males 24.6%; 1976, females 10.5%, males 18.2%. Thus there are about 8% more deaths of females than of males in these three months, or < 3% per month. This slight shift in mortality is what causes the change in sex ratio. It seems possible that a predator preferentially taking larger snails could impose this slight excess of mortality among females. By treating pools on the shore with the anaesthetic Quinaldine (which samples the fish but does not affect invertebrates) rock pool fish were collected for stomach content analysis. Samples were taken in November only, when it was found that the cottid *Taurulus bubalis* (Euphrasen) was preying on both *Lacuna* spp.; of 10 fish taken, 6 had *L. pallidula* in the stomach, numbering 25 snails altogether. There was no evidence of size selection. It is unlikely that comparing the sizes of snails in the stomachs with the prey size–frequency histograms could reveal this effect (presuming it to be present) unless the sample was many times larger than that obtained, and it was not practicable to obtain such large samples. Therefore, the

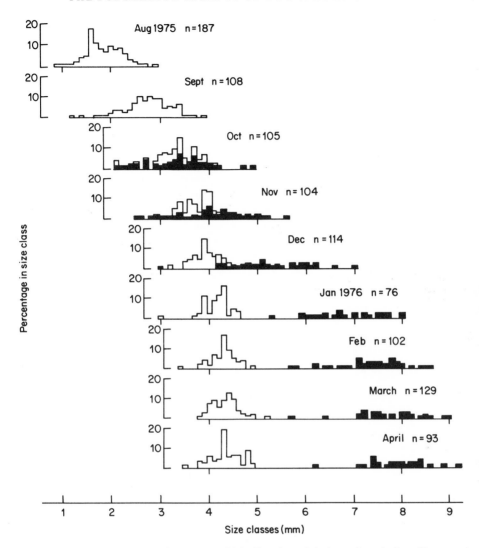

Fig. 9.2. Size class–frequency histograms for *Lacuna pallidula*. Size of sample is shown for each. Open histogram: juveniles (August, September) and males thereafter. Solid histogram: females.

size–selective predation hypothesis remains the best explanation of the differential mortality, but it has not been adequately tested.

The apparent abrupt cessation of mortality between December and January is also unexplained. As predators are still available, it must be due to a change in their behaviour or to the scarcity of the prey rendering it unprofitable, or to a combination of the two factors. No information on fish stomach contents is available for winter months. Larger snails may also be less vulnerable to mortality from physical sources, such as being washed off the substratum and carried away in the water. The possibility of slight immigration to the study site exists (see above), and this would mask continuing mortality, but it seems very unlikely that it could be on such a scale as to conceal mortality occurring at the autumn rate.

9.3.2 *L. vincta*

Fewer data are available for this species – it was sorted and enumerated only between June, 1976, and September, 1977, with a further sample in January, 1978. Population densities (Fig. 9.3) behaved in much the same way as did those of *L. pallidula*, with peak densities in autumn, followed by a rapid decline to low winter and spring levels. Again during January and February there was little sign of decrease in population numbers, but evidence of such decrease from March to May.

Inspection of the size classes (Fig. 9.4) shows different features from those for *L. pallidula*. Taking as juveniles those *L. vincta* of < 3mm shell length (the smallest size at which eggs were spawned in the laboratory), then the population was dominated by juveniles in July (95%), August (100%) and September (94% in 1976, 99% in 1977). However juveniles were always present, even in May forming 6% of total numbers. Adults were present in all months except August and eggs were found on the shore between February and July. Very small snails were seen only in June, July and August during what may be considered to be the main recruitment season. The juveniles present in other months may have been immigrating to the shore from sublittoral populations. The inference for this is strong, since these snails were larger than summer juveniles and were probably too large to have recently settled from the plankton.

The sex ratio (males: females) was examined four times and found to be as follows: February, 1:0.75; April, 1:0.8; May, 1:0.82; June, 1:0.63. None of the chi-square values was significant (P = 0.05), but it does seem nevertheless as if the sex ratio was always male-biased. There was no apparent size difference between the sexes in the Robin Hood's Bay populations.

In *L. vincta* the ratio of maximum to minimum densities was about 6:1, while in *L. pallidula* it was nearer 10:1. However as the population of *L. vincta* is so evidently 'open', with evidence of immigration from sublittoral populations, it is difficult to make meaningful comparisons between the two species.

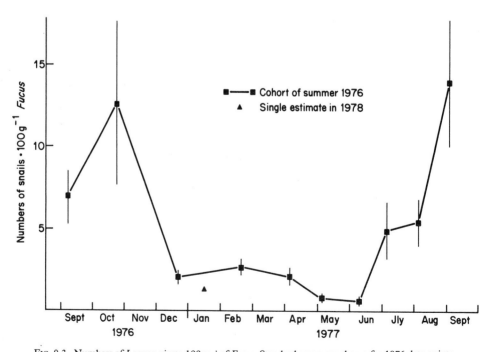

FIG. 9.3. Numbers of *Lacuna vincta*·100 g⁻¹ of *Fucus*. Standard errors are shown for 1976 data points.

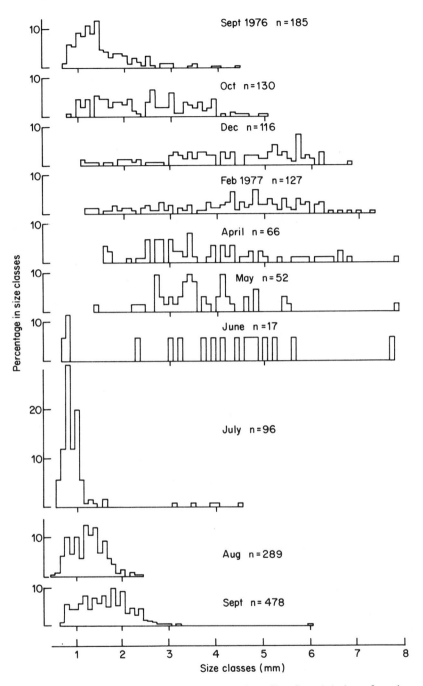

FIG. 9.4. Size class–frequency histograms for *Lacuna vincta*. Size of sample is shown for each.

9.4 Discussion

Both species of *Lacuna* dealt with here maintain their populations at Robin Hood's Bay, generations appearing year after year. The quantitative information given here is part of a longer known history of the species locally (1975 to present), and a very much longer inferred one. Both species are recorded in the unpublished fauna list for the locality, *L. pallidula* in 1948 and *L. vincta* in 1948 and 1950. Both are annual, and depend upon regular recruitment year by year to avoid local extinction. Yet, *L. pallidula* is an *in situ* breeder with very limited powers of dispersal, and *L. vincta* has a long-life planktotrophic larval phase. Clearly, both kinds of life cycle are capable of sustaining populations of annual species. It is known that *L. vincta* may show explosive population increases (Fralick *et al.*, 1974) with devastating effects on their food algae, but this was not seen at Robin Hood's Bay.

It may be speculated that *L. vincta* shows features which are adaptations to a more 'chancy' lifestyle. Although the littoral settlement period is as discrete as recruitment in *L. pallidula*, a continuous flow of juvenile snails into the shore population spreads recruitment there over the whole year. It seems likely that these 'out of season' juveniles are snails which settle sublittorally and subsequently appear on the shore.

The sexual dimorphism and sex ratio of populations of *L. pallidula* have been investigated in several localities (Gallien and de Larambergue, 1939; Rasmussen, 1973; Smith, 1973; Southgate, 1982). The sex ratio of *L. vincta* has attracted less attention. Russell-Hunter and McMahon (1975) studied populations on the coast of Massachusetts, where growth was faster among females, and so the largest snails tended to be female. Mortality was said to be higher among larger snails of both sexes, and also higher among females than males; these factors operated to shift the sex ratio. Between November and March, this was about 1:1 (males:females) but had become about 2:1 by the end of June. The mortality referred to took place after the initiation of spawning, and might have been due to 'physiological exhaustion' of females. However in the laboratory, there was no difference in male and female survivorship, pointing back to a mortality factor operating in the field. The authors do not explain the phenomenon of higher mortality in larger snails: it is reminiscent of the pattern of events in *L. pallidula* at Robin Hood's Bay which could be an effect of size-selective predation. Apparently, the Robin Hood's Bay populations show the same sex ratio as on the coast of Massachusetts. However on the West coast of Ireland populations of this species are female-dominated (Southgate, 1982).

In discussing the sex ratio in *L. vincta*, Russell-Hunter and McMahon (1975) considered that it was anomalous, and that the opposite phenomenon (i.e., greater female survivorship) would be expected to be adaptive. They say, 'the usual patterns with disproportionately more large females surviving are clearly of adaptive value in any situation of competition for food or other limiting resource.' This seems to mean a recourse to untenable ideas of group selection.

In the case of *L. pallidula*, it is common to find the sex ratio biased towards females. This is so on coasts in France (Gallien and de Larambergue, 1939), Denmark (Rasmussen, 1973), the South and West coasts of England, Wales and Scotland (Smith, 1973) and Ireland (Southgate, 1982). Interestingly, *L. parva* also has female-dominated populations in Denmark (Ockelmann and Nielsen, 1981). On the East coast of England, however, a male-dominated population is reported for *L. pallidula* (Smith, 1973; this study).

The mechanisms underlying these sex ratios are unknown. It is clear that the initial sex ratio in *L. pallidula* at Robin Hood's Bay is 1:1, and that the observed ratio of about 1 male to 0.7 females later in the year is a result of some unknown factor or factors operating on the population. It is likely that this is predation on the larger snails, which certainly cannot be adaptive. Further field work is necessary to elucidate the sex ratios in *Lacuna* and the processes involved in producing the observed ratios.

CHAPTER X

THE ECOLOGY OF THE PERIWINKLE, *LITTORINA NEGLECTA* BEAN

J.D. Fish and Lynne Sharp

10.1 Introduction

The abundance and world-wide distribution of the rocky shore winkles has made them popular subjects for study and their importance as components of shore communities has long been acknowledged. Their significance in shore ecology is clearly recognized in schemes of zonation which have universal application (Stephenson and Stephenson, 1972), the 'Littorina zone' extending high on the shore and marking the upper limit of the littoral fringe (terminology from Lewis, 1964). In these high-shore zones littorinids are important grazers (Hawkins and Hartnoll, 1983a) and it is here that the rough periwinkles, members of the *Littorina* 'saxatilis' species-complex, are often abundant. This group of snails is characterized by a highly variable morphology and has achieved some degree of notoriety because of its history of taxonomic confusion. Indeed, such is the significance of recent changes in taxonomy that some ecological research is difficult to interpret for, as pointed out by Raffaelli (1982), it is not always clear which species is under consideration. Recent taxonomic changes in the European species of *Littorina* are shown in Table 10.1. The contribution made by Heller (1975a) was particularly significant in clarifying the taxonomy of the rough periwinkles, for prior to that date the picture was confused by the number of 'subspecies' and 'varieties'. Heller (1975a) concluded that in Wales the 'saxatilis' species-complex was made up of four distinct, sympatric species, one of which was *L. neglecta* which had been given species status by Bean in 1844. Although there have been changes in taxonomy since Heller (1975a) and full agreement on the status of all members of the complex has yet to be reached, *L. neglecta* is accepted as being distinct. The original description by Bean was based on specimens from Scarborough on the east coast of England and was as follows: 'Shell strong, smooth, glossy and nearly globular, volutions four, mostly ending in an obtuse point; body whorl large covered with numerous transverse dark interrupted bands; aperture orbicular, inside pale purple. Diameter, not 2 lines. This small species is found in company with *L. Petraea* and *Fabalis* on large blocks of oolite that have long braved the fury of the elements on the north shore of Scarborough.' (A line is a unit of measurement, derived from the French, *ligne*, equivalent to one-twelfth of an inch (2.1mm). *L. Petraea* = *L. neritoides*; *L. Fabalis* = young of *L. obtusata/mariae*.)

Although Bean's original material has not been located, specimens from the type locality have been examined and compared with those from the West coast of Wales. The following description amplifies those given by Bean (1844), Heller (1975a) and Fretter and Graham (1980) and is based on material from west Wales. The fragile adult shell is 2–5mm in height, generally smooth, though sometimes ridged. Shell colour is variable, usually pale fawn or grey, occasionally red-brown; a tessellated or

Table 10.1

Recent taxonomic changes in European species of *Littorina* (after Raffaelli, 1982).

Pre-1966 status	Sacchi and Rastelli, 1966	Heller, 1975a	Hannaford Ellis, 1978, 1979	Raffaelli, 1979a; Hannaford Ellis, 1979	Smith, 1981	Fretter, 1980	Present status and mode of reproduction
L. neritoides (L.)						→	*L. neritoides* (L.) (pelagic egg capsules)
L. littorea (L.)						→	*L. littorea* (L.) (pelagic egg capsules)
L. obtusata (L.) = *L. littoralis*	*L. obtusata* (L.)					→	*L. obtusata* (L.) (oviparous)
	L. mariae Sacchi and Rastelli						*L. mariae* Sacchi and Rastelli (oviparous)
L. saxatilis (Olivi)		*L. nigrolineata* Gray				→	*L. nigrolineata* Gray (oviparous)
		L. neglecta Bean				→	*L. neglecta* Bean (ovoviviparous)
		L. patula Jeffrys	synonomized	*L. rudis* (Maton)	synonomized(*)		*L. saxatilis* (Olivi) (*) (ovoviviparous)
		L. rudis Maton	*L. rudis* Maton	*L. saxatilis* (Olivi)	*L. saxatilis* (Olivi)		
		L. arcana Hannaford Ellis	*L. arcana* Hannaford Ellis			→	*L. arcana* Hannaford Ellis (oviparous)

(* but see Faller-Fritsch and Emson, this volume)

Editors' note: considerable controversy still surrounds the nomenclature of the *Littorina saxatilis/rudis* entity. Authors have therefore been allowed their individual preference and the use of inverted commas throughout serves as a reminder of this uncertainty.

striped pattern is often imposed on this background. Males have an elongated tip to the penis, the first penial gland being situated more than its width from the penis tip. There are from one to nine penial glands which are large in relation to penis size and arranged in a single row. The species is ovovivi-parous and although some females carry embryos throughout the year, there is a peak of reproductive activity in the spring and summer. Males mature at a shell height of 1.4mm and above, females slightly larger, at 1.6mm. The species is widely distributed round the British Isles where it is found largely within the barnacle zone on exposed shores but it has also been recorded from salt marshes (James, 1968c), *Laminaria* holdfasts and *Corallina* (Fretter and Graham, 1980) and eelgrass meadows in Nova Scotia (Robertson and Mann, 1982).

Although there are a number of recent publications on the demography and reproductive biology of members of the *L. 'saxatilis'* species-complex (Hughes, 1980c; Hughes and Roberts, 1980a, 1981; Roberts and Hughes, 1980; Hart and Begon, 1982; Naylor and Begon, 1982; Hannaford Ellis, 1983; Faller-Fritsch and Emson, this volume), *L. littorea* (Williams, 1964; Fish, 1972) and *L. neritoides* (Hughes and Roberts, 1980b, 1981), there are no comparable data on *L. neglecta* from the rocky shore environment. Robertson and Mann (1982) have described the population dynamics and life history adaptations of the species from an eelgrass meadow in Nova Scotia, but apart from this study, observa-tions on *L. neglecta* are incomplete. That this should be the case is surprising for, as pointed out by Fretter and Graham (1980), 'Never before, . . . has so much effort been put by so many people into the study of one molluscan genus as into that of *Littorina* over the last decade or so, . . .' Clearly, the choice of specific name by Bean in 1844 proved to be not only appropriate at that time but also prophetic, and until this situation is remedied the structure and dynamics of upper shore communities cannot be fully understood. This paper provides data on morphology, population structure, growth and reproduction of the species based on monthly samples from 1979 to 1981 of a population from Borth on the West coast of Wales (O.S. Grid ref. SN 601 885). The shore is moderately exposed, southwesterly facing and dominated by the barnacles, *Chthamalus montagui* Southward and *Semibalanus balanoides* (L.). Samples were also collected at three-monthly intervals from Cullercoats on the east coast of England (O.S. Grid ref. NZ 366 708) where the moderately exposed, east-facing shore is dominated by *S. balanoides*. Samples were also examined from a wide range of localities in the British Isles extending from the Isles of Scilly to the Shetland Islands.

10.2 Morphology

An important feature to emerge from the recent taxonomic discussion of rough periwinkles is the degree of morphological variability which exists both within and between populations as a result of the limited gene flow associated with direct development. In the present study, a range of morphological characters has been investigated and attention paid to intraspecific variation within and between populations, and to interspecific differences with other littorinids, in particular with juvenile specimens of *L. 'saxatilis'*. Unless specifically stated the descriptions given in the following account refer to specimens from west Wales.

10.2.1 Shell colour

Casual observation of *L. neglecta* shows that one of the most distinctive features of the shell is the char-acteristic pattern of bands and tessellations (Fig. 10.1), the banded pattern giving way to tessellations in the larger snails (Hannaford Ellis, 1980). Shell colour was initially scored by the method devised by Pettitt (1973a) for *L. 'saxatilis'* and individuals were finally assigned to one of four morphs based on the colour/pattern of the most recently secreted portions of the body whorl. In practice, because of erosion and encrustation by algae, this was the only part of the shell which was clearly visible in some of the older snails. The morphs were:(i) uniform, pale orange-brown, (ii) shell with one or more bands,

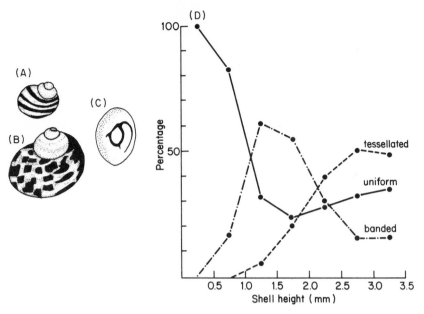

FIG. 10.1. *Littorina neglecta*. (A) banded and (B) tessellated morphs. C, Sub-opercular pattern (not to scale). D, Frequency of uniform = solid line, banded = broken line with dots, and tessellated = broken line morphs at different shell heights at Borth.

(iii) shell with tessellations and (iv) uniform, dark brown.

On release from the brood pouch at 0.35 – 0.40mm shell height, all specimens were a uniform, pale orange-brown colour (morph i). Although snails which can be described as a uniform colour morph (i or iv) are present in the adult population, most develop one or more bands on the shell, the first band appearing at a shell height of about 0.7mm, the banding eventually giving way to a tessellated pattern at a shell height of about 1.5 – 2.0mm (Fig. 10.1). This ontogenetic change has been recorded in all populations of *L. neglecta* examined in the present study and its possible significance is discussed below. Despite a similarity in the shell pattern of adult snails from one locality to the next it was possible to separate the different populations into two types depending on whether the newly emerged snails were a uniform pale colour (morph i typified by the Borth population) or a uniform dark colour (morph iv typified by the Cullercoats population). The distribution of the two types round the British Isles revealed no apparent trend.

When released from the brood pouch, at about 0.5mm shell height, juvenile specimens of *L. 'saxatilis'* were of a uniform orange-brown colour similar to *L. neglecta*. At shell heights of between 1 and 4mm an average of 21% of the population had banded shells, but this value decreased with size such that above 4mm shell height, few snails showed this character, the majority being a dark grey or brown colour. Very few shells had a tessellated pattern and shell pattern is thus a useful character in separating the juveniles of this species from *L. neglecta*.

10.2.2 Shell shape

While difficult to define precisely, certain aspects of shell shape are characteristic of *L. neglecta* and differ from those of juvenile specimens of *L. 'saxatilis'*. The shell aperture of juvenile *L. neglecta* has a downward extension at the junction of the outer lip and columellar lip, a feature which is present from hatching to a shell height of about 1.8mm. Although also present in juveniles of *L. 'saxatilis'*, it is obvious in the latter species from hatching to a shell height of about 4.2mm. The presence or absence of this feature is thus a useful guide in the separation of the species and can be used in conjunction with others such as the less frequently ridged shell of *L. neglecta*, and the sharply convex profile of the body whorl at the junction with the outer lip, when seen in aperture view (Fig. 10.2). This feature is characteristic of *L. neglecta* of about 1.8mm and above in shell height, whereas *L. 'saxatilis'* of similar size generally have a flattened profile (Fig. 10.2). Analysis of shell width/shell height ratios showed no

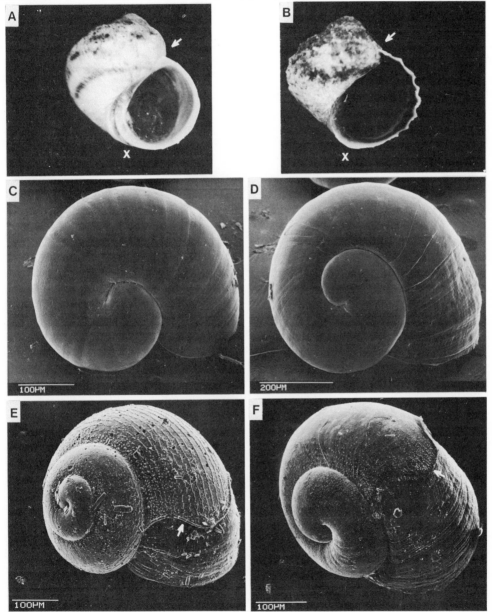

FIG. 10.2. (A) *Littorina neglecta* and (B) *L. 'saxatilis'* of 2.9mm shell height. Note shell profile (arrowed) and shell aperture (X). Scanning electron micrographs of newly emerged *L. neglecta* (C) and *L. 'saxatilis'* (D) and recently metamorphosed *L. neritoides* (E) and *L. littorea* (F). Junction between larval and post-larval shell arrowed in E and F.

significant intraspecific variation in *L. neglecta* from the different localities, nor interspecific variation with *L. 'saxatilis'*.

10.2.3 Sub-opercular pigmentation

The pattern of pigmentation below the operculum has been described for a number of British littorinids by Hannaford Ellis (1980) who considered it to be species-specific for *L. neglecta*. The pattern recorded for *L. neglecta* at Borth (Fig. 10.1) was the same as that recorded by Hannaford Ellis (1980) and was distinct from that of other littorinids but the number of snails showing a pattern was variable. For example, at shell heights of up to 2.0mm, 20% of the population was without a definable sub-opercular pattern and the character must be of limited diagnostic value. At Cullercoats, however, the pattern was evident in all snails greater than 1.0mm shell height and was a useful diagnostic character at this locality.

10.2.4 Penis morphology

The morphology of the penis of rough periwinkles has been used by a number of authors in taxonomic studies and differences between sympatric species suggested as a means whereby reproductive isolation may be maintained. Its form is diagnostic in *L. nigrolineata* (Heller, 1975a) but not in *L. 'rudis'* and *L. arcana* (Hannaford Ellis, 1979). The penis of mature specimens of *L. neglecta* from all localities sampled in the present study had an elongated tip and penial glands which were large in relation to penis size, and distributed in a single row. The number of penial glands varied between localities, for example at Borth the number varied from 1 to 9 (mean 5) and at Cullercoats 1 to 7 (mean 3) but no trend was apparent in the data. Analysis of penial gland number between *L. neglecta* and *L. 'saxatilis'* revealed that although there was a difference in gland number between the species, the data were continuous and the gland number of small *L. 'saxatilis'* and adult *L. neglecta* overlapped at some size categories. The differences were thus characteristic but not diagnostic. Covariate analysis of penis characters confirmed the relatively larger size of the penial glands of *L. neglecta* compared with *L. 'saxatilis'* (Heller, 1975a), a character which is useful in species separation.

10.2.5 Shell ornamentation of juvenile littorinids

L. neglecta occurs sympatrically at Borth with *L. neritoides* and *L. littorea* as well as *L. 'saxatilis'*, and care has to be taken to separate newly emerged/settled specimens of these species which can occur in high densities. The earliest post-metamorphic stages of *L. littorea* can be identified by the ornamentation of the larval shell which consists of bands of scattered tubercles (Fig. 10.2). This ornamentation is quickly eroded after settlement but the young snails can be identified by the outer lip which joins the body whorl tangentially and the early development of a heavily ridged shell. Newly metamorphosed specimens of *L. neritoides* are characterized by longitudinal striae on the body whorl of the larval shell (Fig. 10.2) and although these become eroded after settlement, the species can be identified by the smooth shell and the presence of a periostracal flap along the margin of the outer lip. These features enable identification of the smallest specimens of *L. littorea* and *L. neritoides* and with experience they can be detected under a binocular microscope. Scanning electron microscopy has failed to reveal differences in surface ornamentation of *L. neglecta* and *L. 'saxatilis'*, both of which have a smooth shell (Fig. 10.2).

10.3 Population Structure and Growth

Population structure and growth were determined from monthly samples at Borth. Three $10 \times 10\text{cm}^2$ quadrats were taken at high-, mid- and low- shore levels relative to the previously determined vertical distribution of the species. These levels were 3.5m (M.H.W.N.), 2.8m and 2.0m (M.L.W.N.) above

Chart Datum. Samples were taken by removing all barnacles from within the quadrats and searching through the material under a binocular microscope.

The sex ratio was approximately 1:1 throughout the year at all beach levels. Size–frequency distribution histograms showed a greater number of snails with a shell height larger than 2mm on the high-shore compared with lower beach levels (Fig. 10.3). This pattern of distribution predominated throughout most of the year and was also evident at Cullercoats. Monthly size–frequency histograms revealed a number of components which could be separated using the probability paper method of Harding (1949), as modified by Cassie (1954). Although three components could be detected when observations began in October, 1979, the population was essentially unimodal with the smallest-sized component dominating the sample and accounting for some 92% of the population. There was little change in population structure throughout the winter and early spring and the first recruitment was

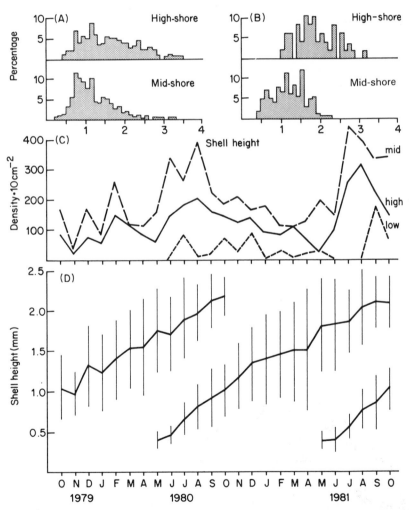

FIG. 10.3. Population structure of high- and mid-shore populations of *L. neglecta* at Borth (A) and Cullercoats (B). C, population density at high- = solid line, mid- = large dashed line and low-shore = broken line. D, Growth rate of *L. neglecta* at Borth; monthly mean shell height ± S.D.

recorded in May, 1980, at a mean shell height of 0.41mm. This component comprised about 30% of the population and the individual snails grew rapidly through the summer and by December, 1980, had reached a shell height of 1.35mm which compared well with the size of the corresponding component in December, 1979. This sequence of events was repeated in 1981 with the first recruitment observed in May at a mean shell height of 0.39mm. Analysis of population structure suggests that longevity is about 18 months, very few animals surviving more than two years. Similar conclusions were reached for the Cullercoats population and growth rates are shown for *L. neglecta* at Borth in Fig. 10.3.

The population density of *L. neglecta* fluctuated throughout the year and, as to be expected, was highest after recruitment (Fig. 10.3). This was particularly evident at the high- and mid-shore stations where maximum density was recorded in July/August. There was a marked decline in density of the newly emerged snails during the first few months on the shore (Fig. 10.4). Both population density and recruitment were erratic on the low-shore; at this level the population is close to its lower limit.

Further information on growth rate was obtained from mark–recapture experiments. Marking small snails poses several problems, not least of which is the extra weight, calculated to be an average 12.3%, which must be borne by the snail when marked with a tiny spot of paint. However, different size categories of snail could be colour-coded and identified in subsequent collections and the calculated growth rates were in good agreement with those estimated from the analysis of population structure. As expected, smaller snails had a faster growth rate than larger ones (Table 10.2) and the reduced growth rate of snails larger than 2.0mm shell height from May to July is believed to result from a slowing of growth during reproduction.

10.4 Reproduction

Monthly collections of snails were separated into mature males and females, immature males and females, and juveniles in which the sex of the individual could not be distinguished. Mature females

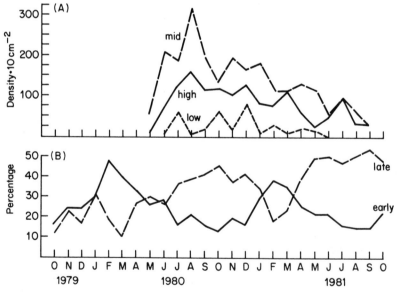

FIG. 10.4. A, survival of the 1980 settlement at high- = solid line, mid- = large dashed line and low-shore = broken line. B, Seasonal variation in early = solid line and late = large dashed line embryos in the brood pouch.

TABLE 10.2

Growth data for *L. neglecta* from mark–recapture experiments.

Size category	Number released	Percentage recovered	Original mean height (mm ± S.D.)	Final mean height (mm ± S.D.)	Mean growth (mm·d^{-1} × 10^{-3})
January–March 1980					
0 – 0.99	14	0			
1.0 – 1.49	315	14.9	1.32 ± 0.12	1.70 ± 0.11	5.03
1.5 – 1.99	923	27	1.75 ± 0.14	2.14 ± 0.20	5.12
2.0 – 2.49	666	23	2.20 ± 0.17	2.53 ± 0.20	4.29
2.5 – 2.99	141	34.8	2.67 ± 0.13	3.03 ± 0.20	4.56
3.0 – 3.49	15	20	3.19 ± 0.15	3.45 ± 0.06	3.67
May–July 1980					
1.0 – 1.49	111	14.4	1.29 ± 0.13	1.76 ± 0.17	5.8
1.5 – 1.99	125	18.4	1.72 ± 0.14	2.14 ± 0.13	5.09
2.0 – 2.49	119	15.1	2.24 ± 0.15	2.42 ± 0.16	1.99
2.5 – 2.99	121	22.3	2.73 ± 0.13	2.86 ± 0.18	1.89
3.0 – 3.49	49	12.2	3.19 ± 0.14	3.28 ± 0.15	1.12
3.5 – 3.99	23	17.4	3.72 ± 0.16	3.86 ± 0.28	1.51

were defined as those containing embryos in the brood pouch and mature males as those with a penis at or above the minimum penis length (0.65mm) recorded for animals with active sperm. Immature animals were those in which the sex could be determined but which were not in reproductive condition and included individuals which had not reached maturity and those which were spent (females without embryos and males showing regression of the penis, see below). In the Borth samples the smallest male had a shell height of 1.12mm, the smallest female, 1.20mm; the smallest mature male and female were recorded at shell heights of 1.4 and 1.6mm respectively. Females attained a larger size than males.

Seasonal variation in the number of mature males and females, expressed as a percentage of the total male and female population respectively, shows a marked seasonal cycle (Fig. 10.5). Highest numbers of mature females occurred in the summer months and in both 1980 and 1981 there was also a suggestion of a peak in September before the decline to winter levels. About 20% of the females carried embryos during the winter and examination of monthly data showed these to be females larger than 2.5mm shell height. The abundance of mature males also showed a sharp seasonal trend with the cycle being slightly in advance of that of the females. Monthly regression analysis of shell height against penis length of a standard animal of 2.0mm shell height showed a clear seasonal trend of increasing penis length throughout the winter and spring (Fig. 10.5). This was followed by a regression in penis length to levels below that at which active sperm were recorded. Interestingly, in spent males of *L. littorea* the penis is shed and reforms for the next breeding season (Grahame, 1970). A seasonal trend was also recorded for animals of a standard shell height of 2.5mm, but in these larger animals penis length remained above the minimum length for mature males throughout the year and it is believed that these snails maintain the low level of reproduction during the winter.

A linear relationship exists between shell height of the female and the number of embryos in the

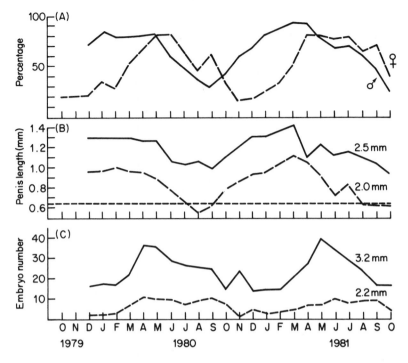

FIG. 10.5. A, Seasonal variation in mature males = solid line and females = large dashed line. B, Seasonal variation in penis length of 2.0mm = large dashed line and 2.5mm = solid line standard height males. The horizontal dashed line indicates minimum penis length recorded for mature males. C, Embryo number of 3.2mm = solid line and 2.2mm = large dashed line standard height females.

brood pouch and there was a seasonal trend in the number of embryos carried by mature females (Fig. 10.5). Females of 2.2mm shell height carried about 10 embryos compared with 30 to 40 at a shell height of 3.2mm. However, few animals reached this latter size category and the bulk of the recruitment must be generated by the smaller animals. The maximum number of embryos recorded was 125 in May, 1981, in a snail of 4.65mm shell height. Although there was some suggestion that females from the mid-shore contained slightly more embryos than snails at other levels, no significant pattern emerged. The pattern of reproduction at Cullercoats was similar to that at Borth but maturity was reached at a smaller shell height; 1.2 and 1.4mm for males and females respectively, and during the winter months only 3% of the females carried embryos.

Embryos in the brood pouch can be separated into five developmental stages as described by Thorson (1946) for *L. saxatilis*. The total number of embryos in early (stage E of Thorson) and late stages of development (stage C of Thorson), expressed as a percentage of the total number of embryos in the brood pouches of mature females showed a seasonal variation with a rise in the percentage of late embryos coinciding with the time of recruitment on the shore (Fig. 10.4).

10.5 Littoral Distribution

L. neglecta inhabits the zone from about M.H.W.N. to M.L.W.N., the species being generally restricted to the mid- and upper zones of the barnacle belt. In an attempt to gain a quantitative assessment of the fundamental niche available to the snail, a 10cm wide vertical transect from just above M.H.W.N. to just below M.L.W.N. was marked on the shore at Borth. It was divided into contiguous quadrats which were photographed and the barnacles and associated fauna collected and analysed for a number of factors.

L. *neglecta* reached its highest density in a narrow belt about mid-way between M.H.W.N. and M.L.W.N. (Fig. 10.6) while the number of dead barnacles (a potential habitat for L. *neglecta*) increased from the top to the middle of the transect and remained at consistently high levels downshore. The mean aperture size of dead barnacles (an indication of the size of the spaces available to L. *neglecta*) showed no significant variation from high- to low-shore, but the density of the larger size categories of dead barnacles increased downshore (Fig. 10.6). Although the number of dead barnacles was high at the lower levels of the transect, the population density of the snail fell and it is at these beach levels that it will be in competition for space with an increasing number of species. Notable amongst these are juvenile specimens of other littorinids, the isopod, *Campecopea hirsuta* (Montagu) and the bivalves *Mytilus edulis* L. and *Lasaea rubra* (Montagu). The latter three species are permanent inhabitants of the lower barnacle zone at Borth and are frequently recorded in densities of several hundred$\cdot 10\ cm^{-2}$.

10.6 Discussion

Littorina neglecta is widely distributed round the British Isles, occurring sympatrically with other littorinids, particularly L. '*saxatilis*', and morphological studies highlight the difficulties experienced in separating the species. At Borth, L. *neglecta* leaves the brood pouch at a shell height of about 0.35mm compared with 0.5mm for L. '*saxatilis*' and there is a critical size range from about 0.5 to 0.9mm shell height at which separation of the species is very difficult and in some cases one has to rely on characters so appropriately described by Evans (1947a) – evaluating the importance of the external surface of the shell in separating species of patellids – as being '. . . too subtle . . . for precise verbal description'. Nevertheless, there are few specimens which cannot be confidently assigned to a species using the characters described earlier. At shell heights above 1.0mm, separation becomes

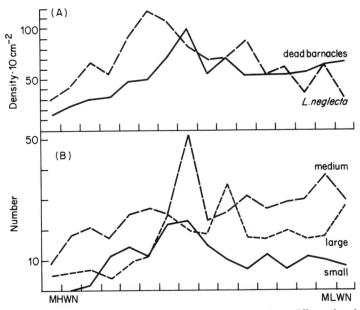

FIG. 10.6. A, Density of L. *neglecta* = large dashed line and dead barnacles = solid line at different shore levels. B, Variation in density of different size categories of dead barnacles. 0–1.49mm = solid line; 1.5–2.99mm = large dashed line; 3.00 + mm = broken line aperture length.

progressively easier using a combination of characters, but the situation is complicated by the fact that there are ontogenetic changes in shell-shape in both species (see also Van Marion, 1981).

The similarity between *L. neglecta* and *L. 'saxatilis'* extends to details of the anatomy and there is a close similarity between the structure of the radula of adult *L. neglecta* and juvenile *L. 'saxatilis'* (Raffaelli, 1976; Sharp, pers. obs.). Details of the ciliated field, an area of cilia between the genital tract and the columellar muscle first described by Hannaford Ellis (1979) and an important character in the identification of *L. arcana*, are the same in *L. neglecta* and *L. 'saxatilis'* (Sharp, pers. obs.). Furthermore although *L. neglecta* has been reported to be the only British littorinid not infected by any digenean parasite (James, 1969), investigations during the present study have shown that adults of the species are infected by the larval stages of *Parvatrema homoeotecnum* James, a parasite which also infects juvenile stages of *L. 'saxatilis'*. Such observations lend support to speculation that *L. neglecta* arose as a neotenous form of *L. 'saxatilis'* through selection for early maturation (see Emson and Faller-Fritsch, 1976) which enabled the species to exploit the security of the barnacle belt throughout life.

The most striking feature of the shell of *L. neglecta* is the pattern of bands and tessellations so clearly seen in the majority of adult specimens. Polymorphism of the molluscan shell must be to some extent under genetic control but the relative proportions of each morph in a population may vary with environmental factors, several of which may operate to cause the observed phenotypes to be cryptic within a habitat. In all populations studied ontogenetic changes of shell morph were observed and the frequency of banded and tessellated morphs varied throughout the year as the population structure changed. Snails which were not severely eroded or obscured by encrusting algae showed the change in pattern, older parts of the shell being banded and the more recently secreted parts tessellated. Ontogenetic change in colour morphs has been recorded in *L. mariae* where juveniles of 'dwarf' *reticulata* morphs with a white apex to the shell closely resemble the tubes of the polychaete *Spirorbis* spp. present on the fronds of *Fucus serratus* L. (Reimchen, 1981). This crypsis was maintained for about the first 4mm of shell growth during which time Reimchen demonstrated that predation by *Blennius pholis* (L.) was less than that in other colour morphs of equivalent size. At larger shell size crypsis would be lost and other morphs selected. In *L. neglecta* the change from one morph type to another takes place over a narrow range of shell height and may be an adaptation to reduce predation. The uniform colour of the tiny, newly emerged snail may be cryptic, but as shell size increases a disruptive pattern may be more adaptive and would seem to be particularly advantageous in the microhabitat associated with the barnacle zone. It is perhaps significant that banded morphs are recorded in the juveniles of other species of littorinids which occupy this zone. Certainly, *L. neglecta* is cryptic to the human eye during both emersion and submersion but to date there is no conclusive evidence that the proportions of the different morphs are maintained in the population through selection by visual predators. (See also Hannaford Ellis (1984) who suggests that the physiological effects of shell colour may be important.)

Despite limited gene flow as a result of its ovoviviparous reproductive habit, *L. neglecta* displays less divergence of shell morphology than do other rough periwinkles. Shell-shape and aperture-shape show no significant trends in variation throughout the range of sites investigated in the British Isles and there is no indication of variation in shell thickness, a parameter which is known to vary in *L. 'saxatilis'*. The separation of populations of *L. neglecta* into two types depending on the intensity of coloration of the newly emerged snails is an interesting phenomenon which requires further study. Results to date show that the occurrence of the morphs is not related to any obvious environmental factor. The relative stability of shell characters shown by *L. neglecta* is believed to result from the uniformity of the habitat from which the snails were collected; in all cases collections were made from the barnacle zone of rocky shores and it may be that selection pressures are similar from one location to the next. It would be particularly interesting to have data on the morphology of specimens from eelgrass meadows and other habitats.

In general small gastropods tend to be short-lived (Underwood and McFadyen, 1983), for example *Lacuna vincta* (Montagu) and *L. pallidula* (da Costa) (D.A.S. Smith, 1973; Grahame, this volume), *Rissoa parva* (da Costa) (Wigham, 1975; and see Underwood and McFadyen, 1983) and *Littorina acutispira* Smith (Underwood and McFadyen, 1983). *Littorina neglecta* conforms to this generalization; maturity at Borth is reached when the snails are about one year old at a shell height of 1.4mm in males and 1.6mm in females, and the majority of individuals (about 90%) die after 18 months, a small number living for 2 to 3 years and reaching a maximum shell height of about 4.6mm. These details are similar to those recorded by Robertson and Mann (1982) working on a population from an eelgrass meadow, and preliminary observations made on populations from the east coast of England show little variation from this pattern. The growth rate of *L. neglecta* is slow in comparison with that determined for other species of rough periwinkle from a number of localities (Berry, 1961; Hughes, 1980c; Hughes and Roberts, 1981; Janson, 1982).

In common with *L. nigrolineata* and *L. arcana*, *L. neglecta* shows a marked reproductive periodicity (Hannaford Ellis, 1983), while *L. 'saxatilis'* maintains a high level of reproductive activity throughout the year, the number of mature animals fluctuating between 54 and 99% at some localities (Roberts and Hughes, 1980). Peak maturity in *L. neglecta* was reached in spring and summer with males maturing before females, a strategy which is common in the genus and would seem to increase the probability of a female being fertilized. Although egg-bearing females were recorded throughout the year, there was no significant recruitment to the population during winter. Embryo development is slow at low temperatures, requiring 83 and 74 days for hatching at 5 and 10°C respectively (Sharp, pers. obs.). In addition, it is possible that fully developed young, which are free from the egg capsule, remain in the brood chamber for prolonged periods during adverse conditions.

Size of *L. neglecta* at hatching is smaller than that recorded for other rough periwinkles (Berry, 1961; Hughes, 1980c; Roberts and Hughes, 1980) and there is little variation in the size at hatching between populations in the British Isles and Nova Scotia (Robertson and Mann, 1982). Although the number of broods produced per female is not known, it can be concluded that size-specific fecundity is high with females of 2.5mm shell height containing up to 30 embryos. The maximum number of embryos recorded during the present study was 125 in a female of 4.65mm shell height but few snails attain such a size and recruitment to the population is largely derived from animals of about 2.0mm shell height which contain about 10 embryos in the brood pouch at any one time. The heavy mortality suffered by the new recruits to the population must be related to competition for food and space, and it is significant that at the time of recruitment the barnacle zone is an important nursery ground for juvenile littorinids of a number of species; the young of *L. 'saxatilis'*, *L. neritoides* and *L. littorea* all find temporary refuge in this zone and a total density as high as 7200 individuals·m^{-2} has been recorded for these species at Borth.

L. neglecta is generally restricted in its littoral distribution to the mid- and upper zones of the barnacle belt and a number of factors are thought to operate in restricting the population density at the lower limits. These include the instability of the habitat resulting from the tall, columnar growth forms of the barnacle, which are common on the low-shore, being removed by wave action (Connell, 1961a); competition for space with *Campecopea hirsuta*, *Mytilus edulis* and *Lasaea rubra*; and increased exposure to predators, principally *Blennius pholis* and small crabs. Preliminary observations have shown that during the summer months *B. pholis* forages over vertical rock faces in densities up to 20·m^{-2} and it has been estimated that these have the potential for removing up to 400 specimens of *L. neglecta* per tidal cycle. Littorinids are consumed whole and there appears to be no selection for size of snail, the population structure of *L. neglecta* taken from the gut of the fish matching that on the shore.

In common with a number of littorinid species (see Branch and Branch, 1981), *L. neglecta* shows an increase in size and decrease in population density upshore. The reasons for this are complex and likely to include both biological interactions and tolerance to physical factors. The population density and size of individuals of *L. 'rudis'* have been related to the size and availability of crevices (Emson and Faller-Fritsch, 1976) and similar conclusions have been reported for *L. neritoides* (Raffaelli and Hughes, 1978) and *L. neglecta* (Raffaelli, 1978b). In *L. acutispira* a high density of snails on exposed shores was related to the protection from wave action afforded by barnacles as opposed to protection from desiccation or high temperatures (Underwood and McFadyen, 1983). One of the problems in attempting to correlate the parameters of the barnacle belt to the population density and to the size of individual specimens of *L. neglecta* is the difficulty in defining and obtaining quantitative data on the precise niche occupied by the snail. *L. neglecta* is principally found inside the shells of dead barnacles and the number in a single empty barnacle shell varies. At times, especially during the breeding season, several young may occupy a single empty barnacle. The snails are also found in the spaces between barnacles, a micro-habitat which varies seasonally with the density and growth of the barnacles. Observations made during the present study failed to demonstrate a relationship between the occurrence and size of dead barnacles and the population structure of *L. neglecta*, but the artificial creation of extra habitats by killing barnacles and leaving only the outer shells, did lead to an increase in the density of littorinids (Sharp, pers. obs.). The species of littorinid showing the greatest increase in population density as a result of such manipulation depended on shore level and will almost certainly depend on the time of year at which the experiments are carried out. Carefully controlled experimental manipulations of this type are clearly an area worthy of further research and should give valuable information on the inter- and intraspecific interactions of littorinids occupying the barnacle belt. They would be particularly informative if carried out in conjunction with studies on the ontogenetic changes in tolerance of the different species to physical factors.

CHAPTER XI

CAUSES AND PATTERNS OF MORTALITY IN *LITTORINA RUDIS* (MATON) IN RELATION TO INTRASPECIFIC VARIATION: A REVIEW

R.J. Faller-Fritsch and R.H. Emson

11.1 Introduction

The studies reviewed in this Chapter concern the causes, incidence and effects of mortality in *Littorina 'rudis'* (Maton), one of four species formerly regarded as a variety of *L. 'saxatilis'* (Olivi). *L. 'rudis'* is the most widespread and undoubtedly the most variable British littorinid. It is abundant on all types of rocky shore, and ovoviviparous reproduction (restricted gene flow) has led to a remarkable degree of local differentiation, providing excellent material with which to study processes of adaptation to littoral environments. Much earlier work on variation concentrated upon aspects of shell morphology and coloration, in an attempt to understand this variation in terms of the habitats occupied. Relative lack of success was due partly to a lack of quantitative methods and partly to insufficient appreciation of the small scale variations in habitat which affect the observed variation. Another major problem was taxonomic confusion. Adaptation to littoral environments in littorinids has involved extensive speciation, particularly where limited larval dispersal has allowed the evolution of locally adapted, relatively isolated populations. Recent developments in taxonomy (Heller, 1975a; Hannaford Ellis, 1979) have made possible a renewed attack on the problem of variation, though it cannot be assumed that the taxonomic position is yet stable (Fretter and Graham, 1980). Interest in *L. 'rudis'* has centred on three main areas: comparative population dynamics, morphological variation and reproductive biology. Such studies are intimately concerned with causes of mortality in contrasting habitats, and the manner in which adaptive responses arise by selection. Mortality studies in *L. 'rudis'* are facilitated by direct development, but made more difficult by the rapidity with which dead animals are removed from the habitat. Quantifying the various causes of mortality has proved enormously difficult. Much of the work referred to is still in progress, so this paper is necessarily an interim report rather than a comprehensive synthesis. Apart from assembling the available information in an accessible form, its main aim is to outline areas where further work is needed and likely to bring about significant advances in knowledge.

There is still confusion surrounding the taxonomy of *L. 'rudis'* and its relatives, and we have no wish to add to it. It is necessary however to outline and justify the taxonomic interpretation that we have adopted, and this is done in the following section.

11.2 Notes on Taxonomy

Following the taxonomic revisions of Heller (1975a) and Hannaford Ellis (1979), L. 'rudis' in Britain includes all ovoviviparous winkles not referrable to the much smaller L. neglecta Bean. This interpretation cannot reliably be applied beyond British shores, while British forms exist whose taxonomic status is uncertain (Fretter and Graham, 1980). Nevertheless, most recent studies adopt this interpretation in comparing various aspects of biology in populations occupying contrasting habitats. Two recent developments should be briefly discussed as they are directly relevant to the present paper. These are the description of L. arcana by Hannaford Ellis (1978, 1979) and the revision by Smith (1981) which recognised two ovoviviparous species rather than one.

Little information concerning the oviparous L. arcana has been published since its original description. Fretter (1980) described the structure of the oviduct, and Atkinson and Warwick (1983) studied colour morph frequencies in L. arcana and L. 'rudis'. In two studies (Caugant and Bergerard, 1980; Hughes and Roberts, 1981) it was suggested that arcana is a reproductive morph of rudis, since the two forms may be otherwise indistinguishable. However it will be shown later that clear differences in size, morphology and zonation are common, even though not consistent from one shore to another. We believe that the idea of two reproductive morphs, involving as it must both structural and behavioural aspects, is pushing the concept of polymorphism too far, and that the two forms are good species. It will be necessary to distinguish them rigorously in future studies if further confusion is to be avoided. Some of the possible interactions between these two species are discussed on p. 168.

A recent taxonomic revision is that of Smith (1981). In a study of 65 Cornish populations, he redescribed two ovoviviparous species. L. 'saxatilis' (thin shell, obviously striated, variably coloured and with a large aperture) was characteristic in exposed habitats and L. 'rudis' (thicker shell, weakly striated, less variably coloured and with a smaller aperture) predominated in sheltered and estuarine localities. Smith demonstrated significant differences in embryonic shell-shape in the two forms, with stabilizing selection for shell-shape in some populations. The two forms seldom occur together; where they do, as at Trevaunance Cove in north Cornwall, they retain their distinct identities. These findings, if confirmed, would fundamentally affect interpretations of much recent work on L. 'rudis', which has tended to contrast exposed and sheltered populations. Concepts of intraspecific variation in L. 'rudis' would also have to be thoroughly revised.

Smith's views have not been generally accepted. Atkinson and Warwick (1983) interpreted the variations as intraspecific adaptation to local conditions, and fertile hybrids between the proposed species have been reported (Atkinson and Newbury, 1984). Fretter and Graham (1980) regarded rudis and saxatilis as members of a cline, a view strongly supported by Smith's own data, in particular the aperture size results from estuarine localities (Fig. 2 in Smith, 1981). These data appear merely to confirm that gradual changes in aperture size take place between exposure and shelter (James, 1968a; Heller, 1975a; Newkirk and Doyle, 1975), and it is impossible to determine, using Smith's own criteria, at what point one 'species' gives way to the other.

Other arguments may be advanced against Smith's scheme. First, neighbouring populations, for example on harbour walls and among nearby boulders, often differ in size, shell-shape and coloration (Faller-Fritsch, 1983 and unpubl. data; Atkinson and Newbury, 1984) and on Smith's argument they would be different species. How L. 'saxatilis' colonizes such exposed situations in the absence of planktonic dispersal poses a problem, and it is surely more likely that colonization of recent artificial habitats is from neighbouring populations, with selection then resulting in the observed morphological differences. This would explain the apparently continuous variation between the proposed species in all the characters studied by Smith, and the absence of constant differences of the sort described by Heller (1975a).

This leaves the observation that at Trevaunance Cove, the two forms meet and retain their specific features, *saxatilis* occupying a cliff habitat and *rudis* boulders at a slightly lower shore level. Our own observations show that this interpretation is incorrect; in particular, the cliff population is dominated by *L. arcana* whose shells have distinctly enlarged apertures. *L. rudis sensu* Heller, though present, is in a minority, making up perhaps 10% of the total population. The shell apertures are conspicuously smaller than those of *arcana*, and since both were included in his analysis (J.E. Smith, pers. comm.) a falsely high estimate of aperture size for *saxatilis* would have been obtained.

Nevertheless, differences in embryonic shell-shape in the two populations (Smith, 1981) remain to be explained (here, of course, the presence of *arcana* is irrelevant). These differences are explicable in terms of the paramount importance of attachment to the cliff, necessitating a large foot area. This does not apply among the boulders where, as Smith remarks, the population is subject to significant levels of crab predation, and smaller shell apertures may be favoured. Comparisons of crab damage in snails from cliff and boulders, made on 19th April, 1984, gave the results shown in Table 11.1. χ^2 analysis shows that there was significantly more damage among 'boulder' *rudis* than among *rudis/arcana* from the cliff ($P < 0.001$). *L. nigrolineata* Gray was also more damaged on the boulders than on the cliff ($P < 0.001$) but significantly less so than *rudis* ($P < 0.01$). The boulder *nigrolineata* are noticeably thick-shelled with very narrow apertures, features commonly found when crabs are abundant (Elner and Raffaelli, 1980; Hughes, 1980c). That *rudis* shows similar adaptations is also well known (Heller, 1976; Raffaelli, 1978a) and it is reasonable that such adaptation would be observable in embryonic shells. It also appears that *L. 'rudis'* may have adapted less successfully in this respect than *L. nigrolineata* (Elner and Raffaelli, 1980). The boulders at Trevaunance are of recent origin, dating from the destruction by wave action of an old quay soon after the 1914–18 war. This emphasises the possibilities of rapid adaptation in the absence of planktonic dispersal.

In summary, there is evidence not of two ovoviviparous species at Trevaunance, but of one species, *L. 'rudis'*, which has adapted to contrasting habitats in which different selective agents have been identified. *L. arcana* is widespread in Cornwall (Table 11.2), often with the patulous shape found at Trevaunance. It is certainly abundant at Kynance Cove and Porthleven, where Smith recorded *saxatilis*, and many of his *saxatilis* populations must be similarly contaminated, invalidating the characters on which his description of *saxatilis* is based. For all the above reasons we regard *L. 'rudis'* as a single, highly variable species.

Concerning nomenclature, most recent authors (but see Raffaelli, 1982; S. Smith, 1982) have adopted the name *L. 'rudis'* following Heller (1975a). We believe this to be correct since, as Heller has pointed out, there is no evidence that *L. 'rudis'* from Britain is conspecific with *L. 'saxatilis'* from the type locality in Venice. Use of the latter name to describe British material would therefore involve

TABLE 11.1

Incidence of shell damage in cliff and boulder populations of L. 'rudis', L. arcana and L. nigrolineata at Trevaunance Cove, North Cornwall (19 April, 1984).

Population	Number (%) damaged	Number (%) undamaged	Total
cliff *rudis/arcana*	17 (12)	124 (88)	141
cliff *nigrolineata*	1 (2)	63 (98)	64
boulder *rudis*	31 (56)	24 (44)	55
boulder *nigrolineata*	28 (30)	65 (70)	93

TABLE 11.2

New records for *Littorina arcana*. For existing records see Hannaford Ellis (1979) and Atkinson and Warwick (1983).

Area	Site	O.S. Grid Reference		
Britain – Dyfed	Broadhaven	SR	977	937
	St Govans	SR	967	929
	Greenala Point	SS	007	965
	Manorbier	SS	050	976
	Castle Beach Bay	SM	820	046
	Watwick	SM	819	036
	Cliff Cottages	SM	822	053
Devon	Peartree Point	SX	819	367
	St Mary's Bay	SX	935	548
Cornwall	Lizard Point	SW	695	118
	Kynance Cove	SW	684	133
	Trevaunance	SW	720	518
	Porthleven	SW	625	255
	Mevagissey	SX	018	449
	Mullion Cove	SW	666	179
	Portholland	SW	958	410
	Port Isaac	SW	995	811
	Polzeath	SW	935	790
France – Brittany	Plogoff			
	Plozévet			
	Pleubian		not applicable	
	Pointe du Raz			
	Trébeurden			
Normandy	Cap de la Hague			

an unjustified taxonomic assumption, apart from adding to the already confusing series of entities associated with the name *saxatilis*. Older references to *L.* '*saxatilis*' in Britain may involve several species, and we will adopt the name *saxatilis* to mean one or more species of the '*saxatilis*' group.

11.3 Patterns of Mortality

Ovoviviparous development allows mortality to be studied at every life history stage. Causes and rates of mortality are likely to be seasonal, and the youngest individuals may be expected to suffer the highest mortality rates. It is therefore important to study mortality in relation to seasonal patterns of recruitment on different shore types. This may be done by recording the proportion of gestating females (Daguzan, 1976; Hannaford Ellis, 1983) or, more sensitively, by regularly counting developing embryos or newly hatched snails (Berry, 1961; James, 1968b; Roberts and Hughes, 1980; Faller-Fritsch, 1983). Most populations reproduce throughout the year, often with a more or less marked seasonal component involving maximum activity in early summer with a lull in midsummer. This is followed by a gradual recovery during the autumn and winter (Berry, 1961; Faller-Fritsch, 1983). Reproductive inactivity in autumn and winter has also been recorded (Raffaelli, 1976) and Guyomarc'h-Cousin (1973) found that ovulation may stop in very cold weather. In some populations there is little seasonal fluctuation (Roberts and Hughes, 1980; Faller-Fritsch, 1983), and Bergerard (1971) argued that reproduction is more markedly seasonal in populations subject to severe emersion conditions via restricted time for feeding.

Protracted recruitment has some important consequences for mortality studies. It is in principle possible to follow the fate of recruits born at different times of year, though no significant differences were found in the only study where this was attempted (Hughes and Roberts, 1981). More detailed knowledge of juvenile survivorship is needed, particularly since maximum abundance of newly hatched snails often coincides with the most severe emersion conditions.

A second consequence of prolonged reproduction is the absence of discrete cohorts on the shore, so that ageing of size–frequency samples using graphical methods (Harding, 1949; Cassie, 1954) is unreliable. The study of survivorship therefore requires indirect methods, involving analysis of size structure and growth rates (Faller-Fritsch, 1983) or mark and recapture procedures (Hughes and Roberts, 1981; Atkinson and Newbury, 1984). Survivorship curves for four populations are shown in Fig. 11.1. In each case very high mortality affects the newly hatched snails and young juveniles. Lower and perhaps approximately constant mortality rates apply after about six months. Despite the fact that these populations are from widely differing habitats, there is general similarity in survivorship, suggesting that whatever the causes of mortality may be, survivorship is very strongly age- (or size-) dependent.

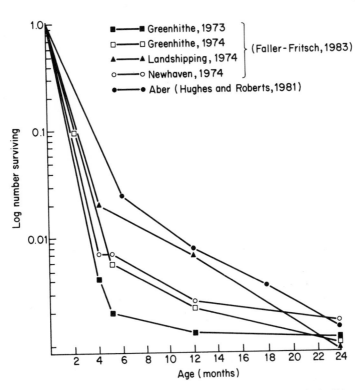

FIG. 11.1. Survivorship over two years of four populations of *Littorina 'rudis'*.

Population structure in *L. 'rudis'* differs greatly between exposed and sheltered habitats. Exposed shore populations characteristically consist of small individuals; in shelter much larger individuals are common, and there is often a dearth of juveniles (Hughes and Roberts, 1981; Faller-Fritsch, 1983). Interpretation of population structure in terms of differential mortality is made difficult by lower growth rates in exposure than shelter (Roberts and Hughes, 1980; Faller-Fritsch, 1983). It is thus probable that mortality regimes and maximum longevity are less variable than size–frequency comparisons suggest. Size-specific crevice-seeking behaviour often leads to significant, very localized, differences in population size-structure (Raffaelli and Hughes, 1978; Faller-Fritsch, 1983), and probably invalidates generalizations concerning shore level and mortality based on size structure analysis (Vermeij, 1972).

11.4 Physical Causes of Mortality

11.4.1 Desiccation, heat death and dislodgement

These three interacting factors must account for the majority of all mortality in *L. 'rudis'*. Their effects depend greatly upon aspect, exposure and microtopography. The importance of these factors is clear from the several adaptations which have evolved to minimize their effects, including shell-shape, crevice-seeking behaviour, activity patterns in relation to environmental factors, and well-developed tolerances of high temperatures and prolonged desiccation (Evans, 1948; Kensler, 1967; Sandison, 1967). Direct evidence of mortality from these and other causes is very hard to obtain, since on most shores dead snails are quickly removed by the incoming tide. On exposed shores the close relationship between both abundance and size structure of *L. 'rudis'* populations and the availability of crevices would indicate that these factors, acting singly or in combination, are of major importance (Emson and Faller-Fritsch, 1976; Raffaelli and Hughes, 1978; Hughes and Roberts, 1981; Atkinson and Newbury, 1984). On the other hand it is possible that wave action may have relatively little effect in areas where suitable crevices are abundant, for instance Hughes and Roberts (1981) found that winter storms caused greater mortality in a saltmarsh than in an exposed cliff population. Unusual wave action at sites where it is normally rare may thus be more dangerous to winkles than a constant predictable pounding. Faller-Fritsch (1983) recorded death from desiccation among newly hatched snails on a sheltered boulder shore, whose stones had been overturned by wave action. Experimental upturning of stones led to the same result. The preference of small snails for damp interstices between small pebbles (Berry and Hunt, 1980; Faller-Fritsch, 1983) cannot ensure protection from desiccation on very unstable substrata. There is some evidence that mortality on such shores is greater in particularly dry summers (Faller-Fritsch, 1983), but further quantitative studies of mortality among newly hatched snails are needed.

Also needed is more information concerning the behavioural responses of winkles to changing physical factors and to different microclimates. This is crucial to our understanding of mortality related to emersion factors, particularly for exposed sites. *L. 'rudis'* is normally inactive during immersion, feeding and copulation taking place after the tide has receded while the shore remains damp (Berry, 1961). On boulder shores, winkles encountering suitable crevices will be relatively safe from high temperatures and desiccation, though not necessarily from predation. On exposed shores the situation is more complex, and there are three behavioural responses shown during emersion (pers. obs.). Activity will continue throughout emersion if conditions are favourable, particularly at night. As conditions become more desiccating, movement stops though animals remain attached to the substratum. Further desiccation leads to production of a mucous holdfast (Boschma, 1948; Bingham, 1972) which anchors the outer lip to the substratum. Shells thus attached are normally orientated aperture-upwards, and the splash from the incoming tide allows reattachment before dislodgement can take place. Shells anchored aperture-downwards are less stable (pers. obs.) and may be less able to achieve reattachment. The three responses described above can usually be found on insolated and shaded sides of gullies, and in channels of water running down the rock surface. More detailed analyses of these traits would reveal more about the incidence of mortality during emersion both in relation to population structure and to the species composition in contrasting microhabitats.

11.4.2 Extreme cold

There is little evidence that extreme cold, as opposed to other factors associated with winter conditions such as storms, is a significant cause of mortality in *L. 'rudis'*. Cold weather delays ovulation, prolongs the gestation period and depresses activity (Berry, 1961; Guyomarc'h-Cousin, 1973; Faller-Fritsch, 1983). More direct effects are perhaps not to be expected in a species which is abundant at high latitudes (Thorson, 1941, 1944; Matveeva, 1974) where sub-zero temperatures are common. *L. 'rudis'* was less affected by cold than lower shore gastropods, particularly limpets and topshells, as shown during the exceptionally cold British winter of 1962/3 (Crisp (ed.), 1964). *L. 'rudis'* was reported to have survived being completely encased in ice.

11.4.3 Burial and crushing

These factors are potentially important on sheltered boulder and muddy shores. Boulder movements during winter gales caused burial and crushing of *L. 'rudis'* and *L. nigrolineata* on a sheltered shore in Wales (Raffaelli and Hughes, 1978; Hughes, 1980c), although this was not evident in their mortality data. The effect was thought to be greater among small snails and at lower shore levels where wave action was greater.

Crushing was also suggested as a cause of mortality by Heller (1976), Raffaelli (1978a) and Faller-Fritsch (1983). It cannot simply be inferred from the presence of damaged shells, since such damage is also, and perhaps more commonly, caused by crabs (Raffaelli, 1978a). In some sheltered and estuarine localities, stones and pebbles lie over a substratum of soft mud, burial in which may be lethal to small individuals (Faller-Fritsch, 1983). Solid structures surrounded by soft mud may also pose a hazard, since dislodgement may result in burial and reattachment be prevented (Atkinson and Newbury, 1984).

11.4.4 Salinity

L. rudis is common in estuaries and other brackish situations, and it has been shown to be tolerant of a wide range of salinities (Avens and Sleigh, 1965; Arnold, 1972; Parsons, 1972). This is to be expected in a high-shore species which is subject to both concentration and dilution of seawater at different stages of the tidal cycle and in varying weather conditions. Brackish habitats have been extensively studied elsewhere in northern Europe (Thorson, 1946; Muus, 1967; Matveeva, 1974), though the specific identity of the winkles studied is open to doubt, e.g. Muus (1967) considered that the brackish form *L. saxatilis tenebrosa* may constitute a separate species.

Salinities in estuaries show marked seasonal variations, with a tidal component if there is incomplete mixing. These variations may be termed predictable, and locally adapted populations of *L. rudis* probably arise, so that generalizations about 'salinity tolerance' in *L. rudis* are of limited value. It has been suggested that low salinities depress reproductive output (Thorson, 1946; Matveeva, 1974), though contrary views were expressed by Muus (1967) and Faller-Fritsch (1983). Of more relevance to the present discussion is the possible connection between low salinities and embryonic abnormality. This was first suggested by Thorson (1946), although studies by Clyne and Duffus (1979) and Faller-Fritsch (1983) suggested that such abnormality was not significant in the overall dynamics of the populations affected. Faller-Fritsch (1983) found a higher incidence of abnormality in the Thames estuary than at an open coast site in Sussex. The Thames population was subject to marked hypo-salinity in winter, when values of 12‰ were frequently recorded. There was no seasonal trend in the incidence of embryonic abnormality as would have been expected if salinity was directly involved. This, taken together with the fact that abnormality also occurred in fully marine habitats, leaves the causes of embryonic abnormality essentially unexplained. Another aspect of salinity is upstream estuarine penetration, discussed by Berry and Hunt (1980). There was poor survival of *L. 'rudis'* of all ages in salinities below about 15‰, though adults were more tolerant in low temperatures. It was thus suggested that the salinity tolerance of juveniles may limit upstream penetration.

11.4.5 Pollution

Some information is available concerning the effects of various pollutants upon littorinid snails and other gastropods. The effects of oil, and of emulsifiers used to disperse it, have been studied in most detail, and it is clear that deleterious sublethal effects may be of more importance than mortality caused as a direct result of chronic levels of pollutants. Gastropods in general are highly susceptible to oil pollution (Nelson-Smith, 1968), although crevices may provide refuges for species like *L. 'rudis'*. The manner in which emulsifiers are used, particularly in relation to the tidal cycle and methods of washing them from the shore, may be of overriding importance. Winkles and dogwhelks are more sus-ceptible to oil when under salinity stress and after starvation (Ottway, 1972). The effects of emulsifiers may vary seasonally, suggesting a relationship with temperature and/or reproductive fatigue (Crapp, 1970). Hargrave and Newcombe (1973) found that rates of crawling and respiration in *L. littorea* (L.) increased in the presence of oil, but were reduced by a low toxicity dispersant, and it appears that dis-persants are potentially much more damaging than the oil itself (Corner *et al.*, 1968; George, 1971).

In polluted estuaries several aspects of pollution may act simultaneously. An estuarine population of *L. 'rudis'* studied by Faller-Fritsch (1983) was subject to thermal pollution and to periodically reduced oxygen tensions. Apart from a low incidence of embryonic abnormality, which could not be positively attributed to pollution, no discernible effects were found. Calabrese and Nelson (1974) have recorded adverse effects on embryonic development in clams caused by heavy metals. *L. 'rudis'* embryos provide excellent material for quantitative pollution studies, although difficulties in culturing them remain to be overcome (Berry, 1956). It is also possible to investigate pollution incidents by analysis of past growth using annual growth interruptions (Black, 1973).

11.5 Biological Causes of Mortality

11.5.1 Predators and parasites

Much older literature concerning predation upon winkles takes the form of isolated field observations and, in the case of birds and fish, analysis of gut contents or faeces. This material has been assembled by Pettitt (1975). Many potentially predatory species are involved and as Pettitt remarks, predation may constitute a major selective agent even if overall rates of predation are low. Of the three main predatory groups (crustaceans, birds and fish) the former, and crabs in particular, have been the most studied. Crabs are important predators of littorinids (Reimchen, 1974; Heller, 1975b, 1976; Smith, 1976; Raffaelli, 1978a) and it has been possible to study their predatory activities both in the field (Hamilton, 1976) and in the laboratory (Elner and Hughes, 1978; Hughes and Elner, 1979; Elner and Raffaelli, 1980). The analysis of shells damaged by crabs, as well as the abundance and size structure of the predator, is also possible, so that the importance of predation can be compared in different winkle populations (Heller, 1976; Raffaelli, 1978a; Elner and Raffaelli, 1980).

The main predator is *Carcinus maenas* (L.), although other species may be locally important. Most predation takes place on boulder shores, where shelter is available for the crabs (Heller, 1976;

Raffaelli, 1978a; Faller-Fritsch, 1983). In the laboratory crabs preferred juvenile snails, perhaps because less energy was expended in extracting the meat (Elner and Raffaelli, 1980). For the same reason, L. 'rudis' was preferred to L. nigrolineata. Four methods of shell breakage were identified, and it is likely that large crabs can successfully attack the largest L. 'rudis'. Smaller and less powerful crabs are more restricted in the prey sizes they can successfully exploit, although they may kill large numbers of newly hatched snails (Hughes and Roberts, 1981). The responses by L. 'rudis' to crab predation depend upon other things than the size structure of the predator population. These responses, including aspects of morphology, colour and life history adaptations, are discussed on p. 170. The importance of other predators is much less well established, because no evidence is left of their activity, which may take place when observation is difficult. Birds are undoubtedly highly significant predators of several littorinid species. Gibb (1956) calculated that a single rock pipit may consume 14,300 winkles per day, and Feare (1966a) gives a figure of 4,600 for the purple sandpiper. It was further calculated that a flock of 40 birds may remove more than 11 million winkles during two months feeding.

There is good evidence that the most important predatory birds choose small shells. Mean shell length (mm) in the guts of three species were 2.25 (rock pipit); 2.72 (purple sandpiper); 2.98 (turnstone) (Gibb, 1956). Summers and Smith (1983) found c. 4mm L. littorea and L. 'saxatilis' shells in the guts of knot in eastern Scotland, and James (1968b) found that oystercatchers fed upon large winkles only when very hungry, normally choosing small winkles. The significance of these data for the dynamics of winkle populations is clear. What should be emphasized is that studies of coloration in relation to predation miss the point if they consider only the adult winkles. It is among the juveniles that we must look for evidence of visual selection.

Concerning the final group of predators, the fish, no quantitative information is available. The studies of Quasim (1957), Reimchen (1974) and Anderson (1974) suggest that the importance of fish should not be discounted, particularly those species associated with rockpools in semi-exposed situations.

L. 'rudis' is an intermediate host for many larval digeneans (James, 1968b,c). Most species infect adult snails, often with a marked seasonal variation in the degree of infestation (Berry, 1961; James, 1964, 1968b). Certain species infect only juvenile hosts and two of them, *Parvatrema homoeotecnum* James and *Microphallus pygmaeus* (Levinsen) form B have final hosts (oystercatcher and rock pipit respectively) which feed preferentially on juvenile winkles. *Microphallus similis* (Jägerskiöld) may be more common in L. 'rudis' than L. nigrolineata because the latter has a thicker shell and is more resistant to attack by crabs (Elner and Raffaelli, 1980).

Sublethal effects of digenean parasites include inhibition of locomotion (James, 1968b; Lambert and Farley, 1968) and disruption of the structure and activities of the digestive gland (James, 1964; Davis and Farley, 1973). Parasitized snails often suffer partial or complete castration (Berry, 1961; Hughes and Roberts, 1981) and this, coupled with high rates of infestation, must significantly depress natality rates. Whether parasites contribute directly to mortality is not clear, though it is likely that they render the host more susceptible to mortality caused by other factors. More work is needed to test this possibility and to establish the seasonal nature of parasitic infection and vertical and horizontal variations in rates of infestation.

11.5.2 Intraspecific competition and population regulation

Little information is currently available concerning the manner in which populations of L. rudis are kept in check. There is some evidence for density-dependent regulation both in populations from bedrock and boulder shores (Emson and Faller-Fritsch, 1976; Hughes and Roberts, 1981; Faller-Fritsch, 1983) although, as Hughes and Roberts pointed out, data covering longer periods of time are needed. Density-dependent mortality is associated with inter- and intraspecific competition, and with predator–prey interactions (or, more broadly, trophic relationships). Current information only allows discussion of intraspecific competition as a possible means of regulation, and so the two subjects are treated together for convenience.

Intraspecific competition occurs when, in exploiting a resource, individuals cause deleterious effects on other individuals of the same species (Birch, 1957). In arguing for the existence of competition it is therefore necessary to demonstrate that a resource is in short supply, preferably by manipulating population densities experimentally. Connell (1974) and Underwood (1979) have discussed these considerations in detail, and Underwood (1979) summarized the available evidence for competition in littoral gastropods.

Two resources which are potentially limiting for a rock-dwelling species such as *L. 'rudis'* are food and space. Castenholz (1961) found that *L. scutulata* Gould and limpets (*Acmaea* spp.) were capable of removing all available diatoms in summer, but not in winter when they were less active. Intraspecific competition among the littorinids cannot be assumed to have occurred. Berry (1961) found that *L. 'rudis'* at higher levels on a boulder shore grew and reproduced more rapidly than those lower downshore. This was due to drainage properties which allowed longer feeding periods at higher levels, and there was no implication of competition. Raffaelli and Hughes (1978) argued, because *L. 'rudis'* often reproduces throughout the year, and is often found at relatively low densities amid abundant food, that food limitation does not generally take place. Emson and Faller-Fritsch (1976) showed that crevices, not food, may be the limiting resource on exposed shores. The addition of artificial crevices resulted in an eight-fold increase in abundance without any reduction in size-specific fecundity. Similar effects of artificial crevices have been found by Raffaelli and Hughes (1978) and Hughes and Roberts (1981), and strongly suggest that exposed populations are generally crevice-limited. This may be true even when crevices are not absolutely in short supply, since the chance of a snail encountering a suitable crevice will decrease as density increases, even though some crevices may be unoccupied (Emson and Faller-Fritsch, 1976; Hughes & Roberts, 1981). This argument assumes that winkles search randomly for crevices, without homing behaviour for which there is no published evidence (Raffaelli and Hughes, 1978). In limpets where such behaviour has been studied intensively, homing has been suggested to reduce desiccation (Davies, 1969b), allow territorial defence (Stimson, 1970; Branch, 1971) or produce regular patterns of dispersion to maximize the efficiency with which food may be exploited (Aitken, 1962; Breen, 1971; MacKay and Underwood, 1977). None of these advantages appears relevant to *L. 'rudis'*, although homing might be advantageous where crevice availability is very severely limited, and the chances of encountering a crevice therefore very low. This situation sometimes prevails on sea or harbour walls made of concrete. Fig. 11.2 shows the contrasting grazing patterns of *L. 'rudis'* and the limpet *Patella vulgata* L. on the sea wall at Lyme Regis, photographed in April, 1984. Some of the limpets move upwards to graze, returning to home scars below the frame. The winkles graze very restricted areas around the crevices in which they shelter during emersion. They are highly aggregated, some crevices being crowded, others unoccupied. The restricted grazing patterns are suggestive of homing. Fig. 11.2 also clearly shows that food is abundant, at least at this time of year. Whether the localized and intensive grazing causes a relative food shortage is not known. The question of homing, and the possibility of relative food shortages resulting from aggregation, should be investigated further.

It is clear that crevices, whether encountered randomly or through homing behaviour, may limit abundance in a density-dependent manner. The abundance and size characteristics of available crevices may limit numbers in different size groups, so influencing local patterns of population structure (Raffaelli and Hughes, 1978). Since juvenile survivorship may be affected by barnacle abundance (Emson and Faller-Fritsch, 1976), the size structure of winkle populations may reflect patterns of

FIG. 11.2. Feeding trails of *Littorina 'rudis'* and *Patella vulgata* on the sea wall at Lyme Regis, Dorset.

settlement, growth and mortality among barnacles. This offers scope for manipulative experiments, since barnacle mortality is relatively easily monitored (Connell, 1961a,b) and experimentally induced. There is also a need for comparative studies of the stability of *L. 'rudis'* populations living in crevices versus those living among barnacles.

Evidence of limiting resources in sheltered populations has been harder to obtain. Hughes (1980c) found that population densities of *L. nigrolineata* changed by a factor of only 2.3 over 3 years. Hughes and Roberts (1981) suggested the presence of a density-dependent regulating factor affecting a saltmarsh population of *L. 'rudis'*, while a boulder population studied by Faller-Fritsch (1983) remained remarkably stable over three years despite seasonally abundant newly hatched snails. Food appeared to be abundant throughout the year, though the time for feeding was limited during periods of emersion in summer.

Mortality rates among small juveniles on sheltered shores are very high, caused by crushing, desiccation and predation, and some workers have assumed that these factors act in a way that is independent of density (Raffaelli, 1976; Hart and Begon, 1982). This may be incorrect. Berry and Hunt (1980) found that newly hatched snails favour the sides of smaller stones, where humidities remain high during emersion. Such small stones, if overturned, may crush small snails and subject them to desiccation. The number of stable sites may be limited, in which case space may have a density-dependent rôle in shelter as well as in exposure, though for different reasons. The lack of numerical fluctuations in sheltered populations needs further investigation. Other possible means of density-dependent regulation need to be investigated, including density-dependent predation, which seems likely to occur in the case of birds and perhaps crabs (pp. 164–5). Other effects recorded in gastropods, though not in littorinids, include those of slime-trail pheromones and density-dependent migration (Williamson *et al.*, 1976; Underwood, 1979).

11.5.3 Interactions with other littorinids

The redescription of *L. 'rudis'* and related species (Heller, 1975a; Hannaford Ellis, 1979) raises questions as to how the littoral environment is partitioned between them, and offers scope for studies of competition and coexistence (see reviews by Connell, 1974, 1983; Underwood, 1979).

On sheltered shores *L. 'rudis'* may overlap with *L. littorea* and, on western shores only, with *L. nigrolineata*. The latter may predominate over *L. 'rudis'* in the mid-shore (Hughes, 1980c), and the possibility of competitive exclusion should be investigated. It is probably significant that *L. littorea* and *L. nigrolineata*, both larger and thicker-shelled than *L. 'rudis'*, are often abundant where *Carcinus* is present and shell damage conspicuous (Table 11.1; Heller, 1976; Raffaelli, 1978a; Elner and Raffaelli, 1980).

On exposed shores *L. 'rudis'* often predominates in the upper barnacle zone, extending up to levels determined by wave splash and microtopography. On western shores other species may coexist with *L. 'rudis'* throughout its vertical range. In the barnacle zone, which Hannaford Ellis (pers. comm.) has aptly described as a winkle nursery, complex littorinid communities may be found (see Fish and Sharp, this volume). Juvenile and adult *L. nigrolineata* and *L. neglecta*, together with juvenile *L. neritoides*, *L. littorea* and *L. arcana* may all accompany *L. 'rudis'*. Resource partitioning between these species depends partly on local microclimates. *L. neritoides* and *L. neglecta* appear to favour sunlit rock surfaces, with *L. nigrolineata* and *L. arcana* being more abundant in shade (pers. obs. at Castlebeach Bay, Dyfed).

Towards its upper limit *L. 'rudis'* is often associated with *L. neritoides* and *L. arcana*. The latter species is widely distributed and often abundant, despite its only recent recognition (Table 11.2; Hannaford Ellis, 1979; Atkinson and Warwick, 1983). Its coexistence with *L. 'rudis'* is particularly problematic where the two entities are externally indistinguishable, and comparative studies of the two species are urgently needed. Current information suggests that *L. arcana* is most abundant towards the upper limit of *L. 'rudis'* (Atkinson and Warwick, 1983) although vertical migration associated with spawning has been reported by Hannaford Ellis (1979).

Table 11.3 shows some aspects of the variable relationship between *L. 'rudis'* and *L. arcana*. The latter species is often dominant at higher shore levels, and where *L. 'rudis'* is absent, as at Pointe du Raz, *L. arcana* appears to replace it. On other shores, e.g. Plozévet and Cap de la Hague, *L. arcana* is zoned above *L. 'rudis'* with only a small area of overlap. The two Dyfed samples are from shores where the two species overlap very considerably, over most if not all of the total range. On both shores the species can be distinguished on the basis of shell size, coloration and striation, and so cannot be regarded as occupying the same niche. Such differences existed on the majority of shores where both species were found, the exceptions being the shores around Dale, where neither structural nor zonational differences were found. There is no doubt that these two species will repay detailed studies of their comparative microhabitats, population dynamics and morphology. New methods must be developed by which different high-shore microhabitats can be distinguished, perhaps involving detailed studies of microalgal communities (Aleem, 1950; Castenholz, 1961, 1963; Underwood, 1984a,b).

11.6 Summary of Mortality Factors in Exposed and Sheltered Winkle Populations

At first sight there are general similarities in both the rates and causes of mortality between exposed and sheltered populations. Dislodgement may be a major factor on exposed shores, though this has yet to be experimentally demonstrated, and predation by crabs is a feature on many sheltered shores. Nevertheless desiccation is probably universally of overriding significance on all shore types, particularly affecting the smallest individuals (Fig. 11.1). With the exception of the possible rôle of empty barnacle shells, the available data allow no definite conclusions concerning the effects of microhabitat upon juvenile mortality rates to be drawn, and further comparative studies are desirable.

TABLE 11.3

Some comparisons between populations of *L. rudis* and *L. arcana* on five shores.

Shore and exposure grade (Lewis, 1964)	Site of collection (rock faces unless otherwise indicated)	Species	Mean shell length (mm)	Sample size	Shell characters	
					Coloration	Development of striation
Broadhaven, Dyfed (3)	at and above barnacle line	*arcana*	10.8	60	pale grey, fawn, yellow or brown	weak
		rudis	5.3	66	orange with brown bands, or fawn	strong
St Govans Dyfed (1–2)	as above	*arcana*	6.7	37	pale grey, fawn, yellow or brown	weak
		rudis	5.2	55	orange unbanded	strong
Plozévet, Brittany (3)	2m above barnacle line	*arcana*	10.3	56	brown, lined or unlined, pale grey or pale fawn	weak
	crevices in barnacle zone	*rudis*	10.6	44	all brown, lined or tesselated	strong
Cap de la Hague, Normandy (4)	harbour wall above barnacles	*arcana*	10.0	69	yellow, fawn or pale grey	variable, weak to strong
	boulders above barnacles	*arcana*	8.6	123		strong
	boulders in barnacle zone	*rudis*	7.0	80	yellow, fawn or pale grey	strong
Pointe du Raz, Brittany (1)	2–3m above barnacle line	*arcana*	6.9	77	fawn or brown ± tessellations, or yellow	weak
	crevices in barnacle zone	*arcana*	4.9	60		

In view of the overall similarities in survivorship in exposure and shelter, how is the enormous variability of L. 'rudis' to be understood? Clearly, significant selective mortality must often involve rates which are far too small to be relevant or measurable in studies of population dynamics. In L. 'rudis' and other species with restricted dispersal, this selection is reflected in spatial variation as well as polymorphism. Recognition of different causes of mortality in contrasting habitats provides a basis on which certain aspects of variation are beginning to be investigated and understood. These investigations are briefly reviewed in the next section.

11.7 Aspects of Variation in Relation to Mortality

11.7.1 Shell morphology

There have been several comparative studies of shell morphology in L. 'rudis'. Shell geometry, thickness and surface patterning differ markedly in exposed and sheltered populations, and conspicuous differences are often evident in closely adjacent samples. The shell characteristics of each population must result from several distinct, and sometimes opposing, selection pressures. For example the need for powerful adhesion may select for large shell apertures, which may inevitably lead to rapid desiccation (Atkinson and Newbury, 1984) and render the shell vulnerable to attack by crabs. Major causes of mortality must therefore be identified if the adaptive significance of shell morphology is to be understood.

Most shell geometry studies have been restricted to measurements of aperture size and shape (Heller, 1975a, 1976; Raffaelli, 1978a, 1979; Smith, 1981). Additional shell parameters are defined by Raup (1966) and Vermeij (1971), some of which have been applied to L. 'saxatilis' by Newkirk and Doyle (1975). Shells from exposed shore populations characteristically have rapidly expanding whorls and large, rounded apertures. As shelter increases and substrata become less stable, the rate of whorl expansion decreases and apertures become smaller and narrower. Shell thickness generally increases in sheltered localities (Raffaelli, 1978a). These differences can be related to the major problems associated with exposure and shelter. Violent wave action selects for shells with large apertures and low resistance to water flow. In such conditions a thick, heavy shell would be both cumbersome and unnecessary. In shelter, where adhesion is less important than resistance to desiccation and predation by crabs, thick shells with small, narrow apertures will be favoured (Vermeij, 1975). Similar responses have been found in L. nigrolineata (Heller, 1976) and dogwhelks (Crothers, 1973, 1974b; Kitching and Lockwood, 1974). The above interpretation is no doubt oversimplified. Atkinson and Newbury (1984) found that L. rudis from exposure and shelter may differ in foot area but not shell aperture area. This underlines the importance of relating shell geometry to the soft tissues.

Though these generalizations concerning shell thickness and exposure appear valid, anomalous data exist which suggest that factors other than crushing and crab predation influence the shell thickness of winkles in sheltered situations (Raffaelli, 1978a). Interpretation of shell thickness data depends upon how thickness is measured. Raffaelli (1978a) rejected measurements based on shell weight relative to shell height, since these are affected by shell-shape. Lip thickness relative to shell height is preferable, although lip thickness may not be the best measure of shell strength or vulnerability to attack, which are presumably the essential factors in many sheltered localities. These factors must be affected by aperture size and shape as well as thickness, and a better measure of shell strength is the relationship between shell weight and dry tissue weight (Currey and Hughes, 1982). The shell of L. 'rudis' appears thinner and weaker than that of L. nigrolineata, and thus more susceptible to predation (Table 11.1; Elner and Raffaelli, 1980). L. 'rudis' probably achieves partial escape from predation by virtue of its position high on the shore. Relationships between the distribution of L. 'rudis' and the presence of L. nigrolineata and Carcinus maenas deserve further study.

An additional observation relevant to shell thickness is that of Burton (1969) who reported slight but measurable water loss through the shells of several littorinids. The significance of such losses is unknown, and these experiments should be repeated.

The studies referred to above have concentrated upon variations in mean values of shell parameters. Of equal importance are measurements of the variances of these parameters. Reduction in variance of a parameter in adult shells compared to that in juveniles is evidence of stabilizing selection (Weldon, 1901; Haldane, 1959; Berry and Crothers, 1968, 1970). Such studies, applied to L. 'rudis', may reveal much about the process and rate of adaptation in recently colonized habitats such as sea walls (Moore and Sproston, 1940). There may be greater variances of shell parameters in exposure than in shelter (Newkirk and Doyle, 1975). Raffaelli (1979a) did not find significant shell-shape differences between shore levels, though the greatest variance was found at the highest level. This suggests a possible relationship between variance and patchiness of the habitat, and further work is needed to explore these possibilities.

Shell surface patterning, taking the form of spiral striations and growth interruptions, also varies between exposure and shelter (James, 1968a; Heller, 1975a). Despite their striking nature, little is known about the adaptive significance of these differences, and adequate methods have yet to be developed for quantitative analyses of shell pattern. Earlier descriptive papers are of little value because several species have almost certainly been confused. However, the following observations are of general occurrence. Sheltered populations are usually smooth-shelled, with striation poorly developed or absent. Growth interruptions are sometimes obvious. Weakly striated shells may also be found on all types of exposed shore, where they are usually accompanied by much more strongly grooved shells; thus there is more variation in sculpturing in exposure, and this variation appears to be continuous (Heller, 1975a). Emson and Faller-Fritsch (1976) suggested that striation aids the tight fitting of shells within crevices. This may also account for the abundance of small juvenile *L. littorea* (which are strongly striated) on exposed shores and the absence of the smoother-shelled large juveniles and adults.

The opposite relationship between shell sculpturing and wave action was reported in *L. picta* Philippi by Struhsaker (1968). Sculptured shells were found at high-shore levels where wave action was limited; lower downshore, smooth shells predominated. Stabilizing selection was evident in some samples. Strongly sculptured shells were less susceptible to desiccation than smooth ones. Struhsaker suggested that sculpturing may be genetically linked with physiological factors, the latter perhaps more important in determining the distributions of the different shell types. However, such linkage would not be expected if selection also operated on sculpturing, and it is difficult to accept that sculpturing is not in itself adaptive. The relationship between sculpturing and turbulence should be further investigated.

A major conclusion from the studies reviewed here is that all aspects of shell morphology appear much more variable in exposed populations. Future studies should take account of the patchiness of many exposed habitats in relation to observed patterns of morphology, investigating adult and juvenile shells from different shore levels.

11.7.2 Shell coloration

The enormous and often very striking variations in shell colour of littorinids have long been a source of interest to visitors to the seashore. Why this variation exists at all, how it is created and maintained, and why shell colours differ from place to place, are questions that can only be answered in the vaguest terms, applying knowledge from better-known situations. The problems posed by colour variation in *L. 'rudis'* are formidable, and considerably more complex than those associated with the flat periwinkles studied by Reimchen (1974, 1981) and Smith (1976). Speculation is very much easier than the

collection of useful data, and this section briefly reviews literature directly relevant to coloration in
L. 'rudis', emphasizing difficulties that must be tackled in future studies. These must inevitably take
account of the very detailed work on *Cepaea*, summarized by Jones *et al.* (1977).

Several interpretations have been applied to shell colour variation in littorinids. Heller (1975b)
showed a convincing relationship between red shells and red background rock in both *L. 'rudis'* and
L. nigrolineata, although the latter produced white and yellow shells where barnacles were abundant.
Heller argued that visual selection by birds and crabs was responsible. Such apparent crypsis is not
restricted to red backgrounds. James (in Fischer-Piette *et al.*, 1964) recorded yellow and fawn shells
among *Pelvetia* and *Fucus spiralis L.*, where such shells are well concealed. However, Heller (1975b)
pointed out that subjective assessment of this type is of limited value, and the desirable step of classifying the background coloration is often impossible.

Apart from these examples of apparent crypsis, it is common to find a large variety of colour morphs
in a single population, the majority of which are not obviously cryptic, and some of which are
exceedingly conspicuous. Many such morphs occur on red sandstone, while red or orange shells are
sometimes found on other backgrounds. The *L. 'rudis'* population at St Govans, Dyfed, quoted by
James (in Fischer-Piette *et al.*, 1964) and Heller (1975b) is so conspicuous that a greater contrast
between shells and background is hard to envisage. Reimchen (1974) has well exposed the dangers of
extrapolation from human visual perception, indeed such extrapolation hindered any real understanding of coloration in *Cepaea* for many years; nevertheless it is hard to believe that all colour morphs in
L. 'rudis' are cryptic. Some authors (Fischer-Piette *et al.*, 1963, 1964) have assumed that coloration is
of no selective importance, or that selection may be acting on factors closely linked with shell colour
(Raffaelli, 1979b). Light coloured shells in high-shore species may have better heat reflecting
properties (Vermeij, 1972). This has been demonstrated in *Cepaea* (Heath, 1975), but not in *Littorina*.
There appear to be general increases in morph diversity from East to West (James, 1968a) and from
shelter to exposure (Fischer-Piette and Gaillard, 1971; Smith, 1981), so that climate and exposure may
be suggested as two further influences on coloration.

The control of colour production has not yet been studied in detail. It has often been assumed to be
genetic (Pettitt, 1973b; Raffaelli, 1979b) and there is some supporting evidence (Atkinson and
Warwick, 1983). The appearance of a shell depends also on the presence or absence of algae, the degree
of erosion and sculpturing, and whether it is viewed wet or dry. The latter point is obviously relevant
where visual predators may be active during immersion (fish, crabs) and emersion (birds). Phenotypes
may also change with age, at least in *L. neglecta* (Hannaford Ellis, 1984) It is clear that more information is needed about the control of colour patterns, and the fate of colour morphs in natural populations, possibly involving controlled transplantation experiments. Whatever the outcome of this work,
it is easy to agree with Atkinson and Warwick (1983) that many factors must simultaneously influence
colour morph frequencies in littorinid populations.

Atkinson and Warwick studied coloration in 41 mixed populations of adult ($\geq$ 5mm shell length)
L. 'rudis' and *L. arcana* – species chosen because of their obvious similarities and sympatric distributions. Convincing evidence of selection was found, though no attempt was made to identify causes. Of
particular interest is the possibility of apostatic selection affecting the brown morphs. When 'brown'
was common in *L. 'rudis'* it tended to be slightly but significantly less so in *L. arcana*. Similar effects
have been observed in *Cepaea nemoralis* (L.) and *C. hortensis* (Müller) (Clarke, 1969). It has been
suggested that if predators cannot or do not distinguish between the two species, removing common
morphs in disproportionate numbers, then in each species there will be selection against morphs
which are common in the other. However, some mixed populations of *Cepaea* behave in the opposite
manner to that predicted by this theory (Jones *et al.*, 1977), and evidence for apostatic selection in
Cepaea is not yet satisfactory (Cain, 1983).

In *L. 'rudis'* and *L. arcana* there is an urgent need for much more refined methods of sampling before such a theory can be critically evaluated, and the following points should be taken into account:

(i) Collections of adult shells usually include several year classes, depending upon size structure and growth rates in the populations sampled. Seasonal changes in fitness of different morphs (Sheppard, 1951) or the abundance of predators selecting different morphs (Cain, 1983) would therefore be masked, limiting the value of such collections.

(ii) In collections from unspecified areas and habitat types (Atkinson and Warwick, 1983), it cannot be assumed that *L. 'rudis'* and *L. arcana* occupy similar microhabitats, or that they are equally available to predators. Differences in population structure, shell-shape and striation, and crevice-seeking behaviour may ensure that this is not the case. More account must be taken of very small scale patchiness in the zone occupied by these species, related for example to the ability of different bird species to perch and feed.

(iii) Even where *L. 'rudis'* and *L. arcana* occupy the same shore level, there is often only partial overlap in their vertical distributions (Table 11.3). Differences in morph frequency in this zone of overlap may result from differing selection acting on each species in its own zone of maximum abundance. Indeed, comparative data for both species occurring separately and together would be essential for a convincing demonstration of apostatic selection.

(iv) There is good evidence (p. 164; Heller, 1975b) that much of the proposed visual selection affects much smaller size-classes than those studied so far. Very little is yet known about the habitats of juvenile *L. arcana*, although seasonal breeding migrations (Hannaford Ellis, 1979) may well ensure separation between them and juvenile *L. 'rudis'*. This would render studies of the adults largely irrelevant, and would certainly invalidate apostatic selection as a basis of any observed differences. Future studies must overcome difficulties in distinguishing the juveniles of these species.

(v) The apparent similarity between *L. 'rudis'* and *L. arcana* may, in view of the reproductive differences, be due to convergent evolution rather than true relationship. If so, similar selection pressures may result in quite different colour morph responses, as has been found in *C. nemoralis* and *C. hortensis* (Jones *et al.*, 1977). This underlines the limitations of classifying colour phenotypes (Pettitt, 1973) without a knowledge of their genetics.

In conclusion, the various difficulties mentioned here, though considerable should not prove insurmountable. Data are needed concerning the relationship between colour morph frequencies and size (age) in habitats more clearly defined than has yet been attempted. Such information, coupled with better understanding of the behaviour of the visual predators, may reveal a great deal about the effects of predation upon natural populations.

11.7.3 Reproductive variation

L. 'rudis' is as highly variable in its reproductive biology as it is in its morphology. These variations include size at maturation, embryo size and reproductive effort, and are of interest because they provide an opportunity to study reproductive adaptations in contrasting habitats. Apart from their relevance to the ecology of *L. 'rudis'*, this variation is also of interest in more general discussions of reproductive strategies and their evolution (Pianka, 1970, 1976; Hirschfield and Tinkle, 1975; Stearns, 1976, 1977; Horn, 1978). These theories are directed at two interrelated problems; first, what factors influence reproductive effort (the proportion of assimilated energy devoted to reproduction) in individuals, populations or species; and second, what factors influence the relationship between numbers of embryos and their size. Stearns (1977) discussed the difficulties posed by these questions. Littorinids offer certain practical advantages, notably the relative ease with which populations can be delimited and at least some aspects of their dynamics studied.

Hughes and Roberts (1980a) and Hart and Begon (1982) have described aspects of life history theories relevant to littorinids. The following predictions are possible:

(i) Large reproductive effort is expected in populations dominated by density-independent mortality, where adult mortality is high and variable, and juvenile mortality low and more constant. Features of such populations may include early maturation, high age-specific fecundity and the production of numerous, small offspring.

(ii) Small reproductive effort is expected in populations whose environment is relatively stable, in which density-dependent mortality predominates, and where adult mortality rates are lower and less variable than those of juveniles. Features may include delayed maturation and production of large, hence (for a given expenditure) fewer embryos.

The reproductive literature concerning L. 'rudis' is presently much too restricted and open to widely differing interpretation to allow much useful generalization. The following discussion summarizes the available data and emphasizes areas where further critical investigation is needed.

The problems of defining and measuring reproductive effort have been discussed by Hughes and Roberts (1980a), who show that the interpretation of data depends upon the chosen definition. Reproductive effort, however defined, in four littorinids could not be correlated with reproductive method (oviparity, ovoviviparity, planktonic development). Hughes and Roberts concluded that different factors influence reproductive effort in each species, and that similar reproductive efforts may result from the operation of different ecological factors. Variation in egg size in L. 'rudis' was thought to reflect predation pressure in some habitats but not others, and it was emphasized that overall reproductive effort may be affected by factors other than those influencing embryo size. If this is true, it is unlikely that natural populations will correspond neatly to the general predictions of life history theories.

Similar general conclusions have been reached by Hart and Begon (1982) and Atkinson and Newbury (1984) who compared crevice and boulder populations of L. 'rudis'. Their results, together with those of Faller-Fritsch (1977, 1983) are summarized below in Table 11.4. The terms 'large' and 'small' are valid only within each study, their values having been calculated using different methods. Apart from certain observations common to each study, Table 11.4 reveals several inconsistencies both in the results and their interpretation. There is general agreement that mean shell length is greater in shelter and/or among boulders, and that size at maturation increases with increasing mean shell length. This relationship holds for widely differing populations (Faller-Fritsch, 1983), and has also been found in L. nigrolineata (Naylor and Begon, 1982). Maturation has been described as being delayed in sheltered populations (Faller-Fritsch, 1977), which may be incorrect as such populations grow more rapidly than those in exposure (Roberts and Hughes, 1980; Faller-Fritsch, 1983). It may however be valid to regard this as a physiological delay (Hart and Begon, 1982) if maturation is a function of size rather than age. Available data concerning age at maturation are insufficient to show whether there is significant variation (Faller-Fritsch, 1983).

Concerning embryo sizes and reproductive effort there are several fundamental differences in the three studies under consideration. Thus, larger embryos may occur in 'boulder' populations or 'crevice' populations, the latter being recorded also by Hughes and Roberts (1980a). Similarly, populations on boulders may show larger or smaller reproductive effort relative to those among crevices. The differing interpretations in each study are partly explicable in terms of these contrasting results, but also reflect fundamentally different assumptions about the rôles of density-dependent and independent mortality in contrasting habitats. There is a need for a critical review of these differences, and of the methods employed in each study.

The embryo size differences found by Faller-Fritsch (1977, 1983) were viewed as adaptive responses to different agents of mortality (crushing and desiccation among boulders, desiccation and dislodge-

TABLE 11.4

Summary of results and their interpretation in three studies of life history variation in *L. 'rudis'*.

Authors	Study site	Mean Shell length (mm)	Size at maturation (mm)	Embryo size	Reproductive effort	Interpretation
Faller-Fritsch (1977, 1983)	a. Greenhithe (sheltered boulders)	7.2	6–7	Large	Large	Large reproductive effort at (a) and (b) due to abundant food. Feeding time limited at (c). Crushing of juveniles at (a) and (b) selects for large embryos and delayed maturation. Need for dispersal at (c) selects for numerous, small embryos. High adult mortality selects for maturation at small size.
	b. Landshipping (sheltered boulders)	5.7	6–7	Intermediate	Large	
	c. Newhaven (exposed crevices)	4.9	4–5	Small	Small	
Hart and Begon (1982)	a. Abraham's Bosom (exposed boulders)	Large	11.4	Small	Small	Density-independent mortality (crushing) among boulders leads to delayed maturation and small reproductive effort allowing more growth. Numerous small young produced. Among crevices, dislodgement and/or desiccation cause density-dependent mortality. Selection favours early maturation and large embryos.
	b. Abraham's Bosom (exposed crevices)	Small	7.0	Large	Large	
Atkinson and Newbury (1984)	a. Cramond Island (sheltered boulders)	9.4	7.4	Large	–	Among crevices, dislodgement and desiccation cause high mortality rates throughout life. Selection favours early maturation. Small embryo size among crevices not discussed.
	b. Cramond Island (exposed crevices)	4.7	3.1	Small	–	

ment on exposed bedrock). The exposed population, and particularly its largest individuals, were shown to be crevice-limited (Emson and Faller-Fritsch, 1976) and the dispersal of young snails among empty barnacle shells was an essential requirement favouring maturation at small size and production of numerous, small offspring. This argument may not apply to crevice populations above the barnacle zone, where dispersal may be unimportant and large offspring may be less susceptible to desiccation. Competition with other species e.g. *L. arcana* may be locally significant; indeed, both Hughes and Roberts (1980a) and Hart and Begon (1982) found *L. arcana* among their crevice populations. Nevertheless, embryo size data from a variety of shores (Fig. 11.3) suggest a possible relationship between size and exposure or substratum stability. Embryos from unstable substrata are significantly larger than those from stable ones ($P < 0.05$ by Mann-Whitney U test), although considerable unexplained variation is clearly present. Reproductive effort in the three populations studied by Faller-Fritsch was seen as a reflection of food availability and feeding time, the latter being restricted on exposed bedrock. Estimation of reproductive effort in each population was based on a mean gestation period of 70 days (Berry, 1961; Roberts and Hughes, 1980). If the period is shorter when small embryos are produced, reproductive effort at Newhaven would have been underestimated. Hart and Begon (1982) showed that embryo size is a function both of initial egg weight and the amount of material absorbed from the broodpouch. Large embryos could therefore result from faster growth or prolonged gestation. Embryo sizes appear to remain constant in transplants of females between shores, suggesting a genetic influence upon embryo size (Faller-Fritsch, 1983).

Hart and Begon (1982) found delayed maturation and low reproductive effort in their boulder population, and interpreted this as a necessary adaptation in a habitat where crushing was a significant cause of mortality. Crushing was viewed as a density-independent factor, favouring the production of numerous, small young. Whether this is the case is arguable (see p. 165), and even if it is, large young would be less susceptible than small ones, so the argument appears contradictory. In addition, the measurement of reproductive effort based on samples at a single time assumes similar reproductive

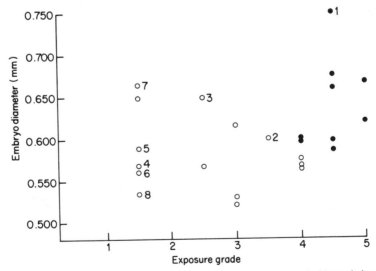

FIG. 11.3. Embryo diameter (mm), site exposure rating (Lewis scale) and substratum type in 24 populations of *L. 'rudis'*. Open circle = stable substratum, closed circle = mud or boulder substratum. Data from Faller-Fritsch (1983) except nos. 1–3 (Hughes and Roberts, 1980a) and 4–8 (new data). 4 = Manorbier, Dyfed; 5 = St Govans, Dyfed; 6 = Greenala Point, Dyfed; 7 = Black Head, Co. Clare; 8 = Lizard Point, Cornwall.

cycles and size-specific respiratory expenditure, which were not studied. In particular, there are as yet no data concerning levels of activity and respiration in contrasting habitats, and significant differences are highly probable.

A recent study (Atkinson and Newbury, 1984) provides yet different interpretations of reproductive variation. The results (maturation at small size, production of numerous small embryos) in a crevice population are very similar to those of Faller-Fritsch, but were interpreted differently. Desiccation was regarded as the major cause of mortality, and high rates of mortality were thought to act on all size classes. Large individuals were not considered to be particularly at risk, and were said to be able to survive well among the crevices, their scarcity being due to low chances of survival to large size. This interpretation is open to several criticisms. First, no evidence is presented that mortality rates in the crevice population are in reality higher than those among the neighbouring boulders. Mortality data were derived only from short-term mark–recapture studies in the crevice population. In other boulder populations of *L. 'rudis'* very high rates of mortality have been recorded (Fig. 11.1). Second, there is no evidence that large individuals were successful among the boulders, except that large *L. littorea* were also present. Favourable surface area: volume ratios and the relatively smaller aperture of *L. littorea* render comparisons with *L. 'rudis'* invalid. The size structure of the crevice *L. 'rudis'* population (Atkinson and Newbury, unpubl. data) shows that individuals larger than 7mm make up only 5% of the population, contrasting with the statement that 'large winkles are able to survive well among the crevices'. Third, high mortality rates due to desiccation would be expected to favour large size at hatching, the opposite of the observed results. Indeed, the significance of the production of numerous small embryos is nowhere discussed.

It is clear from the foregoing that much more work is needed on the problems of reproductive variation in *L. 'rudis'*. Central to this work must be the identification and measurement of causes and rates of mortality in different habitats. Atkinson and Newbury (1984) argued that reproductive strategies 'are best understood by reference to the specific ecology of the population rather than by generalizations such as *r*- and *K*- selection'. It is necessary to add that untested generalizations concerning mortality also stand in the way of such understanding.

11.8 Conclusions

The studies reviewed here show that *L. 'rudis'* and its relatives provide remarkable material with which to study processes of littoral adaptation, although formidable problems remain to be overcome. The variability of *L. 'rudis'* clearly results from limited mobility coupled with patchiness of the habitats occupied. Much previous work has involved comparisons between strongly contrasting habitats. It is now necessary to study variation on a much smaller scale. This will require knowledge of actual (rather than assumed) mobility, and methods of quantifying the features of upper shore micro-habitats. The microflora of the upper littoral zone appears to have been largely neglected since the studies of Aleem (1950) and Castenholz (1961, 1963). Knowledge of this microflora, in conjunction with measurements of physical parameters, may significantly add to our knowledge of factors affecting the littorinid populations of the upper littoral. Indeed, it may even be possible to define the features of this zone on different shores based on the composition of the microflora, in a way analogous with the biological exposure scales of Ballantine (1961b) and Lewis (1964). This would provide a firm basis for studying intraspecific variation in littorinids, as well as being relevant to problems of coexistence, e.g. between *L. 'rudis'* and *L. arcana*.

Previous studies have established quantitative methods by which the complex problems of intra-specific variation in littorinids may be attacked. The continuing interest in this subject encourages the view that the challenge is being taken up.

CHAPTER XII

THE BIOLOGY OF THE LIMPET *PATELLA VULGATA* L. IN THE BRITISH ISLES: SPAWNING TIME AS A FACTOR DETERMINING RECRUITMENT SUCCESS

R.S. Bowman

12.1 Introduction

During the 1960s and early 1970s, the population dynamics of certain 'key' rocky shore species were studied around the British Isles, in order to elucidate the spatial and temporal changes in their communities and to explore some of the ideas propounded by Lewis (1964) on the factors controlling the species' geographical range. Preliminary results on the most 'amenable' species, *Patella vulgata* L., were published by Lewis and Bowman (1975) and Bowman and Lewis (1977), when the following inferences were presented:

(i) Recruitment success varied considerably both geographically and annually, but in spite of considerable recruitment 'noise', caused by biological interactions, the intra-regional success pattern was similar.

(ii) Recruitment failure in N. Yorkshire was attributed to the spat experiencing severe cold within a few weeks of settlement (the 'frost hypothesis'), and regional settlement patterns tended to reinforce this relationship.

(iii) The limited data available suggested considerable annual and geographical differences in the breeding cycle, particularly in the timing and frequency of spawning.

It was then suggested (Bowman and Lewis, 1977) that the geographical limits of *P. vulgata* might be set to the North by reproductive failure or by spat intolerance of low winter temperature, and to the South by desiccation of spat or by their intolerance of high temperatures during autumn or the summer after settlement.

These preliminary conclusions were based on data gathered over seven years from N. Yorkshire, and over four or five years from Scotland and Wales. Since 1974 the geographical coverage of these studies has been expanded to clarify regional differences in recruitment, and to explore some outstanding questions, viz:

Is there regularly a geographical difference in breeding season, and if so how is it achieved? How frequent are multiple spawnings, and how relatively successful are their spatfalls? If timing of spawning is vital to settlement success, what is the spawning stimulus? and to what extent are spat survival and recruitment success influenced by planktonic/hydrographic factors or by conditions during early shore life?

Questions involving survival of the spat demanded a new approach – to detect spat immediately after settlement, i.e. well before they emerged on the observation sites – this was eventually achieved by the use of settlement plates. The programme has inevitably been a compromise between the conflicting needs for simultaneous geographical coverage and intensive local and experimental plate work, and for work on other species. As a result, not until it was felt that regional trends had been sufficiently established was it possible to concentrate on the studies of spat settlement and survival.

Geographical coverage was therefore most extensive from 1974 to 1979, with selectively reduced coverage thereafter, mainly in Scotland. Settlement-plate studies began in 1979 and are still in progress; a detailed account of this work is currently in preparation, but some interim results are presented here where relevant. A further aid to understanding breeding and recruitment patterns has been the development of an *in situ* shore/sea temperature recorder, operative (with occasional lapses) on the shore at Robin Hood's Bay since April, 1981.

12.2 Geographical Variation in Recruitment

Fig. 12.1A shows the regions studied around the British Isles; the numbers in brackets indicate the number of shores visited regularly and the total number of observation sites in each region. Fig. 12.1B shows the principal shores worked in each region; those in brackets were discontinued after 1976, when effort was switched to S.W. England. A preliminary assessment of recruitment variation for these principal shores is presented in Bowman and Lewis (1977). Though the sites were deliberately chosen to minimize habitat variability, and where possible to resemble those found most favourable for settlement and accessibility at Robin Hood's Bay (Lewis and Bowman, 1975), it became clear that

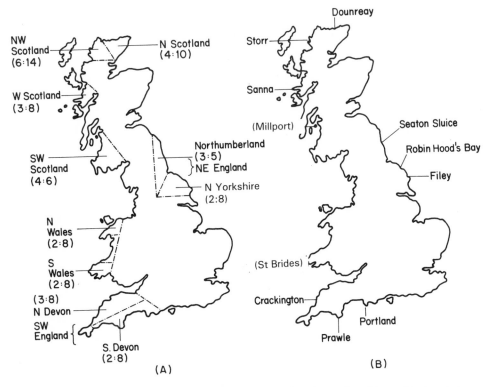

FIG. 12.1. A, Map showing regions studied around the British Isles: brackets give number of shores visited regularly per region and total number of 1m² observation sites. B, Principal shores worked in each region.

elsewhere in Britain biological variability in the mid-shore is greater than at Robin Hood's Bay, with only rare exceptions. This is the result of any combination of a number of factors rarely found on N. Yorkshire shores, namely (i) frequent 'blanket' settlements of *Semibalanus* (= *Balanus*) *balanoides* (L.), capable of filling all available space and ousting limpets from the sites; (ii) greater instability of (exposed-shore) populations of small-sized *Mytilus edulis* L., resulting (a) from their greater growth rate and storm losses, (b) from the higher shore range of their chief predators *Nucella* (= *Thais*) *lapillus* (L.) and *Asterias rubens* L., and (c) additional predation by eider ducks (*Somateria mollissima* (L.)); (iii) less extensive shores and (hence?) lower densities of limpets, resulting in more variable algal cover (mainly *Fucus vesiculosus* L.) and partly a result of (iv) regular, and intermittently catastrophic, predation of limpets by oystercatchers (*Haematopus ostralegus* L.).

Changes in *Mytilus* cover in particular were known to affect site recruitment potential (Lewis and Bowman, 1975) by altering wetness or availability of settlement crannies. In order to counteract this biological 'noise' more shores and sites were included in the study, and spat counts were also taken from large littoral pools and low-shore wet rock, where desiccation would be unaltered. These extra data permitted compensatory interpretation following temporary change in an individual site's recruitment potential resulting from short-term biological or physical aberrations or unusual climatic events. Though strict statistical analysis is not therefore possible, an assessment of recruitment success is presented in Table 12.1. The correlation of settlement success with hard winters and early frosts from 1969 to 1974 was discussed by Bowman and Lewis (1977), and the subsequent years' data broadly supported this correlation. At Robin Hood's Bay there was subsequently a period remarkable for the absence of early autumn frosts, and, as predicted, there were no recruitment failures – see Fig. 12.2B. Settlement totals at Robin Hood's Bay were very variable however: the 1978 input at most sites exceeded by three times the previous ten-year mean, in spite of experiencing the very cold and stormy winter of 1978/9, the worst since 1970. The eventual numbers of spat found on many of the observation sites were undoubtedly reduced in N. and N.W. Scotland and N.E. England by severe cold and storms in this winter (1978/9) and in that of 1981/2, and by excessive heat/desiccation in the summer of 1976, though mainly because of loss of *Mytilus* and *Fucus* cover.

TABLE 12.1

Assessment of regional recruitment success in *Patella vulgata* since the start of monitoring. ++ = very good; + = good; 0 = moderate; − = poor; ? = record incomplete.

Spawning year:	66	67	68	69	70	71	72	73	74	75	76	77	78	79	80	81	82
N. Scotland				+	+	+	+	−	−	0	+	++	+	+	+	0	−
N.W. Scotland					+	+	−	−	−	0	+	+	0	+	+	0	0
W. Scotland					+	0	0	0	−	0	+	++	+	−	0	−	+
S.W. Scotland					−?	−	+	−?									
N.E. England	−	−	0	+	+	−	−	0	0	0	+	+	++	0	0	−	−
S. Wales									−	+	+	+					
N. Devon											+	0	0	0	−	+	++
S. Devon											+	0	0	+	++	0	++

Short data runs from S.W. England and Wales, together with a much smaller mean input per site and lower annual variability in Scotland than in N.E. England (e.g. Dounreay: mean input·m^{-2} ($\pm$ one S.D.) 62 $\pm$ 21; Storr: 20 $\pm$ 18; Sanna: 37 $\pm$ 23; Robin Hood's Bay: 216 $\pm$ 133) make assessment of input success more difficult. It would appear that the pattern of success was broadly similar over northern Britain, being good to moderate from 1975 to 1980, and moderate to poor in 1981 and 1982. There is less agreement with this pattern in S.W. Scotland and a different pattern in southern Britain.

12.3 Geographical Variation in Spawning Time

As shown in Fig. 12.2A, from 1975 onwards spawning in N.E. England tended to start earlier than in the preceding years, i.e. in September in 1976, 1977 and 1978, and in August in 1980 and 1981. There was often considerable redevelopment of gonads (in 1977 and 1978) and one or more subsequent spawnings. This spawning pattern resembled that previously seen in N. and N.W. Scotland and repeated over this period.

At Robin Hood's Bay, weekly or even more frequent gonad sampling was possible – indeed necessary – to ascertain onset and frequency of spawning and redevelopment, but regional gonad sampling was possible only two or three times each autumn, at monthly intervals from August to October. Sampling from S.W. England was further restricted, though occasionally supplemented by preserved samples from the Plymouth Marine Laboratory.

It was possible to detect whether recent spawning had occurred from the colour of the fresh gonads (see Orton *et al.*, 1956) and the amount of loose (= ripe) eggs and sperm. With experience, redevelopment could also be detected using similar criteria; both states can easily be recognized histologically. Orton's Gonad Index classification (*op. cit.*) was used as a subjective measure of gametic output. Although this is a fairly crude measure, it can be done on the spot; quantitative methods using gonad weight or volume, or egg/oocyte size–frequencies proved no better at indicating first release and were markedly less sensitive at detecting small incomplete spawnings and redevelopment, particularly when populations spawned asynchronously, e.g. in secondary spawnings.

In N.E. England it was sometimes possible to pinpoint the day of spawning as it usually occurred during a rough sea, but elsewhere one could determine only whether spawning had occurred before the sampling date, and whether the gonads were still developing or redeveloping. Rarely, a sampling

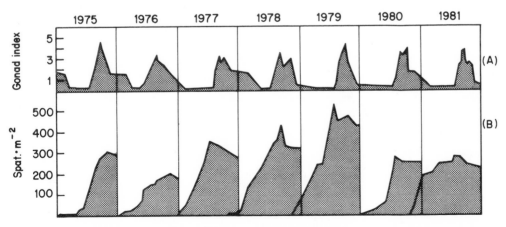

FIG. 12.2. The Gonad Index (A) and recruitment record (B) at Site 2, Robin Hood's Bay. N.B. Recruitment each year is derived from the spawning of the previous autumn.

trip coincided with a storm producing spawning, as in N. Scotland between 24th and 27th August, 1977, and in N. and N.W. Scotland on a Force 11 storm between 16th and 17th September, 1979. Often, however, recently-spawned gonads were found shortly after storms had been reported by local inhabitants or the BBC.

Table 12.2 shows for each region the approximate date of first release of gametes and subsequent (observed) duration of the breeding season. It can be seen that spawning had frequently started before late August or mid-September in N. and N.W. Scotland, a little later (mid-September/October) in W. and S.W. Scotland. There was usually a variable degree of redevelopment and secondary spawning before the 'main' or final release which usually occurred during October for all Scottish populations, except at Millport where spawning could be as late as December. Spawning did not occur in N. Wales before October, or in S.W. England before late October/November, but there the frequency of redevelopment and duration of the breeding period could not be determined. In N.E. England the 'normal' time for first release is now thought to be September/October rather than late October as presumed up to 1974. These data, together with other reports of the breeding period around southern Britain and France (Evans, 1953; Orton et al., 1956; Choquet, 1966; Thompson, 1980) confirm the suspicion (Bowman and Lewis, 1977) that in any given year there is a North–South shift in the time of onset of spawning.

To increase comparability, the gonads examined were all from limpets taken from the mid-shore, as at Robin Hood's Bay, but subsidiary samples were taken from different shore levels to test for synchrony. In no year did gonads from any population fail to develop; the populations showing poorest gonad development (in terms of maximum size) were in N.E. England not, as might have been expected, in N. Scotland. Also, though it was difficult to quantify, redevelopment after first release seemed to be greater in N. and N.W. Scotland than in N.E. England; it was certainly more common-place and possibly of longer duration.

Within the regional pattern of spawning time there could be considerable local variation in the onset of spawning. Whilst first release occurred synchronously (as far as could be ascertained) at all exposed shores within the region (and sometimes over several adjacent regions) limpets on nearby sheltered/embayed shores sometimes did not release until a later general spawning. Early release, redevelopment and asynchrony of gonad development were therefore more commonly found in exposed shore populations than on sheltered shores.

There appears to be a broader pattern of gonad development superimposed on the regional pattern. Thus, first release occurred earlier throughout the North in the years 1977 to 1980, and redevelop-

TABLE 12.2

Estimated time of first release of gametes in *Patella vulgata* and observed spawning period. e = early; l = late; A = August; S = September; O = October; N = November.

Spawning year	Scotland				Wales		Devon	
	N.	N.W.	W.	S.W.	N.	S.	N.	S.
1973	mS	mS	mS	mN	mO–?			
1974	mS	mS	mO	?N	mO–?			
1975	eS–O	eS–O	?lS/O	eO–?	eO–?			
1976	mS–O	mS–O	lS–O	lO–N				
1977	lA–O	lA–O	mS–O	mO–N		lO–N		
1978	eS–N	eS–O	mS–O					
1979	eS–O	eS–O	lS–O			lS/O–?	m/lN	mN–?
1980	lA–?	lA–O	mS–?				O/N–?	lO–?

ment after first release was absent or markedly less than in subsequent years throughout Scotland in 1973 and 1974; gonad development at Robin Hood's Bay in 1974 was the poorest yet recorded (see Bowman and Lewis, 1977).

12.4 The Spawning Stimulus

12.4.1 Regional evidence

Earlier work has linked spawning with autumn storms, not only in *Patella vulgata* but also in *P. aspera* Lamarck (Thompson, 1979, and pers. obs.), *P. depressa* Pennant (Orton and Southward, 1961), various S. African *Patella* spp. (Branch, 1974a), and other littoral gastropods (Grange, 1976). At Robin Hood's Bay, however, the connection was not wholly satisfactory: in particular the first release did not always coincide with the first storm of the autumn. It could be argued that insufficient wave action or gonad ripeness might explain non-release, yet a sea state causing release in only partially-developed gonads at Robin Hood's Bay might not, at another time or place, stimulate release from much more fully-developed gonads. Unsuccessful attempts to stimulate spawning artificially in limpets in the laboratory and on the shore, using powerful jets of seawater, probably demonstrated only the inadequacies of the method.

Although no relation could be demonstrated between spawning and Robin Hood's Bay inshore sea temperatures during 1968 to 1974 (*op. cit.*), the sparse sea-temperature data available for Scotland during 1974 to 1980 suggested that years of earlier spawning (1977–1980, with regional variations) had below-average sea temperatures in August and/or September (see Table 12.3). In particular it was noticed on early autumn sampling trips that when the sea temperature (taken at low tide in deep water off the observation area) was recorded as being at or below 12°C spawning had occurred, but when the sea temperature was well above 12°C either gonads were not spawned or redevelopment was occurring. When spawning was found to have occurred at exposed but not at adjacent embayed/sheltered shores, sea temperature at the latter was found to be 2–4°C higher than at the former.

At Robin Hood's Bay storms were often associated with decreased sea temperature, but as temperatures were unavoidably taken in shallow bay water at low tide, and were known to be warmer than true sea temperatures particularly in summer, no conclusions could be drawn from such data. Examination of Meteorological Office sea temperature records taken at the Humber Light Vessel suggested that

TABLE 12.3

Sea temperature anomalies in Scotland over the breeding seasons 1974–80. Means are for 1965–80; temperatures obtained from the Meteorological Office, local sources and personal visits.

	N. Scotland			N.W. Scotland			W. Scotland		
	Aug	*Sept*	*Oct*	*Aug*	*Sept*	*Oct*	*Aug*	*Sept*	*Oct*
Mean temp. (°C):	12.7	11.8	10.25	13.0	11.7	10.6	13.0	12.7	11.7
1974	+ 0.5	− 0.7	+ 0.8	0	+ 0.1	+ 0.4	− 1.0	+ 0.3	+ 0.6
1975	+ 0.5	− 0.7	+ 0.8	+ 1.0	+ 1.1	+ 1.4	+ 1.0	+ 0.5	+ 0.3
1976	nd	+ 0.2	0	nd	− 0.5	nd		− 0.5	nd
1977	− 0.8	nd	nd	nd	− 0.5	− 0.1		+ 0.3	+ 0.3
1978	nd	− 0.3	0	nd	− 0.7	− 0.6		− 0.2	− 1.0
1979	nd	− 1.3	nd	nd	− 0.2	− 0.1		nd	+ 0.3
1980	− 1.5	nd	nd	− 1.0	+ 0.7	nd		− 0.2	nd

some autumn storms were not accompanied by a drop in sea temperature, but during 'spawning storms' the temperature dropped markedly.

Spawning in response to a *rise* in sea temperature past a critical level has been recorded in a variety of molluscs: the Antarctic limpet *Nacella concinna* Strebel (Picken, 1980; Picken and Allen, 1983); American *Acmaea* spp. (Fritchman, 1962a,b), and several bivalves (Nelson, 1928a; Ansell and Lander, 1967; Lammens, 1967). Only rarely has spawning been linked with a drop in sea temperature past a critical level: in the Bay scallop (Barber and Blake, 1983) and possibly in the S. African *Patella oculus* Born. (Branch, 1974a).

Fig. 12.3A shows the mean monthly sea temperatures around the British Isles. There is a marked similarity between each region's 'typical' time of first release and the month in which its sea temperature first drops below 12°C. In N. Scotland the maximum summer sea temperature is so close to this proposed critical temperature that any storm is likely to cause spawning, given sufficient gonad development, except in areas of inshore warming. It is not impossible that open-coast sea temperatures here might not exceed 12°C in cool summers (i.e. perhaps in 1977 or 1978), but since the Meteorological Office discontinued sea temperature recording in Scotland from 1976 there are insufficient data to resolve this. In contrast, in N. Devon in 1980, two days of very rough seas on 23rd and 24th November reduced the sea temperature only to 13°C: no spawning occurred in limpets whose gonads were full 'to bursting point' (Gonad Index 4.2).

12.4.2 Sea temperature records

However suggestive is the evidence that spawning might be triggered by storms producing a drop in sea temperature to below a critical level, the connection remained tenuous due to a lack of detailed and accurate sea temperature data for the observation shores. Accordingly, a system was devised which was

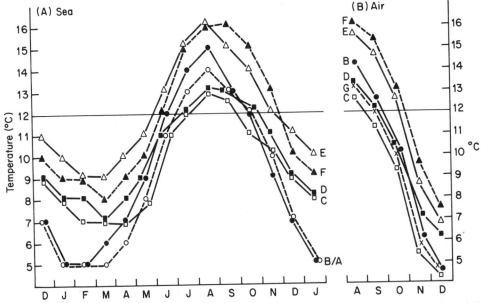

FIG. 12.3. Mean monthly sea and air temperatures in the regions studied. A, Sea temperature means for A) Humber, 1965–80; B) Robin Hood's Bay inshore, 1969–80; C) N. Scotland, 1965–75; D) W. Scotland, 1965–75; E) Sevenstones, 1965–80; F) Channel, 1965–80. B, Air temperature means for B) Whitby (for Robin Hood's Bay), 1962–76; C) Dounreay, 1961–75; D) Tiree (for Sanna), 1961–75; E) Bude (for N. Devon), 1961–72; F) Portland, 1941–70; G) Inverpolly (for Storr), 1963–1972. Data from the Meteorological Office.

capable of recording rock-surface temperature continuously during high and low water. The first version was installed at M.T.L. on the shore at Robin Hood's Bay about 150m (horizontally) from the limpet sampling area, in April, 1981. Briefly, it consisted of a platinum resistance probe cemented onto the shore, the probe end only just below the concrete surface, and connected by several hundred feet of cable (running up the shore inside the Wellcome Marine Laboratory's seawater intake pipe) to a flatbed chart recorder. Because the system's electronics and recording apparatus were inside the Laboratory, they could be mains-operated, but when the Laboratory was closed in December, 1982 a self-contained, battery-operated system had to be devised. The new apparatus comprises a similar probe connected by only a metre of cable to a Grant MR1U solid-state-memory recorder bolted to the shore inside watertight plastic and steel housings. Temperature readings are taken at pre-set intervals (storage capacity 21 days' readings taken at 30 minute intervals) and can be transferred via a transcription unit to either a chart recorder or into a computer. This system has been in operation at Robin Hood's Bay since July, 1983.

The results thus obtained are shown in Fig. 12.4. Record A depicts the maximum and minimum sea temperature at high water over each period of 15 tides, or between gonad samples if this was shorter, during the breeding seasons 1981 to 1983. Comparison of this record with the old method of taking sea temperatures showed that, particularly during fine calm weather, the body of water previously sampled could attain temperatures of 4–6°C above 'true' sea temperature. The probe, situated at exactly M.T.L., recorded these elevated temperatures for only about 30 minutes after the tide first reached it. This spotlights the inadequacy of most shore-based manual sampling methods and the unlikelihood of their detecting temperature-controlled mechanisms in the field.

On the graph, the broken vertical bars show a continuous fall in sea temperature sustained over a minimum of three consecutive night tides (daytime sea temperatures are sometimes elevated a little by insolation). As shown, these drops in sea temperature are usually, *but not always*, associated with rough seas (shown by vertical bars along the baseline: solid blocks indicate continuous stormy conditions). Such drops probably indicate break-up of the summer thermocline in early autumn, and/or the influx of a colder body of offshore water from a seiche produced by gales elsewhere in the North Sea, as was the large drop in mid-August, 1982 (marked * in Fig. 12.4A).

12.4.3 Gonad state

Fig. 12.4B shows the gonad state of Robin Hood's Bay mid-shore limpets, from a population which is sufficiently large to be unaffected by such heavy sampling, but is also representative of other, and more exposed, local populations. Points on the dotted line show the Gonad Index of samples of *c.* 80 individuals, taken as frequently as possible, ideally at weekly or shorter intervals, particularly when spawning was judged to be imminent. The vertical bars show the percentage of limpets spawning or having spawned.

Spawning is seen from the graph as a drop in the Gonad Index (G.I.), or as an increase in numbers spawning, or both. Continued or new development is indicated by a subsequent increase in G.I. or by a decrease in spawners, or both. It is clear that spawning can occur early in the season while the G.I. is still increasing (e.g. in August, 1980 and 1981). Such spawnings can soon be masked by continued gonad development and are therefore likely to be missed by infrequent or mis-timed sampling. In these spawnings, the gametes released are from only partially-developed gonads (Stage 3 or 4 on Orton's scale) and comprise only a small proportion of the limpet's potential output. Since gonad development within the population is not completely synchronized (cf. Orton *et al.*, 1956; Blackmore, 1969a; Workman, 1983), only a small proportion of the population, and particularly of the females, contain gametes ripe enough to be released. The total potential larval production from these early spawnings must be small compared to the output from later releases: the volume ratio of gonad stages 5:4:3:2 in Robin

Hood's Bay limpets is of the order 8:4:2:1, so a decrease from a fully-developed Stage 5 or 4 gonad involves the release of at least half its gametic production.

When early spawnings occur before development is complete, the gonad size (and therefore G.I.) finally reached is sub-maximal, thus years with early release have a lower peak G.I. than when spawning is delayed until after all the gametes are fully developed (cf. G.I.s for 1980–83 with those for 1975 and 1979, Fig. 12.2). Continued development of gametes after early spawning is not to be confused with redevelopment, which is the production of a second generation of gametocytes late in the season. These might develop fully and be released or might remain unspawned over the winter, to be resorbed at the start of the next breeding season. Redevelopment is more common in males but easier to detect, morphologically and histologically, in females: the small decreases in spawners late in the breeding season thus denote female redevelopment.

12.4.4 Initiation of spawning

Comparison of the records in Fig. 12.4A and B show clearly that spawning was triggered not by the first storm or fall in sea temperature of the season, but when the sea temperature first fell below 12°C, whether or not this was accompanied by rough seas. Thus the falls in mid-August, 1981 and 1983, did not produce spawning in gonads at a developmental state almost identical to that in mid-August, 1982, when a small but definite spawning was induced by a fall to just below 12°C.

After the initial release, if sea temperature rose again to above 12°C the gonads continued to increase in size as more gametes became fully developed, and the number of spawners fell or showed no increase (see early September in 1981, 1982; September–October, 1983). Further bursts of spawning were triggered subsequently every time the sea temperature again fell below 12°C (mid- and late September and mid-October, 1981; mid-September, 1982), again with an increase in G.I./decrease in spawners if the sea temperature rose above 12°C again between samples (e.g. between 27th September and 3rd October, 1981). These changes in gonad state, though small, were not caused by sampling error – they occurred in other local population samples.

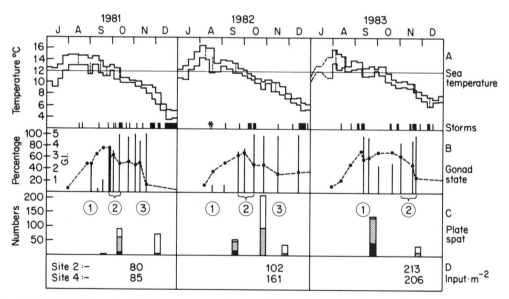

FIG. 12.4. The detailed records of A, Sea temperature and storms; B, Gonad Index and percentage spawning; C, Settlement on plates from each spatfall; D, Site input at Robin Hood's Bay for the 1981–83 breeding seasons. For explanations see text.

By mid-October each year the sea temperature had begun its steady decline to the February winter minimum, and no longer returned above 12°C. By this time, virtually all gametes were fully developed, and further releases were recorded immediately after periods of rough seas not necessarily associated with abrupt drops in sea temperature (cf. November, 1982 and 1983; October and November, 1981). Even so, spells of calm sunny weather in late autumn, often characterized by a halt in the decline of sea temperature, could result in a temporary decrease in spawners or even a small increase in G.I. (October/November, 1982; early November, 1981). These changes were also mirrored in other populations locally.

The triggering of spawning by the first fall to below 12°C is reinforced by data from other North-Eastern shores. Thus in 1983 initial spawning occurred synchronously at all exposed-shore sites examined over *c.* 200km of coastline in N.E. England, and at all these sites the sea temperature had fallen below 12°C for the first time that season. On adjacent embayed shores, where shallow water and restricted tidal movement had led to marked inshore warming, the fall in sea temperature left it above 12°C and spawning did not occur.

It is still arguable whether the same 12°C trigger is operating in other parts of Britain, or whether it varies over the species' geographical range as shown for the Bay scallop (Barber and Blake, 1983). Shore recorders sited in Scotland and Wales should help to answer this question. However, the same storm that produced the above spawning in N.E. England in September, 1983, also produced the autumn's first sea temperature drop to below 12°C in N.W. Scotland: a collecting trip three days later found considerable very recent spawning. In Scotland, it was not the first storm of the autumn. (N.B. The timing of this trip was fortuitous. The temperature data were not received until October. In fact, limpet samples are deliberately examined before the temperature record is checked, to preclude any influence, however unconscious, on categorizing the gonads.)

12.5 Settlement Success

It is clear from this detailed analysis of limpet breeding seasons at Robin Hood's Bay that the various spawnings produce different quantities of gametes, depending on the time elapsing before first release and the amount of redevelopment between later spawnings. Yet even a small early release results in appreciable numbers of young limpets either becoming visible on the shore well before winter (Fig. 12.2: 1977/78, 1978/79 and 1980/81), or, being found after winter at above-usual size, as seen in Scotland after the early spawnings in 1977, 1978 and 1980. These later data re-affirm the conclusion (Bowman and Lewis, 1977) that eventual input is not closely related to maximum attained gonad size, or the amount of gametes liberated at one release.

12.5.1 Settlement on plates

It was previously considered impossible to ascertain the contribution from different spawnings to shore spat totals, because of the lag of up to six months between presumed time of settlement and the emergence of young limpets on the observation sites. To resolve this problem, grooved 10cm square Tufnol settlement plates were fixed on the shore in permanent pools at Robin Hood's Bay, so they could be brought into the laboratory for microscopic examination whenever the tide permitted, daily if necessary. Spat of known age could also be subjected to laboratory or field experimentation without being detached from their plates. This work has yielded a wealth of information on settlement preferences, growth rates and survival of newly-settled spat. Space precludes a detailed account of these findings here, but the results are currently being prepared for publication. Only aspects having a direct bearing on the scope of this paper will be summarized here.

To follow the fate of spat on the shore, plates were positioned in mid-shore 'lithothamnion' pools, where spat settlement and survival were known to be good. Settlement began within 10–14 days of spawning, which confirmed not only the spawning but also earlier estimates of the length of the plank-tonic phase in *P. vulgata* (Smith, 1935; Dodd, 1957). Veligers were 0.25mm in diameter, and numbers continued to increase on the plates for three to four weeks after the start of settlement, partly because the spat tended at first to hide in the sediment and microflora in the base of the grooves. Provided that spawnings were sufficiently separated, it was possible to distinguish their settlements, and to follow the growth and fate of the spat in the different cohorts until they died or moved off the plates. It was possible to distinguish between mortality and emigration by the size, mobility and appearance of the animals lost. Emigration coincided with the emergence of such spat in the pools and later on the observation sites.

The spawnings whose inputs could be separated are shown in Fig. 12.4B. By comparing the sizes of spat on the plates with data on size–frequency of input on the adjacent observation sites, it was possible to determine the contributions of the different settlements to the site total. The results are shown in Table 12.4. The site concerned is the wet-rock M.T.L. site at Robin Hood's Bay (Site 5 in Bowman and Lewis, 1977) which shows the greatest range of recruitment and earliest emergence of spat. At this site it was not possible to separate the settlements from the August and September, 1981, spawnings by June, 1982, when the site measurements were made.

Two features stand out: the total failure of the November, 1981, spawning to contribute to site input after the severe winter of 1981/1982, and the disproportionately large settlement from the first spawning in September, 1983. Because of annual differences in the siting of the settlement plates in this area it is not possible to compare plate-settlement densities directly with site input, but a similarly very heavy settlement occurred in October, 1979. This is a relatively sheltered part of Robin Hood's Bay, unusual among the sites worked there in experiencing sporadic very heavy recruitments (see Bowman and Lewis, 1977) which were suspected to be the result, at least partially, of hydrographic influences. The September, 1983, settlement occurred after spawning had been followed by 10 days of calm sunny weather, possibly minimizing larval dispersal.

12.5.2 Size and fate of settlements

At the exposed headland location of Site 2, Robin Hood's Bay, plate-settlement data were collected each year from the same settlement pool, located at M.T.L. midway between Site 2 and the similar, but lower, Site 4. The settlement on plates resulting from the indicated spawnings are shown in Fig. 12.4C. The overall height of the columns indicates mean total spat settlement per plate per spawning (mean of 4 plates); the columns are positioned over the approximate period of peak numbers.

There would appear to be closer agreement here between the size of spawning and the numbers

TABLE 12.4

Percentage contribution of different spatfalls to the shore input of *Patella vulgata* at Site 5, Robin Hood's Bay. Figures are positioned to indicate the period when each spatfall settled on the plates. Site total is the peak input recorded the year following settlement.

Spatfall in:	Sept	Oct	Nov	Dec	Site spat input·m⁻²
1979		46.6	46.0	7.4	654
1980	60.0	40.0			243
1981	100.0		0.0		319
1982	50.2	40.0	8.8		496
1983	81.7		18.3		3130

settling, though without a quantitative estimate of gametic production no statistical correlation is possible. Even so, there are anomalies, e.g. the size of the first input in 1982 compared to that of the surely greater release in 1981. Each year's input is here of the same order of magnitude; not as at Site 5. This might be because the hydrographic/planktonic effects thought to operate at Site 5 are unlikely to have so much effect at this exposed site, which has deep water and strong tidal currents immediately off the headland, and wind strength and direction have previously provided no explanation of relative settlement success (Bowman and Lewis, 1977).

Fig. 12.4D shows the eventual maximum input numbers per square metre on Sites 2 and 4, obtained during the year after the spawning/settlement records. Clearly, the total settlement on plates bears no relation to the site input, but consideration of the numbers leaving the plates (emigrants) reveals a correlation with eventual site totals. In Fig. 12.4C the solid portion of each column indicates the numbers of spat per plate from that settlement which emigrate from the plate before the onset of winter (= mid-December). The siblings of these emigrants simultaneously emerge from their shore settlement micro-habitats and can be found in pools and, shortly afterwards, on the observation sites. Only fast-growing spat from early inputs are large enough to emerge from their settlement refuges before winter. The hatched portion of each column indicates those which survive the winter on the plates and emigrate in the spring, and the unshaded portion denotes spat which die. Mortality is thus very high in late settlements, hence their generally poor contribution to shore input, regardless of size of settlement. Total survivors do not correlate well with site totals, but this is probably because experimental studies showed that overwinter survival, particularly of small late-settlers, is much higher in these mid-shore pools than in the habitats offered by the observation sites. Fig. 12.5 shows site input (as a mean of Sites 2 and 4) plotted against (A) total survivors per plate from early (August and September) settlements; and (B) pre-winter emigrants. Again there is no relation between site input and total survivors from early settlements, but there is a clear relationship with pre-winter emigrants (r = 0.97, 2 d.f., P < 0.05).

The original premise of the 'frost hypothesis', that success depends on early settlement, can now be re-formulated, viz. success depends on the numbers of spat large enough to emerge from their settlement micro-habitat before the onset of winter. Other spat apparently stand a poor chance of survival, depending on their size and habitat.

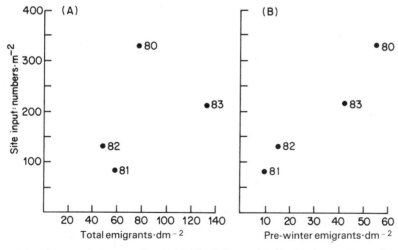

FIG. 12.5. Correlations between site input totals at Robin Hood's Bay and A, Total emigrants from early spatfalls; B, Pre-winter emigrants.

12.5.3 Factors affecting survival

The factors affecting survival which cause this relationship are not as simple as originally believed; they are still being investigated and will be reported in due course. Interim results suggest the following:

(i) There is no evidence of outright frost-kill of spat, as originally hypothesized, though there might be some for veligers (cf. Beaumont and Budd, 1982). Instead the effects of winter cold are apparently cumulative: even in mild winters, spat which fail to reach emergent size remain immobile on settlement plates (and presumably in the shore settlement refuges), and grow little between December and April/May. Their numbers decline slowly, largely because of wash-out from settlement refugia during winter storms and also, probably, because of starvation. In mild winters and on less exposed shores more of these might survive to contribute to the shore population.

(ii) Severe winter cold stunts growth and produces irreversible shell damage which leads ultimately to the animal's death (described briefly in Bowman, 1981). The severity of this effect varies inversely with the size of spat, thus the earlier the cold, and the later the settlement, the greater will be the effect on more spat. Only in very cold and prolonged winters, e.g. 1981/82, are early settlers affected, though they usually survive.

In northern limpet populations, therefore, input success depends on early spawning and settlement, allowing the spat to grow sufficiently to survive the winter. These results do not altogether explain the controlling factors in southern populations, where winters are much milder (see Fig. 12.3A and B). There are however some indications, even at Robin Hood's Bay, of a heat-stress factor operating on the spat, and this is also currently under investigation.

12.6 Discussion

12.6.1 Breeding strategy

a) *Size of release.* In regions subject to hard winters, if spat survival and resultant shore input densities depend on the timing of spawning, it would seem advantageous for the limpet population to spawn as early as possible. Yet it seems logical that the quantity of gametes released must be reflected in the numbers settling, unless masked by over-riding hydrographic/planktonic factors. It is therefore conceivable that in some years later settlements could contribute significantly to shore input. In N.E. England, the very extensive rocky shores and high densities of the limpet breeding population (100–500·m^{-2}), and the synchrony of first release, probably ensure that even a very small early release produces sufficient larvae to result in some settlement, despite undoubted heavy losses in the plankton. In regions with shores of limited extent and/or small breeding populations, particularly towards the extreme edges of the geographical range, very small releases might not produce settlement unless favoured by chance hydrographic/planktonic influences.

Settlement plate data from Robin Hood's Bay cover a period when early releases were relatively small, but it is possible that the very large input at the exposed sites in 1978/79 (see Fig. 12.2) resulted from the unusually large early release: late settlers are very unlikely to have contributed in view of the severity of the winter. The early emergence of spat on Site 2 in spite of these winter conditions tends to support this assumption.

In northern Scotland, where earlier multiple releases are the norm, more than one settlement might regularly contribute to shore recruitment, especially after mild winters. Also, and unexpectedly, the chance of some contribution from late settlements might be better in northern Scotland than in N.E. England, because of the higher winter sea temperatures (see Fig. 12.3). This might tend to damp fluctuations in annual settlement and possibly explain the reduced variability reported on p. 181. These possibilities cannot be resolved except by settlement-plate studies in other regions.

Given that in northern regions the exceptionally good settlement years have all been marked by early emergence of spat, it is fair to assume that in the North early spawning is generally of disproportionate importance. A strategy for producing some ripe gametes for release as soon as possible could therefore be more advantageous to species survival than relying on a later synchronous release of the entire gametic production (putting all eggs in one basket!). To what extent this might apply throughout the limpet's geographical range is uncertain. In southern populations either 'early' spawning (though chronologically later than in the North) might be required to produce spat large enough by summer to withstand desiccation, or, conceivably, a heat-stress effect reducing viability of autumn-settling spat might shift the advantage to later settlements, and favour delayed spawning.

These studies have concentrated to date on northern populations, in which spawning regularly occurs two to three months earlier than in southern populations, to discover how this is brought about. Theoretically it could be achieved by (i) earlier onset of gametogenesis; (ii) faster growth and/or ripening of gametes; or (iii) response to a spawning stimulus guaranteed to occur earlier in the season.

b) *Gametogenesis.* Gametogenesis is reportedly under hormonal control (Choquet, 1965, 1967), being induced by a product from the cerebral ganglion which over-rides an inhibitor produced by the ocular tentacles, while vitellogenesis is initiated by a second cerebral gangliar hormone. There is no evidence on what triggers production of these hormones. Geographical data obtained during these studies, and provided for other years and localities by other workers in this field (*op. cit.*), suggest that in any given year there is probably no significant difference in the time of onset of gamete proliferation over the whole of the British Isles and Eire, and possibly throughout all North-Western Europe. A distinction must be made however between gamete proliferation, evinced by thickening of the gonad and production of gametocytes, which starts everywhere in July/August, and onset of gametogenesis, i.e. the production of the germinal epithelium, which is detectable only by histological examination. In some northern populations of *P. vulgata*, the latter process starts before the end of the previous breeding season, so that there is no truly neuter over-wintering phase as is the rule in southern populations (Orton *et al.*, 1956). A similar difference is found in northern British *P. aspera* (pers. obs.), and such an ability must surely increase the chances of producing ripe gametes earlier in the season than would be possible otherwise. The phenomenon is most easily detectable when associated with sex-change, and as such has been observed in *P. coerulea* L. (Bacci, 1947) and *P. oculus* (Branch, 1974a).

c) *Rate of gonad growth and ripening.* There are insufficient regional data to decide whether the rate of gametogenesis varies either annually or geographically, and investigation is complicated by yearly and regional differences in spring gonad size, caused by the presence of relict gametes and/or over-wintering germinal epithelium, as well as by the result of early releases.

It is known that the total gametic production depends on age, sex and degree of site exposure (Blackmore, 1969a), and on the availability of food and feeding opportunity (Workman, 1983; and cf. Fritchman (1962a) for Californian *Acmaea* spp., Simpson (1982) for the Antarctic *Nacella macquariensis* (Finlay), Ansell (1967) for *Mercenaria*, and Sastry (1968) for *Aequipecten*). Present studies show that maximum gonad size in northern populations is a poor measure of gametic output because of early spawnings, and that continued development or redevelopment may be to some degree dependent on sea temperature. The greater size of gonads in Scottish populations, despite early release, might indicate greater gametic production than in N.E. England, perhaps because the lower densities of limpets mean increased food availability.

All studies on *P. vulgata* show that females produce relatively smaller gonads more slowly than equal-sized males, so that males are ready to spawn before females. The problem confronting northern populations is therefore to produce ripe eggs as early as possible. Choquet (*op. cit.*) demonstrated that vitellogenesis is under independent hormonal control, but whether 'ripeness' – indicated morphologically by the presence of loose eggs in the ventral gonad – requires an external trigger or merely indicates that the eggs are full-grown is unknown and is currently under investigation. The recent Robin Hood's Bay data suggest that as soon as full-sized eggs have developed they can be successfully spawned and fertilized, given the necessary spawning stimulus. The onus would then fall on rapid development of some full-sized eggs. It is worth recording that female gonads from an August, 1974, sample from Tromsø (Norway) revealed patches of well-developed eggs in an undifferentiated matrix. Was this an adaptation to produce a few fully-developed eggs quickly at the expense of total potential output, or was it merely a failure in gonad production at the northern limit of the range?

d) *The spawning stimulus.* Given the need in northern populations to release gametes as far in advance of winter as possible, the use of a sudden drop in sea temperature to indicate the start of the autumn decline and initiate spawning would seem more reliable than merely responding to a rough sea. The evidence strongly indicates the existence of a critical 'trigger' temperature, 12°C, though it is not impossible that this temperature is only proximate to some other environmental change, such as oxygen content, salinity, dissolved organic matter, to which the limpet is ultimately responding. There is however well-substantiated evidence of a similar temperature trigger in other molluscs (*op. cit.*), though many of these are sublittoral or low-littoral species. It is not yet clear how a littoral animal detects a relatively small change in sea temperature against a background of considerable diurnal and tidal variation.

A clue to the mechanism may be provided by some observations made by Jones (1968) on changes in heart-beat rate of *P. vulgata* at Millport. Using electrodes implanted in shore animals he found a steady heart-beat at low water caused by auricular plus ventricular contraction, with a superimposed and stronger, slower rate at high water produced by the *bulbus aortae*. This latter rate varied non-linearly with temperature, i.e. the rate of increase with increased temperature was constant over the range 12°C–20°C, but fell off more sharply between 6–12°C and increased faster over 20°C. Here then is a physiological mechanism responding differentially to temperatures above and below 12°C. It is interesting that limpets in the laboratory did not produce this aortal beat; and no-one has succeeded in producing controlled laboratory spawning in limpets.

Jones suggested that only the aortal beat is strong enough to circulate the blood, and hence provide the oxygen necessary for feeding and movement, the inference being that at low water (and also during storms) the limpet is merely 'ticking over' metabolically. Translocation of metabolites to the gonad might therefore also occur only during submersion, hence the possible link between development and sea temperature.

If this critical-temperature trigger is common to all limpet populations it alone would explain most of the observed regional differences in time of first spawning, and the apparent adaptations in the breeding cycle of northern populations to promote early egg production. A number of questions inevitably remain unanswered:

(i) Is the critical temperature fixed, or does it vary over the geographical range, and what happens if the sea temperature never rises above, or falls below, the limit?

(ii) What environmental (?) stimulus triggers gametogenesis, and is the ability to start next year's production before the end of the current breeding season a genetic adaptation or an ecological accident?

(iii) How frequent are multiple spawnings in southern regions, and what is the fate of their settlements over the winter; and what are the effects of high temperatures on spat survival?

Most of these questions can be answered only by more intensive study of populations in the south of the limpet's range. Meanwhile, the emphasis has switched to the other northern British limpet, *P. aspera*, to determine how far the criteria controlling the biology of *P. vulgata* populations apply to this, or any other, limpet species.

ACKNOWLEDGEMENTS

This volume is a tribute to Dr Jack Lewis and it is a pleasure to be able to acknowledge my indebtedness to him for many years of inspiration and support.

I must also thank the many colleagues, friends and hapless acquaintances prevailed upon to collect limpets and sea temperatures over the course of these studies, and to the technical staff of the late Wellcome Marine Laboratory (R.I.P.) and of Leeds and Newcastle Universities' Electronics and Engineering Depts. for help in devising and producing settlement plates and the shore-temperature recording systems.

CHAPTER XIII

LOCAL AND REGIONAL VARIATION IN SETTLEMENT AND SURVIVAL IN THE LITTORAL BARNACLE *SEMIBALANUS BALANOIDES* (L.): PATTERNS AND CONSEQUENCES

D.S. Wethey

13.1 Introduction

Planktonic larvae act as a dispersal stage in the life cycles of many sedentary marine invertebrates. Dispersal by tidal and wind-driven currents, coastal residual drift and diffusion can lead to the dispersion of larvae from a single parent over a large area (Strathmann, 1974). Theoretically such dispersion may reduce the risk of individual reproductive failure in a spatially unpredictable environment (e.g. Strathmann, 1974; Crisp, 1976b; Barnes and Barnes, 1977; Palmer and Strathmann, 1981). By analogy, temporal variation in larval settlement may reduce risks of reproductive failure in a temporally unpredictable environment (e.g. Fretwell and Lucas, 1970). Temporal variation in settlement may also be advantageous if there is a survival advantage associated with settlement in preferred sites. If larvae actively choose specific kinds of settlement sites like pits, in which individuals have higher survival, then the 'best' sites on a shore should fill up early in the settlement season and larvae that settle late should have low survival. In this case, natural selection should favour parents whose larvae settle early in the settlement season. In contrast if environmental variability overrides the advantages of preferred sites, then early settlers may not show higher survival than later settlers. In the latter case parents whose larvae settle over an extended period should be favoured by natural selection. Thus to determine the importance of spatial and temporal dispersal one must be able to measure both variation in settlement and survival.

Barnacles represent a nearly ideal organism for the study of the consequences of dispersal because their larvae are detectable at settlement and survival of daily cohorts can be measured daily or more frequently until death (Wethey, 1984). Their dispersal range is of the order of 15 to 20km (Crisp, 1958, 1976b; Strathmann, 1974), so it is possible to sample on an appropriate geographical scale. By measuring the similarity in survival patterns of cohorts that settle over 20 to 50km of coast it may be possible to test some of the assumptions of the models of dispersal, specifically that of large regional variation in survival among sites.

Intensity of settlement in barnacles varies locally, regionally and temporally, but the mechanisms responsible for the variation are uncertain. Small-scale local variation includes elements of larval choice (e.g. Knight-Jones, 1953; Crisp and Barnes, 1954; Crisp, 1955; Crisp and Meadows, 1962; Wethey, 1984). A number of different, but not necessarily exclusive, mechanisms have been suggested as causing variation in the rate of settlement. Variation in the supply of competent larvae in the plankton could lead to variation in settlement intensity. Grosberg (1982), for example, related the differences in intensity of settlement at different levels on the shore to the position of larvae in the water column. Winds have been invoked by many authors as affecting larval supply near the shore (e.g. Barnes, 1956; Connell, 1961a; Barnes and Barnes, 1977; Bennell, 1981; Hawkins and Hartnoll, 1982b; Kendall et al., 1982). Larval development could influence settlement intensity. Pyefinch (1948) followed three peaks of all stages of nauplii to three peaks of cyprid larvae in the plankton. The spacing of the peaks varied somewhat between larval stages, but was always resolvable; thus synchrony in larval release can lead to synchrony in settlement several weeks later. Larval behaviour could also affect settlement rate: competent larvae might wait for a lunar cue before moving ashore (see review by DeCoursey, 1983).

In this paper I examine daily patterns of settlement and survival of barnacles on local (10–100m) and regional (25–50km) scales to ask several questions:

(i) What mechanisms may be responsible for daily fluctuations in settlement intensity: larval supply and/or larval behaviour?

(ii) What may be the consequences of dispersal of larvae over a wide geographical area, as seen from the point of view of individual survival (and thereby reproductive success or failure)?

(iii) What may be the consequences of variation in settlement time: do 'good sites' fill up early to the disadvantage of later settlers?

13.2 Material and Methods

The barnacle Semibalanus balanoides (L.) is abundant in the rocky littoral zone in the North Atlantic and has been investigated on both sides of the Atlantic in this study. Adults brood their egg masses after fertilization in autumn, and release nauplius larvae into the plankton in early spring. After four to six weeks in the plankton, non-feeding cyprid larvae settle on the shore.

Permanent quadrats (6 × 9cm) were established in the high- and mid-littoral zone in wave-exposed and sheltered sites along a sloping gabbro bench at East Point, Nahant, Massachusetts, U.S.A. (42°25′ N, 70°54′ W). During the settlement season these sites were sampled on every accessible low tide in 1978 and daily in 1980. Similar quadrats were set up at three localities along the Yorkshire coast, U.K., each separated from the next by 25km. At Staithes (54°33′45″ N, 0°47′10″ W), the quadrats were on nearly vertical limestone surfaces on the southern mouth of the harbour. At Robin Hood's Bay (54°25′45″N, 0°32′15″ W) quadrats were on vertical portions of a shale scar, 100m southeast of the slipway. At Filey Brigg (54°13′50″ N, 0°15′45″ W) quadrats were on horizontal limestone 50m from the end of the Brigg on the northern side. These sites were sampled daily during the settlement season in 1980. Quadrats were marked with stainless steel, flat-head wood screws set in plastic anchors in holes drilled in the rock. Flashlit photographs were taken with a 35mm camera (U.S.A. photos: Nikonos II, 35mm lens, 3:1 extension ring, Panatomic X film; U.K. photos: Zorki 4K, 50mm lens, 3:1 extension ring, Panatomic X film) whose focal framer fitted on the slots of the screws, maintaining registration of camera position from day to day.

Newly settled larvae were identified by their locations on enlargements of the photographs, and were followed until their disappearance. This was done by hand, using plastic transparencies with locations marked in coloured ink, and with computer methods (see Wethey, 1984, for details). The two methods were compared on three sites and the results were indistinguishable.

Weather data for the Massachusetts site were collected at Logan International Airport, Boston (5km from the study area) and were obtained from the National Climatic Data Center. Wind speed and

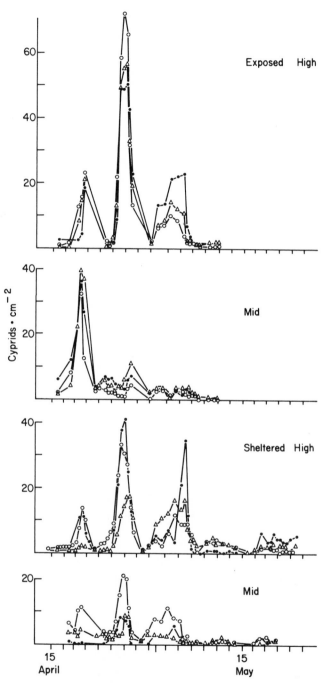

FIG. 13.1. Daily settlement of cyprids in Massachusetts, 1978. Values are the number of cyprids observed in photographs of each of 3 replicates taken every accessible low tide on exposed and sheltered shores in the high- and mid-littoral.

direction for the hour encompassing high tide prior to each sample were used to estimate the influence of wind on settlement intensity (e.g. Hawkins and Hartnoll, 1982b).

Estimates of synchrony of settlement among study areas were made by cross correlation analysis. This method measures the correlations between data series from two sites, considering observations made on the same day (lag = 0), as well as observations made one, two, three and four days apart (lag = 1, 2, 3, 4). If the cross correlations are greatest with a lag of 0, then the series are synchronous. If the cross correlations are highest with a lag of 2, then peaks in the second series occur 2 days after those in the first.

13.3 Results

13.3.1 Daily settlement in Massachusetts
There were distinct waves of settlement in both 1978 and 1980 in Massachusetts (Figs. 13.1 and 13.2). Three large and two small peaks of settlement can be distinguished in 1978, separated by approximately 7.5 days. Three peaks were observed in 1980, also separated by approximately 7 days. There was strong synchrony in settlement in 1978 in replicates within habitats, and among habitats (Fig. 13.1). Of all cross correlations among sites, the highest cross correlations occurred at lags of 0 or 1 day, indicating synchrony (Table 13.1).

The major difference between the years is in the timing of settlement. In 1978 the first major settlement peak was April 19th, and in 1980 the first peak was April 5th. In 1978 the shore filled slowly, with maximum numbers of 10 larvae arriving per square centimetre per tide (Fig. 13.1), while in 1980, 70 larvae arrived per square centimetre in two days on sheltered high littoral sites (Fig. 13.2).

There is no clear pattern of influence of wind on settlement. In 1978 the peaks of April 19th and April 26th were associated with onshore (East) winds, but the peaks of May 3rd and May 11th were associated with offshore (West) winds.

There is a possible association between settlement and a lunar cue. Full moon in 1978 was on April 24th, 1 to 2 days before the second settlement peak. Full moon in 1980 was on March 31st, 4 days before the first peak. The 7.5 day (15 tide) period between the peaks is approximately 0.25 lunar months. The occurrence of the same periodicity in two years lends credence to the hypothesis that some component of the pattern is the result of behaviour.

13.3.2 Daily settlement in Yorkshire
At all sites there were waves of settlement (Fig. 13.3). At the northern site, Staithes, 4 peaks of settle-

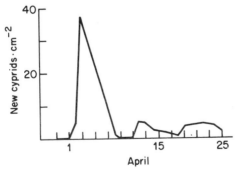

FIG. 13.2. Daily settlement of cyprids in Massachusetts, 1980. Values are the number of cyprids observed in photographs taken daily in the high-littoral on a sheltered shore.

TABLE 13.1

Settlement periodicity: cross correlations among sites. Values are the number of days by which settlement peaks lead or lag behind peaks in other sites, as estimated by the maximum cross correlation values measured. A value of zero indicates synchrony. P Mid = sheltered mid-shore; P High = sheltered high-shore; E mid = exposed mid-shore; E High = exposed high-shore; S = Staithes, R = Robin Hood's Bay, F = Filey Brigg.

Massachusetts Site	P Mid	P High	E Mid	E High		
P Mid	0	0	− 0.5	0		
P High		0	− 1.5	0		
E Mid				0		

Yorkshire Site	S Mid	S High	R Mid	R High	F Mid	F High
S Mid		− 3	0	− 1	2	1
S High		0	1	3	4	0
R Mid				2	4	− 1
R High					− 3	4

ment occurred in a month, separated by 8 days (Staithes mid-shore, Fig. 13.3); on the high shore at this locality there were additional peaks (Fig. 13.3). At Robin Hood's Bay, the intermediate site geographically, there were peaks separated by 5, 6, 6, and 7 days on the mid-shore, and peaks separated by 7, 5, 3, 6, and 7 days on the high-shore. At Filey Brigg, the southern site, there were 4 peaks separated by 8 days. The settlement pattern at Filey was synchronous with that at Staithes, 50km to the North (Fig. 13.3). Robin Hood's Bay shows synchrony on May 30th and June 10th but is offset slightly on the other dates. The first peak at Staithes began 1 day after full moon, the first peak at Robin Hood's bay 3 days before full moon, and the first peak at Filey 1 day after full moon (Fig. 13.3).

13.3.3 Daily survival in Yorkshire

Mortality of newly settled individuals was as high as 90% in 5 days on the high-shore and 60% in 5 days on the mid-shore. In some localities mortality was consistently high (e.g. Staithes high-shore, Fig. 13.4). In other areas mortality was consistently low (e.g. Staithes mid-shore, Filey mid-shore, Fig. 13.4). At Robin Hood's Bay on both the high- and mid-shore, and the high-shore at Filey, mortality was highly variable (Fig. 13.4). Some cohorts suffered very little mortality (June 9th Robin Hood's Bay mid; June 9th Filey high). Other cohorts had precipitous declines soon after settlement (June 4th and 5th Filey high; May 31st and June 2nd Robin Hood's Bay mid).

There is no obvious trend of low mortality among the earliest settlers with higher mortality later, as one might expect if 'good' microsites became pre-empted. Rather some cohorts survive well and others die rapidly (Fig. 13.4). There is no clear synchrony of death. A strikingly high mortality of one cohort may occur at the same time as very low mortality of other cohorts. This makes it very difficult to identify the cause of such selective mortality when the cohorts differ in age by no more than 2 days (e.g. June 7th to June 11th cohorts, Robin Hood's Bay mid-shore).

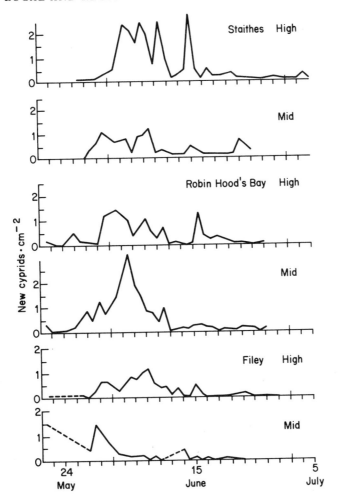

FIG. 13.3. Daily settlement of cyprids in Yorkshire, 1980. Values are the numbers of new cyprids observed in photographs taken daily in the high- and mid-littoral zone at three stations separated from each other by 25km. Staithes is the northern site, Robin Hood's Bay the middle and Filey Brigg the southern site.

The bulk of mortality occurs during the first 5 days after settlement (Fig. 13.4). The only exception to this is the high-shore at Robin Hood's Bay where death was postponed until days 6 to 10 for several cohorts (Fig. 13.4). Metamorphosis occurs within 2 days after settlement so all initial mortality is not uniquely associated with metamorphosis. The risk of death for cyprids appears to be nearly identical with that of uncalcified 1 day old metamorphs. On June 2nd and 4th uncalcified metamorphs and cyprids were followed separately. The mortality rates were indistinguishable. This indicates that there is no clear reduction in mortality risk associated with metamorphosis. Uncalcified barnacles, be they cyprids or metamorphs, have equal mortality risks.

13.4 Discussion

The dispersion of larvae from a single parent has been viewed in the theoretical literature as a mechanism for spreading the risk of mortality in a spatially uncertain environment (e.g. Strathmann,

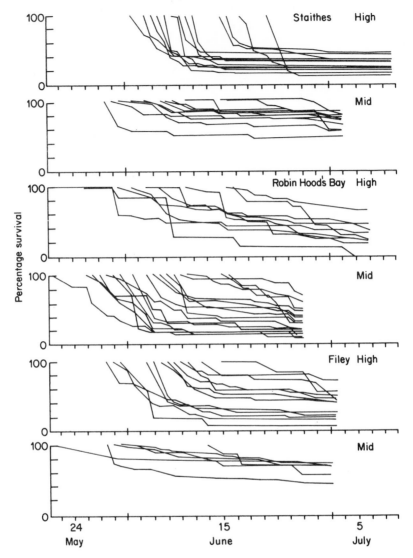

FIG. 13.4. Survival of daily cohorts of larvae in Yorkshire, 1980. Values are the percentage of the cohort remaining over time on the high- and mid-shore at Staithes, Robin Hood's Bay and Filey Brigg.

1974; Crisp, 1976b; Barnes and Barnes, 1977; Wethey, 1985). The data presented here are fully consistent with this view. Mortality was consistently high in some sites (Staithes high-shore), low in others (Staithes mid-shore), and highly variable elsewhere (Fig. 13.4). Temporal dispersion in settlement is also advantageous. Cohorts that settled one day apart showed radically different mortality rates (June 8th versus June 9th, Robin Hood's Bay, Fig. 13.4). Elsewhere I have argued that year-to-year variation in mortality regime should select against habitat specialization (Wethey, 1985). Here, the same argument can be made, based on day-to-day variation in survival.

The mortality data do not support the hypothesis of early settlers pre-empting the most suitable sites, but rather indicate the importance of temporal variation in mortality rates (Fig. 13.4). Given the mortality data, one might expect to see an extended settlement season, with variations in intensity of settlement perhaps driven by physical phenomena. Several authors have invoked the wind in explanations of variations in settlement. Boicourt (1982) showed that a wind stress of 0.5 dynes·cm^{-2} could induce currents of velocity 20cm·s^{-1} in surface waters (to 38m depth), and 10cm·s^{-1} down to 70m on the continental shelf. Thus even organisms which can regulate their position in the water column could be influenced strongly by wind-induced currents. Levin (1983) documented transport of surface drifters at 25cm·s^{-1} in a direction opposite to the normal longshore current as a result of a single winter storm. Based on these empirical data and on theoretical grounds (e.g. Barnes and Barnes, 1977), wind should be expected to have a strong effect on supply of larvae to the shore. Hawkins and Hartnoll (1982b) presented convincing evidence for the importance of wind direction at Port Erin, Isle of Man. Onshore winds were associated with higher settlement. More difficult to explain is the pattern of high settlement with offshore winds documented by Bennell (1981) with data collected during the same season as Hawkins and Hartnoll. The data presented here show inconsistent relations between wind direction and settlement. Half of the settlement peaks in 1978 were associated with onshore and half with offshore winds (Fig. 13.1). Presumably numerous factors such as turbulent mixing in the water column, asynchronous larval release (e.g. Kendall *et al.*, 1982), and larval behaviour, combine to override the effects of wind direction in some cases.

Waves of settlement have been observed by several authors. Connell (1961a and this volume) saw 2 peaks in his daily surveys at Millport, Scotland in 1955, separated by 2 weeks. These were sufficiently widely separated that he attributed them to synchronous release of larvae into the plankton (Connell, 1961a). Chipperfield (1948, cited in Connell, 1961a) observed 3 peaks separated by 16 and 12 days, two of which were at spring tides and one at neap tides. Kendall *et al.* (1982) observed 2 broad peaks in settlement at Robin Hood's Bay in 1978, separated by 25 days. These might be the result of synchronous release, although Kendall *et al.* (1982) noted that naupliar release is prolonged, and may not occur in peaks. Synchrony in development of nauplii to cyprids in 3 separate peaks (separated by 15 and 18 days) was observed by Pyefinch (1948) at Millport. It is therefore possible that waves of settlement could be the result of waves of release. If this were the case, on a coastline with a prevailing residual drift current, one should see progressive waves of settlement offset by several days at stations separated along the coast. The residual drift runs from Staithes southwards to Robin Hood's Bay then Filey in Yorkshire. The tidal excursion is 10km, so if waves of synchronously released larvae were being transported from North to South, there should be peaks of settlement appearing first at Staithes, then a few days later at Robin Hood's Bay, and later still at Filey. I did not find such a pattern. Instead, settlement was synchronous. Kendall (pers. comm.) made a series of plankton tows from Staithes to Robin Hood's Bay during my surveys. He found a single patch of cyprids 1km wide. Such a patch could not encounter all three sites on a single day. The synchrony of settlement observed along this section of shore cannot be accounted for by North–South transport of waves of synchronously released larvae.

The occurrence of approximately 8 day spacing between settlement peaks in 2 years at Nahant, and at 3 sites in Yorkshire lends credence to the hypothesis that some component of the periodicity is behavioural. However there is no obvious synchronizing mechanism. In Massachusetts, the second settlement peak was 1 day after full moon in 1978, but 4 days after full moon in 1980. In Yorkshire, the second settlement peak was 1 day after full moon in 1980 at Staithes and Filey, and 2 days after full moon at Robin Hood's Bay.

The data presented here demonstrate the importance of temporal variation in settlement. Mortality has a strong temporal component and risk appears to be age-, site- and day-dependent (Fig. 13.4). These data underscore the importance of a prolonged settlement period and wide dispersal range. The data on settlement synchrony are less clear. Peaks are present in all years for all geographical locales and are usually approximately one week apart (Figs. 13.1, 13.2 and 13.3). However, neither wind direction nor larval transport by residual drift nor lunar influence adequately explain this periodicity. Lunar and semilunar behavioural periodicities are well known in Crustacea, but this appears to be the first example of a 7.5 day period (DeCoursey, 1983 and pers. comm.).

ACKNOWLEDGEMENTS

The field work for the British portion of this study was carried out during tenure of a National Science Foundation National Needs Postdoctoral Fellowship (SPI 79–14910) at the Wellcome Marine Laboratory, Robin Hood's Bay, Yorkshire. Field assistance in Yorkshire was provided by S.A. Woodin, M.A. Kendall, A. Simpson and C. Wright. J.R. Lewis provided laboratory space, transport and housing at the Wellcome Marine Laboratory. Discussions with M.A. Kendall, R.S. Bowman, P. Williamson and J.R. Lewis were very helpful in putting these results in perspective with data which they had collected in Yorkshire. Jack Lewis was a source of constant stimulation and encouragement during my stay at Robin Hood's Bay. Field work in Massachusetts was supported by National Science Foundation Grant OCE 77–26503. W. Fowle watched for waves during the night tides at Nahant in 1978, and with G. Fowle, took all of the photographs in 1980. M.P. Morse and N.W. Riser provided access to the Massachusetts sites and laboratory space at the Northeastern University Marine Science Institute. Development of methods of analysis of settlement photographs was supported by Office of Naval Research (Contract N00014-K-82-645), the National Science Foundation (Grant OCE 82–08176) and the University of South Carolina. S.A. Woodin made numerous helpful comments on the manuscript.

CHAPTER XIV

REPRODUCTIVE STRATEGIES OF NORTH TEMPERATE ROCKY SHORE INVERTEBRATES

C.D. Todd

14.1 Introduction

This Chapter will attempt to summarize our current understanding of the reproductive strategies of rocky shore invertebrates, drawing particularly upon data from the extensive studies of organisms from Northeast Pacific, Northwest Atlantic and Northeast Atlantic coasts. I have not attempted an exhaustive review of the literature: rather, I have structured this essay as a personal perspective with the intention of attempting to link currently available empirical and analytical data to contemporary life history theory. In particular I address what I believe to be the two major questions within this aspect of rocky shore ecology. First, why is it that (with only very few exceptions) the dominant rocky shore invertebrates – whether they be sessile or sedentary, herbivorous or carnivorous, and micro-phagous or macrophagous – are invariably perennial and iteroparous? Secondly, is there any discernible pattern among the varying larval strategies displayed by these rocky shore invertebrates, and especially what is the ecological significance and what are the implications of larval dispersal?

14.2 Definitions of Terms, and the Theoretical Framework

I differentiate the terms life history strategy, life-cycle strategy and larval strategy and attempt to examine their inter-relationships within the context outlined in Fig. 14.1. *Reproductive strategy* I apply as a general term. *Life-cycle strategy* I define as the duration of the benthic adult phase. *Life history strategy* has a dichotomous basis and refers to organisms as being either semelparous (reproducing once and then dying) or iteroparous (undergoing repeated breeding periods) (Cole, 1954). In the present context I constrain the use of the term *larval strategy* in applying it to the three fundamental larval types. Broadly, all marine invertebrate larvae are primarily divisible into 'pelagic' (or planktonic) versus 'non-pelagic' (or benthic) forms (see Thorson, 1946, 1950; Mileikovsky, 1971; Jablonski and Lutz, 1980, 1983). Pelagic larvae may require to undergo feeding, growth and ontogenetic development in the plankton and, as such, are termed *planktotrophic*. Some, notably polychaetes, are briefly planktonic (a few days or weeks) although most (e.g. cirripedes, gastropods and echinoderms) occupy the plankton for an extended period (weeks or months) in order to complete development and attain competence to metamorphose. Other pelagic larvae (notably some gastropods and ascidians) do not require to feed in the plankton to complete their development since they are provisioned with all their required reserves as an embryo: such larvae are termed *lecithotrophic*. Most pelagic lecithotrophic larvae are planktonic for only a few hours or days and are, as a consequence, only subject to limited

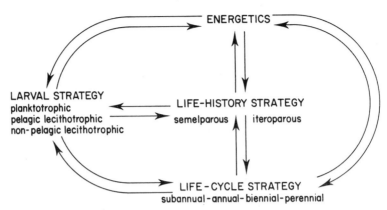

FIG. 14.1. The inter-relationships between reproductive strategy traits considered in the text.

dispersal from the adult micro-habitat in contrast to long-term planktotrophs. This planktonic phase of pelagic lecithotrophs appears to involve an ontogenetically 'preparatory' period prior to settlement and metamorphosis. Many rocky shore invertebrates (notably some gastropods and echinoderms) have eliminated all pelagic phases from their reproduction and display 'non-pelagic' or 'benthic' lecithotrophic development: juveniles either hatch fully-developed from benthic spawn masses or the embryos are retained and brooded, throughout development, by the mother.

Among these larval categories there are a number of ecologically important correlates. In general planktotrophic larvae develop from small ($< 100\mu$m) eggs, with non-pelagic lecithotrophic embryos hatching from large (400–900μm) eggs and pelagic lecithotrophic larvae from intermediate-sized eggs (Thorson, 1946, 1950; Ockelmann, 1965; Steele, 1977; Strathmann, 1977; Hermans, 1979; Turner and Lawrence, 1979; Perron, 1981a; Todd and Doyle, 1981). Individual adult fecundity generally decreases with increasing egg size (Smith and Fretwell, 1974; Wilbur, 1977). Moreover, small eggs (which contain less yolk) generally cleave and develop more rapidly than larger eggs (Jägersten, 1972) and there is thus a complex of relationships between fecundity, egg size, larval type and embryonic development time. Inclusion of the pelagic larval phase may result in major differences in egg-to-benthic juvenile periods and, evidently, dispersal capacity according to the three basic larval strategies. It is invariably assumed to be implicit that there is a consistent trend of decreasing individual probability of larval/juvenile survivorship according to strategy, in the sequence: non-pelagic lecithotrophy > pelagic lecithotrophy > planktotrophy. This arises from both the size at hatching and the time spent in the plankton. Planktonic mortality and losses due to failing to find the correct benthic substratum for metamorphosis are almost certainly very high and variable.

The final definitions to be made, pertinent to Fig. 14.1, refer to 'energetic' considerations. Individual organisms must allocate resources to maintenance, growth, survival and reproduction and, as such, 'energy' satisfies the criteria for providing a 'common currency' in terms of which the functional ecology of diverse organisms (both plant and animal) may be realistically compared. Since the total energy budget of an individual organism is finite, such allocations, which may be considered as 'traits' within a reproductive strategy, are presumed to be subject to selective forces such that these are optimized or maximized by the individual (Williams, 1966a,b; Gadgil and Bossert, 1970; Schaffer, 1974). Reproduction especially has been considered in detail and in isolation for a wide variety of flowering plants (e.g. Harper, 1967; Harper and Ogden, 1970; Gadgil and Solbrig, 1972; Gaines *et al.*, 1974; Abrahamson, 1975) and animals (Hirschfield and Tinkle, 1974; Tinkle and Hadley, 1975; and refs below) and the concept of reproductive 'strategy' has become a central construct of life history theory (see Giesel, 1976; Stearns, 1976, 1977, 1980, for reviews). Montague *et al.* (1981) considered the reproductive strategy of a given organism to be the set of physiological, morphological and behavioural traits that dictate the 'where', 'when', 'how often', 'how many' (and, for marine invertebrates, 'what kind of') tactics of propagule production. Within the broad confines of reproductive strategies the notion of reproductive effort (RE) (i.e. some measure of the proportion of somatic resources (ideally energy) allocated specifically to reproduction) is uppermost (Hirschfield and Tinkle, 1974; Tinkle and Hadley, 1975; Stearns, 1976). The connection of RE to reproductive strategy is self-evident (Primack and Antonovics, 1982) in that allocations to reproductive structures relate to fecundity, while allocations to somatic/vegetative structures relate to survivorship, growth and, ultimately, to future fecundity – or 'reproductive value'. ('Residual reproductive value' (RRV) (*sensu* Fisher, 1930) is defined as the number of offspring an adult female might expect to produce, on average, throughout her lifetime, discounted back to the present. This value will usually be maximal for females just at the age they start to reproduce, and for females beyond the age of reproduction it will normally be zero.)

Cole (1954) sought ecological circumstances under which a semelparous organism 'ought' to become iteroparous. He used 'r', the intrinsic rate of natural increase of the population, as his measure of Darwinian fitness, and considered two idealized situations (which make unrealistic assumptions).

For Cole's ideal semelparous population all adults reproduce and die (no generation overlap), and there is no juvenile mortality. Thus:

(1) $N_{t+1} = N_t \cdot B_s$ where N = Number of individuals at time t or t + 1, and B_s is the (semelparous) birth rate.

Similarly, in Cole's ideal iteroparous population all individuals are immortal since there is, again, no juvenile mortality and each adult survives to breed again. Here,

(2) $N_{t+1} = N_t \cdot B_i + N_t$ where B_i is the iteroparous birth rate or, (3) $N_{t+1} = N_t(B_i + 1)$

Bearing in mind that selection favours that individual which differentially produces the greatest *number* of *viable* offspring the outcome is that an ideal semelparous organism could attain the same fitness as an ideal iteroparous counterpart merely by elevating its fecundity by one. This is known as 'Cole's Result' and begs the question, why should iteroparity ever evolve? Clearly, there are a number of inadequacies in the formulations above. First, organisms are not immortal and there are presumably 'trade-offs' between the investment in present reproduction and future survival to reproduce again. Moreover, adult survivorship is often far greater (*per capita*, and per unit time) than that for larvae or juveniles and there is, in consequence, a considerable potential advantage in reducing current RE in order that the adult might enhance its survival to reproduce again (i.e. iteroparity). Incorporation of such age-specific effects (Charnov and Schaffer, 1973) does, in fact, radically alter the outcome of Cole's equations. Charnov and Schaffer (1973) differentiated the probability of offspring survivorship to maturity (c) from the probability of an iteroparous adult surviving between reproductive seasons (p). The rate of population growth (λ) is given by:

$$\lambda = N_{t+1}/N_t$$

Thus, for a semelparous organism, population growth (λ_s) is given by:

$$N_{t+1} = B_s \cdot c \cdot N_t \text{ or } \lambda_s = B_s \cdot c,$$

while for an iteroparous organism:

$$N_{t+1} = B_i \cdot c \cdot N_t + p \cdot N_t$$
$$= (B_i \cdot c + p)N_t \text{ or } \lambda_i = B_i \cdot c + p$$

Now, if the two populations are to increase at the same rate (i.e. $\lambda_s = \lambda_i$):

$B_s \cdot c \cdot N_t = (B_i \cdot c + p)N_t$ or
$B_s = B_i + p/c$

Thus, *only* if $p = c$ does Cole's Result apply. If $p < c$ then the semelparous strategy is selected for. Conversely, if $p > c$ then selection will favour iteroparity: it does not matter if mortality is density-dependent or density-independent, so long as it is age-specific making p/c large.

Conceptually, we can consider annual population growth (λ) in terms of Schaffer's (1974) simple formulation:

$\lambda = B \cdot c + p$, where, again, c = juvenile survivorship to reproduction, B = births, and p = adult survivorship to reproduce again.

Note that a decrease in c from, say, 0.01 to 0.001 would necessitate either an increase in B of an order of magnitude (from, say, 10,000 to 100,000) or a corresponding increase in p (from, say, 0.001 to 0.01). Since such multiplicative elevations in fecundity are likely to be beyond the energetic capacities of well-adapted organisms, general life history analyses consequential upon these formulations invariably revolve around decreases ($\rightarrow$ semelparity) or increases ($\rightarrow$ iteroparity) in p, in response to fluctuations in c. What such projections fail to account for, however, are the implications of adjusting c by means of altered juvenile quality. As we have already seen (and will pursue below) evolution of marine invertebrates has resulted in radical adjustments in the individual probabilities of larval/juvenile survival by altering egg size, and hence larval strategy.

Thus, even if selection for semelparity/iteroparity were accountable simply in terms of differential juvenile/adult survivorship fluctuations (but see Young, 1981) we must expect (for benthic marine invertebrates) a diverse complex of specific life-cycle, life history and larval strategy combinations.

14.3 Models of Life History Theory

Stearns (1976, 1977) presented in his reviews the two opposing contemporary theoretical bases of life history evolution: the 'deterministic' model or '*r-K* selection theory' (*sensu* MacArthur and Wilson, 1967) and the 'stochastic' or 'bet-hedging' model (Cohen, 1966; Holgate, 1967; Mountford, 1968; Murphy, 1968; Schaffer, 1974). *r-K* theory is based upon determinate schedules of mortality and fecundity and emphasizes the importance of abiotic factors and environmental predictability and their density-independent effects on populations. It predicts that in populations dominated by density-independent mortality and subject to fluctuating environmental conditions there will be ('*r*') selection for early maturity, high RE and large numbers of small offspring. At the other extreme the emphasis is placed upon the connections between environmental predictability, density-dependent mortality and biotic factors, and predicts that ('*K*') selection will favour delayed maturity, low (periodic) RE and small numbers of (large, high quality) offspring (see Grahame, 1977; Hughes and Roberts, 1980a; Suchanek, 1981; Hart and Begon, 1982; Atkinson and Newbury, 1984).

The 'bet-hedging' model recognizes that both mortality and fecundity schedules fluctuate and, indeed, these are the very features which provide its theoretical basis. In this formulation predictions of the life history traits displayed by given organisms result from the fluctuations in pre-reproductive (juvenile) survivorship probabilities relative to those of the adult. Thus, an environment which confers *constant* – even if low level – predictability of juvenile survivorship (relative to adult) should favour species of short life and high RE, which reproduce at an early age (hence, semelparity). Conversely, an environment which confers more variable juvenile survivorship (in contrast to the adult) should favour long-lived, large-bodied species which make small, repeated and temporally extended allocations to reproduction (hence, iteroparity) (but see Caswell, 1980 and King, 1982 who question these generalities). These are the very same conclusions to arise from the descriptive equations in the previous section.

The relative merits of the two approaches have been long contested. In their simplicity they are both irreconcilable and mutually exclusive, for they make diametrically opposed predictions of selectively favoured life history traits given the same environmental circumstances. The present consensus of opinion is, I believe, somewhat against the utility of r-K theory, if only because its assumptions and predictions with respect to density-dependence/independence are untestable (Stearns, 1976; Ebert, 1982). Moreover, unlike r, K cannot be realistically expressed as a function of life history traits (Stearns, 1977). The adoption of the 'bet-hedging' model is recommended if only because it makes intuitively plausible predictions which are, after all, falsifiable. However, I must concur with Ebert (1982) when he suggests that whatever the viewpoint (r-K theory or 'bet-hedging') selection must be linkable to energy budgets to allow optimal allocation of size (= quality), numbers, and timing of off-spring production.

My intention throughout this Chapter is, therefore, to consider the reproductive strategies of rocky shore invertebrates within the broad framework of the stochastic 'bet-hedging' equations above, while acknowledging the importance of energetic considerations. The bulk of the data to be considered here relate to organisms found on rocky shores of the Northwest Pacific (California to Alaska) and North-east Atlantic (New England) coasts of North America and the British Isles. For clarity each specific example is suffixed with an appropriate abbreviation for the respective geographic localities (i.e. PNW, NE, BI). I am concerned primarily with the animals which appear subjectively to be 'dominant', or of major ecological importance. Nevertheless, additional illustrative reference will be made to other species (from these and other geographical localities).

14.4 Life-cycle and Life History Strategies

The major North temperate rocky shore invertebrates, almost without exception, display extended or perennial life-cycles. Biennialism is generally rare among both animals and plants (Hart, 1977) and is not represented among the organisms with which we are concerned. Obligatory annual life-cycles are to be found among, for example, small herbivorous and carnivorous prosobranch and opisthobranch molluscs (e.g. Grahame, 1977; Todd, 1979a), but these organisms are of minor ecological importance. Ephemeral, or subannual, life-cycles are absent.

A clear distinction should be made between *potential* and *realized* longevity in that survivorship of (potentially) long-lived organisms, such as barnacles, may be markedly curtailed by the activity of predators (e.g. Connell, 1970, 1972, 1975) or abiotic factors such as freezing (e.g. Wethey, 1979). In addition, local habitat patches, separated by perhaps only a few metres, may confer very different survivorship and growth probabilities for conspecific individuals (e.g. *Patella vulgata* L., see Lewis and Bowman, 1975).

Among littoral anemones the life-cycle strategy of *Anthopleura xanthogrammica* (Brandt) (PNW) is perhaps the most remarkable. This species attains a basal diameter of 25cm, requires 5–9 years to reach maturity and lives for maybe 100–150 years (Sebens, 1981a,b, 1982). Curiously, littoral anemones are conspicuous in their absence from New England shores although the long-lived *Actinia equina* (L.) is abundant in the British Isles.

Barnacles are characteristic of rocky shores world-wide and all are potentially long-lived and iteroparous. A few boreo-arctic species (such as *Semibalanus* (= *Balanus*) *balanoides* (L.), (see Newman and Ross, 1976) and *B. balanus* (L.)) reproduce only once per year (Barnes and Barnes, 1954); most species (e.g. *Chthamalus stellatus* (Poli) (= *montagui* Southward?), *Elminius modestus* Darwin (see Crisp and Patel, 1969)) however, complete several reproductive cycles at variable intervals depending upon a complex of factors – notably, food availability and ambient temperature (Crisp, 1956; Crisp and Spencer, 1958; Barnes, 1963; Barnes and Barnes, 1968; Crisp and Patel, 1969). In the specific instance of *Semibalanus balanoides*, after copulation and oviposition (within the mantle space) in November (BI) there follows a period when moulting ceases followed by a unique moult in which the penis is lost. The embryos are retained throughout the ensuing winter and held at the naupliar stage of development. Hatching and the liberation of the nauplii the following March/April is dependent upon phytoplankton availability (i.e. the spring diatom bloom) and is mediated by a 'hatching factor' produced by the adult. Gametogenesis in preparation of the next year's brood proceeds immediately after spawning. *Tetraclita squamosa* Darwin (PNW), which requires 2 years to reach maturity, may attain 14 years of age (Hines, 1979) while *Semibalanus balanoides* has a maximum (realized) longevity of only 2 years on New England shores (Wethey, 1979). Nevertheless, *S. balanoides* matures in its first year of benthic life and, on British shores, both this species and *Chthamalus* spp. display considerably greater life-spans than their New England counterparts.

Pollicipes polymerus Sowerby (PNW), a pedunculate 'gooseneck' (as opposed to an 'acorn') barnacle, is a major component of rocky shores from California to Alaska. This species has a maximum life-span of at least 6 (Paine, 1974) and perhaps up to 20 years, but, again, requires 3–6 years to reach maturity (C.A. Lewis, 1975).

The most comprehensively studied littoral invertebrates are the molluscs. Bivalves of the genus *Mytilus* are among the most widespread and abundant of rocky shore invertebrates and invariably dominate temperate 'exposed' coasts. The cosmopolitan (Seed, 1976b) *Mytilus edulis* L. (BI, NE, PNW) may attain sexual maturity within only 1–2 months of settling on the shore and may live as long as 18–24 years (Seed, 1969a; Suchanek, 1981). By contrast, the much larger, faster-growing *M. californianus* Conrad (PNW), which competitively displaces *M. edulis* in exposure (Harger, 1972b; Paine, 1974, 1976a; Suchanek, 1981) may require anything from 4 months to 3 years to mature (depending upon local conditions) (Paine, 1976a; Suchanek, 1981) and certainly lives for 7–20, and possibly as many as 50–100 years (Suchanek, 1981).

On North American Pacific shores chitons occupy the central rôle of the major herbivorous grazers on open coasts (Lewis, 1976; Paine, 1980) – a rôle which is pre-empted by the limpet *Patella vulgata* L. in the British Isles. Among these Pacific chitons are the exceedingly large (1200g), long-lived (16–25 years) *Cryptochiton stelleri* (Middendorff) (MacGintie and MacGintie, 1968; Palmer and Frank, 1974) and the somewhat smaller but more abundant *Katharina tunicata* (Wood). Chitons are of only minor importance on North Atlantic shores.

Branch (1981) has comprehensively reviewed the biology of limpets world-wide, and finds that they invariably display extended perennial life-cycles. Of the 20 species for which there are comprehensive data (see Branch, 1981) all, except one, have life-cycles ranging from in excess of 1 year to approximately 30 years. *Patella oculus* Born. (South Africa), for example, matures after one year but rarely survives beyond a third (Branch, 1974b). *Patella vulgata* (BI) displays a remarkably plastic demography (Thompson, 1980) in relation to local habitat differences (Lewis and Bowman, 1975) but generally appears to survive for approximately 10 years. Some limpets have lower mortality rates (Sutherland, 1970; California) or longer life-spans (Lewis and Bowman, 1975; U.K.) on the high-shore, while others suffer higher mortality rates in the upper shore, at least during the (hot) summer months (Breen, 1972). Whether these local, within-shore variations in growth rate and survivorship are 'strategies' or phenotypic effects in response to, for example, varying quality and/or quantity of food is not clear (see Lewis and Bowman, 1975; Thompson, 1980; Branch, 1981).

Many of the archaeogastropod trochid ('topshell') prosobranchs may be aged from annual growth checks (annuli) on the shell. On this basis Williamson and Kendall (1981) estimated a maximum adult life of more than 10 years for *Monodonta lineata* da Costa (BI). From annular growth checks these same authors concluded that the other major British topshells *Gibbula cineraria* L. and *G. umbilicalis* da

Costa were similarly long-lived, although the annuli in these species are less distinct.

The herbivorous prosobranch genus *Littorina* has been subject to repeated study in the British Isles. Presently, eight species are recognized – *L. neritoides* (L.), *L. littorea* (L.), *L. obtusata* (L.), *L. mariae* (Sacchi et Rast.), *L. nigrolineata* (Gray), *L. neglecta* Bean, *L. 'saxatilis'* (Olivi) (*'rudis' sensu* Heller, 1975a) and *L. arcana* Hannaford Ellis. *L. arcana* (oviparous) was separated from the seemingly intractable *'rudis/saxatilis'* complex by Hannaford Ellis (1979) and this nomenclatural change especially has major consequences on earlier taxonomic and ecological studies (Raffaelli, 1982). Hughes and Roberts (1980) estimated age at maturity and age-specific fecundity on the basis of the von Bertalanffy growth parameter. From these data age at first maturity ranged from 8.5 months (*L. littorea*) to 18 months (*L. nigrolineata*, *L. 'saxatilis'*) to 3 years (*L. neritoides*) while longevity ranged from 8 years (*L. littorea, L. nigrolineata*) to 8–11 years (*L. 'saxatilis'*) to 16 years (*L. neritoides*). These approximations should not be considered absolute because littorinids, like limpets, may display highly plastic demographies between local habitats. Thus, despite their invariably small size (with the exception of *L. littorea*) these abundant and important grazers may be surprisingly long-lived (Hughes and Answer, 1982) (excepting *L. neglecta*, Hannaford Ellis (1983); Fish and Sharp (this volume)).

Predatory dogwhelks of the genus *Nucella* number among the major carnivores on north temperate rocky shores. All have extended life-cycles although there are, of course, specific variations. *Nucella lapillus* (l.) (BI, NE) matures after 2.5–3 years (Feare, 1970b; Hughes, 1972) at which point there is generally cessation of growth, unless parasitized by trematode infection. Individual survivorship beyond 6 years (Hughes and Roberts, 1980a) is unlikely. The three *Nucella* species of Pacific Northwest shores (*N. lamellosa* (Gmelin), *N. canaliculata* (Duclos) and *N. emarginata* (Deshayes)) have been intensively studied (e.g. Connell, 1970, 1975; Stickle, 1973; Spight, 1974, 1975, 1976a,c, 1977b, 1982b; Lambert and Dehnel, 1974; Spight and Emlen, 1976; Palmer, 1983a). *N. canaliculata* is rather shorter-lived than the other two species although *N. emarginata*, which matures after only one year, seldom survives more than two years: this latter species does, however, spawn several times a year (Spight, 1982b). *N. lamellosa* only matures at four years of age and may survive a further six years (Spight, 1982b).

The last, but by no means least important, Phylum to consider is the Echinodermata – notably the classes Echinoidea and Asteroidea. Echinoids are generally restricted to the sublittoral on rocky substrata and are invariably associated with macroalgal kelp forests (for review, see Lawrence, 1975) (e.g. *Echinus esculentus* L., BI (Kain and Jones, 1966; Jones and Kain, 1967), *Strongylocentrotus purpuratus* (Stimson), and *S. franciscanus* (Agassiz), PNW (Pearse and Hines, 1979; Tegner and Dayton, 1981 and refs therein)). However, two species of echinoid – *S. droebachiensis* Müller (PNW, NE) and *Paracentrotus lividus* (Lamarck) (BI) – may be of major littoral importance, especially in rock pools. Autecological data are notably lacking for littoral echinoids although their destructive grazing activity (as a major source of ecological 'disturbance') is well documented.

Asteroid starfish are major predators on most North temperate rocky shores. They are especially so in the Pacific Northwest of North America, and there have probably been an intense selective force in structuring marine benthic communities over evolutionary time (Menge, 1982a). Indeed, in polar and temperate regions sea stars occupy a dominant predatory rôle though in the tropics they are apparently replaced by teleost fish as the top predators (Menge, 1982a). *Pisaster ochraceus* (Brandt) (PNW) may attain 40cm or more and has an estimated life-cycle of, perhaps, 34 years (Menge, 1974, 1975): this species may require up to 5 years to mature. The smaller *Leptasterias hexactis* (Stimson) (sympatric with *P. ochraceus*) probably takes only 2 years to mature and has an estimated longevity from 4–18 years (Menge, 1974, 1975). Feder (1970) has emphasized the impossibility of ageing perennial starfish such as these because of the absence of skeletal growth checks: even measurements of body size are of limited value for post-juvenile asteroids. In the British Isles, *Asterias rubens* L. is the major asteroid predator, and preferentially takes *Mytilus edulis* on rocky shores (Dare, 1982). Littoral *Asterias* appear to comprise the upper fringes of otherwise sublittoral populations, in contrast to *Pisaster* which is clearly littoral (Paine, 1966, 1974, 1976a, 1980; Dayton, 1971), although Nichols and Barker (1984) succeeded in following one cohort of littoral *Asterias* from settlement to 2.25 years of age: they could distinguish 3 year-classes, all less than 65mm in diameter. *Asterias rubens* may attain a diameter of 25cm and is evidently potentially very long-lived. Barker and Nichols (1983) recorded the onset of maturity of littoral *Asterias* at 50mm diameter, towards the end of the second year of life. Similarly, Barker (1979) recorded the onset of maturity in *Stichaster australis* Verrill (New Zealand) at approximately 5mm, or 2.5–3 years of age. Clearly, therefore, littoral starfish – in common with all the other major rocky shore invertebrates – display extended life-cycles and iteroparity.

Rocky shores constitute much less than 1% of the total area of marine benthic habitats and yet carry a vast array of (abundant) specialist species. Along a given stretch of coastline rocky substrata are discontinuous and interspersed by mud, sand, shingle, etc. Recruitment from pelagic larval stages is thus likely to be a highly erratic and variable process. Nevertheless, these shores are frequently densely populated and highly productive habitats. That competition for primary space (bare rock) is generally intense is perhaps intimated by the universal occurrence of distinct faunistic zones.

Perhaps for descriptive purposes we can classify organisms functionally into those whose prime objective is to retain primary space (i.e. rock surface), and those which are more mobile space exploiters. Space-occupiers therefore include barnacles, mussels and anemones (which may clone asexually to form extensive 'colonies', e.g. (PNW) Sebens, 1981a,b, 1982), while the mobile organisms embrace winkles, dogwhelks, starfish and, where applicable, sea urchins.

Competition for space (either for attachment, or for the provision of grazing or prey) is thus likely to be of overriding importance to both groupings. Barnacles, mussels and anemones require attachment; winkles, limpets, topshells, chitons and sea urchins graze rock surfaces for microflora or macroalgae. The algae themselves compete for space. I suggest that the fundamental requirement of the reproductive strategy of these organisms is, once established, to maximize the occupation and retention of space for as long as possible. This is best effected by means of an extended, perennial life-cycle. (This is not to say that *every* individual in *every* micro-habitat is competing inter- and intra-specifically: over ecological time and throughout each species' geographical range competition must be pervasive in this essentially two-dimensional environment.) What of the major predatory taxa – the dogwhelks and starfish? In these cases, the major selection pressure may derive not so much from competition for space as, perhaps indirectly, from competition for food (see, for example, Menge, 1974, 1975). An additional argument I develop on pp. 216–219 attempts to reconcile the apparently widespread selective pressure (of crab predation on juvenile snails) for increasing hatchling/post-larval juvenile size. This is viewed as an evolutionary response on the part of the prey organism to increase juvenile survivorship and appears to be co-adaptive with a perennial life-cycle strategy and iteroparity.

The extended life-cycle strategies of the top predators (e.g. *Pisaster ochraceus* (PNW), *Asterias forbesi* (Desor) (NE), and *A. rubens* (BI)) may, on the other hand, be simply explicable in terms of life history theory outlined above. Juvenile recruitment to echinoid (Ebert, 1982) and asteroid (Menge, 1975) populations is notoriously infrequent and sparse, and here may be instances where all we need invoke is the very variability of larval recruitment necessitating an increased adult longevity (and iteroparity) under the premises of the 'bet-hedging' model. Whatever the viewpoint I find it intriguing that the perennial life-cycle, in conjunction with iteroparity, applies to these diverse dominant organisms regardless of their ecology. Intuitively, we expect perennial life-cycles (and thence iteroparity) in rocky shore invertebrates: imagine the chaotic spatial and temporal dynamics of rocky shore communities were organisms with ephemeral life-cycle strategies dominant. Long-lived (benthic) adult strategies combined with subtle and specific larval settlement behaviour have led to a remarkable degree of order and predictability in these communities. Larvae such as barnacle cyprids (which are offered only one chance of permanent attachment) must ensure the present or future proximity of conspecifics in order to guarantee copulation and fertilization success (Luckens, 1970; C.A. Lewis, 1975): this is best served by the occupation and retention of space, at all other costs, in the face of similarly striving competitors.

14.5 Fertilization and Encapsulation Strategies

For those organisms which release gametes into the water column and fertilize externally there can be no production of spawn-masses. External fertilization invariably is associated with long-term planktotrophic development (e.g. mytilid bivalves, limpets, starfish and sea urchins). Internal fertilization offers the possibility of depositing benthic spawn-masses of encapsulated embryos and of brooding.

Encapsulation concerns the protection of developing embryos within some form of gelatinous, mucopolysaccharide, or proteinaceous matrix – either individually (e.g. *Littorina littorea*, *L. neritoides*) or in a clutch to form a spawn-mass: spawn-masses are always attached to the substratum. Presumably there is considerable advantage in affixing the embryo's capsule to the substratum rather than having it passively cast around the benthos. For *L. littorea* and *L. neritoides* however, individual buoyant capsules – containing usually one or two embryos – are released directly into the plankton and hatch as planktotrophic veligers (e.g. Grahame, 1975). In general, encapsulation may be viewed as a strategy to protect the embryos from the hazards of planktonic life, at least until such time as the larva (e.g. veliger) can fend for itself. Encapsulation, as illustrated by the prosobranch molluscs, does not correlate with any particular larval strategy.

While most embryos subsist entirely on the resources provided by the parent in the egg itself – in addition, perhaps, to planktonic nutrition from particulate feeding and/or uptake of dissolved organic matter (e.g. Manahan, 1983a,b; Manahan and Crisp, 1982, 1983) – others (notably neogastropod dogwhelks) are provided with extra-zygotic resources. These latter usually take the form of 'nurse eggs' which the embryo consumes as it develops within the capsule. 'Nurse egg' provision correlates with benthic encapsulation almost without exception: certainly, a capsule sufficiently large to contain even a single embryo and its complement of 'nurse eggs' would hardly be buoyant (cf. *L. littorea*). Immobile capsules permit hatching of juveniles within the adult's micro-habitat and reduce their exposure to potential predators (Spight, 1975, 1976a,c, 1977b; Rivest, 1983) or adverse abiotic factors (Underwood, 1979).

In the San Juan islands, Washington State, Spight (1977b) observed that 43% of all *Nucella lamellosa* (PNW) spawn capsules failed to hatch. Similarly, Feare (1970b) found anything up to 100% failure for *N. lapillus* (BI); for example, 73% of capsules subject to freshwater runoff in gulleys failed to hatch. In view of the protracted development time of muricid embryos (2.5–4 months, Feare, 1970b; Costello and Henley, 1971; Spight, 1975) and the consequential risks of mortality, it is evidently important that the parent should spawn in reliably productive micro-habitats. Indeed, for such long-lived iteroparous species, females which consistently deposit their spawn in 'good' sites should be selected for. It is, perhaps, surprising that both Feare (1970b; *N. lapillus*, BI) and Spight (1977b; *Nucella lamellosa*, PNW) observed areas with low probability of successful hatching being used more frequently than 'good' sites. Why this should be so is not clear.

Encapsulation of developing embryos is *presumed* to have a protective function (see Spight, 1977b and refs therein; also Pechenik, 1979; Pechenik *et al.*, 1984), but against precisely what is not clear. Certainly capsule production is expensive, in terms of resources, to the parent (Stickle, 1973; Perron, 1981b) and is unlikely to be maladaptive. However, there is as yet little evidence of a nutritional value of spawn-mass jelly matrices, or of protection from heat/desiccation, osmotic change, parasite infestations or predators for a variety of prosobranch gastropods (reviewed by Pechenik, 1979). The capsular fluid of prosobranchs (the so-called 'albumen') could not be shown to have either nutritional or bacteriostatic effects for developing embryos in the case of *Nucella lapillus* (NE) (Pechenik *et al.*, 1984).

Many mesogastropods (notably *Littorina* spp., BI) and asteroid echinoderms (e.g. *Leptasterias hexactis*, PNW; *Leptasterias mulleri* (M. Sars), *Henricia sanguinolenta* (Müller), BI) exhibit brooding behaviour, but here the large eggs themselves provide all the resources necessary for individual embryonic development: the parent merely retains and protects the embryos either within the mantle cavity (*Littorina*) or beneath the adoral surface of the disc (*Leptasterias*). In both cases the juveniles are released when fully formed and are capable of independent life.

Brooding by barnacles is a rather specialized variant on the above pattern. Here is a case of the parent protecting the preliminary (pre-naupliar) phase of development but then releasing the planktotrophic larva to the pelagic system. Feeding, growth and development (through six naupliar moults) leads to the attainment of the non-feeding cypris (settlement) stage of *Semibalanus* within approximately three weeks of release.

Whereas the neogastropods benefit in avoiding the pelagic system (by depositing benthic capsules and provisioning the embryos with extra-zygotic resources) they are, accordingly, subject to reduced gene flow between populations. Admittedly individual pre-juvenile survivorship is enhanced, but at what selective cost in contrast to those organisms which display 'mixed' developmental strategies (such as littorinids and barnacles) with partial protection or parental brooding, or even those which spawn freely into the water column? Do 'mixed' strategies confer an ideal compromise by their temporary protection from the vicissitudes of planktonic mortality, while still ensuring some pelagic dispersal (Pechenik, 1979); or do they result in the 'worst of both worlds', in view of the cost to the parent of protection and the exposure of larvae to pelagic mortality and wastage (Caswell, 1981)?

14.6 Correlates of Reproductive Effort

Reproductive effort (RE) should, ideally, provide a measure of the *total* energy budget fraction apportioned to reproduction by an individual female or hermaphrodite parent (Tinkle and Hadley, 1975). Such a precise measure is largely intractable and most marine workers have, therefore, provided compromise indices based usually upon the expression of egg production as a function of body size, or within gross energy budgets. Available data indicate an absence of predictable patterns or correlations between RE and life history or larval strategy among rocky shore and other marine invertebrates (e.g. Menge, 1974, 1975; Spight and Emlen, 1976; Grahame, 1977, 1983; Todd, 1979b; Hughes and Roberts, 1980a; Todd and Doyle, 1981; Hart and Begon, 1982). But should we expect any such consistent patterns? How comparable are annual, herbivorous, semelparous molluscs weighing only milligrams and perennial iteroparous predatory asteroids which may exceed a kilogram?

Life history theory predicts that current reproduction carries associated costs (in terms of continued adult survival and fecundity) and that RE should increase with age, or 1/RRV (Williams, 1966a,b; Pianka, 1970); also that iteroparous species will exert a lower RE than semelparous counterparts. Furthermore, among long-lived iteroparous species RE should be correlated with extrinsic (non-reproductive) adult mortality and negatively correlated with the variability of juvenile survivorship (Hirschfield and Tinkle, 1975). Perron (1982) presents data for tropical *Conus* spp. which support this latter prediction, and which show increases in RE with age. Taking one of the central premises of the 'bet-hedging' model – notably that fluctuations in juvenile survivorship > adult survivorship leads to iteroparity and low current RE – Hughes and Roberts (1980a) argued that the larval strategies of planktotrophy, non-pelagic lecithotrophy and ovoviviparity ought to provide an increasing trend, in that order, of juvenile survivorship. Accordingly, they predicted that current RE alone should grade the British littorinids *L. 'saxatilis'* < *L. nigrolineata* < *L. littorea* < *L. neritoides* respectively. They could not, however, confirm such a pattern and concluded that, rather than crude demographic features, more specific selection pressures – such as the risk of benthic egg predation, or potential mortality of embryos by desiccation – had led to the patterns observed. Moreover, as Hughes and Roberts (1980a) emphasize, the number and size of eggs (and thence, larval strategy) produced depend only partly on RE, but more on the partitioning of energy resources to individual offspring. Such parental investment per offspring may be influenced by selective pressures totally independent of those affecting RE *per se*. Thus, perhaps expectations of broad correlations and patterns of RE in relation to larval strategy are somewhat naive.

14.7 Larval Dispersal and Models of Larval Strategy

Over the past 60 years it has become axiomatic that pelagic larval forms display 'delay' of metamorphosis in the absence of a specific cue or cues, and that as the delay phase progresses the larva becomes less and less discriminating with regard to its choice of settlement site (see, for example, Bayne, 1965; Meadows and Campbell, 1972; Crisp, 1974a; Strathmann, 1978a; Pechenik, 1984; and other articles in Chia and Rice, 1978).

Another distinction in larval developmental processes which reiterates the point is that between the 'pre-competent' and 'competent' phases (e.g. Crisp, 1974a,b). During the pre-competent phase the larva is morphologically and/or physiologically incapable of settlement and metamorphosis: the competent (= delay) phase commences from the point at which metamorphosis can be undergone upon the acquisition of the appropriate stimuli or cues. This distinction has fundamental implications on reproduction of marine invertebrates. Consider, for example, the larval development of *Semibalanus balanoides* which preferentially settles in the presence of its own species. It matters not how many times the pelagic larva traverses expanses of sand or a multitude of hard substrata occupied by conspecifics during the naupliar (pre-competent) stages: what is crucial, however, is the encounter of the latter substrata by the (competent) cypris stage. It may, therefore, be of adaptive value for the larva to persist in such a competent (delay) phase for as long as possible. The competent phase is not, however, of indefinite duration (see, for example, review by Jackson and Strathmann, 1981). Indeed, Pechenik (1980, 1984) considers the termination of the delay phase of individual larvae to be 'programmed' in that there are clear correlations between the respective pre-competent and competent phases, and between the overall rate of larval development and duration of the competent, or delay, phase. Thus Pechenik (1984) has found that slower-growing larvae of *Crepidula fornicata* (L.) have an extended delay phase, though they require more time to attain competence. At first sight this might suggest that slower-growing (?lower fitness) genotypes might be selected for. However, we must take account of the (presumably) high rates of mortality of pelagic larvae and thus the lower probability of such larvae surviving, attaining competence and successfully metamorphosing.

Available data (e.g. Jackson and Strathmann, 1981) suggest that the delay phases for a range of taxa range from only a few days to many months in duration. A number of authors (e.g. Lucas *et al.*, 1979; Pechenik *et al.*, 1979; Pechenik, 1984) have suggested that an inability to feed on particulates must limit the delay potential of non-feeding pelagic lecithotrophic larvae. While this may be true in, for example, barnacle cyprids this probably does not extend to soft-bodied larval forms, some of which (e.g. veligers) have been shown to take up and utilize dissolved organic matter (e.g. Manahan, 1983b).

Thorson (1946) estimated that approximately 80% of benthic shallow water or littoral marine invertebrates undergo some form of pelagic larval life. All pelagic larvae are subject to dispersal away from the parental micro-habitat and, for specialist rocky shore species, this must be considered detrimental in terms of the individual probabilities of such larvae subsequently locating a suitable substratum. Strathmann (1974) expressed reservations as to the advantages of long-term larval dispersal, while acknowledging as intuitively sensible the benefits to sessile species undergoing short-term dispersal, perhaps by means of pelagic lecithotrophic larvae. Certainly, a major 'cost' of wide dispersal is the reduction in the opportunities of local genetic adaptation (e.g. Strathmann *et al.*,

1981). Nevertheless, in pursuing the problem of long-term dispersal – such as that encountered by littoral barnacles, mussels, gastropods and starfish – Strathmann (1974) deduced a major selective advantage in a parent spreading its sibling offspring both away from the parental source and from one another, thereby reducing parent-offspring and sibling–sibling competition. These deductions, and the model developed, were prompted by his observation that open coast rocky shore invertebrates 'always' undergo large-scale dispersal (perhaps away from *very* favourable circumstances) and few, if any, of the offspring will return to the adult habitat.

Palmer and Strathmann (1981) concluded that planktotrophic larvae (with their inevitably extended pelagic life) receive little, if any, advantage from increased scale of dispersal. Specifically, an extra day spent in the plankton confers little extra spreading of siblings in relation to that already achieved, and the daily rates of pelagic mortality are likely to be pernicious. Accordingly, they deduced that the 'advantages' of the pelagic versus the non-pelagic larval strategy lies not so much in dispersal *per se* as in other traits, such as the ability (or requirement?) to maximize egg numbers.

Chia (1974) had hinted at the latter possibility in suggesting that planktotrophy, which necessitates high fecundity, might confer an enhanced mutation rate to the species. In the case of *Pisaster ochraceus* (planktotrophic) (PNW), Menge (1975) estimated lifetime fecundity at approximately 10^9 eggs in contrast to *Leptasterias hexactis* (non-pelagic lecithotrophic) at approximately 10^3: clearly selection has many more genotypes upon which to work in *Pisaster*.

In modelling the phenomenon of propagule dispersal in general (but with benthic marine invertebrates specifically in mind) Vance (1980, 1984) found the 'spreading of (reproductive) risk' associated with (juvenile) dispersal to stabilize disjunct populations. Moreover, he found populations characterized by such reproductive traits to increase in size under a wide range of (theoretical) conditions. The notion of 'larval colonizing strategies' led Obrebski (1979) to model benthic marine invertebrate reproduction, presuming a series of disjunct adult habitat patches. Obrebski's model links the infrequency of colonization of adult habitat patches with the duration of the pelagic larval stage by combining colonizing success with larval survivorship schedules and adult RE (which determines fecundity). Like Strathmann (1974) he intimated a connection between larval dispersal and the predictability of the adult habitat. An increase in dispersal range necessitates a prolonged larval life (and hence increased fecundity). Conversely, non-pelagic lecithotrophy (with large eggs), while increasing the individual probabilities of 'larval' survival necessarily causes a decrease in both fecundity and dispersal capacity or range. He asks, therefore, if there is such as an 'optimal dispersal range' by relating the frequency and separation of suitable adult habitat patches to dispersal abilities: as might be expected, he concluded that as colonization becomes unfavourable selection should act to reduce larval dispersal.

Crisp (1974a, 1976) has also simulated the effects of larval dispersal on isolated adult populations and concluded a major advantage was conferred by pelagic larvae in cases where there is high density-independent mortality affecting these unequally. Crisp (1976) has also invoked the necessity of high adult fecundity in order to offset the high rates of planktonic mortality. Thus, unlike Strathmann (1974) and Palmer and Strathmann (1981), Crisp (1976) made explicit statements with regard to the advantages commensurate with a pelagic larval phase – notably the potential to increase the species' geographical range, the increase of gene flow, the reduction of local extinctions resulting from density-independent perturbations and (as a result of the necessarily higher fecundity) the increase in potential juvenile offspring per unit RE.

In very general terms Vance's (1973a,b) model views the duration of the pelagic phase (if any) primarily in terms of the maximization of the number of benthic juveniles per unit RE. Thus, the alternatives are the production of large numbers of small eggs, giving rise to feeding planktotrophic larvae, or of fewer, larger eggs provisioned with all necessary resources, and which may therefore avoid development in the pelagic system. The required duration of the pelagic phase is determined by the resource requirements of planktotrophic larvae; selection for the pelagic versus non-pelagic strategies depends upon the differential mortality encountered during planktonic versus benthic development, and goes toward that strategy which maximizes the 'efficiency' of numbers of viable offspring per unit RE. Vance's model in fact predicts only the extremes of egg size (small → planktotrophy; large → lecithotrophy) to be evolutionarily stable. This, in turn, may be interpreted as suggesting that the distribution of egg sizes among marine invertebrates ought to be bimodal: whether or not this is the case is open to some argument (e.g. Christiansen and Fenchel, 1979; Perron and Carrier, 1981; Grant, 1983).

Vance's conceptualizations of larval strategies, and their underlying assumptions, have been subject to not inconsiderable debate (e.g. Crisp, 1974a; Underwood, 1974; Vance, 1974; Steele, 1977; Strathmann, 1977; Christiansen and Fenchel, 1979; Todd, 1979; Perron and Carrier, 1981; Todd and Doyle, 1981; Grant, 1983). Of fundamental consequence is his assumption that selection should favour that strategy which results in the highest reproductive 'efficiency'. Marine invertebrates may, some would argue, be ancestrally 'channelized' in their larval strategy as a result, perhaps, of (evolutionary) historical accident. Thus, for example, Strathmann (1978b) has shown that in a wide variety of marine invertebrate phyla, pelagic-feeding larval stages have been lost during evolution, and that there are apparently barriers to their re-acquisition. It may be that the various larval strategies do not, therefore, present alternative 'options' to many taxa. Consider two genotypes, A and B, which reproduce by means of planktotrophic and pelagic lecithotrophic larvae respectively. Genotype A commits 10 calories to reproduction and produces one viable offspring; genotype B commits 100 calories and has nine surviving offspring. The reproductive 'efficiency' for each respective genotype is therefore 1/10 calories and 1/11.1 calories: Vance's model would dictate that selection ought to favour B, or planktotrophy, but this cannot be so. Selection acts upon the differential production of absolute numbers of viable offspring – even if these are produced 'inefficiently'. It may be that genotype A cannot, for a variety of reasons, alter egg size and switch strategy to adopt planktotrophy: nevertheless, in producing nine viable offspring B must enjoy a selective advantage over A.

Despite the controversies surrounding Vance's (1973a,b) model there can be little doubt that these have made a major contribution in providing a conceptual framework within which marine benthic invertebrate reproductive strategies might be viewed. Christiansen and Fenchel (1979), for example, constructed another model (similar to Vance's) which considered RE a constant in evolution. Their model is based upon the premise that there is an evolutionary trade-off between fecundity and (individual larval) survivorship, and that this trade-off can be formulated with respect to RE. Thus, fecundity is considered directly proportional to RE, but inversely proportional to egg size.

Like Vance's (1973a), Christiansen and Fenchel's model predicts that only the extremes of egg size (and, by implication, larval strategy) are evolutionarily stable. They make the doubtful assertion that it is evolutionarily 'easy' for planktotrophy to be re-acquired from non-pelagic development, and in support of this suggest that (non-pelagic) prosobranchs which utilize nurse-eggs 'only spend longer in the capsule, feeding on provisioned yolk'. Like Vance (1973a), they make no explicit statements with regard to larval dispersal or the significance of (short-term) pelagic lecithotrophy, save to suggest that there is some advantage.

All the above models and formulations still leave us some considerable distance from a clear understanding of the evolution of particular larval strategies and, indeed, the inter-relationships between larval strategy, life-cycle, life history, larval dispersal and energetic considerations. With respect to the question of 'brooding' of non-pelagic young, as opposed to 'broadcasting' of planktotrophic larvae (Menge, 1975), I feel we are somewhat closer. Parental retention and protection of eggs is not uncommon among rocky shore invertebrates such as littorinid prosobranchs, barnacles and asteroid echinoderms. With the latter particularly in mind Strathmann and Strathmann (1982) and Strathmann *et al.* (1984) have indicated the significance of the allometric consequences of body size on egg production (a function of body size) versus brooding capacity (essentially a function of area). They suggest that the capacity for an adult starfish to brood its young beneath the oral disc is considerably constrained relative to the number of eggs which can be produced. Therefore brooding is favoured in smaller organisms, since larger counterparts cannot brood all they can produce. In attempting to resolve the dichotomy in larval strategy between *Pisaster ochraceus* (planktotrophic) and the small (non-pelagic lecithotrophic) *Leptasterias hexactis* (PNW) Menge (1974, 1975) suggested that dispersal of larval offspring allows *Pisaster* the opportunity of exploiting temporally and/or spatially unpredictable areas of high-quality prey (*Mytilus californianus*) resources: small adults (*Leptasterias*) are suggested to be incapable of producing sufficient larvae to offset pelagic mortality and are thus constrained to exploit less variable resources. Although Menge's arguments with respect to larval dispersal appear intuitively sensible there are, as yet, no empirical field data of survivorship and colonization success for the pelagic phases of marine invertebrates upon which tests can be based. The reversal of the question as exemplified by Strathmann and Strathmann (1982) and Strathmann *et al.* (1984) is, perhaps, our only viable alternative at present.

14.8 A Stochastic Model of Non-pelagic Development Co-adaptive with Iteroparity

Reproductive strategies of British littorinids have been investigated repeatedly. Analyses have concentrated particularly upon the relation of certain phenotypic (e.g. shell morphology) and demographic/reproductive traits (e.g. size at first maturity, size/number of offspring, correlates of RE) in local populations subject to contrasting selection regimes.

High/mid-shore littorinids (*L. neritoides, L. 'saxatilis', L. nigrolineata*) frequently take refuge in crevices on tidal emersion. 'Crevice' or 'cliff' populations are often presumed to be subject to intense density-independent mortality pressure from wave-crash dislodgement, lack of refuges and perhaps desiccation stress, whereas 'boulder' shore populations are held to be subject to stone-crushing and perhaps excessive predatory mortality. Thus, 'crevice' winkles are generally found to mature at a smaller size and to exert greater RE (e.g. Faller-Fritsch, 1977; Roberts and Hughes, 1980; Hughes and Roberts, 1981; Hart and Begon, 1982; Atkinson and Newbury, 1984). Faller-Fritsch (1977) found 'crevice' *L. 'rudis'* to produce more, smaller offspring, while Hart and Begon (1982) noted the inverse – 'crevice' offspring > 'boulder' offspring. Size at first reproduction is greater in 'crevice' versus 'boulder' individuals of both *L. 'saxatilis'* (Roberts and Hughes, 1980; Hart and Begon, 1982) and *L. nigrolineata* (Naylor and Begon, 1981), but whether or not age at first reproduction differs here also remains unestablished.

Hughes and Roberts (1980a) observed a cline of variation in (brooded) embryo size for *L. 'saxatilis'*: sheltered saltmarsh > 'cliffs' (or 'crevices') > sheltered boulder shore. This cline of offspring size could not be related to population density differences, or any other demographic feature (Hughes and Roberts, 1981), and it is likely that other selection pressures affect embryo/juvenile size (see also Hart and Begon, 1981; Atkinson and Newbury, 1984). It was suggested that juvenile shore crabs (*Carcinus maenas* (L.)) are a major predator of small littorinids and that in saltmarshes especially, larger eggs (giving rise to larger hatchlings) are selected for, in that they require less time to grow to a 'safe' size. For their 'cliff' *L. 'saxatilis'*, Hughes and Roberts (1980a) suggest that larger offspring tolerate desiccation stress better.

The littorinid studies have provided variously conflicting support both for the *r-K* theory and the 'bet-hedging' model (e.g. Hughes and Roberts, 1980a; Hart and Begon, 1982; Raffaelli, 1982; Atkinson and Newbury, 1984). The subjective classification of habitats into 'crevice', 'cliff' and 'boulders' by diverse authors, however, has certainly not aided comparisons. As Hughes and Roberts suggest, it is perhaps necessary to seek more proximate selective forces (while acknowledging the implications of, for example, the 'bet-hedging' assumptions and predictions), which may affect particularly egg size → hatchling size → larval strategy → life history strategy.

I would argue that mortality from stone-crushing is not such a pervasive selective force on size or shell thickness on juvenile littorinids as is crab or hermit crab predation. The size differences are so minor as to be of questionable adaptive value against wave-shifted rocks but may be of critical consequence in terms of protection from small predators.

Species of gastropods that produce normal eggs have uniform hatchling sizes (Fioroni, 1966) and thus in order for hatchling size to be adjusted in such cases, selection would have to act upon egg size itself. While this apparently applies to the above littorinids there are, presumably, limits to the flexibility of egg size as a variable. Neogastropods which utilize nurse eggs may, however, adjust hatchling size (Gallardo, 1979) by altering the number of nurse eggs per embryo. Thus, for example, *Nucella lapillus* (BI) hatches at 0.3–2.5mm (Risbec, 1937) while *N. emarginata* (PNW) may range from 0.9–1.8mm shell length (Spight, 1976a); this latter doubling of length confers an eight-fold weight difference. Rivest (1983) noted *Searlesia dira* (Reeve) (PNW) to vary at hatching from 1.1mm (eight embryos/capsule) to 2.4mm (only two embryos/capsule).

The advantages of increased hatchling size are, perhaps, best illustrated by age-specific survivorship data for *Nucella lamellosa* (PNW). Spight (1976a) estimated that the newly hatched dogwhelk (1.4mm) had a 1–2% chance of reaching three months of age, then a 35% chance of attaining one year, but then a 40–60% chance of surviving beyond this. Clearly, with such rapid increases in survivorship (with size and age), a small increase in hatching size would confer marked benefit. Rivest (1983) has shown that the numbers of nurse eggs per embryo for a variety of PNW neogastropods represent random statistical samples from a binomial distribution (of a genetically fixed nurse egg: embryo ratio). Thus, the unequal parental investment in provisioning of embryos results in important variance upon which selection may act. However, an increase in hatchling size is only attainable at a selective cost, for larger hatchlings require prolonged intra-capsular development time and, as we have seen, benthic capsules are not risk-free: anomuran hermit crabs and pagurid or hemigrapsid crabs are major predators of juvenile rocky shore snails (Spight, 1976c; Elner and Raffaelli, 1980; Hughes and Roberts, 1980a; Rivest, 1983), and mortality from physical causes is frequent.

Spight (1976c) has noted a steady increase in hatchling (both pelagic and non-pelagic) sizes along the evolutionary line Archaeogastropoda < Mesogastropoda < Neogastropoda. Furthermore, the maximum muricid dogwhelk hatchling size is approximately 2.5mm, while many other (sublittoral) neogastropods hatch as large as 7mm. Indeed, sublittoral muricids from a range of geographical localities hatch bigger than littoral counterparts. The conclusion must be, therefore, that selection for hatchling size is primarily attributable to biological selective forces (such as crab predation) rather than abiotic stress. I argue that there are widespread pervasive predation pressures which have led to increased hatchling size among rocky shore gastropods (and perhaps echinoderms). I further argue that the adoption of non-pelagic 'larval' strategies (as adaptive responses to increase juvenile size) have necessitated the adoption of perennial, iteroparous reproductive strategies as co-adapted traits; this arises from the reduction in fecundity and perhaps the differential product of juvenile/adult survivorship. Certainly, I find no examples of non-pelagic lecithotrophic development correlating with abbreviated life-cycles and semelparity.

The flow chart in Fig. 14.2 summarizes my conjecture. It is largely self-explanatory, but the inferences of demographic responses are drawn from the premises of the 'bet-hedging' model. The model should be followed by interpreting the arrows in accordance with the key. The broad (shaded or black) arrows outline the adaptive pathways which are evolutionarily supportable. The broken circle I consider to be an evolutionary blind alley in that there are self-perpetuating negative influences incurred throughout. The broad shaded pathway is best illustrated by certain muricid neogastropods:

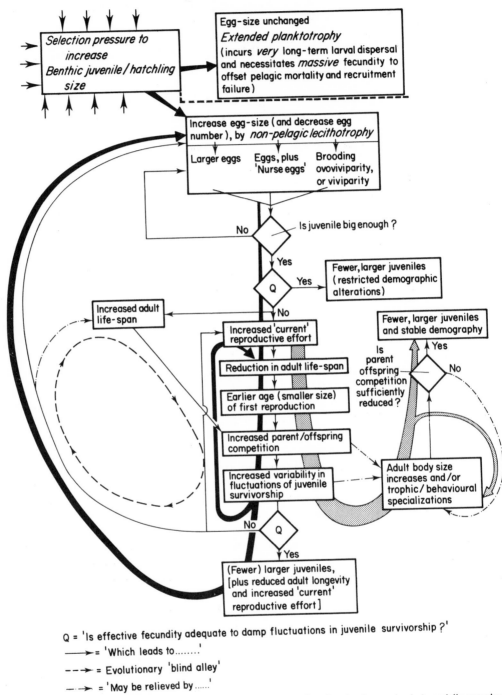

FIG. 14.2. Flow chart illustrating possible reproductive strategy responses of rocky shore animals (especially prosobranch gastropods). The responses are to selection pressures favouring an increase in hatchling size. The diagram should be followed according to the key. See text for additional explanation.

in some species there is ecological separation of cohorts. Thus, for example, juvenile *Thais orbita* (Gmelin) (Australia) (Phillips, 1969; Butler, 1979) migrate up into the littoral, while adults return to the sublittoral; other species, such as *Nucella lapillus* (BI) (Feare, 1970b) make progressive up- and downshore movements throughout the individuals' life-span.

The broad black pathways I envisage as representing littorinids (especially) and other non-migratory species, though the possibilities of the individual 'switching' to the right half of the model remain. Here, increases and decreases in life-span, current fecundity and juvenile survivorship are balanced according to the prevailing selective regime. It is, perhaps, significant that the flow chart model *may* dictate that the final hatchling/juvenile size be bigger (as a result of demographic constraints and implications) than that demanded by the original selection pressure. This depends upon the precise 'route' and number of 'circulations' required to resolve constraints.

14.9 Summary

I have outlined two scenarios to explain the prevalence of perennial life-cycles and iteroparity in rocky shore invertebrates. Neither are to be considered as absolutes – rather as topics for discussion. The first concerns both 'space-occupying' (e.g. barnacles and mussels) and 'space-exploiting' (grazers and predators) taxa. The emphasis here is on the acquisition and retention of primary space in the face of intense inter- and intraspecific competition. (This is not to deny the frequently pervasive influence of predation and physical disturbance as major community-structuring forces.) An intuitively sensible demographic response would be for individuals to occupy such space as long as possible: indeed, the fluctuations and variations in pelagic larval recruitment and (low) juvenile survivorship probably preclude annual, semelparous strategies.

No correlations between adoption of embryonic encapsulation and level of reproductive effort (RE), or between RE and larval strategy, or between larval strategy and life history are detectable. However, perennial life-cycles and iteroparity prevail throughout all dominant rocky shore taxa. The significance of pelagic larval dispersal (and its effects on level and variations in recruitment) remains unclear, but its importance is deducible.

A second conceptual scenario is developed with respect to the incidence of non-pelagic lecithotrophy, and this is related to (predatory) selection pressures to increase hatchling size. The model applies equally to ovoviviparous species and those using nurse eggs. However, there is, as yet, an undetermined connection between the advantages of increased juvenile survivorship (with opportunities of local adaptation) versus the reduction of gene-flow and preclusion of larval dispersal.

ACKNOWLEDGEMENTS

I would like to thank Mr Jon. Havenhand for many thoughtful hours of discussion.

CHAPTER XV

LIFE HISTORY PATTERNS IN ROCK POOL ANIMALS

R.H. Emson

Rock pools are a characteristic and easily accessible feature of almost every rocky shore, yet they have received comparatively little attention from marine ecologists. The explanation for this may reside in their variability. The three major factors causing variation between pools are height on the shore with respect to low water, the degree of wave exposure of the site and the pools' internal dimensions and shape. Each of these features will contribute to variation in physical conditions within a pool. For instance, organisms living in a pool high on a shore are subject to the problems which result from an absence of water exchange for long periods. Equally a shallow pool at any shore level is more likely to suffer more severe temperature fluctuations than is a deep pool and thus temperature-associated problems (such as oxygen availability) will be greater in such pools. The degree of water exchange in pools will be affected markedly by wave action. Complete mixing and exchange is characteristic of pools on exposed shores but on sheltered shores, bottom water layers in pools may remain relatively undisturbed even during the period of inundation. This is most likely to happen in pools near the upper limits of tidal excursion, and again can have important effects on physical conditions.

A fourth component of variability in the physical conditions of pools is the biota, particularly the macroalgae. When present in large quantities, algae affect the environment of the pool significantly. They reduce water movement and create relatively sheltered micro-habitats and refugia in exposed situations, but most importantly they alter (often very considerably) the oxygen content of the pool in a cyclical manner with potential effects on the fauna.

Pools are a part of the wider dynamic environment of rocky shores and drastic physical events such as storms which may fundamentally alter the balance of plants and animals on the open rock surface will also affect pool populations. Storms are a usual winter feature, but their impact may have more radical effects 'out of season'.

Larger pools exhibit biological succession towards a climax flora, which may have marked effects on the availability of habitats for animals, as well as destructive effects on subordinate flora. In some rock pools, this feature is complicated by the intervention of grazers (which may selectively graze dominant forms) and by the unpredictable incursions of 'outside' herbivores and their predators into such pools (Paine and Vadas, 1969). Predictable events include inevitable seasonal changes such as the elevation of temperatures in summer with, for some pools, the consequence of hypersalinity or even complete drying-out. Other seasonal events include migration onshore of various predatory species in the

---

Editors' note: Due to illness and other unforeseen circumstances, Dr Emson has only been able to provide a brief summary of his views on this topic instead of the comprehensive review he had planned.

summer months, and their reverse movements in winter (e.g. crabs, some prawns), and the arrival of sporelings and larvae of plants and animals in the spring and summer. Although the arrival of colonizing sporelings and larvae is predictable, which ones succeed and in what quantities is not. This adds another element to the variability of rock pools. Is it possible then to discern any ecological trends of general significance in the face of all this habitat variability?

Recently, interest in aspects of rock pool ecology has been reawakening. The variations in the physical environment have received attention from Ganning (1971a), Daniel and Boyden (1975), Truchot and Duhamel-Jouve (1980) and Morris and Taylor (1983). Community organization has been studied by Mwaiseje (1977), Goss-Custard et al. (1979) and by Dethier (1980, 1981b, 1984).

It is now becoming apparent that adaptation to rock pool conditions has resulted in predictable physiological capacities (e.g. Emson and Foote, 1980) and life history traits among pool-dwelling species. The physiological attributes of pool species will be reviewed elsewhere (Emson, in prep.); here I will be concerned very briefly with animal reproductive biology and life history pattern.

Rock pool animals can be divided arbitrarily into four categories as follows:

(i)   True pool species which are found only in rock pools and only rarely in any numbers outside.
(ii) Species which are characteristically abundant in rock pools but are also successful in other habitats.
(iii) Species which are occasional in rock pools but have their major populations elsewhere.
(iv) Species which are seasonal immigrants into rock pools for reproductive or other purposes.

Recently Goss-Custard et al. (1979) and Mwaiseje (1977) have listed the species found in two separate Irish rock pool systems and I have overlapping lists for rock pool systems in South Wales and South-West England. A full consideration of these lists here (but see Emson, in prep.) is now precluded, but certain generalizations can be made.

Very few species are entirely restricted to rock pools (British examples include the shrimp *Palaemon elegans* Rathke, the gastropods *Rissoella diaphana* (Alder), *Omalogyra atomus* (Philippi), *Skeneopsis planorbis* (Fabricius) and the starfish *Asterina phylactica* Emson and Crump): the list of characteristically pool-dwelling species is more extensive (species like the anemone *Anemonia viridis* (Pennant), the polychaetes *Fabricia sabella* (Ehrenberg), *Janua pagenstecheri* Quatrefages, *Pomatoceros lamarckii* (Quatrefages), *Spirorbis corallinae* de Silva and Knight-Jones, *S. inornatus* L'Hardy and Quiévreux, the isopods *Idotea pelagica* Leach, *I. granulosa* Rathke, *Jaera* spp., the amphipods *Apherusa jurinei* (Milne-Edw.), *A. cirrus* (Bate), *Stenothoe monoculoides* (Mont.), *Hyale stebbingi* Chevreux, the decapod *Pisidia longicornis* (L.), the molluscs *Patella aspera* Lamarck, *Littorina littorea* L., *Cingula cingillus* (Mont.), *Rissoa parva* (da Costa), the brittle star *Amphipholis squamata* Delle Chiaje, the starfish *Asterina gibbosa* Pennant and the butterfish *Pholis gunnellus* (L.) to name only some). Among such 'typical' rock pool species direct development is favoured and brooding of direct developed eggs is also common. Relatively few species have lecithotrophic or planktotrophic larvae (Jardine, this volume, describes one such species, the prosobranch *Gibbula cineraria* (L.)). The highly unpredictable nature of the rock pool environment has already been stressed. It has been demonstrated that unpredictable environments like the rocky littoral are usually characterized by a predominance of species with a large reproductive potential (Todd, this volume), i.e. planktotrophic development. Furthermore, since rock pools with conditions suitable for a particular species may be separated by significant physical barriers, the 'sensible' reproductive mode for rock pool species would appear at first sight to be to broadcast larvae widely. Since the observed facts are contrary to this expectation, we must review the premises of our argument. The answer is probably simple. The rock pool environment favours small, as well as tolerant, species. Many of the typical pool species are small enough to find shelter in the multiplicity of cryptic habitats within pools, beneath rocks, in crevices, in the cavities within and between encrusting calcareous algae and among the holdfasts and fronds of the turf-forming algae. A significant proportion of rock pool species are thus of phytal origin.

Small size inevitably restricts gonad volume and thus female fecundity. The potential number of larvae possible is therefore low, and since the chances of individual larvae surviving a period of planktonic life are extremely low, species producing small numbers of planktotrophic larvae have little chance of successful recruitment to pools. Such a reproductive mode has been predicted to be evolutionarily unstable (Vance, 1973a), unsatisfactory and unlikely to persist. Many species with these reproductive characteristics either have an alternative 'safer' means of reproduction, that is asexual reproduction (e.g. Mladenov and Emson, 1984), or have modified the planktonic phase in some way. Both of these reproductive patterns are found among rock pool species. Species which utilize asexual reproduction as a means of population increase include *Anemonia viridis*, bryozoans, and species with modified planktonic development, including those with an abbreviated planktonic phase shown by some of the small polychaetes (e.g. *Spirorbis corallinae*). Thus it appears that rock pool species have been forced to adopt modified planktonic development and direct development as a consequence of needing to be small to adapt to the rock pool environment.

The prevalence of brooding in rock pool species may be a consequence of high levels of predation. Such experimental studies as have been made of predation effects in pools indicate that it is a significant selective agency. Dethier (1980) demonstrated the effect of fish on the copepod *Tigriopus*, and Crump and Emson (1978) showed that unprotected eggs of *Asterina gibbosa* were rapidly consumed by prawns (*Palaemon elegans, P. serratus* Pennant), polynoid polychaetes and, in all probability, fish. The value of brooding was demonstrated later in *A. phylactica* (Emson and Crump, 1979). Predators constitute a continuous threat to unprotected eggs. Clearly predation is one reason why brooding of young is such a prominent feature of pool invertebrates, and the same applies even to fishes (see Gibson, 1969, 1982). It has been demonstrated (Strathmann and Strathmann, 1981) that small size and brooding are correlated but no universal explanation as to why this should be so could be given. The disadvantages of direct development are slow dispersal, low rates of recruitment, the possibility of local extinction and (potentially) the effects of inbreeding. The first three of these attributes are certainly features of rock pool populations. Studies of recolonization of pools (Mwaiseje, 1977; Crump, pers. comm. and pers. obs.) have shown that although ephemeral algae are quick to colonize pools and some of the more active pool species, such as amphipods, take up residence quite soon, many less mobile species, particularly those associated with the turf-forming algae, may be several years in establishing themselves.

The scope for studies on reproductive mode as a consequence of small size in pool animals is as yet inadequately realized. The trade-offs between dispersal ability, fecundity, reproductive effort and body size which underpin so much of contemporary life history theory have an ideal testing ground in the rock pools of the world. To re-iterate Pat Boaden's meiofaunal dictum . . . 'Think small!'

CHAPTER XVI

ROCKY SHORE COMMUNITIES: CATALYSTS TO UNDERSTANDING PREDATION

R.N. Hughes

16.1 Introduction

Several rocky shore predators have proved to be good experimental subjects for testing theories about foraging; the way predation shapes community structure on certain rocky shores has elucidated general ecological principles; whilst predation on rocky shore gastropods appears to have important zoogeographical consequences. These aspects of rocky shore biology, each contributing greatly to our understanding of predation as an ecological process, are discussed sequentially.

16.2 Foraging Behaviour

An economics approach to predation, in which foraging behaviour is assessed according to the ensuing return rate or ratio of gain to cost, has attracted vigorous theoretical treatment over the last decade (Pulliam, 1974; Charnov, 1976a,b; McNair, 1979; Winterhalder, 1983), producing a conceptual framework, popularly known as Optimal Foraging Theory, whose simplistic predictions continue to inspire a wealth of experimental studies of foraging both in the laboratory and in the field (reviewed in Pyke *et al.*, 1977; Krebs, 1978; Hughes, 1980a; Townsend and Hughes, 1981). The essentials of Optimal Foraging Theory, however, had been suggested about a decade earlier by MacArthur and Pianka (1966) who sought to predict 'in which patches a species would feed and which items would form its diet if the species acted in the most economical fashion' and by Emlen (1966a, 1968) who developed 'a model which relates optimal food preference relationships and caloric yield per unit time of potential food sources' (see Schoener, 1971, for review of early literature). Emlen (1966a,b) chose dogwhelks, *Nucella emarginata* (Deshayes), and *N. lamellosa* (Gmelin), feeding on the barnacles of rocky shores in Washington State as a system for comparison with his theoretical ideas, and this surely must be the first experimental application of the Optimal Foraging Theory.

Dogwhelks, like other muricaceans, drill the shells of their prey using the accessory boring organ on the propodium, together with radular action (Carriker and van Zandt, 1972), gaining access to the prey's flesh with their extensible proboscis. Drilling and ingestion of barnacles takes at least several hours, almost entirely during high tide, but Emlen (1966b) was able to quantify total handling times by remote time-lapse underwater photography, using an enclosed cine camera fixed about 0.6m from the rock surface at shore levels, -0.6, 0 and $+0.6$m from Chart Datum.

Knowing the handling times associated with different sized dogwhelks and barnacles, together with the allometric relationships between barnacle diameter and dry flesh weight, Emlen (1966b) predicted the yield (flesh per hour of handling) for particular categories of dogwhelk and barnacle. Thus defined, profitability was predicted to increase as barnacles grew bigger and, as expected, *N. emarginata* clearly preferred the largest *Balanus glandula* Darwin available.

Because their flimsier shells can be drilled quicker, *Balanus glandula* were predicted to be more profitable than *Semibalanus cariosus* (Pallas) of similar size; but as they grow larger, *S. cariosus* should equal or exceed the profitability of *B. glandula*. However, *N. emarginata* was estimated to take only about 3h to handle an average-sized *B. glandula* but about 14h to handle a larger *S. cariosus*. Being a relatively small species, there is room for several *N. emarginata* on top of a large *S. cariosus* and a feeding individual tends to attract others, who try to exploit the already drilled prey. 'Hangers-on' were frequently observed on the shore and Emlen (1966b) calculated that an intruder would depress the profitability of a 12mm *S. cariosus* by about 71%, to a level below that of a 1mm *B. glandula* (Fig. 4e of Hughes, 1980a). Consequently, even though *S. cariosus* was abundant lower on the shore where physical conditions were more benign, *N. emarginata* was expected to prefer *B. glandula*, and indeed foraging *N. emarginata* were found to congregate in the *B. glandula* zone at mid-to-high levels on the shore.

Nucella lamellosa, on the other hand, grows larger than *N. emarginata*, leaving little room for intruders even when feeding on large *S. cariosus* and few such cases were observed. Large *S. cariosus*, therefore, should be more profitable to large *N. lamellosa* than to small conspecifics and to *N. emarginata*. Accordingly, the proportion of *S. cariosus* in the diet increased as *N. emarginata* became larger (Emlen, 1966b).

Emlen (1966a,b) was therefore the first to demonstrate quantitatively that a predator, *Nucella*, shows feeding preferences tending to maximize its energy intake per unit foraging time. Since then, approximations to an 'energy-maximizing' foraging behaviour have been demonstrated in a wide variety of taxa (Krebs, 1978; Hughes, 1980a,b), but muricacean gastropods of rocky shores continue to serve as convenient experimental subjects because of their accessibility, robustness and well-defined dietary requirements.

The 'energy maximization premise' – that foraging behaviour maximizing the net rate of energy intake also increases genetic fitness, which is central to the Optimal Foraging Theory – has not been shown directly to hold for any animal, and even indirect tests of this assumption have been made only rarely. Another critical assumption of the Optimal Foraging Theory, that the foraging predator stores information on the average quality and availability of prey types, for use in 'deciding' whether or not to accept an encountered prey item, has also rarely been tested. Indirect tests of both assumptions, however, have been made by Palmer (1984) who, like Emlen (1966b), exploited the observational and manipulative advantages of dogwhelks and their sedentary prey in designing appropriate experiments.

Juvenile *Nucella emarginata*, caged on the shore with different monotypic prey, grew fastest on *Balanus glandula*, less well on *Mytilus edulis* L. and slowest on *Semibalanus cariosus*, which was thought to reflect the relative profitabilities of these prey items since growth occurs only after costs associated with eating a particular kind of prey have been paid (Palmer, 1983a). By comparing the expected profitability of a prey item being eaten by *N. emarginata* with the expected values of all other prey items in the immediate vicinity on the shore, Palmer (1984) showed that there was a strong tendency for dogwhelks to choose the more profitable items among those available. These observations suggested that the categories of prey preferred by *N. emarginata* are those maximizing growth rate and hence fitness.

To see whether average yields of prey experienced during previous foraging periods could influence the future choice of prey items, Palmer (1984) caged groups of *N. emarginata* on the shore with different sized barnacles and mussels representing low and high yield situations. After a month of conditioning within the cages, the dogwhelks were released onto an area of rock to which were glued large and small *Balanus glandula* and *Mytilus edulis*. The freely foraging dogwhelks were observed directly at low tide and by using SCUBA at high tide, showing that those conditioned to a low average yield attacked the different prey in the proportions encountered, whereas those conditioned to a high average yield preferentially attacked the most profitable items, large *Balanus glandula*. It appears, therefore, that the previous foraging experience of *N. emarginata* leads it to 'expect' a certain availability of the more profitable prey, causing it to specialize on them when they are expected to be abundant and to broaden its diet when they are expected to be scarce, in accordance with the Optimal Foraging Theory. Observations on other caged individuals suggested that conditioned *N. emarginata* require more than 14 days to adjust their expectation of average yield in a new prey régime (Palmer, 1984).

As the Optimal Foraging Theory gained application, it became popular to draw attention to constraints, such as risks of mortality while foraging or behavioural requirements other than feeding, that might influence foraging behaviour. In fact the counterbalance of energy maximization while foraging and associated risks from desiccation and wave action had been considered in detail by Emlen (1966b) (see also Spight, 1982a).

A putative example of the effect of a constraint on foraging behaviour was given by J.L. Menge (1974) in her account of dietary selection by the Californian muricacean *Acanthina punctulata* (Sowerby). Laboratory studies had shown that *A. punctulata* prefers *Littorina* spp. to barnacles. When foraging commenced on the falling tide, *A. punctulata* preferentially attacked *Littorina* spp., as expected, but in the last half of the foraging bout the preference was lost and, since barnacles were encountered more frequently, they were more likely to be attacked. Menge (1974) argued that if *A. punctulata* persisted in their search for *Littorina*, they would be at risk from dislodgement by waves at the turn of the tide, but in accepting barnacles they avoided this risk by maintaining a firm attachment to the substratum and remaining immobile while feeding.

Palmer's investigation (1984) on the effect of previous foraging experience on dietary selection by *Nucella emarginata* allowed the influence of conditioning to a specific prey to be discounted. Maintenance of *Nucella* (= *Thais*) *lapillus* (L.) for 2–3 months on either *Semibalanus balanoides* (L.) or *Mytilus edulis*, however, causes them to increase their tendency to attack familiar prey when subsequently offered both (Hughes and Dunkin, 1984b), a result of 'ingestive conditioning' first demonstrated (Wood, 1968) in the oyster-drill, *Urosalpinx cinerea* (Say), and subsequently recorded in a variety of animals.

Nucella lapillus also responds over a shorter time scale to experience with specific prey. Dogwhelks, taken from a population feeding on barnacles and then allowed to consume 6–7 small mussels, achieved about a 27% reduction in penetration time, by drilling in the thinnest area of the mussel shell. No change in penetration time occurred when naive dogwhelks were presented with larger mussels, but they developed a tendency to drill over the digestive gland, gaining direct access to the most nutritious tissues (Hughes and Dunkin, 1984a). In either case, the learned behaviour would increase the profitability of the mussels. Similarly, dogwhelks fed on mussels for 3 months tended to drill through the skeletal plates of the first few barnacles subsequently presented to them, but developed an increasing tendency to gain quicker entry between the opercular plates after about 6 prey items had been eaten. Again, this learned behaviour would increase the profitability of the prey (Dunkin and Hughes, 1984). Because *N. lapillus* can learn to shorten handling times, the profitabilities of large *Semibalanus balanoides* and small *Mytilus edulis* may become transposed as the dogwhelk successively gains experience with each prey (Fig. 16.1A), thus providing a possible mechanism for 'switching' from a diet purely of one prey to that of the other (Hughes, 1979; Hughes and Dunkin, 1984b). Profitabilities would not, of course, be transposed if prey times were too dissimilar in size, as with small *S. balanoides* and large *M. edulis* (Fig. 16.1A).

Switching has not been demonstrated in *Nucella lapillus*, but the first experimental indication of switching in any predator was found in another muricacean, *Acanthina spirata* (Blainville), of Californian rocky shores (Murdoch, 1969). Whilst on average, *A. spirata* showed an equal predilection

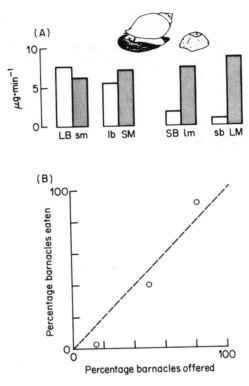

Fig. 16.1. A, Profitability (yield of flesh/handling time) of *Semibalanus balanoides* (open bars) and *Mytilus edulis* (stippled bars) to *Nucella lapillus*. Letters under the bars indicate large or small barnacles and large or small mussels. Capital letters denote prey (barnacles or mussels) to which dogwhelks are trained (from Hughes and Dunkin, 1984b). B, Switching of diet in *Acanthina spirata*. Low datum, snails trained to mussels and offered 16.7% *Balanus glandula* with 83.3% *Mytilus edulis*; middle datum, snails not trained either to barnacles or mussels and offered 50% barnacles; top datum, snails trained to barnacles and offered 83.3% barnacles. Dietary composition expected in the absence of switching is denoted by the broken line (from Murdoch, 1969).

for *Balanus glandula* and comparably sized *Mytilus edulis*, individuals tended to prefer one prey or the other when tested. By prolonged feeding on monospecific diets, Murdoch (1969) induced *A. spirata* to develop a preference for barnacles or mussels, so that when subsequently offered a mixture of prey, the dogwhelks fed disproportionately on those on which they had been maintained (Fig. 16.1B). These simultaneous results with different batches of dogwhelks were thought to reflect temporal dietary changes that would occur within individuals experiencing sequential changes in the relative abundance of barnacles and mussels.

Although the mechanism for changing dietary preferences – whether by learned reduction in handling time, increased attack success rate, or by development of a 'search image' – was not elucidated, Murdoch's (1969) demonstration of dietary responses of *Acanthina spirata* to foraging experience became established as a classic example of frequency dependent predation, a phenomenon hallowed by population ecologists as a potential stabilizing force in predator–prey systems (Murdoch and Oaten, 1975) and by population geneticists as a force maintaining polymorphisms by 'apostatic selection' (Clarke, 1969).

16.3 Effect of Predation on Community Structure

Experimental studies of predation (taken in its widest ecological sense to include herbivory (Lubchenco, 1979; Hughes, 1980b)) in rocky shore communities date back at least to Jones (1948b) and Southward (1953) who, by experimentally removing limpets from a strip of shore on the Isle of Man, showed that intense grazing can prevent the establishment of fucoids. About a decade later, Kitching and Ebling (1961) demonstrated a similar effect of grazing by urchins on sublittoral algae in Lough Ine, Southern Ireland, and Southward (1964) reviewed the work on limpets. Yet it was a contemporary study by Connell (1961a) showing, by the local removal of dogwhelks, how predation ameliorated the intensity of competition among barnacles, that really inspired ecologists to adopt a more experimental approach to rocky shore biology.

This experimental approach has been championed by Paine (1966, 1980) and his students (critically reviewed by Underwood and Denley, 1984). Influenced by the long-established idea that predation may be capable of preventing competitive exclusion (Gause, 1934; Hutchinson, 1941; Lack, 1949; Slobodkin, 1961) and by Connell's experimental demonstration (1961a) that predation can indeed reduce the intensity of competition on the shore, Paine (1966) supposed that predation might be the key to coexistence of the diverse community of sedentary organisms which fully occupy space on exposed rocky shores of Washington, North America. The striking, unequivocal results of Paine's predator-exclusion experiments (1966) – showing how consumption of mussels, *Mytilus californianus* Conrad, by a starfish, *Pisaster ochraceus* (Brandt), can regenerate the primary space used by sedentary organisms – provided ecologists with a rare commodity: a clear, uncomplicated demonstration of an ecological principle operating in nature. In a field where theories germinate profusely, only to become etiolated without the light of appropriate data, the *Mytilus–Pisaster* interaction was quickly established as a favourite example of the diversity-promoting rôle of predation.

Further applications of Paine's experimental techniques to the rocky littoral biota of North America revealed similar patterns of community dynamics in which the local monopoly of space by competitive dominants is repeatedly disturbed, so facilitating the persistence of competitive sub-dominants in the community. Physical factors, such as wave action and impact by water-borne objects, were found to act synergistically with predation (Dayton, 1971, 1975; Paine, 1974) and biological interactions were found to be complex in some cases.

In contrast to the single 'keystone' predator and its competitively dominant prey in the barnacle-mussel zone of exposed Washington coasts, a greater number of 'strongly interacting' (Paine, 1980) 'foundation' species was found to shape the richer, algal-dominated community lower on these shores (Dayton, 1975). The competitively dominant algae, *Hedophyllum sessile* (Ag.) Setchell and (in areas exposed to greater wave action) *Lessoniopsis littoralis* (Farlow and Setchell) Reinke, are heavily grazed by the urchin, *Strongylocentrotus purpuratus* (Stimpson), preventing them from monopolizing the substratum. Urchins, however, graze so intensively that they could eradicate all macroalgae and reduce the flora to a crust of corallines. They are prevented from so doing by the starfish, *Pycnopodia helianthoides* (Brandt), which feeds on the urchins and causes them to vacate local areas. Circumstantial evidence suggests that this set of interactions is contingent on the removal of *Mytilus californianus* from the lower shore by *Pisaster ochraceus*, since *M. californianus* can grow well at these levels and could outcompete the algae (Dayton, 1975).

On the East coast of North America (Menge, 1983) and on British shores (Seed, 1969b) no single predator consistently matches the impact of *Pisaster ochraceus* on certain western North American coasts (Fig. 16.2A). Instead, on New England shores, competitive exclusion of the red alga, *Chondrus crispus* Stackh., by barnacles and mussels is prevented by a guild of predators consisting of two starfish, three crabs and a dogwhelk, any one of which can substitute for another (Menge, 1983). A similar predatory guild affects the barnacle–mussel community on dock-pilings in New Jersey (Peterson, 1979).

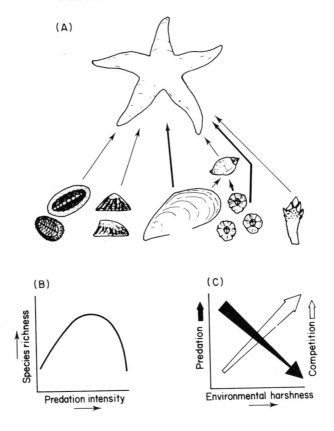

FIG. 16.2.

A. The *Pisaster* dominated subweb in the exposed rocky shore community studied by Paine (1966) on the west coast of North America. Arrows point from prey to predator. From left to right, the prey are two species of chiton, two acmaeid limpets, *Mytilus californianus*, *Nucella emarginata*, three species of sessile barnacle, and *Mitella* (stalked barnacle).

B. The effect of predation intensity on species richness: light predation may be ineffectual in preventing competitive exclusion among prey and heavy predation may eradicate prey, whereas intermediate intensities of predation will promote coexistence of prey (from Lubchenco, 1978).

C. Predation diminishes in importance as a structural force in rocky shore communities, while competition among prey increases in importance, as the physical environment becomes harsher (from Menge and Sutherland, 1976).

   Despite the apparent variety of possible mechanisms, the fundamental process maintaining species richness in these particular rocky littoral communities has proven to be the repeated interruption of competitive exclusion by disturbances, often caused by predation. Further afield, the same was found to be true of a sponge-dominated Antarctic sublittoral community (Dayton *et al.*, 1974), and of the contrasted communities on the Great Barrier Reef and adjacent tropical rain forests of Queensland (Connell, 1978).

   While perhaps not receiving inspiration directly from the experiments of rocky shore ecologists, Horn (1976) elaborated on the rôle of disturbance in shaping communities by suggesting that organisms with appropriate life histories are selected by the periodicity and nature of the disturbance. Thus the short generation time of the colon bacterium is associated with daily evacuation of the gut; annual weeds are phenologically compatible with the ploughing of arable land; chaparral shrubs depend on clearing by fires every 10–50 years, becoming more fire-prone with age in a way that reinforces this periodicity; while eastern white pine are fitted to the 100–300 year intervals between fires or severe hurricanes.

Among marine habitats, it is possible that the predictable periodicity of tropical storms hitting shallow reef-flats has selected for patterns of growth in the branching corals *Acropora* spp. that cause breakage into fragments of shapes and sizes facilitating survivorship and regeneration (Highsmith, 1982). It is questionable, however, whether the schedules of growth, reproduction and longevity of rocky littoral organisms could be interpreted in a similar way, because disturbances at any point on the shore are relatively unpredictable in their extent and timing (Underwood *et al.*, 1983).

In addition to frequency and periodicity, intensity influences the way disturbances affect community structure. This was highlighted by Lubchenco's experimental demonstration (1978) that grazing by *Littorina littorea* (L.) at low densities in high-littoral New England rock pools could not prevent *Enteromorpha* from outcompeting other algae, whilst at high densities the winkles removed all macroalgae except the unpalatable *Chondrus crispus*, which covered the substratum. Only at intermediate grazing intensities was the coexistence of many macroalgae possible (Fig. 16.2B).

Much also depends on the competitive status of the preferred prey. *Enteromorpha*, the preferred 'prey' of *L. littorea*, is competitively dominant in high-shore rock pools whereas outside the pools, *Enteromorpha* and other palatable ephemerals are competitively subdominant to fucoids, which are avoided by *L. littorea*. Grazing therefore enhances the competitive exclusion of ephemerals by fucoids, and this is prevented only in patches cleared by other disturbances such as wave action during storms (Lubchenco, 1978).

Physical conditions also strongly influence the importance of predation as a structuring force in communities. The high littoral zone of exposed New England shores is subject to great variability and extremes of temperature, precipitation and wave action. Sedentary competitors are confined to barnacles and mussels, while predators are rare or absent (Menge, 1976; Peterson, 1979). Competitive exclusion of barnacles by mussels, modified or re-initiated by physically induced local mortality, is the major determinant of community structure. Comparing this with the more diverse barnacle–mussel community of exposed shores of the West coast of America, where the climate is less variable and less extreme, Menge and Sutherland (1976) proposed that rocky shore communities range from the trophically complex in benign physical environments, where predation prevents widespread competitive exclusions, to the trophically simple in harsh physical conditions, where competition remains the dominant structuring force (Fig. 16.2C). Underwood and Denley (1984), however, point out that critical measurements testing this hypothesis have not been made and its applicability may be limited.

The mid-littoral zone of shores experiencing intermediate levels of wave action in New South Wales has an ecological diversity between those of the East and West coasts of North America. Careful experimentation has shown that, while predation has some effect, interactions among all species are important in determining community structure, and that the latter is also strongly influenced by vagaries of recruitment from the plankton (Underwood *et al.*, 1983). Further experiments are needed to clarify the situation in most parts of the world, notably the British Isles.

All the above mentioned examples concern the interruption of competitive exclusions among organisms competing for space as a primary resource. It is less evident that this mechanism operates among non-sedentary species, although it was invoked by Hutchinson (1961), in the form of seasonal environmental changes, to explain the 'paradox' of coexistence among numerous ecologically similar species in the lacustrine phytoplankton. Predation, however, has been shown to change limnetic planktonic community structure without promoting species richness (reviewed in Lynch, 1979) and there is little evidence of 'keystone' species in marine planktonic communities (Dayton, 1984). Experimental manipulation of mobile animals in the field is often extremely difficult, so that progress is unlikely to match that achieved with sedentary organisms. Whether generalizations are transferrable from the one group of organisms to the other remains to be shown: experimental investigations of benthos in soft sediments (Peterson, 1979) suggest that they may not be.

Predation emerges, therefore, as one of a large set of disturbance factors which, if acting within appropriate limits of frequency, periodicity, intensity and selectivity, may promote species richness of communities by locally interrupting competitive exclusions. Outside these limits, predation is likely to reduce species richness or have no effect. Rocky shores have played a large part in developing our understanding of the rôle of predation in this ecological context.

16.4 Biogeographical Rôle of Predation

From the evidence of fossilized biota in sedimentary substrata, from plate tectonics and from oceanic circulation, marine biogeographers have sought geographical and climatological explanations for present global patterns of species diversity and the contemporary distribution of taxa (Ekman, 1953; Valentine, 1973; Briggs, 1974; Kohn, 1983). More recently, biological explanations for these patterns have also been sought, and the evidence comes to a significant degree from rocky shores.

Working principally with tropical rocky shore and shallow sublittoral fish faunas, but applying his ideas more widely to other taxa, Briggs (1974) argued cogently that interspecific competition has influenced the spread of species between centres of origin. Thus the poverty of East Atlantic and East Pacific tropical littoral and shallow sublittoral faunas compared with their Western counterparts, may reflect the difficulty with which eastern immigrants can invade western communities containing more numerous, competitively specialized species that partition resources more finely. Because of this competitive differential, western immigrants are more likely to invade eastern communities successfully, despite less favourable water circulation in that direction (Briggs, 1967).

The idea that predation could strongly influence marine biogeographical patterns stems largely from the experiences of a rocky shore biologist (Vermeij, 1978). Noticing that rocky shore gastropods of the Indo-Malaysian area and western Indian Ocean tend to have more occluded apertures, robust opercula, rounded spires and stronger external shell sculpturing than those elsewhere in the tropics (Fig. 16.3), Vermeij (1974) surmised that these features are anti-predator devices, which have developed further in the Indo-West Pacific centre of species diversity because widespread habitats and climatic stability have facilitated the prolonged co-evolution of predators and prey. To test the idea that the morphological features of Indo-West Pacific shells impart greater resistance to predation, Vermeij (1976) collected neritid, trochid and conid gastropods from Jamaica and transported them to Guam in the West Pacific. Hermit crabs were induced to occupy the Atlantic shells, which were then presented to several species of crab, together with comparable local Pacific shells. In each case, the largest shells yielding to crabs were bigger among the Atlantic than among the equivalent Pacific species. The more occluded apertures, lower spires and thicker shells of the Pacific species did indeed afford greater resistance to crab predation. Moreover, Vermeij (1976) noted that Pacific species of *Eriphia* and *Carpilius*, representing the more important littoral molluscivorous crabs, have relatively stronger master chelae than equivalent Atlantic species (Fig. 16.3), leading him to conclude that co-evolution between Indo-West Pacific rocky shore gastropods and their crab predators is more advanced than among West Atlantic species.

Using similar methods, Reynolds and Reynolds (1977) showed that East Pacific *Nerita* spp. are intermediate between Indo-West Pacific and West Atlantic congeners in their resistance to crab attacks. It was concluded that, although the co-evolutionary 'arms race' in the East Pacific has escalated less than in the Indo-West Pacific, it has escalated more than in the West Atlantic (Fig. 16.3), so that East Pacific species might have a competitive advantage over West Atlantic species should contact occur through a sea-level canal across the Isthmus of Panama. Vermeij (1978) endorsed this view, suggesting that superior survivorship of juveniles could lead to high rates of adult recruitment,

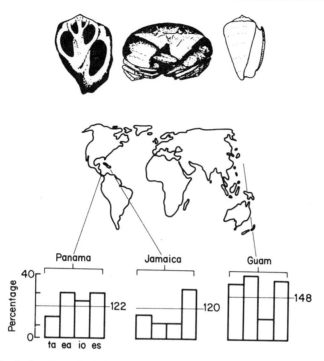

FIG. 16.3. Top left, longitudinal section of *Thais melones* (East Pacific) showing thick walls and strong columella (from Palmer, 1979); top middle, *Carpilius maculatus* crushing *Strombus gibberulus* (West Pacific, from Zipser and Vermeij, 1978); top right, *Strombus gibberulus* (West Pacific) showing elongate aperture (from Zipser and Vermeij, 1978). Bottom, percentages of shells collected from the East Pacific (Panama), West Atlantic (Jamaica) and West Pacific (Guam) showing features that impede crab attacks: ta = toothed apertures; ea = elongate apertures; io = inflexible operculum; es = strong external sculpturing (from Vermeij, 1978). Horizontal lines denote an index of cross-sectional area of the master chela of species of *Eriphia* (from Reynolds and Reynolds, 1977).

and superior adult survivorship to longer mean reproductive life among East Pacific immigrants; but he acknowledged that possible faster growth of West Atlantic species, gained at the expense of less heavily armoured shells, would reduce the competitive advantage of East Pacific species. Such a trade-off remains an interesting possibility requiring experimental investigation.

Whereas thickened walls, reduced spires and occluded apertures of gastropod shells help to repel crabs (Kitching *et al.*, 1966; Kitching and Lockwood, 1974; Vermeij, 1976; Hughes and Elner, 1979; Bertness and Cunningham, 1981), strong external sculpturing in the form of knobs and spines seems less appropriate because crabs can apply their chelae to the weaker areas between the protrusions. By comparing the failure rates of normal shells of *Thais kioskiformis* (Duclos) and *Cymia tecta* (Wood) with those of shells whose spires had been filed down (Fig. 16.4C), Palmer (1979) showed that external sculpturing is an effective defence against puffer fish, *Diodon* spp. Because fish use their mouths to crush gastropods (Fig. 16.4A), knobs and spines may hinder crushing by increasing the effective diameter of the shell (Fig. 16.4B) thus decreasing the mechanical advantage of the fishes' jaws or pharyngeal teeth, by distributing the stress over a larger area of the shell (Fig. 16.4B), by localizing the stress to the thicker parts of the shell and by damaging the predator.

Puffer fish and wrasse, equipped with strong jaws and specialized dentition, are important predators of littoral gastropods throughout the tropics (Palmer, 1979) but not in temperate regions, where external sculpturing of shells is much less pronounced (Vermeij, 1977; Palmer, 1979). This latitudinal

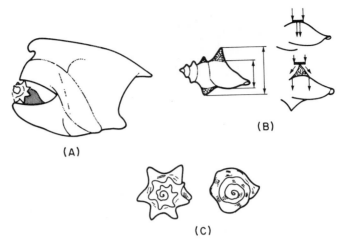

FIG. 16.4. External sculpturing of shells resists crushing by fish jaws: A, *Thais kioskiformis* between the crushing plates (modified teeth) of *Diodon hystrix*. B, Spines resist crushing by increasing the effective diameter (left) and by distributing stress over a broader area (right, arrows indicate direction of stress). C, Normal shell of *Thais kioskiformis* (left) and experimental shell with spines filed down (right) (all figures taken from Palmer, 1979).

gradient in the development of protective mechanisms also involves the features effective against crab predation, leading Vermeij (1978) to consider a causal relationship related to the general abundance of molluscivorous predators. The increased diversity and potency of crabs and fish that feed on littoral gastropods towards the tropics are well documented (Vermeij, 1978; Palmer, 1979; Bertness and Cunningham, 1981) but the latitudinal temperature gradient confounds the interpretation, since colder water impedes calcification and may prevent the development of large, very robust shells (Vermeij, 1977, 1978). Whether or not it results from coincidence or co-evolution, the greater relative thickness of shells from warmer waters certainly confers greater resistance to compression (Vermeij and Currey, 1980) and therefore to crab attack. Shells of *Littorina littorea* harbouring hermit crabs, collected from the cooler hydrographic regime north of Cape Cod, proved to be thicker and more resistant to attacks by *Cancer borealis* Stimpson than those collected from warmer conditions south of Cape Cod (Dudley, 1980).

Evidence favouring a co-evolutionary explanation for latitudinal differences in the resistance of gastropod shells to crab predation was adduced by Vermeij (1982a) from a correlation between increases in the frequency of repaired shells of *Nucella lapillus* (presumed to have survived crab attack) and the colonization of eastern North American shores by the European crab *Carcinus maenas* (L.) Using museum and recent collections of *N. lapillus* from Cape Cod to Halifax, Nova Scotia, Vermeij (1982a) found that repairs to the basal whorl of the shell rose from about 2.5% in samples collected before *C. maenas* was first recorded in the various localities, to about 4.4% in samples collected at least seven years afterwards. The increase in frequency of repairs was accompanied by an increase in relative thickness of the shell.

Whereas local evolutionary responses to crab predation are probably facilitated by the direct development and restricted dispersion ability of *Nucella lapillus*, they may be hindered by the widely dispersing planktotrophic larvae of *Littorina littorea* (Scheltema, 1978; Currey and Hughes, 1982). Accordingly, shell thickness and frequency of repair remained unchanged in *L. littorea* after the immigration of *Carcinus maenas* (Vermeij, 1982b). This supports a physiological, rather than a co-evolutionary, explanation for Dudley's results (1980) described above. Vermeij (1982b), however, suggested that the greater thickness of *L. littorea* in Brittany and southern England compared with those further north in Europe, represents a selective response to increased predation in warmer water.

Clearly plenty of scope remains for the experimental marine biogeographer.

CHAPTER XVII

THE ECOLOGICAL SIGNIFICANCE AND CONTROL OF SHELL VARIABILITY IN DOGWHELKS FROM TEMPERATE ROCKY SHORES

J.A. Kitching

Sea snails of the family Muricidae are widely distributed around the world from Arctic seas to the tropics. In this Chapter I shall discuss the dogwhelks of rocky shores in three temperate but widely separated areas – British Columbia, New Zealand and Western Europe – where these snails occupy similar but not identical niches. I hope to make some progress towards a comparative study of niche occupation by concentrating on the three areas which I have had the good fortune to visit.

Dogwhelks probably evolved in the Pacific, where different species inhabit different geographical areas. On the Pacific coast of North America there are now three common rocky shore species: *Nucella emarginata* (Deshayes), *N. canaliculata* (Duclos), and *N. lamellosa* (Gmelin); and a fourth, *N. lima* (Martyn) is found in Alaska (all shown in Fig. 17.1). In New Zealand there are four common species on rocky shores. *Lepsiella scobina* (Quoy and Gaimard) has two main varieties which overlap geographically: *L. scobina scobina* of more northerly distribution and *L. scobina albomarginata* of more southerly distribution. *Thais orbita* (Gmelin) (in New Zealand formerly *Neothais scalaris*) is of northerly distribution, while *Lepsithais lacunosus* (Bruguière) is of southerly distribution. *Haustrum haustorium* (Gmelin) is widely distributed. All are shown in Fig. 17.2. The cold north Atlantic contains *Nucella lapillus* (L.) (first appearing in the early Pliocene) and *Ocenebra erinacea* (L.), both shown in Fig. 17.3, and the American oyster tingle *Urosalpinx cinerea* (Say), introduced into Britain accidentally (Hancock, 1959). Other species prevail towards warmer climatic conditions.

Dogwhelks bore through the shells of mussels and other shelled prey by means of their radula and accessory boring organ (ABO) (Carriker, 1961). The ABO consists of a small pad mounted in a recess on the underside of the foot. It has a secretory type of epithelial covering, and contains intracellular carbonic anhydrase, which undoubtedly plays a rôle in the secretion of acid by this organ (Chétail and Fournié, 1969). During boring activity, periods of drilling with the radula alternate with periodic application of the ABO to the bored spot, which no doubt softens the shell (Carriker, 1961).

Possession of boring equipment has opened up new opportunities for dogwhelks of cool temperate seas, where mussels and barnacles abound littorally on wave-exposed rocky coasts. Mussels and barnacles feed upon phytoplankton, which is available in enormous quantities. Mussels form great and continuous beds in the mid- and low-littoral region, but are limited below that by predators such as starfish. Mussels form the most important prey for *Nucella lapillus* in the northern North Atlantic and

Thais emarginata

Pachena Point, near Bamfield, B.C.

Bamfield Inlet, B.C.

Thais lamellosa

Brady's Beach, near Bamfield, B.C.

Grappler Inlet, near Bamfield, B.C.

Thais canaliculata

Cape Beale, near Bamfield, B.C.

0 1 2 3 4 5

Cm

Thais lima

Pribilof Islands, Bering Sea

FIG. 17.1. Dogwhelks from sites on the Pacific coast of North America.

Thais orbita

Totaronui

Lepsithais lacunosus

Buller's Point   Vaila Voe, Paterson Inlet

Stewart Island

Lepsiella scobina albomarginata

Ryan's Creek, Stewart Island

Bragg Bay, Stewart Island

Lepsiella scobina scobina

Leigh

Hakahaka Bay, Port Underwood

Haustrum haustorium

Menzies Bay, Banks Peninsula

0   1   2   3   4   5

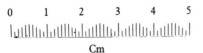

Cm

Tayolor's Mistake, Bank's Peninsula

FIG. 17.2. Dogwhelks from sites in New Zealand.

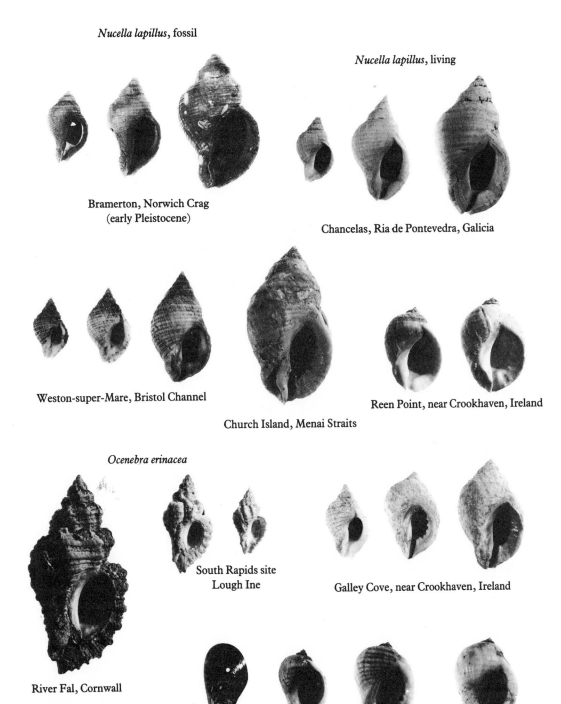

Nucella lapillus, fossil

Nucella lapillus, living

Bramerton, Norwich Crag
(early Pleistocene)

Chancelas, Ria de Pontevedra, Galicia

Weston-super-Mare, Bristol Channel

Church Island, Menai Straits

Reen Point, near Crookhaven, Ireland

Ocenebra erinacea

South Rapids site
Lough Ine

Galley Cove, near Crookhaven, Ireland

River Fal, Cornwall

0 1 2 3 4 5
Cm

Cape Clear, Ireland, with drilled mussel

FIG. 17.3. Dogwhelks from sites in Western Europe.

for corresponding species in other cool temperate seas. Barnacles are often attacked by insertion of the proboscis between the shell plates, but shells are sometimes drilled. Other prey items are sometimes taken by *N. lapillus* (Largen, 1967), and regularly so by various Pacific dogwhelks.

In some areas mussel beds fail to extend into sheltered waters owing to the feeding activity of predators such as crabs and starfish (Kitching *et al.*, 1959), although mussels may reappear in extreme shelter on vertical surfaces such as pilings which are inaccessible to crabs. Dogwhelks are reduced in numbers where mussels and barnacles are scarce.

The egg capsules of dogwhelks each contain a group of viable eggs, together (usually) with nurse eggs upon which the embryos will feed. In *N. lapillus* the young emerge from the capsules as baby snails; there is no planktonic stage. Spight (1977a) has surveyed the development of muricids on rocky shores and has found that species living in the tropics have planktonic larvae, that all species so far investigated living at high latitudes hatch as baby snails, and that there are zones of overlap of hatching types between latitudes 25° and 30° (N and S). This generalization does not apply to muricids in other habitats, and there is no information for dogwhelks in New Zealand. Lack of a dispersal phase has important implications for the control of variation.

Hazards in the littoral region are not evenly distributed. Most physical hazards, such as extremes of temperature, desiccation, or rain water, increase up the shore, while most biological hazards, such as predation and competition, increase downwards (as discussed by Connell, 1972). Wave action gives some protection against various physical and biological factors, but its direct mechanical action is also of great importance.

Maintenance of a population of a species requires survival to maturity of sufficient numbers of individuals to launch the next generation. Studies of life history patterns of dogwhelks have been carried out at Plymouth by Moore (1936b, 1938a, 1938b), at Robin Hood's Bay by Feare (1970a, 1971a), in the San Juan Islands near Seattle by Connell (1970) and Spight (1974, 1976a, 1979), and in Australia by Phillips (1969), Phillips and Campbell (1974) and Phillips, Campbell and Wilson (1973).

On the open coast of British Columbia and Washington State *Nucella emarginata* abounds on the mid-littoral mussel beds. It matures within 1–2 years, and few survive beyond this time (Spight, 1979). It can only grow to a rather small size, and its life pattern is appropriate for a mid-littoral snail not likely to encounter powerful invertebrate predators. At a site studied by Connell (1970), the vertical range of *N. emarginata* was limited by the time for which it could remain out of water. With mixed tides in operation, by which the rise and fall of every alternate tide is less extreme, its prey *Balanus glandula* Darwin found a refuge from it above 'low' high water. In the low littoral region *N. emarginata* is replaced by the spirally ribbed *N. canaliculata*, and towards increasing shelter by the exceedingly variable (Kincaid, 1957) and more heavily armoured *N. lamellosa* (although very occasional sheltered populations of *N. emarginata* are reported by Crothers, 1984). *N. lamellosa* takes four years to reach maturity; it is no doubt better able (than *N. emarginata*) to resist predators, and it moves up and down the shore, avoiding excessive desiccation (Spight, 1979). With its better chances of survival after reaching maturity the breeding season of *N. lamellosa* is restricted.

Little is known about the growth rates of New Zealand dogwhelks. In the south *Lepsiella scobina albomarginata* occupies the mid-littoral region; it is small and lightly armoured, and probably occupies a niche which corresponds with that of *Nucella emarginata*. In the low littoral region it is replaced by the spirally ribbed dogwhelk *Lepsithais lacunosus*, which seems to correspond with *N. canaliculata* of western North America. *Lepsiella scobina scobina*, of more northerly but overlapping distribution, is more heavily armoured than *L. scobina albomarginata*, and extends from open coasts to sites of considerable shelter. Some move down the shore as they grow, and change their diet to oysters, which may form a zone in the low littoral (Walsby, 1979). *Haustrum haustorium* has a very large shell aperture and pounces on its prey, which includes various active marine snails, as well as limpets (Walsby, 1979).

In the cold North Atlantic *Nucella lapillus* appears to occupy a wider niche than *N. emarginata* and *Lepsiella scobina emarginata*. On open coasts it inhabits the mid- and low-littoral region, and it extends considerably into sheltered waters. The lowest littoral levels in sheltered localities may also be inhabited by the heavily armoured *Ocenebra erinacea*, which corresponds with *N. lamellosa* of the North American Pacific coast. In further discussion we shall be concerned with how and why *N. lapillus* can succeed under such a wide range of conditions.

Various methods have been used to summarize shell form. D'Arcy Thomson, following Mosely, treated the turbinate gastropod shell as a logarithmically expanding tube coiled spirally within a right cone (Thompson, 1917). This idealized form is described in terms of the half apical angle (θ), which defines the cone into which the shell just fits, and the spiral angle ($\propto$), which defines the shell spiral within the cone stated. The apical angle is easily measured and directly defines the overall shape of the shell. The spiral angle is the angle between a radius from the shell apex cutting the spiral whorl outline at any convenient point on its course and a tangent to the whorl outline at that point. The spiral angle is not readily measured on a turbinate (rather than on a plane spiral) shell. Accordingly Moore (1936b) measured the ratio of consecutive whorl diameters (R) and used this to calculate the spiral angle from the relation $\tan \propto = \dfrac{2.72 \sin \theta}{\log R}$. R is conveniently estimated as D_0/D_{-1} where D_0 = diameter of body whorl measured from the highest point of the aperture along the shell striae to a point on the opposite side and D_{-1} is exactly one whorl above this (Fig. 17.4) (Kitching and Lockwood, 1974). In view of the fact that the shell-shape of a dogwhelk changes as it grows, Kitching (1977) obtained his measurements from the last two whorls of the shell, as illustrated in Fig. 17.4, and plotted the changing values of R and 2θ against shell height (Fig. 17.6).

Other techniques involve the use of ratios which do not describe the shape of the shell, but which are a consequence of a geometry not fully specified. Spight (1973) assessed shell-shape ('fat' or 'slender') by plotting log fresh weight against log height for *N. lamellosa*, and Crothers (1983, with earlier refs) has used shell height/aperture length to describe many populations of *N. lapillus*. Further

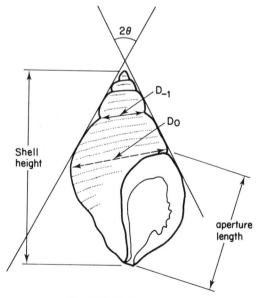

FIG. 17.4. Shell measurements.

developments in the description of shell-shape are given by Raup (1966). Ekaratne and Crisp (1983) have developed a system involving the length of the shell spiral, with a view to its application in studies of shell growth, which can be traced with great refinement from growth lines laid down with every tide (Ekaratne and Crisp, 1982, 1984).

Nucella lapillus has long attracted interest because of its variability. Cooke (1895) and Colton (1922) associated a small shell height, a wide shell aperture, and a large foot with a wave-exposed site, for which these characteristics were presumably beneficial. Shells from shelter were tall and narrow. This was confirmed at Lough Ine (Ebling et al., 1964; Kitching et al., 1966), where it appears also that dog-whelks from shelter have thicker shells. N. lapillus from the open coast and from shelter show a closely similar relation between shell height and shell weight. Regarding each as approximating in shape to a right cone, the surface area of the wide shells from the open coast must be greater for the same weight of shell, and therefore the shell must be thinner. The correlation of wide shell with wave action, although not accepted by Moore (1936b), has been fully confirmed by Crothers (1973) for Pembroke-shire, by Kitching (1977) for Reen Point (very wave-exposed) and Galley Cove (moderately sheltered) near Crookhaven, Co. Cork (Ireland), and by Seed (1978a) and Hughes and Elner (1979) for North Wales. Shape changes progressively with changing wave-exposure (Crothers, 1983). Colton (1916), Moore (1936b), and Berry (1983) have also described the occurrence of dark or banded shells in certain localities. These observations on shell-shape and on colour variations raised the important questions (i) what ecological benefits do these local variations provide? and (ii) to what extent do these variations result from hereditary differences continually subject to a natural selection appropriate for each site, and to what extent to a direct effect of environment on the development of each individual snail? If hereditary characters are the cause of these local differences, genetic differences could develop over short distances for dogwhelks lacking a planktonic stage, and would be expected to do so.

Evidence as to the ecological importance of shell-shape in Nucella lapillus was also provided at Lough Ine. Two possibilities were tested: that a shell with a wide aperture (such as is found on the open coast) accommodates a larger foot, which is better for holding on in rough seas, and that a thick shell with a narrow aperture (such as is found in sheltered situations) is better for resisting predators. A detailed comparison was made between N. lapillus from the open coast on the headland of Carri-gathorna and from a sheltered site with continually but not violently moving water at the south end of the Rapids. Both sites are rocky, but Carrigathorna has extensive mussel beds. 'For shells of cor-responding weight or height, the body weight, the length and breadth of aperture, and the area of foot, are greater for Carrigathorna than for the Rapids' (Kitching et al., 1966). (This statement refers to the sheltered South Rapids site.) All the results are statistically highly significant. Individual N. lapillus from Carrigathorna required greater force to pull them from the rock and from a plastic basin in which they had subsequently been allowed to settle than did individuals from the South Rapids site. Both kinds of N. lapillus were allowed to attach themselves to a slate under water, and this was held in turn in the still water above the Rapids and (edge on to the current) at stations of progressively increasing current along the Rapids quay. Considerably more dogwhelks from the South Rapids site than from Carrigathorna fell off the slate. Finally, 100 N. lapillus from the South Rapids site and 100 from Carri-gathorna were removed, marked and placed together on an area of rock in their proper zone cleared of its original Nucella population. After 5 days of rather rough weather 90 N. lapillus from Carrigathorna remained on the site but only 22 from the South Rapids site.

Other experiments have demonstrated the better protection against predators of N. lapillus native to a sheltered site. Ebling et al. (1964) measured the force necessary to break shells of dogwhelks from Carrigathorna and from the South Rapids site by gradually increasing pressure exerted locally on the shell, as though by a crab's chela, in an apparatus shown in their Fig. 5. The shells from the South Rapids site were substantially more resistant than those from the open coast, height for height, and within each group the taller shells were stronger. Similar tests have been carried out between flat plates by Currey and Hughes (1982), who found that *N. lapillus* from the open coast of Anglesey were weaker than from a sheltered shore, and that these in turn were not as strong as those from a very sheltered habitat. Again, within each group the taller (and presumably older) shells were stronger than the shorter (younger) ones. A turbinate shell might be crushed by the global collapse of the whole arch structure of a whorl, or by the local failure of the shell wall at the point of pressure. In either case an increase in shell thickness would greatly increase the resistance to collapse.

Tests of the ability of the crabs *Liocarcinus puber* (L.) and *Carcinus maenas* (L.) to prey upon *Nucella lapillus* from Carrigathorna and from the sheltered South Rapids site were carried out in cages on the beach (Ebling *et al.*, 1964; Kitching *et al.*, 1966); in some cases *Ocenebra erinacea* (from the South Rapids) were also used. Single crabs of various sizes were each given a range of sizes of both (or of all three) potential prey items together. Both *L. puber* and *C. maenas* were much more successful against *N. lapillus* from Carrigathorna than from the South Rapids site, and against the smaller than the larger dogwhelks. *O. erinacea* was the most resistant of all. The larger crabs smashed the shells of all but the largest *N. lapillus* from Carrigathorna, and crabs of intermediate size tore out the operculum and sometimes the body even of large dogwhelks from that site. Thus dogwhelks from the open coast were doubly vulnerable, with their weaker shells and larger shell apertures. Hughes and Elner (1979) have described the tactics used by large *C. maenas* in breaking dogwhelk shells; the crabs give up unless they are quickly successful.

Two 'field' experiments were carried out in the sheltered creek (North Barloge) which leads out from Lough Ine. In each experiment *Nucella lapillus* from Carrigathorna and from the South Rapids site were transferred together to a sheltered site previously cleared of dogwhelks. Although there were many losses from all groups of dogwhelks, losses were considerably greater for those from the wave-exposed locality (Kitching *et al.*, 1966). Many *Liocarcinus puber* were captured in crab traps at both sites just after the close of the experiments, and *Carcinus maenas* was seen intertidally. Feare (1970a) reported that *Cancer pagurus* L. was a serious predator of dogwhelks at low-shore levels at Robin Hood's Bay. There the juvenile dogwhelks tended to move up from the low- to the middle-shore, but returned to the low shore as their breeding season (at the age of 2.5 years) approached. Thus the danger from crabs was reduced during the growing period.

Nucella lapillus is very variable in the weight of shell used to protect a given body weight or volume of living space. Fig. 17.5, drawn from data of Kitching *et al.* (1966), shows the consistently greater weight of shell, in relation to volume enclosed, for animals from the lower Rapids than from Carrigathorna. The same is also true for shell weight in relation to body weight. *N. lapillus* can thus meet a very wide range of requirements in respect of adhesion and of resistance to predation, as long as these two requirements do not occur in extreme form at the same site. *N. emarginata*, its counterpart in Pacific North America, is also taller and narrower in shelter than on the open coast, but its shell is substantially lighter, in relation to volume enclosed, than that of *N. lapillus* from a comparable site (Table 17.1) (Kitching, 1976). *N. emarginata* occupies a more restricted range of habitats in respect of predation than does *N. lapillus*. It is replaced towards the low littoral of the open coast by *N. canaliculata* and towards shelter by *N. lamellosa*, both of which are more heavily armoured (Table 17.1). On the shores occupied by *N. emarginata* the common shore crab is *Hemigrapsus nudus* (Dana), which reaches little more than half the linear size of a fully grown *Carcinus maenas*, but on sheltered shores there are much larger and more powerful crabs, such as *Cancer productus* Randall, and even *N. lamellosa* is vulnerable to the larger specimens of these. It is not practicable to carry defenses against all potential predators, in view of the energetic cost involved.

In New Zealand the common dogwhelk of rocky shores is *Lepsiella scobina*, which is smaller than *Nucella lapillus* and occurs in two varieties. Of these, the more weakly sculptured, *L. scobina albo-*

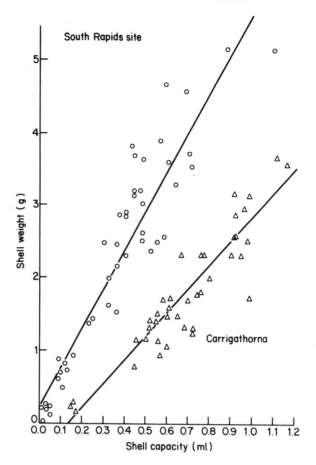

FIG. 17.5. Graph of shell weight: shell capacity for *Nucella lapillus* from Carrigathorna (very wave-exposed) and South Rapids site, Lough Ine area, Ireland. Recalculated and redrawn from data by Kitching *et al.* (1966), with acknowledgements to the *Journal of Animal Ecology*.

marginata, was found to have a shorter, wider shell on steep mussel-inhabited rocks at two wave-exposed localities in the South Island (Whites Bay and Taylor's Mistake) (Fig. 17.2) than at sheltered sites (Hakahaka Bay). The shells from Whites Bay and Taylor's Mistake were substantially lighter for a given shell capacity. (See also Fig. 17.2 for specimens from Bragg Bay (moderately open) and the very sheltered Ryan's Creek, both on Stewart Island.) Tests with the common shore crab *Hemigrapsus edwardsi* (Hilgendorf) were carried out in the tidal tank at the Kaikoura laboratory. A range of sizes of *L. scobina albomarginata* and *L. scobina scobina* from Whites Bay and from a sheltered site (Hakahaka Bay) were kept with *H. edwardsi* for 5 days. Substantial losses were suffered in the smaller sizes of *L. scobina albomarginata* from Whites Bay, and there were very few losses of those in other categories (Kitching and Lockwood, 1974). *L. scobina albomarginata* gives way to the more heavily armoured *Lepsithais lacunosus* in the low littoral region, to which we may presume that more powerful predators may penetrate. This dogwhelk also grows shorter and wider on an open coast than in shelter (Powell, 1979). The shell of both varieties of *L. scobina* is considerably lighter, for a given space enclosed, than that of *N. lapillus*, but *H. edwardsi* only reaches half the linear size of *Carcinus maenas*.

TABLE 17.1

Shell weight (g) ± S.E. for stated shell capacity.

Data from Kitching et al. (1966), Kitching and Lockwood (1974) and Kitching (1976 and unpubl.).

Stated shell capacity (ml)	0.25	0.5	1.0	2.0	4.0
Nucella lapillus					
Carrigathorna	0.48 ± 0.16	1.25 ± 0.10	2.80 ± 0.18	–	–
South Rapids	1.71 ± 0.14	3.01 ± 0.14	4.03 ± 0.76	–	–
Ocenebra erinacea					
South Rapids	0.91 ± 0.07	–	–	–	–
River Fal	–	–	–	6.98 ± 0.48	9.62 ± 0.60
Nucella emarginata					
Cape Beale (B1)	–	0.41 ± 0.05	0.77 ± 0.04	–	–
inside Aguilar Point (G2)	–	0.40 ± 0.11	1.10 ± 0.07	–	–
Nucella canaliculata					
Cape Beale (B1)	–	0.79 ± 0.05	1.46 ± 0.04	–	–
Nucella lamellosa					
Grappler Narrows (J4)	–	1.29 ± 0.17	2.37 ± 0.12	–	–
Lepsiella scobina albomarginata					
Taylor's Mistake	0.27 ± 0.05	0.55 ± 0.01	–	–	–
Whites Bay	0.29 ± 0.04	0.52 ± 0.01	–	–	–
Hakahaka Bay	0.46 ± 0.08	0.96 ± 0.03	–	–	–
Lepsiella scobina scobina					
Robertson Point (Port Underwood)	0.55 ± 0.03	1.07 ± 0.04	2.22 ± 0.08	–	–

In general, dogwhelks from wave-exposed rocky shores tend to stop growing at a lower shell height than those from sheltered sites. This is true of *Nucella lapillus* (Cooke, 1895; Colton, 1922) and also of *N. emarginata* (Kitching, 1976), and *Lepsiella scobina* is quite small anyway. Presumably a tall shell is more likely to project from the substratum and be carried away by waves. How is shell height determined?

An understanding of the mechanisms by which (i) the shell thickness of *N. lapillus* of various ages, (ii) the shell height at maturity, and (iii) the termination of growth are controlled, will require additional biological studies such as those carried out by Moore (1938a) at Plymouth and by Feare (1970a) from the Robin Hood's Bay Laboratory. Moore recorded the growth of marked shells on a sheltered shore. He concluded that they probably reached 10–15mm in their first year, about 21–26mm after two years, and maturity at an average height (at that site) of 29–30mm during their third year.

On a reef near Robin Hood's Bay, egg capsules were deposited during April and May, and juvenile *Nucella lapillus* emerged during September and October. After considerable practice Feare was able to recognize dogwhelk year groups up to (but not after) maturity, when growth stopped. Feare's graph (his Fig. 2), based on sampling and recognition of year groups, shows 1 year old *N. lapillus* reaching an average shell height of 10–15mm (in September–October), and 2 year old dogwhelks around 20mm. At this stage the outer lip of the shell thickened, growth usually ceased, and sexual maturity appeared to have been attained at an age of a little over 2 years. From the evidence of a few marked specimens, *N. lapillus* can live for at least 6 years (Feare, 1970a). Specimens infected with the trematode *Parorchis acanthus* (Nicoll) were parasitically castrated and continued growing to a larger size.

An important aspect of dogwhelk ecology concerns the thickening of the shell and outer lip and the formation of internal teeth, as described by Moore (1936b). By examining a large number of *Nucella lapillus* from his site on Drake's Island in Plymouth Sound, Moore showed a close correlation between sexual maturity and thickening of the shell. He reported that growth normally stops at this stage, but that rarely growth might be resumed and then stop again with the formation of the further definitive set of teeth. Feare (1970a) found that dogwhelks at his Robin Hood's Bay site frequently had two rows of teeth, and sometimes three or four. Bryan (1969), Feare (1970a), and Cowell and Crothers (1970) attributed supernumerary rows to a period of starvation. The evidence is convincing that in immature *N. lapillus* the formation of teeth is phenotypically determined by a period of hunger during which growth is suspended but calcification continues. The definitive set of teeth is formed when growth finally ceases and the dogwhelk begins to breed.

Evidence suggests that in some cases the size attained depends on the availability of food. Large *Nucella lapillus* with thin shells are found at certain very sheltered sites having abundant mussels, and few of these dogwhelks show any indication of thickening of the outer lip. This was true at Connel Bridge across the mouth of Loch Etive (WS24 in Kitching, 1977), Joppa (Fig. 17.6) and Ferry Ness in the Firth of Forth (Cambridge and Kitching, 1982), and in the rias of northwest Spain (SP13 in Kitching, 1977). Moore (1936b) reported very large *N. lapillus* from sublittoral sites, and Hughes and Elner (1979) found large specimens in the sublittoral fringe on Church Island in the Menai Straits (Fig. 17.3). All these are shells which have continued to grow to a large size either by growing faster or by growing for a longer time. According to Spight (1974), the mean adult size of a wild population of *N. lamellosa* increased steadily over a four-year period as food became more abundant. 'Snails reach a maximum size fixed by local growth conditions before becoming adults, but conditions vary from time to time, so growth is, in a sense, indeterminate'. See also Hughes (1972) for growth of *N. lapillus* in relation to food.

It is not immediately clear why *N. lapillus* should reach a smaller shell height on an open coast than in shelter. In the Lough Ine area, those from Carrigathorna (very wave-exposed) were shorter than those from the sheltered south Rapids site, but reached if anything a greater body mass (Fig. 17.5).

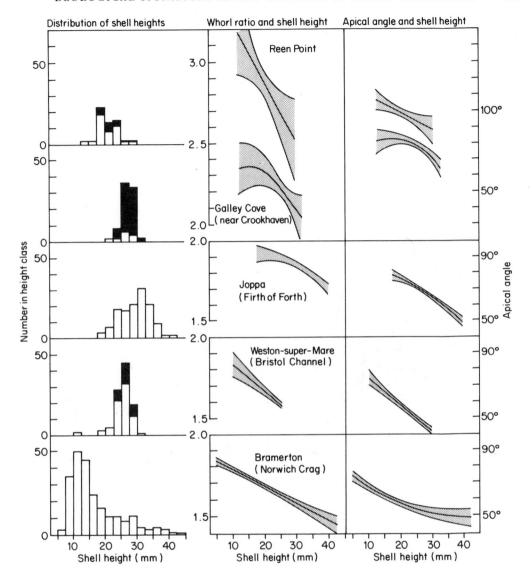

FIG. 17.6. Shell height distribution, whorl ratio and apical angle for *Nucella lapillus* from various sites. Black indicates shells with teeth visible from outside. Regressions for whorl ratio and apical angle are shown with stippled area covering ± 2S.E. Site names also relate horizontally (left and right). Partly redrawn from Cambridge and Kitching (1982) and Kitching (1977) with acknowledgements to the *Journal of Conchology* and the *Journal of Experimental Marine Biology and Ecology*.

Perhaps the difference in shell height is simply the result of attaining maturity within a predetermined time-span, of growing within that time-span in accordance with the local food supply and conditions for feeding, and of achieving the resulting terminal body mass in accordance with the shape appropriate to the site (however that may be determined). Thus the time to reach maturity, in determining the ultimate body size at any particular site, plays a very important part in delimiting the niche which the dogwhelk occupies; and movements up and down the shore, as shown by Feare for *N. lapillus*, by Spight for *N. lamellosa*, and by Walsby for *Lepsiella scobina*, enable these dogwhelks to exploit their niches to best advantage. (See also Butler (1979) for a discussion of the littoral movements of *Thais* spp.)

The poverty of the North Atlantic fauna, relative to that of the Pacific, is attributed to the harsher climate and wide connexion with the Arctic Ocean (Briggs, 1970). The ancestors of *Nucella lapillus* are likely to have originated in the Pacific and to have migrated into the Atlantic during a period or periods of milder climate in Miocene or Pliocene times, in accordance with the general migrations outlined by Briggs.

There are many varieties of preglacial North Atlantic *Nucella*, and their classification into species is problematical. The shell characteristics of fossil populations found in the early Pleistocene Norwich Crag are different from those of living British and Irish west coast specimens. They resemble more closely those from the Firth of Forth (Scotland) or rias of northwest Spain in apical angle, scarcity or lack of teeth, and maximum size attained. Very tentatively, Cambridge and Kitching (1982) suggested that the Norwich Crag *Nucella* lived on the low shore of a sheltered bay or firth.

The exuberance of variation of North Atlantic fossil *Nucella* (or *Purpura*) is reminiscent of the variation in modern *N. lamellosa* on the Pacific coast of North America, as described by Kincaid (1957). It is highly probable that genetic differences are a necessary part of the mechanism, but this does not exclude all possibility of some direct environmental effect on the development of the individual. Experimental tests are required.

In an important study of '*Dicathais*' in Australia and New Zealand, Phillips, Campbell and Wilson (1973) concluded that three Australian and the single New Zealand 'species' were all part of a continuous cline of shell form. Progressing from Western Australia along the south coast to New South Wales, this dogwhelk (now *Thais orbita*, see Powell, 1979) changes from nodulose through smooth or striated to ribbed; and the New Zealand form is also ribbed. *Thais orbita*, as reported by Phillips (1969) for the Western Australian form, has a planktonic larval stage, but even so a cline based on genetic differences could be established over a long distance of coast. However, Phillips *et al.* (1973) found that when the ribbed form from New South Wales was transferred to an aquarium at Western Australian water temperature and fed on a diet of mussels, the new shell growth laid down at the outer lip was first striated (instead of ribbed) and later smooth, as though they had moved westwards along the cline. Western Australian dogwhelks in the same aquarium continued nodulose, as normally. Spight (1973) found that the offspring of short, wide *N. lamellosa* grew up as slender dogwhelks in aquaria, while the offspring of slender *N. lamellosa* stayed slender. He attributed the determination of shape to environmental influences other than food supply.

Genetic differences between populations of dogwhelks such as *N. lapillus* might exist between different geographical areas, such as the North Sea and the west coasts of the British Isles; and they might exist over very short distances, such as between Reen Point and Galley Cove near Crookhaven (see Figs. 17.5 and 17.6). These two possibilities must be treated separately.

The importance of suppression of a motile larval stage for the establishment of genetically controlled differences over short distances has already been emphasized. It would be surprising if lack of a distributive planktonic stage did not encourage the local selection of advantageous, genetically influenced shell and body forms. Moore (1936b) attributed the short wide form of *N. lapillus* found on west coasts of the British Isles to a diet of mussels (which are indeed associated with wave-exposure). However, in the rias of Northwest Spain, on the piers of the Connel Bridge, and at sites in the Firth of Forth (e.g. Joppa in Fig. 17.6) *N. lapillus* lives on mussel beds in very sheltered situations, and is tall and narrow at these sites. It appeared that diet did not determine the shape of dogwhelks. Nevertheless it could be argued that mussels and wave-exposure together determine the short wide 'westerly' shape, or that only a west coast race is able to produce this shape in response to appropriate environmental conditions. *N. lapillus* did not produce very wide shells even at wave-beaten sites in Northwest Spain, and was not very successful there. Changes in apical angle during early growth might possibly be associated with a change in micro-habitat, and posture might influence the shape of the growing shell mouth. Attempts to breed and grow *N. lapillus* from a wave-exposed site in North Devon in aquaria (Crothers, 1980) suggest a hereditary control of shell-shape, but the experiments suffered from heavy mortality. A decrease in variance of the relation shell height/$\sqrt[3]{}$ shell weight with increasing age of *N. lapillus* at wave-exposed sites was attributed by Berry and Crothers (1968) to stabilizing selection, and this was held to imply a genetic control of shell form. However, there remains the possibility that selection is not involved. For instance, there might be a natural tendency to attain a standard ultimate degree of shell thickening, even if the age of onset or rate of thickening varied considerably. Feare (1970a) has also questioned their conclusions. More information is needed.

The potential course of development is determined genetically, but environmental conditions such as temperature and food supply may influence what is actually achieved. The change in shell form along the short distance of coast between Reen Head and Galley Cove (illustrated in Figs. 17.3 and 17.6) is brought about by a change in whorl ratio. Spiral angle does not change significantly. Very speculatively, whorl ratio might be influenced by rate of growth. As maturity is approached, the decline of specific growth rate might lead to a decline in whorl ratio, and with it of apical angle. Whorl ratio, in responding to growth, might be subject to control by environmental conditions such as temperature and the availability of food, but might also be subject to genetic variation. Evidence is wanting as to the relative importance of these two systems of control.

There is also some evidence suggesting the existence of different geographical races of *Nucella lapillus*. The very tall specimens found by Crothers (1974a) in the Bristol Channel are difficult to explain in any other way, and there is some evidence that they breed true in the laboratory (Crothers, 1977). Discontinuities of distribution of shell height/aperture length in relation to wave-exposure are reported in other areas (Crothers, 1981). *N. lapillus* does not appear to grow as short and wide at wave-exposed sites in the North Sea as in the Atlantic (Cambridge and Kitching, 1982), and it is possible that the North Sea dogwhelks are a separate stock, as discussed further below. It can, however, be argued that in the North Sea they are not subject to such prolonged rough weather.

Chromosomal abnormalities were found in *N. lapillus* upon the coast of Brittany by Staiger (1954) and in Dorset and Devon by Bantock and Cockayne (1975). Here the normal haploid number of 13 chromosomes can be increased up to 18 because any one or more of 5 V-shaped 'metacentric' chromosomes can be split into 2 acrocentric rods. It has been suggested that these chromosomal abnormalities are the result of interbreeding of stocks normally or formerly separate (Kitching, 1977), and that perhaps these stocks had previously been kept apart by the land bridge which connected England and France in early post-glacial times (Cambridge and Kitching, 1982). Information from Scottish waters could prove interesting.

In conclusion *Nucella lapillus* of the North Atlantic is an exceedingly variable species, covering a wide range of environmental conditions to which it is locally adapted. The extent to which this species can adjust the shape of the shell and the weight of shell used to enclose a given volume of living space enables it to occupy a wide ecological niche. Opportunities for the migration of dogwhelks from the Pacific to the Atlantic along Arctic shores have been severely limited. *N. lapillus* has fewer rivals in the Atlantic than its counterparts *N. emarginata* in Pacific North America and *Lepsiella scobina albo-marginata* in southern New Zealand. It is most nearly approached, in the range of its habitats, by *L. scobina* (including both varieties), and a combined genetical and ecological study of that species is much to be desired. The relatively small size of *L. scobina* suggests a short time-span to reach maturity, which would be an advantage for breeding experiments.

ACKNOWLEDGEMENTS

I am happy to acknowledge helpful discussion or correspondence with Dr W.J. Ballantine, Dr C.R. Bantock, Professor R.J. Berry, Dr G.M. Hewitt, Professor J. Heyman, and Dr B.F. Phillips. I also wish to thank Mr M.J. Hardy for the photographs of my dogwhelks.

CHAPTER XVIII

BIRDS AS PREDATORS ON ROCKY SHORES

C.J. Feare and R.W. Summers

18.1 Introduction

A wide variety of birds feed on rocky shores. For example, during a three-year period at Robin Hood's Bay, Yorkshire, 47 species were seen feeding in the rocky littoral along a 1.5km stretch of shore. However, of those species only nine were seen to feed regularly on the shore, and only four occurred in appreciable numbers. Rocky shores do not support the large (sometimes immense) flocks of birds seen on estuarine mudflats, and first impressions might suggest that birds do not play an important rôle in rocky shore communities. However, birds have a high metabolic rate, necessitating a high energy intake, and a few studies have shown that large numbers of prey species can be eaten by birds: Gibb (1956) calculated that rock pipits, *Anthus spinoletta petrosus* (Mont.), each ate about 14,300 periwinkles and 3,500 chironomid larvae per day, and Feare (1966a) estimated that a flock of 40 purple sandpipers, *Calidris maritima* (Brünn.), ate about 11.5 million littoral snails during a two-month winter residence. These birds thus take large numbers of prey items but what effect this level of predation has on prey populations has received little study. On soft shores, however, Baird *et al.* (1985) found that birds consumed 6–44% of the annual production of invertebrates, indicating that birds can be important predators in shore habitats.

Similarly, the number of birds involved and their seasonal pattern of abundance on rocky shores is largely unknown, in contrast to the now large volume of data available on estuarine systems (Prater, 1981). The rôle that birds play in the dynamics of rocky shore communities has thus been largely overlooked by littoral ecologists and ornithologists alike. In this Chapter our aim is to review the little that is known about this topic and to suggest research that will help to elucidate the significant contribution that birds undoubtedly make to life on rocky shores.

18.2 The Species Involved

Most of the 47 species seen feeding on the shore at Robin Hood's Bay were passerines but only one of these, the rock pipit, fed there regularly. Foster and Gibb (1950) also found the rock pipit regularly feeding on a rocky shore and it is the only passerine adapted to this habitat in the British Isles. Other passerines feed in the rocky littoral infrequently or irregularly (e.g. Hunt, 1964) although they may be stimulated to do so by food scarcity on land, e.g. as a result of inclement weather (Feare, 1967). Resort to littoral invertebrates for food may, however, place these birds under osmotic stress since most passerines do not appear to possess a functional salt gland, a gland through which excess sodium chloride, taken in with food, can be excreted by marine birds (Shoemaker, 1972). In this context, the ability of rock pipits to eat large quantities of littorinids (Gibb, 1956) suggests that they may possess a mechanism for ridding themselves of excess salt but this has not been investigated.

At Robin Hood's Bay, the remaining eight species that regularly fed on the shore were charadrii-forms, gulls (Larinae) and typical shore-birds or waders (Charadrii); all birds which possess salt glands and are therefore well-adapted to a marine environment (Shoemaker, 1972). Around British coasts gulls and waders form the most conspicuous component of the bird fauna but the number of individuals that occur on rocky shores seems small compared with the numbers seen on estuaries and coastal mudflats. Britain's gull population has increased dramatically during this century (Cramp and Simmons, 1983) but this has probably had little influence on rocky shore faunas since this population expansion has been accompanied by and probably facilitated by greater emphasis on feeding inland (Harris, 1965; Horton *et al.*, 1983) on arable fields and at refuse tips.

While most wader species will feed on rocky shores periodically (e.g. knot, *Calidris canutus* (L.) see Summers and Smith (1983), though this species can occur regularly on some coasts), in Britain few appear to do so with regularity. The purple sandpiper is practically restricted to this habitat (Feare, 1966a,b; Cramp and Simmons, 1983) and while the turnstone, *Arenaria interpres* (L.), might be similarly regarded as a rocky shore specialist it is more versatile and will feed in a variety of habitats in winter (Becuwe, 1971; McKee, 1982). European oystercatchers, *Haematopus ostralegus* (L.), are similarly adaptable and this century have shown an increasing tendency to feed and breed inland (Heppleston, 1971). Their feeding behaviour has been studied intensively on account of their economic importance as predators of commercial cockles, *Cerastoderma edule* (L.) (Drinnan, 1957; Davidson, 1967; Horwood and Goss-Custard, 1977), and mussels, *Mytilus edulis* (L.) (Drinnan, 1958), from sedimentary environments, but their predation on rocky shore organisms has been less inten-sively studied (Feare, 1971b). Redshanks, *Tringa totanus* (L.), are primarily birds of mudflats (Hale, 1980), where their behaviour has received detailed study by Goss-Custard (1969, 1970, 1977a,b), but their feeding habits on rocky shores have received little study (Baker, 1981).

On a world scale and outside the breeding season, the purple sandpiper, and its Pacific coast counter-part the rock sandpiper, *Calidris ptilocnemis* (Coues), are rocky shore specialists restricted to mid to high latitudes of the northern hemisphere. They have the shortest migration distances of all Arctic breeding shore-birds. By contrast, large numbers of turnstones migrate to the tropics and into the southern hemisphere as far as South Africa and New Zealand, where some non-breeding birds remain throughout the year. Turnstones are by no means restricted to rocky shores and in the tropics they feed in diverse habitats, often feeding inland in grassland on coralline islands and even at an altitude of 500m on the floor of tropical rain forest (Feare and High, 1977). On the western seaboard of North America, the black turnstone, *Arenaria melanocephala* (Vigors), and the superficially similar surfbird, *Aphriza virgata* (Gmelin), are both inhabitants of rocky shores outside the breeding season (Peterson, 1961). The oystercatchers (Haematopodidae) are represented in all zoogeographic regions where some species feed on rocky shores. In the Chatham Islands, New Zealand, the rare shore plover, *Thinornis novaeseelandiae* (Gmelin), feeds in rock pools (Falla *et al.*, 1979) and in the Indian Ocean the crab plover, *Dromas ardeola* Paykull, occasionally forages for crabs on the shores of raised reef islands (C.J.F., pers. obs.). On some southern ocean islands, lesser sheathbills, *Chionis minor* Hartlaub, include invertebrates found on rocky shores in their diet (Burger, 1981).

In Britain the grey heron, *Ardea cinerea* (L.), includes rocky shore fish, crustaceans and occasionally molluscs in its diet (Cramp and Simmons, 1977). Elsewhere, especially in the tropics, other members of the Ardeidae, such as the reef herons, *Egretta gularis* (Bosc.) and *E. sacra* (Gmelin), and the green-backed heron, *Butorides striatus* (L.), feed in the rocky littoral in addition to other habitats (Recher and Recher, 1972; Snow, 1974; Hancock and Elliott, 1978).

When the tide is in, the littoral zone becomes available to aquatic birds such as cormorants (Phala-crocoridae), ducks (Anatidae) and gulls and terns (Laridae). The eider duck, *Somateria mollissima* (L.), includes a wide variety of invertebrates in its diet (Cramp and Simmons, 1977) but mussels predominate and where the eider is common, e.g. in western Scotland, low-shore mussels may form an important part of its diet. Other sea ducks that dive in shallow water, e.g. scoters, *Melanitta* spp., eiders, *Somateria* spp., goldeneyes, *Bucephala* spp., and sawbills, *Mergus* spp., eat littoral mussels and gastropods while the last of these, together with cormorants and terns, prey predominantly on fish and crustaceans.

An unusual passerine, the seaside cinclodes, *Cinclodes nigrofumosus* (d'Orbigny and Lafresnaye), of coastal Peru, feeds on rocky shores, often in association with waders. Its diet shows a marked overlap with that of the shore-birds (Atkins, 1980) and it does possess a salt gland to enable it to overcome osmotic problems associated with this diet (Paynter, 1971).

Very few birds graze the seaweeds of rocky shores. One that does, and which lives almost exclusively on seaweeds, is the kelp goose, *Chloëphaga hybrida* (Molina), which inhabits the rocky coasts of southern Chile, Argentina, and the Falklands Islands where it eats *Ulva* spp. and *Porphyra* spp. (Woods, 1975). In order to dilute the large intake of salt, it drinks frequently from streams and also has salt glands to help maintain its salt balance.

Although the kelp forests are usually out of reach of littoral animals they do play an important rôle in the ecology of birds on rocky shores, for they provide an enormous input of stranded detritus on the high water marks. Although the kelps (*Laminaria* spp. in the northern hemisphere) contribute most of this, several other brown and red seaweeds are also important. The fronds are torn from the plant or whole plants are ripped from the rocks during storms and are washed ashore. The strandings of kelp are far from even along the coast, being concentrated in certain areas by the configuration of the coast and by the action of offshore currents. Such banks of stranded kelp on the high water mark can reach a depth of a metre and provide a rich food supply for scavenging amphipods (Talitridae). Banks which have been left high-and-dry by a series of spring tides begin to rot and it is in this slimy mulch that flies, particularly the kelp-fly, *Coelopa frigida* (Fabr.), lay their eggs and in which the resulting larvae feed. When such a bank is again inundated by a series of spring tides an abundance of flies, larvae and pupae and amphipods 'abandoning ship' is revealed to shore-birds. In particular, gulls, especially black-headed gulls, *Larus ridibundus* (L.), turnstones, redshanks, purple sandpipers, wagtails, *Motacilla* spp., wheatears, *Oenanthe oenanthe* (L.), jackdaws, *Corvus monedula* L., magpies, *Pica pica* (L.), rock pipits and starlings–even foraging mallard, *Anas platyrhynchos* L. – feed on these (Backlund, 1945).

This brief account of birds adapted to life on rocky shores suggests that few species have adopted this habitat, a surprising fact considering the extremely high densities at which potential prey can be found. This paucity of species is well illustrated within the shore-bird family Scolopacidae, which includes the sandpipers and snipes: of the 81 species in the family (Gruson, 1976), only five live on rocky shores, the remainder inhabiting sandy or muddy beaches and marshes.

18.3 Number and Distribution of Rocky Shore Birds in Britain

The distribution and numbers of waders on the rocky coasts of Britain are poorly known in comparison with estuaries (Prater, 1981). A few studies that have been carried out have attempted to describe the situation in eastern and northern Britain. The first systematic counts were carried out by Brady (1949), who surveyed the rocky and sandy coast between the Tweed estuary and Holy Island each fortnight for three years, in order to describe the seasonal changes in numbers. Peak counts obtained in spring and autumn were interpreted as indicating migration.

The problems of counting waders on rocky shores have been examined by da Prato and da Prato (1979a,b) who concluded that counts at low tide, rather than at high tide roosts, gave representative figures, though low tide counts were very time consuming because only *c.* 10km of shore could be surveyed in one low tide period (half ebb to half flood). The observer walked the shore, close to the water line where waders tend to concentrate, and counted those birds which flew behind, inland or were passed by the observer. Repeat counts along stretches of coast on consecutive days have shown that it is difficult to obtain precise information on numbers, partly due to the limitations of observers, and partly because several species (lapwing, *Vanellus vanellus* (L.), golden plover, *Pluvialis apricaria* (L.), European oystercatcher, redshank and curlew, *Numenius arquata* (L.)) use grass fields as well as rocky shores for foraging and regularly commute between these habitats (Summers *et al.*, 1984). Only purple sandpipers and turnstones could be counted precisely.

Given the problems in interpreting counts, surveys were carried out from Berwickshire to the Outer Hebrides in winter to describe the numbers and distribution of shore-birds (Table 18.1). Some marked differences occurred between counties. For example, knots were restricted to the southern counties, and curlews were far more abundant in the northern counties. The very large numbers of curlews in Caithness and Orkney were dependent on coastal grasslands, as well as the shore, for feeding, so the high densities on the shore are not a true reflection of the population which depends solely on this habitat. The total densities ranged from 202 to 1258 birds·km^{-2}, with a mean of *c.* 750·km^{-2}. On estuaries the density of waders can be as high as 4940·km^{-2}, but such densities apparently only occur on small estuaries. When all estuaries in Britain are considered the average density in January was only 486·km^{-2} (Prater, 1981). Thus rocky shores apparently support higher densities of waders but direct comparison may not be valid because many rocky shore waders obtain only part of their food on rocky shores.

There are few comparative data for densities of waders in other parts of the world. The abundance (numbers·km^{-1} length of shore) has been estimated at 47 and 7 waders·km^{-1} for the West and South coasts of western Cape, South Africa (Summers *et al.*, 1977). The greater abundance on the West coast has been linked to the nutrient-rich Benguela current which runs along the West coast of southern Africa. The abundance in eastern Scotland is even higher, i.e. 72 waders·km^{-1} (Summers *et al.*, 1975a; da Prato and da Prato, 1979a; Tay and Orkney Ringing Groups, 1984). None of the above estimates include shores with sections of cliff which, having few or no waders, would depress the estimates of abundance had they been included. However, the inclusion of cliff would actually have little effect on estimates of density for the area of the littoral zone along cliffs is very small.

Britain has a very long coastline (about 14,000km) and most of this is in Scotland, due to island groups such as Orkney, Shetland and the Outer Hebrides. As a result, Orkney has a very much larger population of rocky shore waders compared with mainland counties of similar land area (Table 18.1).

Of birds other than waders, only the distribution of the rock pipit, established by the British Trust for Ornithology's Atlas of Breeding Birds, is well known. This species inhabits most rocky shores and Sharrock (1976) estimated that there were around 50,000 pairs in the British Isles. Grey herons are also widely distributed in Britain and feed on all rocky shores, but their utilization of this habitat is greatest in western Scotland and on the Hebrides (Marquiss, pers. comm.). The ducks that feed over rocky shores, such as the eider and the sawbills, are also predominantly northern in their distribution (Sharrock, 1976) and undoubtedly exert their greatest influence around Scottish coasts.

18.4 Seasonal Changes in Bird Activity

There are large seasonal changes in the numbers of waders occurring on rocky shores because most species depart to breed elsewhere. Results from ringing have shown that many of these species migrate long distances to the Arctic regions of Canada, Greenland and Russia (Table 18.2). Waders generally arrive back on British rocky shores during July to October, maintain high numbers over winter, and depart in April and May (Fig. 18.2). The pattern is similar in other parts of the world, such as South Africa, although there waders tend to arrive later and depart slightly earlier (Fig. 18.1). Some species of waders can be seen on rocky shores all the year round. The immature birds of species which do not breed in their first year may remain on rocky shores, and some European oystercatchers remain to

TABLE 18.1

Densities (numbers·km^{-2}) of waders on the rocky shores of eastern and northern Scotland (from Summers et al., 1975a; da Prato and da Prato, 1979; Buxton, 1982; Summers and Buxton, 1983; Tay and Orkney Ring Groups, 1984).

	East Lothian	Fife	Angus	Kincardine	Aberdeenshire	Ross-shire	Sutherland	Caithness	Orkney	Lewis and Harris
Oystercatcher	168	54	170	115	113	52	51	229	46	67
Ringed Plover	24	10	5	3	12			3	16	22
Grey Plover	2				2					
Golden Plover	89	2	121	54			5	7	36	
Lapwing							5	26	59	
Turnstone	158	179	135	191	289	68	56	164	102	81
Snipe	3		1		2				11	
Bar-tailed Godwit									4	
Curlew	32	42	72	33	20	92	7	208	271	34
Redshank	49	38	74	114	197	102	35	87	117	40
Knot	117	46	557		21			3		
Purple Sandpiper	73	55	67	109	175	135	27	225	101	42
Sanderling									6	
Dunlin	113	41	56	19	54		16	10	14	4
Total density	828	467	1258	638	885	449	202	962	784	290
Total number of birds	7719	10160	6164	3440	4607	1169	526	6156	41669	1771

TABLE 18.2

The percentage composition (based on numerical abundance) and breeding localities (Cramp and Simmons, 1983; McLachlan and Liversidge, 1970) **of wader communities on rocky shores in northern and eastern Scotland** (Summers et al., 1975a; Summers and Buxton, 1983) **and in the Cape Province, South Africa** (Summers et al., 1977).

Species	Scotland		South Africa	
	Composition	Breeding localities	Composition	Breeding localities
European Oystercatcher	15.1	Britain, Faeroes, Iceland, Norway		
Black Oystercatcher			9.5	South Africa
White-fronted Plover			4.9	South Africa
Kittlitz's Plover			0.7	South Africa
Three-banded Plover			0.5	South Africa
Ringed Plover	1.5	Britain	0.5	Arctic Russia
Blacksmith Plover			0.2	South Africa
Lapwing	3.4	Britain, Scandinavia		
Golden Plover	3.1	Britain, Iceland, Fenno-Scandia, Russia		
Grey Plover			1.0	Arctic Russia
Turnstone	15.0	Arctic Canada, Greenland	44.0	Arctic Russia?
Curlew Sandpiper			12.0	Arctic Russia
Little Stint			1.6	Arctic Russia
Knot	11.7	Arctic Canada, Greenland	0.1	Arctic Russia
Purple Sandpiper	11.5	Norway, Iceland? Greenland?		
Dunlin	6.2	Fenno-Scandia, Russia		
Sanderling	0.3	Arctic Russia,? Greenland	21.3	Arctic Russia
Common Sandpiper			1.9	Russia
Redshank	12.1	Britain, Iceland		
Greenshank			0.1	Russia
Bar-tailed Godwit	0.4	Arctic Russia		
Whimbrel			1.6	Russia
Curlew	19.1	Britain, Scandinavia		
Snipe	0.6	Britain, Fenno-Scandia, Iceland		
	100.0		100.0	

breed on coastal fields or beaches close to the rocky shores where they spend the rest of the year. Similarly in South Africa, black oystercatchers, *Haematopus moquini* Bonaparte, and white-fronted plovers, *Charadrius marginatus* Vieillot, occur in similar numbers throughout the year and breed just above the high-water mark on the shore (Pringle and Cooper, 1977).

The migrations of the Arctic-breeding waders vary greatly from species to species, and even within populations of the same species. In some species the different sexes migrate at different times, e.g. female purple sandpipers leave the breeding sites before the males and young (Cramp and Simmons, 1983). Those species which start arriving back on rocky shores in July and August begin the post-nuptial moult which involves all feather tracts. Some species, and indeed some populations, moult before migrating to their non-breeding areas, e.g. the populations of purple sandpipers in Spitsbergen (Bengtson, 1975) and Iceland (Morrison, 1976) moult close to their breeding quarters before migrating, whilst the Norwegian population migrates to its non-breeding quarters before moulting (Atkinson et al., 1981). Thus the seasonal pattern of numbers varies regionally depending on which

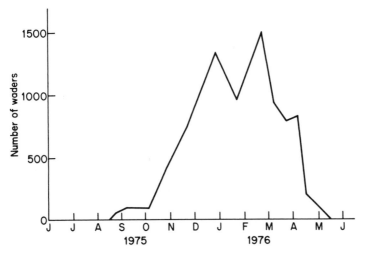

FIG. 18.1. Seasonal changes in the number of Palaearctic waders (Charadrii) in the marine littoral of the Cape Peninsula, South Africa (after Pringle and Cooper, 1977).

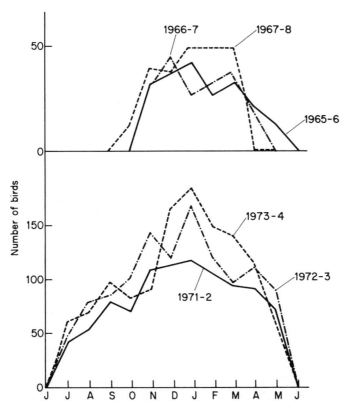

FIG. 18.2. Seasonal changes in the number of purple sandpipers at Robin Hood's Bay, Yorkshire, England (upper graph) (Feare, unpubl. data) and at Arbroath, Angus, Scotland (lower graph) (after Atkinson et al., 1981).

populations occur on the rocky coast, and the period of arrival back on the rocky coasts can span several months. The purple sandpipers in eastern Scotland start arriving in July (Fig. 18.2) whilst those in Yorkshire and northern and western Scotland arrive mainly in October (Tay and Orkney Ringing Groups, 1984).

Post-nuptial moult of most wader species is completed by November and by this time the waders generally increase their body fat levels which reach a peak in December. The changes in fat are reflected in their total body mass (Fig. 18.3 for the turnstone in Scotland). These extra fat levels act as a reserve in case the rate of food intake is insufficient to balance the rate of energy expenditure (Davidson, 1981). Food shortage may be caused by (i) cold weather which may affect the availability of the prey (Goss-Custard, 1969), (ii) strong winds which make feeding less efficient by buffeting the birds (Pienkowski, 1981), or (iii) increased wave action which decreases the amount of shore foraging area available for feeding (Feare, 1966a). Coupled with this, in winter, is the shorter day length when one might expect less time for foraging. However, most waders can feed at night, though the relative amount of food taken by day and night varies from species to species (Dugan, 1981). Some species such as the purple sandpiper do not accumulate additional fat reserves in winter (Fig. 18.3). This is typical of waders spending the non-breeding season in warmer parts of Britain (Pienkowski *et al.*, 1979) or in the southern hemisphere (Summers and Waltner, 1979) (Fig. 18.3, turnstone in South Africa), and thus suggests that purple sandpipers are unlikely to experience food shortage in Britain. The non-breeding range of the purple sandpiper extends further North than any wader but whether they accumulate winter fat reserves in northern Norway or Greenland remains to be established.

In those species that do fatten in winter (e.g. turnstone in Scotland, Fig. 18.3) the fat deposits are reduced in late winter and are maintained at a low level until a few weeks before they migrate back to

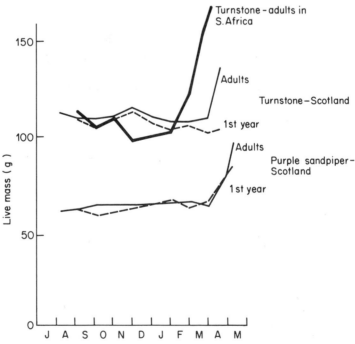

FIG. 18.3. Seasonal changes in the body mass of turnstones and purple sandpipers on rocky coasts in eastern Scotland (after Summers *et al.*, 1975b; (Atkinson *et al.*, 1981) and of turnstones in South Africa (after Summers and Waltner, 1979).

their breeding grounds. The fat reserves accumulated in late April and May are used as fuel during migration.

The turnstones which spend the non-breeding season in South Africa start to accumulate fat reserves about one month before those in Scotland (Fig. 18.3). Those that winter this far South have a migration of 13,000km to the Arctic, and as a load of fat (65g above their lean mass of 100g) will carry them about 4,800km, they will need to stop to replenish their fat load at least twice (Summers and Waltner, 1979). It takes approximately two to three weeks of intensive feeding to attain a full load of fat (Morrison and Wilson, 1972). Most of the turnstones in Britain do not appear to attain the high fat levels observed in South Africa (Fig. 18.3; Branson *et al.*, 1979). They leave in the first half of May and migrate via Iceland where they can 're-fuel' before completing the journey to the breeding grounds in Greenland and Canada (Morrison and Wilson, 1972). Other turnstones remain in Britain until the latter half of May, accumulating larger amounts of fat (similar to the South African birds), sufficient to enable them to fly direct to Greenland (Clapham, 1979). Only a small percentage of the first-year turnstones migrate with the adults (Clapham, 1979); most first-year birds remain on the coast during the summer, and will not breed until their second year. In contrast, both adult and first-year purple sandpipers emigrate and both put on fat for migration (Fig. 18.3).

Ringing studies have shown that oystercatchers, turnstones, redshanks, purple sandpipers, dunlins and curlews are faithful to their non-breeding areas (Hardy and Minton, 1980; Tay Ringing Group, unpubl. data). They tend to remain on the same stretch of rocky coast throughout the winter and return to the same stretch in successive winters. For example, one purple sandpiper trapped on the Isle of May, Fife, was re-trapped there 14 years later. Some birds do move short distances during the winter and movements of 30km and 23km have been recorded for turnstones and purple sandpipers respectively (Summers *et al.*, 1975b; Atkinson *et al.*, 1981).

18.5 Survival

Measurements of survival have not been carried out on rocky shore waders but studies have been made on waders in estuaries, including species which also occur on rocky shores (Evans, 1981). Annual survival rates of waders wintering on the coast of N.E. England are surprisingly high (80–90%), even for the small sandpipers which undertake long migrations to breed in the Arctic. When the annual mortality was divided into mortality during the migration/breeding season and non-breeding season it was apparent that most usually occurred during the non-breeding period, though with the oyster-catcher the opposite was true (Goss-Custard *et al.*, 1982; Evans and Pienkowski, 1984). Years when mortality was greater than normal could be attributed to periods of severe weather during winter; and it was strong winds accompanied by cold temperatures rather than cold temperatures alone which led to depletion of energy reserves and ultimately to death (Evans, 1981).

The above estimates of survival are based on populations of waders in England at a time when the raptor populations were much reduced through pesticide poisoning and persecution by man. In other parts of the world, where raptor populations are at more natural levels, the annual survival of waders can be much lower. For example, populations of dunlin, *Calidris alpina* (L.) in California have been reduced by as much as 21% in a five month period by northern harriers, *Circus cyaneus* (L.), American kestrels, *Falco sparverius* (L.), short-eared owls, *Asio flammeus* Pontoppidan, peregrine falcons, *Falco peregrinus* Tunst, and particularly merlins, *Falco columbarius* Tunst (Page and Whiteacre, 1975). Juvenile dunlins are particularly susceptible to predation by these raptors (Kus *et al.*, 1984) and Whitfield (in prep.) found that juvenile turnstones and redshanks suffered heavier predation, mainly from sparrowhawks, *Accipiter nisus* (L.), than adults in East Scotland.

18.6 The Rocky Shore as a Habitat for Birds

Rocky shores support extremely high densities of potential prey items for birds. For example, Seed (1969a) recorded mussel, *Mytilus edulis*, densities of over $400,000 \cdot m^{-2}$ in the low-shore. Connell (1970) found densities of *Balanus glandula* Darwin exceeding $30,000 \cdot m^{-2}$ and total barnacle (*Semibalanus* and *Chthamalus* species) exceeding $500,000 \cdot m^{-2}$ (Connell, 1961b). Smith and Newell (1955) found *Littorina littorea* (L.) exceptionally living at over $650 \cdot m^{-2}$, while Gibb (1956) considered the average density of *L. neritoides* (L.) on his study area to be about $25,000 \cdot m^{-2}$. Frank (1982) found densities of the limpet, *Notoacmea personata* (Rathke), over $60 \cdot m^{-2}$, and *Patella vulgata* (L.) has been recorded at densities exceeding $1000 \cdot m^{-2}$ (Bowman, pers. comm.).

Such high densities do not necessarily imply a superabundance of food, however, for many constraints restrict its availability to birds. These constraints can be grouped into (i) physical and (ii) biotic factors on the shore and (iii) the feeding behaviour of the birds: these constraints are, of course, interlinked.

18.6.1 Physical factors

The predominant physical factors that affect the ability of birds to feed on rocky shores are the tidal cycle, shore topography, seasonal climatic change and weather.

Apart from the few species, like eiders, that feed over rocky shores by diving to the substratum when it is covered by water, rocky shore birds feed on those parts of the shore which are not covered by water. There is thus a direct relation between height on the shore and the time for which prey at a particular level are susceptible to bird predation: birds can feed at high-shore levels for most of the day but can feed in the low-shore only at low water. During low spring tides the birds can feed further down the shore than during neap tides, but conversely, they are denied feeding at the top of the shore for longer periods during high spring tides. It had been thought previously (Feare, 1966a) that waders such as purple sandpipers would have a more restricted time for feeding if high tide coincided with the middle of the day rather than early and late in the day. However, the purple sandpiper, like many waders (Dugan, 1981), can feed by night so the time of high tide may not be so critical, though the relative feeding efficiencies by day and night are unknown. This simple relationship can be confounded by shore topography, however, for crevices and deep pools provide prey refuges which birds are unable to exploit. Conversely, shallow pools can, for biotic reasons to be mentioned below, provide sites of high risk to bird predation. The area available for feeding is also determined by shore slope, with steeply shelving shores providing smaller feeding areas than flat reef platforms. Wave action, usually most severe in winter, restricts the amount of time that birds can feed undisturbed on the shore. For example, Feare (1966a) found that, in stormy weather, purple sandpipers devoted 48 minutes of their 6h daily feeding time to avoiding waves. This effect is more pronounced on exposed than on sheltered shores and can be exacerbated by onshore winds and low barometric pressure, both of which hold the tide in for longer periods.

Ice on the shore can present a problem in parts of the wintering range of the purple sandpiper. In Nova Scotia (Canada) sheltered shorelines are covered with blocks of ice and few littoral organisms are uncovered. Therefore the purple sandpipers in this area have to spend the winter on exposed points of coast where wind and waves keep the shore free of ice (Smith and Bleakney, 1969). Around British coasts, freezing of the shore is a rare event but low temperatures in winter may nevertheless restrict the birds' abilities to feed through reducing the activity of prey organisms (see below) or by causing them to shelter in crevices and under rocks.

At high tide, birds that have fed in the littoral zone can either roost or feed elsewhere. Waders that roost flock together in single or mixed species associations at protected sites at high water mark or on inland fields. Goss-Custard (1969) and Heppleston (1971) found that, in estuarine situations, redshanks and European oystercatchers were unable to obtain their daily food requirements from the mudflats and had to supplement their intake from the shore by feeding in grass fields at high tide. Rocky shore species behave similarly (Summers and Buxton, 1983) but some species seem more disposed to feed inland at high tide than others. For example, Baker (1981) observed redshanks that fed on a rocky shore at low tide feeding both inland and at night while turnstones were seen to feed only during low tides and by day, even though they did not appear to be able to fulfil their daily requirements by so doing. However, inland feeding may be a tactic to which these birds can resort when conditions are sufficiently severe, as during winter in high latitudes where daylengths are short. Waters (1966) reported both turnstones and purple sandpipers feeding inland at high tide in the Outer Hebrides and Shetland but such behaviour did not occur at Robin Hood's Bay (Feare, 1966b). Such latitudinal variations in winter behaviour might be expected and data on the feeding schedules of purple sandpipers towards the North of their winter geographical range would be especially interesting.

The fish that grey herons eat on rocky shores are generally smaller than those taken from fresh water. Furthermore, most Herons only feed on the shore for up to 3 or 4h around low tide and, while food may be abundant then, some birds are unable to obtain their daily requirement and when breeding must resort to fresh water or terrestrial habitats at high tide to sustain their young (Marquiss, pers. comm.).

18.6.2 Biotic factors

Birds that feed on rocky shores generally seem to prefer to take prey that are active. This aspect of their feeding has received little study in this habitat but the relationship between prey activity and predation has been demonstrated on muddy and sandy beaches (Goss-Custard, 1977a; Pienkowski, 1983a). Since the shells of many littoral organisms offer a strong defence against predation by birds and other animals, the selection of active prey, e.g. a mussel with open valves, or a limpet with its shell raised off the substratum or a dogwhelk that is mobile and not firmly attached, may well reduce the energetic cost to a predator of obtaining a prey item. The energetics of this predator–prey relationship on rocky shores merit study.

The preference for active prey concentrates the activity of many rocky shore birds around the water's edge so that feeding birds move up and down the shore with the tide. This movement imposes dietary switches upon the birds as they pass through the zones occupied by different prey species during each tidal cycle (Feare, 1966a) and necessitates considerable adaptability in the feeding behaviour of the birds – demonstrated by the wide variety of food organisms that each species eats (Table 18.3). In rock pools, lack of emersion enables their inhabitants to remain active, a factor that may account for the tendency of shore-birds to concentrate their activities in shallow pools (Feare, 1966a; 1971b). How birds partition their time between such rocky shore micro-habitats has not been studied.

The extent to which littoral invertebrates can remain active during the tidal cycle determines their growth rates: Seed (1968) found that mussels in the low-shore grew fast and had thin shells, while upper-shore mussels grew slowly and had thick shells. Feare (1971b) found that shells of the limpet *Patella aspera* (Lamarck), living in the low-shore and in mid-shore pools, were softer than those of *P. vulgata* which occupied the mid- and upper-shore. The softer shells of *P. aspera* were considered to be easier for European oystercatchers to break and dislodge, accounting for the birds' preference of this species over *P. vulgata*, and for their apparent selection of shallow pools as favoured feeding sites.

The inter-relationships between temperature, prey activity and shore-bird feeding have been studied on muddy and sandy beaches (Goss-Custard, 1977a; Pienkowski, 1983b) but similar investigations on rocky shores are lacking. Extreme temperatures on rocky shores do, however, produce

TABLE 18.3

Littoral invertebrates (and fish) recorded in the diets of rocky shore waders in Britain. Data from Dewar (1940), Feare (1966a, 1971a), Harris (1979), Cramp and Simmons (1983), Summers and Smith (1983) and S.M. Smith (unpubl.).

	Oystercatcher	Purple Sandpiper	Turnstone	Knot
Annelida	+	+	+	+
Mollusca				
Lepidochitona sp.			+	
Patella vulgata L.	+		+	
Patella aspera (Lamarck)	+			
Lacuna sp.		+		
Nucella lapillus (L.)	+	+		
Littorina littorea (L.)	+	+	+	+
Littorina obtusata (L.)		+		+
Littorina 'saxatilis' (Olivi)		+		+
Littorina neritoides (L.)		+	+	
Littorina neglecta Bean		+		
Littorina mariae Sacchi & Rastelli		+		
Rissoa parva (da Costa)		+		+
Calliostoma sp.			+	
Skeneopsis planorbis (Fabr.)		+		+
Onoba semicostata (Mont.)		+		
Mytilus edulis L.	+	+	+	+
Crustacea				
Balanus sp.		+	+	
Idotea granulosa Rathke		+		
Amphipod spp.			+	+
Carcinus maenas (L.)		+	+	
Pagurus sp.			+	
Echinodermata				
Psammechinus miliaris (Gmelin)			+	
Pisces		+	+	

responses in invertebrates that could affect their vulnerability to predation by birds. In hot weather, the avoidance of desiccation necessitates the closure of the valves of emersed mussels and the clamping down of limpets, thereby simultaneously increasing their protection against predators such as oystercatchers. In winter, extreme cold and wave action may stimulate more mobile animals to seek refuge in crevices and pools or to migrate down the shore (Feare, 1970a). Where climatic extremes cause mortality of shore invertebrates, however, a temporary food abundance for birds may result. The aggregation of dogwhelks, especially in winter, may confer some protection from avian predators (Feare, 1971a) and in this context it is significant that the parasitic castration of dogwhelks *Nucella lapillus* (L.) by the trematode *Parorchis acanthus* (Nicoll) leads infected hosts to lead a more solitary life on the open shore, rather than join in aggregations. This behaviour renders them more susceptible to predation by oystercatchers (and possibly other birds) which are final hosts of the parasite (Feare, 1971b). Other parasites of littoral invertebrates that include avian hosts in their cycles (Harris, 1964; Pettitt, 1975) may also prove to affect the behaviour of their invertebrate hosts.

On rocky shores in Scotland, grey herons prefer to feed among seaweed (Marquiss, pers. comm.) and some of the best habitat is on gently shelving shores in sheltered sea lochs with a dense cover of weed, especially *Ascophyllum nodosum* (L.) Le Jol. Herons are more abundant on shores with continuous rather than broken weed cover (Carss, 1983) and in Fife, Smith (1984) found that the density of adult herons on the shore was directly correlated with the percentage cover of brown algae. Their food consists primarily of fish typical of weed-covered shores, notably fifteen-spined sticklebacks, *Spinachia spinachia* (L.), long-spined sea scorpions, *Taurulus bubalis* (Euphrasen), greater pipefish, *Syngnathus acus* (L.), and butterfish, *Pholis gunnellus* (L.).

A further biotic effect upon shore-bird feeding has been postulated by Hockey (1983b), who considered that nutrient enrichment of waters around islands off South Africa led to an enhanced littoral community. This enrichment resulted from the guano produced by dense sea-bird colonies. The ensuing high productivity of green algae and, subsequently, of gastropods and crustaceans on the shores of the islands led to higher populations of the South African black oystercatcher, *Haematopus moquini*, than on mainland coasts which were relatively nutrient poor: however, other factors, such as predation of coastal birds by mammals, will also contribute to lower oystercatcher populations on the mainland.

18.6.3 Feeding behaviour of the birds

While those birds that follow the movements of the tides show considerable adaptability in their diets (Table 18.3), they nevertheless restrict their selection of food items within certain size ranges so that many of the apparently superabundant items on rocky shores do not constitute *available* prey. There is a tendency for different species to take different sizes of prey, generally with prey size being proportional to predator size and leading to a degree of ecological segregation of species that may compete for the same species on rocky shores (Gibb, 1956; Feare, 1966a; Pettitt, 1975). Furthermore, the size of prey in the diet often differs from the size distribution of the prey population on the shore, again indicating size selection by the predator (Gibb, 1956; Feare, 1966a, 1971b; Hartwick, 1976; Frank, 1982). The size of prey taken by a species of shore-bird can, however, vary both geographically (Summers and Smith, 1983) and temporally (O'Connor and Brown, 1977) depending upon prey availability and upon the availability of alternative prey species. This variation in prey size has implications with respect to the net rate of energy gain, for prey of different sizes may require widely differing handling and ingestion times. For example, Butler and Kirbyson (1979) observed that black oystercatchers, *Haematopus backmani* Audubon, took longer to open and eat large (than small) oysters, *Crassostrea gigas* (Thunberg). In comparison with other habitats, there have been very few rocky shore studies designed to test optimal foraging models (Hartwick, 1976) although recently there have been a few investigations of some of the parameters that contribute to successful feeding in the rocky littoral (Baker, 1981; Fleischer, 1983; Metcalfe and Furness, 1984). This is clearly an area where further studies of this kind are required.

In addition to the selection of different prey sizes by different species of predator, prey item size may vary intraspecifically according to the sex and age of the birds. Fig. 18.4 shows that female purple sandpipers take larger mussels than do males and a similar trend exists for their predation of littorinids. Among calidrine sandpipers, purple sandpipers exhibit an unusually large sexual size dimorphism which includes the bill, with the female being the larger (Cramp and Simmons, 1983). This may be an example of ecological release facilitated by this species' specialization to the rocky shore habitus: the main habitats of other calidrine sandpipers outside the breeding season are soft sediment shores.

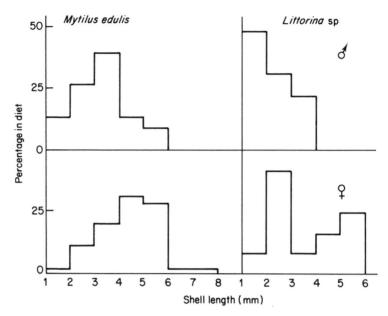

FIG. 18.4. The size–frequency (%) distribution of *Mytilus edulis* and *Littorina* sp. in the guts of 4 male and 4 female purple sandpipers on 17 December, 1973 at Arbroath, Scotland (Tay Ringing Group, unpubl. data). For *Mytilus edulis*, Kolmogorov-Smirnov two sample test, $D = 0.44$, $n_1 = 23$, $n_2 = 35$, $\chi^2 = 10.7$, $P < 0.02$; differences for *Littorina* sp. are not significant, $P > 0.05$.

Further intraspecific prey selection has been demonstrated during the breeding season. Adult black oystercatchers (*H. bachmani*) eat small to medium limpets during the breeding season but they select larger individuals to take back to the nest for the young (Hartwick, 1981). This oystercatcher also selects different proportions of prey species for its chicks and for its own consumption (Hartwick, 1976). Groves (1978) noted higher rates of feeding by adult, than by juvenile, turnstones and intra-specific differences in prey selection may also be implicated here.

A major consequence for prey organisms of size selection by the predator is that, once a prey individual has grown out of the range of sizes taken by a specific predator, the prey is then immune to predation by that species. Frank (1982) has termed this release from predation as 'refuge in large size' and concluded that it could protect some limpet species from oystercatcher predation at the expense of other limpet species (cf. Seed and Brown, 1978). However, the taking of different sizes of prey could lead to competition between bird species, for those that take young individuals of a prey species could leave fewer individuals for birds that eat older age-groups. Similarly, the predation of older cohorts may affect the reproductive capacity of the prey population, thereby reducing recruitment to the young age-classes.

Further constraints are placed upon birds' efficiencies in exploiting rocky shore invertebrates by both the birds' own activities and the activities of their neighbours. The effects of the birds' depletion of their own food supplies and of interference between neighbours in flocks have been studied on sandy and muddy beaches (e.g. O'Connor and Brown, 1977; Goss-Custard, 1980) and it is likely that similar effects will occur on rocky shores, although investigations have not yet been directed to these aspects. However, it is known that shore-birds can locally deplete at least some of the prey species available to them (Feare, 1969; Frank, 1982) but the effect of this depletion on the birds' food intake or selection has not been established. Similarly, aggression between neighbours in flocks has been recorded in rocky shore waders (e.g. Feare, 1966a; Groves, 1978) but whether this interference influences prey selection or intake rates is unknown. A competing demand on birds' time while feeding is vigilance for potential predators, and possibly other birds that might steal prey, and recent studies have shown that vigilance does occupy significant amounts of time, but that in flocks (both single and mixed species) the requirement for an individual to remain alert decreases, leaving more time available for feeding (Metcalfe, 1984a,b).

While flocking may permit more efficient exploitation of food resources it nevertheless carries increased risks of mutual interference, both by birds impeding one anothers' movements and by disturbing potential prey so that the prey can take evasive action. Further, flocking concentrates the activities of feeding birds into small areas, increasing the risk of depleting food stocks in those areas but leaving other areas untouched. Flocking species might therefore be expected to prey upon resources that are rapidly renewed or redistributed, while dispersed feeders might take prey from more stable populations. This prediction does not appear to apply to rocky shores, however, since purple sandpipers, which almost invariably feed in small flocks, have been found to deplete juvenile dogwhelks on a restricted area of a rocky shore during winter when redistribution of this dogwhelk age-class was minimal and recruitment had ceased (Feare, 1969).

Some species of shore-bird defend territories on rocky shores during the non-breeding season. Myers et al. (1979) observed territorial behaviour in whimbrel, Numenius phaeopus (L.), spotted sandpipers, Actitis macularia (L.), wandering tattlers, Heterosceles incanus (Gmelin), and willets, Catoptrophus semipalmatus (Gmelin), but not in sanderlings, Calidris alba (Pallas), turnstones or surfbirds. In some species, both flock and territorial feeding occurs. In pied wagtails, Motacilla alba yarrelli Gould, Davies (1976) found that the strategy adopted by a particular individual depended upon its social status and upon the predictability of food resources: high-ranking birds defended territories when food was predictably abundant but rejoined flocks when food became scarce. Such a relationship has not been investigated for rocky shore waders and any study should also take into account the risk of predation (Metcalfe, 1984b). Herons feed solitarily on rocky shores and at least some individuals have been shown to defend territories (Recher, 1972; Snow, 1974; Smith, 1984).

18.7 The Impact of Birds on Littoral Ecosystems

Very few studies have attempted to integrate the disciplines of ornithology and littoral invertebrate ecology and the extent to which birds impose selective forces on saxicolous invertebrates is therefore largely unknown. Some studies, however, report heavy predation on some prey species, suggesting that birds can be important agents in the dynamics of rocky shore communities.

In Britain, Feare (1969) estimated that purple sandpipers were responsible for 93% of the 89% winter mortality observed for first-year dogwhelks. This level of mortality was inflicted on a local dogwhelk population living on the low-shore on an exposed reef at Robin Hood's Bay and the birds had access to this shore level on only 33 days between January and April. At a nearby locality, Lewis and Bowman (1975) recorded an 81% reduction in the limpet, Patella vulgata, population of one of their study sites in two months following the winter influx of oystercatchers.

The selective nature of bird predation can lead to reductions in particular size categories, thus affecting the age structure of the population (Horwood and Goss-Custard, 1977; O'Connor and Brown, 1977) and Moore (1983b) deduced that size selection by rock pipits of the amphipod, Hyale nilssoni (Rathke), could be an important determinant of the sex ratio of the population that survived the winter. Pettitt (1975) inferred that birds may also be involved in the maintenance of colour polymorphisms in some littoral gastropods and while Colton (1916) claimed that gulls might act as agents of selection on dogwhelk populations, this has been doubted, for South-West Wales at least, by Berry and Crothers (1968).

In Britain, bird predation on rocky shores is mainly a winter phenomenon, since the shore-birds that constitute numerically the most important predators generally breed away from the shore. Where oystercatchers do breed close to the shore, however, their diet during the breeding season can include components of the rocky shore fauna (Harris, 1967). In America, the effects of predation by black oystercatchers has received more intensive investigation. Hartwick (1981) found that these birds had little effect on limpets (*Collisella digitalis* Rathke) before and during the early breeding season because the oystercatchers then foraged away from their territories and subsequently devoted much of their time on the shore to territorial defence and mating. Later, after the chicks hatched, adult birds ate small limpets themselves and carried large ones back to the nest for the chicks. In the autumn, both adults and young concentrated on small and medium-sized limpets, but when large limpets were available they were heavily exploited, to the extent that large limpets became restricted to areas inaccessible to oystercatchers. Frank (1982) recorded over-winter population reductions of 99% for the limpet, *Notoacmea persona* (Rathke), and 97% for *N. scutum* (Rathke) while *Collisella pelta* (Rathke) suffered a 53% loss. Most of these losses were attributed to black oystercatcher predation and Frank considered that *C. pelta* ceased being vulnerable when they had grown to sizes beyond the birds' capabilities. Hockey and Branch (1984) concluded that a similar situation prevailed on rocky shores of southern Africa. Here, those limpets, *Patella granularis* L., that had grown sufficiently large to avoid predation by South African black oystercatchers, *Haematopus moquini*, were responsible for 86% of the gamete formation by the limpet population; it was therefore these large limpets that maintained high levels of recruitment in areas of severe oystercatcher predation.

These birds clearly exert major effects on these limpet populations and further studies may illustrate similar influences of other bird species. Studies of birds must, however, be more closely integrated with more classical studies of littoral communities, for the predation by birds of dominant components of the littoral fauna will have far-reaching effects on the structure of these communities in space and time (Paine, 1974; Hawkins, 1981a). The local nature of much bird predation (Lewis and Bowman, 1975) and the survival of prey species in refuges provided by micro-habitat, shore level or body size can lead to selection pressures producing adaptive behaviour in the prey. This can produce variable, often unpredictable, patterns of distribution in the prey and in other littoral biota that are dependent upon the presence or absence of these prey species.

ACKNOWLEDGEMENTS

We are grateful to Drs M. Marquiss, P.G. Moore, M.W. Pienkowski and R. Seed for valued comments on the manuscript and to N. Metcalf, Shelagh M. Smith and P. Whitfield for allowing us to quote their unpublished data.

CHAPTER XIX

THE USE OF *PATELLA VULGATA* L. IN ROCKY SHORE SURVEILLANCE

A.M. Jones and J.M. Baxter

19.1 Introduction

The search for biological elements of the marine ecosystem suitable for use in surveillance, often with pollution impacts in mind, has provided the stimulus for much recent ecological research. Since, as Jack Lewis has stressed, an adequate knowledge of the interactions between abiotic and biotic factors is a necessary pre-requisite for evaluating changes which may be ascribed to pollutants, much of this activity has been directed initially, not at the effects of pollutants, but at fundamental aspects of species and community biology. It is still debatable whether current knowledge is yet adequate for any species in this context. A few species, however, by virtue of their widespread distributions and important ecological rôles, have received particular attention. The limpet, *Patella vulgata* L., is one such species and it is the aim of this paper to consider the biology of this species critically with particular reference to its potential for inclusion in biological surveillance programmes.

19.2 Ecological Rôle

Patella vulgata is considered to be a 'keystone' species (Lewis, 1976) and its rôle in the structuring of communities in the rocky littoral was never more dramatically demonstrated than in the various studies which followed the 'Torrey Canyon' incident (J.E. Smith, 1968; Southward and Southward, 1978). Experimental manipulations of limpet densities and population structures (Jones, 1948b; Lodge, 1948; Southward, 1956; Hawkins, 1981b; Hawkins and Hartnoll, 1983a,b) have demonstrated a delicately balanced shore ecosystem (Fig. 19.1), in which changes in density and structure of the adult component of limpet populations may result in major changes in community structure: Fig. 19.2 illustrates the consequences of experimentally reducing the population density of adult limpets from $80 \cdot m^{-2}$ to $35 \cdot m^{-2}$ in Orkney. Similar changes in community structure do occur naturally but their periodicity and the resulting floral and faunal composition vary in a manner dependent on many different environmental factors and the time of year when such changes take place. It is clear, therefore, that any factor which directly or indirectly modifies the population structure or the grazing activities of *P. vulgata* can be expected to cause marked changes in community structure. Such changes need not be detrimental however, since they may represent only a change from one stable condition to another but they can serve as indicators of change whose cause can then be considered.

19.3 Distribution

P. vulgata has an extensive geographical range within the Palaearctic region (de Beaufort, 1951) being found on rocky shores from the Mediterranean northwards to the Lofoten Islands, off Norway (Fretter and Graham, 1976): in the British Isles, therefore, *P. vulgata* is towards the centre of its

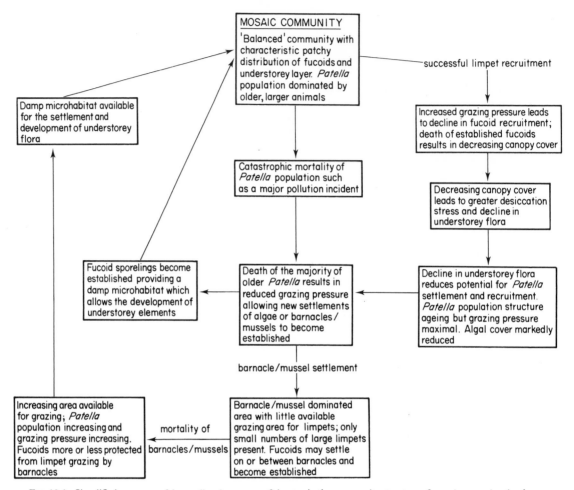

FIG. 19.1. Simplified summary of the predicted sequence of changes in the community structure of a semi-exposed rocky shore.

geographical range and the impact of climatic factors might be expected to be less dramatic than at its northern or southern limits of distribution. Two more southerly species of *Patella* compete with *P. vulgata* in Britain; *P. aspera* Lamarck is reaching its northern limits in Scotland where it becomes increasingly restricted to the low-shore regions of exposed shores while *P. depressa* Pennant reaches its northern extreme in Anglesey (Fretter and Graham, 1976) but is found in the mid-shore.

P. vulgata is common on all rocky shores from the most sheltered ones dominated by *Ascophyllum nodosum* (L.) Le Jol. to the most exposed, mussel/barnacle-dominated types but its ecological rôle is markedly reduced in significance towards the sheltered end of this spectrum: it is most important on the 'mosaic' semi-exposed shores. Its upper shore limit varies with exposure from near M.H.W.S. on exposed shores to c. M.H.W.N. on sheltered ones while the lower limit normally extends to c. E.L.W.S. Adult population densities are usually greatest around M.T.L. but both distribution and density are modified by micro-habitat factors (Lewis and Bowman, 1975). This results in spatial distributions of individuals ranging from the more usual dispersed pattern shown in Fig. 19.3A to the markedly clumped pattern shown in Fig. 19.3B, a feature which has important implications for the selection of sampling procedures whenever distributions are being described or compared.

FIG. 19.2. Plate showing the fucoid-dominated area which resulted from experimentally reducing the limpet densities in a small area of shore at Sandwick Bay in Orkney.

The widespread distribution and abundance of *P. vulgata* populations is of great value in a surveillance context since it offers considerable choice of site and the possibility of control sites with an acceptable degree of similarity.

19.4 Behaviour

P. vulgata is a grazer feeding on detritus, organic films and algal sporelings growing on the rock surface (Lodge, 1948; Southward, 1956; Hawkins and Hartnoll, 1983a). The feeding excursions of adult limpets take place from a fixed point, known as the 'homescar', to which the individual returns and homing behaviour and scar formation have been demonstrated for many *Patella* spp. (Cook *et al.*, 1969; Branch, 1975, 1981). Rigid homing has been recorded for *P. vulgata* by several workers (Morgan, 1894; Cook *et al.*, 1969), but in very moist habitats, or on very smooth surfaces, homing may be less rigid (Orton, 1929; Lewis, 1954). Where homing and homescar formation does occur, the residence time at a homescar may be very considerable; marked animals in Orkney have been recorded at precisely the same location over a five-year period (Baxter, pers. obs.). The adult component of *P. vulgata* populations, therefore, is effectively sessile under many conditions; a requirement for a useful 'sentinel' species (Baker, 1976). This effectively sessile mode of existence allows repeated non-destructive sampling of the same groups of individuals to be used for the study of population dynamics in fixed areas (Baxter, 1982, 1983a) and it means that problems due to avoidance behaviour are negligible.

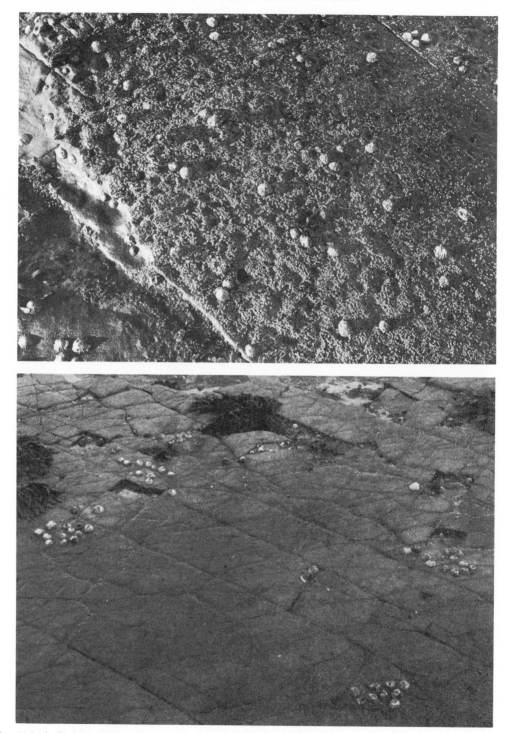

FIG. 19.3. A, Typical, dispersed distribution of limpets. B, Markedly clumped distribution of limpets on a smooth, well-drained rock platform.

19.5 Reproduction

The gonads of *P. vulgata* are easily assessed for gross reproductive condition (Orton *et al.*, 1956) and the reproductive cycle has been studied by various workers in different localities (Ballantine, 1961a; Blackmore, 1969a,b; Bowman and Lewis, 1977; Baxter, 1983a). Spawning is highly synchronized at the more exposed sites and typically takes place over a period of a few weeks between late September and February, the time varying with geographical location (Orton *et al.*, 1956; Ballantine, 1961a; Bowman and Lewis, 1977; Baxter, 1983a); this provides the potential for a discrete year-class settlement. Recent studies of limpet populations from more sheltered habitats (Baxter, 1982), however, have revealed that these animals have a greatly protracted spawning period extending over a number of months with (potentially) a much less well-defined population year-class structure. Limpet spawning is apparently triggered by the occurrence of violent onshore storms (Orton *et al.*, 1956; Ballantine, 1961a; Bowman and Lewis, 1977; Baxter, 1983a). Clearly by their very definition, sheltered shores do not experience these events and this explains the reduced spawning synchrony of limpet populations at these sites. The potential for studies of sub-lethal effects of pollutants on reproductive capability is reduced by the non-linearity of the gonad condition index (Orton *et al.*, 1956), the phenomenon of sex change (Orton, 1928) and the paucity of knowledge about the planktonic phase of the life-cycle. Dodd (1957) studied larval development and metamorphosis under laboratory conditions but no information regarding the time scale of these processes in the natural environment is available.

19.6 Growth and Longevity

Growth rates of *P. vulgata* in different populations vary considerably (Lewis and Bowman, 1975) depending on the biological and tidal characteristics of the habitat, although studies in Orkney have shown growth rates to be consistent from year to year at any particular site (Baxter, 1982). Characteristically, *P. vulgata* growth rates are fastest in the first year, ranging from 5–15 mm·y^{-1} (Bowman, 1981) declining by their third year to 3–10mm·y^{-1} (Lewis and Bowman, 1975). The growth rate then tends to remain relatively constant for several years before the virtual cessation of growth, typical of older animals, is observed. Faster growing individuals tend to attain greater maximum sizes. Longevity and growth rate appear to be inversely related (Lewis and Bowman, 1975) as found for many bivalve species (Jones, 1979) although difficulties in ageing limpets make definitive statements impossible; the identification of internal shell growth lines (Ekaratne and Crisp, 1982, 1984) may be of considerable value both for studies of growth rate and for assessment of age.

The shell morphology of various species of *Patella* has been studied and differences both between species (Davies, 1969a; Bannister, 1975) and between different populations of the same species (Branch, 1975; Branch and Marsh, 1978) have been described. The differences of *P. vulgata* shell form associated with micro-habitat type and beach level (Davies, 1969a; Lewis and Bowman, 1975; Baxter, 1983a) suggest that the study of allometry of shell and soft body dimensions might offer a means of detecting and describing changes in the environment. The parameters monitored must be selected carefully and the existence of seasonal cycles of variable amplitude and duration (Blackmore, 1969b; Jones *et al.*, 1979; Baxter, 1983a,b) make interpretation more difficult unless long-term seasonal studies are undertaken; single samples are of little or no value and inter-site comparisons may be meaningless. The differences in growth form and allometric relationships mean that the conventional measure of growth, namely unit increase in shell length, is inadequate since shell height may be very different in different populations (Lewis and Bowman, 1975; Baxter, 1983a,b). A simple measure of shell length may not give a true estimate of the energetic expenditure involved in growth; a unit increase in length of a 'tall' shell requires the deposition of much more shell material than the equivalent increase in a 'flat' shell. In differently shaped shells with identical shell lengths, the available body space and/or body size may be very different and the development of a condition index relating shell volume to soft tissue dry weight by Jones *et al.* (1979) was an attempt to overcome such difficulties.

19.7 Population Structure

The structure of a population is a reflection of many aspects of a species' biology. *P. vulgata* population structures vary markedly with habitat (Lewis and Bowman, 1975; Thompson, 1980; Baxter, 1982, 1983a). Only those with suitable settlement areas will show the polymodal pattern (Fig. 19.4A) resulting from regular settlement and recruitment; this situation is quite frequently found in the mid to low level mosaic communities on semi-exposed shores. A suitable habitat for spat settlement and survival is one that is moist and cool (Southward, 1956; Lewis and Bowman, 1975); it may be provided by barnacle/mussel stands or by an understorey flora of *Laurencia* spp./*Corallina officinalis* L., with or without a fucoid canopy. Where extensive areas of beach are dominated by this type of habitat the population structure shown in Fig. 19.4B is commonly found; here successful settlement and recruitment take place, but as the animals grow they must migrate to regions with large 'open' grazing areas and so the adult population is numerically insignificant. These regions of the beach can be regarded as 'nursery' areas. They provide the potential recruitment for adjacent populations in habitats unsuitable for settlement by desiccation-sensitive spat. In regions where settlement is minimal and recruitment at best sporadic the population structure is often unimodal (Fig. 19.4C), dominated by one or a small number of successful year-classes, and any significant loss of individuals due to adverse environmental conditions will result in a major change in community composition. Fig. 19.4D shows a population structure often found in the higher regions of the shore where the older, larger and more desiccation-tolerant individuals dominate the community as a mode comprising several merged year-classes. Such a population appears to be relatively stable in spite of very sporadic recruitment and it is maintained by a small-scale upward migration of adult animals: but if a significant proportion of the individuals were killed by a catastrophic event a major change in community structure would probably occur.

19.8 Physiology

The physiological ecology of *P. vulgata* has been studied by Davies (1966, 1969a,b) and its energetics have been considered by Wright and Hartnoll (1981) and by Workman (1983). *P. vulgata* is very tolerant of environmental extremes of both temperature and salinity, avoiding desiccation problems by its ability to cling tightly to the rock surface – a feature enhanced by the homing behaviour and homescar formation which enable it to form a virtually water-tight seal between shell and rock surface. This represents a form of avoidance behaviour which allows for short-term escape from pollutants, adverse environmental conditions and predators. Feeding excursions typically take place only during periods of immersion with the animals returning to their homescars before the tide retreats and subjects them to the air (Orton, 1929; Jones, 1948b) although modifications to this pattern can occur under certain environmental conditions. Under moist conditions such as those existing beneath a dense fucoid canopy, or at night, grazing activities often continue even when the animals are emersed.

This tolerant physiology combined with a form of avoidance behaviour may be considered disadvantageous for sensitive surveillance studies but it could also be useful, since it will act as a form of damping mechanism removing 'noise' from the system, tending to smooth out small-scale perturbations so that only the more significant ones are observed. The value or otherwise of this aspect of *P. vulgata* biology depends very much on the objectives of any particular study.

19.9 Pollutant Sensitivity

P. vulgata has been shown to be sensitive to oil and dispersants (Crapp, 1970; Dicks, 1973; Crothers, 1983b) in that even sub-lethal concentrations cause limpets to detach from the rock and this will result

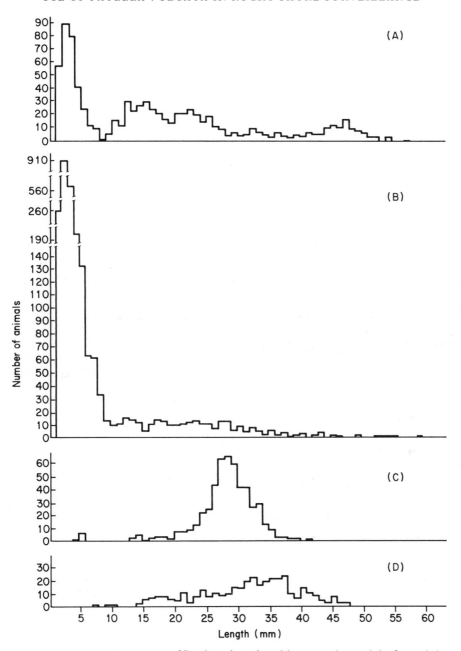

FIG. 19.4. Some common population structures of *P. vulgata*. A, a polymodal structure characteristic of a population receiving regular, annual recruitment. B, structure in an area particularly suitable for settlement. C, unimodal structure characteristic of an area with markedly sporadic recruitment. D, structure of an upper shore population dominated by relatively large individuals and maintained principally by small-scale upward migration.

in a large proportion dying through predation and/or physiological disturbance; such a result was clearly demonstrated following the 'Torrey Canyon' incident (J.E. Smith, 1968; Southward and Southward, 1978). More subtle changes in gill ultrastructure have also been shown to occur with crude oil and dispersant contact (Nuwayhid *et al.*, 1980, cf. Nuwayhid *et al.*, 1978) but these less easily detectable but important sub-lethal responses have been little studied. The potential for using *P. vulgata* as a monitoring agent for heavy metals has been shown (Navrot *et al.*, 1974; Howard and Nickless, 1977), but again there have been few other studies on this aspect of the species' response to pollutants.

19.10 Discussion

The broad problems associated with the use of rocky shore communities for surveillance and/or monitoring have been described by Lewis (1976, 1977b, 1978a,b, 1982) and by Hartnoll and Hawkins (1980). The particular problems involved in our ability to differentiate between a pollution-induced change and a natural change have been discussed at length by Hawkins and Hartnoll (1983b). The complex, often cyclic nature of natural changes (Gray and Christie, 1983; Baxter *et al.*, 1985) themselves lead to a requirement for more fundamental research if such long-term changes are to be understood while the identification of pollution-induced change can only be effected by a combination of ecological and chemical techniques. No ecological study in the field can prove cause and effect except under exceptional circumstances of gross pollution where the effect is very obvious. The exclusive use of chemical monitoring also suffers from serious deficiencies: sampling considerations are no less difficult than for biological studies while the identification of chemical contamination is of limited value unless a biological/environmental effect can be demonstrated. Ecological studies properly undertaken are of value for detecting unexpected change whose cause may then be sought using chemical analyses where considered necessary; this paper wishes to draw attention to the significant potential of *P. vulgata* for the ecological component of such studies.

The attributes desirable in a species to be used as the focal point of a target monitoring programme may be summarized as follows:

a) It should be widely distributed and numerous throughout the area of interest.

b) It should have either a key rôle in the community or be especially sensitive to the environmental parameters of concern to the investigation.

c) It should have a sedentary habit to avoid problems of avoidance behaviour and migration.

d) It should have a size range and population density sufficient to allow a variety of destructive sampling techniques.

e) It should have an interpretable population structure ideally based upon regular recruitment, reasonable growth rates and a longevity greater than the period over which change may be expected to occur.

f) It should have a well-known physiology and have predictable responses to environmental variables.

g) It should be accessible, easy to sample and be sufficiently resistant to allow at least short-term laboratory experimentation.

h) If the objective is pollution-orientated, it should have either a proven record of sensitivity to the pollutant/s or the ability to accumulate a measurable body burden of the pollutants without being killed by the environmental levels of that substance.

P. vulgata complies with the majority of these requirements although there is much scope for further understanding and research on even the most fundamental aspects of its biology; however, as one of the most intensively studied littoral species it is at the present time one of the best bets. The main problems in using *Patella* populations for surveillance/monitoring derive from the adaptability of the species, the very feature which gives it a widespread distribution. The variations which result from this adaptability may be physiological, behavioural or ecological (population structure differing in different micro-habitats) and for use in surveillance, great care must be taken to select the appropriate sites for the specific requirements and objectives of the situation under investigation. The optimum *Patella* sites comprise mid- to low-shore mosaic communities with a balanced combination of discrete 'nursery' areas to provide for regular recruitment and sufficient open rock surface to support a sizable adult population. When carrying out long-term studies on a population of *P. vulgata* the size of the sample area is determined by a number of factors, namely limpet density, topographical features and the need to minimize the chances of sampling anomalies as a result of the inherent patchiness in the flora and fauna of these mosaic communities (Hawkins and Hartnoll, 1983b). Too little attention tends to be given to the difficulties of sampling *P. vulgata* populations in a sufficiently representative manner. Seasonal records of population structure are essential if growth rates, recruitment and mortality rates are to be assessed accurately. It is also important that any monitoring programme includes an element devoted to measuring those environmental factors which might be expected to influence the animals' responses.

CHAPTER XX

LEVELS OF HETEROGENEITY AND THE AMPHIPOD FAUNA OF KELP HOLDFASTS

P.G. Moore

20.1 Introduction

The heterogeneity of the rocky littoral, so extensively commented upon in recent years by Dr J.R. Lewis (Lewis and Bowman, 1975; Lewis, 1976, 1977a,b, 1980a, 1982) is no less a feature of the sub-littoral zone. Heterogeneity is a scaled feature of all environments (the prefix 'local' adding little precision, see Moore, 1975), and an understanding of the effects of spatial heterogeneity at different levels is clearly necessary if ecological data are to serve any useful environmental 'baseline' function. The choice of any circumscribed area for intensive work, for instance, inevitably prompts questions of representativeness.

Earlier work by the author on North Sea coasts, generated (*inter alia*) the hypothesis that the kelp-dwelling amphipods *Corophium bonnellii* Milne-Edwards and *Lembos websteri* Bate are susceptible to waters made turbid by the erosion products of clay lithologies (Moore, 1972, 1973a,b; see also Sheader, 1978). This hypothesis gained subsequent support from a wide-ranging survey of kelp holdfast amphipods in Wales and S.W. England (Moore, 1978).

The development in the lower Clyde (by the British Steel Corporation) of an iron ore terminal at Hunterston (Fig. 20.1), with associated risk of dust contamination of coastal waters, highlighted the desirability of gaining a detailed understanding of the local status and ecological performance (see Moore, 1981) of these two potentially useful 'indicator' species, before operations began (in late 1979). In view of the hazards to accurate interpretation associated with isolated studies of one or two con-stituents of complicated faunas, coverage was once again (see Moore, 1978) expanded to encompass the entire amphipod component. This goes some way towards alleviating such problems: it does not, however, eliminate them.

This descriptive paper sets the scene for the quantitative analyses of seasonal variations in numerical abundance and diversity which will form the basis of additional contributions. Together, these data will have application as a local baseline. Equally fundamentally, however, this intensive study can be considered, and was conceived, as a basic biological analysis of an important segment of the kelp holdfast ecosystem.

This treatment begins by considering heterogeneity at successively finer levels of resolution. Then, having placed the study area in its spatial context, the author sets out a prognosis for Lewisian sur-veillance of this complex ecosystem.

20.2 Sampling and Methods

Samples were not random. Acceptable holdfasts were single, large and growing on horizontal or gently sloping, flat surfaces; they were symmetrical and evenly branched all round. In formal terms sampling can be regarded as stratified random. On occasions, departures from the 'ideal' became acceptable as sea conditions worsened, air supplies diminished, diver's temperatures dropped unacceptably or when no 'ideal' plants could be found.

The main series of samples was taken from a small area (O.S. grid ref: NS 17225395) off the S.E. sector of Farland Point, Gt Cumbrae (Fig. 20.1). No samples were taken from the Kames Bay side, nor from any further North than the second major ridge before the stone jetty-head on the East side of the Point. Samples (all of *Laminaria hyperborea* (Gunn.) Foslie) were taken by SCUBA diving, usually in the morning (0800–1000 G.M.T.), from the depth range 1 to 3m below C.D. (back checked from Keppel Pier tide gauge), using standard methods and treated as previously (Moore, 1971, 1978). Samples from other areas (Fig. 20.1) were usually of *L. hyperborea*, except in very sheltered situations, where *L. saccharina* (L.) Lamour. exclusively (as at L. Fyne, L. Striven, Hunterston, Downcraig Ferry, Wishing Well, White Bay), or *L. digitata* (Huds.) Lamour. (Lochaline, Linne Mhuirich rapids – L. Sween) or a mixture of *L. hyperborea* and *L. saccharina* (Fintray Bay, Eileans – Millport) perforce had to be sampled. Ten individual holdfasts (usually) were sampled fortnightly at Farland Point over one year from May, 1974, with less numerous (always at least five) samples being taken less frequently (*c.* monthly) for nearly a subsequent year (until February, 1976). Over 150,000 amphipods from W. Scottish sites were hand sorted from the extracted material, identified and counted.

FIG. 20.1. The West coast of Scotland showing kelp survey sites. Inset, the Isles of Cumbrae. Key to site lettering: FP = Farland Point, J = Iron ore jetty, W = Wishing Well, D = Downcraig Ferry, WB = White Bay, F = Fintray Bay, E = Outer Eilean.

TABLE 20.1

Occurrences of Amphipoda in kelp holdfasts from sites in W. Scotland.

Species \ Site No	1 Linne Mhuirich	2 S.W. Iona	3 St Kilda	4 Islay (N. Portnahaven)	5 Islay (The Ard)	6 Macrihanish	7 Mull of Galloway	8 Ailsa Craig	9 L. Cumbrae Site 1	10 Gt Cumbrae Farland Pt	11 Gt Cumbrae outer Eilean	12 Gt Cumbrae Wishing Well	13 Gt Cumbrae Downcraig	14 Gt Cumbrae White Bay	15 Gt Cumbrae Fintray Bay	16 Hunterston SMBA Buoy	17 Claonig Bay	18 L. Fyne (N. Furness)	19 L. Sirveen (The Craig)	20 Lochaline (Old Jetty)	21 L. Aline (Sgeir nam Balg)
Nannonyx goesi (Boeck)	+									+			+		+			+		+	
Lysianassa ceratina (A.O. Walker)			+	+	+	+				+					+		+	+		+	
L. plumosa Boeck																				+	
Orchomene humilis (A. Costa)																				+	
Tryphosa sarsi (Bonnier)	+			+	+	+	+			+	+				+	+	+	+	+	+	+
Ampelisca tenuicornis Liljeborg					+																
Urothoe marina (Bate)													+			+					
U. elegans Bate																					
Harpinia cremulata Boeck					+								+							+	
Amphilochus manudens Bate	+																				
Gitana sarsi Boeck	+	+		+	+	+	+	+	+		+		+	+	+	+	+	+	+	+	+
Leucothoe spinicarpa (Abildgaard)							+														+
Metopa pusilla G.O. Sars										+											
Stenothoe monoculoides (Montagu)	+	+		+		+	+	+	+	+	+	+		+			+	+	+		
Colomastix pusilla Grube		+	+			+	+														
Iphimedia minuta (G. O. Sars)	+	+			+				+	+			+		+	+		+	+	+	
Liljeborgia kinahani (Bate)	+																				
Apherusa bispinosa (Bate)			+						+	+	+	+	+	+	+	+		+	+	+	+
A. jurinei (Milne Edwards)			+	+		+			+	+	+	+	+	+	+			+	+	+	
Parapleustes assimilis (G.O. Sars)						+	+								+						
Atylus swammerdami (Milne Edwards)																+					
A. vedlomensis (Bate & Westwood)										+											
Gammarellus carinatus (Rathke)		+		+																	
Echinogammarus sp. indet.										+											
Cheirocratus sundevalli (Rathke)																		+		+	

TABLE 20.1 *Cont'd*

Species	Linne Mhuirich	St Kilda	S.W. Iona	Islay (N. Portnahaven)	Islay (The Ard)	Macrihanish	Mull of Galloway	Ailsa Craig	L. Cumbrae Site I	Gt Cumbrae Farland Pt	Gt Cumbrae outer Eilean	Gt Cumbrae Wishing Well	Gt Cumbrae Downcraig	Gt Cumbrae White Bay	Gt Cumbrae Fintray Bay	Hunterston SMBA Buoy	Claonig Bay	L. Fyne (N. Furness)	L. Striven (The Craig)	Lochaline (Old Jetty)	L. Aline (Sgeir nam Balg)
Site No	1	2	3	4	5	6	7	8	9	10	11	12	13	14	15	16	17	18	19	20	21
Dexamine thea Boeck		+	+							+	+	+	+	+	+	+		+	+	+	+
D. spinosa (Montagu)		+	+	+						+			+		+	+	+	+		+	+
Tritaeta gibbosa (Bate)		+	+	+	+	+	+		+	+	+	+	+	+	+		+	+		+	
Hyale nilssoni (Rathke)				+						+											
H. pontica Rathke						+															
Aora gracilis (Bate)				+	+	+	+			+	+	+	+	+	+	+		+	+	+	+
Lembos websteri Bate	+	+	+	+	+	+	+	+	+	+	+	+	+	+	+	+	+	+	+	+	+
Microdeutopus sp. (prob. *anomalus*)																		+		+	+
M. versiculatus (Bate)	+																				
Photis pollex Walker						+															
Gammaropsis maculata (Johnston)			+	+	+	+															
Megamphopus cornutus Norman																				+	
Amphithoe rubricata (Montagu)	+		+	+	+	+	+		+	+	+	+	+	+	+	+		+	+	+	+
Amphithoe (*Pleonexes*) *gammaroides* (Bate)	+	+							+	+				+		+					
Sunamphithoe pelagica (Milne Edwards)																	+		+		
Jassa falcata (Montagu)	+	+	+	+	+	+	+	+	+	+	+	+	+	+	+	+					
Parajassa pelagica (Leach)		+		+	+	+		+		+					+						
Ischyrocerus anguipes Krøyer		+	+	+	+	+	+														
Ericthonius punctatus (Bate)	+				+		+						+	+			+			+	+
Corophium bonnellii Milne Edwards	+		+			+			+		+	+	+	+	+	+		+	+	+	+
C. crassicorne Bruzelius											+		+			+					
Phtisica marina Slabber	+	+		+	+					+			+					+		+	
Caprella acanthifera Leach			+	+	+	+				+	+	+	+			+		+			
C. linearis (L.)	+	+							+						+		+				

West Scottish occurrences of holdfast-dwelling amphipods, as well as taxonomic authorities, are given in Table 20.1.

20.3 Habitat Factors and Species Composition

20.3.1 Geographical

The list of species presently recorded at Farland Point (see Table 20.1) differs predictably from that given in Moore (1978, Appendix I) by the omission of the extreme southwestern element therein defined, viz., *Podocerus variegatus* Leach, *Amphilochus neapolitanus* Della Valle, *Corophium sextonae* Crawford, *Parametopa kervillei* Chevreux, *Apherusa cirrus* (Bate), *Caprella fretensis* Stebbing, *Elasmopus rapax* Costa, *Microdeutopus chelifer* (Bate). (Note: the entity *Microdeutopus* spp. in Moore (1978), thought originally to be a mixture of *M. chelifer* and *M. damnoniensis*, can now with reasonable confidence be assigned solely to *M. chelifer*. Dr A.A. Myers kindly examined male material for me and referred my *M? damnoniensis* to *M. chelifer*. He regards the specific identity of *M. damnoniensis* as possibly dubious.)

The consistent holdfast-inhabiting species at Farland Point, i.e. *Gitana sarsi*, *Stenothoe monoculoides*, *Apherusa bispinosa*, *A. jurinei*, *Dexamine thea*, *Tritaeta gibbosa*, *Aora gracilis*, *Lembos websteri*, *Amphithoe rubricata*, *Jassa falcata*, *Corophium bonnellii*, *Phtisica marina* and *Caprella linearis* are very much those species which occur country-wide (cf. Moore, 1973b, 1978), whilst *Caprella acanthifera* is widely distributed on the West coast (especially further North, see Harrison, 1944).

Within this geographical range the overriding factor influencing the fauna is undoubtedly water movement (see also Lewis, 1968, 1980a; Fenwick, 1976; Hiscock, 1983).

20.3.2 Water movement

The presence–absence data for amphipods from W. Scottish sites (Table 20.1) have been classified (after exclusion of species occurring in < 10% of sites) using Jaccard's simple coefficient of community, with the resultant similarity matrix sorted by average cluster linkage (Fig. 20.2). The technique, if rather crude, is still effective (Hellawell, 1978), and the data do result from highly dissimilar sampling intensities at different sites and include data from sites visited in different years (St Kilda, 1973; Linne Mhuirich, 1969 and 1974). The major dichotomies nevertheless can be associated with water movement differences. Cluster B, for the most part, are sites sheltered or extremely sheltered from wave action. Cluster A are sites of intermediate exposure, while clusters C and D represent the most extreme wave-stressed sites (S.W. Iona, Portnahaven (Islay) and St Kilda) grouped, it is interesting to note, together with Linne Mhuirich rapids (L. Sween). These tidal rapids are extremely sheltered from wave action. A degree of functional comparability of water movement (the key feature) between these apparently dissimilar sites is thus suggested. Interestingly, Linne Mhuirich also clustered with Portnahaven and St Kilda when the analysis was re-run to include all species. Figs. 20.3 and 20.4 show the relative abundance of eight numerically significant species and their distribution in the West of Scotland. The dominance of three species *Amphithoe rubricata* (cf. Dommasnes, 1968), *Lembos websteri* (see also Hiscock and Mitchell, 1980) and *Jassa falcata* (see also Moore, 1973c) is enhanced by increasing exposure to wave action (as may *Apherusa jurinei*), while *Gitana sarsi*, *Dexamine thea* and *Corophium bonnellii* (see also Dommasnes, 1968; Hiscock and Mitchell, 1980; Peattie and Hoare, 1981) are inhibited by energetic water movement and flourish instead in quieter, wave-sheltered environments. *Stenothoe monoculoides* is largely indifferent to the water movement regime (see also Dommasnes, 1968). There is evidence of a greater site catholicity in *Caprella acanthifera* than *C. linearis* (Fig. 20.4; Table 20.1), with the former penetrating into sheltered areas to a greater degree (note Sloane *et al.*, 1961) and the latter preferring tidal streams (see below; also Hughes, 1975; Knight-

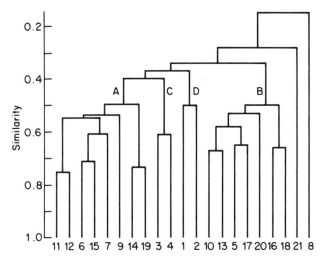

FIG. 20.2. Similarity dendrogram based on presence–absence data for kelp holdfast Amphipoda from W. Scottish sites, calculated using Jaccard's coefficient (species occurring in < 10% of sites excluded). See text for explanation.

Jones and Nelson-Smith, 1977; Peattie and Hoare, 1981; Pipe, 1982; Hiscock, 1983). The propensity for living in wave-exposed situations shown by *Parajassa pelagica* (Dommasnes, 1968; Moore, 1973c) is presently underlined, with records from Ailsa Craig, St Kilda and Islay, although only two individuals were ever collected from Farland Point. Yet the possibility previously raised (Moore, 1973c) that *P. pelagica* might be sensitive to slight changes in exposure grade, is contradicted by the species' not infrequent occurrence at Fintray Bay (Gt Cumbrae), a site experiencing considerably less wave action than Farland Point (see also Lewis and Powell, 1960, but note Round *et al.*, 1961).

20.3.3 Proximity of mobile material

On Gt Cumbrae, *Laminaria hyperborea* is only found growing in significant quantities at the most exposed headland (Farland Point). There, it grows on solid rock, conforming to the usual British situation. This was one reason (it is also close to the Hunterston development) for originally selecting the site for detailed study. The dominant kelp on Cumbrae, however, is *L. saccharina*. It may be attached to solid rock, but generally it grows on stones and boulders; these latter being frequently sand-bound in the bays (as at Fintray Bay, White Bay, Downcraig Ferry). At these sites, periodic redistribution of sand by storms can inundate (and sometimes completely bury) holdfasts attached to protruding boulders. Certain amphipods thrive in these situations, particularly *Corophium bonnellii* at Fintray Bay and *Dexamine thea* at White Bay (see also Dommasnes, 1968). At Fintray Bay, *Corophium* tubes can be so dense as to form a readily visible honeycomb between the haptera branches, making it an exceptional site for large collections of this species (Shillaker and Moore, 1978). *D. thea* was also abundant (with *Ericthonius punctatus*) at Lochaline (Old Jetty) (note Sloane *et al.*, 1961), near the site of a silica sand factory whose operations result in run-off and spillage of fine siliceous particles which (in such sheltered waters) settle all over the kelp forest. *C. bonnellii* was also noted (summer, 1979) to have established itself in the environmental lake adjacent to the iron ore terminal at Hunterston, where it appeared to co-dominate the bottom along with dipteran larvae (J.J.P. Clokie, pers. comm.).

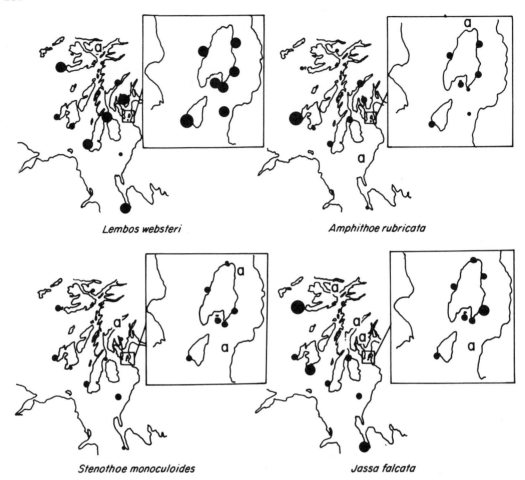

Lembos websteri   *Amphithoe rubricata*

Stenothoe monoculoides   *Jassa falcata*

FIG. 20.3. Abundance of *Lembos websteri*, *Amphithoe rubricata*, *Stenothoe monoculoides* and *Jassa falcata* in kelp holdfasts at W. Scottish sites (assessed on a five point scale: a = absent).

20.3.4 Topographical variation

The rock at Farland Point is current-bedded Old Red Sandstone of characteristic strike and dip (178°/30°). Erosion has produced a terraced scarp/dip configuration across an E.–W. line which dips seawards (south): these features continue sublittorally. As a result, four separable micro-environments are produced (Fig. 20.5): (i) near vertical (70°–80°) scarp walls (facing E.S.E.), usually of no great height (2m max.) and often undercut, supporting little or no kelp growth and with a macrofauna generally dominated by *Alcyonium digitatum* (L.), *Echinus esculentus* L. and *Asterias rubens* L.; (ii) scarp crests, the transitional zone between the vertical walls and the dip slope beyond. Kelp holdfasts may overlap this edge. Rock surface pitting is greatest along these edges, and this, together with greater water turbulence (which results from stronger tidal shear and wave overspill effects), selects for strong adhesion. As a result edge-growing plants have a more densely branched and less symmetrical shape, and are certainly more difficult to dislodge; (iii) dip slopes, dominated by *L. hyperborea* with a seasonal understorey of red algae. The density of kelp plants declines gradually downslope towards the next vertical, with (iv) a relatively barren area at the junction of the dip and scarp slopes. These gullies

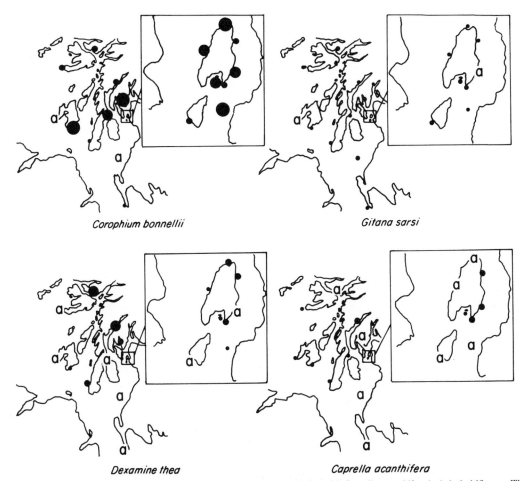

Corophium bonnellii

Gitana sarsi

Dexamine thea

Caprella acanthifera

FIG. 20.4. Abundance of *Corophium bonnellii*, *Gitana sarsi*, *Dexamine thea* and *Caprella acanthifera* in kelp holdfasts at W. Scottish sites (assessed on a five point scale: a = absent).

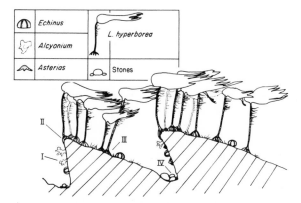

FIG. 20.5. Diagrammatic representation of topography of the substratum at Farland Point (not to scale) with conspicuous organisms and discernible micro-habitats (I–IV) indicated.

accumulate stones, ranging in size from cobbles to pebbles (amongst which *Cancer pagurus* L. may be found) which, during rough weather, move up and down channels acting as a scouring agent. The bedrock of these gullies in consequence is largely bereft of sedentary organisms (see also Gulliksen, 1978).

The bulk of the samples was deliberately taken from dip slopes (88%) to reduce the impact of this variable to a minimum. Nevertheless, occasional recourse had perforce to be made to 'scarp crest' plants. Such holdfasts were readily identifiable (by their characteristic underside conformation) during subsequent sample processing. Consideration of holdfast amphipods from the 'scarp crest' group compared with the 'dip slope' holdfasts revealed that in only five species did relative abundance differ by more than 1%. Of these five, three showed enhanced relative abundances in 'scarp crest' plants, namely *Gitana sarsi*, *Lembos websteri* and *Caprella linearis* (this latter showing a factor of × 2 difference: *vide* Hughes, 1975; Hiscock, 1983). Conversely, *Jassa falcata* and *Corophium bonnellii* showed an increased relative abundance in 'dip slope' holdfasts. The *Caprella* result was largely contributed by a single holdfast, in which *C. linearis* represented 50.8% of the amphipod fauna. Exclusion of this plant from the 'crest' series brought the relative abundance of *C. linearis* down to 3.3%, i.e. lower than the 'dip slope' mean. This treatment modified the figures for *Gitana*, *Lembos*, *Jassa* and *Corophium* too; but in no other case was the above relationship overturned. In the case of sample 2 (29.7.74), prominent hydroid growth (noted) was probably responsible for the high caprellid density (*C. acanthifera* contributed over 10% of this plant's amphipods too) (Round *et al.*, 1961; Hughes, 1975; Pipe, 1982).

Within the small sampling plot, the main scope for distributional discontinuity would be in response to topographical variation: with its micro-hydraulic consequences. Such effects as are apparent, either support the wider-scale water movement hypothesis, e.g. with *Lembos websteri* profiting and *Corophium bonnellii* losing out on current-scoured ridges (cf. Hiscock and Mitchell, 1980; Peattie and Hoare, 1981); or else conflict with it, e.g. *Gitana* increasing and *Jassa* decreasing in ridge crest holdfasts. Such inconsistencies may, however, arise from an ignorance of the distribution of other essential attributes of particular species' micro-habitats.

20.3.5 Micro-habitat interspersion in the kelp forest

Whilst an understanding of the holdfast fauna of *Laminaria hyperborea* is central to any explanation of British kelp forest ecology, the latter cannot be achieved exclusively with reference to the former. The potential importance of habitat interspersion and microtopographical factors to colonization and migratory processes merits examination.

Except at the sublittoral fringe, where *L. digitata* is dominant, the major laminarians coexisting with *L. hyperborea* at Farland Point were *Saccorhiza polyschides* (Lightf.) Batt. and *L. saccharina*. Preliminary comparison of *Saccorhiza* vs *L. hyperborea* revealed significant differences in emphasis amongst the commoner holdfast-dwelling amphipods (McKenzie and Moore, 1981, Fig. 3). Particular note may be taken of the enhanced dominance of *Lembos websteri*, *Corophium bonnellii* and *Caprella linearis* in *L. hyperborea* holdfasts, and of *Amphithoe* (*Pleonexes*) *gammaroides* from *Saccorhiza* bulbs (note Robertson, 1894). The very close comparability of the *L. hyperborea* amphipod pattern on the relevant sampling date (19.12.75) with the overall pattern from all pooled *L. hyperborea* data for Farland Point, lends extra weight to the belief that these differences between kelps are real.

Conceivably, these differences may relate to the different requirements of *L. websteri* and *C. bonnellii* versus *A. (P.) gammaroides* in terms of tube building materials or acceptable crevice morphology (cf. Shillaker and Moore, 1978), or to the reduced availability and diversity of small branched structures (haptera, epifauna and epiflora) suitable for caprellids to cling to (note Hughes, 1975) on a short-lived *Saccorhiza* compared with a perennial *L. hyperborea* substratum, or to different water movement

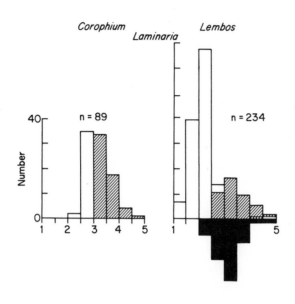

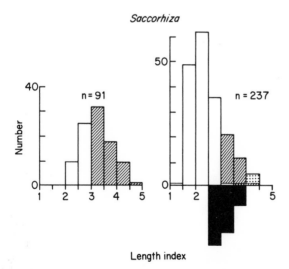

FIG. 20.6. Population histograms for the amphipods *Corophium bonnellii* (left) and *Lembos websteri* (right) at Farland Point (19 December, 1975). Top, from *Laminaria hyperborea* holdfasts; bottom, from *Saccorhiza polyschides* bulbs. Length index, see Moore (1981). Open = juveniles; diagonal stripe = non-ovigerous females; dotted = ovigerous females, solid = males.

characteristics of the sites occupied by the different kelps.

Although the relative abundance of *L. websteri* and *C. bonnellii* is reduced in *Saccorhiza* holdfasts, no major differences were apparent in the population structure of these amphipods from *Saccorhiza* or *Laminaria* holdfasts at the same site (Fig. 20.6). By implication, the amphipods' rate of growth would seem not to be dependent on plant species or on the composition of the coexisting amphipod fauna. As size–frequency distributions are the same, and since at any one place, depth and time, light and temperature effects will be constant, it seems legitimate to assume an equivalence (perhaps a general superabundance) of food in both situations, such that growth is unimpeded by observed changes in relative density of amphipods, and substratum an irrelevance. Perspicuous comparisons of absolute density are precluded. Simple comparisons, for example, of density per unit mass, between two such dissimilar structures as a *Saccorhiza* and a *Laminaria* holdfast would be entirely arbitrary. Density per unit of real living space is the tantalisingly missing key parameter (Moore, 1977c) which, to date, may best be approached using surface area-based standardization procedures (Hicks, 1980). Even these, however, do not produce complete definitions of habitable space.

The above theory of the irrelevance of plant substratum to population structure of individual species is borne out by data relating to *Corophium bonnellii* from L. Striven (Fig. 20.7), where a general

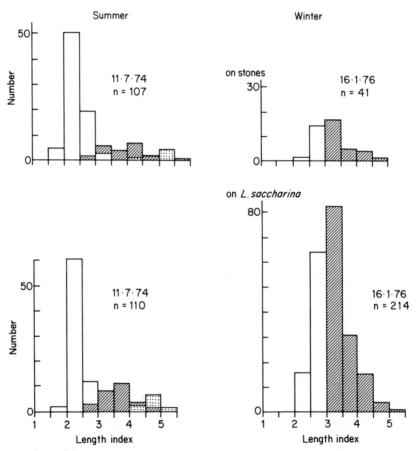

Fig. 20.7. Population histograms for the amphipod *Corophium bonnellii* at The Craig, L. Striven in summer (11 July, 1974) and winter (16 January, 1976). Top, from small stones; bottom, from *Laminaria saccharina* holdfasts. Other details as for Fig. 20.6.

equivalence is seen between the population structure of *Corophium* in *L. saccharina* holdfasts and on small stones.

Both *C. bonnellii* and *L. websteri* have been recorded from a variety of habitats; algae (Moore, 1973b, 1978, 1981), stones (Robertson, 1888; pers. obs.), rock faces (Hiscock and Hoare, 1975; Hiscock and Mitchell, 1980), shells, (pers. obs.) and on sponges (Peattie and Hoare, 1981; M. Costello, pers. comm.). Whilst they consistently and commonly occurred in *L. hyperborea* holdfasts, this 'preference' may be no more than a reflection of an increased availability of suitably-sized nooks and crannies per unit volume in such complex perennial structures (see Sloane *et al.*, 1961; Shillaker and Moore, 1978; Peattie and Hoare, 1981).

To conclude however, that the interspersion of habitats has few repercussions on population dynamics of holdfast amphipods would be precipitate (note Edgar, 1983d). Future faunal studies on the potential rôle of ephemeral understorey weeds as 'overspill' and nursery habitats during the amphipod breeding season are needed to illuminate this question. In the littoral zone, moisture-retaining filamentous algae act as nursery grounds for a variety of invertebrate species (Moore, 1977c). Whether such an arrangement is found in amphipod populations sublittorally is not known. Clearly, in the absence of emersion, juvenile desiccation ceases to be a problem: maintaining a hold on, or nestling between, suitably-sized algal filaments however, may still be a significant consideration (see Bayne, 1964). Certainly all size classes of resident amphipods from post-marsupial juveniles upwards are represented in kelp holdfasts (Moore, 1981). Many phytal amphipods are motile (Haage and Jansson, 1970), especially at night (Edgar, 1983d), but with the exception of Edgar's Tasmanian data, insufficient is known about whether colonists of new substrata are primarily juveniles, or adults whose emigration might have been prompted by population expansion from established nuclei (like kelp holdfasts), or random individuals inadvertently translocated, e.g. on drifting weed fragments. Whether space ever becomes limiting in holdfasts is unknown. The regulatory processes which impinge on holdfast amphipod populations cannot yet be quantified, nor with certainty can we ascribe such properties to agencies internal or external to the holdfast microcosm (see Gordon, 1983). The question of dispersal is certainly crucial if stable populations are to be maintained in a heterogeneous environment (Roff, 1975).

20.3.6 Inter- and intraholdfast variability

Holdfast size is a function of plant age, but by ignoring the processes of succession leading to the acquisition of diversity, it is possible to reduce data heterogeneity by selective sampling (as here). Holdfast branching creates spatial complexity which will aid or abet the foraging ability of different vertebrate (Stoner, 1982; Coull and Wells, 1983; Edgar, 1983a; Gordon, 1983) and invertebrate predators (Edgar, 1983d); it also affects silt accumulation (Moore, 1972, 1973a), which may modify the acceptability of particular holdfasts to different amphipod species. Many other space-occupying sedentary organisms will presumably compete with tubicolous amphipods (Moore, 1978) for hapteron attachment sites (barnacles, zoophytes, saddle oysters, tubeworms, etc.); others will occlude the voids between hapteron branches (sponges, anemones, tubeworms, bivalves, etc.). Alternatively they may provide necessary substrata for inquilinous species. Sponge-associated amphipods (Moore, 1978 and below) are a case in point. We have also seen groups of the isopod *Janiropsis breviremis* G.O. Sars living in particular holdfast crevices in close juxtaposition to (guarded by?) individual sagartiid anemones (*Actinothoe sphyrodeta* (Gosse)) in holdfasts from Fintray Bay (P.G. Moore and R.O. Shillaker, unpubl.; cf. Rubin, 1980, Fig. 2). Holdfast amphipods may also utilize the permanent artifacts (e.g. tubes) of similar or dissimilar organisms, usually, but not always after the demise of the original occupant. Thus, old *Pomatoceros* tubes have been seen housing *Corophium bonnellii*, and Hamond (1967) has reported *C. bonnellii* actually tube-sharing with *Ampelisca tenuicornis* Lilljeborg.

Old cavities beneath holdfasts, excavated by *Patina pellucida* (L.) may also be colonized secondarily. The occurrence of such cavities in Farland Point holdfasts was of a low order (7%), compared with exceptionally high infestations (<67%: Isle of Man) reported elsewhere (Kain, 1979; Kain and Svendson, 1979). Infestation levels <20% seem to be typical of *in situ* (i.e. not drift) collections country-wide (Kain, 1979) and this figure accords with my earlier North Sea data (14%).

The additional significance of *Patina* cavities in a related context (Moore, in prep.), however, is that they modify the surface:mass relationships of holdfasts and in so doing, contribute to the heterogeneity of numerical abundance data after weight-standardization procedures.

20.3.7 Biological interactions between amphipod species

The possibility of territorial exclusion, especially between tubicolous species, remains real (Connell, 1963; Moore, 1978; Edgar, 1983d). Differences in the micro-habitat characteristics of selected construction sites (Shillaker and Moore, 1978; McKenzie and Moore, 1981), however, could well lessen the impact of this phenomenon particularly at low population densities. The significance of such interactions, especially at peak densities, remains to be seen. In addition, the possibility of aggressive encounters amongst amphipod species, especially involving caprellids (Lewbel, 1978; Hiscock, 1983), cannot be ignored. This whole area is in considerable need of attention.

20.3.8 Rarities and chance occurrences

The list of amphipods which occur occasionally in W. Scottish holdfasts includes *Hyale nilssoni, H. pontica, Ampelisca tenuicornis, Harpinia crenulata, Liljeborgia kinahani, Urothoe marina, U. elegans, Echinogammarus marinus, Corophium crassicorne, Lysianassa plumosa, Cheirocratus sundevalli, Megamphopus cornutus, Dexamine spinosa* and *Gammarellus carinatus*. Such individuals represent chance displacements, generally from adjacent littoral rock (*Echinogammarus, Hyale*) or sublittoral sandy habitats (*C. crassicorne, Cheirocratus, Ampelisca, Liljeborgia, Harpinia, Urothoe, D. spinosa*), whose intermittent occurrence in holdfasts is of no real significance.

Amphithoe (*Pleonexes*) *gammaroides*, although rare in *L. hyperborea* holdfasts at Farland Point, dominated *Saccorhiza* bulbs there (McKenzie and Moore, 1981). *Nannonyx goesi* and *Tryphosa sarsi* are established, if rare, components of the kelp fauna (Jones, 1948a; Moore, 1973b, 1978), whose biology is uncertain. *Tryphosa* may be a sponge feeder or scavenger (Jones, 1948a). *Metopa pusilla* is even more enigmatic. It is very rare at Farland Point, but the author has never found it in holdfasts elsewhere. Excepting a possible relationship with hydroids (Jones, 1948a; Hamond, 1967), the specific requirements of *M. pusilla* are unknown. It is interesting, however, that another stenothoid, *Stenothoe marina*, showed an analagous distribution. It is certainly not a regular holdfast dweller (Hughes (1975) found it commonly amongst *Nemertesia*), but on one occasion only it was conspicuous in *L. saccharina* holdfasts from near Keppel Pier (Millport) (hydroid cover not noted).

Iphimedia minuta and *Apherusa bispinosa* seem likely to lead active, vagrant lives (see below, also Colman and Segrove, 1955). It cannot be discounted entirely, that habitat disturbance during sample collection might provoke the flight of vagile calliopiids and lysianassids (although received opinion suggests that most phytal animals cling tightly to the substratum when it is disturbed, see Colman (1940)).

Aora gracilis and *Amphithoe rubricata* occurred consistently at Farland Point, but their overall contribution to the fauna was slight. *Amphithoe* may require more exposed conditions (Fig. 20.3) and *Aora* more sheltered. *Aora* was increasingly evident in *L. saccharina* holdfasts from L. Striven and L. Fyne. Both species, however, are often found in the Clyde area inhabiting sea-bed accumulations of rotting macroalgae (Bedford and Moore, 1984), so perhaps their primary requirement hinges on detrital quantity and/or quality.

Ericthonius punctatus occurred rarely at Farland Point. This species was best represented in more sheltered waters (Downcraig Ferry, L. Fyne (on hydroids), Lochaline (Old Jetty), The Ard (Islay), Claonig Bay) (note Hughes, 1975), although significant numbers were found at the Mull of Galloway.

The caprellid *Phtisica marina* was infrequent in kelp holdfasts universally. It has a wide habitat range however, penetrating into deeper water than *Caprella* spp. (Jones, 1948a).

20.3.9 Absences

Apart from theoretical considerations of asymmetry, the issue of presence and absence is usually plagued by practical reservations over sampling adequacy (Lewis, 1980a). Since holdfast amphipods at no other site have been examined with such sampling intensity (112,236 individuals, 267 holdfasts) as at Farland Point, misgivings over sampling may perhaps be set aside. Thoughts addressed to the question: why have certain 'holdfast' species never been recorded there? may thus be uniquely apt.

The absence from Farland Point of the spongicolous (see Moore, 1978) species *Lysianassa ceratina* (found in only one sample), *Colomastix pusilla* and *Leucothoe spinicarpa* is interesting. No geographical barrier exists for these species: *L. ceratina* has been recorded from holdfasts elsewhere within the Clyde Sea area; *Leucothoe* exists both to the North (L. Aline) and South (Moore, 1978): so does *Colomastix*, my northernmost record is for Iona. Lincoln (1979) recorded it from Shetland (so Scarratt (1961) was incorrect in maintaining that *C. pusilla* did not occur as far North as Scotland). The habitual sponge-dwelling species *Tritaeta gibbosa*, which does occur at Farland Point, has not proved to be any deterrent to these species elsewhere (Moore, 1978). Sponge-specificity however, may exert a strong influence (Alexander, 1969; Frith, 1976). The conspicuous sponges in holdfasts at Farland Point were *Halichondria panicea* (Pallas) and *Hymeniacidon perleve* (Montagu). Frith (1976) thought that these sponges secreted chemicals which were attractive to the amphipods *Microdeutopus damnoniensis*, *M. anomalus* (*vide intra*) and *Corophium sextonae* (and *Caprella linearis*, see Peattie and Hoare (1981)) but she did not record the species above. Hopefully, work in progress in Lough Ine (Eire) will shed further light on these matters soon (Mr M. Costello, pers. comm.). *Lysianassa ceratina*, *Tritaeta gibbosa*, *Colomastix pusilla*, *Leucothoe spinicarpa* and *Tryphosa sarsi* regularly co-occurred in holdfasts from Macrihanish, a site where kelps support an outstanding diversity of sponges.

Neither *Atylus swammerdami* nor *Gammarus locusta* made any contribution to the Farland Point holdfast fauna, although large swarms of both species occur intermittently around the kelp bed perimeter offshore, where they are often taken in sea-bed accumulations of decaying drift kelp (Watkin, 1941; Steen, 1951; Colman and Segrove, 1955; Bedford and Moore, 1984). Appreciable numbers of *A. swammerdami* have been recorded in holdfasts elsewhere (Moore, 1973b,c). Although these species are less bound to the kelp forest proper, and exist largely beyond its margins, they are tied ultimately to its energetic bounty. It is possible that fast-swimming forms like *Apherusa* spp. and *Gammarellus carinatus* occupy similar niches beneath the kelp canopy. Any special food requirement in such organisms though might create distributional restrictions.

The absence of *Gammaropsis maculata* from Farland Point is mirrored throughout the Firth of Clyde in my experience. It occurred in holdfasts from the oceanic seaboard at sites such as Macrihanish, Islay and Iona, (but never in Scotland in such extraordinary numbers as at Bracelet Bay, S. Wales (Moore, 1978)). The mechanism which allows the tubicolous species *Jassa falcata*, *Gammaropsis maculata*, *Lembos websteri* and *Amphithoe rubricata* to coexist in wave-beaten situations offers scope for future interesting work.

Ischyrocerus anguipes apparently is another such exposed shore species, with W. Scottish records only from Macrihanish, Islay, Iona, Mull of Galloway, S. Arran and St Kilda. It co-dominated the kelp fauna on the exposed coast of N.E. Britain (Moore, 1973b,c), but made no significant impact within the Firth of Clyde. Further South, its appearances at Aberystwyth, Porth Cwyfan and Bigbury Bay (all in Wales) add further weight to an 'exposed shore' categorization, although it also occurred in the relative shelter of Quarter Wall Bay, Lundy (Moore, 1978). *I. anguipes* will be coming increasingly towards its southern geographical limit in southern England (Truchot, 1963, did not list it from Roscoff), so southern English sites may be atypical.

The converse situation is illustrated by *Microdeutopus* spp. These aorids have never been recorded at Farland Point and have never been taken from open coast sites. Extreme shelter, as at Lochaline and L. Fyne appears to be a mandatory requirement for this genus (possibly associated with a spongicolous preference? see Frith, 1976; M.J. Costello, pers. comm.). Competition with *Lembos websteri* may thus be avoided. The identification to species of microdeutopids is amongst the most difficult of tasks in the British amphipod fauna. With preserved, often damaged material and without fully mature males, it is well-nigh impossible. Some good material (alive and intact) has been examined from L. Fyne and attributed to *M. anomalus*. The biggest problem (see Myers, 1969) is over the distinction between *M. anomalus* and *M. damnoniensis* (if the latter really is a valid species – therefore note Frith, 1976). The true situation within the genus is as yet improperly resolved and in this contribution the principal W. Scottish entity remains unspecified as *Microdeutopus* sp. My feeling though, and that of Dr Myers, is that this will prove to be *M. anomalus*. The distinctive *M. versiculatus* has only been taken in Scotland from holdfasts at Linne Mhuirich rapids (L. Sween).

20.4 Heterogeneity – a Conspectus

From within a restricted species repertoire, an individual site assumes its distinctive character by virtue of sufficient and consistent differences in emphasis between species. Diagnostic species may or may not be dominant. Thus, Fintray Bay holdfasts are notable for *Corophium bonnellii*; White Bay and Loch Fyne (N. of Furnace) for *Dexamine thea*; Lochaline (Old Jetty) for *D. thea* and *Ericthonius punctatus*; L. Striven (The Craig) for *Aora gracilis* and *Sunamphithoe pelagica*; L. Fyne (N. of Furnace) for *Caprella acanthifera*; Linne Mhuirich rapids for *Microdeutopus versiculatus* and *Amphilochus manudens*; Farland Point for *Gitana sarsi* and *Metopa pusilla* (though the latter is rare). Whether such sites represent increasingly optimal conditions for each species, or whether what is perceived is a spatial mosaic built up and maintained by differential fecundity and dispersion tendencies of species and subject to flux, is not clear.

Intensive sequential sampling of kelp holdfast Amphipoda at Farland Point, over a period of nearly two years, gave no indication of invasive elements (Moore, in prep.). Rather, the author is struck by the general constancy of relative species composition with time (cf. the status of *Corophium bonnellii* at Menai Bridge, commented on earlier by Moore (1978), see also Hoare and Peattie (1979); Hiscock and Mitchell (1980); Peattie and Hoare (1981); Sebens (this volume)). In the normal course of events then, site-to-site differences seem to be maintained.

In supporting all the 'standard' holdfast amphipods, Farland Point typifies northern British sites. The ecological interpretation of the amphipod complement supports a site categorization of inter-mediate exposure to wave action (high numbers of *Lembos*, *Stenothoe* and *Jassa* on the one hand, low abundance of *Amphithoe*, *Gammaropsis*, *Parajassa*, *Ischyrocerus* and high abundance of *Corophium* and *Gitana* on the other, with no *Microdeutopus*). Such an interpretation is consistent with the site grading arrived at from a consideration of littoral biota on the same shore, *vide* the presence of the 'exposed shore' species *Littorina neritoides* (L.), *Chthamalus montagui* Southward, *Alaria esculenta* (L.) Grev. and *Patella aspera* Lamarck, as well as more typically 'sheltered shore' algae, such as *Pelvetia canaliculata* (L.) Dcne et Thur., *Ascophyllum nodosum* (L.) Le Jol., *Laminaria digitata* and *L. saccharina* (Lewis, 1964).

With the gradual acquisition of biological data on individual species, it becomes possible to understand patterns of distribution and to interpret community organization. From such an under-standing flows a capacity for prediction which is central to any baseline application (Lewis, 1980). Gross changes in the relative status of 'standard' species, or incursions by 'foreign' species would point readily to unusual causes. However, sufficient grounds for optimism are now emerging, to suggest that predictive statements of known statistical probability about the pattern of seasonal variation of numerical abundance (Moore, in prep.) at Farland Point will soon be forthcoming. From experience gained, both (Lewis, 1980a) in earlier extensive (Moore, 1973a,b,c, 1978) and more recent highly intensive programmes (Moore, 1981, present report and in prep.), recommendations will emerge for the efficient use of kelp holdfast fauna in monitoring schemes (Moore, in prep.). Our background understanding of one element of this system (at least) has now reached a sufficiently high level for sub-littoral kelp fauna not to be considered intrinsically too complicated to play a useful rôle in surveillance contexts (*vide* Lewis, 1976, 1980a). As stated before (Lewis, 1975, 1980a; Moore, 1983a), the need for experimental verification of field hypotheses (Underwood, this volume) is assumed throughout.

Finally, however, it should be re-iterated forcefully that no precise and fully rounded understanding of species interactions in little-known, complex ecosystems will be forthcoming without a major contribution from, and a return to respectability of, forgotten subjects – notably natural history (Lewis, 1975, 1980a; Southward, Foreword to this volume) and functional morphology (Fryer, 1971).

ACKNOWLEDGEMENTS

The foundations of my obsessions were laid by Dr J.R. Lewis 'when all the world was young' for which I will always be grateful. The present work was supported primarily by a research grant from the Natural Environment Research Council. Additional monies on divers occasions from the Royal Society of London and the University of London Central Research Fund also facilitated travelling and the purchase of equipment. Mr K.S. Cameron is thanked for his conscientious, cheerful assistance both underwater and in the laboratory. Mr G.A. Fisher kindly made the computer program available. Mr R. Coyne (Ardtornish Estates) kindly looked after us at Lochaline and our visit to St Kilda was made possible via the good offices of the Nature Conservancy Council and the Ministry of Defence. Mr R. Brant is thanked for facilities put at our disposal there, as are the Royal Artillery and Royal Corps of Transport. Dr J.S. Buchanan, Dr R.O. Shillaker, Dr S.J.F. Gorzula and Dr R.J.A. Atkinson acted as buddy divers on countless occasions, and are thanked for their generosity.

CHAPTER XXI

ASPECTS OF THE ECOLOGY OF ROCKY SUBLITTORAL AREAS

K. Hiscock

21.1 Introduction

The history of biological surveys in rocky sublittoral areas of the British Isles is much more recent than that of the rocky littoral. Although Jack Kitching used 'hard hat' diving to undertake work off South Devon and western Scotland before 1940 (Kitching *et al.*, 1934; Kitching, 1941), the full exploration of this rather inaccessible part of our coast was only started when self-contained diving apparatus (SCUBA) became available. Then, Bob Forster undertook observations of areas around Plymouth (Forster, 1954, 1955, 1961) and Wyn Knight-Jones worked at Bardsey and in the Menai Strait (Knight-Jones and Jones, 1955; Knight-Jones *et al.*, 1957). During the 1960s and subsequently, Joanna Kain, working in the Isle of Man, used SCUBA diving for a variety of studies of algal populations, particularly of *Laminaria hyperborea* (Gunn.) Fosl. (reviewed in Kain, 1979). Extensive surveys were also being carried out off the coast of Brittany, though by remote sampling, by Louis Cabioch (Cabioch, 1968). Since about 1970, a wide range of underwater studies has been undertaken along the coasts of the Northeast Atlantic to describe nearshore sublittoral communities and to investigate ecological relationships between species and their environment. Of particular importance in Britain have been the surveys commissioned by the Nature Conservancy Council as a part of their programme of work to assess the nature conservation importance of marine sites. Since about 1977 a large amount of work has been accomplished, and our knowledge of the composition, distribution and dynamic ecology of rocky sublittoral communities is now substantial, albeit based mainly on information contained in limited-circulation reports or in field notebooks. Some of this information is already summarized: viz. an assessment of the community concept in relation to sublittoral nearshore areas in Hiscock and Mitchell (1980), and the ecology of sublittoral areas in relation to various environmental factors in a volume edited by Earll and Erwin (1983).

The aim of this Chapter is to bring together some of the main conclusions of work from Northeast Atlantic coastal areas (Fig. 21.1) and give an outline of the rocky sublittoral ecology of the coast of the British Isles and nearby areas. In doing this, I am aware of the many parallels between the way in which Jack Lewis studied and described rocky littoral areas and the way in which sublittoral sites have been studied. Both exercises have been necessarily descriptive initially and concerned mainly with conspicuous rather than cryptic species in order to provide a comparison between many different sites. I have based my presentation on *The Ecology of Rocky Shores*, Lewis's classic work published in 1964. However, I cannot offer such a detailed description as he did and the following summary must ignore many fascinating elements of the communities to be encountered on sublittoral rocks in Britain and many of the intricate combinations of environmental conditions which lead to their development. One day, I hope that their detailed description will make a volume in its own right.

Fig. 21.1. Location of places mentioned in the text. Fig. 21.5 gives a more detailed map of Southwest Britain.

21.2 Zonation on Open Coasts

21.2.1 Introduction

Just as on the shore, different communities occupy distinct horizontal bands along a sublittoral rock slope. The diver-biologist descending such a slope observes that the shallow rocks are dominated by algae, usually a forest of large kelps, and that with increasing depth the kelps disappear, being replaced by dense growth of foliose red algae which in turn grade into animal-dominated communities. Fig. 21.2 illustrates this zonation and the terms applied to the main subzones of the sublittoral. This terminology is mainly derived from that suggested by Pérès and Molinier (1957). A full discussion of the various schemes of nomenclature applied to sublittoral zonation has been given in Hiscock and Mitchell (1980). By strict definition, the sublittoral zone extends from the upper limit of large kelps to the greatest depth to which photosynthetic plants can grow. However, for practical purposes the sub-littoral is considered here to include all depths below the littoral in nearshore areas. The types of communities which characterize each of the subzones are described below.

21.2.2 The sublittoral fringe

This, the upper part of the sublittoral zone, shares species with both the littoral and the permanently submerged sublittoral zones but also has a characteristic flora and fauna of its own. Lewis (1964) has already described in general terms the species which occur in this area, and which can be reached on the lowest spring tides. On most open coasts, the sublittoral fringe extends from about 1m above the lowest spring tide level to about that level and is above the main *Laminaria hyperborea* population. On sites exposed to very strong wave action, the communities characteristic of the sublittoral fringe extend further upshore and a little deeper into the area below extreme low water level. The most conspicuous elements of the community are the large brown kelps *Laminaria digitata* (Huds.) Lam. and *Alaria esculenta* (L.) Grev. and pink encrusting coralline algae covering the rock below. The coralline algae

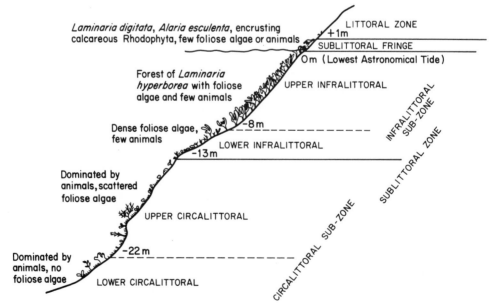

FIG. 21.2. Zonation of sublittoral communities. Depths given are for Lundy Island.

are most often *Phymatolithon lenormandii* (Areschoug) Adey and *P. calcareum* (Pallas) Adey et McKibbin but also include the non-calcareous crustose red algae, *Cruoria pellita* (Lyngb.) Fries and *Hildenbrandia rubra* (Sommerf.) Menegh. The encrusting algae are largely bare of foliose species and erect animals, most likely as the result of sweeping by kelp fronds. However, some encrusting animal species, including the sponges, *Halichondria panicea* (Pallas), *Amphilectus fucorum* (Esper) and *Myxilla incrustans* (Johnston), small varieties of the anemones, *Sagartia elegans* (Dalyell) and *Metridium senile* (L.), the barnacle, *Balanus crenatus* Brug., and the bryozoan *Umbonula littoralis* Hastings, are often present in large amounts. In some geographical areas, mussels also thrive in the sublittoral fringe where wave action is most likely too vigorous for starfish predators to survive. *Corallina officinalis* (L.) may be present in large amounts in exposed areas or *C. officinalis*, together with *Mesophyllum lichenoides* (L.) Lemoine, in sheltered areas. A very few outliers of the main limpet (*Patella* spp.) populations of the eulittoral are often present, but the usual limpets living on encrusting coralline algae are *Acmaea virginea* (Müller) and small *Patina pellucida* (L.). The ascidians *Diplosoma listerianum* (Milne Edwards) and *Botryllus schlosseri* (Pallas) are often present in the fringe. Castric-Fey *et al.* (1973) also listed *Trididemnum cereum* (Giard) as characteristic of the fringe at Glénan, off Brittany. The hydroids *Plumularia setacea* (Ellis and Solander) and *Aglaophenia pluma* (L.), together with the bryozoan *Scrupocellaria reptans* (L.), are also present, though usually in concavities. Of the foliose algae, species such as *Chondrus crispus* (Stackh.) are outliers of the main eulittoral populations while species such as *Plocamium cartilagineum* (L.) Dixon, *Callophyllis laciniata* (Huds.) Kütz, *Gastroclonium ovatum* (Huds.) Papenf., *Delesseria sanguinea* (Huds.) Lamour., *Heterosiphonia plumosa* (Ellis) Batt., *Brongniartella byssoides* (Good. et Woodw.) Schm. and *Odonthalia dentata* (L.) Lyngb. are predominantly sublittoral species. Few algae are characteristic of the fringe, although *Phyllophora pseudoceranoides* (S.G. Gmel.) Newr. et Taylor, *Jania rubens* (L.) Lamour, *Chaetomorpha melagonium* (Web. et Mohr) Kütz, *Pikea californica* Harv. (recently discovered in Britain) are predominantly found in the sublittoral fringe and just deeper.

21.2.3 The infralittoral

The infralittoral subzone is that part of the sublittoral zone dominated by photophilous algae (Pérès and Molinier, 1957). For practical purposes, the infralittoral is considered to be the area where upward-facing rocks are dominated by erect algae. Distinctive communities occur both in the depth range dominated by large brown algae (mainly *Laminaria hyperborea*, *L. ochroleuca* Pyl., *L. saccharina* (L.) Lamour, and *Saccorhiza polyschides* (Lightf.) Batt.) and where these brown algae are absent and foliose algae thrive: these are the upper and lower infralittoral. However, foliose algae do not thrive where large numbers of grazing *Echinus esculentus* (L.) occur. Here rocks are dominated by encrusting red algae, especially *Phymatolithon calcareum*, *P. polymorphum* (L.) Fosl., *P. laevigatum* (Fosl.) Fosl. and *Cruoria pellita*, and by the encrusting brown algae *Pseudolithoderma extensum* (Crouan frat.) S. Lund and *Cutleria multifida* (Sm.) Grev. ('Aglaozonia' phase), particularly in Scotland. The descriptions below are for less-grazed areas:

a) *The upper infralittoral.* In the shallow, well-lit areas of the sublittoral, there is sufficient light for the growth of Laminariales which form a dense canopy, reducing the level of light on the sea-bed beneath. Species which are found only (or predominantly) in this zone are mainly associated with the kelp plants, in particular those living on the stipes and fronds. Species of foliose algae often encountered on the rocks in this area include *Bonnemaisonia asparagoides* (Woodw.) C.Ag., *Plocamium cartilagineum*, *Phyllophora crispa* (Huds.) Dixon, *Dilsea carnosa* (Schmidel) O. Kuntze, *Callophyllis laciniata*, *Kallymenia reniformis* (Turn.) J.Ag., *Acrosorium uncinatum* (Turn.) Kylin, *Cryptopleura ramosa* (Huds.) Kylin ex Newton, *Delesseria sanguinea*, *Drachiella spectabilis* Ernst et J. Feldm., *Heterosiphonia plumosa*, *Brongniartella byssoides*, *Odonthalia dentata*, *Desmarestia* spp., *Halopteris filicina* (Grat.) Kütz, *Dictyopteris membranacea* (Stackh.) Batt. and *Dictyota dichotoma* (Huds.) Lamour. Species of algae occurring mainly on kelp stipes, and therefore largely restricted to this depth range, include *Palmaria palmata* (L.) O. Kuntze, *Membranoptera alata* (Huds.) Stackh., *Phycodrys rubens* (*L.*) Batt. and *Ptilota plumosa* (Huds.) C.Ag.

Animals present are mainly those occurring in deeper water with a few individuals living among algal-dominated populations of the kelp forest. A few species are particularly abundant, or are only found in the infralittoral, including anemones with symbiotic algae: *Aiptasia mutabilis* (Gravenhorst) and *Anemonia viridis* (Forskal). Erect Bryozoa of the genus *Scrupocellaria* are also often present in large amounts and sometimes dominate the sea-bed below the kelp canopy. Kelp also provides cover for fish, particularly corkwing wrasse, *Crenilabrus melops* (L.), and ballan wrasse, *Labrus bergylta* Ascanius, together with pollack, *Pollachius pollachius* (L.), which swim over the kelp.

b) *The lower infralittoral.* Here, the kelp forest becomes a kelp park and, with further increase in depth, Laminariales disappear leaving the rock dominated by foliose algae. Often there is a belt of *Halidrys siliquosa* (L.) Lyngb. at this depth. The foliose species present in abundance are usually those described for the upper infralittoral but include species found in much deeper water and described for the upper circalittoral: *Dictyopteris membranacea* and *Dictyota dichotoma* are often present in particularly large amounts and the southern alga *Carpomitra costata* (Stackh.) Batt. occurs here. Animal species are generally few, although they include the anemones mentioned above and a few more circalittoral species, often in shaded areas.

21.2.4 The circalittoral

The circalittoral subzone is that part of the sublittoral zone that extends below the levels dominated by photophilous algae, taken here as below the area dominated by the foliose algae. Here rock surfaces are covered by animal species, usually as a turf of erect bryozoans and hydrozoans amongst which live large sponges, anthozoans, echinoderms and tunicates. The subzone is divided into upper and lower areas where foliose algae are present and absent respectively.

a) *The upper circalittoral.* This area is distinguished by the presence of scattered foliose algae. Several of the species also found in shallow depths extend towards the lower limits of this area including various encrusting coralline algae, *Delesseria sanguinea*, *Plocamium cartilagineum*, *Phyllophora crispa*, *Schottera nicaeensis* (Lamour. ex Duby) Guiry et Hollenberg, *Cryptopleura ramosa*, *Dictyopteris membranacea* and *Dictyota dichotoma*. Some algae are particularly abundant or are only found in the upper circalittoral, including *Lithothamnion sonderi* (Hauck), *Rhodymenia holmesii* Ardiss., *Hypoglossum woodwardii* (Kütz), *Myriogramme bonnemaisonii* (C.Ag.) Kylin, *Polyneura gmelinii* (Lamour.) Kylin, and *Rhodomela confervoides* (Huds.) Silva. The animals present are those of the circalittoral in general, although often at these depths some species are restricted to vertical surfaces.

b) *The lower circalittoral.* The animal communities of the lower circalittoral vary enormously from site to site, partly depending on the local physical environment and partly on other factors such as geographical location and the considerable local patchiness caused by biological interaction. Communities are described more fully in the sections on local distribution (page 300).

21.2.5 Factors determining distribution of communities with depth

a) *Light.* In the rocky sublittoral, light is the predominant factor determining which communities occur at different depths. The intensity of light is attenuated with increasing depth and the spectral composition also changes. Several studies, including those published by Boutler *et al.* (1974), Norton *et al.* (1977) and Lüning and Dring (1979), have indicated that the critical depth below which kelp plants fail to grow is where about 1% of surface illumination is reached. For the foliose red algae, the critical depth is that at which *c.* 0.1% of surface illumination penetrates. These critical light levels occur at different depths in water of different turbidity; Fig. 21.3 illustrates the downward extent of these algal-dominated zones in relation to different water types. The clarity of water generally decreases from open coastal areas, near to oceanic water, to enclosed areas such as the Bristol Channel and English Channel. Fig. 21.4 shows the maximum downward extent of each of the main algal community types at locations along the northern coasts of Cornwall, Devon and Somerset. On the open coast where the water is clear, the zonation of algal species can be seen clearly and may be subdivided further than I have suggested above. However, in enclosed coastal waters where turbidity is high, the different subzones are difficult to define and algal species may not be present in the sublittoral at all.

The absence, or low abundance of many animals in, shallow water is doubtless partly an effect of competition for space with algae, but the majority probably choose to settle in the darker waters below the zone of algal domination. Obvious exceptions are few and include anemones such as *Anemonia viridis*, *Aiptasia mutabilis* and *Anthopleura ballii* (Cocks) together with the hydroid *Aglaophenia pluma* which have symbiotic algae in their tissues.

Although light must be considered to be the main factor determining changes in community with depth in the nearshore rocky sublittoral, its influence is modified by several other factors which also vary with or are related to depth; these include the strength of wave action, rock slope, stratification of temperature, salinity and oxygen and biological interactions.

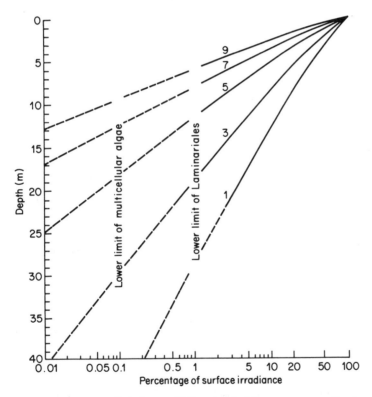

FIG. 21.3. The expected downward extent of kelp forest and foliose algae in different water types. Based on Jerlöv (1970) (solid lines) projected (broken lines) for lower light levels. The critical light levels for penetration of algae are from Lüning and Dring (1979). As a guide to water types, each is approximately represented in the following areas: 1 (clear oceanic) = Glénan Archipelago (Brittany); 3 = Isles of Scilly, Southwest Ireland, Western Scotland; 5 = Lundy, West Wales; 7 = Helgoland; 9 (turbid coastal water) = North Devon.

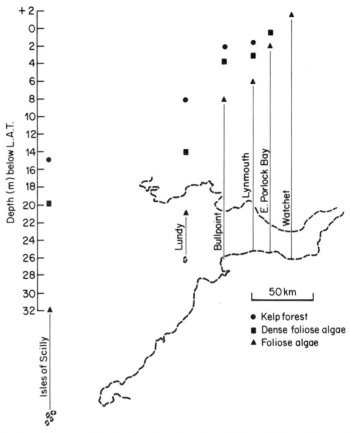

FIG. 21.4. The penetration of algae to critical depths at locations from the Isles of Scilly to Watchet in the upper Bristol Channel. Closed circle = lower limit of kelp forest; closed square = lower limit of dense foliose algae; closed triangle = lower limit of foliose algae (L.A.T. = Lowest Astronomical Tide).

b) *Wave action.* The strength of wave action is rapidly attenuated with depth. Shallow-water communities must therefore be tolerant of potentially very destructive forces, and only tough, strongly attached species will survive. On some headlands and offshore islands exposed to prevailing winds and swell, kelp plants may not survive and shallow rocks are dominated by foliose algae with perhaps only a few small, widely scattered kelps present. In such areas an upper infralittoral cannot be defined. At such wave-exposed locations and in areas subjected to strong tidal streams, water currents bring a plentiful supply of food to passive suspension-feeding animals. In such situations, sponges, hydroids and barnacles in particular may out-compete algae for living space in shallow depths and effectively reduce the downward penetration of algae, thus affecting the downward extent of the infralittoral subzone. In the extreme shelter of sea lochs (loughs), a forest of *Laminaria hyperborea* is again often absent, making the definition of an upper infralittoral difficult. Also, despite often very clear water, erect algae do not extend to deep water and the lack of water movement there is apparently affecting the downward penetration of these algae. In sheltered conditions, the deposition of silt is also important and may limit the downward extent of algae.

c) *Rock slope.* On steep rock slopes the downward penetration of algae is also reduced, thus decreasing the extent of the different subzones. On vertical and almost-vertical rock, algal penetration may only be to half the extent seen on nearby upward-facing surfaces. The effect is one of shading although settlement and establishment of species may also be important. Many circalittoral species also penetrate into the infralittoral in gullies and under overhangs although there are also many species, particularly some sponges and anthozoans, which are not found in shallow depths, possibly because of the effect of wave action.

d) *Salinity stratification.* Salinity stratification is an unusual feature around the British coast although many sea lochs have lowered salinity near to the surface for much of the year. On the Skagerrak coast of Norway, the outflow from the Baltic is of low-salinity water and its effects extend to a depth of 10 to 12m in places. The kelp forest may be absent or, where present, plants may be covered by epibiota, particularly encrusting bryozoans. Other algae are similarly affected and species diversity in shallow depths is low. Littoral species such as *Fucus serratus* (L.) often penetrate into the sublittoral in such places. Below the halocline, diverse communities similar to the open coast are present. Although the basic characteristics of the infralittoral and circalittoral zones remain intact in such situations, the lowered surface salinity and its effects impose a zonal separation of different communities in addition to that resulting from the effects of light attenuation.

e) *Temperature and oxygen stratification.* Temperature stratification is usually a feature of waters deeper than have generally been investigated in nearshore areas. The thermocline of those open oceanic waters which approach the western part of Britain and nearby Europe is present at a depth of 70 to 80m, although it might rise to 40m under calm conditions. On the open coast, Castric-Fey *et al.* (1973) and Könnecker (1977) have distinguished different communities from those of shallow depths on rocks below 40m off the Glénan Archipelago and Galway Bay respectively. Off Glénan, characteristic species include the sponges *Axinella egregia* Ridley, *Phakellia ventilabrum* (Johnston), the anthozoans *Dendrophyllia cornigera* (Lamarck), *Swiftia rosea* (Grieg), *Hormathia coronata* (Gosse), the hydroid *Thecocarpus myriophyllum* (L.) and the bryozoan *Porella compressa* (Sowerby). Könnecker (1977), studying mainly sponges, described *Thetyopsilla zetlandica* (Carter) and *Tetilla cranium* (O.F. Müller) as characteristic species with other sponges including *Phakellia ventilabrum* and the brachiopods *Crania anomala* (O.F. Müller) and *Terebratulina retusa* (L.) present. The temperature range experienced by the Galway Bay communities was suggested to be between 8° and 11°C. Cabioch (1968) also separated 'coastal' and 'offshore' circalittoral zones but at the 80m isobath off Brittany.

Thermoclines form in shallow depths in extremely sheltered areas such as sea lochs. The depth of such thermoclines in the Scottish lochs is often about 15m. However, there have been few studies of the importance of temperature stratification to the zonation of rock-living communities in such situations. It is notable that the brachiopods *Crania anomala* and *Terebratulina retusa*, mentioned above, are often present in large numbers below the thermocline.

The thermocline at Abereiddy Quarry in Pembrokeshire effectively separates deep from shallow waters during summer, and any effects of temperature on zonation there are masked by the severe oxygen depletion which occurs below a depth of about 13m. The ecological effects have been fully described by Hiscock and Hoare (1975). Deoxygenation resulted in an extremely marked zonal boundary. Above this boundary, rocks were colonized by the tunicate *Ascidia mentula* O.F. Müller, the fanworm, *Bispira volutacornis* (Montagu), and a variety of other species. Below the boundary, rocks appeared bare and only a few species survived – including the entoproct *Barentsia elongata* Jullien and Calvert, the ciliate *Folliculina* sp., the hydroid *Melicertum octocostatum* (M. Sars) and a few harpacticoid copepods – all species very rarely encountered on the open coast.

f) *Biological interactions.* Biological interactions in the form of competition for living space must occur throughout the rocky sublittoral, and the eventual pattern of algae dominating in shallow water and animals deeper down is largely unaffected by the actual species which make up that pattern. However, one important biological interaction which can greatly affect the extent of the zones around the British Isles is grazing by the sea urchin, *Echinus esculentus*. Jones and Kain (1967) demonstrated, by clearing urchins from an area of the Port Erin breakwater, that the lower limit of *Laminaria hyperborea* and other algae could be extended. High densities of *E. esculentus* also remove cover of foliose algae almost completely and make the definition of the infralittoral subzone difficult.

21.3 The Distribution of Different Communities

21.3.1 Geographical distribution

The British Isles and adjacent coasts of western Europe and Scandinavia lie at the meeting point of two major biogeographical provinces: the Arctic-Boreal and Mediterranean-Atlantic with, in addition, the Boreal province centred in the North Sea (Ekman, 1953). A slightly different classification was proposed by Briggs (1974), who regarded regions to the South of the British Isles as a 'warm-temperature Lusitanean province', while the eastern English Channel, the whole North Sea and Scandinavian coasts were classed as a 'cold-temperature Boreal province'. The presence of this overlap of biogeographical areas means that many of the species which characterize, or are dominant in, sublittoral communities differ from North to South in the British Isles. The biogeographical divisions are not based solely on latitude. Residual currents carry water masses northwards along the West coast of the British Isles and various other factors (such as lower seawater temperatures in the enclosed North Sea) mean that communities on the western Scottish coast may have species which are more southern in character than North Sea sites of equivalent latitude. Some of the species which characterize or dominate mainly rocky sublittoral communities in different geographical areas are listed in Table 21.1. A greater diversity of species is found in the South. Some species have a discontinuous distribution in the shallow sublittoral, and it is interesting to find *Swiftia rosea*, *Porella compressa* and *Terebratulina retusa* (as *T. caputserpentis*) listed by Castric-Fey *et al.* (1973) for the Glénan Archipelago but not recorded from coasts of the British Isles further South than western Ireland or western Scotland.

Many areas also show a strong regional character because of the prominence of particular species. Examples include the presence of dense populations of feather-stars, *Antedon bifida* (Pennant), in West Wales but not elsewhere in Southwest Britain; the presence of dense encrustations of the bryozoan *Cellepora pumicosa* (Pallas) in South Pembrokeshire; the presence of extensive areas dominated by the sponge *Phorbas fictitius* (Bowerbank) in North Wales; and the presence of dense erect Bryozoa in the circalittoral in some coastal areas but not others; the presence of beds of the ascidian *Molgula manhattensis* (De Kay) dominating rocks in some areas; the domination of some areas of sea-bed by the bivalve *Musculus discors* L. recorded off Brittany, Lundy and Galway Bay, and the absence or low abundance of many Porifera, Hydrozoa, Anthozoa, Decapoda, Opisthobranchia, Bryozoa, Echinodermata and Ascidiacea in the Isles of Scilly. Some of these features can be explained by the status of a known variable, such as low numbers of the sea urchin *Echinus esculentus* which would allow dense growths of erect Bryozoa to flourish, or by the isolation of areas such as the Isles of Scilly from sources of larvae of coastal species. Many more features have no clear cause.

It is possible to divide a geographical area into minor provinces based on different community characteristics which may be related to the biogeographical distribution of species, to changes in water quality, changes in substratum type or to some undefinable reason. The boundaries of such provinces are not usually strong but often occur at headlands or across large bays. At headlands, tidal streams often sweep offshore possibly carrying larvae with them. Extensive stretches of sand in large bays often cause a marked difference in rock communities on either side of the bay where otherwise there may have been a gradual transition. Provinces have been defined for South-West Britain in the final report

TABLE 21.1

Conspicuous rocky sublittoral species restricted to major biogeographical areas of the British Isles.

Southwest coasts only	Southwest and western coasts only	Northern coasts only
Dictyopteris membranacea	Anemonia viridis	Callophyllis cristata
Carpomitra costata	Corynactis viridis	Phyllophora truncata
Cystoseira baccata	Parazoanthus axinellae	Ptilota plumosa
Laminaria ochroleuca	Alcyonium glomeratum	Rhodomela lycopodioides
Axinella polypoides	Palinurus elephas	Odonthalia dentata
Gymnangium montagui	Antedon bifida	Protanthea simplex
Aiptasia mutabilis	Marthasteris glacialis	Bolocera tuediae
Anthopleura ballii	Holothuria forskali	Modiolus modiolus
Balanophyllia regia		Lithodes maja
Leptopsammia pruvoti		Cucumaria frondosa
Caryophyllia inornatus		Strongylocentrotus droebachiensis
Eunicella verrucosa		
Maia squinado		
Pentapora foliacea		
Paracentrotus lividus		
Pycnoclavella aurilucens		
Archidistoma aggregatum		
Distomus variolus		
Stolonica socialis		

of the Nature Conservancy Council/Field Studies Council South-West Britain Sublittoral Survey and in Cabioch *et al.* (1977). These boundaries are shown in Fig. 21.5.

21.3.2 Local distribution – introduction

The distribution of species into different communities in a limited biogeographical area is determined by local environmental factors. As in the littoral, the strength of wave action is very important in the sublittoral zone. So also is the strength of tidal streams. Other factors which help to determine the local distribution of communities within any particular depth include topographical features, the type of substratum present, the stability of substrata, siltation and the supply of silt, scouring, proximity of sediments, and the water quality characteristics of an area. The relationship between all of these factors and the communities present is often only clear in extreme environmental conditions such as in the shelter of sea lochs, on exposed headlands facing the Atlantic, in the tidal sounds between land masses where currents in excess of 400 cm·s^{-1} (8 knots) occur, or in estuaries where sublittoral rock surfaces are exposed to salinities of less than 30‰. On sublittoral bedrock in open coastal areas of intermediate exposure, the number of species able to colonize rocks is very large, and distinctly different communities may develop under apparently very similar conditions. This can occur even over a very short distance (Hiscock and Mitchell, 1980).

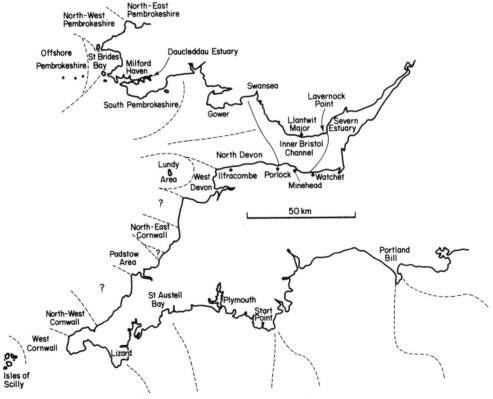

FIG. 21.5. Minor geographical provinces defined for Southwest Britain. The boundaries drawn off the south coast of Cornwall, Devon and Dorset mark the eastern limits of groups of sublittoral species defined by Cabioch *et al.* (1977). Within the area surveyed during the NCC/FSC South-West Britain Sublittoral Survey, boundaries are based on changes in species distribution, community types and substrata. Most boundaries are areas of transition but unbroken lines indicate strong boundaries.

The following sections provide an outline description and examples of the types of distinctive communities which develop under particular physical conditions.

21.3.3 Local distribution in relation to water movement

a) *Introduction.* Underwater the dominant physical factors determining the communities present on rock slopes include wave action and tidal streams. The interaction of these two different types of water movement makes the definition of simple relationships difficult, although in a previous publication (Hiscock, 1983) I presented diagrams illustrating (i) the changes in communities of conspicuous species which occur from very exposed to extremely sheltered sites, and (ii) the distribution of some sublittoral species which have distinctive preferences or tolerances for a range of tide and wave exposure conditions.

b) *Areas exposed to strong tidal streams.* At locations such as Ramsey Sound, the Menai Strait, Strangford Lough Narrows, the Sound of Islay and the Gulf of Corryvreckan, tidal streams reach speeds of over 400 cm·s^{-1} (8 knots) or higher, and distinctive communities develop. In both shallow and deep waters, the number of species which survive such strong tidal streams is small, although those which are capable of withstanding the mechanical stresses of flowing water benefit greatly by the enhanced food supply (suspension-feeding animals) and the considerable supply of nutrients (plants). In shallow depths, kelp plants are often very long with a dense stipe flora and the undergrowth turf of algae and animals below is very prolific. Growths of *Palmaria palmata* are often dense on kelp stipes and rock surfaces. In deeper water, similar communities are often seen in widely different geographical areas. A '*Halichondria panicea–Tubularia indivisa*' association is often present, although in some areas the barnacle, *Balanus crenatus*, may dominate rocks to the exclusion of almost all other sessile species. These barnacles are often overgrown by other species. The hydroids *Abietinaria abietina* (L.), *Sertularia argentea* (L.), *S. cupressina* (L.), *Hydrallmania falcata* (L.) and, in the strongest tidal streams, *Amphisbetia operculata* (L.), *Garveia nutans* Wright and *Eudendrium rameum* (Pallas), are also often abundant. Swarms of caprellid, and often jassid, amphipods occur on erect growths, and the usually littoral prosobranch *Nucella lapillus* (L.) is sometimes abundant, feeding on dense stands of *Balanus crenatus*. Sponges other than *Halichondria panicea* may be present in large amounts, particularly *Pachymatisma johnstonia* (Bowerbank) and *Amphilectus fucorum*. The anthozoans *Sagartia elegans* and *Actinothoe sphyrodeta* (Gosse) are often present in large groups at such exposed locations, although sea-fingers *Alcyonium digitatum* (L.) do not occur in such large numbers as in tide-stressed areas on the open coast. Erect Bryozoa often found include *Flustra foliacea* (L.) and, in Scotland, *Eucratea loricata* (L.). The butterfish *Pholis gunnellus* (L.) is usually present in large numbers in tideswept sounds. In the Gulf of Corryvreckan, famous for its whirlpools and overfalls, circalittoral rocks were dominated in places by a crust of *B. crenatus* accompanied by *Tubularia indivisa* (L.) which, in other parts of the Sound, were overgrown by a turf of the erect bryozoan *Securiflustra securifrons* (Pallas) with large numbers of the rarely-encountered tunicate *Synoicum pulmonaria* (Ellis and Solander). Other species were almost entirely restricted to holes and crevices in the rock.

Table 21.2 lists the species found at different depths in the Sound of Islay and in the Gulf of Corryvreckan in the Western Isles of Scotland.

c) *Areas exposed to strong wave action.* Distinctive exposed-coast communities occur in areas open to the full force of Atlantic wind-driven waves and swell. In shallow water, there is a downward extension of a few metres of species usually characteristic of the narrow sublittoral fringe above the lowest level of spring tides. In the upper infralittoral, where kelp plants are often sparse on extremely exposed coasts, species characteristic of exposed conditions occur including *Tubularia indivisa*, *Sagartia elegans*, *Actinothoe sphyrodeta*, *Alcyonium digitatum* and extensive colonies of *Corynactis viridis* (Allman). Mussels, *Mytilus edulis* (L.), may also dominate to considerable depths, most likely because

TABLE 21.2

Communities of conspicuous species at sites exposed to strong tidal streams in the Western Isles of Scotland.

	Sound of Islay (Beinn na Cille) Exposed to very strong tidal streams, sheltered from wave-action		Gulf of Corryvreckan (Carraig Mhòr) Exposed to extremely strong tidal streams, sheltered from wave-action	
	Infralittoral boulders and pebbles at 8.5 to 10.5m. * = algae on boulders + = on fronds of L. hyperborea Encr. calc. algae	Circalittoral boulders and bedrock at 39m	Infralittoral large boulders with some small boulders at 9m * = on stipes of L. hyperborea	Circalittoral steep bedrock slope at 23 to 25m
Abundant species	Pseudolithoderma extensum*	Tubularia indivisa Alcyonium digitatum		Sertularia cupressina Balanus crenatus Securiflustra securifrons
Common species	Encr. Rhodophyta indet.	Sertularia cupressina Balanus crenatus	'Trailiella intricata' Plocamium cartilagineum Cryptopleura ramosa Myriogramme bonnemaisonii Phycodrys rubens Laminaria hyperborea Alcyonium digitatum	Synoicium pulmonaria
Frequent species	Calliblepharis ciliata Rhodophyllis divaricata Plocamium cartilagineum Phyllophora traillii* Chondrus crispus Callophyllis lacineata Antithamnion plumula Cryptopleura ramosa* Odonthalia dentata Pterosiphonia parasitica Porphyropsis coccinea* Desmarestia aculeata* Desmarestia ligulata Chorda tomentosa Laminaria hyperborea	Pachymatisma johnstonia Halichondria sp. Encr. Porifera indet. Actinothoe sphyrodeta Echinus esculentus	Bonnemaisonia asparagoides Callophyllis lacineata Nitophyllum punctatum Pterosiphonia parasitica Odonthalia dentata Encr. red/brown algae Scypha ciliatum Sertularia argentea Pomatoceros triqueter Paguridae indet. Calliostoma zizyphinum Bugula sp.	Pachymatisma johnstonia Alcyonium digitatum Hydrallmania falcata Pholis gunnellus

TABLE 21.2 Cont'd

Sound of Islay (Beinn na Cille)		Gulf of Corryvreckan (Carraig Mhòr)	
Exposed to very strong tidal streams, sheltered from wave-action		*Exposed to extremely strong tidal streams, sheltered from wave-action*	
Infralittoral boulders and pebbles at 8.5 to 10.5m. * = algae on boulders + = on fronds of *L. hyperborea* Encr. calc. algae.	Circalittoral boulders and bedrock at 39m	Infralittoral large boulders with some small boulders at 9m * = on stipes of *L. hyperborea*	Circalittoral steep bedrock slope at 23 to 25m
Laminaria saccharina *Saccorhiza polyschides* *Obelia geniculata*+ *Sertularia cupressina* (10m) *Actinothoe sphyrodeta* *Gibbula cineraria* *Membranipora membranacea* *Antedon bifida*	*Bonnemaisonia asparagoides* *Furcellaria fastigiata* *Halarachnion ligulatum* *Phyllophora crispa* *Gymnogongrus crenulatus* *Phyllophora truncata* *Peyssonnelia dubyi* *Peyssonnelia immersa* *Cordylecladia erecta* *Griffithsia flosculata* *Spermothamnion repens* *Brongniartella byssoides* *Porphyra* sp. *Dictyota dichotoma* *Eudendrium rameum* *Abietinaria abietina* *Hydrallmania falcata* *Sagartia elegans venusta* *Pomatoceros triqueter* *Calliostoma zizyphinum*	*Occasional species* *Lomentaria orcadensis* *Kallymenia reniformis* *Antithamnion plumula* *Callithamnion* sp. *Membranoptera alata** *Desmarestia aculeata* Encr. Porifera indet. *Urticina felina* *Balanus crenatus* Crisiidae indet. *Sidnyum* sp. *Pomatoschistus pictus*	*Myxilla incrustans* ?*Haliclona* sp. *Alcyonidium gelatinosum*

TABLE 21.2 *Cont'd*

Sound of Islay (Beinn na Cille)		Gulf of Corryvreckan (Carraig Mhór)	
Exposed to very strong tidal streams, sheltered from wave-action		*Exposed to extremely strong tidal streams, sheltered from wave-action*	
Infralittoral boulders and pebbles at 8.5 to 10.5m. * = algae on boulders + = on fronds of *L. hyperborea* Encr. calc. algae	Circalittoral boulders and bedrock at 39m	Infralittoral large boulders with some small boulders at 9m. * = on stipes of *L. hyperborea*	Circalittoral steep bedrock slope at 23 to 25m
Halidrys siliquosa *Urticina felina* *Pomatoceros triqueter* *Balanus crenatus* *Calliostoma zizyphinum* *Echinus esculentus* *Clavelina lepadiformis*	*Amphilectus fucorum* *Nemertesia antennina* *Hyas coarctatus* *Henricia* sp. *Asterias rubens* *Crossaster papposus* *Pholis gunnellus* *Ctenolabrus rupestris*	*Rare species* *Desmarestia ligulata* *Desmarestia viridis* *Saccorhiza polyschides* *Hyas coarctatus* *Cancer pagurus* *Echinus esculentus* *Asterias rubens* *Crossaster papposus* *Pholis gunnellus*	*Haliclona oculata* *Haliclona* sp. 1 *Haliclona* sp. 5 *Tubularia indivisa* *Eudendrium rameum* *Sertularia rugosa* *Halecium ?beanii* *Nemertesia ramosa* *Urticina felina* *Corynactis viridis* *Hyas coarctatus* *Cancer pagurus* *Crisia eburnea* *Asterias rubens*
Scinaia turgida* *Delesseria sanguinea* *Sagartia elegans nivea* *Sagartia elegans venusta* *Sabella pavonina* *Balanus balanus* *Hyas* sp. *Pecten maximus* Encr. Bryozoa indet. Crisiidae indet. *Alcyonidium gelatinosum* *Henricia* sp. *Asterias rubens* *Crossaster papposus*	Additional species in samples: *Myxilla* sp. *Haliclona* sp. 1 and 3 *Celleporina hassallii* *Cellepora* sp.		

the starfish *Asterias rubens* (L.) is swept off by wave action in shallow water. Another ecologically important species, *Echinus esculentus*, is also restricted to deeper water at wave-exposed sites and may not be seen shallower than 20m. The reduced grazing pressure which must result from the restricted distribution of this grazer allows the development of dense populations of foliose algae. In the circalittoral the strength of wave action is much reduced but may still exceed an oscillatory velocity of 200 cm·s⁻¹ at 20m depth. On open rock surfaces, large erect species such as branching sponges and seafans are usually absent and the rock, in areas not heavily grazed by sea urchins, is covered by a turf of erect Bryozoa and Hydrozoa, particularly species of Crisiidae, *Scrupocellaria* spp., *Flustra foliacea*, *Aglaophenia tubulifera* (Hincks), *Nemertesia* spp. and many others. Encrusting sponges, tunicates and barnacles are often present in large amounts together with more solitary species characteristic of strong water movement such as *Actinothoe sphyrodeta*. The sponge *Polymastia boletiforme* (Lamarck) and the bryozoan *Pentapora foliacea* (Ellis and Solander) are often common. Where topographical features such as rock pinnacles to the West or gullies provide local shelter, large erect species and species characteristic of wave-sheltered areas occur. Strong wave action is an irregularly occurring force and, particularly during summer, communities on open coasts may be subjected to a high degree of siltation and poor food supply for passive suspension feeding. This is in contrast to sites subjected to strong tidal streams where rocks and organisms are clean of silt and a regular supply of suspended food is assured. Table 21.3 shows examples of wave-exposed communities from the outlying rocks of the Isles of Scilly.

d) *Areas exposed to strong wave action: surge gullies.* Shallow parts of narrow, steep-sided gullies facing into areas of strong wave action are often colonized by a highly distinctive community already described in Hiscock and Mitchell (1980) as the '*Dendrodoa grossularia–Clathrina coriacea*' community. The tunicate *Dendrodoa grossularia* (van Beneden) is often dominant and is always present in this community and the calcareous sponge *Clathrina coriacea* (Montagu) is also to be expected. *Pachymatisma johnstonia*, *Amphilectus fucorum*, *Myxilla* spp., *Halichondria panicea*, *Tubularia indivisa*, *Actinothoe sphyrodeta*, *Corynactis viridis* and *Alcyonium digitatum* are species found in different regimes of strong water movement which also occur in the '*Dendrodoa–Clathrina*' community. Also often present are the sponge, *Stelleta grubii* (Schmidt), the hydroid *Aglaophenia pluma* and, surprisingly, delicate colonies of the tubeworm, *Salmacina dysteri* (Huxley) (referred in previous years to *Filograna implexa* (Berkeley)).

Any remaining available space is occupied by erect Bryozoa: *Scrupocellaria* spp. and species of Crisiidae. At one location in North Cornwall, *Dendrodoa grossularia* was replaced by *Distomus variolosus* Gaertner. Table 21.4 lists species present in this community from widely different geographical areas.

e) *Open-coast sites sheltered from strong wave action and tidal streams.* Within this section are included the majority of sites likely to be encountered by biologists investigating nearshore rocky areas. Here, because water movement conditions are more moderate with many other environmental variables to influence the composition of communities, the types of community likely to be encountered are very varied. The composition of algal communities in the infralittoral is generally similar from site to site and it is in the circalittoral of these largely sheltered coasts that the very varied community types are particularly noticeable. The richest communities are found in Southwest Britain where many Mediterranean-Atlantic species are present. Here, circalittoral rocks are often dominated by a turf of erect Bryozoa with larger and often very colourful species of Porifera, Anthozoa, Ascidiacea and other groups scattered over the rock. These rich communities are often best-developed off East-facing coasts where tidal streams are moderate (up to about 130 cm·s⁻¹ (1.5 knots) surface velocity). The Mediterranean-Atlantic species which make these areas so attractive include the sponge, *Axinella polypoides* Schmidt, the hydroid *Gymnangium montagui* (Billard), the sea-fan, *Eunicella verrucosa*

TABLE 21.3

Communities of conspicuous species at sites exposed to very strong wave action in the Isles of Scilly.

	Jolly Rock, Western Rocks			*Maiden Bower Ledges*	
	Sublittoral fringe at −0.5m * on calcareous substrata	Upper infralittoral at 8m * vertical surfaces only	Lower infralittoral at 18–21m * on algae	Upper circalittoral Horizontal surfaces of very large boulders at 24m	Upper circalittoral Vertical bedrock surfaces at 21m
Abundant species	Encr. Rhodophyta indet. Pikea californica Patina pellucida (juv.)	Cryptopleura ramosa Diplosoma listerianum Haliclona 'rosea'* Laminaria hyperborea			Alcyonium digitatum Corynactis viridis
Common species	Chondrus crispus Cryptopleura ramosa Brongniartella byssoides Encr. brown/red algae	Polysiphonia urceolata Amphilectus fucorum Alcyonium digitatum*	Bonnemaisonia asparagoides Encr. Rhodophyta indet. Cryptopleura ramosa Polyneura gmelinii Encr. red/brown algae Desmarestia viridis Dictyopteris membranacea Dictyota dichotoma Echinus esculentus Labrus bergylta Pollachius pollachius	Alcyonium digitatum Caryophyllia smithii Corynactis viridis Echinus esculentus Labrus bergylta	Asterias rubens
Frequent species	Plocamium cartilagineum Corallina officinalis Callophyllis laciniata Ceramium sp. Delesseria sanguinea Desmarestia ligulata Laminaria hyperborea Alaria esculenta Pomatoceros triqueter Acmaea virginea Encr. Bryozoa indet. Labrus bergylta	Cruoria pellita Bonnemaisonia asparagoides Callophyllis laciniata Kallymenia reniformis Polyneura gmelinii Pterosiphonia parasitica Dictyota dichotoma Tubularia indivisa Actinothoe sphyrodeta Corynactis viridis Echinus esculentus Botryllus schlosseri	Plocamium cartilagineum Phyllophora crispa Hypoglossum woodwardii Brongniartella byssoides Pterosiphonia parasitica Electra pilosa Membranipora membranacea* Echinus esculentus	Hemimycale columella Haliclona 'rosea' Sertularia argentea Alcyonium glomeratum Asterias rubens Marthasterias glacialis Clavelina lepadiformis	Actinothoe sphyrodeta Caryophyllia smithii Crisiidae indet. Bugula flabellata Clavelina lepadiformis

TABLE 21.3 Cont'd

Jolly Rock, Western Rocks			Maiden Bower Ledges	
Sublittoral fringe at −0.5m * on calcareous substrata	Upper infralittoral at 8m * vertical surfaces only	Lower infralittoral at 18–21m * on algae	Upper circalittoral Horizontal surfaces of very large boulders at 24m	Upper circalittoral Vertical bedrock surfaces at 21m
Kallymenia reniformis Nitophyllum punctatum Lomentaria articulata Polysiphonia urceolata Alaria esculenta Dictyota dichotoma Amphilectus fucorum Obelia geniculata ?Sarsia eximea Sertularella sp. Corynactis viridis Diplosoma listerianum	Plocamium cartilagineum Drachiella spectabilis Compsothamnion thuyoides Myriogramme bonnemaisonii Sagartia elegans (small)* Caryophyllia smithii* Pomatoceros triqueter Crisia eburnea* Marthasterias glacialis	Kallymenia reniformis Sphondylothamnion multifidum Delesseria sanguinea Laminaria ochroleuca Obelia geniculata* Alcyonium digitatum Sagartia elegans Caryophyllia smithii Corynactis viridis Marthasterias glacialis Clavelina lepadiformis	Hypoglossum woodwardii Encr. Rhodophyta indet. Chiona celata Halichondria panicea Encr. Porifera indet. Phorbas fictitius Nemertesia antennina Actinothoe sphyrodeta Pomatoceros triqueter Crisiidae indet. Alcyonidium gelatinosum	Alcyonium glomeratum Echinus esculentus

Occasional species

Dilsea carnosa Saccorhiza polyschides	Dictyopteris membranacea Hemimycale columella Trivia arctica			

Rare species

		Axinella polypoides ?Halichondria panicea Holothuria forskali Labrus mixtus	Cryptopleura ramosa Polyneura gmelnii Dictyopteris membranacea Scypha ciliatum Amphilectus fucorum Dysidea fragilis Nemertesia ramosa Urticina felina Bicellariella ciliata Bugula plumosa Cellepora pumicosa Pentapora foliacea Luidia ciliaris Antedon bifida Labrus mixtus	Axinella polypoides Halecium beanii Bicellariella ciliata Cucumaria sp.

Specimens collected from this station but not recorded in situ were:
Leucosolenia botryoides, Modiolus phaseolinus, Hiatella arctica, Anomiidae indet., Celleporina hassalli, Celleporella hyalina and Electra pilosa.

Specimens collected at this site but not recorded in situ were:
Campanularia flexuosa, Eudendrium capillare, Plumularia setacea, Capmella tuberculata, Arcturella damnoniensis, Musculus sp., Scrupocellaria reptans, Crisia ?eburnea, Bugula flabellata, Aetea anguina and Sidnyum turbinatum

TABLE 21.4

Communities of conspicuous species in shallow wave-surge gullies.

	N. Round Island and Men-a-vaur, Isles of Scilly. Walls of steep-sided gullies at 3 to 5m (records of algae are mainly from the Round Island Gully)	Ogof Goch, Lleyn Peninsula. Wall of steep sided/over-hanging gully at 0 to 2m (records of algae are for gully walls and boulders in the gully)	South of Traigh Bhàn, West Islay. Wall of steep-sided gully at 2 to 3m
Abundant species	Encr. Rhodophyta indet. *Dendrodoa grossularia*		Encr. Rhodophyta indet. *Clathrina coriacea* *Dendrodoa grossularia*
Common species	*Corynactis viridis*	Encr. Rhodophyta indet. *Spondylothamnion multifidum* *Cryptopleura ramosa* *Hypoglossum woodwardii* *Delesseria sanguinea* *Polyneura gmelinii* *Pterosiphonia parasitica* *Desmarestia ligulata* *Laminaria saccharina* ?*Syncoryne eximea* *Actinothoe sphyrodeta* *Dendrodoa grossularia*	*Corallina officinalis* *Heterosiphonia plumosa* *Odonthalia dentata* *Pterosiphonia parasitica* *Scypha ciliata* *Scypha compressa* *Gibbula cineraria* Crisiidae indet. ?*Escharoides coccinea* *Botryllus schlosseri*
Frequent species	*Phyllophora crispa* *Rhodymenia holmesii* *Halurus equisetifolius* *Delesseria sanguinea* *Clathrina coriacea* *Tubularia indivisa* *Metridium senile* (dwarf) *Potamilla reniformis* *Crisidia cornuta* *Crisia denticulata*	*Schottera nicaeensis* *Corallina officinalis* *Dilsea carnosa* *Brongniartella byssoides* *Rhodomela confervoides* *Laminaria hyperborea* *Clathrina coriacea* *Halichondria panicea* *Amphilectus fucorum* *Myxilla incrustans* *Dysidea fragilis* *Tubularia indivisa* *Aglaophenia pluma*	*Furcellaria lumbricalis* *Rhodophyllis* sp. *Plocamium cartilagineum* *Dilsea carnosa* *Lomentaria orcadensis* *Delesseria sanguinea* *Nitophyllum punctatum* *Rhodomela lycopodioides* Filamentous brown algae *Pachymatisma johnstonia* *Halichondria panicea* Terebellidae indet. *Balanus crenatus*

TABLE 21.4 Cont'd

N. Round Island and Men-a-vaur, Isles of Scilly. Walls of steep-sided gullies at 3 to 5m (records of algae are mainly from the Round Island Gully)	Ogof Goch, Lleyn Peninsula. Wall of steep sided/over-hanging gully at 0 to 2m (records of algae are for gully walls and boulders in the gully)	South of Traigh Bhàn, West Islay. Wall of steep-sided gully at 2 to 3m
Rhodophyllis divaricata	Corynactis viridis	Calliostoma zizyphinum
Plocamium cartilagineum	Umbonula littoralis	Nucella lapillus
Corallina officinalis	Bugula turbinata	Encr. Bryozoa indet.
Kallymenia reniformis	Bugula flabellata	Henricia sp.
Haematocelis fissurata	Didemnidae indet.	Didemnidae indet.
Lomentaria orcadensis		Diplosoma listerianum
Callithamnion sp.		
Acrosorium uncinatum		
Drachiella spectabilis		
Polyneura gmelinii		
Heterosiphonia plumosa		
Laurencia pinnatifida	Occasional species	
Pterosiphonia complanata	Bonnemaisonia asparagoides	Callophyllis lacineata
Pterosiphonia parasitica	Chondrus crispus	Acrosorium uncinatum
Dictyota dichotoma	Callophyllis lacineata	Brongniartella byssoides
Cladophora sp.	Griffithsia flosculosa	Rhodomela confervoides
Pachymatisma johnstonia	Acrosorium uncinatum	Desmarestia ligulata
Halichondria panicea	Desmarestia viridis	Dysidea fragilis
Amphilectus fucorum	Saccorhiza polyschides	Salmacina dysteri
?Eudendrium sp.	Alaria esculenta	Anomiidae indet.
Plumularia setacea	Dictyota dichotoma	Trivia arctica
Diadumene cincta	Haliptysema tumanowiczi	Trivia monacha
Sagartia elegans	Pachymatisma johnstonia	Buccinum undatum
Pomatoceros triqueter	Encr. Porifera indet.	Paguridae indet.
Scrupocellaria reptans	Microciona atrasanguinea	Cancer pagurus
Encr. Bryozoa indet.	Alcyonium digitatum	Liocarcinus puber
	Sagartia elegans	Hyas sp.
	Potamilla reniformis	Alcyonidium sp.
	Balanus crenatus	
	Jassidae indet. (tubes)	
	Calliostoma zizyphinum	
	Crisiidae indet.	
	Bugula plumosa	
	Scrupocellaria sp.	
	Henricia oculata	
	Clavelina lepadiformis	
	Diplosoma listerianum	

TABLE 21.4   *Cont'd*

N. Round Island and Men-a-vaur, Isles of Scilly. Walls of steep-sided gullies at 3 to 5m (records of algae are mainly from the Round Island Gully)	*Ogof Goch, Lleyn Peninsula.* Wall of steep sided/over-hanging gully at 0 to 2m (records of algae are for gully walls and boulders in the gully)	*South of Traigh Bhàn, West Islay.* Wall of steep-sided gully at 2 to 3m
Marthasterias glacialis		
Botryllus schlosseri		
Diplosoma listerianum		
	Rare species	
Kallymenia sp.	*Cladostephus spongiosus*	Galatheidae indet.
Cladophora pellucida	*Scypha ciliata*	*Facelina coronata*
Dysidea fragilis	*Dercitus bucklandi*	
Sertularia argentea	*Tethya aurantium*	
Cancer pagurus	*Bicellariella ciliata*	
Bugula sp.		
Asterias rubens		
Didemnidae indet.		

(Pallas), the sea-finger, *Alcyonium glomeratum* (Hassall), the coral *Leptopsammia pruvoti* Lacaze-Duthiers, the zoanthid anemone, *Parazoanthus axinellae* (Schmidt), and the tunicate *Stolonica socialis* Hartmeyer. In the North these species are absent, and very few Arctic-Boreal species take their place – part of a general decline in the variety of species on moving from South to North. Here, on the open coast, the horse-mussel, *Modiolus modiolus* (L.), may dominate some rock surfaces while, in Shetland, the northern sea urchin, *Strongylocentrotus droebachiensis* (O.F. Müller), is an important grazer at some localities. Other species characteristic of the North include the sea-cucumber, *Cucumaria frondosa* (Gunnerus), found in Shetland and the sea anemone, *Bolocera tuediae* Johnston, and the hydroid *Thujaria thuja* (L.) found on the Northeast coast. Some species occur around most of our coasts and may dominate areas of rocky seabed; these include the brittlestar, *Ophiothrix fragilis* (Abild.), and the tunicate *Molgula manhattensis*. Amongst the conspicuous species colonizing sublittoral rocks in these fairly sheltered conditions, the majority are passive suspension-feeders relying on food carried by water movements. Sponges are an exception in that they create their own feeding currents, but even these are enhanced by external currents. Large predators are few but include several species of starfish such as *Asterias rubens*, *Marthasterias glacialis* (L.), *Henricia oculata* (Pennant) and *Luidia ciliaris* (Philippi). Small but very conspicuous predators are the sea-slugs. The sea-cucumber, *Holothuria forskali* (Delle Chiaje), is an unusual species in that it feeds on deposited silt. The many large crustaceans are generally scavengers and sometimes predators. The great scourge of sublittoral communities on many coasts is, again, *Echinus esculentus*. In parts of Southwest Britain, western Ireland, western Scotland, Orkney, Shetland and the Northeast coast of Britain, rocks are grazed clear of erect species leaving a layer of pink or brown encrusting algae and a few scattered large erect species. Erect bryozoans and foliose seaweeds are largely confined to crevices and overhangs.

Communities of conspicuous species from four distinctly different circalittoral sites are shown in Table 21.5, although the lists there can only represent a small proportion of the very wide range of communities which occur around our coasts.

f) *Sea lochs and other extremely sheltered areas.* The sea lochs of western Scotland and locations such as Lough Ine (Hyne) in Southwest Ireland, Abereiddy Quarry in Pembrokeshire and Easdale Quarry in Scotland are exceptionally sheltered habitats with rocky sublittoral communities very different from those of the open coast. Lough Ine has been studied for many years by Professor J.A. Kitching and his co-workers and there is a great deal of information published on the shallow sublittoral areas of the Lough. The most recent paper, Kitching and Thain (1983), describes species present in the shallow parts of Lough Ine. A list of species present on circalittoral cliff surfaces in the most sheltered part of the Lough is given in Hiscock and Mitchell (1980). Abereiddy Quarry in West Wales has also been thoroughly described (Hiscock and Hoare, 1975). The communities on rock surfaces in the most sheltered Scottish lochs await a detailed study, although I have recently completed a brief visit to some sites.

In the shallowest parts of the sublittoral zone in these sheltered areas, there is usually a narrow band of *Laminaria saccharina* and, more rarely, *L. digitata*. The dominant or most conspicuous species in the infralittoral include a few large algae such as *Chorda filum* (L.) Stackh. and *Codium fragile* (Sur.) Hariot subsp. *tomentosoides* (Goor) Silva, and many species with narrow often filamentous fronds forming a loosely attached blanket over the rock, e.g. species of *Polysiphonia*, *Antithamnion*, *Ceramium*, *Gelidium* and *Enteromorpha*, *Bonnemaisonia hamifera* (Hariot), ('Trailliella' phase), *Griffithsia corallinoides* (L.) Batt., *Stilophora rhizoides* (Turn.) J.Ag. and *Sphacelaria cirrosa* (Roth) C.Ag. In Lough Ine, the southern alga *Laurencia platycephala* (Kützing) is important and shallow rocks are dominated by *Lithophyllum incrustans* Philippi, a southern rock pool species. In some of the Scottish sea lochs, *Phycodrys rubens* and *Membranoptera alata* (species usually found only on kelp stipes on the open coast) are often present in large amounts on rock. However, the variety of algae is

TABLE 21.5

Communities of conspicuous species on circalittoral bedrock and boulders at four open coast sites.

	Bedrock sheltered from wave-action and tidal streams at 20m off Darrity's Hole, Isles of Scilly * = on vertical rock only. + = on horizontal/upward facing rock	Upward-facing bedrock exposed to strong wave-action, sheltered from strong tidal streams at 19 to 21m off Battery Point, Lundy	Bedrock forming an extensive broken plain. Exposed to strong wave-action and tidal streams at 16 to 17m Northwest of Bardsey Island * = under other animals + = on pebbles	Boulders exposed to wave-action, semi-exposed to tidal streams, at 18 to 22m (including records of algae in the upper circalittoral at 18m) west of Glengarrisdale, Northwest Jura
Abundant species		Alcyonium digitatum Balanus crenatus*	Balanus crenatus	
Common species	Suberites carnosus + Caryophyllia smithii Corynactis viridis* Crisiidae indet.*	Nemertesia ramosa Aplysia punctata Bugula plumosa Scrupocellaria sp(p). Cellaria sp(p). Flustra foliacea	Flustra foliacea Antedon bifida	
Frequent species	Polyneura hilliae + Brongniartella byssoides + Dictyopteris membranacea + Theocarpus myriophyllum + Alcyonium glomeratum Holothuria forskali Clavelina lepadiformis* Stolonica socialis* Labrus mixtus Labrus bergylta	Polymastia boletiforme Ciocalypta penicillus Nemertesia ramosa Caryophyllia smithii Balanus crenatus Crisiidae indet. Bugula plumosa Cellaria sp(p). Scrupocellaria sp(p). Marthasterias glacialis	Plocamium cartilagineum Rhodymenia holmesii Rhodymenia sp. ('spiky') Polyneura gmelinii Tethya aurantium Polymastia boletiforme Haliclona 'rosea' Nemertesia antennina Gymnangium montagui Actinothoe sphyrodeta Bugula turbinata Bugula flabellata Pentapora foliacea	Pachymatisma johnstonia Halecium halecinum Alcyonium digitatum Securiflustra securifrons Echinus esculentus Ascidia mentula

TABLE 21.5 *Cont'd*

Bedrock sheltered from wave-action and tidal streams at 20m off Darrity's Hole, Isles of Scilly. * = on vertical rock only. + = on horizontal/upward facing rock	Upward-facing bedrock exposed to strong wave-action, sheltered from strong tidal streams at 19 to 21m off Battery Point, Lundy	Bedrock forming an extensive broken plain. Exposed to strong wave-action and tidal streams at 16 to 17m Northwest of Bardsey Island * = under other animals + = on pebbles	Boulders exposed to wave-action, semi-exposed to tidal streams, at 18 to 22m (including records of algae in the upper circalittoral at 18m) west of Glengarrisdale, Northwest Jura
		Occasional species	
Plocamium cartilagineum +	Cliona celata	Encr. Rhodophyta indet. +	'Trailliella intricata'
Encr. Rhodophyta indet.	Suberites carnosus	Delesseria sanguinea	Rhodophyllis sp.
Hemimycale columella*	Tethya aurantium	Pachymatisma johnstonia	Antithamnion plumula
Haliclona 'rosea'*	Axinella polypoides	Axinella polypoides	Compsothamnion thuyoides
Polymastia boletiforme +	Homaxinella subdola	Phorbas fictitius	Phycodrys rubens
Polymastia mamillaris +	Raspailia hispida	Dysidea fragilis	Sertularia argentea
Cliona celata +	Raspailia ramosa	Sertularia argentea	Kirchenpaueria pinnata
Axinella infundibuliformis +	Dysidea fragilis	Aglaophenia tubulifera	Bicellariella ciliata
Axinella polypoides +	Halichondria panicea	Caryophyllia smithii	Alcyonidium sp.
Homaxinella subdola +	Tethyspira spinosa	Corynactis viridis	Crossaster papposus
Raspailia hispida +	Encr. Porifera indet.	Pomatoceros triqueter	Polycarpa sp.
Raspailia ramosa +	Halecium halecinum	Asterias rubens	Polyclinidae indet.
Dysidea fragilis*	Plumularia setacea	Henricia oculata	Labrus mixtus
Encr. Porifera indet.	Nemertesia antennina	Echinus esculentus	
Nemertesia antennina +	Aglaophenia tubulifera	Clavelina lepadiformis	
Nemertesia ramosa +	Aglaophenia kirkenpaueri	Polyclinidae indet.	
Alcyonium digitatum +	Gymnangium montagui	?Aplidium sp.	
Leptopsammia pruvoti*	Alcyonium digitatum	Labrus bergylta	
Parazoanthus axinellae*	Eunicella verrucosa		
Actinothoe sphyrodeta*	Actinothoe sphyrodeta		
Urticina felina +	Bugula turbinata		
Polycera sp. +	Bugula flabellata		
Crisiidae indet. +	Flustra foliacea		
Bugula sp(p). *	Pentapora foliacea		
Cellaria sp. +	Parasmittina trispinosa		
Antedon bifida*	Encr. Bryozoa indet.		
Marthasterias glacialis	Alcyonidium gelatinosum		

TABLE 21.5 Cont'd

Bedrock sheltered from wave-action and tidal streams at 20m off Darrity's Hole, Isles of Scilly. * = on vertical rock only. + = on horizontal/upward facing rock	Upward-facing bedrock exposed to strong wave-action, sheltered from strong tidal streams at 19 to 21m off Battery Point, Lundy	Bedrock forming an extensive broken plain. Exposed to strong wave-action and tidal streams at 16 to 17m Northwest of Bardsey Island * = under other animals + = on pebbles	Boulders exposed to wave-action, semi-exposed to tidal streams, at 18 to 22m (including records of algae in the upper circalittoral at 18m) west of Glengarrisdale, Northwest Jura
Echinus esculentus +	Asterias rubens +		
Cucumaria sp. +	Echinus esculentus		
Stolonica socialis +	Clavelina lepadiformis		
Polyclinidae indet. +	Pycnoclavella aurilucens		

Rare species

?Pytheus rosea	Pachymatisma johnstonia	Polymastia mamillaris	Bispira volutacornis
Ciocalypta penicillus +	Axinella infundibuliformis	Myxilla incrustans	Hyas araneus
Tethya aurantium*	Hydrallmania falcata	Halecium halecinum	Cucumaria ?lefevrei
Eunicella verrucosa +	Schizotricha frutescens	Sertularella polyzonias	
Isozoanthus sulcatus*	Thymosia guernei	Aglaophenia pluma	
Cereus pedunculatus +	Urticina felina	Bispira volutacornis	
Macropipus puber +	Pomatoceros triqueter	Cancer pagurus	
Pentapora foliacea +	Salmacina dysteri	Omalosecosa ramulosa	
Henricia oculata +	Cancer pagurus	Botryllus schlosseri	
Asterias rubens +	Gibbula cineraria	Scyliorhinus canalicula	
Luidia ciliaris +	Trivia sp(p).	Ctenolabrus rupestris	
Diazonia violacea*	Greilada elegans		
Ascidia mentula +	Boverbankia sp.		
Thorogobius ephippiatus	Henricia oculata		
Scyliorhinus canalicula +	Luidia ciliaris		
	Cucumaria lefevrei		
	Archidistoma aggregatum		
	Molgula manhattensis		
	Botryllus schlosseri		
	Labrus mixtus		
	Labrus bergylta		
	Ctenolabrus rupestris		

small compared to the open coast. Erect algae do not extend as deep as might be expected considering the clarity of the water, although encrusting algae can still be found dominating rocks to considerable depths, even under a layer of silt. In extreme shelter, some sponges grow in massive rather than encrusting forms, for example, *Hymeniacidon perleve* (Mont.) and *Halichondria panicea*. *H. panicea* demonstrates the most spectacular morphological change, with massive colonies often having large exhalent oscula at the tops of chimney-like growths. In the upper few metres of these extremely sheltered sites, the prosobranch *Bittium reticulatum* (da Costa) and sea urchin *Psammechinus miliaris* (Gmelin) (*Paracentrotus lividus* (Lamarck) in Lough Ine) are often abundant. Saddle oysters, *Anomia ephippium* (L.) are sometimes abundant and the ascidian *Clavelina lepadiformis* (Müller) may be present in large amounts. Many of the larger ascidians that are usually only found in deep water extend into very shallow depths.

The animal communities on rocks below the infralittoral are very characteristic and are usually dominated by large ascidians (*Ascidiella aspersa* (Müller), *A. scabra* (Müller), *Ascidia mentula*, *A. virginea* Müller, *Corella parallelogramma* (Müller) and, in areas of slightly lowered salinity, *Ciona intestinalis* (L.)), with large numbers of sabellid tubeworms (*Sabella pavonina* (L.) and *Bispira volutacornis*), serpulid worms (particularly *Pomatoceros triqueter* (L.), *Hydroides norvegica* (Gunnerus), Spirorbidae and smaller worms such as *Josephella marenzelleri* (Caullery and Mesnil)), and the scyphistomae of *Aurelia aurita* (L.). The brachiopods *Crania anomala* and, less consistently, *Terebratulina retusa*, also colonize the cliffs of such extremely sheltered sites. Sponges are often present in large amounts, including encrusting species and erect species such as *Tethya aurantia* (Pallas), *Suberites carnosus* (Johnston) and *Stelligera stuposa* (Mont.). Almost all of the hydroid species, so common on the open coast, are absent from extreme shelter, but *Eudendrium ramosum* (L.), some species of *Obelia* and *Kirchenpaueria pinnata* (L.) are characteristic of extreme shelter and are often very common in sea lochs. Likewise, the many erect bryozoans so conspicuous on the open coast are mainly absent from extreme shelter although *Scrupocellaria scruposa* (L.) may be abundant, together with a much smaller amount of Crisiidae and other Scrupocellaridae. One of the most spectacular and characteristic species of sea lochs in Scotland and fjords in Scandinavia is the anemone, *Protanthea simplex* Carlgren. Table 21.6 lists the conspicuous species found at a site near to the head of Loch Long in Scotland.

21.3.4 Local distribution in relation to substratum

a) *Introduction.* 'Rocky' surfaces include many different geological types, many different topographical features, and may be bedrock, boulders, cobbles or pebbles. Also, it is appropriate to include artificial hard substrata such as jetties and wrecks in the 'rocky' part of the sublittoral, since they are colonized by the same species. Communities may also differ depending on whether they are growing on rock or on other organisms, although the only such community to be described here is that present on kelp plants. Substratum mobility (in the case of boulders, cobbles and pebbles) and the scour caused by suspension of nearby sediments are very important. The presence or absence of silt or sand on the rock also has a considerable effect on the communities present. The influences of substratum on the community composition are often complex and are mixed in with those of other environmental factors such as the strength of water movement at a site. Only a few examples of the effects of substratum are given here.

b) *Geology.* The type of rock present seems less important than might be imagined. However, limestone is a particular exception where several species not occurring elsewhere bore into the rock and others live in the holes left by these species. The large bivalve species in the Pholadacea together with *Hiatella arctica* (L.) are particularly important boring organisms, and the holes they leave may be colonized by anemones such as *Cereus pendunculatus* (Pennant) and *Edwardsiella carnea* (Gosse) or by small crustaceans.

TABLE 21.6

Communities of conspicuous species on rock surfaces in an extremely sheltered location at South of Ardmay, Loch Long, Western Scotland (unpubl. data from field records).

Upward-facing rock on bedrock outcrops at 2m (upper infralittoral)	Upward-facing rock or very large boulders at 15m (lower circalittoral)	Steeply-sloping to vertical bedrock at 21m (lower circalittoral)
Abundant species		
Encr. Rhodophyta indet. (pink)	Encr. Rhodophyta indet.	*Protanthea simplex*
Common species		
Antithamnion sp.		*Sabella pavonina*
Polysiphonia sp(p).		Serpulidae indet.
Encr. Rhodophyta indet. (dark red)		
Metridium senile		
Asterias rubens		
Labrus exoletus		
Frequent species		
Phycodrys rubens	*Eudendrium ramosum*	Terebellidae indet.
Laminaria saccharina	*Protanthea simplex*	*Chaetopterus variopedatus*
Phaeophyta indet. (filamentous)	*Sagartiogeton undata*	*Pomatoceros triqueter*
Alcyonium digitatum	*Edwardsiella carnea*	*Crania anomala*
Pomatoceros triqueter	*Pomatoceros triqueter*	*Asterias rubens*
Lepidochitona cinerea	*Lepidochitona cinerea*	*Corella parallelogramma*
Ophiocomina nigra	*Ophiocomina nigra*	*Ascidia mentula*
Psammechinus miliaris	*Asterias rubens*	
Ctenolabrus rupestris	*Psammechinus miliaris*	
	Ciona intestinalis	
On *Laminaria* fronds:	*Corella parallelogramma*	
?*Elachista* sp.		
Clytia johnstoni		
Spirorbinidae indet. (2 spp.)		
Gibbula cineraria		
Crisia aculeata		
Cellepora hyalina		
Callopora lineata		
Tubulipora flabellaris		

TABLE 21.6 *Cont'd*

Upward-facing rock on bedrock outcrops at 2m (upper infralittoral)	Upward-facing rock or very large boulders at 15m (lower circalittoral)	Steeply-sloping to vertical bedrock at 21m (lower circalittoral)
	Occasional species	
Membranoptera alata	Haliclona sp. ('stalked')	Encr. Porifera indet. (white)
Polysiphonia elongata	Encr. Porifera indet. (white)	Eudendrium ramosum
Suberites carnosus	Eudendrium ramosum	Lepidochitona cinerea
Hymeniacidon perleve	Metridium senile	Anomia ephippium
Gobiusculus flavescens	Aurelia aurita (scyphistomae)	Modiolus modiolus
Ctenolabrus rupestris	Chaetopterus variopedatus	Psammechinus miliaris
	Echinus esculentus	?Pyura tessellata
	Ctenolabrus rupestris	Ciona intestinalis
	Rare species	
Suberites domuncula	Kirchenpaueria pinnata	Clathrina coriacea
Eudendrium ramosum	Alcyonium digitatum	Caryophyllia smithii
Kirchenpaueria pinnata	Urticina loftensis	Buccinum undatum
Acmaea tessulata	Protula tubularia	Ophiocomina nigra
Blenniidae indet.	Paguridae indet.	Henricia sp.
	Cancer pagurus	Didemnidae indet.
	Crania anomala	Ctenolabrus rupestris
	Botrylloides leachii	Scophthalmidae indet.

Many polychaete worms also bore into limestone, including *Polydora* spp., *Pseudopotamilla reniformis* (O.F. Müller) and *Perkinsiana rubra* (Langerhans). One of the most conspicuous species found living in limestone is the phoronid, *Phoronis hippocrepia* Wright, which forms extensive colonies both on limestone rock and in encrusting calcareous algae growing over harder rocks. Sponges of the genus *Cliona* also bore into limestone rock.

Other features of the geology of rock surfaces such as their friability or the presence of crevices in slate substrata are doubtless of importance. Further work on these aspects would be very rewarding.

c) *Cobbles and pebbles.* The cobbles and pebbles which often form extensive plains near to the shore and offshore in tideswept areas have a distinctive algal community in shallow depths. The foliose species of algae present are often only found on pebbles or are very rarely encountered on stable rock and include *Scinaia turgida* Chemin, *Stenogramme interrupta* (C.Ag.) Mont., *Schmitzia neapolitana* (Berth.) Lagerh. ex Silva, *S. hiscockiana* (sp. ined.), *Dudresnaya verticillata* (With.) Le Jol., *Radicilingua thysanorhizans* (Holm.) Pagenf. and *Naccaria wiggii* (Turn.) Endl. The rock itself is encrusted with calcareous algae including *Cruoria pellita*, *Cruoriella armorica* (Crouan frat.), *Hildenbrandia rubra*, *Peyssonnelia harveyana* J.Ag. and *P. dubyi* Crouan frat. In deeper water, where animals mainly colonize rock surfaces, cobbles and pebbles are usually dominated by encrusting bryozoans, particularly *Escharoides coccinea* (Abild.), but with many other species present. *Balanus crenatus* or *Verruca stroemia* (O.F. Müller) is often present and *B. crenatus* may dominate stones in some areas. *Pomatoceros triqueter* is usually present in large amounts. *Sabellaria spinulosa* Leuckart dominates tideswept cobbles and pebbles. The cobbles and pebbles are also colonized by erect animals including species of *Nemertesia*, *Sertularia*, *Bugula* and *Scrupocellaria*, *Alcyonidium gelatinosum* (L.) and polyclinid tunicates. Both algae and animals are probably fast-growing species which colonize surfaces soon after disturbance by storms and it is most likely this periodic disturbance which results in the presence of a characteristic flora and fauna. Many animals grow in the finer substrata between cobbles and pebbles or live under them including *Urticina felina* (L.), *Sabella pavonina*, *Lanice conchilega* (Pallas), Terebellidae, *Chaetopterus variopedatus* (Renier), *Galathea* spp. and *Munida bamffica* (Pennant). Echinoderms such as *Asterias rubens* and *Marthasterias glacialis* are often present but *Echinus esculentus* is rarely observed. Some areas of cobbles and pebbles, particularly in moderate tidal streams, are colonized by beds of feather stars *Antedon bifida* or brittle stars *Ophiocomina nigra* (Abild.) and *Ophiothrix fragilis*. The latter species occurs in densities of over several thousand $\cdot m^{-2}$ and any species attached to rock are obscured.

Table 21.7 gives examples of communities present on cobbles from the Isles of Scilly and Bardsey Island.

d) *Sandy rock.* There are several species of algae and animals which thrive where rocks extend to, and submerge into, sand – particularly mobile sand – and do not appear nearby on rock surfaces well clear of the sand. On vertical rock in areas of vigorous wave action, there is clearly a high degree of scouring with rock surfaces dominated by encrusting calcareous algae with scattered *Pomatoceros triqueter*, encrusting Bryozoa, encrusting sponges and a few small erect foliose algae, anemones and erect hydrozoans and bryozoans in concavities or cracks in the rock. On upward-facing scoured surfaces at a few sites, some of the species more usually characteristic of cobbles or pebbles including *Scinaia turgida* and *Naccaria wiggii* may be found. Where upward-facing rock is subject to occasional covering by sand, the effect is less severe. In the infralittoral, several large foliose algae thrive in such conditions. From studies in the Isles of Scilly, Northeast Cornwall, Lundy, South Pembrokeshire and Islay, the following species of foliose algae are suggested as being particularly abundant on or characteristic of sandy rocks in the sublittoral: *Asparagopsis armata* Harv., *A. armata* ('Falkenbergia' phase), *Bonnemaisonia hamifera*, *B. hamifera* ('Trailliella' phase), *Furcellaria lumbricalis* (Huds.) Lamour., *Polyides rotundus* (Huds.) Grev., *Gracilaria verrucosa* (Huds.) Papenf., *Ahnfeltia plicata* (Huds.) Fries,

TABLE 21.7

Communities of conspicuous species present on pebbles.

Smith Sound, Isles of Scilly. Infralittoral at 13m, pebbles on clean sand	Pen Cristin, Bardsey Island. Upper circalittoral at 15 to 17m
Abundant species	
Bacillariophyceae indet.	
Common species	
Stenogramme interrupta	Balanus crenatus
Cereus pedunculatus	Bugula plumosa
	Alcyonidium gelatinosum
Frequent species	
Scinaia turgida	Schmitzia hiscockiana
'Falkenbergia rufolanosa'	Encr. Rhodophyta indet.
Halarachnion ligulatum	Lomentaria clavellosa
Rhodophyllis divaricata	Griffithsia flosculosa
Gracilaria verrucosa	Radicilingua thysanorhizans
Phyllophora crispa	Heterosiphonia plumosa
Encr. Rhodophyta indet.	Polysiphonia urceolata
Dudresnaya verticillata	Polysiphonia elongata
Antithamnion plumula	Dictyota dichotoma
Brongniartella byssoides	Dictyopteris membranacea
'Aglaozonia parvula'	Bugula flabellata
Carpomitra costata	Scrupocellaria sp(p).
Dictyota dichotoma	Cellaria sp(p).
Pomatoceros triqueter	Ophiura texturata
Encr. Bryozoa indet.	
Diplosoma listerianum	
Occasional species	
Bonnemaisonia asparagoides	Scinaia turgida
Callithamnion ciliata	Schmitzia neopolitana
Ahnfeltia plicata	Bonnemaisonia asparagoides
?Cryptonemia seminereis	Halarachnion ligulatum
Lithothamnion glaciale	Callithamnion ciliata
Lomentaria clavellosa	Rhodophyllis divaricata
Lomentaria orcadensis	Phyllophora crispa
Cordylecladia erecta	Schottera nicaeensis
Griffithsia flosculosa	Rhodymenia holmesii
Acrosorium uncinatum	Rhodymenia pseudopalmata
Nitophyllum punctatum	Antithamnion plumula
Pterosiphonia parasitica	Ceramium rubrum
Desmarestia aculeata	Sphondylothamnion multifidum
Porphyropsis coccinea	Acrosorium uncinatum
Desmarestia ligulata	Acrosorium reptans
Laminaria saccharina	Cryptopleura ramosa
Cystoseira foeniculacea	Drachiella spectabilis
Ulva sp.	Myriogramme heterocarpum
Sagartia sp.	Polyneura gmelinii
Chaetopterus variopedatus	Heterosiphonia plumosa
Lanice conchilega	Brongniartella byssoides
Terebellidae indet.	Cutleria multifida
Sabella pavonina	Arthrocladia villosa
Sertularia cupressina	Sporochnus pedunculatus
Cancer pagurus	Scypha ciliata
Asterias rubens	Nemertesia ramosa
Marthasterias glacialis	Alcyonium digitatum
Clavelina lepadiformis	Pomatoceros triqueter
	Antiopella cristata
	Cellepora pumicosa
	Valkeria uva
	Vesicularia spinosa
	Eucratea loricata
	Clavelina lepadiformis
	Archidistoma aggregatum

TABLE 21.7 Cont'd

Smith Sound, Isles of Scilly. Infralittoral at 13m, pebbles on clean sand		Pen Cristin, Bardsey Island. Upper circalittoral at 15 to 17m	
Schmitzia neopolitana	Encr. Porifera indet.	*Rare species*	
Plocamium cartilaginum	Tubularia indivisa	Sertularia argentea	Henricia sp.
Gymnogongrus crenulatus	Nemertesia antennina	Nemertesia antennina	Luidia ciliaris
Rhodymenia delicatula	Nemertesia ramosa	Urticina felina	Ophiothrix fragilis
Callithamnion sp.	Alcyonium digitatum	Crossaster papposus	Morchellium argus
Sporochnus pedunculatus	Sagartia elegans	Asterias rubens	Didemnidae indet.
Desmarestia dresnayi	Actinothoe sphyrodeta		
Codium sp.	Facelina coronata		
Halicystis ovalis	Gibbula cineraria		
Suberites domuncula	Holothuria forskali		
Polymastia boletiforme	Marthasterias glacialis		

Gymnogongrus crenulatus (Turn.) J.Ag., *Phyllophora crispa, Chondrus crispus, Jania rubens, Grateloupia filicina* (Lamour.) C.Ag., *Cordylecladia erecta* (Grev.) J.Ag., *Compsothamnion thuyoides* (Sm.) Schmitz, *Dasya hutchinsiae* (Harv. in Hook), *Chondria dasyphylla* (Woodw.) C.Ag., *Asperococcus compressus* (Griff. ex Hook), *A. turneri* (Sm.) Hook, *Desmarestia aculeata* (L.) Lamour., *Alaria esculenta, Laminaria saccharina, Laminaria* sp. sporelings, *Cladostephus spongiosus* (Huds.) C.Ag., *Halidrys siliquosa, Enteromorpha* sp. and *Ulva* sp. The large brown algae listed are characteristic of the fast-growing community which develops after disturbance. *J. rubens* and the 'Falkenbergia' phase of *A. armata* grow on *C. spongiosus*. In the circalittoral, a few animal species appear to occur mainly or only on sandy rock and include the commonly encountered sponge *Ciocalypta penicillus* and the much more rarely seen *Adreus fasicularis* (Bowerbank). *Urticina felina* is also often abundant adjacent to, or partly covered by, coarse sand. The small ascidian, *Pycnoclavella aurilucens* Garstang, is particularly common on rocks with a sprinkling of sand.

e) *Kelp plants.* Kelp plants, particularly the longer-lived *Laminaria hyperborea*, provide a habitat for distinctive communities in the holdfasts (Moore, 1971, 1973b,c,d, 1978, 1981, this volume; Hoare and Hiscock, 1974; McKenzie and Moore, 1981) on the stipes and on the fronds (Seed, this volume). The communities present on stipes vary from site to site but are usually dominated by algae. *Palmaria palmata, Lomentaria articulata* (Huds.) Lyngb., *Ptilota plumosa, Membranoptera alata* and *Phycodrys rubens* are usually present only on kelp stipes in the sublittoral. Table 21.8 lists algal species present in large amounts on kelp stipes in widely different geographical areas of the British Isles. The animal species present on stipes commonly include *Balanus crenatus* and *Electra pilosa* (L.). Rich groups of animal species are mainly restricted to areas of strong tidal flow. Here, *Halichondria panicea* and other encrusting sponges may dominate stipes. *Scypha ciliata* (Fabr.) and *S. compressa* (Fabr.) are often present. Lobed colonies of *Alcyonidium hirsutum* (Fleming) and *Botryllus schlosseri* may be attached to the stipes together with several erect hydrozoan and bryozoan species including *Amphisbetia operculata* which only grows in the strongest tidal streams. Kelp stipes are also subject to grazing by *Echinus esculentus*. Kelp fronds are colonized characteristically by the hydroid *Obelia geniculata* (L.) and the bryozoan *Membranipora membranacea* (L.), but several other species occur including, amongst the algae *Callithamnion tetragonum* (With.) S.F. Gray, *Porphyropsis* sp. and Ectocarpoidea, and amongst the animals *Diplosoma listerianum*.

f) *Man-made structures.* Although the species living on man-made structures such as jetty piles, pontoons and wrecks are the same as those which occur on rock surfaces, the communities are often very distinctive and quite similar from one type of artificial structure to another. Shallow structures are often colonized by dense stands of *Metridium senile* and *Mytilus edulis* or *Balanus crenatus*. Hard surfaces, including primary colonizers, are often overgrown by hydroids especially *Tubularia larynx* (Ellis and Solander) and by tunicates such as *Diplosoma listerianum, Botrylloides leachii* (Savigny) and *Botryllus schlosseri*. Sponges such as *Halichondria panicea* and *Amphilectus fucorum* are often common and hydroids such as *Aglaophenia pluma* and *Plumularia setacea* also occur. Feather stars, *Antedon bifida*, and brittlestars, *Ophiothrix fragilis*, also occur. Often, hard surfaces are covered by the tubes of amphipods, particularly *Jassa falcata* (Mont.). Algae are usually sparse even in shallow depths on these structures partly because of overhead shading and partly because of the usually vertical nature of the sides of pontoons and jetty piles. *Laminaria saccharina* and *L. digitata* are often present as a fringe at the low water mark with a small variety of foliose red algae and some green algae, for instance *Ulva lactuca* (L.), present. Very shaded or deeper parts of shallow structures are often dominated by large ascidians, species of *Ascidiella* and *Ciona intestinalis* in particular.

Wrecks in deep water are sometimes rich in marine life very different from that of nearby rocks. In most cases, the variety of species is much lower on wrecks although some of the communities can be spectacular with large areas covered by *Metridium senile* or *Antedon bifida*. On one wreck described by

TABLE 21.8

Species of algae commonly recorded from kelp stipes in different geographical areas around the British Isles. Species present in small amounts at only one or two sites or present at only one site within a survey area have been excluded from the table. All records of separate *Polysiphonia* species are listed in one line. Records are from survey reports, Norton *et al.* (1977), Hiscock and Hiscock (1980) and Tittley *et al.* (1976).

+ = present in small amounts, + + = present in large amounts at any single location within the area studied.

	Isles of Scilly	Lundy	Southwest Ireland	Bardsey and Lleyn	Jura and Islay	Shetland	St Abbs, S.E. Scotland
Rhodophyllis divaricata	+ +	–	+	+ +	–	–	–
Plocamium cartilagineum	+ +	+	+	+ +	+	+ +	+ +
Encrusting calcareous Rhodophyta	+	–	–	–	+	–	–
Phyllophora sicula	–	+ +	–	–	–	–	–
Callophyllis lacineata	+ +	+	+	+	+	+ +	+ +
Palmaria palmata	+ +	+ +	+ +	+ +	+ +	–	–
Lomentaria articulata	+ +	–	–	+	–	–	–
Rhodymenia pseudopalmata	+ +	+	–	–	+	+	+
Ptilota plumosa	–	–	–	–	–	+	–
Acrosorium uncinatum	+	–	–	+	–	–	+
Cryptopleura ramosa	+ +	+ +	+ +	+ +	+ +	+	–
Delesseria sanguinea	+	–	–	+	+	+	+
Hypoglossum woodwardii	–	–	–	+	+	–	+
Membranoptera alata	+ +	+ +	+ +	+ +	+ +	+	–
Myriogramme bonnemaisonii	+	–	–	+	+	–	–
Phycodrys rubens	+ +	+ +	+ +	+ +	+ +	+ +	+ +
Brongniartella byssoides	+ +	+ +	+ +	+	–	+	–
Polysiphonia spp.	+ +	+ +	+ +	+	+ +	+ +	+
Ectocarpoidea indet.	–	+ +	–	–	+	+ +	–
Desmarestia aculeata	–	+	+	–	+	–	–
Desmarestia viridis	–	+	+	–	+	+	–
Laminaria spp. (young plants)	+	+	–	+	+	–	+
Dictyota dichotoma	+	+	–	–	–	–	–
Ulva lactuca	+	–	–	–	–	+	–

Hiscock (1980) and Rostron and Hiscock (in prep.), the sides of the hull had been initially colonized by *Balanus crenatus* and *Sabellaria spinulosa* followed by a wide variety of erect hydrozoans and bryozoans in particular. The hold of the vessel was like a large cave covered mainly by solitary ascidians. Wrecks are rarely colonized by the erect sponges, sea fans and anthozoans which characterize rock surfaces.

Table 21.9 lists conspicuous species present on jetty piles in Milford Haven and the wreck of the M.V. Robert off Lundy.

21.3.5 Local distribution in relation to water quality

On moving from open coastal areas near to oceanic water to enclosed coastal waters such as the upper Bristol Channel, eastern English Channel and Liverpool Bay, many aspects of water quality change. Turbidity is higher, the temperature range of seawater through the year is greater, nutrient concentrations are generally higher and salinity is more variable. All of these factors (and several others) result in the presence of communities which are impoverished compared to open coastal areas and which have several characteristics of their own. Similar changes occur over a shorter distance in flooded river valleys (the rias of Southwest Britain) where rocks continue to be present even in highly estuarine conditions.

In the Bristol Channel, the main changes which occur from West to East are listed below:

(i) The downward extent and the number of species of algae are reduced. Significant boundaries occur across Swansea Bay and Porlock Bay where *Laminaria* spp. and many other species of algae disappear, and at Minehead and probably Lavernock Point east of which no sublittoral algae are found.

(ii) All major animal groups (except for conspicuous polychaetes) show a reduction in the number of species, with particularly large reductions in the abundance and numbers of species of sponges, hydrozoans, bryozoans, echinoderms and ascidians. A major change in animal communities occurs across Swansea Bay and Porlock Bay.

(iii) The tube-building polychaetes *Sabellaria alveolata* (L.) and *Sabellaria spinulosa* are locally abundant on hard substrata east of Swansea Bay and Porlock Bay.

(iv) The rock-boring worm *Polydora*, the bryozoan *Vesicularia spinosa* (L.) and the ascidian *Dendrodoa grossularia* are particularly abundant in the Inner Channel in comparison with the open coast.

(v) The dogwhelk *Nucella lapillus* and the barnacle *Elminius modestus* (Darwin), which are usually found only in the littoral zone on the open coast, are present in the sublittoral zone in the Inner Channel.

The fall in numbers of conspicuous species observed during surveys of nearshore rocky areas was from 145 at sites near the entrance to Milford Haven to 64 near Llantwit Major along the South Wales coast and from 128 near Ilfracombe to 62 east of Porlock and to only 13 near Watchet along the English coast. In Milford Haven and its eastern part, the Daucleddau estuary, the fall in the number of species was from 134 at the entrance to the Haven to 25 in the region of Black Tar, 25km from the mouth of the Haven. In this area, the reason for a fall in species numbers is much clearer since there is a strong salinity gradient east of the Cleddau bridge at Pembroke Dock. At the location where numbers of species fell below about 50 in the Daucleddau estuary, minimum surface salinity reaches about 20‰ and at the furthest sites surveyed with rock present, about 12‰ (Nelson-Smith, 1965).

Species which are often encountered in these stressed areas but which are rarely seen on sublittoral rock and open coasts include *Sabellaria spinulosa*, *Elminius modestus*, *Carcinus maenas* (L.), *Mytilus edulis* and *Dendrodoa grossularia*. *S. spinulosa*, *M. edulis* and *D. grossularia* are often dominant species. Spionid worms of the genus *Polydora* are also present in large numbers on limestone rock.

Table 21.10 lists species present on rocky substrata at two sites on the southern shore of the Inner Bristol Channel.

TABLE 21.9

Communities of conspicuous species on jetty piles in Milford Haven (taken from surveys of nine separate piles on the Amoco jetty in June, 1981) and on the wreck of the M.V. Robert at Lundy (from Hiscock, 1980).

	Jetty piles		M.V. Robert	
	Infralittoral fringe at +0.3m	Circalittoral at 2m	Horizontal surface (port side) at 14m	Vertical surface (underside of hull) at 15–18m
Abundant species	Balanus crenatus		Sabellaria spinulosa	
Common species	Ectocarpaceae indet. Laminaria sp(p) (sporelings) Aglaophenia pluma Ascidiella sp.	Metridium senile Antedon bifida Ascidiella sp.	Metridium senile	Metridium senile
Frequent species	Antithamnion plumula Polyneura gmelinii Laminaria digitata Laminaria hyperborea Halichondria panicea Suberites domuncula Amphilectus fucorum Liocarcinus puber Didemnidae indet. Botrylloides leachii Botryllus schlosseri	Suberites domuncula ?Mycale macilenta ?Halichondria sp. Tubularia larynx Urticina felina Balanus crenatus Bugula plumosa Bicellariella ciliata Botrylloides leachii Botryllus schlosseri Didemnidae indet.	Nemertesia antennina Nemertesia ramosa Metridium senile Cellaria spp. Crisiidae indet.	Nemertesia antennina Pomatoceros triqueter Bugula plumosa Ascidia mentula
Occasional species	Palmaria palmata Lomentaria clavellosa Callithamnion sp. ?Pleonosporium sp. Hypoglossum woodwardii Leucosolenia botryoides Tubularia larynx Urticina felina Sagartia elegans	Leucosolenia botryoides Sagartia elegans Liocarcinus puber Ascidia mentula	Rhodymenia holmesii Antithamnion plumula Antithamnion cruciatum Ceramium tenuissium Hypoglossum woodwardii Myriogramme bonnemaisonii Polyneura gmelinii Delesseria sanguinea Radicilingua thysanorhizans	Dysidea fragilis Encr. Porifera indet. Nemertesia ramosa Urticina felina Eubranchus tricolor ?Jassidae indet. (tubes) Crisiidae indet. Cellaria spp. Cellepora pumicosa

TABLE 21.9 *Cont'd*

Jetty piles		M.V. Robert	
Infralittoral fringe at +0.3m	Circalittoral at 2m	Horizontal surface (port side) at 14m	Vertical surface (underside of hull) at 15–18m
Terebellidae indet.		Dictyopteris membranacea	Pentapora foliacea
Antedon bifida		Dictyota dichotoma	Encr. Bryozoa indet.
Styela coriacea		?Dysidea fragilis	Berenicea patina
Cottus sp.		Tubularia indivisa	Asterias rubens
		Sertularia argentea	Antedon bifida
		Plumularia setacea	Botryllus schlosseri
		Aglaophenia tubulifera	Diplosoma listerianum
		Sagartia troglodytes	Didemnum maculosum
		Urticina felina	
		Sabella penicillus	
		?Jassidae indet. (tubes)	
		Inachus sp.	
		Eubranchus tricolor	
		Polycera faeroensis	
		Scrupocellaria sp(p)	
		Bugula plumosa	
		Flustra foliacea	
		Pentapora foliacea	
		Omalosecosa ramulosa	
		Amathia lendigera	
		Antedon bifida	
		Asterias rubens	
		Luidia ciliaris	
		Labrus bergylta	
		Pollachius pollachius	
Rhodophyllis divaricata	*Cliona celata*	*Rare species*	*Halecium halecinum*
Encr. red/brown algae	*Dysidea fragilis*	*Tubularia larynx*	*Abietinaria abietina*
Lomentaria orcadensis	*Encr. Porifera indet.*	*Hydrallmania falcata*	*Antennella secundaria*
Griffithsia flosculosa	*Inachus sp.*	*Sertularella polyzonias*	*Caryophyllia smithii*
Cryptopleura ramosa	*Cancer pagurus*	*Sagartia elegans*	*Corynactis viridis*
Delesseria sanguinea	*Trivia monacha*	*Pomatoceros triqueter*	*Bugula turbinata*
Brongniartella byssoides	*Scrupocellaria sp.*	*Cancer pagurus*	*Bugula flabellata*
		Liocarcinus puber	

TABLE 21.9 *Cont'd*

Jetty piles

Infralittoral fringe at +0.3m	Circalittoral at 2m	Horizontal surface (port side) at 14m	*M.V. Robert* Vertical surface (underside of hull) at 15–18m
Porphyra sp.	Ciona intestinalis	Parasmittina trispinosa	Maia squinado
Laminaria saccharina	Styela clava	Alcyonidium gelatinosum	
Dictyota dichotoma	Clavelina lepadiformis·	Marthasterias glacialis	
?Mycale macilenta	Polyclinidae indet.	Echinus esculentus	
Encr. Porifera indet.	Cottus scorpius		
Obelia dichotoma	Pholis gunnellus		
Plumularia setacea			
Jassidae indet. (tubes)			
Cancer pagurus			
Pholis gunnellus			

TABLE 21.10

Communities of conspicuous species on infralittoral and circalittoral hard substrata at sites in the Inner Bristol Channel.

	Infralittoral bedrock at + 1.4m at Hurlstone Point on the East side of Porlock Bay	Circalittoral large boulders in nearshore areas at 0 to 5m at Hurlstone Point on the East side of Porlock Bay	Circalittoral small boulders and cobbles in offshore areas at 1.2 to 4m in East Porlock Bay	Circalittoral small boulders and stones consolidated by Sabellaria alveolata at 5 to 12m at Greenaleigh Point west of Minehead
Abundant species	Phyllophora pseudoceranoides	Sabellaria spp. *Balanus crenatus*	Sabellaria spp. *Balanus crenatus*	Sabellaria spp. (mostly *S. alveolata*)
Common species	*Chondrus crispus* *Mastocarpus stellatus*	*Pagurus* sp. *Flustra foliacea* *Dendrodoa grossularia*	*Pagurus* sp. *Flustra foliacea* *Dendrodoa grossularia*	
Frequent species	*Polyides rotundus* *Cladostephus spongiosus* Bacillariophyceae indet. Sabellaria spp. *Bicellariella ciliata* *Alcyonidium hirsutum* *Flustrellidra hispida* *Dendrodoa grossularia*	*Urticina lofotensis* *Pomatoceros triqueter* Sabellaria spp. *Balanus crenatus* *Pagurus* sp. *Bicellariella ciliata* *Flustra foliacea* *Henricia oculata* *Dendrodoa grossularia*	*Urticina lofotensis* *Pomatoceros triqueter* *Buccinum undatum* *Henricia oculata* *Dendrodoa grossularia*	*Pagurus* sp. *Vesicularia spinosa* *Bicellariella ciliata* *Alcyonidium gelatinosum*
Occasional species	*Ceramium* sp. *Hypoglossum woodwardii* Encr. Rhodophyta indet. *Palmaria palmata* *Polyneura gmelinii* *Rhodomela confervoides* *Bugula plumosa* *Alcyonidium gelatinosum* *Asterias rubens*	*Elminius modestus* *Nucella lapillus* *Buccinum undatum* *Calliostoma zizyphinum* *Electra pilosa* *Asterias rubens* *Polycarpa pomaria*	*Pomatoceros triqueter* *Nucella lapillus* *Calliostoma zizyphinum* *Flustra foliacea* *Lichenopora hispida* *Berenicea patina* Encr. Bryozoa indet. *Asterias rubens* *Echinus esculentus*	*Haliclona oculata* *Tubularia indivisa* *Plumularia setacea* *Urticina lofotensis* *Pomatoceros triqueter* *Balanus crenatus* *Calliostoma zizyphinum* *Berenicea patina* *Electra pilosa* *Dendrodoa grossularia* *Polycarpa pomaria*
Rare species	*Membranoptera alata* *Nucella lapillus* *Calliostoma zizyphinum* *Crisia eburnea*	*Haliclona oculata* *Dysidea fragilis* *Gibbula cineraria* Encr. Bryozoa indet.	*Dysidea fragilis* *Tubularia indivisa* *Sertularia argentea* *Amphisbetia operculata* *Homarus vulgaris* *Crossaster papposus*	*Cliona* sp. *Halichondria panicea* *Halecium halecinum* *Hydrallmania falcata* *Nemertesia antennina* *Sertularia argentea* *Sertularia cupressina* *Bugula plumosa* Encr. Bryozoa indet. *Henricia oculata* *Crossaster papposus*

21.4 Conclusion

The outline I have tried to provide in this Chapter should give readers a reasonable feel for the main types of communities of conspicuous species and some of the ecological relationships to be encountered in the very heterogeneous area known as the nearshore rocky sublittoral. Most of the descriptions have resulted from surveys commissioned by the Nature Conservancy Council over the past seven years. However, if the conservation of marine sites of high scientific interest is to be successful, much more survey work comparing sites and identifying those of nature conservation importance must be carried out. I would like to plead that, in Britain, it should not fall entirely to the Nature Conservancy Council to undertake studies in nearshore rocky sublittoral areas. The communities present are an important part of the natural environment of the British Isles and more academic studies are needed (i) to investigate the quantitative composition of these communities, (ii) to elucidate aspects of the biology of component species or species groups, and (iii) to monitor natural and pollution-induced temporal change. Academic institutes and funding bodies have been slow to acknowledge the enormous gap in our knowledge of marine ecosystems that exists for sublittoral rocky areas. There remain many elements of rocky sublittoral ecosystems to investigate and I encourage all serious students of marine ecology to learn to dive and view for themselves this rich and fascinating part of the rocky coast.

ACKNOWLEDGEMENTS

Most of the conclusions reached in this Chapter, together with examples given in the figures and tables are from work I have carried out or supervised. However, its preparation has drawn on unpublished information from many reports with a large number of contributors. Colleagues who have unwittingly assisted me through the reports they have written include Frances Dipper, Bob Earll, Sue Hiscock, Annette Little, Christine Maggs, Bernard Picton and Dale Rostron. I have been greatly helped in editing my manuscript by Sue Davies, Lucille Evans, Sue Hiscock and Geoff Moore.

CHAPTER XXII

DETECTION OF LONG-TERM TRENDS IN ROCKY SUBLITTORAL COMMUNITIES: REPRESENTATIVENESS OF FIXED SITES

T. Lundälv

'To record change is no problem. There is too much, and it would be a remarkable investigation that showed none. The major need is to ensure that the change recorded is real and relevant.'　　　　J.R. Lewis, 1976

22.1 Introduction

A basic problem in most ecological studies is that of representativeness of samples in relation to some larger entity, e.g. population, community or geographical area. The utility of a sample differs markedly depending on what sampling strategy is employed.

For most types of communities in the marine environment various strategies based on destructive random sampling have been used. This approach has the advantage of providing a standardized technique for the calculation of confidence limits or other estimates of precision. Among its disadvantages and problems, however, may be mentioned (i) that the sampling procedure in itself introduces variation (e.g. Lewis, 1976), (ii) that it is often uncertain whether the basic requirements for the use of various statistical techniques are fulfilled and (iii) that the final measures obtained are often coarse, thereby offering only limited opportunities for the study of subtle or slow biological change and/or detailed analysis of population-dynamic features.

In certain marine habitats, especially the rocky littoral and sublittoral, there are good opportunities for the use of alternative sampling strategies such as non-destructive sampling of fixed sites (e.g. Lundälv, 1971; Lewis, 1976; Hartnoll and Hawkins, 1980). Advantages of this technique include (i) reduced variability between consecutive samples since many environmental factors are kept constant (e.g. Lundälv, 1971, 1974; Lewis, 1976), (ii) the opportunity of obtaining exact (within the limits of methodological accuracy) measures of dynamic processes pertaining to well-defined communities, populations or individuals and (iii) ideal conditions for experimental manipulation (e.g. Connell, 1972, 1974).

Pertinent questions relating to fixed-site sampling strategies include (i) how to choose fixed test areas and (ii) what these test areas represent in relation to some larger entity (population, community, geographical area).

As pointed out by Hawkins and Hartnoll (1983b), studies involving quantitative analysis of change within rocky littoral communities have largely been made by means of three basic sampling strategies:

(i) fixed belt transects, (ii) fixed quadrats in selected areas and (iii) repeated random sampling in set areas.

The use of the second of these strategies, with emphasis on selected 'key' species, has been discussed and recommended by Lewis (1976). It has been employed in long-term studies on the dynamics of littoral (e.g. Lewis and Bowman, 1975; Lewis, 1976, 1977b; Bowman and Lewis, 1977) as well as sublittoral rocky-bottom communities (Lundälv, 1971; Svane and Lundälv, 1981, 1982a,b; Christie and Green 1982; Christie, 1983; Svane, 1983, 1985) and it forms the basis of this study.

When it comes to the more detailed decisions, such as the positioning and size of test squares and the frequency of sampling, required to set up a sampling programme, a wide variety of approaches has been used. A useful discussion of the advantages and disadvantages of various possibilities pertaining especially to rocky shores has been given by Hartnoll and Hawkins (1980).

The key problem is perhaps that of representativeness of test areas as a function of positioning and size. In the past, the issue of the relationship between test-area size and the qualitative representation of studied communities received much attention and led to the classical concept of 'minimal area' (e.g. Goodall, 1952; Gounot, 1969; Hawkins and Hartnoll, 1980). Attempts have also been made to incorporate a quantitative component, usually based on indices of similarity or diversity, in the determination of 'minimal area' (e.g. Gounot, 1969; Boudouresque, 1974; Niell, 1977; Weinberg, 1978; Fuentes and Niell, 1981).

A common limitation of the vast majority of past studies is that they have been dealing with sample representativeness in a static sense. By this, I mean that they have been considering the representativeness of a sample on one particular occasion or on a number of occasions treated separately. Many ecological studies, however, are primarily concerned with dynamic processes. As has been pointed out by Lewis (1978b), by Hartnoll and Hawkins (1980) and by Hawkins and Hartnoll (1983b) there is the possibility that the representativeness of a specific sample can change with time due to a phenomenon termed 'mosaic recycling' (see also Burrows and Lodge, 1950; Southward, 1964). Basically, smaller parts of a community may change in an unsynchronized way as a result of random events leading to chain reactions involving various kinds of biological interactions in a mosaic pattern. If mosaic recycling is a common phenomenon it should be of particular concern when fixed-site sampling strategies are employed. In a study dealing to some extent with this problem on a moderately exposed rocky shore, Hawkins and Hartnoll (1983b) concluded that test squares measuring $2 \times 1m$ were not large enough to eliminate the effects of mosaic recycling for all components of the studied communities. This conclusion was largely based on subjective criteria, however, as well as on a relatively short period of observation (30 months).

The present study aimed to provide additional information on the representativeness of fixed test squares in a long-term dynamic context, with special reference to sublittoral rocky-bottom communities on the Swedish West coast.

22.2 Material and Methods

The material for this study was obtained by means of photogrammetrical analysis of stereophotographs from fixed sites on sublittoral rock walls along the Swedish West coast. The selection of sites was based on pre-determined criteria. The sites should (i) cover a horizontal gradient from a sheltered fjord environment to an exposed outer archipelago environment, (ii) cover a gradient of depth: pre-determined depth levels (5, 10, 15, 20 and, when possible, 25m) were used at each locality, and (iii) the exact positioning of sites would be based on the occurrence of a standard type of substratum, involving the presence of near-vertical, relatively smooth rock faces at the required depth levels. As soon as these criteria were met, fixed test squares were marked.

Four localities (Fig. 22.1), meeting the stated criteria, were monitored photographically at intervals

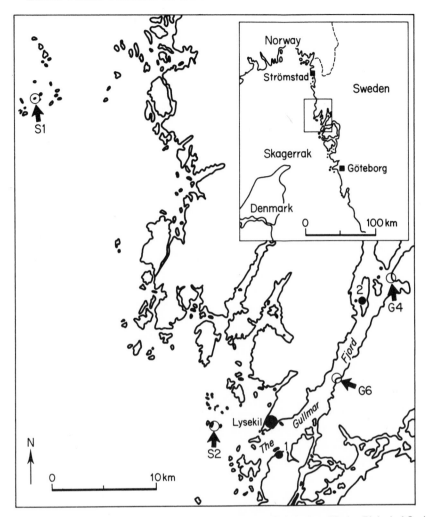

FIG. 22.1. Map of the studied area showing the investigated localities: 1. Kristineberg Marine Biological Station, 2. Bornö Hydrographical Station, Inset: position of the studied area in the Skagerrak.

over a thirteen-year period (1969–82). Station G4 is a sheltered locality facing W in the inner part of the Gullmarsfjord (Smörkullen 58°23′.7N; 11°37′.9E). Station G6 is a semi-sheltered locality facing N.W. in the central part of the Gullmarsfjord (Gåsklåvan 58°23′.7N; 11°32′.4E). Station S2 is a moderately exposed locality facing E.S.E. (Gäven, 58°16′.3N; 11°21′.2E) in the archipelago outside the Gullmarsfjord. Station S1 is an exposed locality facing S.S.E. (St. Sundskär, 58°32′.7N; 11°3′.3E) in an isolated group of islands (Väderöarna) outside the northern part of the Swedish West coast. The shortest distance by sea between the two most distant localities (Stations S1 and G4) is approximately 62km.

At each station and depth level a horizontal strip of six consecutive test quadrats, each measuring 0.5 × 0.5m (making a total of 1.5m²) was utilized for photographic monitoring. The test areas were defined by two plastic dowels, separated by a horizontal distance of 3m and attached to the rock by means of previous rock drilling. A rod was suspended between the plastic dowels on each sampling occasion and a photography frame could be moved along the rod at 0.5m intervals. In this way, test squares defined to an accuracy of *c.* 10mm could be relocated at intervals. Mean inclinations of the chosen test squares varied between 60° and 120°.

Stereophotographs were obtained by means of Hasselblad SWC-cameras fitted with corrective front ports. During the period 1971–77 a single camera was used that was moved between two positions 0.2m apart (the stereo-base) by means of a support on the photography frame. From 1978 and onwards a motorized and synchronized pair of cameras was utilized. Prior to 1971 a Hasselblad 500C camera without corrective front port was used and only part of the photographs were stereoscopic. Positive 70mm colour film (Ectachrome MS and Ectachrome 64) was used throughout the study.

During the period 1969–75 the test squares were photographed at a frequency of 4–7 times per year. Later, the frequency was lowered to 2–4 times per year.

Stereophotographs were analysed in a Wild Microstereocomparator, MSTK or in a stereoscope constructed from two aligned stereomicroscopes. Single photographs were analysed in a stereomicroscope. Determinations of faunal density were made by careful examination of the colour transparencies at a magnification between 12–25X. For some of the species considered (*Ascidia mentula* O.F. Müller, *Pyura tessellata* (Forbes) and *Boltenia echinata* (L.)) the determinations were based on continuous observation of all individuals through their observable benthic stages (cf. Svane and Lundälv, 1980, 1982a,b; Svane, 1985). This yields a high degree of accuracy for individuals of a size greater than 5mm. For other species (*Ciona intestinalis* (L.) and *Protanthea simplex* Carlgren) determinations were based on direct counts for each sampling occasion. This technique is less accurate for small individuals but still produces comparable results between stations and sampling occasions. A more detailed account of the photogrammetrical technique and its limitations is given by Lundälv (1971, 1974) and by Torlegård and Lundälv (1974).

Several persons were involved in picture analysis. Possible personal bias has not been tested in all cases. In tests performed to date, such error has not normally been found to exceed 5%. Furthermore, for most of the comparisons presented, compared time intervals were analysed by the same person.

Analysis of correlation between long-term variation patterns in different test squares was performed by means of Spearman's rank correlation coefficient (cf. Siegel, 1956). In some cases, the correlation coefficients were clustered according to Mountford (1962) and depicted as dendrograms.

All computations of correlation between test squares from the same station were based on actual numbers. However, when different stations were compared the correlation was based on pairs of interpolated data in order to eliminate effects of varying sampling times. In this case, four interpolated values per year (weeks 13, 26, 39 and 52) were used. Their derivation was based on the assumption of linear change between actual sampling occasions. In one case (comparison of *Ciona intestinalis* between sites) the variation curves were smoothed according to Velleman and Hoaglin's (1981) method 4253H, prior to computation of correlation coefficients.

22.2.1 Notes on hydrographical properties of the studied sites

Daily recordings of water temperature and salinity every 5th metre between the surface and 25m were obtained from Bornö Hydrographical Station (Fig. 22.1) in the inner part of the Gullmarsfjord (courtesy of the Fishery Board of Sweden).

The studied sites are influenced by two water masses, separated by a halocline (often coinciding with a thermocline) which could be subject to rapid vertical displacements of considerable magnitude. The upper water mass, the so-called 'Baltic water', is influenced by run-off from the Baltic Sea (S < 30‰ and variable). The lower water mass (S 31–34‰) is the so-called 'Skagerrak water', ultimately originating from the North Sea.

The mean depth of the halocline is between 10 and 15m. It penetrates below the 15m depth level frequently and occasionally impinges below 20m but very rarely reaches 25m. Monthly means and deviations of temperature and salinity at the 15 and 20m depth horizons over a twelve-year period are given in Svane (1985).

There are also horizontal gradients of hydrographical properties between the inner part of the Gullmarsfjord and the open coast archipelago. The most obvious one is that of increased exposure. The archipelago sites (Stations S1 and S2) are frequently affected by open sea swell which penetrates down to 25m during storms. This is not the case in the fjord sites. There is also a gradient of submarine daylight, which is normally reduced inside the fjord. This is due to the frequent occurrence of a thin surface layer of brackish and highly turbid water, influenced by local run-off in the fjord.

According to Gislén (1929), winter temperatures at 20m depth in the inner part of the Gullmarsfjord are generally 1° to 2°C higher than at the fjord mouth and summer temperatures 0.5° to 2°C lower. This tendency was supported by present observations.

In summary then, the stability of the hydrographic regime tended to increase from the exposed sites (Stations S1 and S2) towards the inner part of the Gullmarsfjord (Stations G6, G4) and from the shallowest (15m) to the deepest (25m) test squares considered.

22.2.2 Notes on dominating organisms in the compared test squares

There were marked differences in community structure between certain of the compared fixed sites, especially between the archipelago (Stations S1 and S2) and the fjord sites (Stations G4 and G6).

A general feature was a tendency towards submarine emergence in many species along a gradient from the outermost archipelago towards the inner parts of the Gullmarsfjord. One example, considered below, is the solitary ascidian, *Ascidia mentula*. In the fjord localities, this species occurred periodically at the 5m level and was a permanent resident at 15m and below. In the outer archipelago localities (Station S1 and S2) *A. mentula* occurred periodically at the 15m level but can be considered as a permanent resident only at 20m and below.

The most stable, long-term space occupiers at the considered depth levels (20 and 25m) of the outer archipelago localities were crust-forming algae (*Lithothamnion* spp.) and the octocoral *Alcyonium digitatum* L. More variable long-term residents were the ascidians, *Ascidia mentula* and *Boltenia echinata*. Finally, these communities were characterized to different degrees by highly variable populations of solitary ascidians, e.g. *Corella parallelogramma* (O.F. Müller), *Ascidiella* spp. and *Ciona intestinalis* (only Station S2), the sedentary polychaete *Pomatoceros triqueter* (L.) and a few hydrozoan and bryozoan species.

The fjord sites were characterized by more diverse communities. Among important long-term residents at the 15m levels may be mentioned the anthozoans *Metridium senile* (L.) and *Protanthea simplex* (the latter with a trend of decreasing abundance), the sedentary polychaete *Pomatoceros triqueter*, the ascidians, *Ascidia mentula* and *Dendrodoa grossularia* (Van Beneden), and a number of crust-forming sponges. Variable populations of the annual ascidians, *Ciona intestinalis* and *Corella parallelogramma*, as well as several species of hydrozoans and bryozoans, were important or dominating at times. At greater depths (20 and 25m) the importance of *Protanthea simplex* increased. Several species of sedentary polychaetes (*Sabella penicillus* L., *Chaetopterus variopedatus* (Renier), *Serpula vermicularis* L. and *Hydroides norvegica* (Gunnerus)), two species of brachiopods (*Crania anomala* (O.F. Müller) and *Terebratulina retusa* (L.)), the solitary ascidian *Pyura tessellata* as well as several species of sponges could be regarded as important long-term residents.

The most important benthic predator at all sites considered was the starfish, *Asterias rubens* L. Grazing effects from the echinoid, *Echinus esculentus* (L.), were evident in the outer archipelago sites and, to a lesser extent, in the central fjord locality (Station G6). *E. esculentus* was never recorded at the inner fjord locality (Station G4).

22.3 Results

Long-term patterns of density variation in a limited number of sessile species with differing life cycles and ecological characteristics were compared between fixed test squares of differing sizes representing a range of local environments. The aim was to study the degree of agreement between patterns as a function of time, space and test area size.

Two basic approaches were used: (i) abundance data for the largest size fixed sites studied (1.5m²) were compared between localities and depth levels, and (ii) abundance data for single, or groups of the six, 0.25m² quadrats comprising each site were compared with each other.

22.3.1 Inter-site comparisons

a) *Ascidia mentula.* The largest data runs for long-term, inter-site comparisons related to the perennial solitary ascidian, *Ascidia mentula.* More detailed accounts of the population dynamics of this species have been given by Svane and Lundälv (1981) and Svane (1983; 1985).

Variations (log scale) in *A. mentula* density over a thirteen-year period at 7 sites are presented in Fig. 22.2. In the three localities where data from two depth levels were available (Stations G4, G6 and S1), there was generally a high degree of conformity in basic patterns between the depth levels of each locality (Fig. 22.2A,B,C). There was also, however, a tendency towards an increased range of variation with decreasing depth.

Comparisons between localities again revealed a high degree of conformity between the two fjord stations (Fig. 22.2A,B). All four sites in these two localities showed the same main features. These included a minimum density in the autumn of 1970 followed by an increase and a period of stasis with a more or less well-developed depression in 1974, another increase towards a total maximum in 1976–77, then another depression in 1979–80, a peak in 1981 and a trend of decreasing abundance towards the end of the study period.

Patterns of variation at the two outer archipelago localities (Fig. 22.2C,D) were less uniform, with certain features held in common but also a number of discrepancies. Among features common to both localities may be mentioned the marked minimum in the autumn of 1970 and the general patterns exhibited between the autumn of 1972 and the autumn of 1975 and over the period 1979–82. Major discrepancies occurred over the period 1970–72 when a marked increase was recorded in the autumn at Station S1 (Fig. 22.2C) which was later followed by a decrease in 1971. In contrast, an increase was recorded at Station S2 only in 1971 (Fig. 22.2D). It should be noted, however, that the increase at Station S1 was recorded between September and December, 1970. Since no recording was made at Station S2 in December, it cannot be excluded that an increase followed by a decline in early 1971 was overlooked. Also, a major increase in the autumn of 1975 at Station S1 followed by a slow decline over the following years was in contrast to a decrease at Station S2 followed by a static period. The decline at Station S2 in the autumn of 1975 was caused by heavy mortality of unknown origin.

Finally, when the fjord sites (Fig. 22.2A,B) are compared with the outer archipelago sites (Fig. 22.2C,D) it is again evident that certain features, such as a minimum in 1970 and a decline in 1982 following a peak, were common to all sites. Other features, such as an increase in late 1975 followed by a peak, were common only to Station S1 and the fjord sites. There were also a number of discrepancies and mis-matches in the timing of events which will not be described in detail.

A quantitative evaluation of the degree of conformity between the sites was made by means of Spearman's rank correlation analysis. The results are summarized in the form of a cluster dendrogram in Fig. 22.3 and are given in full in Table 22.1. The dendrogram clearly illustrates the close relationship between the four fjord sites, with the 15m sites showing the highest correlation. Another closely correlated group was formed by the two depth levels (20 and 25m) at Station S1, while Station S2, 20m exhibited the lowest average relationship with the other sites.

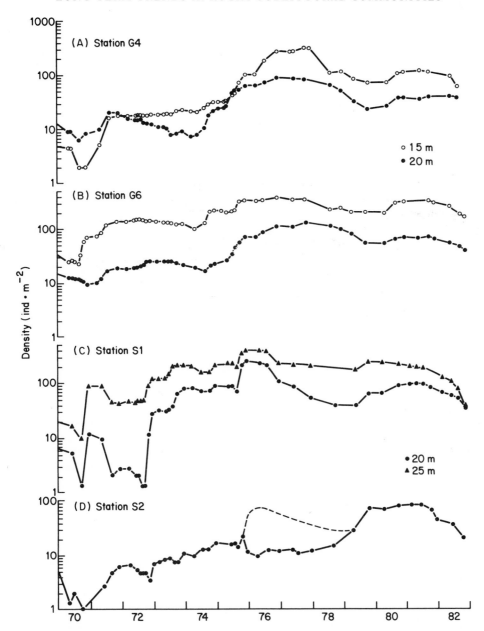

FIG. 22.2. Population density variations in *Ascidia mentula* over the period 1970–82 at seven sites. Symbols indicate sampling times and depths. See text for further information.

Significance testing of the correlation coefficients may not be strictly valid since the variables are not independent (for reference purposes only: all inter-site correlations were 'significant' at $P \leqslant 0.01$). b) *Ciona intestinalis. Ciona* is a solitary ascidian whose abundance exhibited marked temporal variation (both seasonally and over the long-term) in the area studied. In boreal waters it is essentially an annual (Dybern, 1965) but in the inner and deeper fjord sites (Station G4, 15 and 20m; Station G6, 20

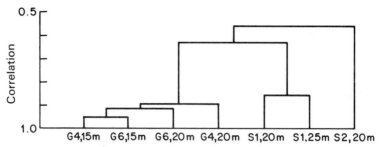

FIG. 22.3. Cluster dendrogram of correlations (Spearman's rho) between seven sites with respect to population density variations in *Ascidia mentula*. See text for further explanation.

TABLE 22.1

Correlation coefficients (Spearman's rho) between seven sites with respect to population density variations in *Ascidia mentula*. See text for further explanation.

	G4,15m	G4,20m	G6,15m	G6,20m	S2,20m	S1,20m
G4,20 m	0.891					
G6,15 m	0.952	0.915				
G6,20 m	0.940	0.885	0.890			
S2,20 m	0.624	0.471	0.584	0.558		
S1,20 m	0.710	0.527	0.722	0.563	0.580	
S1,25 m	0.691	0.546	0.673	0.615	0.555	0.860

TABLE 22.2

Correlation coefficients (Spearman's rho) between six 0.25m² quadrats in Station G4, 20m. The correlation analysis was based on population density variations in four different species as indicated. The numbers of samples are given in Fig. 22.6.

A. *Boltenia echinata*	1	2	3	4	5	6	B. *Ascidia mentula*	1	2	3	4	5	6
2	0.869						2	0.790					
3	0.103	0.198					3	0.719	0.866				
4	0.817	0.932	0.254				4	0.614	0.749	0.875			
5	0.790	0.796	-0.038	0.813			5	0.251	0.493	0.605	0.726		
6	0.717	0.897	0.336	0.911	0.722		6	0.597	0.745	0.844	0.933	0.681	
Σ	0.911	0.966	0.259	0.947	0.822	0.897	Σ	0.765	0.904	0.746	0.938	0.691	0.927

C. *Ciona intestinalis*	1	2	3	4	5	6	D. *Protanthea simplex*	1	2	3	4	5	6
2	0.928						2	0.808					
3	0.919	0.928					3	0.870	0.927				
4	0.899	0.910	0.919				4	0.954	0.885	0.947			
5	0.898	0.927	0.901	0.917			5	0.912	0.920	0.976	0.965		
6	0.933	0.955	0.937	0.911	0.922		6	0.884	0.898	0.978	0.954	0.966	
Σ	0.960	0.973	0.964	0.953	0.958	0.974	Σ	0.905	0.933	0.986	0.971	0.990	0.983

and 25m) it may attain an age of approximately two years (Lundälv, unpubl.). Additional accounts of its biology in the studied area have been given by Dybern (1965) and Svane (1983). Variations (log scale) in *Ciona* density at three sites (the 20m depth levels of Stations G4, G6 and S2, Fig. 22.1) over a thirteen-year period are shown in Fig. 22.4. The graphs clearly illustrate that the seasonal patterns at the three sites differed substantially, as did certain short-term inter-annual features. Regarded in the long-term, however, the three sites conformed closely to a common bi-modal pattern with one major peak centred around 1973, a depression in 1975–76 and another, minor peak centred around 1980. Existing data thus indicate a seven-year cyclical pattern in density variations of *Ciona* (cf. Gray and Christie, 1983). It should be noted, that the lower frequency of observations after 1975 probably precluded the accurate representation of true variability in such a dynamic species as *Ciona*.

Unpublished data from the 15m depth levels of the same localities (Stations G4, G6 and S2) over the period 1969–75 conformed closely to the same basic pattern as that above for 20m.

At Station S1 (Fig. 22.1) *Ciona* never occurred in large numbers. At the 20 and 25m levels of this locality, however, a different group of annual ascidians (*Corella parallelogramma* and *Ascidiella* spp.) exhibited a similar long-term pattern (cf. Svane and Lundälv, 1982a).

The results of a correlation analysis based on the data in Fig. 22.4 after interpolation and 'smoothing' (Velleman and Hoaglin, 1981) are included in that Figure. The two fjord sites exhibited the closest correlation, while G6, 20m and S2, 20m were most different. Once again, significance testing (see p. 335) yielded correlations with $P \leqslant 0.01$ between all sites.

c) *Protanthea simplex*. *Protanthea* is a 'primitive' anthozoan measuring a few centimetres in size. It occurred abundantly below 15m on steep rock walls in the Gullmarsfjord. No published accounts of the ecology of this species have yet appeared.

Variations in *Protanthea* density at five fjord sites (Station G4, 15 and 20m; Station G6, 15, 20 and 25m) are shown in Fig. 22.5. Again, all sites conformed to a common long-term trend of decreasing densities with time. The magnitude of this trend was inversely related to depth. At the 15m sites the density reduction from maximum to minimum was 97–98%. At the 20m sites, the reduction was 68% and at the 25m site 36%. The trend was thus dampened in the hydrographically more stable, deeper

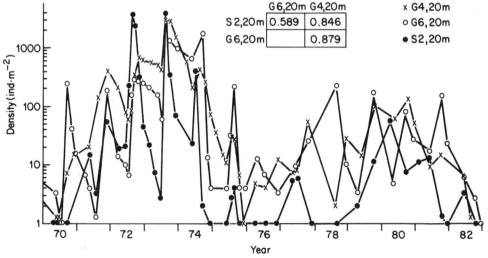

FIG. 22.4. Population density variations in *Ciona intestinalis* over the period 1970–82 at three sites. Symbols indicate sites and sampling times. Inset: Correlation (Spearman's rho) between the sites. See text for further explanation.

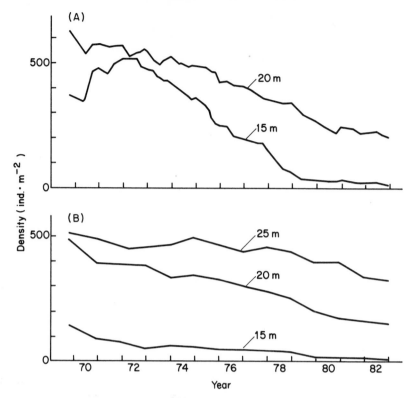

FIG. 22.5. Population density variations in *Protanthea simplex* over the period 1969–82 at five sites: A = station G4. B = Station G6. Only one census per year (November-December).

sites. Correlation analysis of the *Protanthea* data was not undertaken, since only one census per year (November-December) was obtained from the central fjord sites (Station G6) and since the trends were very obvious.

d) *Previously published data.* Data on long-term population dynamics of the solitary ascidian, *Pyura tessellata*, at two fjord sites (Stations G4, 20m and G6, 20m) were reported by Svane and Lundälv (1982b). The population density at Station G4 was 99·m^{-2} at the start of the study in 1971 and 78·m^{-2} at the termination in 1980. At Station G6, the corresponding figures were 51 and 39·m^{-2}. The two populations were thus reduced by 21 and 24% respectively. Both data sets were essentially rectilinear and showed parallel trends throughout the studied period, constituting another example of the high degree of conformity between two fjord sites.

In another study (Svane and Lundälv, 1982a) population dynamics of the solitary ascidian, *Boltenia echinata*, were compared between a fjord site (Station G4, 20m) and an exposed archipelago site (Station S1, 20m). At the exposed site, the speed of population turnover was found to be approximately twice that of the sheltered one. One result of this was a pattern of seasonal density oscillations at the exposed site which was not apparent at the sheltered site. However, the basic long-term patterns in both populations were very similar (cf. also Svane, 1983), and were probably influenced to a large extent by interference competition.

22.3.2 Intra-site comparisons

In order to investigate the relationship between test-square size and patterns of long-term variation two approaches were used: (i) data from single test quadrats (0.25m²) within a site were compared against each other, and (ii) long-term patterns in single or groups of 0.25m² quadrats were compared with complete sites (1.5m²) by means of correlation analysis.

For the first approach, long-term density variations in four species (*Boltenia echinata, Ascidia mentula, Ciona intestinalis* and *Protanthea simplex*) were compared between the six test quadrats comprising the 20m site at Station G4 (Fig. 22.1) by means of correlation analysis. The results are depicted as cluster dendrograms in Fig. 22.6 and are given in full in Table 22.2.

For *Boltenia* (Fig. 22.6A) square 3 showed little relationship with the other squares; especially little with square 5 (r_s = − 0.038). For *Ascidia mentula* (Fig. 22.6B) square 5 was most distant from the others and especially so from square 1 (r_s = 0.251). For *Ciona* and *Protanthea* (Fig. 22.6C,D) all squares were highly correlated.

It may be concluded that the relationship between individual test quadrats differed depending on what species was considered. No clear trend was found indicating that particular squares differed consistently from each other irrespective of species. The two species showing the highest average correlation between the test squares (*Ciona* and *Protanthea*) also had the highest mean densities (412 and 659·m⁻² respectively). The corresponding figures for *Boltenia* and *Ascidia mentula* were 80 and 44·m⁻² respectively.

The relationship between variation patterns in individual test quadrats from two sites in differing environments (Stations G4 and S2, 20m) are illustrated for *Ascidia mentula* in Fig. 22.7. The diagrams indicate a lower degree of conformity between individual quadrats in the exposed archipelago site (Station S2). The graphs also indicate a higher degree of conformity during periods of increased density in both sites, e.g. over the period 1979–82 in S2, 20m (Fig. 22.7B) and over the period 1975–78 in G4, 20m (Fig. 22.7A).

The relationship between test-square size and conformity in variation patterns was studied by the

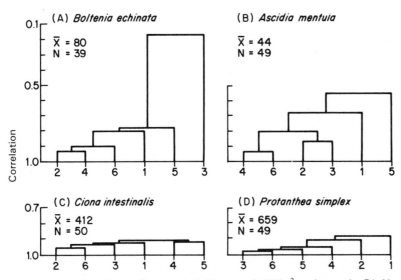

FIG. 22.6. Cluster dendrograms of correlations (Spearman's rho) between six 0.25m² quadrats at site G4, 20m. The correlations were based on population density variations of four species. Mean densities over the studied period and number of samples are indicated.

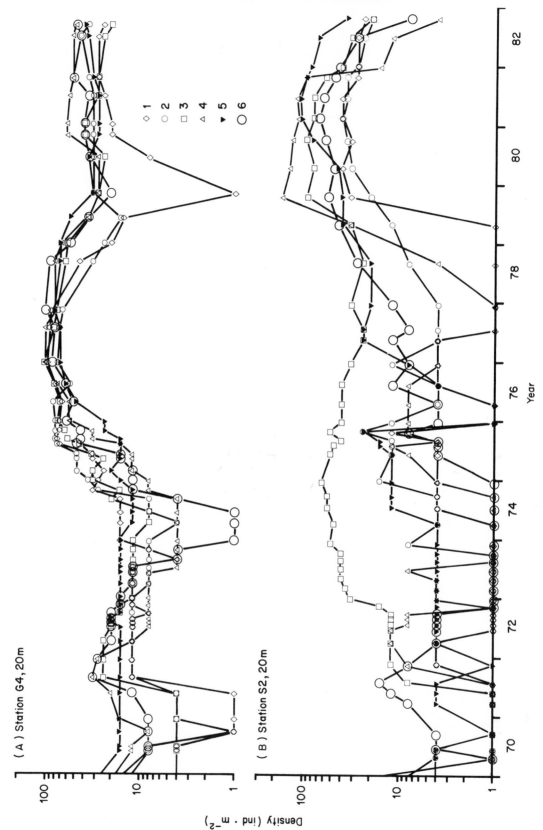

FIG. 22.7. Population density variations in *Ascidia mentula* over the period 1970–82 in six 0.25m² quadrats at two sites. Symbols indicate quadrat number and sampling times.

following procedure: for all the species and sites where adequate density data was available, the correlation (r_s) between each 0.25m² quadrat and the complete site (1.5m²) was calculated. Once this was done, the analysis was extended by running the two quadrats with lowest correlation against the complete site, then the three quadrats with lowest correlation and so on. The results were depicted as cumulative correlation curves, starting with the least correlated quadrat, and are shown in Fig. 22.8.

In most cases, even the 0.25m² quadrat that differed most was highly correlated with the complete site. Only in two cases out of twelve did the lowest correlation coefficients fall significantly below 0.7.

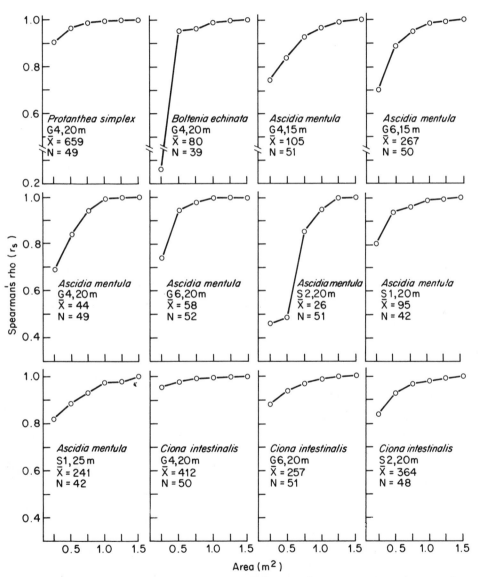

FIG. 22.8. Cumulative correlation curves between increasing numbers of 0.25m² quadrats and complete sites (1.5m²). Species, site, mean density over the studied period and number of observations are indicated for each curve. See text for further explanation.

This was the case for *Boltenia echinata* at Station G4, 20m (r_s = 0.259) and *Ascidia mentula* at Station S2, 20m (r_s = 0.459).

When the area was increased the correlation with complete sites rapidly increased. For two quadrats (0.5m²) the correlation exceeded 0.8 in eleven cases out of twelve and 0.9 in seven cases. For three quadrats (0.75m²) the correlation exceeded 0.8 in all cases and 0.9 in eleven cases. For four quadrats (1.0m²) the correlation coefficients were at or above 0.95 in all twelve cases considered. It may be noted that the one case showing the slowest increase in correlation (*Ascidia mentula* at Station S2, 20m) had the lowest mean density (26·m⁻²) over the study period.

22.4 Discussion

The representativeness of samples can be viewed from several starting points. It could, for example, be looked upon as the qualitative representation of species composition or as the quantitative representation of population densities in a specified community or geographical area. If representativeness in either of these respects is the main objective, then fixed sites would probably not be the best choice of sampling strategy. At any rate, fixed sites cannot be assumed to be representative of a larger entity unless they are compared with this entity by means of a random sampling programme. This has not been done in the present study.

Often, however, the major concern lies with the detection of relative change with time as a basis for the understanding of the processes leading to change. When this is the case, it is essential to know what the change recorded by a sampling programme represents. If, for example, change was largely due to small-scale random processes, then there would be little hope of reaching a level of understanding that could lead to predictive ability. Furthermore, recording this kind of change would provide a poor basis for the detection of possible pollution effects, which is an important aim of many long-term surveillance programmes (Hartnoll and Hawkins, 1980; Hawkins and Hartnoll, 1983b). Small-scale change has also been found by some workers to present a major obstacle to the interpretation of rocky shore data (op. cit.). Clearly, the situation would be more hopeful if change, as recorded by sampling, could be related to more general, large-scale processes.

22.4.1 Inter-site comparisons

In the present study, the degree of co-variation in observed density patterns was assessed by comparison of a number of sites covering a geographical range of approximately 62km. Two major types of environment, a sheltered fjord and the exposed outer archipelago, with great structural differences between the studied communities, were considered.

All the compared sites were positioned below the mean depth of a major pycnocline, separating 'Baltic water' from 'Skagerrak water'. They were, however, depending on depth and exposure, affected to varying degrees by the more variable 'Baltic water'.

The comparison revealed a high degree of conformity in long-term variability between all compared fjord sites (2–5) for all four species considered. This result suggests that the observed changes were largely brought about by factors operating on a 'fjord scale' at least.

When the comparison is extended to the outer archipelago sites (Stations S1 and S2) the picture gets more complicated. For *Ascidia mentula* (Figs. 22.2 and 22.3) all sites showed a high degree of conformity during certain periods, notably at the beginning and end of the study. The two depth levels at Station S1 also showed a high degree of conformity over the entire period. However, there were also periods when patterns of variation differed, both between the two outer archipelago localities and between one or both of these in relation to the fjord sites.

Probably, all sites were influenced commonly, by large-scale factors, and these structured much of the basic pattern of variability. This interpretation is supported by the correlation analysis which showed significantly positive correlations between all sites. Hydrographical factors such as temperature and salinity, in turn influenced by climatic events, are the most likely original causes of the common large-scale patterns. It is not the purpose of this paper, however, to examine these cause–effect possibilities in detail.

The differences between sites could be interpreted as the result of factors operating on a more local scale. The archipelago sites, for example, could be affected by water turbulence during storms, leading to mechanical dislodgement of animals. The activity of sea urchins (*Echinus esculentus*), also causing mechanical dislodgement of sessile species during their grazing activities, is another example of an influence that differed between the studied sites. The highest mean density of *Echinus* over the period 1972–82 was recorded at Station S2, 20m ($0.78 \cdot m^{-2}$). This site also differed most from the others. Corresponding mean densities of *Echinus* were $0.26 \cdot m^{-2}$ at G6, 15m; $0.33 \cdot m^{-2}$ at G6, 20m; $0.43 \cdot m^{-2}$ at S1, 20m and $0.36 \cdot m^{-2}$ at S1, 25m. At Station S2, the highest densities of *Echinus* were recorded over the period 1972–75. At Stations S1 and G6, the highest densities were recorded over the period 1980–82. *Echinus* was not observed at Station G4.

An illustration of the possible significance of a local influence is provided by an instance in the autumn of 1975, when Station S2, 20m showed a small increase in density of *Ascidia mentula* followed by a sharp decline (Fig. 22.2D), when all other sites showed a steady increase. The cause of the decline at Station S2 is uncertain, but sea urchin activity is a possibility since relatively high densities of *Echinus* were observed during this period. A possibility, as indicated by the hypothetical broken curve in Fig. 22.2D, is that this short-term mortality caused much of the departure (of Station S2, 20m) from the basic patterns shown by the other sites. The potential risk for misinterpretation of short-term local influences is greatly reduced, however, when several sites from similar environments can be compared.

Further support for the idea of large-scale influences, structuring much of the basic patterns of variation, was provided by the data on *Ciona intestinalis* (Fig. 22.4) and *Boltenia echinata* (Svane and Lundälv, 1982a; Svane, 1983). For both species, outer archipelago sites (S2, 20m and S1, 20m respectively) conformed closely to basic long-term patterns that were repeated in fjord sites. Again, differences in seasonal and short-term, inter-annual patterns could be interpreted as the result of local influences.

A further point, illustrated by the data presented, refers to the range of variation in different sites. In all localities and species where data were available from more than one depth level, there was a marked tendency towards an increased range of variation with decreasing depth. Possibly, much of the change recorded was related to factors associated with the upper water mass ('Baltic water') since the influence of this water mass is inversely related to depth. A similar trend of increased range of variation, most clearly illustrated by the *Ascidia mentula* data from the 20m sites (Fig. 22.2), was associated with the gradient from sheltered fjord sites to exposed archipelago sites.

Between sites, there were often great differences in mean densities of the same species. Examples are provided by the *Ascidia mentula* data, where mean densities between the two depth levels of each locality always differed by more than a factor of two (Figs. 22.2 and 22.8). In spite of this, the high degree of similarity in long-term variation patterns between the depth levels of each locality seems to indicate that intrinsic, density-dependent factors were of minor importance for the basic structuring of these patterns.

22.4.2 Test-square size

On the basis of the above, it can be concluded that the $1.5m^2$ sites employed in this study were generally adequate to reflect large-scale processes in the studied area reliably. If this is accepted, what happens when the test-square size is reduced?

The comparison of variation patterns in four species between six 0.25m² quadrats at Station G4, 20m (Fig. 22.6 and Table 22.2) showed that the correlations differed greatly between species. In the two species with highest mean densities (*Ciona* and *Protanthea*) there was generally a high correlation between all quadrats. In the other two species (*Ascidia mentula* and *Boltenia*), occurring in lower densities, different combinations of quadrats yielded highly different correlations without a clear common pattern.

The single-quadrat variation patterns in *Ascidia mentula* at two sites, illustrated in Fig. 22.7, further indicated a positive relationship between density and conformity in variation patterns. A lower degree of conformity between quadrats was also indicated at the exposed site (S2, 20m).

From these results it may be concluded that 0.25m² quadrats were not large enough to yield reliable estimates of general long-term changes under all circumstances. Their representativeness, however, seemed to increase with increasing densities and stability of the physical environment. The importance of density seems to indicate that phenomena such as 'mosaic recycling' were probably not very significant. Had they been, it is unlikely that density would have made much difference. A more plausible interpretation is that small-scale, random events were taking place inside the studied quadrats at a rate related to environmental stability. The impact of such events could be expected to increase with decreasing densities, since perturbations affecting only a few individuals would then significantly influence total density figures.

The correlation analysis between progressively summated 0.25m² quadrats and complete sites showed a rapid increase of correlation for all species when the area was increased (Fig. 22.8). Thus in most cases little information would be lost, cf. complete sites, when 0.75m² were analysed. The same was true in all cases when 1.0m² was analysed. In consequence, 1.0m² could be regarded as the 'dynamic minimal area' (DMA) for all the species and sites studied, under the circumstances described. A difference between this concept and the classical 'minimal area' is that 'DMA' integrates representativeness over a period of time, thereby reducing the risk of misinterpretation when test areas are used to study dynamic processes.

It is difficult, however, to formulate a rigorous definition for such a concept. Several problems would have to be solved: (i) how do we define the dynamic representativeness of the basic area, against which the 'DMA' is compared? (ii) how are the differences associated with species and densities accounted for? (iii) how is the importance of the time-scale over which the comparison is made accounted for? (iv) what exact criterion (correlation coefficient?) would be used to define the 'DMA'?

22.4.3 Significance of time-scale

Most of the results and conclusions presented in this study were based on data covering a thirteen-year period (or slightly less). No more than a superficial look at some of the data is needed, however, to demonstrate that certain conclusions might have been very different had only a shorter time period been covered. If, for example, the variation patterns in *Ascidia mentula* had been compared between Station S1 and the fjord stations (G4 and G6) over the period 1971–74 (Fig. 22.2), the conclusion would certainly have been that no co-variation existed at all. Likewise, a comparison of the 15 and 20m depth levels at Station G4 over the period September, 1971–June, 1974 would have indicated a negative correlation rather than a positive one. Several similar examples could be found.

Only when the variation patterns were regarded in a long-term perspective, did it become apparent that many or all basic features were common to all sites, in spite of frequent short-term deviations of variable magnitude. On these grounds, far-reaching negative conclusions concerning the representativeness of samples and the validity of monitoring studies on rocky shores, based on 30 months of data (Hartnoll and Hawkins, 1980; Hawkins and Hartnoll, 1983b), can be challenged.

Without questioning the value of fashionable short-term experimentation (where applicable), it is the belief of the present author that the currently widespread bad reputation of monitoring studies would largely be revoked if the importance of time-scale, as well as sampling design, were to be more fully realized. Without long-term observation of natural communities many important relationships will never be discovered or even suspected. Furthermore, many hypothetical relationships, e.g. those connected with long-term climatic change or the combined effects of many diluted pollutants on complex ecosystems, can never be fully evaluated experimentally. Instead, they call for empirical testing by the recording of relevant long-term biological data in the field.

ACKNOWLEDGEMENTS

The start of the study, of which this paper is one result, owes much to the late Professor B. Swedmark, former director of the Kristineberg Marine Biological Station. Continued favourable working conditions and willing assistance have been provided by Professor J.-O. Strömberg, the present director, as well as the technical staff of Kristineberg.

Many persons assisted in the field work, as well as in the biological analysis of the photographic material. Special thanks are due to A. Holme, C. Larsson, K. Lindahl and I. Svane.

Valuable discussions, as well as substantial help with computer runs of the correlation analysis, were contributed by Professor J.S. Gray and Dr O.-J. Lønne, Institute of Marine Biology and Limnology, University of Oslo. Helpful comments on the first draft of the manuscript were provided by Drs T.H. Pearson, R. Rosenberg and J.-O. Strömberg.

Financial support for this study was provided through many research contracts with the National Swedish Environment Protection Board and the Swedish Natural Science Research Council. To all I am grateful.

This study is a contribution within a cooperative European research programme (COST 47 – Coastal Benthic Ecology) organized by the European Commission and largely inspired by Dr J.R. Lewis.

CHAPTER XXIII

COMMUNITY ECOLOGY OF VERTICAL ROCK WALLS IN THE GULF OF MAINE, U.S.A.: SMALL-SCALE PROCESSES AND ALTERNATIVE COMMUNITY STATES

K.P. Sebens

23.1 Introduction

Sublittoral rock wall communities throughout the temperate zones of the world have common characteristics that make them very different from rocky littoral communities (Lundälv, 1971; Gulliksen, 1978, 1980; Vance, 1979, in review; Grange et al., 1981; Sebens, in press a, in review). The conspicuous zonation of littoral rock in the sublittoral is greatly broadened, and zones extend for ten metres depth or more. Monopolization of space by single zone-forming sessile species is also less evident. In addition, physical abrasion creating large areas of newly cleared rock, a predictable feature of rocky shore communities (Dayton, 1971; Paine and Levin, 1981; Lubchenco and Menge, 1978), is much less common on sublittoral rock walls (Sebens, in press a, in review; Vance, in review). Newly cleared patches tend to be small, on the order of a few centimetres in area, and are produced by predators removing single individuals or parts of colonial organisms. Even extreme storm conditions fail to create large cleared patches on sublittoral rock walls (Sebens, in review). Despite the lack of large-scale physical disturbance, the diversity of species on such walls is often striking even where the physical heterogeneity of the substratum is not. Large smooth expanses of wall usually harbour a number of species all in close contact with others. Time-series photography of marked quadrats (Sebens, in press a) indicates that such assemblages are very dynamic, with species constantly being overgrown, recruiting into cleared space, and often growing rapidly before losing space to better competitors.

The community ecology of sublittoral rock surfaces has been investigated in situ in only a few parts of the world. Much of the information on sublittoral encrusting species comes from 'fouling' community research, where artificial settling plates have been emplaced (e.g. Sutherland, 1974, 1978; Sutherland and Karlson, 1977; Osman, 1977, 1978; Shin, 1981; Harris and Irons, 1982) or where piling surfaces have been examined (e.g. Russ, 1980, 1982; Kay and Keough, 1981; Kay and Butler, 1983). Both surface types may differ substantially from nearby natural rock surfaces. Sublittoral rock walls have been studied intensively in Southern California (Vance, 1978, 1979, in review), Sweden (Lundälv, 1971, this volume), Norway (Gulliksen, 1978, 1980), Australia (rock slopes – Ayling, 1981), New Zealand (Grange et al., 1981), Massachusetts, U.S.A. (Sebens, 1982, 1983c, in press a, in review), and New Brunswick, Canada (Noble et al., 1976; Logan et al., 1984). There are, however, far fewer data and experiments on sublittoral rock walls than exist for littoral rock surfaces, and any generalizations are necessarily premature. Nevertheless, the similarities between widely separated areas are striking. The purpose of this chapter is to review research on rocky sublittoral communities in the Gulf of Maine, U.S.A., with particular reference to the species assemblages on vertical and undercut rock surfaces.

23.2 Rocky Sublittoral Communities in the Gulf of Maine

There is a clear depth zonation on rocky substrata in the Gulf of Maine. The shallowest sublittoral zone often has a band of kelp (*Laminaria saccharina* (L.) Lam., *L. digitata* (Huds.) Lam., *Alaria esculenta* (L.) Grev., *Agarum cribosum* (Mertens)) from the littoral zone to a depth of a few metres. The common littoral mussel, *Mytilus edulis* L., forms isolated and temporary beds within this zone; these are usually removed by predators including fish, sea stars, crabs, lobsters and sea urchins. The understorey below the kelp canopy includes crustose coralline algae, erect corallines and foliose red algae. Lamb and Zimmermann (1964), Hehre and Mathieson (1970), Miller and Mann (1973) and Mathieson and Hehre (1982) have described algal assemblages along this coast.

The sea urchin, *Strongylocentrotus droebachiensis* (Müller), forms extensive aggregations (Garnick, 1978; Bernstein *et al.*, 1983), beginning at 1–3m depth, that can occupy the same approximate location for many years. The edges of urchin 'herds' are 'feeding fronts' where urchins devour erect algae and encrusting invertebrates (Breen and Mann, 1976a,b; Lang and Mann, 1976; Himmelman *et al.*, 1983; Witman, 1984). At sites where urchins have been abundant for several years, horizontal and sloping rock surfaces support a pavement of crustose coralline algae (*Lithothamnion glaciale* Kjellman, *Clathromorphum circumscriptum* (Strömfelt) Foslie, *Phymatolithon rugulosum* Adey, *Phymatolithon laevigatum* (Foslie) Foslie, *Leptophytum laeve* (Strömfelt) Adey), and very little else (Adey, 1966; Steneck, 1978, 1982; Logan *et al.*, 1984). These coralline algal surfaces are also continuously grazed by molluscs, including the limpet, *Acmaea testudinalis* (= *A. tessulata*) (Müller) (Steneck, 1982, 1983), and the chiton, *Tonicella marmorea* (Fabricius), although these are far less common than the urchins. At a few sites in Maine the periwinkle *Littorina littorea* (L.), the most important littoral herbivore (Lubchenco, 1978; Lubchenco and Menge, 1978), also grazes sublittoral substrata to at least 10 metres depth.

The foliose algal community ends at 1–3m where sea urchins are abundant but extends to at least 15m depth at sites where urchins are scarce. In northern Massachusetts, horizontal and sloping rock surfaces at such sites are dominated by beds of *Chondrus crispus* (Stackhouse), *Phyllophora* spp., *Phycodrys rubens* (L.) Batt., *Euthora cristata* (L.), many ephemeral red and green algae, and several of the common kelps, *Laminaria saccharina*, *L. digitata*, *Agarum cribosum* and *Alaria esculenta*. The understorey below the 10–20cm thick red algal canopy comprises crustose corallines, the branched coralline, *Corallina officinalis* L., patches of tunicates, *Aplidium pallidum* (Verrill) and *Molgula citrina* Alder and Hancock, and mats of tubicolous amphipods (e.g. *Jassa falcata* (Montagu), *Corophium bonnellii* (Milne-Edwards)) and polychaete worms (*Polydora* spp., *Nicolea zostericola* (Œrsted)). Small crustaceans (gammarid and caprellid amphipods, shrimps, juvenile crabs) are also abundant in and below the canopy. This type of assemblage is found on the protected (inner East Point) side of Nahant, Massachusetts (Sebens, in review) and in protected sites all along the coast of Maine.

The large horse mussel, *Modiolus modiolus* (L.), often encrusted with the same coralline algal species as is the rock surface, can form extensive beds in shallow sublittoral habitats, offering shelter to a diverse group of invertebrates that live in the gaps between the mussels (Witman, 1984). Large sea stars (*Asterias vulgaris* Verrill) are also common, sometimes feeding on *Modiolus* (Hulbert, 1980; Witman, 1984).

Vertical or slightly undercut rock walls below 3m depth support a very different biotic assemblage (Fig. 23.1), dominated by encrusting invertebrates. Walls at sites from northern Massachusetts (Figs. 23.2 and 23.3) to central Maine are dominated by various combinations of the following: the octocoral,

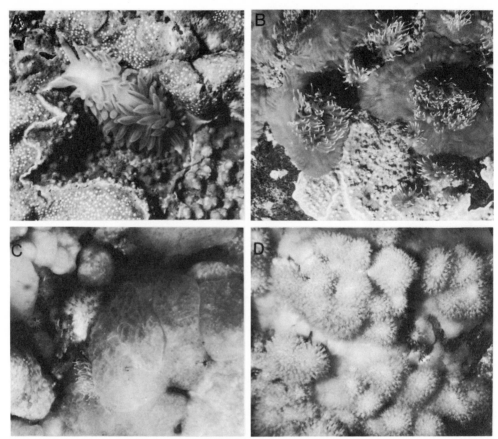

FIG. 23.1. Vertical surfaces at Nahant, Massachusetts (8m depth). Vertical or undercut surfaces are dominated by crustose coralline algae where urchins are abundant or by invertebrate assemblages where urchins are less common. Locally stable states of the vertical rock wall community include domination by: (A) coralline algae, *Lithothamnion* (rough), *Phymatolithon* (with white spots), (B) *Metridium senile*, (C) *Aplidium pallidum*, or (D) *Alcyonium siderium*. Note that *Aplidium* is overgrowing small *M. senile* and *A. siderium* in (C). Nudibranch in (A) is *Coryphella salmonacea*. Scale is 5cm across (A) and (C), 20cm across (B) and (D).

Alcyonium siderium (Verrill), the colonial tunicates, *Aplidium pallidum* and *Didemnum albidum* (Verrill), the solitary ascidians, *Molgula citrina*, *M. manhattensis* (DeKay), *Dendrodoa carnea* (Agassiz), and *Halocynthia pyriformis* (Rathke), the encrusting sponges, *Halichondria panicea* (Pallas), *H. bower-bankii* Burton, *Halisarca dujardini* Johnston, *Cliona celata* Grant, *Leucosolenia cancellata* Verrill and the tall branched sponges, *Isodictya* spp. and *Haliclona oculata* (Pallas). Other common invertebrates on vertical walls include barnacles (*Balanus balanus* (da Costa)), tubeworms (*Spirorbis* spp.), encrusting bryozoans (*Electra pilosa* (L.), *Celleporella* (= *Hippothoa*) *hyalina* (L.), *Schizomavella auriculata* (Hassell), *Porella concinna* (Busk) and others), and the holothurians, *Psolus fabricii* Duben and Koren, and *Cucumaria frondosa* (Gunnerus). The sea anemone *Metridium senile* (L.) and the octocoral *Alcyonium* form dense aggregations that exclude most other species on certain walls. The anemone *Tealia crassicornis* (Müller) occurs on boulders and rock walls infrequently in northern Massachusetts but can be quite common in northern Maine and in deeper water. Usually, only small fronds of erect red algae can be found on walls, but crustose algae are ubiquitous. The non-coralline red alga (*Peyssonnelia* sp. or '*Waernia* sp.', Wilce, proposed n. gen., n. sp.) grows as a millimetre thick crust often

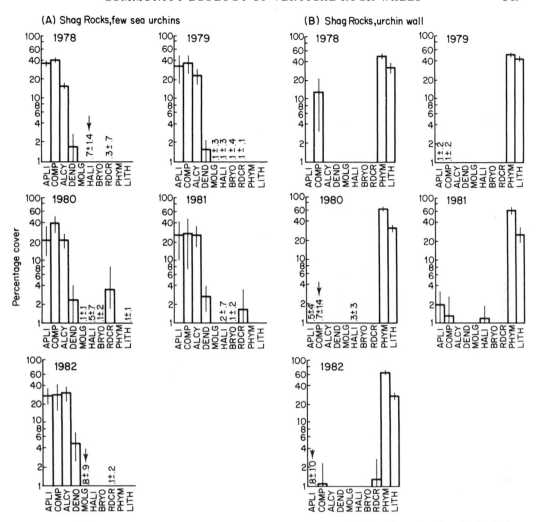

FIG. 23.2. Histograms of percentage cover for all organisms on two vertical rock walls at the Shag Rocks, Nahant, Massachusetts (1978–82). A, An invertebrate-dominated wall with few sea urchins ($< 1 \cdot m^{-2}$). B, A coralline algae-dominated wall with high urchin density ($52 \pm 31 \cdot m^{-2}$ for five years). Bars are mean values, lines are $\pm$ one S.D. for N (3–6) samples taken in that year. Numbers are means $\pm$ S.D. off the scale of the figure. Percentage cover determined by projecting slides of quadrats onto grids of 300 random dots per $0.15m^2$ per month. Monthly data are presented in Sebens (in review). Species abbreviations (see also Fig. 23.3) are as follows: APLI = *Aplidium*; COMP = amphipod tubes and bound detritus (complex); ALCY = *Alcyonium*; DEND = *Dendrodoa*; MOLG = *Molgula*; HALI = *Halichondria*; BRYO = encrusting bryozoans; RDCR = fleshy red crustose alga; PHYM = *Phymatolithon*; LITH = *Lithothamnion*; METR = *Metridium*; DIDE = *Didemnum*; BOLT = *Boltenia*; HYDR = hydroids.

buried beneath thick encrusting invertebrates where it may be able to persist indefinitely (Sebens, in press a) until uncovered again when predators remove the invertebrates.

Erect bryozoan and hydroid colonies form a temporary canopy above some of the encrusting organisms, especially during the summer and autumn. The amphipods *Corophium* and *Jassa* and several species of spionid polychaete worms (*Polydora* spp.) build tubes ($< 1cm$ long) that bind sediment and detritus thus forming a mat that encrusts rock surfaces and grows over some of the other

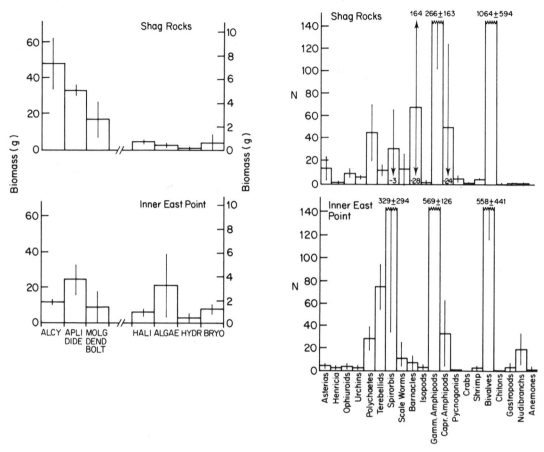

FIG. 23.3. Biomass and numerical histograms for: A, sessile organisms and B, mobile organisms identified from vertical rock walls at the Shag Rocks and at inner East Point (1978–80), monthly airlift samples from 500cm² area per month. Bars are mean values per 500cm², lines are ± one S.D. (N = 3 years). Species abbreviations as for Fig. 23.2.

invertebrates and algae. Detritus, flocculent sediment, and microalgae sometimes form a layer obscuring the encrusting invertebrates but which is not consolidated by tubicolous animals. This mat will be referred to throughout this discussion as a 'complex' (as in Sebens, in press a, in review) when it is thick and at least partially bound by tubes. Mobile predators found on the vertical walls (Fig. 23.3) include decorator crabs (*Hyas coarctatus* Leach, *H. araneus* (L.)), several nudibranch species (e.g. *Coryphella verrucosa* (M. Sars), *C. salmonacea* (Couthouy), *Aeolidia papillosa* (L.), *Onchidoris aspera* (Alder and Hancock) and sea stars (*Asterias vulgaris*, *A. forbesi* (Desor), *Henricia sanguinolenta* (Müller), *Leptasterias* spp.). Descriptions of rocky substratum assemblages from various depths in this area can be found in Harris (1976b), Hulbert *et al.* (1982), Sebens (1983c, in press a, in review), Witman (1984) and Logan *et al.* (1984).

The community changes perceptibly below about 18 metres depth. Light penetration is usually poor and fewer erect algae (e.g. *Ptilota serrata* Kützing) are present; encrusting corallines cover less area and invertebrates are much more common on horizontal surfaces than in the shallower zones. There are dense stands of erect sponges (*Isodictya*, *Haliclona*), mussel beds (*Modiolus modiolus*) and colonies of the octocoral, *Gersemia rubiformis* (Ehrenberg). The sea anemones *Metridium senile* and

Tealia crassicornis can be locally abundant. The tunicates *Aplidium pallidum, Didemnum albidum, Halocynthia pyriformis, Boltenia ovifera* (L.) and others are very common here as well. Brachiopods (*Terebratulina septentrionalis* (Couthouy)) are found frequently on the vertical walls and form small beds in places (Witman and Cooper, 1983) as they do in shallower areas of the Bay of Fundy (Noble *et al.*, 1976; Logan *et al.*, 1984). The large brilliant orange sea star *Hippasteria phrygiana* (Parelius), a predator on octocorals and other coelenterates, and suspension-feeding basket stars, *Gorgonocephalus* spp., are also found here. Deep water assemblages (to 30m) in the Gulf of Maine have been described by Hulbert *et al.* (1982), Logan *et al.* (1984) and Witman (1984).

Much of the field research discussed in this paper (Sebens, 1983c, in press a, in review) was conducted at two sites (6–9m depth) on opposite sides of East Point, Nahant, Massachusetts (42°25′N: 70°54′W). The inner East Point site (just South of Dive Beach) is protected from the strongest ocean swells, which normally come from the East to Northeast, but it does receive heavy wave action when the wind and waves come from the North. The substratum is a series of rock ledges, steps, and boulders from above the high tide line to approximately 10m depth. Most of the area at this site lacks sea urchin aggregations and thus develops a lush canopy of erect red algae and kelp on horizontal and sloping surfaces.

The exposed side of East Point (Shag Rocks) faces the incoming swells during most wind conditions. Wave action and thus surge effects are generally greater here and are easily felt by divers even at 6–9m depth (Sebens, in press b). Tidal currents are also more evident at this site, sometimes strong enough to make swimming at the surface difficult; this is never the case at the inner site. The Shag Rocks are solid ledges and steps with a few very large boulders extending from just at the high tide line (+ 3m) to a flat sand bottom with scattered boulders at 11m. Horizontal and sloping surfaces are almost completely covered by crustose coralline algae. Sea urchin aggregations are ubiquitous on horizontal and sloping surfaces, and on some vertical walls. The study sites at Nahant appear to be characteristic of the southern Gulf of Maine although Nahant is probably near the southern limit of this fauna; comparatively little shallow rock substratum is present further South.

Storm waves can be extreme at these sites. In February, 1978, a severe storm and blizzard produced waves estimated to be over 5m from trough to crest. Beach rocks were thrown across the access road and onto the lawn of the Marine Science Institute at Nahant (> 10m from the beach). Such storms pile urchins, crabs, kelp, lobsters, ascidians, mussels, sponges and many other sublittoral organisms on or above the beach and are an important source of mortality to sublittoral organisms (Witman, 1984). Another extreme storm occurred in October, 1982. However, no obvious change was noted in vertical rock wall assemblages before and after either storm (Sebens, in review). Boulders and cobbles moved around and scoured horizontal sublittoral surfaces during storms but they did not seem to affect the vertical surfaces except at their base. Plots of wave height versus season for the three sites show maximum values during the autumn, winter and early spring and calm water during summer and early autumn. Wave energy, and thus water movement in the sublittoral, increases from Inner East Point to the Shag Rocks to Halfway Rock, a very exposed site three kilometres offshore (Sebens, in press b).

The Gulf of Maine experiences one of the most extreme annual temperature ranges in the world. In February and March water temperature often drops below 0°C and sea ice forms on the shore. In contrast, August and early September temperatures are often > 20°C. Minimum/maximum recording thermometers placed at each of the three sites above showed no substantial difference in the temperature regime, but there were often large day-to-day differences within any one month (Sebens, 1983c, in review). In August, cold water from offshore flows landward with a rising tide and drops the temperature to about 8°C. The falling tide can bring water warmed in the shallow harbours and bays past the Nahant sites, with temperatures above 20°C.

Underwater visibility is greatest during winter months (to > 10m) and least during late summer and autumn ($<$ 4m) at all sites. Studies off Nova Scotia, at the northern end of the Gulf of Maine, show strong spring peaks in chlorophyll concentration and thus in phytoplankton, an important food resource for benthic suspension feeders (Mayzaud *et al.*, 1984). Zooplankton was quantified for two years at bi-weekly intervals at Nahant, and no large differences were found between the three sites ranging from protected to very exposed conditions (Sebens, in press b). Zooplankton concentrations during the six warmest months were, however, 3–5 times greater than during the six coldest months.

23.3 Competition for Space on Vertical Rock Walls

Sessile organisms are often limited by the space available for attachment and thus competition for such space is intense (Dayton, 1971, 1975; Paine, 1974; Sutherland, 1974, 1975, 1978; Jackson and Buss, 1975; Menge, 1976; Jackson, 1979; Lubchenco and Menge, 1978; Buss and Jackson, 1979; Russ, 1982; Quinn, 1982; reviewed in Connell, 1971, 1972, 1975; Jackson, 1977; Paine, 1977; Dayton, 1984; cf. Seed, this volume). Competitive success can result from physical or chemical aggression (Francis, 1973; Lang, 1973; Jackson and Buss, 1975; Sebens, 1976, 1984; Wellington, 1980), bull-dozing or smothering (Connell, 1961a,b, 1970; Harger, 1972; Paine, 1966, 1974; Jackson, 1979; Stebbing, 1973a,b; Osman, 1977, 1978; O'Connor *et al.*, 1980; Sebens, 1982, in press a), shading (Dayton, 1975), and possibly by localized food depletion (Buss, 1979; Buss and Jackson, 1981). Thicker colonies or species often have an advantage (Buss, 1980; Russ, 1982; Sebens, in press a) and can overtop thinner ones when they meet. Overgrowth may also lead to epizooism, however, (Rützler, 1970; Sarà, 1970; Dayton, 1971; Vance, 1978; Sebens, in press a) where the overgrown organism may be unharmed and may even receive some benefit from the relationship (Osman and Haugsness, 1981).

Certain sessile organisms form flat sheets on surfaces while others retain a small point of attachment and grow upward, forming a canopy above the substratum (hydroids, bryozoans, foliose algae). Erect forms may temporarily escape direct competition for rock surface and these two growth forms can thus coexist (Jackson, 1977). This is one possible form of 'niche partitioning' on homogeneous rock surfaces. If canopy-forming organisms become very abundant, however, they may compete for space or for food. Water flow through the canopy may be reduced and prey might thus be removed from the water before adjacent individuals had a chance to capture them (Buss and Jackson, 1979; Buss, 1979) thus slowing the growth of smaller neighbours (Sebens, 1983c). Erect algae may shade each other, resulting in competition for canopy space or light (Dayton, 1975).

The rock wall species at Nahant cover most available space and are clearly in competition (Sebens, in press a). To determine competitive relationships, areas were marked and photographed (10cm across each photograph) for two years (1979–81). All organism boundaries were traced from a projection of each photograph and the direction of edge overlap between organisms noted. Maps made from photographs taken a month or more apart were overlaid and aligned using recognizable fixed objects. Changes in space occupation were then outlined. An edge contact between the tunicates *Aplidium* and *Dendrodoa*, for example, might move over a month such that along 10mm of shared border *Aplidium* advanced over *Dendrodoa*, taking several square millimetres surface and burying part of the *Dendrodoa*. Some borders showed no movement in a month, resulting in at least temporary 'stand-offs'. Stand-offs are common occurrences among encrusting organisms in many littoral and sublittoral communities (Stebbing, 1973a,b; Karlson, 1980; Seed and O'Connor, 1981a; Russ, 1982). They may indicate either a tied competitive ability or that one or both of the organisms in contact grew in another direction where space was less strongly contested. Of 2254 interactions mapped and measured in this study, 934 (41%) were stand-offs that persisted for at least one month each (Sebens, in press a).

A hierarchy of competitive abilities was constructed from the 1320 interactions where changes

Kite-diagram panels (right side), labeled: Competitive rank (axis: 1 11, rank), Thickness (axis: >2 1 0 1 >2, cm), Resistance to grazing (axis: H N H, res), Resilience (axis: <1 2 3 2 <1, yrs).

Won: APLI, METR, ALCY, MOLG, DEND, COMP, BRYO, HALI, LITH, RDCR, PHYM

LOST: (Won ↓)	APLI	METR	ALCY	MOLG	DEND	COMP	BRYO	HALI	LITH	RDCR	PHYM
APLI	IN (3133)	S (N)	96 (908)	96 (397)	70 (196)	72 (3785)	100 (118)	90 (309)	–	100 (1910)	100 (20)
METR		S (10)	S (5)	S (11)	–	100 (15)	–	–	–	100 (20)	100 (8)
ALCY			S (166)	S (42)	S (90)	100 (893)	100 (28)	100 (196)	–	100 (217)	100 (37)
MOLG				IN (14)	S (39)	71 (313)	–	76 (21)	S (17)	100 (257)	–
DEND					S (16)	81 (215)	100 (10)	–	–	100 (124)	100 (7)
COMP						M	95 (181)	72 (546)	100 (15)	100 (1805)	100 (20)
BRYO							–	100 (12)	–	100 (214)	100 (40)
HALI								M	–	100 (90)	–
LITH									S (10)	100 (1070)	100 (1070)
RDCR										M	S (248)
PHYM											S (166)

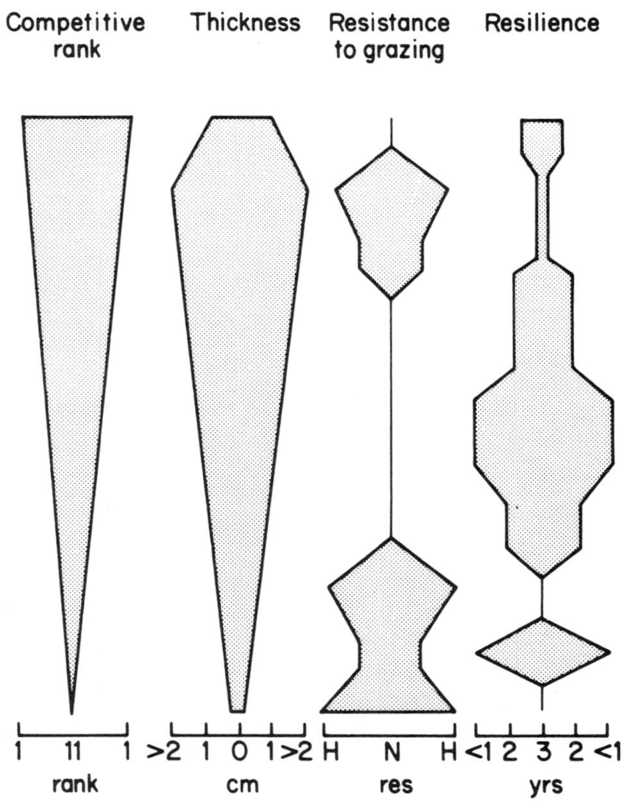

FIG. 23.4. Competitive interactions among encrusting species on vertical rock walls at Nahant, Massachusetts. The species or groups that won interactions (space taken per monthly sampling interval) are listed down the right from highest to lowest competitive ability. Lines connect species whose competitive ability could not be separated by this analysis alone. Entries in the matrix are percentage of interactions won, and amount of contact scored (mm shared border, in parentheses) over a two year period (1980–2). S = standoffs only, no wins or losses; (–) = no contacts observed; IN = intraspecific contacts with distinct borders, M = no zones of contact visible, borders merged. Kite-diagrams at right indicate ecological characteristics of each species or group. H = high resistance to grazing, N = low resistance. Resilience is measured in years to recolonize cleared areas. All data from Sebens (in press a). Species abbreviations as in Fig. 23.2.

occurred (Fig. 23.4). The colonial ascidian *Aplidium* overgrew all other species except the anemone *Metridium* and the larger *Alcyonium* colonies. *Alcyonium* and the two solitary tunicates *Molgula* and *Dendrodoa* were almost equal in competitive ability, but all three displaced most other species. The sponge *Halichondria* was overgrown predictably by all other invertebrates except encrusting bryozoans. Bryozoans overgrew encrusting algae, and the thicker coralline alga *Lithothamnion* predictably overgrew the thinner coralline *Phymatolithon*; the non-coralline red crustose alga was at the bottom of the hierarchy. Not enough active encounters occurred among some of the species to determine each one's exact standing.

Species with thick and massive growth forms were at the top of the hierarchy. Thin colonies ranked lower but may have an energetic advantage because of their high food-capturing surface to biomass ratio; the energy captured can be used to fuel rapid lateral growth. Such species, however, are at a clear disadvantage when they meet a thicker organism. Dominant species grew over inferior ones with no sign of damage by toxic substances (allelochemicals) or aggressive behaviour to aid the process. Only the anemone, *Metridium senile*, displays an aggressive behaviour, inflating specialized 'catch-tentacles' that can damage other anemones (Purcell, 1977) and the octocorals as well (K. Sebens, pers. obs.). Most competitive interactions in this system were hierarchical. Completely non-transitive 'network' relationships such as those noted by Buss and Jackson (1979) for cryptic coral reef fauna were not evident in this community. There were, however, several cases where two species or groups each overgrew the other a significant number of times (reversals) especially between *Aplidium*, *Dendrodoa*, tubicolous amphipods (complex), *Halichondria* and *Molgula*.

On vertical surfaces with sea urchins, the urchins prevent succession from proceeding to a 'climax' state (Fig. 23.5) which would comprise invertebrates that easily overgrow the crustose coralline algae (Sebens, in press a, in review). There is some evidence that crustose corallines can deter settlement of other algae or invertebrates directly onto their surfaces (Breitburg, 1984; Padilla, pers. comm.), but they are very susceptible to lateral overgrowth once the former organisms become established adjacent to them. In addition, the crustose algae can serve as a settlement cue for particular species (e.g. *Alcyonium* – Sebens, 1983a,b). Among the encrusting algae, *Lithothamnion* overgrew *Phymatolithon* and the red crust (Sebens, in press a). Overgrowth between the latter two species was difficult to observe, but the edge of *Phymatolithon* can advance when the red crust is present adjacent to it. When urchins have stopped grazing an area for a few weeks, tubicolous amphipods recruit rapidly and develop a 'complex' on the surface of the coralline algae and on rock. This complex is quickly removed when urchins return, leaving the buried algae unharmed.

Lithothamnion, the competitive dominant among the encrusting algae in this assemblage (Steneck, 1981; Sebens, in press a), is susceptible to attack from at least two sources. Urchins break off the growing edges of *Lithothamnion* and boring invertebrates (e.g. polychaetes, *Dodecaceria* sp.) weaken the thick skeleton causing it to exfoliate; *Phymatolithon* does not suffer from this disturbance. Large fragments of exfoliated *Lithothamnion* are often seen attached to urchins. Within this simplified assemblage, succession proceeds from rock to red crustose algae to *Phymatolithon* then to *Lithothamnion* with 'complex' appearing temporarily at any stage. Competitive ability increases with successional stage but the true 'climax' (an invertebrate assemblage on rock walls) is prevented by continuous grazing. This dependence of coralline algae on their grazers to prevent the establishment of better competitors is a widespread mutualistic association (Steneck, 1982, 1983). The other herbivores on coralline algae (*Tonicella marmorea*, *Acmaea testudinalis*), common at some sites in the Gulf of Maine, were very rare at Nahant.

For a given species of encrusting organism there are basically four categories of other species that it can potentially recognize and react to: (i) superior or approximately equal competitors that pose a direct threat of overgrowth, (ii) inferior competitors that can be overgrown predictably, (iii) inferior

Vertical wall with few or no sea urchins

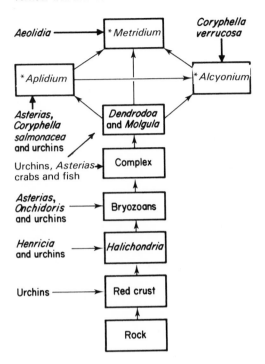

Vertical wall with urchins

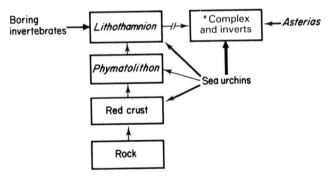

FIG. 23.5. Block diagram of succession, competition, and predation on sublittoral rock walls at sites in Northern Massachusetts. Succession begins with cleared rock and moves upward to one or more alternative 'climax' stages (*) which would persist indefinitely without physical disturbance or predation on that species. Competitive abilities of sessile species are indicated by arrows pointing from poorer to better competitors. Disturbance (physical scraping or predation) can set succession back to cleared rock at any stage. Important predators are indicated by arrows impinging laterally on each stage (thicker arrows indicating more intense predation). A high diversity of encrusting species is maintained on vertical walls with few or no sea urchins, but with some sea stars and other predators, by frequent small-scale disturbances (predation). Heavy sea urchin predation on vertical walls results in a simple community of encrusting coralline algae that is prevented from reaching its climax stage.

competitors than can be used as settlement substrata or as cues to appropriate habitat, and (iv) epibionts that can or cannot be tolerated. There is accumulating evidence that certain sessile species can recognize and react to the first category (e.g. corals – Lang, 1973; Wellington, 1980; bryozoans – Jackson, 1979). Clearly not all species can recognize superior competitors, or do anything to deter their advance even if they are recognized. Competitors of approximately equal ability can often be deterred by construction of raised colony edges (Buss, 1980). One appropriate response when a superior competitor is detected is movement away from that point (e.g. sea anemones – Sebens, 1976) or growth in a new direction (e.g. bryozoans – Jackson, 1979). The Pacific reef coral *Pocillopora damicornis* (L.), once damaged by mesenterial filament extrusion from the 'superior' competitors *Pavona* spp. responds by developing 'sweeper tentacles' with nematocysts that can damage *Pavona* and can thus prevent overgrowth or displacement (Wellington, 1980). Recognition of superior competitors may also occur at the settling larva stage. Certain bryozoan larvae avoid settling near ascidians that are known to overgrow the established bryozoan colonies (Grosberg, 1981; Young and Chia, 1981). There is some evidence that larvae of the octocoral, *Alcyonium siderium*, will delay metamorphosis in the presence of the colonial ascidian, *Aplidium pallidum* (Sebens, 1983a), which can overgrow small octocoral colonies (Sebens, 1982b).

The second group, inferior competitors, may be 'recognized' only in that they put up little or no resistance to overgrowth; growth rates over such species may not differ from those over bare rock (Sebens, in press a). However, larvae may be able to distinguish between the surfaces of inferior competitors and the rock surface (Sebens, 1983b). Since bare rock surfaces are soon fouled by a variety of algal and bacterial films, the surfaces of crustose algae (coralline, fleshy red algae) may be easier to recognize chemically and may thus serve as cues to appropriate habitat.

Finally, epibionts can generally be discouraged by sloughing or by chemical exudation. However, certain epibionts may be tolerated because they are harmless (Sarà, 1970), provide tactile camouflage (Vance, 1978), or have a more direct rôle in discouraging competitors (Osman and Haugsness, 1981) or predators (West, 1976). The sponge *Leucosolenia* grows loosely attached to *Aplidium* and to amphipod tubes on the New England sublittoral rock walls, and does no obvious damage (Sebens, in press a) although it may interfere with filtration by the former. The large sublittoral mussel *Modiolus modiolus* often supports an invertebrate and algal community (Witman, 1984) that makes it seem like part of the rock itself. Although there is as yet no experimental evidence, this covering may camouflage the mussel from its most important predator, the sea star, *Asterias vulgaris*. Sometimes epibionts cannot be prevented from establishing themselves and thus result in damage to the host organism. This occurs when kelp plants attach to *Modiolus* and cause the mussels to be pulled from the substratum during storms (Witman, 1984). There are no obvious examples of this effect among the rock wall biota; however both crustose corallines and fleshy red crusts are often overgrown by invertebrates which are later removed by predators such as sea urchins (Sebens, in press a). The ability to persist underneath other organisms, at very low light levels and for at least several months, is an important feature of these crusts that allows them to occupy significant amounts of space even though they are very low on the competitive hierarchy.

23.4 Predation on Vertical Rock Wall Organisms

Predation modifies the results of competition in benthic communities. Better competitors are often preferred by selective predators (Connell, 1961a,b, 1970; Paine, 1966, 1974; Paine and Vadas, 1969; Dayton, 1971; Menge, 1976; Lubchenco, 1978; reviewed in Paine, 1966; Connell, 1971, 1972, 1975; Menge and Sutherland, 1976), and groups of species may suffer more generalized predation or grazing (Karlson, 1978; Vance, 1978, 1979). Physical disturbance and non-selective predation may have similar effects (Dayton, 1971, 1975; Paine, 1974; Menge, 1976; Paine and Levin, 1981; reviewed in

Levin and Paine, 1974; Connell and Slatyer, 1977; Whittaker and Levin, 1977). A cleared patch forms when a competitive dominant or an entire assemblage is removed; a replacement series or 'succession' then ensues. The best recruits generally arrive first and the better competitors arrive later in both marine and terrestrial assemblages (Horn, 1974; Levin and Paine, 1974; Armstrong, 1976; Connell and Slatyer, 1977; Whittaker and Levin, 1977; Paine and Levin, 1981; Sebens, in press a). Such a replacement or successional series can be permanently or temporarily arrested at an intermediate stage if a species that may not be the best competitor can, however, monopolize a patch of space indefinitely (Sutherland, 1974, 1978; Jackson, 1977; Denley and Underwood, 1979; Dean and Hurd, 1980; Sebens, 1982; modelled in Connell and Slatyer, 1977). An array of such patches at different stages of 'succession' can produce a very heterogeneous spatial pattern (MacArthur and Levins, 1964; Levins and Culver, 1971; Horn and MacArthur, 1972; Smith, 1972; Slatkin, 1974; Connell, 1975; Whittaker and Levin, 1977). Most real substrata with diverse assemblages probably reflect this mechanism as well as a 'niche separation' of species that can utilize different substratum features (crevices, platforms, etc.) (Lewis, 1964; Jackson, 1977).

23.5 Sea Urchin Predation

Where sea urchin aggregations have been present for one or more years, the substratum is a coralline algal pavement comprising the knobbed coralline algae *Lithothamnion glaciale* and *L. lemoinae* and one or more species of smooth corallines (Breen and Mann, 1976a,b; Steneck, 1978, 1982). Urchin 'herds' and their feeding fronts can stretch for hundreds of metres (Miller and Mann, 1973; Mann, 1977; Garnick, 1978; Bernstein *et al.*, 1981, 1983; Chapman, 1981) and there is little that the urchins do not consume. Foliose algae (e.g. Larson *et al.*, 1980) and most encrusting invertebrates (Sebens, in review) are grazed rapidly and completely. The coralline crusts are continually grazed, although tissue is left alive between the knobs of *Lithothamnion*, and within the calcium carbonate layers of smooth species, such as *Clathromorphum* and probably *Phymatolithon*, that can regenerate the surface cells (Steneck, 1978, 1982, 1983).

In 1979 we added urchins to a vertical rock wall that was previously devoid of urchins; the effect was striking. Within 2–3 months all *Aplidium* and the mat of amphipod and polychaete tubes (complex) had been stripped from the wall and only bare rock, a few of the larger *Alcyonium* colonies, and the fleshy red crustose alga remained (Sebens, in review). The urchins were removed the following year after which the complex and *Aplidium* returned within the next year to approximately pre-experiment percentage cover. This experiment illustrates the importance of sea urchin grazing on invertebrate rock wall assemblages and the differential impact that urchins can have on their prey. *Alcyonium* and the red crustose alga were affected far less than all other species in this experiment. Topography modifies the effect of urchins; echinoids apparently have a difficult time remaining on vertical or undercut areas where there is development of a thick invertebrate cover probably because the urchins' tube feet cannot adhere well to such surfaces. Thus, there is an abrupt transition from coralline algae-dominated walls, when such surfaces slope even slightly outward, to invertebrate-dominated walls where the walls are vertical to undercut (Sebens, in review). Karlson (1978) and Vance (1979) have also shown similar effects of urchin grazing on invertebrate assemblages in sublittoral areas of the Southeast and Southwest coasts of North America, respectively (see also Sammarco, 1980, and reviews by Lawrence, 1975; Moore, 1983a).

The common predators on sea urchins at Nahant are crabs (*Cancer borealis* Stimpson), fish (*Macrozoarces americanus* (Bloch and Schneider)), sea stars (*Asterias vulgaris*) and to a lesser extent lobsters (*Homarus americanus* Milne-Edwards) (Sebens, in review). The fish and crabs have the greatest effect on urchin populations. The eelpout (*Macrozoarces*) appears in late spring and packs its gut with hundreds of small urchins. Crabs (*Cancer*) have been observed breaking apart and feeding on large adult urchins. Wave action and rolling cobbles or boulders may also account for high pulses of adult urchin mortality during storms, after which many dead urchins and broken tests wash up on beaches.

Sea urchin populations have apparently expanded over the past century or less (Mann and Breen, 1972; Breen and Mann, 1976b; Mann, 1977; Wharton and Mann, 1981) although quantitative 'baseline' data for this assertion are lacking. This was also the period of time during which a great increase in lobster harvesting occurred, leading Mann and Breen (1972) to postulate a link between declining lobster numbers and increased urchin populations, assuming lobsters to be the most important urchin predators. Lobster diets in the field and in laboratory choice experiments (Himmelman and Steele, 1971; Ennis, 1973; Evans and Mann, 1977; Elner, unpubl.; Sebens, in review), however, suggest that urchins are a relatively small and unpreferred part of lobster diets. Lobster diets consist primarily of crabs, other lobsters, mussels and sea stars. On the other hand, decreased lobster populations may have allowed crab populations (*Cancer borealis* particularly) to expand. Crabs compete with lobsters for refuge holes (Cooper and Uzmann, 1980), and are the main prey of lobsters at our study sites in northern Massachusetts (Sebens, in review). Crabs are important predators on urchins and thus declining lobster populations may just as easily have increased rather than decreased the overall predation pressure on urchins.

Something must check the expansion of urchin populations, and both predators and disease have been implicated. Massive urchin mortality, possibly caused by microbial infection, was observed at our sites in northern Massachusetts in September, 1980. The urchins' ectoderm and spines are lost and they finally lose their ability to cling to rocks and are washed into crevices where they rot or are eaten by *Asterias* and crabs. This phenomenon has occurred several times in other parts of their range (e.g. Nova Scotia – Scheibling and Stevenson, 1984), and may be amoeboid in origin.

23.6 Other Common Predators

The sea star, *Asterias vulgaris*, and its close relative, *Asterias forbesi*, can be found in dense aggregations at the lower edge of littoral mussel beds in the southern Gulf of Maine (Menge, 1979, 1982a, 1983). Mussels are the preferred prey of both species at Nahant (Gonzales, unpubl. quoted in Sebens, in review). Most *Asterias* migrate to the sublittoral late in the autumn and some individuals are sublittoral year-round, preying on *Modiolus*, *Aplidium*, barnacles, urchins, polychaetes, bryozoans, and on each other (Menge, 1979, 1982a; Hulbert, 1980; Sebens, in review). Their major effect on the sublittoral rock wall community may be the removal of barnacles (*Balanus balanus*) and juvenile mussels (*Mytilus*, *Modiolus*) that recruit each year and the clearing of space on rock walls by preying on *Aplidium* and other ascidians. However, *Aplidium* is low on the preference hierarchy of *Asterias*, which will lose weight on a diet solely of *Aplidium* (Gonzales, unpubl. quoted in Sebens, in review).

The crabs *Cancer borealis*, *C. irroratus* Say, *Hyas coarctatus* and *H. araneus* all forage both on vertical walls and over horizontal surfaces. Only the two *Hyas* species seem to spend most of their time on rock walls and may thus have a potential effect on the encrusting invertebrates. *Hyas* grazes on algal fronds and polychaetes and tears into the *Aplidium*, extracting worms underneath and doing damage to the tunicate; it may also eat the *Aplidium*. The large predatory snail, *Buccinum undatum* L., can be locally common, feeding on molluscs (e.g. *Modiolus*, *Mytilus*), or on dead fish and crabs with aggregations of *Asterias vulgaris* (see also Nielsen, 1975). Wave action and predator foraging loosen patches of littoral mussels (*Mytilus edulis*) and wash them into the sublittoral where they collect in rock crevices; *Asterias*, crabs, urchins, and the snail *Buccinum* congregate there and exploit this adventitious resource (Table 23.1).

The common shallow sublittoral fish like the lumpfish, *Cyclopterus lumpus* (L.), the sculpin, *Myoxycephalus aeneus* (Mitchill), the gunnel, *Pholis gunnellus* (L.), the shanny, *Ulvaria subbifurcata* (Storer), the clingfish, *Liparis liparis* (L.), pollack, *Pollachius virens* (L.), and juvenile cunner, *Tautogolabrus adspersus* (Walbaum) (Table 23.1) feed primarily on small crustaceans. *Ulvaria* preys on polychaetes somewhat more frequently than on crustaceans. The flounders (winter flounder, *Pseudopleuronectes americanus* (Walbaum), yellowtail, *Limandia ferruginea* (Storer)) are broad generalists feeding on tunicates (*Aplidium, Molgula*), algae (*Chondrus*), bryozoans (*Electra*), polychaetes, and crustaceans. *Tautogolabrus* migrate to the littoral zone daily and feed primarily on mussels (Chao, 1973; Edwards *et al.*, 1982), although juveniles pick many small crustaceans off sublittoral surfaces.

TABLE 23.1

Predators of the common encrusting species or groups on vertical rock walls at Nahant, Massachusetts (condensed from Sebens, in review). Numbers in parentheses are observations of that prey type followed by total prey identified for that predator species. Sea urchins (*S. droebachiensis*) are divided into groups foraging on a sublittoral mussel bed (M) and those on coralline algal pavement (C). N = numerous observations, not quantified. Data on *L. liparis, U. subbifurcata, P. gunnellus* and *M. aeneus* from S. Norton (unpubl.) given as percentage of diet.

Species or group	Predators
Aplidium pallidum	*Coryphella salmonacea* (45/45), *Asterias vulgaris* (33/362), *Limanda ferruginea* (5/19), *Cancer borealis* (16/450), *Pseudopleuronectes americanus* (455/723), *Strongylocentrotus droebachiensis* (N)
Alcyonium siderium	*Coryphella verrucosa* (330/478), *Tritonia* sp. (60/60)
solitary ascidians (*Molgula, Dendrodoa*)	*Cancer borealis* (16/450), *S. droebachiensis* (N)
Metridium senile	*Aeolidia papillosa* (120/120)
Halichondria panicea	*Henricia sanguinolenta* (14/50)
encrusting bryozoans	*Onchidoris aspera* (115/115), *Polycera dubia* (6/6), *Asterias vulgaris* (N – Hulbert, 1980)
red crustose alga	*S. droebachiensis* (N)
Lithothamnion glaciale	*S. droebachiensis* C (499/677)
Phymatolithon rugulosum	*S. droebachiensis* C (172/677), *Tonicella marmorea* (50/50), *Acmaea tessulata* (80/80)
Halisarca dujardini	*Cadlina laevis* (8/8)
gammarid amphipods (tubicolous and others)	*Pseudopleuronectes americanus* (43/723), *Pollachius virens* (N), *Tautogolabrus adspersus* (30/300), *Liparis liparis* (29%), *Ulvaria subbifurcata* (15%), *Pholis gunnellus* (49%), *Myoxycephalus aeneus* (46%)
Modiolus modiolus	*Buccinum undatum* (7/21), *Asterias vulgaris* (18/362)
Mytilus edulis	*Asterias forbesi* (100/104), *Asterias vulgaris* (174/362), *Buccinum undatum* (14/21), *S. droebachiensis* M (200/200), *Homarus americanus* (298/585), *Cancer borealis* (131/450), *Tautogolabrus adspersus* (370/394), *Macrozoarces americanus* (68/3414), *Pseudopleuronectes americanus* (123/723)

The most specialized predators in this community are nudibranchs (Table 23.1): *Onchidoris aspera* feeds on the bryozoan *Electra* (Smith and Sebens, 1983), *Aeolidia papillosa* on the anemone *Metridium* (Harris, 1973), *Cadlina laevis* (L.) on the sponge *Halisarca*, and *Coryphella salmonacea* (Couthouy) on the ascidian *Aplidium* (Sebens, in review). *Coryphella verrucosa* (Sars) has a slightly less specialized diet, preying on *Alcyonium*, the hydroids *Tubularia* spp., and a few other hydroid and ascidian species (Morse, 1969; Kuzirian, 1979; Sebens, 1983c, in review). The limpet, *Acmaea testudinalis*, is also highly specialized (Steneck, 1982); in the sublittoral zone it lives and feeds only on smooth crustose coralline algae (e.g. *Clathromorphum*, *Phymatolithon*) (note also Farrow and Clokie, 1979).

The specialist predators may limit some of their prey populations. Examples include *Coryphella verrucosa* feeding on hydroids (Morse, 1969; Macleod and Valiela, 1975) and on *Alcyonium* (Sebens, 1983c) and *Aeolidia papillosa* on *Metridium*. Hydroids are abundant from mid-summer to late autumn and their virtual disappearance corresponds with the appearance of numerous predatory nudibranchs in the autumn. The hydroids and some of their predators become scarce by winter, although *Coryphella verrucosa* persists in large numbers until spring. When the hydroid prey species are depleted, *Coryphella* begins feeding on the octocoral *Alcyonium* more frequently. Hydroids (*Tubularia* sp.) were strongly preferred to *Alcyonium* in laboratory choice experiments (Sebens, unpubl.) and the switch to *Alcyonium* probably occurs only when *Tubularia* are depleted. Predation by *Coryphella* may also be the cause of much of the mortality of *Alcyonium* (10–15% annual colony disappearance – Sebens, in press b) although the smaller colonies can also be grazed off by sea urchins or overgrown by other encrusting organisms, such as the tunicate *Aplidium* (Sebens, 1982).

The anemone, *Metridium senile*, suffers heavy mortality each year, primarily from the nudibranch, *Aeolidia papillosa* (Harris, 1973, 1976a; Sebens, in review). Even the largest *Metridium* are attacked by *Aeolidia*, which feeds singly or in groups of 2–12 or more individuals. In most years, *Aeolidia* may be the only important source of mortality to *Metridium* in areas free of rocks or boulders that could move and scrape during storms. However, in September, 1984, the temperature at Halfway Rock reached 21°C even at 16m depth. This site had never experienced temperatures greater than 15°C from July, 1978, to July, 1984 (max./min. thermometer records – Sebens, in review). Many *Metridium* (10–50% of populations) were dead, decaying, or falling off the rock substratum. Given the position of *Metridium* at the top of the competitive hierarchy and its rapid proliferation by basal fragmentation, it is surprising that it is so limited in extent; annual predation by *Aeolidia* may prevent new aggregations from forming and persisting and infrequent physical catastrophes may periodically decimate established populations.

The specialist consumer of ascidians, *Coryphella salmonacea*, is less common and feeds slowly in aquarium experiments. This nudibranch probably does not have a significant effect on its prey, the tunicate *Aplidium*, at these sites. *Onchidoris aspera* can be locally abundant, and specializes on the bryozoan, *Electra pilosa*, growing on algae and more rarely on rock surfaces (Smith and Sebens, 1983). It is possible that *Onchidoris* limits the *Electra* populations to some extent although this bryozoan becomes the most common species on algal fronds each year.

At a community level, specialist predators may limit the populations of some of the large, long-lived, competitively dominant species such as *Metridium* and *Alcyonium*. The ephemeral hydroids and erect bryozoans, on the other hand, are consumed at a season when declining water temperatures would impair their growth and survival in any case. In general, species with defenses against generalist predators may in fact become both common and predictable enough to support specialist predator populations. When the prey organisms are patchily distributed, they can coexist with their predators; the predators can then cause only local extinction of their prey (as in sea pens – Birkeland, 1974). Specialist predators may have a diversifying effect on the assemblage as a whole by limiting their prey to a small fraction of the total available substratum (as for mussels – Paine, 1966, 1974). This effect is often directed toward common or dominant species, possibly because it is impossible for specialist predators to persist on very rare prey species.

23.7 Disturbance and Species Diversity

Any small fraction of a square metre of vertical wall predictably harbours twenty or more sessile species, each represented by at least a few individuals or colonies. This species diversity persists each year even though the actual rock substratum below is smooth and free of discernibly different micro-habitats. How can this number of species maintain coexisting populations on what appears to be a single resource? There are few possible ways to divide up the available physical habitat. However, species may subdivide this spatial resource temporally. For example, the seasonal erect bryozoans and hydroid colonies appear in the summer and disappear by late autumn. The encrusting species are less clearly seasonal, but can be considered along a longer, successional, time span.

When an individual or colony is preyed on or physically dislodged (termed 'disturbance', as in Dayton, 1971; Connell and Slatyer, 1977; Connell, 1978; Sousa, 1979a,b; Paine and Levin, 1981), 'free' space is generated in recognizable 'patches'. This 'free' space may be bare rock or may be covered by any of the crustose algae, which can be grown over by most of the invertebrates, and is therefore considered 'available space'. These patches are colonized (i) by species whose larvae are abundant in the plankton, (ii) by lateral growth of bordering organisms, (iii) by juveniles produced by nearby adults, or (iv) by asexually produced fragments. The earliest colonists are often overgrown by later arrivals or by colonies growing laterally into the patch (Sebens, in press a). Recolonization of cleared patches in littoral communities involves a fairly predictable sequence of species that depends on the season when the patch was created and on the size of the patch (Dayton, 1971, 1975; Lubchenco and Menge, 1978; Paine and Levin, 1981). Without disturbance, a single species or a very few species high in the competitive hierarchy could theoretically monopolize all available space and diversity would be low. At the highest rate of disturbance the species which recruit or grow slowly, and which are likely to be the better competitors, are prevented from becoming established and only the early successional species could persist. Diversity would again be low. If there are particular species able to resist the disturbance (e.g. coralline algae with constant urchin grazing) it will be these species that dominate the substratum rather than early successional species in the latter case. Continuous disturbance by physical or biological factors is therefore necessary to provide free space for early successional species and to maintain a high diversity of species on this homogeneous resource. Any area of rock wall thus consists of a distribution of patches, each at a different stage of recovery, and each with different species groups (as described by Paine and Levin, 1981, for rocky shore communities).

Disturbance rates within some intermediate range allow early successional 'fugitive' species, later successional 'dominant' species, and disturbance-resistant species to coexist (e.g. theoretical models – Levins and Culver, 1971; Horn and MacArthur, 1972; Levin and Paine, 1974; Armstrong, 1976; Levin, 1976; Hastings, 1980; cf. Connell, this volume). There will thus be some intermediate rate of disturbance that maximizes diversity by allowing the coexistence of many species whose rates of recruitment and competitive abilities are inversely related (Levin and Paine, 1974; Connell, 1978; Hastings, 1980). This relationship has been found in a number of marine habitats (Paine and Vadas, 1969; Lubchenco, 1978; Osman, 1978; Sousa, 1979a,b; Paine and Levin, 1981; Sebens, in review). If the space-clearing factor acts preferentially on the competitively dominant species (e.g. selective predators – Paine, 1966, 1974; Menge and Sutherland, 1976), then lower total rates of disturbance might produce the maximum diversity.

Vertical walls at Nahant cover the entire range from low species diversity with low disturbance rate (*Aplidium*-dominated), to high diversity with intermediate disturbance rate (several invertebrate species, Fig. 23.1), to low diversity with high disturbance rate, via urchins (coralline algae, Fig. 23.1).

Winter storms do not appear to inflict serious physical disturbance on these walls. Urchins and the sea star, *Asterias vulgaris*, are probably the major causes of space clearing. Both species are common and active much of the year. All vertical walls are frequented by *Asterias*, while only those at the Shag Rocks and Halfway Rock sites are grazed by urchins. However, the diversities of species on certain walls at both sites are very similar. At the protected site, only the *Aplidium*-dominated wall has a very low diversity. This wall lacks a population of *Alcyonium* but also has no urchins and fewer *Asterias* than do the nearby walls with *Alcyonium* populations (Sebens, in review) and thus probably experiences the lowest total rate of space clearing. The relationship between species abundance or diversity and number of predators shows a maximum at intermediate predator densities although there are several sites with low species number or diversity even at intermediate predator densities (Sebens, in review).

A second measure of disturbance rate is the amount of 'clear space' being generated on rock surfaces (Huston, 1979; Quinn, 1979). The standing percentage of clear space represents a balance between disturbance (physical and biological) and recovery; in this case recovery occurs by settlement and by lateral growth of encrusting organisms. When encrusting invertebrates or fleshy algae are removed by urchins, sea stars or other predators, the underlying substratum is often covered by the fleshy red crustose alga or by crustose corallines, and only rarely is it bare rock (Sebens, in press a). Even intense urchin grazing on coralline crusts rarely scrapes them down to bare rock; only the upper cell layers are removed. Thus, the annual mean percentage cover of rock and crustose algae combined (= 'cleared space') may well be the best overall measure of 'disturbance' since, without such disturbance, all of these surfaces would be rapidly overgrown (e.g. < 1–3 months – Sebens, in press a, in review). The greatest number of coexisting sessile species on rock walls in northern Massachusetts also occurs at intermediate rates of space clearing (Fig. 23.7). Clear space on vertical surfaces with few or no sea urchins seems to form on a very fine-grained scale: newly cleared patches are generally only a few millimetres across. These vertical walls are thus a good example of communities with small-scale frequent disturbance (*sensu* Connell and Slatyer, 1977).

Disturbance also allows the larvae or asexual propagules of certain species to recruit and survive without being rapidly overgrown (e.g. *Alcyonium* larvae, Sebens, 1983c). This can result in a stable coexistence between a dominant competitor (e.g. *Aplidium*) and a species which is an inferior competitor when small, but which can hold its acquired space when it has grown to some threshold (e.g. *Alcyonium* – Sebens, 1982b). Once the disturbance rate has increased beyond this level, species abundance and diversity steadily decrease. The persistence of a species such as *Alcyonium* probably depends on a disturbance rate that is neither too high nor too low.

23.8 Alternative Locally Stable States of the Vertical Wall Community

The vertical rock wall assemblages described in this study showed year-to-year variability in percentage cover of component species (Fig. 23.2), but never drastically changed composition or overall character (Sebens, in review). They represent 'alternative stable states' of the shallow sublittoral community within the time frame of this study (1978–84), as defined by Sutherland (1974, 1975, 1978), Sutherland and Karlson (1977) and Kay and Butler (1983) (see also Connell and Sousa, 1983 for alternative definitions).

Each of the characteristic states of this community is, in many ways, self-perpetuating. Small local perturbations (e.g. cleared areas) are followed by a return to the previous state (Sebens, in press a, in review). Temporary reduction of urchin grazing on coralline algal surfaces allows colonization by invertebrates, as in exclosure experiments. When urchins are allowed access again, they return the substratum to its pre-perturbation state. Similarly, temporary increases in urchin grazing on vertical walls change the assemblages drastically (e.g. urchin addition experiments – Sebens, in review), yet they return to almost the previous state within a year when urchins are removed. Areas of vertical wall dominated by the octocoral *Alcyonium* or the anemone *Metridium* are able to maintain themselves indefinitely, in part by protecting the developing juveniles within from predation (Sebens, 1983c). However, if most of an *Alcyonium* bed were removed, it might never recover and could become locally extinct. When predators are few, the ascidian, *Aplidium pallidum*, dominates space. Neither *Metridium* nor *Alcyonium* can become established on such walls because *Aplidium* easily overgrows small individuals of both species (Fig. 23.1). Large scale perturbations, on the other hand, could cause a portion of the community to switch to another state and to approach a new stable state. For example, movement of an urchin 'herd' into a new area dominated by foliose algae or invertebrates will turn that area into a coralline algal pavement that will persist as long as the urchins remain (Himmelman *et al.*, 1983; Witman, 1984; Sebens, in review).

Once a small area of rock wall becomes dominated by any single species of encrusting organism, it may gradually be replaced by other species or it may be able to defend the space acquired from such encroachment. Connell and Slatyer (1977) noted that succession may stop at any pre-climax stage if the species present are able to prevent the potential 'climax' species from successfully recruiting and establishing itself. Encrusting coralline algae can dominate space on vertical rock walls where sea urchins are very abundant. The urchins prevent the larvae of invertebrates and the propagules of other algae from becoming established. In additon, crustose corallines may be able to discourage settlement of some species by their own surface properties (Breitburg, 1984). In this case, the species that can persist under heavy grazing pressure can hold space indefinitely, although removal of the grazers would allow succession to continue to a macroalgal bed on sloping surfaces or to an invertebrate assemblage on vertical walls.

If neither *Alcyonium siderium* nor *Metridium senile* is abundant nearby, it is most likely that rock walls with few sea urchins will become dominated by the colonial ascidian, *Aplidium pallidum* (Sebens, in press a) which is competitively superior to all other invertebrate and encrusting algal species, including small *Alcyonium* (Sebens, 1982b) and small *Metridium* (unpubl. obs.). *Aplidium* has several

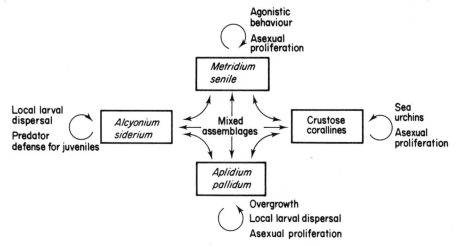

FIG. 23.6. Four alternative locally stable states of the vertical rock wall community at Nahant, Massachusetts, in which one species dominates > 50% of the primary substratum. Positive feedback loops indicate processes that maintain each state. High levels of predation on *Alyconium, Metridium* or *Aplidium* could destabilize those populations and precipitate a change to a mixed assemblage or to one of the other locally stable states. A massive sea urchin mortality event (e.g. disease) or lateral movement of an urchin 'herd' would destabilize the crustose coralline state causing a switch to one of the invertebrate-dominated assemblages.

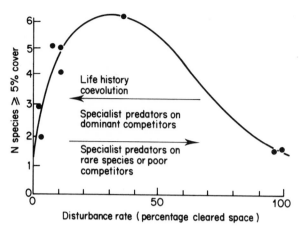

FIG. 23.7. The effect of small-scale biological disturbance on a vertical rock wall community (from Sebens, in review). The number of species consistently accounting for > 5% cover over 5yr is plotted against the disturbance rate measured as the percentage cover of recently cleared space (bare rock, red crustose algae, and crustose coralline algae, all of which are rapidly overgrown without a clearing event). The evolution of life histories that allow positive density-dependent feedback (stabilizing patches of one organism) will decrease local (within wall) but increase large-scale (between wall) diversity because separated walls can be monopolized by different species. Increasing the abundance of specialist predators on dominant competitors will cause the highest local diversity at lower overall disturbance rates (via generalist predators and physical scraping), while increasing the abundance of specialist predators on poor competitors will push the diversity peak to the right; greater overall disturbance rates would be necessary to open space for recruitment by these species (graphical model modified from Paine, 1977; Connell, 1978; Lubchenco, 1978).

predators in addition to sea urchins, and reaches its greatest percentage cover where the combination of urchin and sea star predators is rare (Sebens, in review). However, if a rock wall is very near another with established populations of *Metridium*, the small anemones produced asexually by pedal laceration may be able to migrate and establish a new clonal aggregation that can exclude *Aplidium* and *Alcyonium*. *Metridium* uses its elongate 'catch-tentacles' to defend acquired space from other anemones (Purcell, 1977) and from encroachment by *Alcyonium* (Sebens, unpubl.). Given the large size and dense packing of *Metridium* it is unlikely that it would ever lose space in purely competitive encounters. Only massive physical disturbance, such as boulders rolling during storms, temperature shock, or a large influx of the nudibranch, *Aeolidia papillosa* (a specialist predator of *Metridium*), could remove most of a local population. This nudibranch recruits during the late autumn or winter and consumes large numbers of *Metridium* each year (Harris, 1973, 1976a; Sebens, in review).

The last distinct state of the vertical rock wall community is domination by the octocoral, *Alcyonium siderium*, which can cover more than half of the primary substratum (Fig. 23.6) and can persist for many years (Sebens, in press a, in review). *Alcyonium* can persist even when *Aplidium* is abundant because even moderately large colonies ($\geq$ 15mm diameter) are immune to overgrowth (Sebens, 1982b). It is less clear how *Alcyonium* persists when adjacent to dense *Metridium* populations, although it appears that *Metridium* does best under high water flow conditions, often at the tops of rock walls. *Alcyonium*, which also does best under high flow conditions (Sebens, in press b), is relegated to lower levels on rock walls when *Metridium* is abundant. There may therefore be some degree of habitat partitioning between these two potentially dominant species.

There are at least four alternative states of the rock wall community in which one species dominates (*Metridium*, *Alcyonium*, *Aplidium*, or crustose corallines) and many mixed assemblages (Fig. 23.6). Each of the four alternatives is locally stable in a 'density-dependent' manner. When *Metridium* populations are dense, the anemones can probably swamp their specialist predator *Aeolidia* by local asexual proliferation and can prevent competitors from encroaching by a combination of overgrowth and agonistic behaviour using their tentacles. *Alcyonium* can maintain space by growing too tall to be overgrown, by dispersing larvae locally, and by protecting those larvae from predators. *Aplidium* maintains dense populations by overgrowth of competitors, local colony fragmentation and expansion, and short range larval dispersal. All three species have processes that function best at high population density, thus maintaining a stable community 'state' until a major catastrophic disturbance causes a state change. The coralline algae/urchin community state is also locally stable but this condition depends more on the continued high density of urchins than on the abundance of coralline algae themselves. A population crash of the urchins would cause this state to become unstable. This system of isolated patches of habitat (rock walls) with several locally stable states is very similar to that described for littoral rock pools in Washington State by Dethier (1984), where each of the states (seagrass, sea anemones, red algae) was stable and could prevent competitors encroaching until there was a massive physical disturbance.

For the observed assemblages really to be 'alternative' states within a single community, there should be a means of interconverting the states. Exclosure experiments (Sebens, in review) have been used to test the effects of predators, substratum angle, shading and prior space occupation on the assemblages (Paine, 1977 reviewed similar manipulations). Plastic mesh cages were effective in excluding the large predators including fish, lobsters, crabs and sea urchins although small sea stars could squeeze through the mesh or between the cage top and frame and were not as effectively excluded. Since urchins are by far the most abundant predators, most of the exclusion results on horizontal surfaces are probably due to their absence.

Excluding urchins and other large predators from invertebrate-dominated vertical surfaces for two years had little effect on those assemblages. Scraped areas, and areas both scraped and caged, returned to an approximation of the previous state within the two years. Some invertebrates, such as *Aplidium* and *Halichondria*, were somewhat more abundant inside some cages than in control plots. The caging effects were much greater on horizontal surfaces. Predator exclosures developed significant foliose algal cover. Exclosures with shade-producing roofs developed invertebrate assemblages similar to those on vertical walls, including *Aplidium*, *Halichondria*, complex and bryozoans but lacking *Alcyonium*. Shading alone had no effect. From this set of experiments it appears that invertebrate communities develop when there are low light levels and few urchin predators; this is exactly the situation on most vertical walls. Substratum angle itself may be unimportant except as it reduces light or urchin grazing. Without shade or urchins, erect fleshy algae dominate. These experiments provide evidence that at least some of the observed states of the community can in fact be interconverted by manipulating only two factors, light and urchin density.

The recruitment rates of each species also determine the resilience of the rock wall assemblages. The most rapid colonizers include *Spirorbis*, encrusting bryozoans, the red crustose alga, complex and the erect hydroids and bryozoans. These species covered scraped areas within one to four months in spring, summer and autumn. The tunicates, *Dendrodoa*, *Molgula* and *Aplidium*, came in less rapidly but achieved significant cover during the first year of monitoring. *Aplidium*, *Halichondria* and *Leucosolenia* approached their pre-removal percentage cover only after two years or more. *Alcyonium*, *Metridium* and *Balanus* have had only a few individuals become established after four years of community development in a large number of experimental removal areas. This sequence of colonization agrees with the community positions of species as described in Fig. 23.4; there is a strong inverse correlation between time required to recolonize and the position in the competitive hierarchy (Sebens, in press a). Early colonists are, in fact, inferior competitors. Such a relationship has often been assumed in generalized models of community dynamics and species coexistence (MacArthur and Levins, 1964; Levins and Culver, 1971; Levin and Paine, 1974; Armstrong, 1976; Connell and Slatyer, 1977) but there are few quantified examples from field studies. The life history characteristics of any one species place it in the categories of (i) rapid or slow colonizers, (ii) good or poor overgrowers, and (iii) susceptible or resistant to predators or physical disturbance. Given that the species pool contains species that differ along these gradients, any particular habitat will select species from that pool according to their availability and their life history characteristics. The local physical habitat characteristics, predator load, and prior occupants will determine the subset of the species pool that can coexist. It is interesting in this respect, that the habitats studied for five years in northern Massachusetts had such predictable assemblages year after year. Habitats which suffer infrequent catastrophic (or experimental) disturbances may change characteristics completely, as in the urchin addition experiment, yet the assemblages are resilient and return to their former composition in a relatively short time.

Is the composition of species on any single patch of substratum determined by their competitive interactions, or are the assemblages at this scale randomly composed and determined more by the vagaries of planktonic recruitment? In some ways, isolated vertical rock walls can be considered as habitat islands. Walls with small surface areas contain fewer species than more extensive walls, just as small islands are usually depauperate. Connor and Simberloff (1979) suggested that many of the patterns of species diversity and extinction rates on islands can be explained by chance processes that are not the result of local competitive exclusion. Sale (1977) has developed similar arguments for coral reef fish assemblages. While chance factors play a very large part in the early succession on sublittoral rocky substrata, competition is easily observed at growing edges of encrusting organisms (Sebens, in press a) and a competitive hierarchy is evident. These community states are resilient enough to return to their original composition a few years after complete clearing (Sebens, in press a, in review). Vance (in review) found the same result on sublittoral rock walls in Southern California. However, the three community states represented by *Aplidium*, *Alcyonium*, or *Metridium* may in fact originate as random events then persist indefinitely through positive density-dependent feedback.

23.9 Larval Ecology, Asexual Reproduction and Local Population Stability

Life history characteristics such as type of larval dispersal, number of larvae produced, local recruitment rate, seasonality, growth rate and mortality rate can determine where a species fits into the successional sequence and the competitive hierarchy. For instance, there is a general trend of increasing susceptibility to disturbance, and lower rates of recolonization, with higher competitive ranking (Sebens, in press a). There is no single 'best' life history for a sessile invertebrate or alga; any life history pattern that allows the species to persist given a particular set of potential space competitors, predators, and physical factors will be a successful adaptation at that instant. In an assemblage of organisms characterized by high offspring production and rapid recruitment rates, a species that holds energy back from reproduction and puts that energy into lateral growth or colony thickness (and thus competitive superiority) might be favoured. It would be able to coexist with the former species as long as its recruitment rate was greater than the mortality associated with its specialist and generalist predators, and physical disturbance.

Specific life histories and growth forms may allow species coexistence in other ways. Recent studies on sublittoral invertebrates indicate that the larvae of common species may not disperse very far from their point of origin (e.g. Keough and Downes, 1982). Demersal larvae crawling on the substratum may travel only a few centimetres (e.g. hydrocorals – Ostarello, 1976; corals – Gerodette, 1981; octocorals – Sebens, 1983a,b,c), but even swimming larvae are often ready to settle as soon as they find an appropriate substratum, sometimes within minutes of release (e.g. ascidians – Olson, 1983; bryozoans – Grosberg, 1981; Young and Chia, 1981). One important factor reducing dispersal distance is the local pattern of water movement. While larvae released in uni-directional flow could travel hundreds of metres in an hour or two, larvae released in bi-directional surge are more likely to be wafted back and forth with their actual horizontal displacement being very small. Also, because larvae are released very close to the substratum they tend to remain in the slower moving 'boundary layer' and thus have a high probability of contacting the substratum by random swimming or by eddy entrapment. Sebens and Koehl (1984) noted that the octocoral, *Alcyonium siderium*, and the sea anemone, *Metridium senile*, captured many ascidian larvae, which were abundant at 1–3cm from the substratum but which were virtually absent at 80cm away from the rock wall. Projections such as hydroid stems, erect bryozoans and algae can also form downstream eddies that may cause entrapment and substratum contact by larvae.

Several of the common sessile species on sublittoral rock walls in the Gulf of Maine have larvae of very limited powers of dispersal (Table 23.2). The octocoral, *Alcyonium siderium*, has demersal crawling larvae. The ascidians, *Aplidium pallidum*, *Molgula citrina* and *Dendrodoa carnea*, all have swimming tadpole larvae that can settle within a few minutes to hours after release. The crustose coralline algae have pelagic propagules but may also retain some that later move across the rock surface (Steneck, pers. comm.). The common species whose larvae spend weeks to months in the plankton also have some means of colonizing local substratum. Lateral growth (sponges, red crustose algae) and asexual proliferation by fragmentation (*Metridium senile*) are two such methods. It is a general

TABLE 23.2

Dispersal characteristics of all common species or groups of encrusting invertebrates on sublittoral rock walls at Nahant, Massachusetts. Observations are from this study unless noted. L = lecithotrophic planktonic larva, P = planktotrophic planktonic larva, D = demersal larva, A = algal spore or zygote. Colonization rate is time to return to original percentage cover after removal. Data on ascidian larval types from Millar (1971) and Plough (1978).

Species or group	Larval type	Pre-metamorphosis period	Probable dispersal distance (m)	Asexual proliferation (local)	Colonization rate (years)
Aplidium pallidum	L	hours	1–100	Y	2–4
Alcyonium siderium	D	1 day	<0.1	N	5–10
Tubicolous amphipods:					
Corophium bonnellii	D	hours	<1	N	<0.1
Jassa falcata	D	hours	<1	N	<0.1
Molgula citrina	L	hours	1–100	N	< 1
Dendrodoa carnea	L	hours	1–100	N	< 1
Didemnum albidum	L	hours	1–100	Y	?
Metridium senile	L	months	>10,000	Y	5–10
Balanus balanus	P	weeks	>10,000	N	5–10
Spirorbis spp.	L, D	hours	1–100	N	<0.1
Halichondria panicea	L	days	>10,000	Y	2–5
Halisarca dujardini	L	days	>10,000	Y	2–5
bryozoans	L	hours	1–100	Y	<0.1
hydroids	P	weeks	>10,000	Y	<0.1
red crustose alga	?	?	?	Y	<1
Lithothamnion glaciale	A	weeks	>10,000	Y	3
Phymatolithon rugulosum	A	weeks	>10,000	Y	3

observation that all of the common species in this system have some way, through either sexual or asexual means, of colonizing nearby substratum (Table 23.2). One effect of this ability is that patches of one species, once established, can maintain themselves by locally swamping competitors and/or predators. The second important result, especially for those species that can only disperse locally, is to produce a very patchy distribution. Certain patches of suitable substratum will be heavily populated and will be locally stable for many years while nearby areas, apparently just as suitable for that species, will lack stability altogether. The initial colonization may have been a chance event that occurred when there was abundant clear space after a storm or after a temporary urchin grazing event. When these disturbances coincide with the larval release by any one particular species, that species can establish a locally dense population. Chance factors, such as particularly good or bad physical conditions at the time of potential larval recruitment, may in fact influence the population structure of particular species for many years (Lewis *et al.*, 1982; Sebens and Lewis, 1985).

Substratum selectivity by settling larvae of sessile organisms may also lead to patchy distributions of the adult organism, based on the distribution of suitable substratum types which may be patchily distributed themselves. These may include particular inorganic surfaces, bacterial films (Brancato and Woollacott, 1982), adults of the same species, other encrusting organisms (Sebens, 1983a,b), or microhabitat types (irradiance levels – Olson, 1983; Sebens, 1983a – water flow speed). Substratum selectivity can produce aggregations of larvae settling together, or can provide a continuous recruitment of larvae into habitats that are suitable for that species' growth and survival. The presence of adults, or of other organisms that act as cues to the appropriate habitat, ensures this process.

Alcyonium siderium (Fig. 23.8) has another important life history feature that affects its persistence and spatial distribution. Its larvae are large (2mm), crawling planulae that do not disperse far from the parent colony. They crawl a few centimetres then settle on one of several surfaces that they recognize as suitable, for example the fleshy red crustose alga and coralline algae (Sebens, 1983a,b). Growth is inhibited if the juveniles are too close to adult colonies (< 2cm) but survivorship is enhanced in the range of 2 to 4 centimetres from adult colonies (Sebens, 1983c). The growth reduction near large colonies could be caused either by food depletion or by water flow reduction near large colonies, thus allowing the juveniles to capture fewer prey. Increased survivorship near adult colonies appears to result from the protection offered by these colonies against urchin grazing. Urchins avoid grazing within aggregations of *Alcyonium*; possibly they are deterred by the stinging nematocyst cells of the octocorals or simply by the presence of obstructions in their path and lack of solid attachment surfaces. The result is that *Alcyonium* forms dense aggregations that persist for many years, but they have a difficult time colonizing new space even tens of centimetres away. Vertical walls a few metres from walls with dense stands of *Alcyonium* often lack the octocoral altogether (Sebens, 1983c).

The sea anemone *Metridium senile* also forms dense aggregations on certain walls and is almost absent on others. This species has a very different set of life history characteristics. Fragments of the anemone's base break off and give rise to new anemones (pedal laceration). This asexual proliferation results in clones of genetically identical individuals, all with the same colour pattern (Hoffmann, 1977), sometimes forming thickets metres across. Although they also release gametes annually, forming planktonic planulae, successful recruitment by these larvae seems to be rare. Once a *Metridium* clone becomes established it can keep that space in the face of competition with other clones, or with *Alcyonium*, by direct aggressive behaviour. The elongate 'catch-tentacles' of *Metridium*, often >10cm long, can be used to recognize and damage anemones of other clones (Purcell, 1977) or octocorals, using batteries of specialized nematocysts. This behaviour, combined with local asexual proliferation, results in a very patchy distribution of the anemone. Its specialist predator *Aeolidia* attacks each winter and dense aggregations may be able to survive this onslaught and repopulate the local rock surface where scattered individuals are removed.

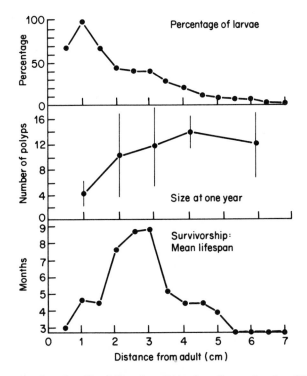

FIG. 23.8. Settlement, growth and survivorship of *Alcyonium siderium* juveniles as a function of distance to the nearest adult colony: percentage settlement is the number of settled larvae as a percentage of the greatest larval density (45 individuals at 2cm from adults, 238 total individuals). Note that larvae settled primarily near the parent colony even though the surface area available for larval settlement increased with distance from the adults. Size after 1 yr (no. of polyps ± S.D.) increased with distance from the adult colonies (1cm to 2cm) then reached a plateau. Survival (mean life span in months) was poor when juveniles were < 2cm or > 3cm from adults. Individuals still alive at the end of a year were given life spans of one year for this analysis, although some may live well beyond one year. Figure redrawn from Sebens (1983c).

23.10 Water Movement, Population Structure and Community Composition

Water movement is one of the most important physical habitat characteristics affecting the composition of vertical rock wall communities in the Gulf of Maine. Extreme water movement during storms is an important source of mortality to sublittoral organisms (e.g. Witman, 1984), and periods of strong wave surge may limit urchin grazing on vertical wall invertebrates (Sebens, in review). In addition to the adverse effects of extreme water movement on particular species, the general flow regime of a particular rock wall will influence the growth rates and population structure of species that depend on water flow for suspension feeding. Hiscock (1983) lists both positive and negative effects of increased water movement for benthic organisms. He also reviews studies showing that community composition can change drastically between sublittoral habitats with different flow regimes.

The greatest biomass of encrusting fauna on vertical rock walls in northern Massachusetts occurs at the sites with the greatest water movement. The outer side of Halfway Rock has the largest colonies of the octocoral *Alcyonium* yet encountered, thick colonies of *Aplidium*, and large and densely packed sea anemones (*Metridium*). The maximum and mean colony diameters of *Alcyonium* are smallest at the inner East Point site, larger at the more exposed Shag Rocks site, and largest at Halfway Rock (Fig. 23.9). Growth rates of *Alcyonium* were also much greater at Halfway Rock than at inner East Point,

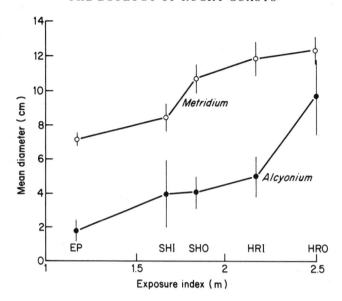

FIG. 23.9. Maximum sizes of the anemone, *Metridium senile*, and the octocoral, *Alcyonium siderium*, at three sites in Northern Massachusetts that differ in water movement. Exposure to wave action, and thus surge in the sublittoral zone, is measured as the vertical extension (m) of the littoral barnacle zone (*Semibalanus balanoides* (L.)) above mean low water (wave height observations and *in situ* flow meter readings confirm the ranking of water movement at the three sites – Sebens, in press b). Values plotted are the means (± one S.D.) of the largest 20 *M. senile* (basal diameter) measured in a 5m² area of vertical rock wall (of > 200 individuals), and the largest 10% of *Alcyonium* colonies (mean expanded colony diameter) measured in 1–2m² (of > 1000 individuals) (*Alcyonium* data from Sebens, in press b). EP = East Point, SHI = inner Shag Rocks, SHO = outer Shag Rocks, HRI = inner Halfway Rock, HRO = outer Halfway Rock. Note that SHO has no intertidal and is thus estimated to be at a slightly greater exposure than SHI which does have an intertidal barnacle zone.

although mortality rates were approximately twice as great at the latter, most exposed, site (Sebens, in press b). Zooplankton concentrations, measured over two years, did not differ greatly between these sites. Therefore, water movement alone, bringing more zooplankton into contact with *Alcyonium* tentacles per unit time (Patterson, 1985), is the most likely factor accounting for increased growth at the exposed site. The combined effects of increased growth rate and higher mortality rate result in a population that has a few very large colonies and many of lesser size at the Halfway Rock site. At inner East Point, the population is more narrowly distributed and contains only the smaller size classes (Sebens, in press b).

Metridium senile also reaches larger maximum diameters with increasing water movement (Fig. 23.9), probably also because of greater prey capture with more water movement. However, the size of *Metridium* depends on a balance between growth and asexual reproduction by pedal laceration. Shick and Hoffmann (1980) found that *Metridium* sizes were smaller in a tidal channel with very rapid flow than in nearby areas with less flow and smallest in areas of very low flow, although pedal laceration was greater in the first habitat. None of the sites in this study has this type of rapid, constrained flow and thus *Metridium* sizes only increase with greater exposure. At some high flow speed, the passive suspension feeding mechanisms of *Metridium* and *Alcyonium* may become less efficient, resulting in lower food capture and slower growth. However, it appears that even the most exposed habitats in Fig. 23.9 are still below that point. At Halfway Rock and at the Shag Rocks, *Metridium* reaches almost 100% cover on certain areas of rock wall, usually near the top edge. At the more protected inner East Point site percentage cover is always less than 10% and large clonal aggregations are absent.

The combined effects of water movement on particular species effect a change in the rock wall community with increasing exposure. The percentage cover and biomass of large passive suspension feeders such as *Alcyonium* and *Metridium* become much greater at more exposed sites (note biomass comparison in Fig. 23.3). This increase occurs at the expense of the smaller, active suspension feeders such as ascidians, sponges, and bryozoans which are much less massive, and consequently competitively inferior, to the former species. The same pattern can often be seen on any single vertical wall. The size and cover of *Metridium* is usually, though not always, greatest at the top, followed by *Alcyonium* and *Aplidium* somewhat lower, then by sponges and bryozoans near the bottom. The structure of these rock wall communities is thus determined by a combination of differences in physical habitat characteristics, such as water flow, and continuous biological interactions, competition and predation, all of which occur on a fine spatial scale resulting in distinct coexisting species assemblages that are stable for many years, until the occurrence of a catastrophic physical disturbance to either the dominant sessile species or to their predators.

ACKNOWLEDGEMENTS

I thank R. Aiello, C.S. Briscoe, M. Ashenfelter, G. Davis, D. Denninger, D. Levitan, R. Merva, S. Norton, R. Olson, M. Patterson, J. Resing, J. Sigda, D. Smith, W. Stotz and T. Van Wey for field and laboratory assistance, and C.S. Briscoe and B.L. Thorne and the editors of this volume for reading and commenting on the manuscript. The interpretation of sublittoral community dynamics benefitted greatly from discussions with P.K. Dayton, L. Harris, J.R. Lewis, M.P. Morse, R. Olson, R.T. Paine, M. Patterson, R. Steneck, R.R. Vance and J. Witman. I also thank R. Steneck and R. Wilce for identifying algal specimens and A. Kuzirian for identifying nudibranchs. This research was supported by grants OCE 78 08482, OCE 80 07923 and OCE 83 08958 from the National Science Foundation and the Milton Fund of Harvard University. I also thank the Marine Science and Maritime Studies Center of Northeastern University, Nahant, Massachusetts, the Museum of Comparative Zoology, and the Biological Laboratories of Harvard University for the use of their facilities. This is M.S.M.S.C. Contribution No. 139.

CHAPTER XXIV

PHYSICAL FACTORS AND BIOLOGICAL INTERACTIONS: THE NECESSITY AND NATURE OF ECOLOGICAL EXPERIMENTS

A.J. Underwood

24.1 Introduction

The rôle of physical environmental factors in determining patterns of vertical distribution, and seasonal and other patterns of abundance of littoral organisms has been widely discussed for rocky shores world-wide (e.g. Doty, 1946; Evans, 1947b; Dakin, 1950; Ricketts *et al.*, 1968; Stephenson and Stephenson, 1972; Morton and Miller, 1973). Lewis (1964) provided the descriptive synthesis which has been the standard for many years. With the advent of more recent experimental investigations of the interactions among littoral organisms, however, particularly those which shed light on the causes and influences of patterns of distribution, there has been a tendency to play down some of the earlier emphasis on physical aspects of the environment, even though the general importance of physical factors has usually been acknowledged; see particularly the reviews by Connell (1972, 1975) and the detailed experimental work of Menge (1978a,b). Nevertheless, there have been several different types of study from which it can be concluded fairly that physical factors associated with different heights on the shore and different periods of emersion during low tide are inadequate as explanations for many patterns of littoral zonation of groups of species, or as proximate factors causing the upper and/or lower limits of distribution of individual species (see for particular examples Chapman, 1973; Wolcott, 1973; Underwood, 1978; Underwood and Denley, 1984).

   Connell (1974) and Paine (1977) have previously extolled the great virtues of well-planned experimental manipulations of organisms in rocky shore systems as invaluable tools for unravelling the complexities of the ecology of these communities. The need for experimental tests of logically developed hypotheses should, by now, be obvious and no further advocacy of properly conducted experiments should be necessary. The success of experimental studies in elucidating the precise nature of the distributional limits of littoral barnacles in Britain (Connell, 1961a,b) and on the West coast of the U.S.A. (Connell, 1970), in unravelling the complexities of interactions in successional sequences on shores of the Pacific Coast (Dayton, 1971; Sousa, 1979a), and in demonstrating the crucial rôles of littoral predators and grazers (Paine, 1966, 1974; Lubchenco, 1978; Menge, 1978a,b; Underwood, 1980) are examples of the power of experimental analyses of the structure of rocky shore communities sufficient to convince the most dubious observer.

   What may not be so apparent, however, is the vital need for experimentation in littoral systems wherever physical factors are invoked as explanations for, or causes of, observed patterns of distribution and abundance. There is an obverse of this coin, in that wherever biological interactions (particularly competition and predation) are investigated, the generality of the results to other situations and other times of the year presupposes knowledge of the influence of physical factors in the environment. Obviously, differences in physical variables from place to place and time to time will influence the behaviour of the interacting organisms, their rates of movement and feeding, and the physiological stresses that might influence the outcome of inter-individual encounters.

The aim of the present contribution is therefore to illustrate these two points about the need for integrated experimentation on physical environmental variables in analyses of interactions among littoral species. In addition, the formulation of appropriate hypotheses about the existence of, or influences of, physical factors in patterns of distribution and abundance of littoral organisms will be considered by examples. Finally, the types of experimental design that have proved efficient in the analysis of some aspects of physical variability in rocky shore communities will be considered.

The examples stem from experimental analyses of processes affecting consumers, i.e. grazers and predators, which can exert a range of indirect effects on other components of the system (see, particularly, the arguments developed by Paine, 1980). A second series of situations concerns competitive interactions among grazing gastropods. Here, the physical environment has been demonstrated to have marked effects on the magnitude of interactions. Finally, the patchiness of distribution of some littoral organisms can be directly related to responses to various forms of physical stress, even though these do not necessarily determine the actual limits of distribution on the shore. The only studies to be considered here are those where there has been experimental evaluation of the relative importance of different hypotheses.

24.2 The Upper Limits of Distribution of Macroalgae
On rocky coasts in New South Wales, there is often a reasonably abrupt upper limit of distribution of foliose macroalgae above low-shore areas completely dominated by plants (Underwood, 1980, 1981a). With the exception of some species (that appear and disappear sporadically or seasonally), above this limit foliose plants are generally scarce, except in pools or among barnacles, but grazing gastropods and encrusting algae are abundant (Underwood, 1981a; Jernakoff, 1983). The vertical distribution of algae varies seasonally, tending downshore in warmer periods of the year, and up again in winter. Also, there is a general trend for algae to extend to higher levels where there is great exposure to wave-action – a pattern of wide generality (e.g. Lewis, 1964; Sze, 1980; Underwood, 1981a; Underwood and Jernakoff, 1984). These observations strongly suggest that physical variables associated with periods of emersion during low tide are important factors influencing the upper limit of algal distribution.

One model to account for the general lack of foliose species above a certain level in any place on the coast of New South Wales is that the plants can only withstand the desiccation, great temperatures and bright sunshine experienced during low tide for a certain period of time. Longer periods of emersion, such as they would have to tolerate at higher shore levels, are fatal. This model of physiological intolerance to the physical factors prevailing during low tide has often been proposed to account for upper limits of distribution. Although this is a likely explanation for many species, it has often been accepted without any enquiry into alternative processes (e.g. Doty, 1946; Lewis, 1964). There have, of course, also been studies that provide evidence for this proposition. For example, Moore (1939), Castenholz (1961) and Dayton (1971) have all demonstrated higher extensions of algae where moist conditions or running water ameliorated the physical environment. Frank (1965b) built experimental rock pools at high tidal levels that would drain slowly causing water to seep downshore as the experimental pools drained during low tide. These experiments were designed to test the hypothesis that if physical conditions were experimentally ameliorated (by keeping areas damp during low tide), algae would be able to grow at higher levels on the shore. These experiments were successful in the sense that algae did indeed grow more profusely in the experimentally damp areas than in surrounding control areas, thus supporting the model.

A second type of experimental evidence used to support the model of physiological intolerance comes from transplants of algae to higher shore levels than those at which they are normally found (e.g. Hatton, 1938; Foster, 1971; Schonbeck and Norton, 1978). Here, the hypothesis being examined is that if plants are intolerant of physical conditions prevailing at some high level on the shore, algae taken there will die at a faster rate than control plants (removed from and transplanted back into the lower areas where they normally grow). Again, these experiments have proved successful at rejecting the null hypothesis that moving plants to higher levels makes no difference to their survival. Thus, the results support the contention that physical factors are responsible for the observed upper limit of distribution of the seaweeds.

There is, however, a problem with the latter type of experiment – that the hypothesis under test does not directly address the question of why plants are not found at higher levels, even though the hypothesis is a logical prediction from the stated model of physiological intolerance of the physical conditions prevailing at high-shore levels (Underwood and Denley, 1984). Consider a different model to account for the observed patterns of vertical distribution of algae. This is that the plants are absent from higher levels because they do not recruit there, as planktonic dispersive propagules. Recruitment at higher levels could be difficult because of limited powers of dispersal of the spores – as demonstrated, for example, for the brown alga *Postelsia palmaeformis* Ruprecht by Dayton (1973) and Paine (1979). Secondly, at higher levels on a shore, there is a decreasing period of time during each tidal cycle when the area is submerged by the tide. Thus, the number of planktonic spores and propagules that float into a high-shore area, and attach to the substratum, will, on average, be less than the numbers at lower levels. The reduction in potential numbers of recruits per tide, and in time available for attachment, are plausible reasons for decreasing numbers of plants at higher levels on the shore. This model is clearly not eliminated by experimental analyses of the fate of adult plants transplanted to higher levels of the shore (see also Underwood and Denley, 1984). Under natural circumstances, adult plants are not likely to be transplanted to, nor to be able to re-attach in, areas higher on the shore than their natural distribution. Their fate is largely irrelevant to the causes of limits of distribution of algae. Thus, the stages of the life history that need to be moved upshore in experiments are the most juvenile stages – not the adult plants. Of course, for the upper limit of the algae to be determined by a failure of recruitment at higher levels, the hypothesis to be examined is that young sporelings taken to higher levels will be able to survive and grow to adult sizes. Data from experimental transplants of adults suggest that such survival would be unlikely, even if the young stages were taken upshore. It is, never-theless, possible that sporelings, if they are able to survive the earliest period of development in the new, higher location, may acclimate, and grow into adults also able to withstand the prevailing conditions there. Thus, a better experiment to distinguish between the two models (physiological intolerance and lack of recruitment) would include transplantation of juvenile, not adult, plants.

Then there is an important third model to account for observed patterns of vertical distribution of some littoral algae. This is that grazing is more intense (because grazers are more numerous, more voracious, more efficient, or whatever) at higher levels on the shore, and thus prevent algae from growing there. From this model, a simple predictive hypothesis can be derived that experimental removal of grazers from levels above the normal distribution of the plants should result in the success-ful colonization and growth of algae higher on the shore than they are normally found. Note that this hypothesis should be examined in conjunction with the previous two. If removal of grazers did not result in an upward extension of the algae, this must be because either the algae did not recruit into the higher areas (the second model above), or because even though recruits arrived at the higher levels, they were quickly killed by physical factors (in accord with the first model proposed – but with particular reference to the juvenile stages of the plants).

Experiments to test this hypothesis have been done in various parts of the world. Notably, however, experimental analyses of the rôles of littoral grazers seem to have been done in isolation from studies on the responses of algae to physiological stress. There is no reason why either aspect of the biology of seaweeds should not be investigated in its own right, independently of other ecological or physiological processes. But, as suggested above, if the results of the experiments are to be related to the patterns of natural distribution of the species on a shore, there is every reason to hope that the various models, and the various hypotheses derived from them might be considered together.

Studies in New South Wales indicate that littoral grazers (mostly molluscs) play a major rôle in determining the vertical distribution of foliose plants (Underwood, 1980). The design of these experiments, done at levels above the regions usually occupied by various species of plants, was as indicated in Table 24.1. Two different factors were manipulated: the grazers themselves were excluded from some areas, and the physical environment of patches of shore was modified by shading some areas with roofs or cages. As indicated in Table 24.1, the relative importance of each factor could be gauged by including the two levels of each variable (grazing and physical environment) in orthogonal combinations. This allowed assessment of the overall effect of each factor independently, and also enabled evaluation of the synergistic or antagonistic interactions between the two potential influences on abundance of algae (see, for example, Winer, 1971; Underwood, 1981b, for discussion of the rôle of orthogonal contrasts in experimental designs).

There are other possible models to account for the lack of foliose algae at higher levels on the shore. For example, pre-emption of space, preventing recruitment of other species, or some allelopathic effect by the crusts on the sporelings after they attach, could prevent foliose plants from invading higher areas on the shore (although clearly this model begs the question of why there are no encrusting forms at lower levels, and therefore why there are foliose plants *anywhere* on the shore). Evidence for both processes exists for seaweeds. Sousa (1979a) demonstrated very clearly that an existing cover of the late-successional species, the red alga, *Gigartina canaliculata* Harv., prevented colonization of littoral boulders by more opportunistic species such as *Ulva* spp. Similarly, Lubchenco (1980) convincingly made out a case for pre-emptive competition by low-shore *Chondrus crispus* Stackh. as an important reason for the absence of species of *Fucus* at lower levels on the shore. Sieburth and Conover (1966) have demonstrated some allelopathic effects of encrusting algae on the newly settled forms of various marine invertebrates; such effects have potentially important influences on other species of plants.

Therefore, with respect to the experimental design in Table 24.1, a fourth model to explain the absence of foliose algae at higher levels was also examined. This was that these algae are absent from higher levels on the shore because they are prevented from recruiting or surviving there by the existing cover of encrusting algae (such species as *Hildenbrandia prototypus* Nardo being particularly common in the areas investigated by Underwood (1980)). To examine this model, it was hypothesized that if foliose plants are prevented from settling or colonizing higher levels of the shore because encrusting plants are present, the removal of the crusts should allow establishment of species which would not appear in adjacent, untouched control sites. To this end, therefore, the experimental treatments in Table 24.1 were repeated in plots cleared of all crusts and in plots where the natural cover of encrusting algae was left intact (the total set of experiments was even more complicated than this, but the other aspects are not relevant to this discussion).

The results were clear-cut and consistent. Wherever grazers were excluded by fences or cages, foliose algae colonized the surfaces. There was little to no long-term effect of the presence of encrusting algae on the rock surfaces (Underwood, 1980). Thus, the second and fourth models suggested to explain the absence of foliose plants from mid-shore levels can be eliminated: clearly,

TABLE 24.1

Design of an experiment to investigate the rôles of physical harshness and grazing in the distribution of low-shore algae.

	Experimental treatment			
	1	2	3	4
	Open (Control)	Fence	Roof	Cage
Grazers	Allowed in	Excluded	Allowed in	Excluded
Physical environment	Normal	Normal	Shaded	Shaded

Possible comparisons:	*Effect examined:*
(1 + 3) vs. (2 + 4)	Presence versus absence of grazers
(1 + 2) vs. (3 + 4)	Normal versus shaded environment
1 vs. 2	Grazing in a normal environment
3 vs. 4	Grazing in a shaded environment
1 vs. 3	Shade in the presence of grazers
2 vs. 4	Shade in the absence of grazers

several low-shore species could recruit into the higher areas (so failure of recruitment was not the cause of their absence, as required by the second model above) and encrusting algae made no difference to the rate or success of this colonization (as suggested by the fourth model above). In fenced plots, with a similar degree of environmental stress during low tide to that in control plots (see Table 24.1), algae colonized in profusion, but did not grow to adult sizes. Only where grazers were excluded, and the areas had some degree of shade from the direct effects of sunlight and temperature, did some of the plants grow up to normal adult condition. Thus, the third model (that grazing prevents the upper extension of low-shore species) does explain the absence of plants from the higher levels. Only where grazers were removed did foliose algae appear in experimental plots. Thus, grazing clearly determines the upper limit of distribution for some species on rocky shores in New South Wales. At the same time, however, the physical factors associated with emersion (probably desiccation, sunlight and temperature) influence greatly the growth and abundance of those plants that manage to colonize where grazers are removed. So, the first model proposed (physiological intolerance of stress during prolonged emersion during low tide) is an important influence on the growth, size, maturity, biomass and overall abundance of foliose plants on sandstone platforms in New South Wales. Physical factors, however, are not directly responsible for the upper limit of distribution of the plants; that is controlled by the activities of invertebrate grazers.

What general principle might be learned from this example? First, and of overwhelming importance, is the demonstration that it is not necessarily a simple matter to explain patterns of distribution of organisms in nature. In this instance, four very different models could be proposed that were entirely consistent with, and could potentially explain, the observed patterns of vertical distribution of low-shore foliose algae. By direct, manipulative experimentation, two of these were shown to be wrong (i.e. failure of recruitment by propagules and pre-emption of space by encrusting algae at high levels were eliminated as processes limiting the upwards spread of low-shore species). The first and often the most readily accepted model proposed (that of physiological intolerance of low-tide conditions) was demonstrated to have important influences on the well-being and abundance of plants, but to be of only secondary importance in the distribution of the algae, which was primarily controlled by the activities of grazers. Parallel findings about the distribution of fucoid algae have been obtained in experiments by Lubchenco (1980), who found that competition with other species prevented the downshore extension of the plants, and that grazing by snails (mostly *Littorina littorea* (L.)) affected the abundance of *Fucus* spp. at lower levels in areas where competing algae had been experimentally removed.

These examples demonstrate two important principles about the valid investigation of ecological patterns. First, untested models about the factors limiting the vertical distributions of species are not necessarily valid. Untested models or assumptions are simply guesses and have no great status until they are subjected to some form of critical appraisal. Here, acceptance of the notion that physical factors are responsible for the upper limit of distribution of foliose algae on rocky shores in New South Wales would have been erroneous, even though the original observations were compelling. Second, any attempt to evaluate the validity of a particular model (or explanation) for the factors determining a pattern should involve the construction and assessment of a variety of alternative models, provided only that each of the alternatives is also capable of explaining the original observations. Distinguishing among the various models may, in theory, be done by any logical process. It is, however, becoming increasingly obvious that manipulative experiments on the shore, designed to test conflicting hypotheses derived from each of the models, are the most powerful, and probably most efficient method available for eliminating some of the competing models from further contention (see also Connell, 1974; Paine, 1977; Dayton, 1979; Underwood and Denley, 1984).

24.3 The Distribution of Littoral Grazers

Whenever studies are completed that suggest the validity of a particular model, or group of models, new problems are raised. First, any subsequent construction of new models (previously unthought of, or missed), that have not yet been eliminated by acquisition of evidence from observations or experiment, requires that new studies are undertaken to evaluate the new versus the previously validated model. This is common sense, and forms the basis for philosophical discussions about the growth of scientific knowledge (see particularly Popper, 1963; Kuhn, 1970; Feyerabend, 1975). Secondly, however, the finished study may, itself, throw up new problems. As an example, if the upper limit of spread of low-shore species of littoral foliose macroalgae is limited by the actions of grazing invertebrates at higher levels, why don't the grazers extend downshore to lower levels, and eliminate the algae altogether from the shore? This question follows naturally from the results discussed above. Several models, again, can be proposed to account for the observed lower limit of distribution of the grazers. Three models immediately spring to mind (each almost a mirror image of one of those proposed to account for the upper limit of distribution of the algae). First, the grazers may be physiologically intolerant of the conditions prevailing at lower levels on the shore where periods of submersion are prolonged (this has occasionally been suggested in the literature, but rarely documented; see the review by Connell, 1972). Second, the presence of low-shore predators might eliminate individuals that happen to wander lower than they are normally found. An example is Paine's (1969b) study of the littoral snail, *Tegula funebralis* (A. Adams), which is rapidly consumed at low levels by the predatory starfish, *Pisaster ochraceus* Brandt. The third model is that the dense algal beds at low-shore levels themselves prevent grazers from moving further downshore. As before, different hypotheses can be deduced from each of these models, and subjected to experimental test to eliminate some or all of these models (see Underwood and Jernakoff, 1981). From that study, it appears that limpets are prevented from invading dense stands of foliose macroalgae (primarily because they are swept away by waves if they try to move over the plants). Nevertheless, if placed in clearings within the low-shore beds of algae, the limpets either move away to higher, free space (if it is accessible without them having to move over algae), or gradually the clearings are invaded by rapidly growing algae and the limpets eventually starve to death, because they cannot forage efficiently on the grown plants, but require the microscopic algal sporelings. The limpets are therefore kept out of low-shore areas by the rapid colonization and growth of algae at low levels on the shore, resulting in domination of free space, and the demise of the microalgal grazers.

What matters for the present discussion is that this model suggests a dynamic tension between the efficiency or activities of grazers at higher levels (which prevent the microsocopic stages of the algae from becoming established) and the rapidity of colonization and growth of the algae at lower levels, that prevents grazers from invading, or staying in, the lower areas. What rôle might physical environmental factors play in this dynamism? They might influence the activity, or rates of grazing of the gastropods (as, for example, demonstrated for predatory whelks by Menge (1978a, b); see later). Certainly, during periods when physical conditions prevail that favour rapid growth of the plants, their distribution ought to rise to higher levels on the shore. When harsher physical conditions prevail, algal growth should be slowed, and grazers should be able to keep the plants clear from even lower regions of the shore. Thus, the position of the upper limit of the algae and the lower limit of the majority of the grazers is now to be explained by a complex model, involving not only the effects of grazers and the plants themselves, but also variations in these two processes brought about by differences in the physical environment. From this model, several specific hypotheses can be proposed. For example, if splash and spray are thought to promote algal growth (by keeping plants damper and cooler during low tide), algal distributions ought to extend to higher levels in wave-exposed areas, and grazers ought to be less effective at eliminating plants where wave-action leads to increased splash and spray. Similarly, plants in rock pools ought to be more profuse than on surrounding areas of rock, which are dried during low tide. Coupled with this, grazers should be less effective in rock pools than outside them, because of more rapid growth of sporelings of the plants inside the pools . . . and so forth – several more predictions can be made. Yet again, these can be subjected to experimental test (see Underwood and Jernakoff, 1984), by use of experimental rock pools, and by experimental exclusions of grazers from areas of shore at different tidal heights and with different degrees of wave-exposure. The results of these experiments indicated both the nature and the effects of physical factors on the distribution of littoral foliose algae in New South Wales (see Table 24.2 where some of the results are summarized). A notable feature of the results is the complexity of interactions among the different physical variables. For example, note that the effect of continuous submersion in shallow rock pools is a function of the height of the pools on the shore, and of the season of the year (Table 24.2). Similarly, the seasonal effects of temperature, insolation, etc., are more marked at lower than at higher levels, but are also related to the degree of exposure to wave-action. In general, therefore, there is great complexity in the effects of physical factors on recruitment success and rates of growth of littoral algae. These, in turn, influence the probability of algae escaping from being grazed, and therefore modify the impact of grazers on the distribution and abundance of the plants.

24.4 Effects of Physical Factors and Grazing on the Diversity of Algae

There are, however, other, more subtle consequences of these physical variables interacting with grazing systems. One is the effect on other components of rocky shore communities (discussed below). The other is the principle identified by Lubchenco (1978) – that under different environmental conditions, grazers can have very different effects on the diversity of algal assemblages. This study repays careful consideration. Lubchenco (1978) demonstrated that grazing snails (*Littorina littorea*) in rock pools mostly fed on ephemeral green algae (*Entermorpha intestinalis* (L.) Link), but were ineffective at removing those algae with tougher thalli, such as *Chondrus crispus*. The net effect of the activities of grazers was therefore to enhance the variety of species of algae found in pools. Without grazers, space was dominated by the rapidly-growing green algae, which then eliminated other species by

TABLE 24.2

Effects of physical environmental variables on abundance of littoral foliose macroalgae in grazed (unfenced) plots on shores in New South Wales (see Underwood and Jernakoff, 1984, for details). Level 1 = top of low-shore algal beds; Level 2 = 11–13cm higher than Level 1; Level 3 = 26–31cm higher than Level 1; tidal range is approximately 2m.

Variable	*Effect on percentage cover of algae*
Rainfall (in 10-day periods)	Level 1: No effect Level 2: 2mm rainfall per day increased mean algal cover from 20% to 60%
Wave-action and associated splash and spray	Level 1: Increased cover of algae associated with greater exposure to wave-action Level 2: Very marked increase in cover of algae with increased exposure to wave-action
Seasonal pattern of temperature, sunlight, etc.	Level 1: Greater algal cover during autumn/winter than spring/summer; range of seasonal variation greater than at Level 2 Level 2: Greater algal cover during autumn/winter than spring/summer; no algae in sheltered locations during the warmer seasons
Submersion in shallow rock pools	Levels 1 and 3: No effect during winter months Level 1: Greatly increased algal cover in pools during summer months Level 3: Very slightly increased algal cover in pools during summer months

over-growing or shading them from the light. While grazers were preventing this domination by their major food species, other algae were able to colonize, grow or persist in the pools. In contrast, in areas that were emersed during low tide, larger, tougher forms of plants predominated, and occupied much of the substratum. Green algae such as *Enteromorpha intestinalis* are still favoured by grazing snails, but their consumption now contributes to a decline in diversity of species of plants – because the grazers eliminate their food-plants from the system. The outcome of grazing is therefore dependent upon which plants the grazers consume (and, as discussed below, the conditions under which grazing occurs). As Lubchenco (1978) pointed out, the preference by consumers for the competitively dominant species of plants will lead to enhanced diversity wherever grazers are active or efficient (because they are preventing competitive elimination of other species). In contrast, where grazers are focussing on competitively inferior species of plants, their activities cause decreased species diversity. Thus, the 'choices' or 'preferences' exercised by the grazers will determine whether grazing causes increased or decreased diversity in a community – and Lubchenco's (1978) studies provide a useful synthesis allowing some prediction to be made for various grazing systems. She has also enabled rational unravelling of the rather different results about the diversity of species obtained from different studies of grazing and predation in different places.

What also underlies her study, in so far as it relates to the diversity of areas of a rocky shore, is that the competitive rôle of the plants is, at least partially, determined by the prevailing physical conditions. In pools, fast-growing, rather 'weedy' species such as *Enteromorpha*, can rapidly colonize and occupy space to the detriment of hardier, tougher species that grow and reproduce more slowly. Where physical factors, associated with the period of emersion during low tide (desiccation, light, temperature, etc.) are more extreme (such as outside rock pools), the less tough species of plants tend to be reduced in growth rate, survival and possibly colonization (see also the experimental work of Hruby and Norton, 1979). Thus, the outcome of grazing, in terms of species diversity, is a function of the competitive status of the plants that are preferred, or most rapidly consumed, by the grazers. This, in itself, is at least partially determined by the suite of physical environmental variables prevailing in any place and time. This aspect of the effects of physical factors on the rôle of littoral consumers will be considered further, with respect to predators and sessile prey, below.

These examples demonstrate the value of comparative experimentation under different environmental regimes. They also indicate the need to consider the less direct effects of physical factors associated with low tide in the design and interpretation of manipulative experiments.

24.5 Effects of Algae and Grazers on Sessile Animals

It has long been known that sessile species of animals interact in various ways to compete for space on which to live. Overgrowth of one species by another (e.g. Jackson, 1977; Russ, 1982) is extremely common among some organisms, such as bryozoans, sponges and tunicates. Undercutting, smothering or crushing are common among other forms, such as barnacles (Hatton, 1938; Connell, 1961a,b; Dayton, 1971). In addition, barnacles are commonly smothered by algae, which cause increased siltation, decreased feeding and respiration, and often the death of the cirripedes (see Hatton, 1938; Barnes, 1955; Dayton, 1971; Denley and Underwood, 1979). In addition to direct overgrowth and smothering of established organisms, algae and other sessile species can often prevent the recruitment of some species that require bare space on which to settle (Denley and Underwood, 1979; Sousa, 1979a; reviewed by Schoener, 1983; Underwood and Denley, 1984). Thus, wherever there are algae present in profusion, interactions with the distribution and abundance of barnacles might be expected.

Another source of mortality of small barnacles is due to them being accidentally crushed or consumed by large foraging limpets (e.g. Hatton, 1938; Lewis, 1954; Connell, 1961a). Dayton (1971) appears to have coined the term 'bulldozing' to describe the effect of limpets on small barnacles.

From both of these considerations, it is obvious that any interactions between algae and grazing gastropods could have potentially large effects on the distribution and abundance of, and further interactions among, other sessile species on the shore. Dayton (1971) completed several series of experiments to demonstrate the various effects of foliose algae on the settlement and subsequent survival of small barnacles. In some experiments, he excluded limpets (*Acmaea* spp.) from areas of the shore (by using plastic fences and cages). Limpets were enclosed inside other fenced plots, and the resulting recruitment or cover of barnacles was recorded. Dayton (1971) was thus able to demonstrate that, in some areas, barnacles (*Balanus glandula* Darwin and *Semibalanus cariosus* (Pallas)) were deleteriously affected by the presence of the limpets. Fewer barnacles recruited where limpets were present, although limpets made no difference to the recruitment of another barnacle, *Chthamalus dalli* Pilsbry. In some places, the limpets had positive effects on the survival of *C. dalli*.

In New South Wales, one of the major occupiers of space at mid-shore levels is the coronuloid barnacle *Tesseropora rosea* (Krauss), which mostly settles on rocky shores where there is some degree of wave-action, and usually settles on bare rock. It is thus rare on sheltered shores, and is rarely found on the shells of adults. It is also overgrown by algae and tubeworms, and will not settle in areas occupied by foliose algae (Denley and Underwood, 1979). In areas dominated by gastropods, barnacles of all species are rare, or absent. In contrast, where there are many barnacles, large species of gastropods are sparse or absent, although several small species of grazing gastropods are found amongst the barnacles (see Creese, 1982; Underwood *et al.*, 1983; Jernakoff, 1983). Finally, there is considerable patchiness in the abundance of the barnacles from place to place and time to time, some of which – at least – is related to physical factors such as wave-shock and temperature that prevail at the time of settlement, or act shortly after cyprids settle and metamorphose.

In parallel with some other studies (e.g. Dayton, 1971; Southward, 1953, 1964; Hawkins, 1983) various models can be proposed to account for the patterns and patchiness observed on shores in New South Wales. One obvious model to account for the negative relationship between the number of limpets and the number of barnacles present in different places is that barnacles are negatively affected by the limpets (perhaps by being 'bulldozed' off the rocks in areas where limpets are abundant or active). It is clear from this that the appropriate hypothesis to test is that removal of limpets should allow greater survival of small barnacles than in control areas where limpets are allowed to forage naturally (noting that this hypothesis can only be examined in areas where barnacles actually settle from the plankton!). There are, of course, many other models that could be proposed to account for the observations. One is that barnacles are unaffected by limpets, but that limpets are deleteriously affected by the presence of many barnacles, and thus migrate away to areas with more bare space, or die. Alternatively, there may be some predator of limpets that is found in greater abundance hiding amongst barnacles than on open rock surfaces. This latter situation has been demonstrated to be the case for predatory whelks, *Nucella* spp., on the coast of Washington in Dayton's (1971) studies; the whelks hid among sea anemones, where they could remain damp during low tide. A more neutral model (i.e. one that presupposes no interactions among the barnacles and limpets) is that small limpets tend to settle in different habitats from those chosen by the barnacle cyprids, and thus the observed patterns of distribution are the result of habitat selection by larvae. Many other models can be proposed too.

In experiments attempting to unravel some of the complexities of these various models, the effects of adult limpets (the patellid *Cellana tramoserica* (Sowerby)) on the settlement and subsequent survival of juvenile *Tesseropora rosea* was examined in a number of places (Underwood *et al.*, 1983). Fenced enclosures containing natural densities of limpets, and similar, nearby enclosures with reduced densities (including zero limpets) were used; the settlement and subsequent survival of barnacles was monitored. The major difference between the experiments in New South Wales and those done by previous workers was that the later experimental designs could incorporate comparisons with different densities of limpets, rather than the simple removal of all naturally occurring limpets, and comparison with control, untouched plots. As a consequence, experiments at mid-shore levels revealed a non-linear effect of *Cellana* on the settlement of *Tesseropora* (see Underwood *et al.* (1983), Fig. 2 and Fig. 24.1 here). At natural densities (8 per enclosure of 400cm^2), limpets had a deleterious effect on settlement of barnacles (counted within three days of settlement). At smaller limpet densities, therefore, more barnacles settled in the experimental plots, except that there were, again, reduced numbers of newly settled barnacles in experimental plots with no limpets. The decline in numbers where there are many limpets is directly attributable to the effects of limpets crushing and 'bulldozing' the newly settled spat off the rocks (as discussed, among others, by Hatton, 1938; Lewis, 1954; Connell, 1961a; Dayton, 1971; Denley and Underwood, 1979). The reduction in numbers of newly settled barnacles where there are no limpets is attributable to the growth of algae in plots with no grazers (see also Denley and Underwood, 1979; Underwood, 1980; Hawkins, 1983). Thus, at some densities, limpets have a positive effect on the settlement of barnacles because they remove algal species that would otherwise pre-empt the space, and make it unavailable for settlement. The subsequent survival of the barnacles in plots with different densities of limpets was also non-linear (Underwood *et al.*, 1983, Fig. 3), because barnacles were smothered by algae in plots where there were no grazers, and continued to be crushed by the foraging limpets wherever these were active. The result of the experiments was to show that high numbers of limpets have deleterious effects on survival of barnacles; low numbers of limpets presumably still crush and 'bulldoze' small barnacles, but this source of mortality is less than that of overgrowth by algae when limpets are absent. Hence, the low numbers of limpets are, overall, beneficial. The results of experiments on survival of limpets match those obtained by Dayton (1971) for *Chthamalus dalli*, which is overgrown and smothered by *Balanus glandula* at some levels on the shore. Where acmaeid limpets are present, they tend to crush and dislodge the *Balanus* in greater numbers than any effect they might have on *Chthamalus*, thus enhancing the survivorship of the *Chthamalus* by removing a potential competitor for space.

Note, however, that the results of experiments on survival of the barnacles (Underwood *et al.*, 1983) would have appeared very different if only the natural density (8 per enclosure) and plots with no limpets had been compared; there would have been no significant difference, because the negative effects of large numbers of limpets on survival were of very similar magnitude to the negative effects of algae where there were no grazers. Only by having experimental plots with a range of densities of limpets was it possible to interpret this interaction.

What would happen where physical environmental factors were different? It is already clear that the effectiveness of grazing limpets depends, at least partially, on the rate of growth of foliose algae. Therefore, environmental conditions that enhance the rate of growth of algae should also increase the rate of overgrowth of newly settled barnacles. Thus, where algae grow rapidly, limpets at greater densities are needed to keep the areas free from plants. It might reasonably be expected, therefore, that the relationship between positive and negative effects of grazing by limpets on the recruitment or survival of barnacles will depend on the rates of growth of algae, and therefore, in turn, on the prevailing environmental conditions. An example demonstrating precisely this was described by Underwood *et al.* (1983, Fig. 4) at low levels on a shore, where algal growth was much more rapid than at higher levels. Limpets in small numbers were ineffective at keeping the areas clear of algae, and even at relatively high densities continued to exert a positive, enhancing effect on the settlement of barnacles.

This is illustrated here in Fig. 24.1. The results of experiments on the effect of limpets on settlement and survival of barnacles should be variable depending on the rates of recruitment and growth of competitors for space at the time, and in the sites of the experiment. For example, where algae grow rapidly and profusely, limpets can be expected to have positive effects on barnacles, even at very high densities. In contrast, where algal growth is sparse, or slow, limpets will have negative effects on barnacles, even at low densities. Finally, there are bound to exist conditions where any single experiment, involving only the removal of natural numbers of limpets and comparison with an untouched control, might result in a positive effect of limpets, a negative effect, or no discernible interaction. In Fig. 24.1C, for example, if the natural density of limpets in some site is X, their removal will result in a negative effect on numbers of barnacles, compared with control areas (compare zero limpets with X limpets in Fig. 24.1C). In contrast, if the natural density happens to be Z, the same experiment should result in a positive effect, and, if the natural density is Y, there will be no effect of limpets.

Better experiments can be designed, provided that non-linearities in the interactions are anticipated. Improved experimental designs would evaluate the effects of limpets at high and low densities, relative to different sources of mortality of barnacles. Such experiments will need to be repeated in different habitats and at different times of the year, if the processes affected by limpets are themselves subject to influences of physical variables. Thus, limpets could be expected to have more positive (facilitatory) effects at lower levels on the shore, or during cooler periods of the year – conditions when algal growth is likely to be faster. In contrast, where algae (or other occupiers of and competitors for space) are held

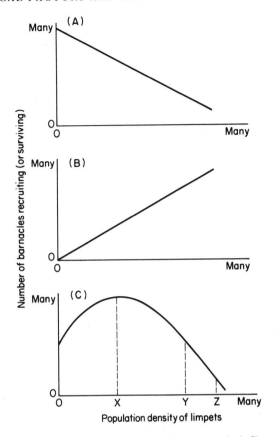

FIG. 24.1. Diagram illustrating the potential effects of limpets on recruitment or survival of barnacles under different environmental conditions. The same range of densities of limpets is shown in all graphs.
A. Harsh conditions that prevent algal growth: limpets at increasing densities crush or 'bulldoze' newly settled and small
barnacles, and thus exert a negative effect (e.g. at high levels on a shore).
B. Benign conditions that allow profuse algal growth: limpets at increasing densities keep the substratum free from algae, and
thus enhance the recruitment or survival of barnacles more than they 'bulldoze' or crush the small barnacles (e.g. at low
levels on a shore).
C. Intermediate conditions that allow some algal growth: at small densities limpets promote recruitment and survival of
barnacles by clearing algae from the substratum (as in B); at great densities, limpets kill many small barnacles (as in A). X, Y
and Z are three densities of limpets discussed in the text.

in check by the weather (as at high levels on some shores, or during hot, summer periods), limpets are
more likely to only have direct, deleterious effects. Finally, in any situation where the facilitatory and
negative effects cancel each other out, numerically, at a given density of limpets, there will be no
observed interaction between grazers and sessile species. These situations are illustrated in Fig. 24.1.

Again, the rôle of physical environmental factors is to modify biological interactions, leading to
different outcomes under different conditions. The final outcome of biological interactions such as
that between sessile species competing for space, and grazers feeding over the same substrata, will
depend not only on the densities of the interacting species, but also on the prevailing environmental
conditions.

24.6 Physical Variables and Littoral Predators

It was suggested earlier, with respect to Lubchenco's (1978) study of preferences of grazers and the diversity of algae, that algal–herbivore interactions involved complex responses to physical factors, and to the choices exercised by consumers in different habitats. The same arguments can be developed for the effects of predators on the diversity, distribution and abundance of sessile prey species (e.g. Paine, 1966, 1974, 1980; Dayton, 1971; Connell, 1975; Menge and Sutherland, 1976; Fairweather *et al.*, 1984). Several studies of the activity and rates of feeding of predatory whelks in response to physical factors have shed light on some of the complexity of ecological relationships among species under different environmental regimes.

The dogwhelk, *Nucella lapillus* (L.), has been particularly widely studied in Britain and on the East coast of the United States. It is well known that dogwhelks often cease feeding and aggregate, usually in crevices, at certain times of the year. For example, Connell (1961a) noted that dogwhelks sheltered in crevices during gales and periods of cold weather. Feare (1971a) described more complex patterns of aggregation, during summer, during winter, and before the onset of reproductive activity. Menge (1978a,b) has studied the activities of dogwhelks on a number of shores of different degrees of exposure to wave-action, to determine the effects of wave-exposure and desiccation on the intensity of predation on its principal prey species. On the eastern seaboard of the United States, the major species of prey were the barnacle, *Semibalanus balanoides* (L.), and the mussel, *Mytilus edulis* L.

Menge noted that intensity of predation was variable among shores, and among seasons of the year, with generally more predation on sheltered shores, and during the warmer months of the year (May to October). The reduced amount of predation recorded at wave-exposed sites was not attributable to the absence of dogwhelks from these areas – the snails were abundant there. Menge (1978a) hypothesized that, on exposed shores, wave-shock was restricting the foraging movements of the dogwhelks, keeping them confined to areas near cracks and crevices, which provided shelter. In contrast, on sheltered shores, where splash and spray from waves are less common, desiccation during low tide might influence the activities of the whelks. The gradients of desiccation and wave-exposure should be negatively correlated (see also Dayton, 1971; Underwood and Denley, 1984). Evidence from dogwhelks in experimental cages on different shores and in different habitats examined these propositions, and supported the hypothesis that desiccation killed dogwhelks in sheltered habitats, particularly at higher levels on the shore. Mortality was greater during warm periods. Where there was a canopy of fucoid algae (*Fucus distichus* L., *F. vesiculosus* L. and *Ascophyllum nodosum* (L.) Le Jol.), mortality due to desiccation was reduced on sheltered shores (means of 18.9% mortality of dogwhelks in cages in open situations versus 3.6% dying where cages were under a canopy). In contrast, the presence of a canopy made no difference to mortality on exposed shores, where little effect of desiccation was found (mean mortalities 4% and 3.6% in open and canopy-covered situations, respectively). In contrast, during storms, mortality of dogwhelks was greater in exposed sites than on sheltered shores. Furthermore, dogwhelks on exposed shores were very much confined to foraging near crevices, presumably because of the direct effects of waves, which killed whelks in experimental cages. Thus, during the period of active feeding by dogwhelks (May to October), the snails remained in or near crevices on the exposed shores, but spread out over the entire habitat on sheltered shores.

From these observations, Menge (1978a,b) constructed a model to account for the observed variations in intensity of predation in different places. This was that the efficiency (or the intensity) of predation by the whelks would be reduced by desiccation (on sheltered shores) and by wave-action (on exposed shores). From this, he hypothesized that rates of consumption of prey (*Semibalanus* and *Mytilus*) would be higher at greater distances from crevices on sheltered shores – where there was a canopy to protect the whelks from desiccation – than in similar regions without a canopy. He also predicted that rates of consumption of prey on exposed shores would be inversely related to the distance from suitable crevices (which provide shelter from the effects of waves), because wave-shock prevents the dogwhelks from efficiently consuming their prey.

To test this hypothesis, Menge (1978a) enclosed some areas of shore inside cages, to prevent dogwhelks from foraging, and used experimental roofs and untouched areas (which allowed access by the dogwhelks) as controls. The difference in cover of barnacles and mussels in the areas with and without dogwhelks allowed an estimate of the intensity of predation.

The results were intriguing. First, they supported the hypothesis that wave-action prevents effective predation outside crevices on exposed shores. There was no measurable effect of predation on cover of prey species at any distance from a crevice. The presence or absence of an algal canopy over the experimental areas made no difference to this result. Simply, wave-action was too severe to allow any predation by the dogwhelks, and they were forced to subsist on prey within a few centimetres of the crevices. On the sheltered shore, in contrast, there was a major effect of algal canopy on the intensity of predation. During the first few months of the experiments (Menge, 1978, Fig. 4B), there were more prey at distances of 1 and 2m from crevices where there was no algal canopy. After 7 months, however, this effect disappeared, and eventually there was 100% cover of prey inside cages, where dogwhelks were excluded, but only 0–27% in areas where dogwhelks had foraged up to 2m from crevices. Under an algal canopy, there were, on average, less prey at all times during the experiment than in similar areas without a canopy. Eventually, there were 0–19% covers of prey in plots without cages under a canopy. Clearly, wave-action seriously disrupted the activities of predators on exposed shores, and algal cover made little to no difference. On sheltered shores, the algal canopy provided protection from the extreme rigours of desiccation, and thus prey species fared worse under the canopy.

Menge (1978b) followed this study by an evaluation of the actual rates of predation inside experimental cages at different distances from crevices, under algal canopies and out in the open on sheltered and exposed shores. Here, enormous complexity of interactions between height on the shore (i.e. a correlate of increasing desiccation), presence of an algal canopy (which moderated desiccation), month of the year (associated with different temperatures and insolation during low tide) and exposure to wave-action influenced the rates of consumption of mussels by the whelks. In addition, the origin of the dogwhelks, i.e. their previous feeding history and general morphology (see Moore, 1936b; Kitching et al., 1966), also influenced their rate of predation. In general, dogwhelks from an exposed locality consumed mussels faster than those from a sheltered shore, and dogwhelks at low levels on the shore fed more quickly than those higher up. Similarly, whelks caged under a canopy of fucoid algae were more rapid consumers than those in open localities. Nevertheless, the intensity of predation varied from place to place in complex ways as a result of all the physical factors examined. For example, on the exposed shore, the effect of an algal canopy depended upon the height on the shore. Dogwhelks at low-shore levels under a canopy were more effective predators than those at the same tidal height where there was no algal cover. At a higher level on the shore, the presence of an algal canopy made less difference to the rates of consumption of prey by dogwhelks.

Menge (1978b) concluded that various aspects of the physical environment caused non-linear variations in the rates of feeding by dogwhelks, and that some aspects of past history or individual's phenotype were also important. These studies demonstrate the need for rigorous experimental appraisal of the rôles of physical factors before any sensible interpretation of the intensity of predation is possible. They also reveal that the various influences of the physical environment are complex, variable and unpredictable – because combinations of physical factors are not linear, nor simply additive.

Other whelks are influenced by desiccation and wave-action, but not in the same manner as that described for Nucella lapillus. For example, Morula marginalba Blainville is an important predator on shores in New South Wales, and consumes a variety of prey types (Fairweather and Underwood, 1983;

Fairweather *et al.*, 1984; Moran *et al.*, 1984). It also forms large aggregations, but not at particular times of the year. These are usually in crevices, shallow pools, or in depressions at low levels on the shore. Whelks are either out of shelter, feeding on a variety of prey, or are clustered in shelters. Whelks are also swept away by waves when out of crevices on wave-exposed shores (Moran, 1980). Within limits, however, on sheltered shores, the proportion of whelks feeding at any given time is increased by increased splash and spray due to waves. This is illustrated in Fig. 24.2. Thus, the proportion aggregating is a negative function of the degree of wave-action. Moran (1980 and in prep.) proposed, as a model to account for the variations in observed pattern of dispersion, that the aggregating behaviour was controlled by the susceptibility of whelks to desiccation on shores sheltered from waves. From this, he hypothesized that whelks should respond to greater desiccatory stress by staying in crevices. Where numbers of whelks are large, and availability of suitable shelter is limited, whelks will inevitably form aggregations in crevices. Where whelks are in lower densities, they will retreat to crevices, but not be in sufficient numbers to appear as aggregations.

To test this in the field, Moran (1980) chose an area with abundant food (mostly barnacles), some 500 whelks and many crevices. He then recorded the numbers of whelks in and out of crevices each day for a month, and the time of low tide during daylight on each day. The rationale behind this was that when low tide is near mid-day, the potential stress of desiccation is greater, because the sun is directly overhead during the period of emersion. In contrast, when low tide occurs near dawn or dusk, insolation and desiccation are less extreme throughout low tide (see also Dayton, 1971; Wolcott, 1973). The final proviso was that the length of period of emersion (and submersion) was similar even though the tidal cycle moved from neaps to springs and back to neaps. Note that above mid-tidal level, there is a longer relative period of submersion during spring than during neap tides; at heights below mid-tidal level, there is a longer period of submersion during neaps than during springs. By choosing a mid-tidal level, Moran was able to ensure that whelks would not be influenced on different days by differences in the potential time available to forage whilst the tide was in. The results demonstrated a striking correlation between the proportion of whelks in crevices and the time of day of low tide on the previous day (see Fig. 24.3). Thus, when low tides were in the middle of the day, more whelks were aggregating in shelter; when low tides were in the early morning or late evening, more whelks came out of shelter and fed. That this influences the rates of mortality of prey was also demonstrated. Moran (1980) had

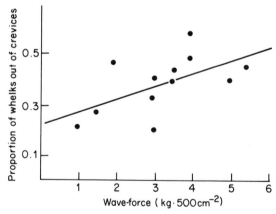

FIG. 24.2. Proportion of whelks (*Morula marginalba*) out of crevices and feeding during low tide, as a function of force of waves during the previous high tide (during October, 1978). Data are from Moran (1980); wave-force was measured by the device described by Jones and Demetropoulos (1968). Spearman's rank correlation coefficient; $r_s = 0.58$; 10 df; $P < 0.05$.

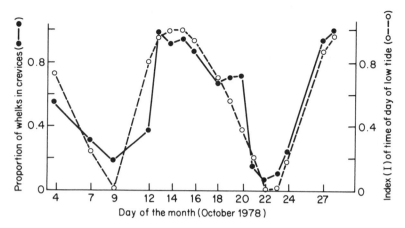

FIG. 24.3. Proportion of whelks (*Morula marginalba*) in crevices each day during October, 1978, and an index (I) of time of day of the previous day-time low tide. This index is $I = \sin((T - 6) \times 90°/6)$ where T is time of low tide (from 0600 to 1800 hours). When low tide is at mid-day, $I = 1$; when low tide is at 6.00 a.m. or 6.00 p.m., $I = 0$. Relationship between proportion sheltering and the value of the index was significant (proportion sheltering $= 0.12 + 0.8\,I$; $r^2 = 0.80$; 15 df; $P < 0.01$). Data are from Moran (1980).

experimental cages around the study site which contained whelks in fixed densities. He counted the numbers of barnacles (*Tesseropora rosea*) that had been drilled by the whelks; these data showed a negative correlation between number being eaten and an index of degree of stress due to desiccation and air temperature during low tide (Fig. 24.4).

As discussed earlier for grazers, the effectiveness of littoral predators is influenced in complex ways by the prevailing physical environment. The studies of Menge (1978a,b) and Moran (1980 and in prep.) demonstrate that the responses of whelks to alterations of the physical regime during low tide are complex. In Menge's experiments, these effects were ameliorated in some places and at some times by the presence of an algal canopy. In Moran's study, there were no, or very few foliose macroalage nearby that could provide any cover during low tide (see Underwood, 1980, 1981a). It is notable that the results of the two studies are similar in only some aspects. *Morula* retreated to crevices on sheltered shores during periods when stress due to desiccation was potentially great. Whelks emerged from the shelters in response to increased wave-action, which effectively reduced the degree of desiccation by causing splash and spray. *Morula* is not usually found in large numbers on exposed shores where wave-action is more extreme, and foraging whelks can be washed away (Moran, 1980). *Nucella lapillus*, in contrast, is found in large densities on wave-exposed shores, but often shows morphological modifications that are adaptive to these environments (see Kitching *et al.*, 1966; Kitching and Lockwood, 1974; Kitching, this volume).

In both cases, the intensity of predation, and the effects of the predators on the distribution and abundance of prey were complicated by the interactions with the physical environment. The proximity and availability of crevices were also important considerations. During the major period of foraging, *Nucella* on sheltered shores were not confined to crevices (Menge, 1978a). *Morula*, in contrast, at all times of the year can only forage near crevices. The effects of crevices on some species of prey have also been investigated in more recent experiments by Fairweather *et al.* (1984) and, for grazers, by Levings and Garrity (1983). The general conclusion from studies where physical factors have been investigated is that they play important rôles in the relationship between predators and their prey, but these are made complex by the interplay of several different environmental gradients operating at once (e.g. desiccation and wave-shock usually being inversely related) and by complex

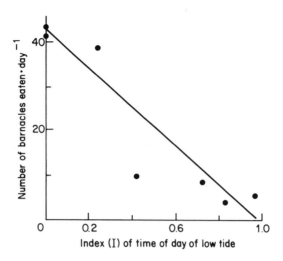

FIG. 24.4. The mean number of barnacles (*Tesseropora rosea*) killed by *Morula* per day, as a function of the time of day of the previous daylight low tide (I; see Fig. 24.3 for details). Spearman's rank correlation coefficient: $r_s = -0.94$; 5 df; $P < 0.01$. Data are from Moran (1980).

non-linearities in the effects of modifying factors, such as the presence of algal canopies or shelter provided by other organisms (see Dayton (1971) for a situation where whelks were able to shelter among sea anemones during periods of inclement weather). Such complexities make it very difficult to generalize (as for example in Connell, 1975; see Underwood and Denley, 1984), and require that physical variables must be examined carefully, and their effects unravelled experimentally before much sense could be made of the activities of littoral predators, and their interactions with their prey.

24.7 Intensity of Competition for Food of Littoral Grazers

It is generally recognized that competition for limited resources of space and food is a widespread feature influencing the structure of rocky shore communities, or, at least, modifying the dynamics of some littoral populations (see reviews by Connell, 1983; Schoener, 1983). There has, however, also been considerable debate about the general importance of competition as an organizing force in natural communities, and about the reliability of some of the experimental evidence available to demonstrate the existence, or magnitude, of competition (e.g. Simberloff, 1983; Underwood, 1985). In fact, as Wiens (1977) reminds us, competition will only be intense (and therefore only detectable) in those places and at those times when resources are in short supply. Widespread experimental studies exist to demonstrate the effects of inter- and intraspecific competition in the life histories of littoral gastropods, particularly limpets (e.g. Sutherland, 1970; Haven, 1973; Underwood, 1976, 1978, 1985; Black, 1977; Creese, 1980; Creese and Underwood, 1982). Despite this, little attention has been paid so far to any influences that variations in physical factors may have on the abundance or availability of food resources of littoral gastropods. Yet, production of littoral algae is very dependent on combinations of physical variables, in addition to the presence, activities and preferences of the grazers (see the earlier discussion of recruitment and growth of macroalgae). Relatively few experimental studies of competition in the field have measured the abundances of resources, and even fewer of the studies have investigated seasonal or other temporal variations in resources and intensity of competition (see the reviews by Connell (1983) and Schoener (1983)).

In studies of supplies of microalgal food for rocky shore grazers in New South Wales, two major gradients of microalgal abundance were identified – more microalgae were present at lower levels on the shore and there were generally greater abundances during cooler periods of the year (Underwood, 1985). These gradients in abundance of food correlate with gradients in physical factors such as desiccation, insolation and temperature during low tide. Previous experiments had revealed intense intraspecific competition at increased densities of the limpet, *Cellana tramoserica*, and the snail, *Nerita atramentosa* Reeve, and interspecific effects of *Nerita* on *Cellana*, causing decreased tissue-weights and increased mortality of limpets (Underwood, 1976, 1978b; Creese and Underwood, 1982). On the basis that competitive interactions should be most intense when resources are least abundant, it was hypothesized that competition among *Cellana*, and between *Nerita* and *Cellana*, would be more extreme at high levels on the shore, and during the summer. Limpets were caged at natural and increased densities at three heights on the shore in two series of experiments, during winter and summer (see Underwood, 1984c for full details). The abundance of food was measured as

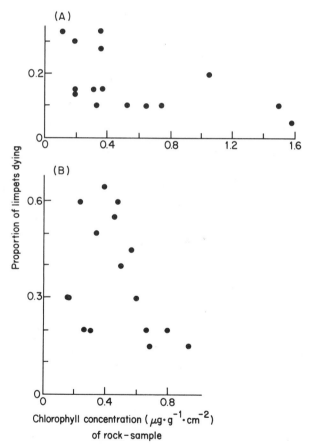

FIG. 24.5. Mortality of limpets (*Cellana tramoserica*) as a function of the amount of microalgal food (measured as concentration of chorophyll in the substratum) in experimental cages during (A) winter and (B) summer series of experiments. Data are mean proportional mortality and mean chlorophyll concentration from two replicate cages at each of three heights on the shore during each season; data are from cages with 10, 20 or 40 *Cellana*, and 10 *Cellana* with 10 or 30 snails (*Nerita atramentosa*). In each season, mortality was negatively correlated with chlorophyll concentration: Spearman's rank correlation coefficient, r_s = -0.57; 13 df; $P < 0.05$ in winter; r_s = -0.53; 13 df; $P < 0.05$ for summer data. For full details, see Underwood (1984c).

the concentration of chlorophyll on and in the substratum, which provides a reliable estimate of the number of microalgal cells present (see Underwood, 1984a).

The major differences in intensity of competitive interactions between seasons are illustrated in Fig. 24.5. There were differences in the negative correlation between mortality of limpets and amount of food present in the cages at the end of each series of experiment. In these graphs, the smaller amounts of food and the generally increased proportional mortality of the limpets during summer are easily seen (compare Fig. 24.5A with B).

From this experimental analysis, it is clear that variations in the intensity of competition among mobile grazing gastropods can be predicted from knowledge of the density of the grazers, and abundance of food resources. It is also clear that abundance and productivity of littoral algae are influenced by physical factors (Castenholz, 1961; Underwood, 1984a). Many of these influences are complex and subtle (see Castenholz, 1963), and therefore variations in competition for microalgal food will also be complex.

24.8 Conclusions

The foregoing brief discussion of selected experimental studies of biological interactions in rocky shore communities demonstrates conclusively the importance of physical factors as modifying influences on patterns and processes on sea-shores. More importantly, however, many of the studies demonstrate that there are several possible models for patterns of distribution and abundance of littoral species. Thus, the influence of physical environmental factors should never be assumed without direct evidence to support hypotheses based on models invoking physical factors. Wherever possible, experimental evidence should also be available to eliminate alternative models before the direct impact of physical factors is accepted (see also Dayton, 1979; Underwood and Denley, 1984).

Examples have been presented to demonstrate that virtually all aspects of the structure and dynamics of rocky shore communities are affected by complex suites of inter-related physical factors. In all case, the rôles of the physical factors could only be identified and interpreted in the light of results of manipulative experiments in the field. From the foregoing comments and examples, it should be obvious that it will only become possible to understand fully the processes governing the distribution, abundance and rates of change of littoral species where experiments are done in a range of habitats, at different times of the year, and with due regard to the complex physical gradients existing in the environment.

ACKNOWLEDGEMENTS

The preparation of this manuscript was aided by funds from the Australian Research Grants Committee and the University of Sydney Research Grant, and by the assistance of P. Scanes. I am grateful for the advice and help of Professor D.T. Anderson, Dr P.A. Underwood, M.G. Chapman and my students and colleagues in the Ross Street Laboratories, especially P.G. Fairweather and K.A. McGuinness.

RETROSPECT

THE WELLCOME MARINE LABORATORY, ROBIN HOOD'S BAY

(photo: A.E. Simpson)

'*The zoological departments of Leeds and Sheffield Universities had decided to open a marine biological Station in the village. They had bought the old Coastguard Station, which forms one of the village ramparts against the sea by the Slipway. They were equipping it with benches and tanks for keeping live marine animals, and they wanted someone to act as a sort of curator-caretaker, preferably someone who knew the beaches and would be able to assist in the collection of specimens. I got the job. They could only pay five shillings a week, but. . . . there were no specified hours. . . . the Leeds professor Walter Garstang. . . . certainly looked like a real scientist. He was untidy and always wore rough tweeds and heavy boots. He didn't mind wading into pools. . . . We cleared one of the cupboards of the students' things and arranged all this new gear on the shelves. Then Sam opened a case which contained nothing but books, and scientific journals and papers. One, a very big volume, was called* British Nudibranchiata; *and Sam handled it almost as though it were sacred. . . . 'What about this chap,* Ancula cristata?' Ancula *was even more beautiful than* Doto. . . . *Sam went on turning the plates. The pictures themselves were beautifully engraved and tinted. . . . what a dull subject geology was compared with this!. . . . We found a specimen of* Ancula, *the nudibranch with the orange-tipped papillae. When it had unfolded itself in the tube and started moving I thought it looked more beautiful than any flower or butterfly I had ever seen. No wonder the man who had drawn and painted them hadn't found time to paint ordinary pictures. . . .*
. . . . We'd discuss things like this by the hour while we worked at the bench or sat smoking our pipes like venerable philosophers in front of the laboratory fire. When the weather was bad and the sea rough, it was like being in a lighthouse. The big waves thundered on the outer wall making the whole building tremble, and we'd see the spray swishing up over the windows and hear it splashing on the roof, and rushing down again. At high tide in such weather it wasn't safe to leave the laboratory to go into the cottage, for everything would be awash outside, and even the fishing cobles had to be hauled from the Dock far up the main street, and the cottages here had to have their ground-floor windows barred to stop flooding. On such occasions we'd have a meal in the laboratory, and when we got tired of talking, Sam would pick up his accordion. . . . I'd. . . . started hob-nobbing with the 'queer folk' at the laboratory.'

Leo Walmsley (1945) *So Many Loves,*
Wm Collins & Sons

REFERENCES

Abbott, R.T. (1974) *American Seashells.* (2nd edn), Van Nostrand Reinhold Co., New York, 663 pp.

Abrahamson, W.G. (1975) Reproductive strategies in dewberries. *Ecology*, **56**, 721–726.

Adey, W.H. (1966) The genera *Lithothamnium, Leptophytum* (nov. gen.) and *Phymatolithon* in the Gulf of Maine. *Hydrobiologia*, **28**, 321–370.

Aitken, J.J. (1962) Experiments with populations of the limpet *Patella vulgata* (L.). *Ir. Nat. J.*, **14**, 12–15.

Aleem, A.A. (1950) Distribution and ecology of British marine littoral diatoms. *J. Ecol.*, **38**, 75–106.

Alexander, D.W. (1969) The study of the biology of animals living on and in littoral sponges with special reference to *Halichondria* (Pallas). Ph. D. Thesis, University of London, 359 pp.

Alheit, J. and Scheibel, W. (1982) Benthic harpacticoids as a food source for fish. *Mar. Biol.*, **70**, 141–147.

Allan, J.D. (1975) The distributional ecology and diversity of benthic insects in Cement Creek, Colorado. *Ecology*, **56**, 1040–1053.

Allen, F.E. (1955) Identity of breeding temperature in southern and northern hemisphere species of *Mytilus* (Lamellibranchia). *Pacif. Sci.*, **9**, 107–109.

Allen, J.A. (1983) Ch. 2. The ecology of deep-sea molluscs. In, *The Mollusca*, Vol. 6, *Ecology*, ed. W.D. Russell-Hunter, Academic Press, London, pp. 29–75.

Al-Ogily, S.M. and Knight-Jones, E.W. (1977) Antifouling role of antibiotics by marine algae and bryozoans. *Nature, Lond.*, **265**, 728–729.

Alveal, K. (1970) Estudios ficoecologicos en la region costera de Valparaiso. *Revta Biol. Mar.*, **14**, 7–88.

Anderson, A. (1974) Studies in the ecogenetics of *Littorina neglecta* Bean, a member of the rough winkle aggregate of species. M. Sc. Thesis, University of Liverpool, 85 pp.

Andrewartha, H.G. and Birch, L.C. (1954) *The Distribution and Abundance of Animals.* University of Chicago Press, Chicago, 782 pp.

Ansell, A.D. (1967) Egg production of *Mercenaria mercenaria. Limnol. Oceanogr.*, **12**, 172–176.

Ansell, A.D. and Lander, K.F. (1967) Studies on the hard-shell clam, *Venus mercenaria*, in British waters. III. Further observations on the seasonal biochemical cycle and on spawning. *J. Appl. Ecol.*, **4**, 425–435.

Aracena, O., Yañez, R., Lozada, E. and Lopez, M.T. (1974) Crecimiento de *Choromytilus chorus* en Talcan, Chiloe (Mollusca, Bivalvia, Mytilidae). *Boln Soc. Biol. Concepción*, **48**, 347–357.

Armstrong, R.A. (1976) Fugitive species: experiments with Fungi and some theoretical considerations. *Ecology*, **57**, 953–963.

Arnaud, P.M. (1974) Contribution à la bionomie marine benthique des régions antarctiques et subantarctiques. *Téthys*, **6**, 471–653.

Arnold, D.C. (1957) The response of the limpet *Patella vulgata* L., to waters of different salinities. *J. Mar. Biol. Ass. U.K.*, **36**, 121–128.

Arnold, D.C. (1972) Salinity tolerances of some common prosobranchs. *J. Mar. Biol. Ass. U.K.*, **52**, 475–486.

Athersuch, J. (1979) The ecology and distribution of the littoral ostracods of Cyprus. *J. Nat. Hist.*, **13**, 135–160.

Atkins, N. (1980) Possible competition between Seaside Cinclodes (*Cinclodes nigrofumosus*) and Ruddy Turnstones (*Arenaria interpres*). *Condor*, **82**, 107–108.

Atkinson, N.K., Summers, R.W., Nicoll, M. and Greenwood, J.J.D. (1981) Population, movements and biometrics of the Purple Sandpiper (*Calidris maritima*) in eastern Scotland. *Ornis Scandinavica*, **12**, 18–27.

Atkinson, W.D. and Newbury, S.F. (1984) The adaptations of the rough winkle, *Littorina rudis* to desiccation and dislodgement by wind and waves. *J. Anim. Ecol.*, **53**, 93–106.

Atkinson, W.D. and Warwick, T. (1983) The role of selection in the colour polymorphism of *Littorina rudis* Maton and *Littorina arcana* Hannaford Ellis (Prosobranchia: Littorinidae). *Biol. J. Linn. Soc.*, **20**, 137–151.

Avens, A.C. and Sleigh, M.A. (1965) Osmotic balance in gastropod molluscs – I. Some marine and littoral gastropods. *Comp. Biochem. Physiol.*, **16**, 121–141.

Ayling, A.M. (1981) The role of biological disturbance in temperate subtidal encrusting communities. *Ecology*, **62**, 830–847.

Bacci, G. (1947) L'inversione dell sesso ed il ciclo stagionale della gonade in *Patella coerulea* L. *Pubbl. Staz. Zool. Napoli*, **21**, 183–217.

Bachelet, G. (1981) Application de l'équation de von Bertalanffy à la croissance du bivalve *Scrobicularia plana*. *Cah. Biol. Mar.*, **22**, 291–311.

Backlund, H.O. (1945) Wrack fauna of Sweden and Finland: ecology and chorology. *Opusc. Ent.*, **5** (suppl.), 1–236.

Bainbridge, I.P. and Minton, C.D.T. (1978) The migration and mortality of the Curlew in Britain and Ireland. *Bird Study*, **25**, 39–50.

Baird, D., Evans, P.R., Milne, H. and Pienkowski, M.W. (1985) Utilization by shorebirds of benthic invertebrate production in intertidal areas. *Oceanogr. Mar. Biol. Ann. Rev.*, (IN PRESS).

Baird, R.H. (1966) Factors affecting the growth and condition of mussels (*Mytilus edulis*). *Fishery Invest., Lond.*, Ser. II, **25**(2), 1–33.

Baird, R.H. and Drinnan, R.E. (1957) The ratio of shell to meat in *Mytilus* as a function of tidal exposure to air. *J. Cons. Perm. Int. Explor. Mer*, **22**, 329–336.

Baker, J.M. (1976) Biological monitoring – principles, methods and difficulties. In, *Marine Ecology and Oil Pollution*, ed. J.M. Baker, Applied Science Publishers, London, pp. 41–53.

Baker, J.M. (1981) Winter feeding rates of Redshank *Tringa totanus* and Turnstone *Arenaria interpres* on a rocky shore. *Ibis*, **123**, 85–87.

Ballantine, W.J. (1961a) The population dynamics of *Patella vulgata* and other limpets. Ph.D. Thesis, University of London, 236 pp.

Ballantine, W.J. (1961b) A biologically-defined exposure scale for the comparative description of rocky shores. *Fld Stud.*, **1**, 1–19.

Bannister, J.V. (1975) Shell parameters in relation to zonation in Mediterranean limpets. *Mar. Biol.*, **31**, 63–67.

Bantock, C.R. and Cockayne, W.C. (1975) Chromosomal polymorphism in *Nucella lapillus*. *Heredity, Lond.*, **34**, 231–245.

Barber, B.J. and Blake, N.J. (1983) Growth and reproduction of the bay scallop, *Argopecten irradians* (Lamarck) at its southern distributional limit. *J. Exp. Mar. Biol. Ecol.*, **66**, 247–256.

Barkati, S. and Ahmed, M. (1974) Reproductive cycle of the marine mussel *Perna viridis*. *Pakistan J. Zool.*, **6**, 31–40.

Barker, M.F. (1979) Breeding and recruitment in a population of the New Zealand starfish *Stichaster australis* (Verrill). *J. Exp. Mar. Biol. Ecol.*, **41**, 195–211.

Barker, M.F. and Nichols, D. (1983) Reproduction, recruitment and juvenile ecology of the starfish *Asterias rubens* and *Marthasterias glacialis*. *J. Mar. Biol. Ass. U.K.*, **63**, 745–766.

Barnes, H. (1955) The growth rate of *Balanus balanoides* (L.). *Oikos*, **6**, 109–113.

Barnes, H. (1956) *Balanus balanoides* (L.) in the Firth of Clyde: the development and annual variation of the larval population, and the causative factors. *J. Anim. Ecol.*, **25**, 72–84.

Barnes, H. (1963) Light, temperature and the breeding of *Balanus balanoides*. *J. Mar. Biol. Ass. U.K.*, **43**, 717–727.

Barnes, H. and Barnes, M. (1954) The general biology of *Balanus balanus* (L.) da Costa. *Oikos*, **5**, 63–76.

Barnes, H. and Barnes, M. (1956) The general biology of *Balanus glandula* Darwin. *Pacif. Sci.*, **10**, 415–422.

Barnes, H. and Barnes, M. (1968) Egg numbers, metabolic efficiency of egg production and fecundity: local and regional variations in a number of common cirripedes. *J. Exp. Mar. Biol. Ecol.*, **2**, 135–153.

Barnes, H. and Barnes, M. (1977) The importance of being a 'littoral' nauplius. In, *Biology of Benthic Organisms*, ed. B.F. Keegan, P. ÓCéidigh & P.J.S. Boaden, Pergamon Press, Oxford, pp. 45–56.

Barnes, H. and Powell, H.T. (1950) The development, general morphology and subsequent elimination of barnacle populations, *Balanus crenatus* and *B. balanoides*, after a heavy initial settlement. *J. Anim. Ecol.*, **19**, 175–179.

Barnes, H. and Powell, H.T. (1953) The growth of *Balanus balanoides* (L.) and *B. crenatus* Brug. under varying conditions of submersion. *J. Mar. Biol. Ass. U.K.*, **32**, 107–127.

Bartsch, I. (1979) Verbreitung der Halacaridae (Acari) im Gezeitenbereich der Bretagne-Küste, eine ökologische Analyse. II. Quantitative untersuchungen und Faunenanalyse. *Cah. Biol. Mar.*, **20**, 1–28.

Bartsch, I. (1982) Halacaridae (Acari) von der Atlantikküste des borealen Nordamerikas: Ökologische und tiergeographische Faunenanalyse. *Helgoländer Wiss. Meeresunters.*, **35**, 13–46.

Batham, E.J. (1958) Ecology of southern New Zealand exposed rocky shore at Little Papanui, Otago Peninsula. *Trans. R. Soc. N.Z.*, **85**, 647–658.

Baxter, J.M. (1982) Population dynamics of *Patella vulgata* in Orkney. *Neth. J. Sea Res.*, **16**, 96–104.

Baxter, J.M. (1983a) Annual variations in soft-body dry weight, reproductive cycle and sex ratios in populations of *Patella vulgata* at adjacent sites in the Orkney Islands. *Mar. Biol.*, **76**, 149–157.

Baxter, J.M. (1983b) Allometric relationships of *Patella vulgata* L. Shell characters at three adjacent sites at Sandwick Bay in Orkney. *J. Nat. Hist.*, **17**, 743–755.

Baxter, J.M., Jones, A.M. and Simpson, J.A. (1985) Rocky shores in Orkney: a long-term study. *Proc. R. Soc. Edinb.*, B, **75**, (IN PRESS)

Bayne, B.L. (1964) Primary and secondary settlement in *Mytilus edulis* (Mollusca). *J. Anim. Ecol.*, **33**, 513–523.

Bayne, B.L. (1965) Growth and delay of metamorphosis of the larvae of *Mytilus edulis* (L.). *Ophelia*, **2**, 1–47.

Bayne, B.L. (1975) Reproduction in bivalve molluscs under environmental stress. In, *Physiological Ecology of Estuarine Organisms*, ed. F.J. Vernberg, University of South Carolina Press, Columbia, pp. 259–277.

Bayne, B.L. (1976) Ch. 4. The biology of mussel larvae. In, *Marine Mussels: their ecology and physiology*, ed. B.L. Bayne, Cambridge University Press, Cambridge, pp. 81–120.

Bayne, B.L., Thompson, R.J. and Widdows, J. (1976) Ch. 5. Physiology: I. In, *Marine Mussels: their ecology and physiology*, ed. B.L. Bayne, Cambridge University Press, Cambridge, pp. 121–206.

Bean, W. (1844) A supplement of new species. In, *British Marine Conchology*, C. Thorpe, Lumley, London, pp. 263–267.

Beaumont, A.R. and Budd, M.D. (1982) Delayed growth of mussel (*Mytilus edulis*) and scallop (*Pecten maximus*) veligers at low temperatures. *Mar. Biol.*, **71**, 97–100.

Beckley, L.E. (1982) Studies on the littoral seaweed epifauna of St Croix Island. 3. *Gelidium pristoides* (Rhodophyta) and its epifauna. *S. Afr. J. Zool.*, **17**, 3–10.

Beckley, L.E. and McLachlan, A. (1980) Studies on the littoral seaweed epifauna of St Croix Island. 2. Composition and summer standing stock. *S. Afr. J. Zool.*, **15**, 170–176.

Becuwe, M. (1971) Het voorkomen van de Steenloper, *Arenaria interpres* (L.) en de Paarse Strandloper, *Calidris maritima* (Brunnich) in Belgie en in Zeeuws- Vlaanderen (Nederland). *De Giervalk*, **61**, 175–223.

Bedford, A.P. and Moore, P.G. (1984) Macrofaunal involvement in the sublittoral decay of kelp debris: the detritivore community and species interactions. *Estuarine Coastal Shelf Sci.*, **18**, 97–111.

Bell, S.S. and Coen, L.D. (1982) Investigations on epibenthic meiofauna. II. Influence of microhabitat and macroalgae on abundance of small invertebrates on *Diopatra cuprea* (Bosc) (Polychaeta: Onuphidae) tube-caps in Virginia. *J. Exp. Mar. Biol. Ecol.*, **61**, 175–188.

Bellido, A. (1981) Les biocoenoses du littoral rocheux aux Isles Kerguelen. *Com. Nat. Fr. Rech. Antarct.*, **51**, 81–92.

Bengtson, S.-A. (1975) Timing of the moult of the Purple Sandpiper, *Calidris maritima* in Spitsbergen. *Ibis*, **117**, 100–102.

Bennell, S.J. (1981) Some observations on the littoral barnacle populations of North Wales. *Mar. Environ. Res.*, **5**, 227–240.

Bennett, I. and Pope, E.C. (1953) Intertidal zonation of the exposed rocky shores of Victoria, together with a rearrangement of the biogeographical provinces of temperate Australian shores. *Aust. J. Mar. Freshwat. Res.*, **4**, 105–159.

Bennett, I. and Pope, E.C. (1960) Intertidal zonation of the exposed rocky shores of Tasmania and its relationship with the rest of Australia. *Aust. J. Mar. Freshwat. Res.*, **11**, 182–221.

Bérard-Therriault, L. and Cardinal, A. (1973) Importance de certains facteurs écologiques sur la résistance à la desiccation des Fucacées (Phaeophyceae). *Phycologia*, **12**, 41–52.

Berge, J.A. and Hesthagen, I.H. (1981) Effects of epibenthic macropredators on community structure in an eutrophicated shallow water area, with special reference to food consumption by the common goby *Pomatoschistus microps*. *Kieler Meeresforsch.*, **5**, 462–470.

Bergerard, J. (1971) Facteurs écologiques et cycle sexuel de *Littorina saxatilis* (Olivi) (Mollusques, Gastéropodes). *Cah. Biol. Mar.*, **12**, 187–193.

Bernstein, B.B. and Jung, N. (1979) Selective pressures and coevolution in a kelp canopy community in Southern California. *Ecol. Monogr.*, **49**, 335–355.

Bernstein, B.B., Schroeter, S.F. and Mann, K.H. (1983) Sea urchin *Strongylocentrotus droebachiensis* aggregating behavior investigated by a subtidal multifactorial experiment. *Can. J. Fish. Aquat. Sci.*, **40**, 1975–1986.

Bernstein, B.B., Williams, B.E. and Mann, K.H. (1981) The role of behavioral responses to predators in modifying urchins' (*Strongylocentrotus droebachiensis*) destructive grazing and seasonal foraging patterns. *Mar. Biol.*, **63**, 39–49.

Berry, A.J. (1956) Some factors affecting the distribution of *Littorina saxatilis* (Olivi). Ph. D. Thesis, University of London, 163 pp.

Berry, A.J. (1961) Some factors affecting the distribution of *Littorina saxatilis* (Olivi). *J. Anim. Ecol.*, **30**, 27–45.

Berry, A.J. and Hunt, D.C. (1980) Behaviour and tolerance of salinity and temperature in new-born *Littorina rudis* (Maton) and the range of the species in the Forth estuary. *J. Moll. Stud.*, **46**, 55–65.

Berry, P.F. (1978) Reproduction, growth and production in the mussel *Perna perna* (L.) on the East coast of South Africa. *S. Afr. Ass. Mar. Res., Oceanogr. Res. Inst., Invest. Rep.* No. 48, pp. 1–28.

Berry, R.J. (1983) Polymorphic shell banding in the dog-whelk, *Nucella lapillus* (Mollusca). *J. Zool., Lond.*, **200**, 455–470.

Berry, R.J. and Crothers, J.H. (1968) Stabilizing selection in the dog-whelk (*Nucella lapillus*). *J. Zool., Lond.*, **155**, 5–17.

Berry, R.J. and Crothers, J.H. (1970) Genotypic stability and physiological tolerance in the dog-whelk (*Nucella lapillus*). *J. Zool., Lond.*, **162**, 293–302.

Berry, S.S. (1954) On the supposed stenobathic habitat of the California sea-mussel. *Calif. Fish. Game*, **40**, 69–73.

Bertness, M.D. (1980) Growth and mortality in the ribbed mussel *Geukensia demissa*. *Veliger*, **23**, 62–69.

Bertness, M.D. (1981) Competitive dynamics of a tropical hermit crab assemblage. *Ecology*, **62**, 751–761.

Bertness, M.D. and Cunningham, C. (1981) Crab shell-crushing predation and gastropod architectural defense. *J. Exp. Mar. Biol. Ecol.*, **50**, 213–230.

Bertness, M.D., Garrity, S.D. and Levings, S.C. (1981) Predation pressure and gastropod foraging: a tropical-temperate comparison. *Evolution, Lancaster, Pa.*, **35**, 995–1007.

Bertness, M.D. and Grosholz, E. (in prep.) Pattern and dynamics in a population of the ribbed mussel, *Geukensia demissa*.

Biebl, R. (1938) Trockenresistenz und osmotische Empfindlichkeit der Meeresalgen verschieden tiefer Standorte. *Jb. Wiss. Bot.*, **86**, 350–386.

Biebl, R. (1952) Resistenz der Meeresalgen gegen sichtbares Licht und gegen Kurzwellige UV-Strahlen. *Protoplasma*, **41**, 353–377.

Biebl, R. (1956) Lichtresistenz von Meeresalgen. *Protoplasma*, **46**, 63–89.

Biebl, R. (1958) Temperatur-und osmotische Resistenz von Meeresalgen der bretonischen Küste. *Protoplasma*, **50**, 217–242.

Bingham, F.O. (1972) The mucus holdfast of *Littorina irrorata* and its relationship to relative humidity and salinity. *Veliger*, **15**, 48–50.

Birch, L.C. (1957) The meanings of competition. *Am. Nat.*, **91**, 5–18.

Birkeland, C. (1974) Interactions between a sea pen and seven of its predators. *Ecol. Monogr.*, **44**, 211–232.

Black, R. (1973) Growth rates of intertidal molluscs as indicators of effects of unexpected incidents of pollution. *J. Fish. Res. Bd Can.*, **30**, 1385–1388.

Black, R. (1976) The effects of grazing by the limpet, *Acmaea insessa*, on the kelp, *Egregia laevigata*, in the intertidal zone. *Ecology*, **57**, 265–277.

Black, R. (1977) Population regulation in the intertidal limpet *Patelloida alticostata* (Angas, 1865). *Oecologia (Berlin)*, **30**, 9–22.

Black, R. (1978) Tactics of whelks preying on limpets. *Mar. Biol.*, **46**, 157–162.

Black, R. (1979) Competition between intertidal limpets: an intrusive niche on a steep resource gradient. *J. Anim. Ecol.*, **48**, 401–411.

Blackmore, D.T. (1969a) Studies of *Patella vulgata* L. I. Growth, reproduction and zonal distribution. *J. Exp. Mar. Biol. Ecol.*, **3**, 200–213.

Blackmore, D.T. (1969b) Studies of *Patella vulgata* L. II. Seasonal variation in biochemical composition. *J. Exp. Mar. Biol. Ecol.*, **3**, 231–245.

Blanco, G.J. (1973) Status and problems of coastal aqua-culture in the Philippines. In, *Coastal Aquaculture in the Indo-Pacific Region*, ed. T.V.R. Pillay, Fishing News (Books) Ltd., London, pp. 60–67.

Blankley, W.O. (1981) Marine food of kelp gulls, lesser sheathbills and imperial cormorants at Marion Island (Subantarctic). *Cormorant*, **9**, 77–84.

Blankley, W.O. and Branch, G.M. (1984) Cooperative prey capture and unusual brooding habits of *Anasterias rupicola* (Verrill) (Asteroidea) at Sub-Antarctic Marion Island. *Mar. Ecol. Prog. Ser.*, **20**, 171–176.

Blankley, W.O. and Branch, G.M. (1985) Ecology of the limpet *Nacella delesserti* (Philippi) at Marion Island in the sub-Antarctic southern ocean. *J. Exp. Mar. Biol. Ecol.*, (IN PRESS).

Boaden, P.J.S., O'Connor, R.J. and Seed, R. (1975) The composition and zonation of a *Fucus serratus* community in Strangford Lough, County Down. *J. Exp. Mar. Biol. Ecol.*, **17**, 111–136.

Boaden, P.J.S., O'Connor, R.J. and Seed, R. (1976a) The fauna of a *Fucus serratus* L. community: ecological isolation in sponges and tunicates. *J. Exp. Mar. Biol. Ecol.*, **21**, 249–267.

Boaden, P.J.S., O'Connor, R.J. and Seed, R. (1976b) Some observations on the size of the sponges *Grantia compressa* (Fabr.) and *Sycon ciliatum* (Fabr.) in Strangford Lough, County Down. *Proc. R. Ir. Acad.* B, **76**, 535–542.

Bocquet, C. (1953) Sur un copépode harpacticoide mineur, *Diarthrodes feldmanni* n.sp. *Bull. Soc. Zool. Fr.*, **78**, 101–105.

Boicourt, W.C. (1982) Estuarine larval retention mechanisms on two scales. In, *Estuarine Comparisons*, ed. V.S. Kennedy, Academic Press, New York, pp. 445–457.

Boschma, H. (1948) Thread spinning in *Littorina scabra*. *Proc. Malac. Soc. Lond.*, **27**, p. 223 only.

Boucher, D.H., James, S. and Keeler, K.H. (1982) The ecology of mutualism. *Annu. Rev. Ecol. Syst.*, **13**, 315–347.

Boudouresque, C.-F. (1974) Aire minima et peuplements algaux marins. *Bull. Soc. Phycol. Fr.*, **19**, 141–157.

Bousfield, E.L. (1955) Ecological control of the occurrence of barnacles in the Miramichi estuary. *Bull. Natn. Mus. Can.*, **137**, 1–69.

Boutler, J., Cabioch, L. and Grall, J.-R. (1974) Quelques observations sur la pénétration de la lumière dans les eaux marines au voisinage de Roscoff et ses conséquences écologiques. *Bull. Soc. Phycol. Fr.*, **19**, 129–140.

Bowman, R.S. (1981) The morphology of *Patella* spp. juveniles in Britain, and some phylogenetic inferences. *J. Mar. Biol. Ass. U.K.*, **61**, 647–666.

Bowman, R.S. and Lewis, J.R. (1977) Annual fluctuations in the recruitment of *Patella vulgata* L. *J. Mar. Biol. Ass. U.K.*, **57**, 793–815.

Brady, F. (1949) The fluctuations of some common shore-birds on the North Northumberland coast. *Br. Birds*, **42**, 297–307.

Brancato, M.S. and Woollacott, R.M. (1982) Effect of microbial films on settlement of bryozoan larvae (*Bugula simplex*, *B. stolonifera* and *B. turrita*). *Mar. Biol.*, **71**, 51–56.

Branch, G.M. (1971) The ecology of *Patella* Linnaeus from the Cape Peninsula, South Africa. I. Zonation, movements and feeding. *Zool. Afr.*, **6**, 1–38.

Branch, G.M. (1974a) The ecology of *Patella* Linnaeus from the Cape Peninsula, South Africa. 2. Reproductive cycles. *Trans. R. Soc. S. Afr.*, **41**, 111–160.

Branch, G.M. (1974b) The ecology of *Patella* L. from the Cape Peninsula, South Africa. 3. Growth rates. *Trans. R. Soc. S. Afr.*, **41**, 161–193.

Branch, G.M. (1974c) *Scutellidium patellarum* n.sp., a harpacticoid copepod associated with *Patella* spp. in South Africa, and a description of its larval development. *Crustaceana*, **26**, 179–200.

Branch, G.M. (1975a) Ecology of *Patella* species from the Cape Peninsula, South Africa. IV. Desiccation. *Mar. Biol.*, **32**, 179–200.

Branch, G.M. (1975b) Intraspecific competition in *Patella cochlear* Born. *J. Anim, Ecol.*, **44**, 263–282.

Branch, G.M. (1975c) Mechanisms reducing intraspecific competition in *Patella* spp.: migration, differentiation and territorial behaviour. *J. Anim. Ecol.*, **44**, 575–600.

Branch, G.M. (1976) Interspecific competition experienced by South African *Patella* species. *J. Anim. Ecol.*, **45**, 507–529.

Branch, G.M. (1978) The responses of South African patellid limpets to invertebrate predators. *Zool. Afr.*, **13**, 221–232.

Branch, G.M. (1979) Aggression by limpets against invertebrate predators. *Anim. Behav.*, **27**, 408–410.

Branch, G.M. (1981) The biology of limpets: physical factors, energy flow and ecological interactions. *Oceanogr. Mar. Biol. Ann. Rev.*, **19**, 235–379.

Branch, G.M. (1984a) Competition between marine organisms: ecological and evolutionary implications. *Oceanogr. Mar. Biol. Ann. Rev.*, **22**, 429–593.

Branch, G.M. (1984b) Changes in populations of intertidal and shallow water communities in South Africa during the 1982/83 temperature anomaly. *S. Afr. J. Sci.*, **80**, 61–65.

Branch, G.M. (1985a) Limpets: evolution and adaptation. In, *The Mollusca*, Vol. 10, ed. E.R. Trueman & M.R. Clarke, Academic Press, London, (IN PRESS)

Branch, G.M. (1985b) The impact of predation by kelp gulls *Larus dominicanus* on the sub-Antarctic limpet *Nacella delesserti*. *Polar Biol.*, **4**, (IN PRESS).

Branch, G.M. (1985c) Competition: its role in ecology and evolution in intertidal communities. *Transvaal Museum Monogr.*, (IN PRESS)

Branch, G.M. and Branch, M.L. (1980) Competition between *Cellana tramoserica* (Sowerby) (Gastropoda) and *Patiriella exigua* (Lamarck) (Asteroidea), and their influence on algal standing stocks. *J. Exp. Mar. Biol. Ecol.*, **48**, 35–49.

Branch, G.M. and Branch, M.L. (1981) Experimental analysis of intraspecific competition in an intertidal gastropod, *Littorina unifasciata*. *Aust. J. Mar. Freshwat. Res.*, **32**, 573–589.

Branch, G.M. and Cherry, M.I. (1985) Activity rhythms of the pulmonate limpet *Siphonaria capensis* Q. & G. as an adaptation to osmotic stress, predation and wave action. *J. Exp. Mar. Biol. Ecol.*, (IN PRESS).

Branch, G.M. and Marsh, A.C. (1978) Tenacity and shell shape in six *Patella* species: adaptive features. *J. Exp. Mar. Biol. Ecol.*, **34**, 111–130.

Branson, N.J.B.A., Ponting, E.D. and Minton, C.D.T. (1978) Turnstone migrations in Britain and Europe. *Bird Study*, **25**, 181–187.

Branson, N.J.B.A., Ponting, E.D. and Minton, C.D.T. (1979) Turnstone populations on the Wash. *Bird Study*, **26**, 47–54.

Breen, P.A. (1971) Homing behavior and population regulation in the limpet *Acmaea (Collisella) digitalis*. *Veliger*, **14**, 177–183.

Breen, P.A. (1972) Seasonal migration and population regulation in the limpet *Acmaea (Collisella) digitalis*. *Veliger*, **15**, 133–141.

Breen, P.A. and Mann, K.H. (1976a) Changing lobster abundance and the destruction of kelp beds by sea urchins. *Mar. Biol.*, **34**, 137–142.

Breen, P.A. and Mann, K.H. (1976b) Destructive grazing of kelp by sea urchins in eastern Canada. *J. Fish. Res. Bd Can.*, **33**, 1278–1283.

Breitburg, D.L. (1984) Residual effects of grazing: inhibition of competitor recruitment by encrusting coralline algae. *Ecology*, **65**, 1126–1143.

Brenko, M.H. and Calabrese, A. (1969) The combined effects of salinity and temperature on larvae of the mussel *Mytilus edulis*. *Mar. Biol.*, **4**, 224–226.

Bretsky, P.W. (1969) Evolution of Paleozoic benthic marine invertebrate communities. *Palaeogeogr. Palaeoclimatol. Palaeoecol.*, **6**, 45–59.

Briggs, J.C. (1967) Dispersal of tropical marine shore animals: Coriolis parameters or competition? *Nature, Lond.*, **216**, p. 350 only.

Briggs, J.C. (1970) A faunal history of the North Atlantic Ocean. *Syst. Zool.*, **19**, 19–34.

Briggs, J.C. (1974) *Marine Zoogeography.* McGraw-Hill, New York, 475 pp.

Brousseau, D.J. (1979) Analysis of growth rate in *Mya arenaria* using the von Bertalanffy equation. *Mar. Biol.*, **51**, 221–227.

Brown, R.A. and Seed, R. (1977) *Modiolus modiolus* (L.) – an autecological study. In, *Biology of Benthic Organisms*, ed. B.F. Keegan, P. ÓCéidigh & P.J.S. Boaden, Pergamon Press, Oxford, pp. 93–100.

Brown, R.A., Seed, R. and O'Connor, R.J. (1976) A comparison of relative growth in *Cerastoderma* (= *Cardium*) *edule, Modiolus modiolus* and *Mytilus edulis* (Mollusca: Bivalvia). *J. Zool., Lond.*, **179**, 297–315.

Browne, R.A. (1978) Growth, mortality, fecundity, biomass and productivity of four lake populations of the prosobranch snail *Viviparus georgianus. Ecology*, **59**, 742–750.

Bryan, G.W. (1969) The effects of oil-spill removers ('detergents') on the gastropod *Nucella lapillus* on a rocky shore and in the laboratory. *J. Mar. Biol. Ass. U.K.*, **49**, 1067–1092.

Bullock, T.H. (1953) Predator recognition and escape responses of some intertidal gastropods in presence of starfish. *Behaviour*, **5**, 130–140.

Burger, A.E. (1981) Food and foraging behaviour of Lesser Sheathbills at Marion Island. *Ardea*, **69**, 167–180.

Burrows, E.M. and Lodge, S.M. (1950) A note on the inter-relationships of *Patella, Balanus* and *Fucus* on a semi-exposed coast. *Rep. Mar. Biol. Stn Port Erin*, **62**, 30–34.

Burrows, E.M. and Lodge, S.M. (1951) Autecology and the species problem in *Fucus. J. Mar. Biol. Ass. U.K.*, **30**, 161–176.

Burton, J.C. (1969) Desiccation and intertidal zonation in *Littorina* spp. *Bios*, **3**, 58–65.

Buss, L.W. (1979) Bryozoan overgrowth interactions – the interdependence of competition for space and food. *Nature, Lond.*, **281**, 475–477.

Buss, L.W. (1980) Competitive intransivity and size-frequency distributions of interacting populations. *Proc. Natn. Acad. Sci. U.S.A.*, **77**, 5355–5359.

Buss, L.W. and Jackson, J.B.C. (1979) Competitive networks: nontransitive competitive relationships in cryptic coral reef environments. *Am. Nat.*, **113**, 223–234.

Buss, L.W. and Jackson, J.B.C. (1981) Planktonic food availability and suspension-feeder abundance: evidence of *in situ* depletion. *J. Exp. Mar. Biol. Ecol.*, **49**, 151–161.

Butler, A.J. (1979) Relationships between height on the shore and size distributions of *Thais* spp. (Gastropoda: Muricidae). *J. Exp. Mar. Biol. Ecol.*, **41**, 163–194.

Butler, R.W. and Kirbyson, J.W. (1979) Oyster predation by the Black Oystercatcher in British Columbia. *Condor*, **81**, 433–435.

Buxton, N.E. (1982) Wintering coastal waders of Lewis and Harris. *Scott. Birds*, **12**, 38–43.

Cabioch, L. (1968) Contribution à la connaissance des peuplements benthiques de La Manche occidentale. *Cah. Biol. Mar.*, **9** (Suppl.), 493–720.

Cabioch, L., Gentil, F., Glaçon, R. and Retière, C. (1977) Le macrobenthos des fonds meubles de la Manche: distribution générale et écologie. In, *Biology of Benthic Organisms*, ed. B.F. Keegan, P. ÓCéidigh & P.J.S. Boaden, Pergamon Press, Oxford, pp. 115–128.

Caffey, H.M. (1982) No effect of naturally-occurring rock types on settlement or survival in the intertidal barnacle, *Tesseropora rosea* (Krauss). *J. Exp. Mar. Biol. Ecol.*, **63**, 119–132.

Caffey, H.M. (in press) Spatial and temporal variation in settlement and recruitment of an intertidal barnacle. *Ecol. Monogr.*

Cain, A.J. (1983) *Cepaea nemoralis* and *hortensis. Biologist*, **30**, 193–200.

Calabrese, A. and Nelson, D.A. (1974) Inhibition of embryonic development of the hard clam, *Mercenaria mercenaria*, by heavy metals. *Bull. Environ. Contam. & Toxicol.*, **11**, 92–97.

Calow, P. (1973) On the regulatory nature of individual growth: some observations from freshwater snails. *J. Zool., Lond.*, **170**, 415–428.

Cambridge, P.C. and Kitching, J.A. (1982) Shell shape in living and fossil (Norwich Crag) *Nucella lapillus* (L.) in relation to habitat. *J. Conch., Lond.*, **31**, 31–38.

Cancino, J.M. (1983) Demography of animal modular colonies. Ph. D. Thesis, University of Wales, 117 pp.

Carricker, M.R. (1961) Comparative morphology of boring mechanisms in gastropods. *Am. Zool.*, **1**, 263–286.

Carricker, M.R. and Van Zandt, D. (1972) Predatory behavior of a shell-boring muricid gastropod. In, *Behavior of Marine Animals: current perspectives in research*, Vol. 1. Invertebrates, ed. H.E. Winn & B.L. Olla, Plenum Press, New York, pp. 157–244.

Carss, D.N. (1983) The relationship between Grey Herons (*Ardea cinerea*) and their food supply in a littoral environment. B.Sc. Thesis, University of Edinburgh, 51 pp.

Carvajal, R.J. (1969) Fluctuación mensuel de las larvas y crecimiento del mejillón *Perna perna* (L.) y las condiciones ambientales de la ensenada de Guatapanare, Edo, Sucre, Venezuela. *Boln Inst. Oceanogr., Univ. Oriente (Venez.)*, **8**, 13–20.

Cassie, R.M. (1954) Some uses of probability paper in the analysis of size-frequency distributions. *Aust. J. Mar. Freshwat. Res.*, **5**, 513–522.

Castenholz, R.W. (1961) The effect of grazing on marine littoral diatom populations. *Ecology*, **42**, 783–794.

Castenholz, R.W. (1963) An experimental study of the vertical distribution of littoral marine diatoms. *Limnol. Oceanogr.*, **8**, 450–462.

Castilla, J.C. (1981) Perspectivas de investigacion en estructura y dinamica de communicades intermareales recosas de Chile central. II. Depredadores de alto nivel trofico. *Medio Ambiente*, **5**, 190–215.

Castric-Fey, A., Girard-Descatoire, A., Lafargue, F. and L'Hardy-Halos, M.T. (1973) Étagement des algues et des invertebrés sessiles dans l'Archipel de Glénan. Définition biologique des horizons bathymétriques. *Helgoländer Wiss. Meeresunters.*, **24**, 490–509.

Caswell, H. (1980) On the equivalence of maximizing reproductive value and maximizing fitness. *Ecology*, **61**, 19–24.

Caswell, H. (1981) The evolution of 'mixed' life histories in marine invertebrates and elsewhere. *Am. Nat.*, **117**, 529–536.

Caugant, D. and Bergerard, J. (1980) The sexual cycle and reproductive modality in *Littorina saxatilis* Olivi (Mollusca: Gastropoda). *Veliger*, **23**, 107–111.

Chan, G.L. (1973) Subtidal mussel beds in Baja California, with a new record size for *Mytilus californianus*. *Veliger*, **16**, 239–240.

Chao, L.N. (1973) Digestive system and feeding habits of the cunner, *Tautogolabrus adspersus*, a stomachless fish. *Fishery Bull. U.S. Natn. Ocean. Atmos. Admn.*, **71**, 565–586.

Chapin, D. (1968) Some observations of predation on *Acmaea* species by the crab *Pachygrapsus crassipes*. *Veliger*, **11**, 67–72.

Chapman, A.R.O. (1973) A critique of prevailing attitudes towards the control of seaweed zonation on the seashore. *Botanica Mar.*, **41**, 80–82.

Chapman, A.R.O. (1974) The ecology of macroscopic marine algae. *Annu. Rev. Ecol. Syst.*, **5**, 65–80.

Chapman, A.R.O. (1981) Stability of sea urchin dominated barren grounds following destructive grazing of kelp in St. Margaret's Bay, eastern Canada. *Mar. Biol.*, **62**, 307–311.

Chapman, A.R.O. (1984) Reproduction, recruitment and mortality in two species of *Laminaria* in southwest Nova Scotia. *J. Exp. Mar. Biol. Ecol.*, **78**, 99–109.

Chapman, G. (1955) Aspects of the fauna and flora of the Azores. VI. The density of animal life in the coralline alga zone. *Ann. Mag. Nat. Hist.*, Ser. 12, **8**, 801–805.

Chapman, V.J. (1966) The physiological ecology of some New Zealand seaweeds. *Proc. Vth Int. Seaweed Symp., Halifax, Nova Scotia*, Pergamon Press, Oxford, pp. 29–54.

Charnov, E.L. (1976a) Optimal foraging: attack strategy of a mantid. *Am. Nat.*, **110**, 141–151.

Charnov, E.L. (1976b) Optimal foraging: the marginal value theorem. *Theor. Populat. Biol.*, **9**, 129–136.

Charnov, E.L. and Schaffer, W.M. (1973) Life history consequences of natural selection: Cole's result revisited. *Am. Nat.*, **107**, 791–793.

Chétail, M. and Fournié, J. (1969) Shell-boring mechanism of the gastropod *Purpura (Thais) lapillus*: a physiological demonstration of the role of carbonic anhydrase in the dissolution of $CaCO_3$. *Am. Zool.*, **9**, 983–990.

Chia, F.-S. (1974) Classification and adaptive significance of developmental patterns in marine invertebrates. *Thalassia Jugosl.*, **10**, 121–130.

Chia, F.-S. and Rice, M.E. (1978) *Settlement and Metamorphosis of Marine Invertebrate Larvae.* Elsevier/North-Holland Biomedical Press, New York, 290 pp.

Chia, F.-S. and Warwick, R.M. (1969) Assimilation of labelled glucose from seawater by marine nematodes. *Nature, Lond.*, **224**, 720–721.

Chipperfield, P.N.J. (1948) A simultaneous study of the breeding, settlement and growth of several sedentary marine organisms in a number of geographically distinct localities. Ph. D. Thesis, University of Liverpool, 293 pp.

Chipperfield, P.N.J. (1953) Observations on the breeding and settlement of *Mytilus edulis* (L.) in British waters. *J. Mar. Biol. Ass. U.K.*, **32**, 449–476.

Choat, J.H. (1977) The influence of sessile organisms on the population biology of three species of acmaeid limpets. *J. Exp. Mar. Biol. Ecol.*, **26**, 1–26.

Choat, J.H. and Black, R. (1979) Life histories of limpets and the limpet-laminarian relationship. *J. Exp. Mar. Biol. Ecol.*, **41**, 25–50.

Choat, J.H. and Kingett, P.D. (1982) The influence of fish predation on the abundance cycles of an algal turf invertebrate fauna. *Oecologia (Berlin)*, **54**, 88–95.

Choquet, M. (1965) Recherches en culture organotypique, sur la spermatogenèse chez *P. vulgata* L. Rôle des ganglions cérébroides et des tentacules. *C. R. Hebd. Seanc. Acad. Sci., Paris*, **261**, 4521–4524.

Choquet, M. (1966) Biologie de *Patella vulgata* L. dans le Boulonnais. *Cah. Biol. Mar.*, **7**, 1–22.

Choquet, M. (1967) Gamétogenèse in vitro au cours du cycle annuel chez *Patella vulgata* L. en phase mâle. *C. R. Hebd. Séanc. Acad. Sci., Paris*, **265**, 333–335.

Christiansen, F.B. and Fenchel, T.M. (1974) Evolution of marine invertebrate reproductive patterns. *Theor. Populat. Biol.*, **16**, 267–282.

Christie, H. (1983) Natural fluctuations in a rocky subtidal community in the Oslo Fjord (Norway). *Actes 17e Symp. Europ. de Biol. Mar., Brest, Oceanol. Acta*, No. SP, 69–73.

Christie, H. and Green, N.W. (1982) Changes in the sublittoral hard bottom benthos after a large reduction in pulp mill waste to Iddefjord, Norway, Sweden. *Neth. J. Sea Res.*, **16**, 474–482.

Clapham, C. (1979) The Turnstone populations of Morecambe Bay. *Ringing and Migration*, **2**, 144–150.

Clark, W.C. (1958) Escape responses of herbivorous gastropods when stimulated by carnivorous gastropods. *Nature, Lond.*, **181**, 137–138.

Clarke, B. (1969) The evidence for apostatic selection. *Heredity*, **24**, 347–352.

Clokie, J.J.P. and Boney, A.D. (1980a) *Conchocelis* distribution in the Firth of Clyde: estimates of the lower limits of the photic zone. *J. Exp. Mar. Biol. Ecol.*, **46**, 111–125.

Clokie, J.J.P. and Boney, A.D. (1980b) Ch. 7. The assessment of changes in intertidal ecosystems following major reclamation work: framework for interpretation of algal-dominated biota and the use and misuse of data. In, *The Shore Environment*, Vol. 2, *Ecosystems*, ed. J.H. Price, D.E.G. Irvine & W.F. Farnham (Syst. Ass. Spec. Vol. **17**a), Academic Press, London, pp. 609–675.

Clyne, P.M. and Duffus, J.H. (1979) A preliminary study of variation in reproduction of *Littorina rudis* (Maton). *J. Moll. Stud.*, **45**, 178–185.

Coe, W.R. (1945) Nutrition and growth of the California bay-mussel (*Mytilus edulis diegensis*). *J. Exp. Zool.*, **99**, 1–14.

Coe, W.R. (1946) A resurgent population of the California bay-mussel (*Mytilus edulis diegensis*). *J. Morph.*, **78**, 85–101.

Coe, W.R. (1957) Fluctuations in littoral populations. *Mem. Geol. Soc. Am.*, **67**, 935–940.

Cohen, D. (1966) Optimizing reproduction in a randomly varying environment. *J. Theor. Biol.*, **12**, 119–129.

Cole, L.C. (1954) The population consequences of life history phenomena. *Q. Rev. Biol.*, **29**, 103–137.

Coleman, N. (1973) Water loss from aerially exposed mussels. *J. Exp. Mar. Biol. Ecol.*, **12**, 145–155.

Coleman, N. and Trueman, E.R. (1971) The effect of aerial exposure on the activity of the mussels *Mytilus edulis* L. and *Modiolus modiolus* (L.). *J. Exp. Mar. Biol. Ecol.*, **7**, 295–304.

Collins, L.S. (1976) Abundance, substrate angle and desiccation resistance in two sympatric species of limpets. *Veliger*, **19**, 199–203.

Colman, J. [S.] (1933) The nature of the intertidal zonation of plants and animals. *J. Mar. Biol. Ass. U.K.*, **18**, 435–476.

Colman, J. [S.] (1940) On the faunas inhabiting intertidal seaweeds. *J. Mar. Biol. Ass. U.K.*, **24**, 129–183.

Colman, J.S. and Segrove, F. (1955) The tidal plankton over Stoupe Beck Sands, Robin Hood's Bay (Yorkshire, North Riding). *J. Anim. Ecol.*, **24**, 445–462.

Colton, H.S. (1916) On some varieties of *Thais lapillus* in the Mount Desert region. A study of individual ecology. *Proc. Acad. Nat. Sci. Philad.*, **68**, 440–454.

Colton, H.S. (1922) Variation in the dogwhelk, *Thais (Purpura* auct.) *lapillus. Ecology*, **3**, 146–157.

Comely, C.A. (1978) *Modiolus modiolus* (L.) from the Scottish West coast. I. Biology. *Ophelia*, **17**, 167–193.

Comely, C.A. (1981) The physical and biochemical condition of *Modiolus modiolus* (L.) in selected Shetland voes. *Proc. R. Soc. Edinb.*, **80**B, 299–321.

Connell, J.H. (1956) A study of some factors which determine the density and survival of natural populations of the intertidal barnacle, *Balanus balanoides* (L.). Ph. D. Thesis, University of Glasgow, 126 pp.

Connell, J.H. (1961a) Effects of competition, predation by *Thais lapillus* and other factors on natural populations of the barnacle *Balanus balanoides. Ecol. Monogr.*, **31**, 61–104.

Connell, J.H. (1961b) The influence of interspecific competition and other factors on the distribution of the barnacle *Chthamalus stellatus. Ecology*, **42**, 710–723.

Connell, J.H. (1963) Territorial behavior and dispersion in some marine invertebrates. *Researches Popul. Ecol. Kyoto Univ.*, **5**, 87–101.

Connell, J.H. (1970) A predator-prey system in the marine intertidal region. I. *Balanus glandula* and several predatory species of *Thais. Ecol. Monogr.*, **40**, 49–78.

Connell, J.H. (1971) On the role of natural enemies in preventing competitive exclusion in some marine animals and rain forest trees. In, *Dynamics of Populations, (Proc. Adv. Study Inst. Dynamics Numbers Popul. (Oosterbeck, 1970))*, ed. P.J. den Boer & G.R. Gradwell, Centre for Agricultural Publishing and Documentation, Wageningen, The Netherlands, pp. 298–312.

Connell, J.H. (1972) Community interactions on marine rocky intertidal shores. *Annu. Rev. Ecol. Syst.*, **3**, 169–192.

Connell, J.H. (1974) Ch. 2. Ecology: field experiments in marine ecology. In, *Experimental Marine Biology*, ed. R. Mariscal, Academic Press, New York, pp. 21–54.

Connell, J.H. (1975) Ch. 16. Some mechanisms producing structure in natural communities: a model and evidence from field experiments. In, *Ecology and Evolution of Communities*, ed. M.L. Cody & J.M. Diamond, Belknap Press, Cambridge, Mass., pp. 460–490.

Connell, J.H. (1978) Diversity in tropical rain forests and coral reefs. *Science*, **199**, 1302–1310.

Connell, J.H. (1983) On the prevalence and relative importance of inter-specific competition: evidence from field experiments. *Am. Nat.*, **122**, 661–696.

Connell, J.H. (in prep.) Effect of initial settlement on distribution and abundance of marine rocky shore populations.

Connell, J.H. and Keough, M.J. (1985) Disturbance and patch dynamics of subtidal marine animals on hard substrata. In, *Natural Disturbance: the patch dynamics perspective*, ed. S.T.A. Pickett & P.S. White, Academic Press, New York, pp. 125–151.

Connell, J.H. and Slatyer, R.O. (1977) Mechanisms of succession in natural communities and their role in community stability and organization. *Am. Nat.*, **111**, 1119–1144.

Connell, J.H. and Sousa, W.P. (1983) On the evidence needed to judge ecological stability or persistence. *Am. Nat.*, **121**, 789–824.

Connor, E.F. and McCoy, E.D. (1979) The statistics and biology of the species-area relationship. *Am. Nat.*, **113**, 791–833.

Connor, E.F. and Simberloff, D. (1979) The assembly of species communities: chance or competition? *Ecology*, **60**, 1132–1140.

Connor, M.S. (1975) Niche apportionment among the chitons *Cyanoplax hartwegii* and *Mopalia muscosa*, and the limpets *Collisella limatula* and *Collisella pelta* under the brown alga *Pelvetia fastigiata. Veliger*, **18** (Suppl.), 9–17.

Conover, J.T. and Sieburth, J.McN. (1966) Effect of tannins excreted from Phaeophyta on planktonic animal survival in tide pools. *Proc. Vth Int. Seaweed Symp., Halifax, Nova Scotia*, Pergamon Press, Oxford, pp. 99–100.

Cook, S.B. (1980) Fish predation on pulmonate limpets. *Veliger*, **22**, 380–381.

Cook, S.B. and Cook, C.B. (1981) Activity patterns in *Siphonaria* populations: heading choice and the effects of size and grazing interval. *J. Exp. Mar. Biol. Ecol.*, **49**, 69–79.

Cooke, A.H. (1895) Molluscs. In, *Molluscs and Brachiopods*, by A.H. Cooke, A.E. Shipley & F.R.C. Reed, *The Cambridge Natural History* Vol. III., Macmillan & Co., London, 1–459.

Cooper, R.A. and Uzmann, J.R. (1980) Ch. 3. Ecology of juvenile and adult *Homarus*. In, *The Biology and Management of Lobsters*, ed. J.S. Cobb & B.F. Phillips, Vol. II. Ecology and Management, Academic Press, New York, pp. 97–142.

Corliss, J.B., Dymond, J., Gordon, L.I., Edmond, J.M., von Herzen, R.P., Ballard, R.D., Green K., Williams, D., Bainbridge, A., Crane, K. and Andel, T.H. van (1979) Submarine thermal springs on the Galapagos Rift. *Science*, **203**, 1073–1083.

Cornelius, P.F.S. (1972) Thermal acclimation of some intertidal invertebrates. *J. Exp. Mar. Biol. Ecol.*, **9**, 43–53.

Corner, E.D.S., Southward, A.J. and Southward, E.C. (1968) Toxicity of oil-spill removers ('detergents') to marine life: an assessment using the intertidal barnacle *Elminius modestus. J. Mar. Biol. Ass. U.K.*, **48**, 29–47.

Costello, D.P. and Henley, C. (1971) *Methods for Obtaining and Handling Marine Eggs and Embryos.* (2nd edn) Marine Biological Laboratory, Woods Hole, Mass., U.S.A., 247 pp.

Coull, B.C., Creed, E.L., Eskin, R.A., Montagna, P.A., Palmer, M.A. and Wells, J.B.J. (1983) Phytal meiofauna from the rocky intertidal at Murrells Inlet, South Carolina. *Trans. Am. Microsc. Soc.*, **102**, 380–389.

Coull, B.C. and Wells, J.B.J. (1983) Refuges from fish predation: experiments with phytal meiofauna from the New Zealand rocky intertidal. *Ecology*, **64**, 1599–1609.

Cowell, E.B. and Crothers, J.H. (1970) On the occurrence of multiple rows of 'teeth' in the shell of the dog-whelk *Nucella lapillus. J. Mar. Biol. Ass. U.K.*, **50**, 1101–1111.

Cramp, S. and Simmons, K.E.L. (eds) (1977) *The Birds of the Western Palaearctic.* Vol. I., Oxford University Press, Oxford, 722 pp.

Cramp, S. and Simmons, K.E.L. (eds) (1983) *The Birds of the Western Palaearctic.* Vol. III., Oxford University Press, Oxford, 913 pp.

Crapp, G. (1970) The biological effects of marine oil pollution and shore cleaning. Ph. D. Thesis, University of Wales, 384 pp.

Creese, R.G. (1980) An analysis of distribution and abundance of populations of the high-shore limpet *Notoacmea petterdi* (Tenison-Woods). *Oecologia (Berlin)*, **45**, 252–260.

Creese, R.G. (1982) Distribution and abundance of the acmaeid limpet *Patelloida latistrigata* and its inter-action with barnacles. *Oecologia (Berlin)*, **52**, 85–96.

Creese, R.G. and Underwood, A.J. (1982) Analysis of inter- and intra-specific competition amongst intertidal limpets with different methods of feeding. *Oecologia (Berlin)*, **53**, 337–346.

Crisp, D.J. (1955) The behaviour of barnacle cyprids in relation to water movement over a surface. *J. Exp. Biol.*, **32**, 569–590.

Crisp, D.J. (1956) A substance promoting hatching and liberation of young in cirripedes. *Nature, Lond.*, **178**, p. 263 only.

Crisp, D.J. (1958) The spread of *Elminius modestus* Darwin in North-West Europe. *J. Mar. Biol. Ass. U.K.*, **37**, 483–520.

Crisp, D.J. (ed.) (1964) The effects of the severe winter of 1962–63 on marine life in Britain. *J. Anim. Ecol.*, **33**, 165–210.

Crisp, D.J. (1974a) Energy relations of marine invertebrate larvae. *Thalassia Jugosl.*, **10**, 103–120.

Crisp, D.J. (1974b) Ch. 5. Factors influencing the settlement of marine invertebrate larvae. In, *Chemoreception in Marine Organisms*, ed. P.T. Grant & A.M. Mackie, Academic Press, New York, pp. 177–265.

Crisp, D.J. (1976a) Settlement responses in marine organisms. In, *Adaptation to Environment: essays on the physiology of marine animals*, ed. R.C. Newell, Butterworths, London, pp. 83–124.

Crisp, D.J. (1976b) The role of the pelagic larva. In, *Perspectives in Experimental Biology*, Vol. 1. *Zoology*, ed. P.S. Davies, Spec. Symp. Soc. Exp. Biol., Pergamon Press, Oxford, pp. 145–155.

Crisp, D.J. and Barnes, H. (1954) The orientation and distribution of barnacles at settlement with particular reference to surface contour. *J. Anim. Ecol.*, **23**, 142–162.

Crisp, D.J. and Meadows, P.S. (1962) The chemical basis of gregariousness in cirripedes. *Proc. R. Soc. Lond.*, B, **156**, 500–520.

Crisp, D.J. and Patel, B. (1969) Environmental control of the breeding of three Boreo-Arctic cirripedes. *Mar. Biol.*, **2**, 283–295.

Crisp, D.J. and Southward, A.J. (1958) The distribution of intertidal organisms along the coasts of the English Channel. *J. Mar. Biol. Ass. U.K.*, **37**, 157–208.

Crisp, D.J. and Spencer, C.P. (1958) The control of the hatching process in barnacles. *Proc. R. Soc. Lond.*, B, **149**, 278–299.

Crisp, D.J. and Williams, G.B. (1960) Effect of extracts from fucoids in promoting settlement of epiphytic Polyzoa. *Nature, Lond.*, **188**, 1206–1207.

Crothers, J.H. (1973) On variation in *Nucella lapillus* (L.): shell shape in populations from Pembrokeshire, South Wales. *Proc. Malac. Soc. Lond.*, **40**, 318–327.

Crothers, J.H. (1974a) On variation in *Nucella lapillus* (L.): shell shape in populations from the Bristol Channel. *Proc. Malac. Soc. Lond.*, **41**, 157–170.

Crothers, J.H. (1974b) On variation in the shell of the dog-whelk *Nucella lapillus* (L.). I. Pembrokeshire. *Fld Stud.*, **4**, 39–60.

Crothers, J.H. (1977) Some observations on the growth of the common dog-whelk, *Nucella lapillus* (Prosobranchia: Muricacea) in the laboratory. *J. Conch., Lond.*, **29**, 157–162.

Crothers, J.H. (1980) Further observations on the growth of the common dog-whelk, *Nucella lapillus* (L.), in the laboratory. *J. Moll. Stud.*, **46**, 181–185.

Crothers, J.H. (1981) On variation in *Nucella lapillus* (L.): shell shape in populations from the Solway Firth. *J. Moll. Stud.*, **47**, 11–16.

Crothers, J.H. (1983a) Some observations on shell-shape variation in North American populations of *Nucella lapillus* (L.). *Biol. J. Linn. Soc.*, **19**, 237–274.

Crothers, J.H. (1983b) Field experiments on the effects of crude oil and dispersant on the common animals and plants of rocky sea shores. *Mar. Environ. Res.*, **8**, 215–239.

Crothers, J.H. (1984) Some observations on shell shape variation in Pacific *Nucella*. *Biol. J. Linn. Soc.*, **21**, 259–281.

Crozier, W.J. (1918) Growth and duration of life in *Chiton tuberculatus*. *Proc. Natn. Acad. Sci. U.S.A.*, **4**, 322–325.

Crump, R.G. and Emson, R.H. (1978) Some aspects of the population dynamics of *Asterina gibbosa* (Asteroidea). *J. Mar. Biol. Ass. U.K.*, **58**, 451–466.

Cubit, J.D. (1984) Herbivory and the seasonal abundance of algae on a high intertidal rocky shore. *Ecology*, **65**, 1904–1917.

Cundell, A.M., Sleeter, T.D. and Mitchell, R. (1977) Microbial populations associated with the surface of the brown alga *Ascophyllum nodosum*. *Microb. Ecol.*, **4**, 81–91.

Currey, J.D. and Hughes, R.N. (1982) Strength of the dogwhelk *Nucella lapillus* and the winkle *Littorina littorea* from different habitats. *J. Anim. Ecol.*, **51**, 47–56.

Daguzan, J. (1976) Contribution a l'écologie des Littorinidae (mollusques gastéropodes prosobranches). 1. *Littorina neritoides* (L.) et *Littorina saxatilis* (Olivi). *Cah. Biol. Mar.*, **17**, 213–236.

Dahl, E. (1948) On the smaller Arthropoda of marine algae, especially in the polyhaline waters off the Swedish West Coast. *Unders. över Öresund.*, **35**, 1–193.

Dakin, W.J. (1950) *Australian Seashores*. Angus and Robertson, Sydney, 372 pp.

Daly, J.M. (1978) Growth and fecundity in a Northumberland population of *Spirorbis spirorbis* (Polychaeta: Serpulidae). *J. Mar. Biol. Ass. U.K.*, **58**, 177–190.

Damant, G.C.C. (1937) Storage of oxygen in the bladders of the seaweed *Ascophyllum nodosum* and their adaptation to hydrostatic pressure. *J. Exp. Biol.*, **14**, 198–209.

Daniel, M.J. and Boyden, C.R. (1975) Diurnal variations in physico-chemical conditions within intertidal rockpools. *Fld Stud.*, **4**, 161–176.

da Prato, E.S. and da Prato, S.R.D. (1979a) Counting wintering waders on rocky shores in East Lothian, Scotland. *Wader Study Group Bulletin*, No. 25, 19–23.

da Prato, E.S. and da Prato, S.R.D. (1979b) Wader counting on the rocky shores of East Lothian. *Scott. Birds*, **10**, 184–186.

Darby, R.L. (1964) On growth and longevity in *Tegula funebralis* (Mollusca: Gastropoda). *Veliger*, **6**, 6–7.

Dare, P.J. (1982) Notes on the swarming behaviour and population density of *Asterias rubens* L. (Echinodermata: Asteroidea) feeding on the mussel, *Mytilus edulis* L. *J. Cons. Int. Explor. Mer.*, **40**, 112–118.

Darnell, R.M. (1967) Organic detritus in relation to the estuarine ecosystem. In, *Estuaries*, ed. G.H. Lauff, Amer. Ass. Adv. Sci., **83**, 376–382.

Davidson, N.C. (1981) Survival of shorebirds (Charadrii) during severe weather: the role of nutritional reserves. In, *Feeding and Survival Strategies of Estuarine Organisms*, ed. N.V. Jones & W.J. Wolff, Plenum Press, New York, pp. 231–249.

Davidson, P.E. (1967) A study of the Oystercatcher (*Haematopus ostralegus* L.) in relation to the fishery for cockles (*Cardium edule* L.) in the Burry Inlet, South Wales. *Fishery Invest., Lond.*, Ser II, **25** (7), 1–28.

Davies, G. (1970) Mussels as a world food resource. In, *Proceedings of the Symposium on Mollusca*, Mar. Biol. Ass. India, pp. 873–884.

Davies, N.B. (1976) Food, flocking and territorial behaviour of the Pied Wagtail (*Motacilla alba yarrellii* Gould) in winter. *J. Anim. Ecol.*, **45**, 235–253.

Davies, P.S. (1966) Physiological ecology of *Patella*. I. The effect of body size and temperature on metabolic rate. *J. Mar. Biol. Ass. U.K.*, **46**, 647–658.

Davies, P.S. (1969a) Effect of environment on metabolic activity and morphology of Mediterranean and British species of *Patella*. *Pubbl. Staz. Zool. Napoli*, **37**, 641–656.

Davies, P.S. (1969b) Physiological ecology of *Patella*. III. Desiccation effects. *J. Mar. Biol. Ass. U.K.*, **49**, 291–304.

Davis, D.S. and Farley, J. (1973) The effect of parasitism by the trematode *Cryptocotyle lingua* (Creplin) on digestive efficiency in the snail host, *Littorina saxatilis* (Olivi). *Parasitology*, **66**, 191–197.

Davis, M.B. (in press) Climatic instability, time lags and community disequilibrium. In, *Community Ecology*, ed. T. Case, J. Diamond, J. Roughgarden & T. Schoener.

Dawson, E.Y. (1959) A primary report on the benthic marine flora of southern California. In, *Oceanographic Survey of the Continental Shelf Area of Southern California*, State Water Pollution Control Board, Sacramento, Ca., Publ. No. 20, 169–218.

Dayton, P.K. (1971) Competition, disturbance and community organization: the provision and subsequent utilization of space in a rocky intertidal community. *Ecol. Monogr.*, **41**, 351–389.

Dayton, P.K. (1973) Dispersion, dispersal, and persistence of the annual intertidal alga, *Postelsia palmaeformis* Ruprecht. *Ecology*, **54**, 433–438.

Dayton, P.K. (1975) Experimental evaluation of ecological dominance in a rocky intertidal algal community. *Ecol. Monogr.*, **45**, 137–159.

Dayton, P.K. (1979) Ecology: a science and a religion. In, *Ecological Processes in Coastal and Marine Systems*, ed. R.J. Livingstone, Plenum Press, New York, pp. 3–18.

Dayton, P.K. (1984) Processes structuring some marine communities: are they general? In, *Ecological Communities: conceptual issues and the evidence*, ed. D.R. Strong, Jr., D. Simberloff, L.G. Abele & A.B. Thistle, Princeton University Press, Princeton, New Jersey, pp. 181–200.

Dayton, P.K. and Oliver, J.S. (1980) An evaluation of experimental analyses of population and community patterns in benthic marine environments. In, *Marine Benthic Dynamics*, ed. K.R. Tenore & B.C. Coull, University of South Carolina Press, Columbia, pp. 93–120.

Dayton, P.K., Robilliard, G.A., Paine, R.T. and Dayton, L.B. (1974) Biological accommodation in the benthic community at McMurdo Sound, Antarctica. *Ecol. Monogr.*, **44**, 105–128.

Dayton, P.K., Rosenthal, R.J., Mahen, L.C. and Antezana, T. (1977) Population structure and foraging biology of the predaceous Chilean asteroid *Meyenaster gelatinosus* and the escape biology of its prey. *Mar. Biol.*, **39**, 361–370.

Dean, T.A. and Hurd, L.E. (1980) Development in an estuarine fouling community: the influence of early colonists on later arrivals. *Oecologia (Berlin)*, **45**, 295–301.

de Beaufort, L.F. (1951) *Zoogeography of the Land and Inland Waters*. Sidgwick and Jackson, London, 208 pp.

de Block, J.W. and Geelen, H.J. (1958) The substratum required for the settling of mussels (*Mytilus edulis* L.). *Archs Néerl. Zool.*, Jubilee Vol., pp. 446–460.

de Burgh, M.E. and Fankboner, P.V. (1979) A nutritional association between the bullkelp *Nereocystis luetkeana* and its epizooic bryozoan *Membranipora membranacea*. *Oikos*, **31**, 69–72.

de Coursey, P.J. (1983) Ch. 3. Biological timing. In, *Biology of the Crustacea*, Vol. 7, ed. F.J. Vernberg & W.B. Vernberg, Academic Press, London, pp. 107–162.

Dehnel, P.A. (1956) Growth rates in latitudinally and vertically separated populations of *Mytilus californianus*. *Biol. Bull. Mar. Biol. Lab., Woods Hole*, **110**, 43–53.

Denley, E.J. and Underwood, A.J. (1979) Experiments on factors influencing settlement, survival, and growth of two species of barnacles in New South Wales. *J. Exp. Mar. Biol. Ecol.*, **36**, 269–293.

de Schweinitz, E.H. and Lutz, R.A. (1976) Larval development of the northern horse mussel *Modiolus modiolus* (L.), including a comparison with the larvae of *Mytilus edulis* L. as an aid in planktonic identification. *Biol. Bull. Mar. Biol. Lab., Woods Hole*, **150**, 348–360.

Dethier, M. (1980) Tidepools as refuges: predation and the limits of the harpacticoid copepod *Tigriopus californicus* (Baker). *J. Exp. Mar. Biol. Ecol.*, **42**, 99–111.

Dethier, M. (1981a) Heteromorphic algal life histories: the seasonal pattern and response to herbivory of the brown crust, *Ralfsia californica*. *Oecologia (Berlin)*, **49**, 333–339.

Dethier, M. (1981b) The natural history and community structure of Washington tidepools: disturbance, herbivory and maintenance of pattern in intertidal microcosms. Ph. D. Thesis, University of Washington, 165 pp.

Dethier, M. (1984) Disturbance and recovery in intertidal pools: maintenance of mosaic patterns. *Ecol. Monogr.*, **54**, 99–118.

Dewar, J.M. (1940) Identity of specialized feeding-habits of the Turnstone and Oystercatcher. *Br. Birds*, **34**, 26–28.

de Wolfe, P. (1973) Ecological observations on the mechanisms of dispersal of barnacle larvae during planktonic life and settling. *Neth. J. Sea Res.*, **6**, 1–129.

Deysher, L. and Norton, T.A. (1982) Dispersal and colonization in *Sargassum muticum* (Yendo) Fensholt. *J. Exp. Mar. Biol. Ecol.*, **56**, 179–195.

Dick, W.J.A., Pienkowski, M.W., Waltner, M. and Minton, C.D.T. (1976) Distribution and geographical origins of Knot *Calidris canutus* wintering in Europe and Africa. *Ardea*, **64**, 22–47.

Dickie, L.M. (1958) Effects of high temperature on survival of the giant scallop. *J. Fish. Res. Bd Can.*, **15**, 1189–1211.

Dicks, B. (1973) Some effects of Kuwait crude oil on the limpet, *Patella vulgata*. *Environ. Pollut.*, **5**, 219–229.

Dieckman, G.S. (1980) Aspects of the ecology of *Laminaria pallida* (Grev.). J. Ag. of the Cape Peninsula, South Africa. I. Seasonal growth. *Botanica Mar.*, **23**, 579–585.

Dixon, J., Schroeter, S.C. and Kastendiek, J. (1981) Effects of the encrusting bryozoan, *Membranipora membranacea* on the loss of blades and fronds by the giant kelp, *Macrocystis pyrifera* (Laminariales). *J. Phycol.*, **17**, 341–345.

Dodd, J.M. (1957) Artificial fertilisation, larval development and metamorphosis in *Patella vulgata* L. and *Patella coerulea* L. *Pubbl. Staz. Zool. Napoli*, **29**, 172–186.

Dommasnes, A. (1968) Variations in the meiofauna of *Corallina officinalis* L. with wave exposure. *Sarsia*, **34**, 117–124.

Dommasnes, A. (1969) On the fauna of *Corallina officinalis* L. in western Norway. *Sarsia*, **38**, 71–86.

Doty, M.S. (1946) Critical tide factors that are correlated with the vertical distribution of marine algae and other organisms along the Pacific coast. *Ecology*, **27**, 315–328.

Doyle, R.W. (1975) Settlement of planktonic larvae: a theory of habitat selection in varying environments. *Am. Nat.*, **109**, 113–126.

Dring, M.J. (1982) *The Biology of Marine Plants*. Edward Arnold, London, 199 pp.

Dring, M.J. (1984) Mean irradiance levels at different heights in the intertidal and upper subtidal zones: a general model and its application to shores in the Bristol Channel. *Br. Phycol. J.*, **19**, p. 192 only.

Drinnan, R.E. (1957) The winter feeding of the Oystercatcher (*Haematopus ostralegus*) on the edible cockle (*Cardium edule*). *J. Anim. Ecol.*, **26**, 441–469.

Drinnan, R.E. (1958) The winter feeding of the Oystercatcher (*Haematopus ostralegus*) on the edible mussel (*Mytilus edulis*) in the Conway Estuary, North Wales. *Fishery Invest., Lond.*, Ser II., **22** (4), 1–15.

Dromgoole, F.I. (1980) Desiccation resistance of intertidal and subtidal algae. *Botanica Mar.*, **23**, 149–159.

Dudley, R. (1980) Crab-crushing of periwinkle shells, *Littorina littorea*, from two adjacent geographical provinces. *Nautilus*, **94**, 108–111.

Dugan, P.J. (1981) The importance of nocturnal foraging in shorebirds: a consequence of increased invertebrate prey activity. In, *Feeding and Survival Strategies of Estuarine Organisms*, ed. N.V. Jones & W.J. Wolff, Plenum Press, New York, pp. 251–260.

Dungan, M. (1984) An experimental analysis of processes underlying the structure of a rocky intertidal community in the northern Gulf of California. Ph. D. Thesis, University of Arizona, Tucson.

Dungan, M.L., Miller, T.E. and Thomson, D.A. (1982) Catastrophic decline of a top carnivore in the Gulf of California rocky intertidal zone. *Science*, **216**, 989–991.

Dunkin, S. de B. and Hughes, R.N. (1984) Behavioural components of prey-selection by dogwhelks, *Nucella lapillus* (L.) feeding on barnacles, *Semibalanus balanoides* (L.) in the laboratory. *J. Exp. Mar. Biol. Ecol.*, **79**, 91–103.

Dunstone, M.A., O'Connor, R.J. and Seed, R. (1979) The epifaunal communities of *Pelvetia canaliculata* and *Fucus spiralis*. *Holarct. Ecol.*, **2**, 6–11.

Dybern, B.I. (1965) The life cycle of *Ciona intestinalis* (L.) f. *typica* in relation to the environmental temperature. *Oikos*, **16**, 109–131.

Earll, R. and Erwin, D.G., eds. (1983) *Sublittoral Ecology: the ecology of the shallow sublittoral benthos*. Clarendon Press, Oxford, 277 pp.

Ebling, F.J., Kitching, J.A., Muntz, L. and Taylor, C.M. (1964) The ecology of Lough Ine. XIII. Experimental observations of the destruction of *Mytilus edulis* and *Nucella lapillus* by crabs. *J. Anim. Ecol.*, **33**, 73–82.

Edgar, G.J. (1983a) The ecology of south-east Tasmanian phytal animal communities. I. Spatial organization on a local scale. *J. Exp. Mar. Biol. Ecol.*, **70**, 129–157.

Edgar, G.J. (1983b) The ecology of south-east Tasmanian phytal animal communities. II. Seasonal change in plant and animal populations. *J. Exp. Mar. Biol. Ecol.*, **70**, 159–179.

Edgar, G.J. (1983c) The ecology of south-east Tasmanian phytal animal communities. III. Patterns of species diversity. *J. Exp. Mar. Biol. Ecol.*, **70**, 181–203.

Edgar, G.J. (1983d) The ecology of south-east Tasmanian phytal animal communities. IV. Factors affecting the distribution of ampithoid amphipods among algae. *J. Exp. Mar. Biol. Ecol.*, **70**, 205–225.

Edwards, D.C., Conover, D.O. and Sutter, F., III (1982) Mobile predators and the structure of marine intertidal communities. *Ecology*, **63**, 1175–1180.

Edwards, P. (1977) An investigation of the vertical distribution of selected benthic marine algae with a tide-simulating apparatus. *J. Phycol.*, **13**, 62–68.

Edwards, R.L. (1984) The reproductive and percentage solids cycles of *Mytilus edulis* and *Mytilus californianus* in Humboldt County, California. M.S. Thesis, Humboldt State University, Arcata, Calif., 57 pp.

Egerton, F.N. (1973) Changing concepts of the balance of nature. *Q. Rev. Biol.*, **48**, 322–350.

Eggleston, D. (1972) Factors influencing the distribution of sublittoral ectoprocts off the south of the Isle of Man (Irish Sea). *J. Nat. Hist.*, **6**, 247–260.

Ekaratne, S.U.K. and Crisp, D.J. (1982) Tidal micro-growth bands in intertidal gastropod shells, with an evaluation of band-dating techniques. *Proc. R. Soc. Lond.* B, **214**, 305–323.

Ekaratne, S.U.K. and Crisp, D.J. (1983) A geometric analysis of growth in gastropod shells, with particular reference to turbinate forms. *J. Mar. Biol. Ass. U.K.*, **63**, 777–797.

Ekaratne, S.U.K. and Crisp, D.J. (1984) Seasonal growth studies of intertidal gastropods from shell micro-growth band measurements, including a comparison with alternative methods. *J. Mar. Biol. Ass. U.K.*, **64**, 183–210.

Ekman, S. (1953) *Zoogeography of the Sea*. Sidgwick and Jackson, London, 417 pp.

Elliott, M.N. (1982) Composition and seasonal changes in the sedentary epifaunal communities associated with the serrated wrack *Fucus serratus* (L.) in Strangford Lough, Northern Ireland. M. Sc. Thesis, The Queen's University, Belfast, 113 pp.

Elner, R.W. (1978) The mechanics of predation by the shore crab, *Carcinus maenas* (L.), on the edible mussel *Mytilus edulis* L. *Oecologia (Berlin)*, **36**, 333–344.

Elner, R.W. and Hughes, R.N. (1978) Energy maximization in the diet of the shore crab, *Carcinus maenas*. *J. Anim. Ecol.*, **47**, 103–116.

Elner, R.W. and Raffaelli, D.G. (1980) Interactions between two marine snails, *Littorina rudis* Maton and *Littorina nigrolineata* Gray, a predator, *Carcinus maenas* (L.), and a parasite, *Microphallus similis* Jagerskold. *J. Exp. Mar. Biol. Ecol.*, **43**, 151–160.

Elofson, O. (1941) Zur Kenntnis der mariner Ostracoden Schwedens mit besonderer Berücksichtigung des Skageraks. *Zool. Bidr., Upps.*, **19**, 215–534.

Elvin, D.W. (1975) Oogenesis in *Mytilus californianus*. Ph. D. Thesis, Oregon State University, Corvallis, 171 pp.

Elvin, D.W. (1976) Observations on the effects of light and temperature on the apparent neurosecretory cells of *Mytilus edulis*. *Biol. Bull. Mar. Biol. Lab., Woods Hole*, **151**, p. 408 only.

Elvin, D.W. and Gonor, J.J. (1979) The thermal regime of an intertidal *Mytilus californianus* Conrad population on the central Oregon coast. *J. Exp. Mar. Biol. Ecol.*, **39**, 265–279.

Emlen, J.M. (1966a) The role of time and energy in food preference. *Am. Nat.*, **100**, 611–617.

Emlen, J.M. (1966b) Time, energy and risk in two species of carnivorous gastropods. Ph. D. Thesis, University of Washington, Seattle, 138 pp.

Emlen, J.M. (1968) Optimal choice in animals. *Am. Nat.*, **102**, 385–389.

Emson, R.H. and Crump, R.G. (1979) Description of a new species of *Asterina* (Asteroidea) with an account of its ecology. *J. Mar. Biol. Ass. U.K.*, **59**, 77–94.

Emson, R.H. and Faller-Fritsch, R.J. (1976) An experimental investigation into the effect of crevice availability on abundance and size-structure in a population of *Littorina rudis* (Maton): Gastropoda: Prosobranchia. *J. Exp. Mar. Biol. Ecol.*, **23**, 285–297.

Emson, R.H. and Foote, J. (1980) Environmental tolerances and other adaptive features of two inter-tidal pool echinoderms. In, *Echinoderms Present and Past*, ed. M. Jangoux, A.A. Balkema, Rotterdam, pp. 163–169.

Engle, J.B. and Loosanoff, V.L. (1944) On season of attachment of larvae of *Mytilus edulis* L. *Ecology*, **25**, 433–440.

Ennis, G.P. (1973) Food, feeding and condition of lobsters, *Homarus americanus*, throughout the seasonal cycle in Bonavista Bay, Newfoundland. *J. Fish. Res. Bd Can.*, **30**, 1905–1909.

Evans, P.D. and Mann, K.H. (1977) Selection of prey by American lobsters (*Homarus americanus*) when offered a choice between sea urchins and crabs. *J. Fish. Res. Bd Can.*, **34**, 2203–2207.

Evans, P.R. (1981) Migration and dispersal of shorebirds as a survival strategy. In, *Feeding and Survival Strategies of Estuarine Organisms*, ed. N.V. Jones & W.J. Wolff, Plenum Press, New York, pp. 275–290.

Evans, P.R. and Pienkowski, M.W. (1984) Population dynamics. In, *Behavior of Marine Animals: current perspectives in research*, Vol. 5, *Shorebirds*, ed. J. Burger & B.L. Olla, Plenum Press, New York, pp. 83–123.

Evans, R.G. (1947a) Studies on the biology of British limpets. Part 1. The genus *Patella* in Cardigan Bay. *Proc. Zool. Soc. Lond.*, **117**, 411–423.

Evans, R.G. (1947b) The intertidal ecology of selected localities in the Plymouth neighbourhood. *J. Mar. Biol. Ass. U.K.*, **27**, 173–218.

Evans, R.G. (1947c) The intertidal ecology of Cardigan Bay. *J. Ecol.*, **34**, 273–309.

Evans, R.G. (1948) The lethal temperatures of some common British littoral molluscs. *J. Anim. Ecol.*, **17**, 165–173.

Evans, R.G. (1949) The intertidal ecology of rocky shores in South Pembrokeshire. *J. Ecol.*, **37**, 120–139.

Evans, R.G. (1953) Studies on the biology of British limpets. The genus *Patella* on the south coast of England. *Proc. Zool. Soc. Lond.*, **123**, 357–376.

Evans, R.G. (1957) The intertidal ecology of some localities on the Atlantic coast of France. *J. Ecol.*, **45**, 245–271.

Evans, S. (1983) Production, predation and food niche segregation in a marine shallow soft-bottom community. *Mar. Ecol. Prog. Ser.*, **10**, 147–157.

Fahrenbach, W.H. (1962) The biology of a harpacticoid copepod. *Cellule*, **62**, 301–376.

Fairweather, P.G. and Underwood, A.J. (1983) The apparent diet of predators and biases due to different handling times of their prey. *Oecologia (Berlin)*, **56**, 169–179.

Fairweather, P.G., Underwood, A.J. and Moran, M.J. (1984) Preliminary investigations of predation by the whelk *Morula marginalba*. *Mar. Ecol. Prog. Ser.*, **17**, 143–156.

Falla, R.A., Sibson, R.B. and Turbott, E.G. (1979) *A Field Guide to the Birds of New Zealand*. Collins, London, 254 pp.

Faller-Fritsch, R.J. (1977) Reproductive strategies of the winkle *Littorina rudis* in relation to population dynamics and size structure. In, *Biology of Benthic Organisms*, ed. B.F. Keegan, P.Ó. Céidigh & P.J.S. Boaden, Pergamon Press, Oxford, pp. 225–231.

Faller-Fritsch, R.J. (1983) Comparative studies on the ecology of *Littorina rudis* (Maton 1797) (Gastropoda: Prosobranchia). Ph. D. Thesis, University of London, 283 pp.

Farrow, G.E. and Clokie, J. (1979) Molluscan grazing of sub-littoral algal-bored shells and the production of carbonate mud in the Firth of Clyde, Scotland. *Trans. R. Soc. Edinb.*, **70**, 139–148.

Fava, G. and Volkmann, B. (1975) *Tisbe* (Copepoda: Harpacticoida) species from the Lagoon of Venice. I. Seasonal fluctuations and ecology. *Mar. Biol.*, **30**, 151–165.

Fawcett, M.H. (1984) Local and latitudinal variation in predation on an herbivorous marine snail. *Ecology*, **65**, 1214–1230.

Feare, C.J. (1966a) The winter feeding of the Purple Sandpiper. *Br. Birds*, **59**, 165–179.

Feare, C.J. (1966b) Purple Sandpipers feeding above the littoral zone. *Br. Birds*, **59**, 346–348.

Feare, C.J. (1967) Terrestrial birds feeding in the littoral zone. *Br. Birds*, **60**, 412–414.

Feare, C.J. (1969) The dynamics of an exposed shore population of dogwhelks *Thais lapillus*. Ph. D. Thesis, University of Leeds, 159 pp.

Feare, C.J. (1970a) Aspects of the ecology of an exposed shore population of dogwhelks *Nucella lapillus* (L.). *Oecologia (Berlin)*, **5**, 1–18.

Feare, C.J. (1970b) The reproductive cycle of the dog whelk (*Nucella lapillus*). *Proc. Malac. Soc. Lond.*, **39**, 125–137.

Feare, C.J. (1971a) The adaptive significance of aggregation behaviour in the dogwhelk *Nucella lapillus* (L.). *Oecologia (Berlin)*, **7**, 117–126.

Feare, C.J. (1971b) Predation of limpets and dogwhelks by oystercatchers. *Bird Study*, **18**, 121–129.

Feare, C.J. and High, J. (1977) The status of migrant shorebirds in the Seychelles. *Ibis*, **119**, 323–338.

Feder, H.M. (1963) Gastropod defensive responses and their effectiveness in reducing predation by starfishes. *Ecology*, **44**, 505–512.

Feder, H.M. (1970) Growth and predation by the ochre sea star, *Pisaster ochraceus* (Brandt) in Monterey Bay, California. *Ophelia*, **8**, 161–185.

Fenwick, G.D. (1976) The effect of wave exposure on the amphipod fauna of the alga *Caulerpa brownii*. *J. Exp. Mar. Biol. Ecol.*, **25**, 1–18.

Feyerabend, P. (1975) *Against Method*. Humanities Press, Atlantic Highlands, New Jersey, 339 pp.

Field, I.A. (1922) Biology and economic value of the sea mussel *Mytilus edulis*. *Bull. U. S. Bur. Fish., Wash.*, **38**, 127–259.

Field, J.G., Griffiths, C.L., Griffiths, R.J., Jarman, N., Zoutendyk, P., Velimirov, B. and Bowes, A. (1980) Variation in structure and biomass of kelp communities along the South-West Cape coast. *Trans. R. Soc. S. Afr.*, **44**, 145–203.

Filion-Myklebust, C. and Norton, T.A. (1981) Epidermis shedding in the brown seaweed *Ascophyllum nodosum* (L.) Le Jolis and its ecological significance. *Mar. Biol. Letters*, **2**, 45–51.

Fioroni, P. (1966) Zur Morphologie und Embryogenese des Darmtraktes und der transitorischen Organe bei Prosobranchieren (Mollusca, Gastropoda). *Revue Suisse Zool.*, **73**, 621–876.

Fischer, E. (1929) Recherches de bionomie et d'océanographie littorale sur la Rance et le littoral de La Manche. *Annls Inst. Océanogr., Monaco*, (N.S.) **5**, 203–429.

Fischer-Piette, E. and Gaillard, J.-M. (1971) La variabilité (morphologique et physiologique) des *Littorina saxatilis* (Olivi) ibérique et ses rapports avec l'écologie. *Mém. Mus. Natn. Hist. Nat., Paris*, Ser. A (Zool), **70**, 1–90.

Fischer-Piette, E., Gaillard, J.-M. and James, B.L. (1963) Études sur les variations de *Littorina saxatilis*. V. Sur des [Deux] cas de variabilité extrême. *Cah. Biol. Mar.*, **4**, 1–22.

Fischer-Piette, E., Gaillard, J.-M. and James, B.L. (1964) Études sur les variations de *Littorina saxatilis*. VI. Quelques cas qui posent de difficiles problèmes. *Cah. Biol. Mar.*, **5**, 125–171.

Fish, J.D. (1972) The breeding cycle and growth of open coast and estuarine populations of *Littorina littorea*. *J. Mar. Biol. Ass. U.K.*, **52**, 1011–1019.

Fisher, R.A. (1930) *The Genetical Theory of Natural Selection*. Clarendon Press, Oxford, 291 pp.

Fishlyn, D.A. and Phillips, D.W. (1980) Chemical camouflaging and behavioral defenses against a predatory seastar by three species of gastropods from the surfgrass *Phyllospadix* community. *Biol. Bull. Mar. Biol. Lab., Woods Hole*, **158**, 34–48.

Fleischer, R.C. (1983) Relationships between tidal oscillations and Ruddy Turnstone flocking, foraging and vigilance behaviour. *Condor*, **85**, 22–29.

Fletcher, R.L. (1975) Heteroantagonism observed in mixed algal cultures. *Nature, Lond.*, **253**, 534–535.

Fletcher, W.J. (1984a) Variability in the reproductive effort of the limpet, *Cellana tramoserica*. *Oecologia (Berlin)*, **61**, 259–264.

Fletcher, W.J. (1984b) Intraspecific variation in the population dynamics and growth of the limpet, *Cellana tramoserica*. *Oecologia (Berlin)*, **63**, 110–121.

Fletcher, W.J. and Day, R.W. (1983) The distribution of epifauna on *Ecklonia radiata* (C. Agardh) J. Agardh and the effect of disturbance. *J. Exp. Mar. Biol. Ecol.*, **71**, 205–220.

Forster, G.R. (1954) Preliminary note on a survey of Stoke Point rocks with self-contained diving apparatus. *J. Mar. Biol. Ass. U.K.*, **33**, 341–344.

Forster, G.R. (1955) Underwater observations off Stoke Point and Dartmouth. *J. Mar. Biol. Ass. U.K.*, **34**, 197–199.

Forster, G.R. (1961) An underwater survey on the Lulworth Banks. *J. Mar. Biol. Ass. U.K.*, **41**, 157–160.

Foster, B.A. (1971) On the determinants of the upper limit of intertidal distribution of barnacles (Crustacea: Cirripedia). *J. Anim. Ecol.*, **40**, 33–48.

Foster, J. and Gibb, J.A. (1950) Shore feeding ecology. *Bird Notes*, **24**, 83–86.

Fralick, R.A., Turgeon, K.W. and Mathieson, A.C. (1974) Destruction of kelp populations by *Lacuna vincta* (Montagu). *Nautilus*, **88**, 112–114.

Francis, L. (1973) Intraspecific aggression and its effect on the distribution of *Anthopleura elegantissima* and some related sea anemones. *Biol. Bull. Mar. Biol. Lab., Woods Hole*, **144**, 73–92.

Frank, P.W. (1965a) Shell growth in a natural population of the turban snail *Tegula funebralis*. *Growth*, **29**, 395–403.

Frank, P.W. (1965b) The biodemography of an intertidal snail population. *Ecology*, **46**, 831–844.

Frank, P.W. (1968) Life histories and community stability. *Ecology*, **49**, 355–357.

Frank, P.W. (1969) Growth rates and longevity of some gastropod mollusks on the coral reef at Heron Island. *Oecologia (Berlin)*, **2**, 232–250.

Frank, P.W. (1982) Effects of winter feeding on limpets by black oystercatchers *Haematopus bachmani*. *Ecology*, **63**, 1352–1362.

Fraser, J.H. (1936) The distribution of rock pool Copepoda according to tidal level. *J. Anim. Ecol.*, **5**, 23–28.

Fretter, V. (1980) Observations on the gross anatomy of the female genital duct of British *Littorina* spp. *J. Moll. Stud.*, **46**, 148–153.

Fretter, V. and Graham, A. (1962) *British Prosobranch Molluscs*. Ray Society, London, 755 pp.

Fretter, V. and Graham, A. (1976) The prosobranch molluscs of Britain and Denmark. Part 1 – Pleuroto-mariacea, Fissurellacea and Patellacea. *J. Moll. Stud.*, Suppl. 1, 1–37.

Fretter, V. and Graham, A. (1977) The prosobranch molluscs of Britain and Denmark, Part 2 – Trochacea. *J. Moll. Stud.*, Suppl. 3, 39–100.

Fretter, V. and Graham, A. (1980) The prosobranch molluscs of Britain and Denmark. Part 5 – Marine Littorinacea. *J. Moll. Stud.*, Suppl. 7, 243–284.

Fretter, V. and Manly, R. (1977) Algal associations of *Tricolia pullus, Lacuna vincta* and *Cerithiopsis tuber-cularis* (Gastropoda) with special reference to the settlement of their larvae. *J. Mar. Biol. Ass. U.K.*, **57**, 999–1017.

Fretwell, S.D. and Lucas jr, H.L. (1970) On territorial behavior and other factors influencing habitat distri-bution in birds. I. Theoretical development. *Acta Biotheoretica*, **19**, 16–36.

Fritchman II, H.K. (1962a) A study of the reproductive cycle in the California Acmaeidae (Gastropoda). Part II. *Veliger*, **3**, 95–101.

Fritchman II, H.K. (1962b) A study of the reproductive cycle in the California Acmaeidae (Gastropoda). Part IV. *Veliger*, **4**, 134–140.

Frith, D.W. (1976) Animals associated with sponges at North Hayling, Hampshire. *J. Linn. Soc. (Zool.)*, **58**, 353–362.

Fryer, G. (1971) Functional morphology and niche specificity in chydorid and macrothricid cladocerans. *Trans. Am. Microsc. Soc.*, **90**, 103–104.

Fuentes, J.M. and Niell, F.X. (1981) Spatial structure of a mid level intertidal community. Some comments on sampling. *Botanica Mar.*, **24**, 135–138.

Fuhrer, B., Christianson, I.G., Clayton, M.N. and Allender, B.M. (1981) *Seaweeds of Australia*. Reed, Sydney, 112 pp.

Fulcher, R.G. and McCully, M.E. (1969) Laboratory culture of the intertidal brown alga *Fucus vesiculosus*. *Can. J. Bot.*, **47**, 219–222.

Gadgil, M. and Bossert, W. (1970) Life history consequences of natural selection. *Am. Nat.*, **104**, 1–24.

Gadgil, M. and Solbrig, O.T. (1972) The concept of *r*- and *K*-selection: evidence from wild flowers and some theoretical considerations. *Am. Nat.*, **106**, 14–31.

Gaillard, J.M. (1965) Aspects qualitatifs et quantitatifs de la croissance de la coquille de quelques espèces de mollusques prosobranches en fonction de la latitude et des conditions écologiques. *Mém. Mus. Natn. Hist. Nat., Paris*, **38**, 1–55.

Gaines, M.S., Vogt, K.J., Hamrick, J.L. and Caldwell, J. (1974) Reproductive strategies and growth patterns in sunflowers (*Helianthus*). *Am. Nat.*, **108**, 889–894.

Gallardo, C.S. (1979) Developmental pattern and adaptations for reproduction in *Nucella crassilabrum* and other muricacean gastropods. *Biol. Bull. Mar. Biol. Lab., Woods Hole.*, **157**, 453–463.

Gallien, L. and de Larambergue, M. (1939) Biologie et sexualité de *Lacuna pallidula* (da Costa) (Littorinidae). *Trav. Stn Zool. Wimereux*, **13**, 293–306.

Ganning, B. (1970) Population dynamics and salinity tolerance of *Hyadesia fusca* (Lohmann) (Acarina, Sarcoptiformes) from brackish water rockpools, with notes on the microenvironment inside *Enteromorpha* tubes. *Oecologia (Berlin)*, **5**, 127–137.

Ganning, B. (1971a) Studies on chemical, physical and biological conditions in Swedish rockpool ecosystems. *Ophelia*, **9**, 51–105.

Ganning, B. (1971b) On the ecology of *Heterocypris salinus, H. incongruens* and *Cypridopsis aculeata* (Crustacea: Ostracoda) from Baltic brackish-water rockpools. *Mar. Biol.*, **8**, 271–279.

Garnick, E. (1978) Behavioural ecology of *Strongylocentrotus droebachiensis* (Müller) (Echinodermata: Echinoidea). *Oecologia (Berlin)*, **37**, 77–84.

Garrity, S.D. (1984) Some adaptations of gastropods to physical stress on a tropical rocky shore. *Ecology*, **65**, 559–574.

Garrity, S.D. and Levings, S.C. (1983) Homing to scars as a defense against predators in the pulmonate limpet *Siphonaria gigas* (Gastropoda). *Mar. Biol.*, **72**, 319–324.

Gause, G.F. (1934) *The Struggle for Existence*. Williams and Wilkins, Baltimore, 163 pp.

George, J.D. (1971) The effects of pollution by oil and oil-dispersants on the common intertidal polychaetes, *Cirriformia tentaculata* and *Cirratulus cirratus*. *J. Appl. Ecol.*, **8**, 411–420.

Geraci, S. and Romairone, V. (1982) Barnacle larvae and their settlement in Genoa harbour (North Tyrrhenian Sea). *P. S. Z. N. I.: Mar. Ecol.*, **3**, 225–232.

Gerrodette, T. (1981) Dispersal of the solitary coral *Balanophyllia elegans* by demersal planular larvae. *Ecology*, **62**, 611–619.

Gersch, M. (1936) Der Genitalapparat und die Sexualbiologie der Nordseetrochiden. *Z. Morph. Ökol. Tiere*, **31**, 106–150.

Gibb, J. (1956) Food, feeding habits and territory of the Rock-Pipit *Anthus spinoletta*. *Ibis*, **98**, 506–530.

Gibson, R.N. (1969) The biology and behaviour of littoral fish. *Oceanogr. Mar. Biol. Ann. Rev.*, **7**, 367–410.

Gibson, R.N. (1982) Recent studies on the biology of intertidal fishes. *Oceanogr. Mar. Biol. Ann. Rev.*, **20**, 363–414.

Giesel, J.T. (1970) On the maintenance of a shell pattern and behavior polymorphism in *Acmaea digitalis*, a limpet. *Evolution, Lancaster, Pa.*, **24**, 98–119.

Giesel, J.T. (1976) Reproductive strategies as adaptations to life in temporally heterogeneous environments. *Annu. Rev. Ecol. Syst.*, **7**, 57–79.

Gislén, T. (1929) Epibioses of the Gullmar Fjord. I. Geomorphology and hydrography. *Skriftser. K. Sv. Vetenskapsakad.*, **3**, 1–123.

Glassow, M.A. (in prep.) The red abalone midden layers of the northern Channel Islands: a preliminary report on their chronology and implications for environmental change.

Goodall, D.W. (1952) Quantitative aspects of plant distribution. *Biol. Rev.*, **27**, 194–245.

Gordon, J.C.D. (1983) Some notes on small kelp forest fish collected from *Saccorhiza polyschides* bulbs on the Isle of Cumbrae, Scotland. *Ophelia*, **22**, 173–183.

Gosling, E.M. (1984) The systematic status of *Mytilus galloprovincialis* in western Europe: a review. *Malacologia*, **25**, 551–568.

Gosling, E.M. and Wilkins, N.P. (1981) Ecological genetics of the mussels *Mytilus edulis* and *M. galloprovincialis* on Irish coasts. *Mar. Ecol. Prog. Ser.*, **4**, 221–227.

Goss-Custard, J.D. (1969) The winter feeding ecology of the Redshank *Tringa totanus*. *Ibis*, **111**, 338–356.

Goss-Custard, J.D. (1970) The responses of Redshank (*Tringa totanus* (L.)) to spatial variations in the density of their prey. *J. Anim. Ecol.*, **39**, 91–113.

Goss-Custard, J.D. (1977a) Predator responses and prey mortality in Redshank *Tringa totanus* (L.), and a preferred prey *Corophium volutator* (Pallas). *J. Anim. Ecol.*, **46**, 21–35.

Goss-Custard, J.D. (1977b) Optimal foraging and the size selection of worms by Redshank *Tringa totanus*, in the field. *Anim. Behav.*, **25**, 10–29.

Goss-Custard, J.D. (1980) Competition for food and interference among waders. *Ardea*, **68**, 31–52.

Goss-Custard, J.D., Le V. dit Durell, S.E.A., Sitters, H.P. and Swinfen, R. (1982) Age-structure and survival of a wintering population of Oystercatchers. *Bird Study*, **29**, 83–98.

Goss-Custard, S., Jones, J., Kitching, J.A. and Norton, T.A. (1979) [The ecology of Lough Ine. XXI.] Tide pools of Carrigathorna and Barloge Creek. *Phil. Trans. R. Soc. Lond.*, B, **287**, 1–44.

Gounot, M. (1969) *Méthodes d'Étude Quantitative de la Végétation*. Masson et Cie, Paris, 314 pp.

Grahame, J. (1970) Shedding of the penis in *Littorina littorea*. *Nature, Lond.*, **221**, p. 967 only.

Grahame, J. (1975) Spawning in *Littorina littorea* (L.) (Gastropoda: Prosobranchiata). *J. Exp. Mar. Biol. Ecol.*, **18**, 185–196.

Grahame, J. (1977) Reproductive effort and *r*- and *K*-selection in two species of *Lacuna* (Gastropoda: Prosobranchia). *Mar. Biol.*, **40**, 217–224.

Grahame, J. (1982) Energy flow and breeding in two species of *Lacuna*: comparative costs of egg production and maintenance. *Int. J. Invertebr. Reprod.*, **5**, 91–99.

Grange, K.R. (1976) Rough water as a spawning stimulus in some trochid and turbinid gastropods. *N.Z. J. Mar. Freshwat. Res.*, **10**, 203–216.

Grange, K.R., Singleton, R.J., Richardson, J.R., Hill, P.J. and Main, W. deL. (1981) Shallow rock wall biological associations of some southern fjords of New Zealand. *N. Z. J. Zool.*, **8**, 209–227.

Grant, A. (1983) On the evolution of brood protection in marine benthic invertebrates. *Am. Nat.*, **122**, 549–555.

Gray, J.S. and Christie, H. (1983) Predicting long-term changes in marine benthic communities. *Mar. Ecol. Prog. Ser.*, **13**, 87–94.

Green, G. (1977) Ecology of toxicity in marine sponges. *Mar. Biol.*, **40**, 207–215.

Green, J. (1958) *Dactylopusioides macrolabris* (Claus) (Copepoda: Harpacticoida) and its frond mining nauplius. *Proc. Zool. Soc. Lond.*, **131**, 49–54.

Greenway, J.P.C. (1969a) Surveys of mussels (Mollusca: Lamellibranchia) in the Firth of Thames, 1961–67. *N.Z. Jl Mar. Freshwat. Res.*, **3**, 304–317.

Greenway, J.P.C. (1969b) Settlement and growth of a colony of the large green mussel from a pontoon in Te Kouma Harbour, Coromandel. *N. Z. Mar. Dept, Fish. Tech. Rep.*, No. 43, 14 pp.

Greenway, J.P.C. (1975) Development of a colony of green mussels, *Perna canaliculus*, in Coromandel Harbour, 1971–72. *N. Z. Min. Agr. Fish., Fish. Tech. Rep.*, No. 141, 22 pp.

Grenon, J.-F. and Walker, G. (1978) The histology and histochemistry of the pedal glandular system of two limpets, *Patella vulgata* and *Acmaea tessulata* (Gastropoda: Prosobranchia). *J. Mar. Biol. Ass. U.K.*, **58**, 803–816.

Grenon, J.-F. and Walker, G. (1980) Biochemical and rheological properties of the pedal mucus of the limpet, *Patella vulgata* L. *Comp. Biochem. Physiol.*, **66**B, 451–458.

Grenon, J.-F. and Walker, G. (1981) The tenacity of the limpet, *Patella vulgata* L.: an experimental approach. *J. Exp. Mar. Biol. Ecol.*, **54**, 277–308.

Griffiths, C.L. and King, J.A. (1979a) Some relationships between size, food availability and energy balance in the ribbed mussel *Aulacomya ater*. *Mar. Biol.*, **51**, 141–149.

Griffiths, C.L. and King, J.A. (1979b) Energy expended on growth and gonad output in the ribbed mussel *Aulacomya ater*. *Mar. Biol.*, **53**, 217–222.

Griffiths, C.L. and Seiderer, J.L. (1980) Rock-lobsters and mussels – limitations and preferences in a predator-prey interaction. *J. Exp. Mar. Biol. Ecol.*, **44**, 95–109.

Griffiths, R.J. (1977) Reproductive cycles in littoral populations of *Choromytilus meridionalis* (Kr.) and *Aulacomya ater* (Molina) with a quantitative assessment of gamete production in the former. *J. Exp. Mar. Biol. Ecol.*, **30**, 53–71.

Griffiths, R.J. (1980a) Filtration, respiration and assimilation in the black mussel *Choromytilus meridionalis*. *Mar. Ecol. Prog. Ser.*, **3**, 63–70.

Griffiths, R.J. (1980b) Natural food availability and assimilation in the bivalve *Choromytilus meridionalis*. *Mar. Ecol. Prog. Ser.*, **3**, 151–156.

Griffiths, R.J. (1981a) Population dynamics and growth of the bivalve *Choromytilus meridionalis* (Kr.) at different tidal levels. *Estuarine Coastal Shelf Sci.*, **12**, 101–118.

Griffiths, R.J. (1981b) Production and energy flow in relation to age and shore level in the bivalve *Choromytilus meridionalis* (Kr.). *Estuarine Coastal Shelf Sci.*, **13**, 477–493.

Griffiths, R.J. (1981c) Predation on the bivalve *Choromytilus meridionalis* (Kr.) by the gastropod *Natica* (*Tectonatica*) *tecta* Anton. *J. Moll. Stud.*, **47**, 112–120.

Griffiths, R.J. (1981d) Aerial exposure and energy balance in littoral and sublittoral *Choromytilus meridionalis* (Kr.) (Bivalvia). *J. Exp. Mar. Biol. Ecol.*, **52**, 231–241.

Griffiths, R.J. and Buffenstein, R. (1981) Aerial exposure and energy input in the bivalve *Choromytilus meridionalis* (Kr.). *J. Exp. Mar. Biol. Ecol.*, **52**, 219–229.

Grosberg, R.K. (1981) Competitive ability influences on habitat choice in marine invertebrates. *Nature, Lond.*, **290**, 700–702.

Grosberg, R.K. (1982) Intertidal zonation of barnacles: the influence of planktonic zonation of larvae on vertical distribution of adults. *Ecology*, **63**, 894–899.

Groves, S. (1978) Age-related differences in Ruddy Turnstone foraging and aggressive behaviour. *Auk*, **95**, 95–103.

Gruson, E.S. (1976) *A Checklist of the Birds of the World*. Collins, London, 212 pp.

Guiler, E.R. (1950) The intertidal ecology of Tasmania. *Pap. Proc. R. Soc. Tasm.*, 1949, 135–201.

Guiler, E.R. (1951) Notes on the intertidal ecology of the Freycinet Peninsula. *Pap. Proc. R. Soc. Tasm.*, 1950, 53–70.

Guiler, E.R. (1955) Australian intertidal belt-forming species in Tasmania. *J. Ecol.*, **43**, 138–148.

Gulliksen, B. (1978) Rocky bottom fauna in a submarine gulley at Loppkalven, Finnmark, Northern Norway. *Estuarine Coastal Shelf Sci.*, **7**, 361–372.

Gulliksen, B. (1980) The macrobenthic rocky-bottom fauna of Borgenfjorde, North-Tröndelag, Norway. *Sarsia*, **65**, 115–136.

Gunnill, F.C. (1982a) Macroalgae as habitat patch islands for *Scutellidium lamellipes* (Copepoda: Harpacticoida) and *Ampithoe tea* (Amphipoda: Gammaridae). *Mar. Biol.*, **69**, 103–116.

Gunnill, F.C. (1982b) Effects of plant size and distribution on the numbers of invertebrate species and individuals inhabiting the brown alga *Pelvetia fastigiata*. *Mar. Biol.*, **69**, 263–280.

Gunnill, F.C. (1983) Seasonal variations in the invertebrate faunas of *Pelvetia fastigiata* (Fucaceae): effects of plant size and distribution. *Mar. Biol.*, **73**, 115–130.

Guyomarc'h-Cousin, C. (1973) Étude de la discontinuité de la ponte ovulaire chez *Littorina saxatilis* (Olivi) gastéropode prosobranche gonochorique. *Cah. Biol. Mar.*, **14**, 519–528.

Haage, P. and Jansson, B.-O. (1970) Quantitative investigations of the Baltic *Fucus* belt macrofauna. 1. Quantitative methods. *Ophelia*, **8**, 187–195.

Hagerman, L. (1966) The macro- and microfauna associated with *Fucus serratus* L., with some ecological remarks. *Ophelia*, **3**, 1–43.

Hagerman, L. (1968) The ostracod fauna of *Corallina officinalis* L. in western Norway. *Sarsia*, **36**, 49–54.

Haldane, J.B.S. (1954) The measurement of natural selection. *Proc. 9th Int. Congr. Genetics*, 480–487.

Hale, W.G. (1980) *Waders*. Collins, London, 320 pp.

Hamilton, P.V. (1976) Predation on *Littorina irrorata* (Mollusca: Gastropoda) by *Callinectes sapidus* (Crustacea: Portunidae). *Bull. Mar. Sci.*, **26**, 403–409.

Hamond, R. (1967) The Amphipoda of Norfolk. *Cah. Biol. Mar.*, **8**, 113–152.

Hancock, D.A. (1973) The relationship between stock and recruitment in exploited invertebrates. *Rapp. P.-V. Reun. Cons. Perm. Int. Explor. Mer*, **164**, 113–131.

Hancock, D.S. (1959) The biology and control of the American whelk tingle *Urosalpinx cinerea* (Say) on English oyster beds. *Fishery Invest., Lond.*, Ser. II, **22** (10), 1–66.

Hancock, J. and Elliott, H.F.I. (1978) *The Herons of the World*. London Editions, London, 304 pp.

Hannaford Ellis, C.J. (1978) *Littorina arcana* sp. nov.: a new species of winkle (Gastropoda: Prosobranchia: Littorinidae). *J. Conch., Lond.*, **29**, p. 304 only.

Hannaford Ellis, C.[J.] (1979) Morphology of the oviparous rough winkle, *Littorina arcana* Hannaford Ellis, 1978, with notes on the taxonomy of the *L. saxatilis* species-complex (Prosobranchia: Littorinidae). *J. Conch., Lond.*, **30**, 43–56.

Hannaford Ellis, C.J. (1980) British rough winkles: aspects of their anatomy, taxonomy and ecology. Ph. D. Thesis, University of Liverpool, 163 pp.

Hannaford Ellis, C.J. (1983) Patterns of reproduction in four *Littorina* species. *J. Moll. Stud.*, **49**, 98–106.

Hannaford Ellis, C.J. (1984) Ontogenetic change of shell colour patterns in *Littorina neglecta* Bean (1844). *J. Conch.*, **31**, 343–347.

Harding, J.P. (1949) The use of probability paper for the graphical analysis of polymodal frequency distributions. *J. Mar. Biol. Ass. U.K.*, **28**, 141–153.

Harding, J.P. (1954) The copepod *Thalestris rhodymeniae* (Brady), and its nauplius, parasitic in the seaweed *Rhodymenia palmata* (L.) Greve. *Proc. Zool. Soc. Lond.*, **124**, 153–161.

Hardy, A.R. and Minton, C.D.T. (1980) Dunlin migration in Britain and Ireland. *Bird Study*, **27**, 81–92.

Hargens, A.R. and Shabica, S.V. (1973) Protection against lethal freezing temperatures by mucus in an Antarctic limpet. *Cryobiology*, **10**, 331–337.

Harger, J.R.E. (1968) The role of behavioral traits in influencing the distribution of two species of sea mussel *Mytilus edulis* and *Mytilus californianus*. *Veliger*, **11**, 45–49.

Harger, J.R.E. (1970a) The effect of wave impact on some aspects of the biology of sea mussels. *Veliger*, **12**, 401–414.

Harger, J.R.E. (1970b) Comparisons among growth characteristics of two species of sea mussel, *Mytilus edulis* and *Mytilus californianus. Veliger*, **13**, 44–56.

Harger, J.R.E. (1970c) The effect of species composition on the survival of mixed populations of the sea mussels *Mytilus californianus* and *Mytilus edulis. Veliger*, **13**, 147–152.

Harger, J.R.E. (1972a) Variation and relative 'niche' size in the sea mussel *Mytilus edulis* in association with *Mytilus californianus. Veliger*, **14**, 275–283.

Harger, J.R.E. (1972b) Competitive co-existence: maintenance of interacting associations of the sea mussels *Mytilus edulis* and *Mytilus californianus. Veliger*, **14**, 387–410.

Harger, J.R.E. and Landenberger, D.E. (1971) The effect of storms as a density dependent mortality factor on populations of sea mussels. *Veliger*, **14**, 195–201.

Hargrave, B.T. and Newcombe, C.P. (1973) Crawling and respiration as indices of sublethal effects of oil and a dispersant on an intertidal snail *Littorina littorea. J. Fish. Res. Bd Can.*, **30**, 1789–1792.

Harper, J.L. (1967) A Darwinian approach to plant ecology. *J. Ecol.*, **55**, 247–270.

Harper, J.L. and Ogden, J. (1970) The reproductive strategy of higher plants. I. The concept of strategy with special reference to *Senecio vulgaris* L. *J. Ecol.*, **58**, 681–698.

Harris, L.G. (1973) Nudibranch associations. In, *Current Topics in Comparative Pathobiology*, **2**, 213–315.

Harris, L.G. (1976a) Comparative ecological studies of the nudibranch *Aeolidia papillosa* and its anemone prey *Metridium senile* along the Atlantic and the Pacific coasts of the United States. *J. Moll. Stud.*, **42**, p. 301 only.

Harris, L.G. (1976b) *Field studies on benthic communities in the New England Offshore Mining Environmental Study (NOMES)*. Final Rep., Envir. Res. Lab., Natn Oceanic Atmos. Admin., 130 pp.

Harris, L.G. and Irons, K.P. (1982) Ch. 5. Substrate angle and predation as determinants of fouling community succession. In, *Artificial Substrates*, ed. J. Cairns, Ann Arbor Science Publishers Inc., Ann Arbor, pp. 131–174.

Harris, M.P. (1964) The incidence of some species of Trematoda in three species of *Larus* gulls in Wales. *Ibis*, **106**, 532–536.

Harris, M.P. (1965) The food of some *Larus* gulls. *Ibis*, **107**, 43–53.

Harris, M.P. (1967) The biology of Oystercatchers *Haematopus ostralegus* on Skokholm Island, South Wales. *Ibis*, **109**, 180–193.

Harris, P.R. (1979) The winter feeding of the Turnstone in North Wales. *Bird Study*, **26**, 259–266.

Harrison, R.J. (1944) *Caprellidea (Amphipoda, Crustacea)*. Linn. Soc., London, *Synopses of the British Fauna*, No. 2, 27 pp.

Hart, A. and Begon, M. (1982) The status of general reproductive-strategy theories, illustrated in winkles. *Oecologia (Berlin)*, **52**, 37–42.

Hart, R. (1977) Why are biennials so few? *Am. Nat.*, **111**, 792–799.

Hartnoll, R.G. and Hawkins, S.J. (1980) Monitoring rocky-shore communities: a critical look at spatial and temporal variation. *Helgoländer Wiss. Meeresunters.*, **33**, 484–494.

Hartwick, E.B. (1976) Foraging strategy of the Black Oystercatcher (*Haematopus bachmani* Audubon). *Can. J. Zool.*, **54**, 142–155.

Hartwick, E.B. (1981) Size gradients and shell polymorphism in limpets with consideration of the role of predation. *Veliger*, **23**, 254–264.

Harvey, P.H., Ryland, J.S. and Hayward, P.J. (1976) Pattern analysis in bryozoan and spirorbid communities. II. Distance sampling methods. *J. Exp. Mar. Biol. Ecol.*, **21**, 99–108.

Haskin, H.H. (1954) Age determination in molluscs. *Trans. N.Y. Acad. Sci.*, **16**, 300–304.

Hastings, A. (1980) Disturbance, coexistence, history and competition for space. *Theor. Populat. Biol.*, **18**, 363–373.

Hatton, H. (1938) Essais de Bionomie explicative sur quelques espèces intercotidales d'algues et d'animaux. *Annls Inst. Océanogr., Monaco*, **17**, 241–348.

Haukioja, E. and Hakala, T. (1979) Asymptotic equations in growth studies – an analysis based on *Anodonta piscinalis* (Mollusca, Unionidae). *Ann. Zool. Fenn.*, **16**, 115–122.

Hauspie, R. and Polk, Ph. (1973) Swimming behaviour patterns in certain benthic harpacticoids (Copepoda). *Crustaceana*, **25**, 95–103.

Haven, S.B. (1973) Competition for food between the intertidal gastropods *Acmaea scabra* and *Acmaea digitalis*. *Ecology*, **54**, 143–151.

Havinga, B. (1956) Mussel culture in the Dutch Waddensea. *Rapp. P.-V. Réun. Cons. Perm. Int. Explor. Mer*, **140**, 49–52.

Hawkins, S.J. (1981a) The influence of *Patella* grazing on the fucoid/barnacle mosaic on moderately exposed rocky shores. *Kieler Meeresforsch.*, **5**, 537–543.

Hawkins, S.J. (1981b) The influence of season and barnacles on the algal colonization of *Patella vulgata* exclusion areas. *J. Mar. Biol. Ass. U.K.*, **61**, 1–15.

Hawkins, S.J. (1983) Interactions of *Patella* and macroalgae with settling *Semibalanus balanoides* (L.). *J. Exp. Mar. Biol. Ecol.*, **71**, 55–72.

Hawkins, S.J. and Hartnoll, R.G. (1980) A study of the small-scale relationship between species number and area on a rocky shore. *Estuarine Coastal Mar. Sci.*, **10**, 201–214.

Hawkins, S.J. and Hartnoll, R.G. (1982a) The influence of barnacle cover on the numbers, growth and behaviour of *Patella vulgata* on a vertical pier. *J. Mar. Biol. Ass. U.K.*, **62**, 855–867.

Hawkins, S.J. and Hartnoll, R.G. (1982b) Settlement patterns of *Semibalanus balanoides* (L.) in the Isle of Man (1977–1981). *J. Exp. Mar. Biol. Ecol.*, **62**, 271–283.

Hawkins, S.J. and Hartnoll, R.G. (1983a) Grazing of intertidal algae by marine invertebrates. *Oceanogr. Mar. Biol. Ann. Rev.*, **21**, 195–282.

Hawkins, S.J. and Hartnoll, R.G. (1983b) Changes in a rocky shore community: an evaluation of monitoring. *Mar. Environ. Res.*, **9**, 131–181.

Hawkins, S.J. and Hartnoll, R.G. (1985) Factors determining the upper limits of intertidal canopy-forming algae. *Mar. Ecol. Prog. Ser.*, **20**, 265–271.

Hay, C.H. (1979) Some factors affecting the upper limit of the southern bull kelp *Durvillea antarctica* (Chamisso) Hariot on two New Zealand shores. *J. R. Soc. N.Z.*, **9**, 279–289.

Hay, M.E. (1981) The functional morphology of turf-forming seaweeds: persistence in stressful marine habitats. *Ecology*, **62**, 739–750.

Hayashi, I. (1980) Structure and growth of a shore population of the ormer *Haliotis tuberculata*. *J. Mar. Biol. Ass. U.K.*, **60**, 431–437.

Hayward, B.W. (1981) Ostracod fauna of an intertidal pool at Kawerua, Northland. *Tane*, **27**, 159–168.

Hayward, P.J. (1980) Ch. 11. Invertebrate epiphytes of coastal marine algae. In, *The Shore Environment*, Vol. 2, *Ecosystems*, ed. J.H. Price, D.E.G. Irvine & W.F. Farnham (Syst. Ass. Spec. Vol. **17**a), Academic Press, London, pp. 761–787.

Hazlett, A. and Seed, R. (1976) A study of *Fucus spiralis* and its associated fauna in Strangford Lough, County Down. *Proc. R. Ir. Acad.* B, **76**, 607–618.

Heath, D.J. (1975) Colour, sunlight and internal temperatures of the land snail *Cepaea nemoralis* (L.). *Oecologia (Berlin)*, **19**, 29–38.

Hehre, E.J. and Mathieson, A.C. (1970) Investigations of New England marine algae. III. Composition, seasonal occurrence and reproductive periodicity of the marine Rhodophyceae in New Hampshire. *Rhodora*, **72**, 194–239.

Heip, C., Vincx, M., Smol, N. and Vranken, G. (1982) The systematics and ecology of free-living marine nematodes. *Helminth. Abstr.*, Ser. B, *Plant Nematology*, **51**, 1–31.

Hellawell, J.M. (1978) *Biological Surveillance of Rivers. A biological monitoring handbook*. Water Research Centre Publication, Stevenage, England, 332 pp.

Heller, J. (1975a) The taxonomy of some British *Littorina* species, with notes on their reproduction (Mollusca: Prosobranchia). *Zool. J. Linn. Soc.*, **56**, 131–151.

Heller, J. (1975b) Visual selection of shell colour in two littoral prosobranchs. *Zool. J. Linn. Soc.*, **56**, 153–170.

Heller, J. (1976) The effects of exposure and predation on the shell of two British winkles. *J. Zool., Lond.*, **179**, 201–213.

Henderson, J.T. (1929) Lethal temperatures of Lamellibranchiata. *Contr. Can. Biol. Fish.*, **4**, (n.s.), 397–410.

Heppleston, P.B. (1971) The feeding ecology of Oystercatchers (*Haematopus ostralegus* L.) in winter in northern Scotland. *J. Anim. Ecol.*, **40**, 651–672.

Hermans, C.O. (1979) Polychaete egg sizes, life histories and phylogeny. In, *Reproductive Ecology of Marine Invertebrates*, ed. S.E. Stancyk, University of South Carolina Press, Columbia, pp. 1–9.

Hewatt, W.G. (1935) Ecological succession in the *Mytilus californianus* habitat as observed in Monterey Bay, California. *Ecology*, **16**, 244–251.

Hickman, R.W. and Illingworth, J. (1980) Condition cycle of the green-lipped mussel, *Perna canaliculus* in New Zealand. *Mar. Biol.*, **60**, 27–38.

Hicks, G.R.F. (1971) Checklist and ecological notes on the fauna associated with some littoral corallinacean algae. *Bull. Nat. Sci. (Wellington)*, **2**, 47–58.

Hicks, G.R.F. (1976) Ecological studies on marine algal-dwelling Copepoda (Harpacticoida) from Wellington, New Zealand. Ph. D. Thesis, Victoria University of Wellington, 211 pp.

Hicks, G.R.F. (1977a) Observations on substrate preference of marine phytal harpacticoids (Copepoda). *Hydrobiologia*, **56**, 7–9.

Hicks, G.R.F. (1977b) Species composition and zoogeography of marine phytal harpacticoid copepods from Cook Strait, and their contribution to total phytal meiofauna. *N. Z. Jl Mar. Freshwat. Res.*, **11**, 441–469.

Hicks, G.R.F. (1977c) Species associations and seasonal population densities of marine phytal harpacticoid copepods from Cook Strait. *N. Z. Jl Mar. Freshwat. Res.*, **11**, 621–643.

Hicks, G.R.F. (1977d) Breeding activity of marine phytal harpacticoid copepods from Cook Strait. *N. Z. Jl Mar. Freshwat. Res.*, **11**, 645–666.

Hicks, G.R.F. (1979) Pattern and strategy in the reproductive cycles of benthic harpacticoid copepods. In, *Cyclic Phenomena in Marine Plants and Animals*, ed. E. Naylor & R.G. Hartnoll, Pergamon Press, Oxford, pp. 139–147.

Hicks, G.R.F. (1980) Structure of phytal harpacticoid copepod assemblages and the influence of habitat complexity and turbidity. *J. Exp. Mar. Biol. Ecol.*, **44**, 157–192.

Hicks, G.R.F. (1982) Habitat structure, disturbance, and equilibrium in crustacean communities. *P. S. Z. N. I.: Mar. Ecol.*, **3**, 41–51.

Hicks, G.R.F. (1984) Spatio-temporal dynamics of a meiobenthic copepod and the impact of predation-disturbance. *J. Exp. Mar. Biol. Ecol.*, **81**, 47–72.

Hicks, G.R.F. and Coull, B.C. (1983) The ecology of marine meiobenthic harpacticoid copepods. *Oceanogr. Mar. Biol. Ann. Rev.*, **21**, 67–175.

Hicks, G.R.F. and Grahame, J. (1979) Mucus production and its role in the feeding behaviour of *Diarthrodes nobilis* (Copepoda: Harpacticoida). *J. Mar. Biol. Ass. U.K.*, **59**, 321–330.

Highsmith, R.C. (1982) Reproduction by fragmentation in corals. *Mar. Ecol. Prog. Ser.*, **7**, 207–226.

Himmelman, J.H., Cardinal, A. and Bourget, E. (1983) Community development following removal of urchins, *Strongylocentrotus droebachiensis*, from the rocky subtidal zone of the St. Lawrence estuary, eastern Canada. *Oecologia (Berlin)*, **59**, 27–39.

Himmelman, J.H. and Steele, D.H. (1971) Foods and predators of the green sea urchin *Strongylocentrotus droebachiensis* in Newfoundland waters. *Mar. Biol.*, **9**, 315–322.

Hines, A.H. (1979a) Effects of a thermal discharge on reproductive cycles in *Mytilus edulis* and *Mytilus californianus*. *Fish. Bull., Natn Mar. Fish. Serv. U.S.*, **77**, 498–503.

Hines, A.H. (1979b) The comparative reproduction ecology of three species of intertidal barnacles. In, *Reproductive Ecology of Marine Invertebrates*, ed. S.E. Stancyk, University of South Carolina Press, Columbia, pp. 213–234.

Hirschfield, M.F. and Tinkle, D.W. (1974) Natural selection and the evolution of reproductive effort. *Proc. Natn. Acad. Sci. U.S.A.*, **72**, 2227–2231.

Hiscock, K. (1980) Marine life on the wreck of the M.V. 'Robert'. *Rep. Lundy Fld Soc.*, **33**, 40–44.

Hiscock, K. (1983) Ch. 3. Water movement. In, *Sublittoral Ecology: the ecology of the shallow sublittoral benthos*, ed. R. Earll & D.G. Erwin, Clarendon Press Oxford, pp. 58–96.

Hiscock, K. and Hiscock, S. (1980) Sublittoral plant and animal communities in the area of Roaringwater Bay, South-West Ireland. *J. Sherkin Is.*, **1**, 7–48.

Hiscock, K. and Hoare, R. (1975) The ecology of sublittoral communities at Abereiddy Quarry, Pembrokeshire. *J. Mar. Biol. Ass. U.K.*, **55**, 833–864.

Hiscock, K. and Mitchell, R. (1980) Ch. 1. The description and classification of sublittoral epibenthic ecosystems. In, *The Shore Environment*, Vol. 2, *Ecosystems*, ed. J.H. Price, D.E.G. Irvine & W.F. Farnham (Syst. Ass. Spec. Vol. **17**a), Academic Press, London, pp. 323–370.

Hoare, R. and Hiscock, K. (1974) An ecological survey of the rocky coast adjacent to a bromine extraction works. *Estuarine Coastal Mar. Sci.*, **2**, 329–348.

Hoare, R. and Peattie, M.E. (1979) The sublittoral ecology of the Menai Strait. 1. Temporal and spatial variation in the fauna and flora along a transect. *Estuarine Coastal Shelf Sci.*, **9**, 663–675.

Hockey, P.A.R. (1983a) Feeding techniques of the African Black Oystercatcher *Haematopus moquini* on rocky shores. In, *Proc. Symp. Birds Sea and Shore*, 1979, ed. J. Cooper, African Seabird Group, Cape Town, pp. 99–115.

Hockey, P.A.R. (1983b) The importance of birds in controlling the structure of rocky intertidal communities: a southern African perspective. (Abstract) *Wader Study Group Bulletin*, No. 39, pp. 41–51.

Hockey, P.A.R. and Branch, G.M. (1983) Do oystercatchers influence limpet shell shape? *Veliger*, **26**, 139–141.

Hockey, P.A.R. and Branch, G.M. (1984) Oystercatchers and limpets: impact and implications. A preliminary assessment. *Ardea*, **72**, 199–206.

Hockey, P.A.R. and Underhill, L.G. (1984) Diet of the African black oystercatcher *Haematopus moquini* on rocky shores: spatial, temporal and sex-related variation. *S. Afr. J. Zool.*, **19**, 1–11.

Hoffman, R.J. (1981) Genetics and asexual reproduction of the sea anemone *Metridium senile*. *Biol. Bull. Mar. Biol. Lab., Woods Hole*, **151**, 478–488.

Holgate, P. (1967) Population survival and life history phenomena. *J. Theor. Biol.*, **14**, 1–10.

Horn, H.S. (1974) Markovian processes of forest sucession. In, *Ecology and Evolution of Communities*, ed. M.L. Cody & J.M. Diamond, Belknap Press, Cambridge, Mass., pp. 197–213.

Horn, H.S. (1976) Succession. In, *Theoretical Ecology: principles and applications*, ed. R.M. May, Blackwell Scientific Publications, Oxford, pp. 187–204.

Horn, H.S. (1978) Optimal tactics of reproduction and life history. In, *Behavioural Ecology: an evolutionary approach*, ed. J.R. Krebs & N.B. Davies, Blackwell Scientific Publications, Oxford, pp. 411–429.

Horn, H.S. and MacArthur, R.H. (1972) Competition among fugitive species in a harlequin environment. *Ecology*, **53**, 749–752.

Hornsey, I.S. and Hide, D. (1976) The production of antimicrobial compounds by British marine algae. 3. Distribution of antimicrobial activity within the algal thallus. *Br. Phycol. J.*, **11**, 175–181.

Horton, N., Brough, T. and Rochard, J.B.A. (1983) The importance of refuse tips to gulls wintering in an inland area of South-East England. *J. Appl. Ecol.*, **20**, 751–765.

Horwood, J.W. and Goss-Custard, J.D. (1977) Predation by the Oystercatcher *Haematopus ostralegus* (L.), in relation to the cockle, *Cerastoderma edule* (L.), fishery in the Burry Inlet, South Wales. *J. Appl. Ecol.*, **14**, 139–158.

Hoshiai, T. (1960) Synecological study on intertidal communities III. An analysis of interrelation among sedentary organisms on the artificially denuded rocky surface. *Bull. Biol. Stn Asamushi*, **10**, 49–56.

Hoshiai, T. (1961) Synecological study of intertidal communities IV. An ecological investigation on the zonation in Matsuchima Bay concerning the so-called covering phenomenon. *Bull. Biol. Stn Asamushi*, **10**, 203–211.

Hoshiai, T. (1964) Synecological study on intertidal communities VI. A synecological study on the intertidal zonation of the Asamushi coastal area with special reference to its re-formation. *Bull. Biol Stn Asamushi*, **12**, 93–126.

Hoshiai, T., Yamamoto, G. and Nishihira, M. (1964) A general outline of the zonation on the rocky shore of the Shimokita Peninsula (1). From Wakinosawa to Sai. *Bull. Biol. Stn Asamushi*, **12**, 127–136.

Hosomi, A. (1977) An ecological study of the mussel *Mytilus galloprovincialis* (Lamarck). I. On the fluctuation of its coverage. *Jap. J. Ecol.*, **27**, 311–318.

Hosomi, A. (1978) A note on the vertical distribution of mussel *Mytilus galloprovincialis* Lamarck. *Venus, Kyoto*, **37**, 205–216.

Hosomi, A. (1980) Studies on the spat recruitment and age structure in the population of the mussel, *Mytilus galloprovincialis* Lamarck, with special reference to the cause of the extinction of population. *Venus, Kyoto*, **39**, 155–166.

Howard, A.G. and Nickless, G. (1977) Heavy metal complexation in polluted molluscs. I. Limpets (*Patella vulgata* and *Patella intermedia*). *Chemico-Biol. Interactions*, **16**, 107–114.

Hruby, T. and Norton, T.A. (1979) Algal colonization on rocky shores in the Firth of Clyde. *J. Ecol.*, **67**, 65–77.

Hubbs, C.L. (1955) Water, fish and man in southern California. *Bull. Sth. Calif. Acad. Sci.*, **54**, 167–168.

Hughes, R.G. (1975) The distribution of epizoites on the hydroid *Nemertesia antennina* (L.). *J. Mar. Biol. Ass. U.K.*, **55**, 275–294.

Hughes, R.N. (1970) Population dynamics of the bivalve *Scrobicularia plana* (da Costa) on an intertidal mudflat in northern Wales. *J. Anim. Ecol.*, **39**, 333–356.

Hughes, R.N. (1972) Annual production of two Nova Scotian populations of *Nucella lapillus* (L.). *Oecologia (Berlin)*, **8**, 356–370.

Hughes, R.N. (1979) Optimal diets under the energy maximization premise: the effects of recognition time and learning. *Am. Nat.*, **113**, 209–221.

Hughes, R.N. (1980a) Optimal foraging in the marine context. *Oceanogr. Mar. Biol. Ann. Rev.*, **18**, 423–481.

Hughes, R.N. (1980b) Ch. 9. Predation and community structure. In, *The Shore Environment*, Vol. 2, *Ecosystems*, ed. J.H. Price, D.E.G. Irvine & W.F. Farnham (Syst. Ass. Spec. Vol. 17a), Academic Press, London, pp. 699–728.

Hughes, R.N. (1980c) Population dynamics, growth and reproductive rates of *Littorina nigrolineata* Gray from a moderately sheltered locality in North Wales. *J. Exp. Mar. Biol. Ecol.*, **44**, 211–228.

Hughes, R.N. and Answer, P. (1982) Growth, spawning and trematode infections of *Littorina littorea* (L.) from an exposed shore in North Wales. *J. Moll. Stud.*, **48**, 321–330.

Hughes, R.N. and Dunkin, S. de B. (1984a) Behavioural components of prey-selection by dogwhelks, *Nucella lapillus* (L.) feeding on mussels, *Mytilus edulis* L., in the laboratory. *J. Exp. Mar. Biol. Ecol.*, **77**, 45–68.

Hughes, R.N. and Dunkin, S. de B. (1984b) Effect of dietary history and selection of prey, and foraging behaviour among patches of prey, by the dogwhelk, *Nucella lapillus* (L.). *J. Exp. Mar. Biol. Ecol.*, **79**, 159–172.

Hughes, R.N. and Elner, R.W. (1979) Tactics of a predator, *Carcinus maenas*, and morphological responses of the prey, *Nucella lapillus*. *J. Anim. Ecol.*, **48**, 65–78.

Hughes, R.N. and Roberts, D.J. (1980a) Reproductive effort of winkles (*Littorina* spp.) with contrasted methods of reproduction. *Oecologia (Berlin)*, **47**, 130–136.

Hughes, R.N. and Roberts, D.J. (1980b) Growth and reproductive rates of *Littorina neritoides* (L.) in North Wales. *J. Mar. Biol. Ass. U.K.*, **60**, 591–599.

Hughes, R.N. and Roberts, D.J. (1981) Comparative demography of *Littorina rudis*, *L. nigrolineata* and *L. neritoides* on three contrasted shores in North Wales. *J. Anim. Ecol.*, **50**, 251–268.

Hughes, R.N. and Seed, R. (1981) Size selection of mussels by the blue crab *Callinectes sapidus*: energy maximizer or time minimizer? *Mar. Ecol. Prog. Ser.*, **6**, 83–89.

Hulbert, A.W. (1980) The functional role of *Asterias vulgaris* Verrill (1866) in three subtidal communities. Ph. D. Thesis, University of New Hampshire, 170 pp.

Hulbert, A.W., Pecci, K.J., Whitman, J.D., Harris, L.G., Sears, J.R. and Cooper, R.A. (1982) *Ecosystem definition and community structure of the macrobenthos of the NEMP Monitoring Station at Pigeon Hill in the Gulf of Maine*. N. O. A. A. Technical Memorandum, NMFS-F/NEC14, 143 pp.

Hunt, O.D. (1964) Song thrushes feeding on periwinkles. *Brit. Birds*, **57**, 253–254.

Huston, M. (1979) A general hypothesis of species diversity. *Am. Nat.*, **113**, 81–101.

Hutchinson, G.E. (1941) Ecological aspects of succession in natural populations. *Am. Nat.*, **75**, 406–418.

Hutchinson, G.E. (1961) The paradox of the plankton. *Am . Nat.*, **95**, 137– 145.

Jablonski, D. and Lutz, R.A. (1980) Ch. 9. Molluscan larval shell morphology: ecological and paleontological applications. In, *Skeletal Growth of Aquatic Organisms: biological records of environmental change*, ed. D.C. Rhoads & R.A. Lutz, Plenum Press, New York, pp. 323–377.

Jablonski, D. and Lutz, R.A., (1983) Larval ecology of marine benthic invertebrates: palaeobiological implications. *Biol. Rev.*, **58**, 21–89.

Jackson, G.A. and Strathmann, R.R. (1981) Larval mortality from offshore mixing as a link between precompetent and competent periods of development. *Am. Nat.*, **118**, 16–26.

Jackson, J.B.C. (1977) Competition on marine hard substrata: the adaptive significance of solitary and colonial strategies. *Am. Nat.*, **111**, 743–767.

Jackson, J.B.C. (1979) Overgrowth competition between encrusting cheilostome ectoprocts in a Jamaican cryptic reef environment. *J. Anim. Ecol.*, **48**, 805–823.

Jackson, J.B.C. and Buss, L.W. (1975) Allelopathy and spatial competition among coral reef invertebrates. *Proc. Natn. Acad. Sci. U.S.A.*, **72**, 5160–5163.

Jackson, L.F. (1976) Aspects of the intertidal ecology of the East coast of South Africa. *S. Afr. Ass. Mar. Biol. Res., Invest. Rep.*, No. 46, 72 pp.

Jägersten, G. (1972) *Evolution of the Metazoan Life Cycle: a comprehensive theory.* Academic Press, London, 282 pp.

James, B.L. (1964) Studies on larval trematodes from some littoral molluscs. Ph. D. Thesis, University of Wales, 156 pp.

James, B.L. (1968a) The characters and distribution of the subspecies and varieties of *Littorina saxatilis* (Olivi, 1792) in Britain. *Cah. Biol. Mar.*, **9**, 143–165.

James, B.L. (1968b) The occurrence of *Parvatrema homoeotecnum* James, 1964 (Trematoda: Gymnophallidae) in a population of *Littorina saxatilis tenebrosa* (Mont.). *J. Nat. Hist.*, **2**, 21–37.

James, B.L. (1968c) The distribution and keys of species in the family Littorinidae and of their digenean parasites, in the region of Dale, Pembrokeshire. *Fld Stud.*, **2**, 615–650.

James, B.L. (1969) The Digenea of the intertidal prosobranch, *Littorina saxatilis* (Olivi). *Z. Zool. Syst. & Evolutionsforsch.*, **7**, 273–316.

Janson, K. (1982) Genetic and environmental effects on the growth rate of *Littorina saxatilis. Mar. Biol.*, **69**, 73–78.

Jansson, A.-M. (1967) The food-web of the *Cladophora*-belt fauna. *Helgoländer Wiss. Meeresunters.*, **15**, 574–588.

Jansson, A.-M. (1974) Community structure, modelling and simulation of the *Cladophora* ecosystem in the Baltic Sea. *Contrib. Askö Lab., Univ. Stockholm.*, No. 5, pp. 1–30.

Jara, H.F. and Moreno, C.A. (1984) Herbivory and structure in a midlittoral rocky community: a case in southern Chile. *Ecology*, **65**, 28–38.

Jensen, P. (1981) Phyto-chemical sensitivity and swimming behaviour of the free-living marine nematode *Chromadorita tenuis. Mar. Ecol. Prog. Ser.*, **4**, 203–206.

Jensen, P. (1982) Diatom-feeding behaviour of the free-living marine nematode *Chromadorita tenuis. Nematologica*, **28**, 71–76.

Jensen, P. (1984) Ecology of benthic and epiphytic nematodes in brackish waters. *Hydrobiologia*, **108**, 201–217.

Jerlöv, N.G. (1970) Ch. 2. Light: general introduction. In, *Marine Ecology*, Vol. I, *Environmental Factors*, Part 1, ed. O. Kinne, Wiley-Interscience, London, pp. 95–102.

Jernakoff, P. (1983) Factors affecting the recruitment of algae in a midshore region dominated by barnacles. *J. Exp. Mar. Biol. Ecol.*, **67**, 17–31.

Jessee, W.N. (1976) The effects of water temperature, tidal cycles, and intertidal position on spawning in *Mytilus californianus* (Conrad). M.A. Thesis, Humboldt State College, Arcata, Calif., 146 pp.

Johnson, M.W. and Miller, R.C. (1935) The seasonal settlement of shipworms, barnacles and other wharf-pile organisms at Friday Harbor, Washington. *Univ. Wash. Publs Oceanogr.*, **2**, 1–18.

Johnson, S.E. (1975) Microclimate and energy flow in the marine rocky intertidal. In, *Perspectives of Biophysical Ecology*, ed. D.M. Gates & R.B. Schmerl, Springer-Verlag, Berlin, pp. 559–587.

Jones, A.M. (1979) Structure and growth of a high-level population of *Cerastoderma edule* (Lamellibranchiata). *J. Mar. Biol. Ass. U.K.*, **59**, 277–287.

Jones, A.M., Jones, Y.M. and Baxter, J.M. (1979) Seasonal and annual variations in the allometric relationships of shell and soft-body characters of *Patella vulgata* L. In, *Cyclic Phenomena in Marine Plants and Animals*, ed. E. Naylor & R.G. Hartnoll, Pergamon Press, Oxford, pp. 199–206.

Jones, H.D. (1968) Aspects of the physiology of *Patella vulgata*. Ph. D. Thesis, University of Hull, 120 pp.

Jones, H.G. and Norton, T.A. (1979) Internal factors controlling the rate of evaporation from fronds of some intertidal algae. *New Phytol.*, **83**, 771–781.

Jones, H.G. and Norton, T.A. (1981) The role of internal factors in controlling evaporation from intertidal algae.

In, *Plants and their Atmospheric Environment*, ed. J. Grace, E.D. Ford & P.G. Jarvis, Blackwell Scientific Publishers, Oxford, Brit. Ecol. Soc. Symp., No. 21, pp. 231–235.

Jones, J.S., Leith, B.H. and Rawlings, P. (1977) Polymorphism in *Cepaea*: a problem with too many solutions? *Annu. Rev. Ecol. Syst.*, **8**, 109–143.

Jones, N.S. (1948a) The ecology of the Amphipoda of the South of the Isle of Man. *J. Mar. Biol. Ass. U.K.*, **27**, 400–439.

Jones, N.S. (1948b) Observations and experiments on the biology of *Patella vulgata* at Port St. Mary, Isle of Man. *Proc. Trans. Lpool. Biol. Soc.*, **56**, 60–77.

Jones, N.S. and Kain, J.M. (1967) Subtidal algal colonization following the removal of *Echinus*. *Helgoländer Wiss. Meeresunters.*, **15**, 460–466.

Jones, S. and Alagarswami, K. (1968) Mussel fishery resources in India. In, *Symposium on the Living Resources of the Seas around India*, Ind. Counc. Agric. Res., Cochin, Dec. 1968, Abstract No. 51, p. 28 only.

Jones, W.E. and Demetropoulos, A. (1968) Exposure to wave action: measurements of an important ecological parameter on rocky shores on Anglesey. *J. Exp. Mar. Biol. Ecol.*, **2**, 46–63.

Jones, W.E. and Dent, E.S. (1971) The effect of light on the growth of algal spores. *Proc. 4th Europ. Mar. Biol. Symp.*, ed. D.J. Crisp, Cambridge University Press, Cambridge, pp. 363–374.

Jordan, T.E. and Valiela, I. (1982) A nitrogen budget of the ribbed mussel, *Geukensia demissa*, and its significance in nitrogen flow in a New England salt marsh. *Limnol. Oceanogr.*, **27**, 75–90.

Kain, J.M. (1975a) Algal recolonization of some cleared subtidal areas. *J. Ecol.*, **63**, 739–765.

Kain, J.M. (1975b) The biology of *Laminaria hyperborea*. VII. Reproduction of the sporophyte. *J. Mar. Biol. Ass. U.K.*, **55**, 567–582.

Kain, J.M. (1979) A view of the genus *Laminaria*. *Oceanogr. Mar. Biol. Ann. Rev.*, **17**, 101–161.

Kain, J.M. and Jones, N.S. (1966) Algal colonization after removal of *Echinus*. *Proc. Vth Int. Seaweed Symp.*, *Halifax, Nova Scotia*, Pergamon Press, Oxford, pp. 139–140.

Kain, J.M. and Svendson, P. (1979) A note on the behaviour of *Patina pellucida* in Britain and Norway. *Sarsia*, **38**, 25–30.

Kangas, P. (1978) On the quantity of meiofauna among the epiphytes of *Fucus vesiculosus* in the Askö area, northern Baltic Sea. *Contrib. Askö Lab., Univ. Stockholm.*, No. 24, pp. 1–32.

Kanter, R.G. (1978) Structure and diversity in *Mytilus californianus* (Mollusca: Bivalvia) communities. Ph. D. Thesis, University of Southern California, 113 pp.

Kanwisher, J.W. (1955) Freezing in intertidal animals. *Biol. Bull. Mar. Biol. Lab., Woods Hole.*, **109**, 56–63.

Karlson, R. (1978) Predation and space utilization patterns in a marine epifaunal community. *J. Exp. Mar. Biol. Ecol.*, **31**, 225–239.

Karlson, R.H. (1980) Alternative competitive strategies in a periodically disturbed habitat. *Bull. Mar. Sci. Gulf Caribb.*, **30**, 894–900.

Kastendiek, J. (1982) Competitor-mediated coexistence: interactions among three species of benthic macroalgae. *J. Exp. Mar. Biol. Ecol.*, **62**, 201–210.

Kato, M., Hirai, E. and Kakinuma, Y. (1967) Experiments on the coaction among hydrozoan species in the colony formation. *Sci. Rep. Tohuku Univ. Ser 4. (Biol.)*, **33**, 359–373.

Kato, M., Nakamura, K., Hirai, E. and Kakinuma, Y. (1961) The distribution pattern of Hydrozoa on seaweed with a note on the so called coaction among hydrozoan species. *Bull. Biol. Stn Asamushi*, **10**, 195–202.

Kaufmann, K.W. (1981) Fitting and using growth curves. *Oecologia (Berlin)*, **49**, 293–299.

Kautsky, N. (1974) Quantitative investigations of the red algal belt in the Askö area, northern Baltic proper. *Contrib. Askö Lab., Univ. Stockholm.*, No. 3, pp. 1–29.

Kautsky, N. (1982) Quantitative studies on gonad cycle, fecundity, reproductive output and recruitment in a Baltic *Mytilus edulis* population. *Mar. Biol.*, **68**, 143–160.

Kautsky, N. and Wallentinus, I. (1980) Nutrient release from a Baltic *Mytilus* – red algal community and its role in benthic and pelagic productivity. *Ophelia*, **1** (Suppl.), 17–30.

Kay, A.M. and Butler, A.J. (1983) 'Stability' of the fouling communities on the pilings of two piers in South Australia. *Oecologia (Berlin)*, **56**, 70–78.

Kay, A.M. and Keough, M.J. (1981) Occupation of patches in the epifaunal communities of pier pilings and the bivalve *Pinna bicolor* at Edithburgh, South Australia. *Oecologia (Berlin)*, **48**, 123–130.

Kelly, R.N., Ashwood-Smith, M.J. and Ellis, D.V. (1982) Duration and timing of spermatogenesis in a stock of the mussel *Mytilus californianus*. *J. Mar. Biol. Ass. U.K.*, **62**, 509–519.

Kendall, M.A., Bowman, R.S., Williamson, P. and Lewis, J.R. (1982) Settlement patterns, density and stability in the barnacle *Balanus balanoides*. *Neth. J. Sea Res.*, **16**, 119–126.

Kenk, V.C. and Wilson, B.R. (1985) A new mussel (Bivalvia; Mytilidae) from hydrothermal vents in the Galapagos Rift zone. *Malacologia*, (IN PRESS)

Kennedy, V.S. (1976) Desiccation, higher temperatures and upper intertidal limits of three species of sea mussels (Mollusca: Bivalvia) in New Zealand. *Mar. Biol.*, **35**, 127–137.

Kennedy, V.S. (1977) Reproduction in *Mytilus edulis aoteanus* and *Aulacomya maoriana* (Mollusca: Bivalvia) from Taylors Mistake, New Zealand. *N. Z. J. Mar. Freshwat. Res.*, **11**, 255–267.

Kennedy, V.S. and Mihursky, J.A. (1971) Upper temperature tolerances of some estuarine bivalves. *Chesapeake Sci.*, **12**, 193–204.

Kensler, C.B. (1967) Desiccation resistance of intertidal crevice species as a factor in their zonation. *J. Anim. Ecol.*, **48**, 65–78.

Keough, M.J. and Butler, A.J. (1983) Temporal changes in species number in an assemblage of sessile marine invertebrates. *J. Biogeogr.*, **10**, 317–330.

Keough, M.J. and Downes, B.J. (1982) Recruitment of marine invertebrates: the role of active larval choices and early mortality. *Oecologia (Berlin)*, **54**, 348–352.

Khafaji, A.K. and Boney, A.D. (1979) Antibiotic effects of crustose germlings of the red alga *Chondrus crispus* Stackh. on benthic diatoms. *Ann. Bot.*, **43**, 231–232.

Kincaid, T. (1957) *Local races and clines in the marine gastropod Thais lamellosa Gmelin. A population study.* Calliostoma Press, Seattle, 140 pp.

King, C.E. (1982) The evolution of life-span. In, *Evolution and Genetics of Life-Histories*, ed. H. Dingle & J.P. Hegmann, Springer-Verlag, New York, pp. 121–138.

Kitching, J.A. (1941) Studies in sublittoral ecology. III. *Laminaria* forest on the west coast of Scotland: a study of zonation in relation to wave action and illumination. *Biol. Bull. Mar. Biol. Lab., Woods Hole*, **80**, 324–337.

Kitching, J.A. (1976) Distribution and changes in shell form of *Thais* spp. (Gastropoda) near Bamfield, B.C. *J. Exp. Mar. Biol. Ecol.*, **23**, 109–126.

Kitching, J.A. (1977) Shell form and niche occupation in *Nucella lapillus* (L.) (Gastropoda). *J. Exp. Mar. Biol. Ecol.*, **26**, 275–287.

Kitching, J.A. and Ebling, F.J. (1961) The ecology of Lough Ine. XI. The control of algae by *Paracentrotus lividus* (Echinoidea). *J. Anim. Ecol.*, **30**, 373–383.

Kitching, J.A. and Ebling, F.J. (1967) Ecological studies at Lough Ine. *Adv. Ecol. Res.*, **4**, 197–291.

Kitching, J.A. and Lockwood, J. (1974) Observations on shell form and its ecological significance in thaisid gastropods of the genus *Lepsiella* in New Zealand. *Mar. Biol.*, **28**, 131–144.

Kitching, J.A., Macan, T.T. and Gilson, H.C. (1934) Studies in sublittoral ecology. I. A submarine gulley in Wembury Bay, South Devon. *J. Mar. Biol. Ass. U.K.*, **19**, 677–705.

Kitching, J.A., Muntz, L. and Ebling, F.J. (1966) The ecology of Lough Ine. XV. The ecological significance of shell and body forms in *Nucella*. *J. Anim. Ecol.*, **35**, 113–126.

Kitching, J.A., Sloane, J.F. and Ebling, F.J. (1959) The ecology of Lough Ine. VIII. Mussels and their predators. *J. Anim. Ecol.*, **28**, 113–126.

Kitching, J.A. and Thain, V.M. (1983) The ecological impact of the sea urchin *Paracentrotus lividus* (Lamarck) in Lough Ine, Ireland. *Phil. Trans. R. Soc. Lond.*, B, **300**, 513–552.

Kito, K. (1975) Preliminary report on the phytal animals in the *Sargassum confusum* region in Oshoro Bay, Hokkaido. *Jour. Fac. Sci. Hokkaido Univ. Ser. VI, Zool.*, **20**, 141–158.

Kito, K. (1977) Phytal animals in the *Sargassum confusum* region in Oshoro Bay, Hokkaido: phenology of harpacticoid copepods. *Jour. Fac. Sci. Hokkaido Univ. Ser. VI, Zool.*, **20**, 691–696.

Kito, K. (1982) Phytal marine nematode assemblage on *Sargassum confusum* Agardh, with reference to the structure and seasonal fluctuations. *Jour. Fac. Sci. Hokkaido Univ. Ser. VI, Zool.*, **23**, 143–161.

Kitting, C.L. (1980) Herbivore-plant interactions of individual limpets maintaining a mixed diet of intertidal marine algae. *Ecol. Monogr.*, **50**, 527–550.

Knight, M. (1947) A biological study of *Fucus vesiculosus* and *Fucus serratus*. *Proc. Linn. Soc. Lond.*, **159**, 87–90.

Knight, M. and Parke, M. (1950) A biological study of *Fucus vesiculosus* L. and *Fucus serratus* L. *J. Mar. Biol. Ass. U.K.*, **29**, 439–514.

Knight-Jones, E.W. (1953) Laboratory experiments on gregariousness during setting in *Balanus balanoides* and other barnacles. *J. Exp. Biol.*, **30**, 584–598.

Knight-Jones, E.W. and Jones, W.C. (1955) The fauna of rocks at various depths off Bardsey. I. Sponges, coelenterates, bryozoans. *Rep. Bardsey Observ.*, **3**, 23–30.

Knight-Jones, E.W., Jones, W.C. and Lucas, D. (1957) A survey of a submarine rocky channel. *Rep. Challenger Soc.*, **3**(9), 20–22.

Knight-Jones, E.W., Knight-Jones, P. and Al-Ogily, S.M. (1975) Ecological isolation in the Spirorbidae. In, *Proc. 9th Europ. Symp. Mar. Biol.*, ed. H. Barnes, Aberdeen University Press, Aberdeen, pp. 539–561.

Knight-Jones, E.W. and Nelson-Smith, A. (1977) Sublittoral transects in the Menai Straits and Milford Haven. In, *Biology of Benthic Organisms*, ed. B.F. Keegan, P. ÓCéidigh and P.J.S. Boaden, Pergamon Press, Oxford, pp. 379–389.

Knox, G.A. (1953) The intertidal ecology of Taylor's Mistake, Banks Peninsula. *Trans. R. Soc. N. Z.*, **81**, 189–220.

Knox, G.A. (1960) Littoral ecology and biogeography of the southern oceans. *Proc. R. Soc. Lond.*, B, **152**, 577–624.

Knox, G.A. (1963) The biogeography and intertidal ecology of the Australasian coasts. *Oceanogr. Mar. Biol. Ann. Rev.*, **1**, 341–404.

Kohn, A.J. (1983) Marine biogeography and evolution in the tropical Pacific: zoological perspectives. *Bull. Mar. Sci.*, **33**, 528–535.

Kohn, A.J. and Leviten, P.J. (1976) Effect of habitat complexity on population density and species richness in tropical intertidal predatory gastropod assemblages. *Oecologia (Berlin)*, **25**, 199–210.

Könnecker, G. (1977) Epibenthic assemblages as indicators of environmental conditions. In, *Biology of Benthic Organisms*, ed. B.F. Keegan, P. ÓCéidigh & P.J.S. Boaden, Pergamon Press, Oxford, pp. 391–395.

Korringa, P. (1976) *Farming Marine Organisms Low in the Food Chain*. Developments in Aquaculture and Fisheries Science, Vol. 1. Elsevier Scientific Publishing Co., Amsterdam, 264 pp.

Krebs, J.R. (1978) Optimal foraging: decision rules for predators. In, *Behavioural Ecology: an evolutionary approach.*, ed. J.R. Krebs & N.B. Davies, Blackwell Scientific Publications, Oxford, pp. 23–63.

Kristensen, I. (1968) Surf influence on the thallus of fucoids and the rate of desiccation. *Sarsia*, **34**, 69–82.

Kuenzler, E.J. (1961a) Structure and energy flow of a mussel population in a Georgia salt marsh. *Limnol. Oceanogr.*, **6**, 191–204.

Kuenzler, E.J. (1961b) Phosphorus budget of a mussel population. *Limnol. Oceanogr.*, **6**, 400–415.

Kuhn, T.S. (1970) *The Structure of Scientific Revolutions*. (2nd edn), University of Chicago Press, Chicago, 210 pp.

Kus, B.E., Ashman, P., Page, G.W. and Stenzel, L.F. (1984) Age-related mortality in a wintering population of Dunlin. *Auk*, **101**, 69–73.

Kuzirian, A.M. (1979) Taxonomy and biology of four New England coryphellid nudibranchs (Gastropoda: Opisthobranchiata). *J. Moll. Stud.*, **45**, 239–261.

Kuznetzov, V.V. and Mateeva, T.A. (1948) Details of the bioecological features of marine invertebrates of eastern Murman. *Trudÿ Murmansk. Biol. Sta.*, **1**, 241–260.

Lack, D. (1949) The significance of ecological isolation. In, *Genetics, Paleontology and Evolution*, ed. G.L. Jepsen, G.G. Simpson & E. Mayr, Princeton University Press, Princeton, U.S.A., pp. 299–308.

Lamb, M. and Zimmermann, M. (1964) Marine vegetation of Cape Anne, Massachusetts. *Rhodora*, **66**, 217–254.

Lambert, L. (1939) *La Moule et La Mariculture*. A. Guillot, Versailles, 55 pp.

Lambert, P. and Dehnel, P.A. (1974) Seasonal variations in biochemical composition during the reproductive cycle of the intertidal gastropod *Thais lamellosa* Gmelin (Gastropoda, Prosobranchia). *Can. J. Zool.*, **52**, 305–318.

Lambert, T.C. and Farley, J. (1968) The effect of parasitism by the trematode *Cryptocotyle lingua* (Creplin) on zonation and winter migration of the common periwinkle, *Littorina littorea* (L.). *Can. J. Zool.*, **46**, 1139–1147.

Lammens, J.J. (1967) Growth and reproduction in a tidal flat population of *Macoma balthica* (L.). *Neth. J. Sea Res.*, **3**, 315–382.

Lang, C. and Mann, K.H. (1976) Changes in sea urchin populations after the destruction of kelp beds. *Mar. Biol.*, **36**, 321–336.

Lang, J. (1973) Interspecific aggression by scleractinian corals. II. Why the race is not only to the swift. *Bull. Mar. Sci. Gulf Caribb.*, **23**, 260–279.

Lang, K. (1965) Copepoda Harpacticoidea from the Californian Pacific coast. *K. Svenska Vetensk. - Akad. Handl.*, **10**, 1–560.

Langley, S., Guzman, L. and Rios, C. (1980) Aspectos dinamicos de *Mytilus chilensis* (Hupe, 1840) en el Estrecho de Magellanes. *Apart. Inst. Patagonia*, **11**, 319–332.

Largen, M.J. (1967) The diet of the dog-whelk, *Nucella lapillus* (Gastropoda Prosobranchia). *J. Zool., Lond.*, **151**, 123–127.

Larson, B.R., Vadas, R.L. and Keser, M. (1980) Feeding and nutritional ecology of the sea urchin *Strongylocentrotus droebachiensis* in Maine, U.S.A. *Mar. Biol.*, **59**, 49–62.

Lawrence, J.M. (1975) On the relationships between marine plants and sea urchins. *Oceanogr. Mar. Biol. Ann. Rev.*, **13**, 213–286.

Lawrence, J.M. and McClintock, J.B. (in prep.) Structure of the intertidal community on the rocky shores of the Bay of Morbihan, Kerguelen (South Indian Ocean).

Lebednik, P.A. (1973) Ecological effects of intertidal uplifting from nuclear testing. *Mar. Biol.*, **20**, 197–207.

Leigh, E.G., Paine, R.T., Quinn, J.F. and Suchanek, T.H. (in prep.) Wave energy and intertidal productivity.

Lent, C.M. (1967) Effect of habitat on growth indices in the ribbed mussel, *Modiolus (Arcuatula) demissus*. *Chesapeake Sci.*, **8**, 221–227.

Lent, C.M. (1968) Air-gaping by the ribbed mussel, *Modiolus demissus* (Dillwyn): effects and adaptive significance. *Biol. Bull. Mar. Biol. Lab., Woods Hole*, **134**, 60–73.

Lent, C.M. (1969) Adaptations of the ribbed mussel, *Modiolus demissus* (Dillwyn) to the intertidal habitat. *Am. Zool.*, **9**, 283–292.

Lepez, I.M. (1974) Algunos aspectos de la biologia de la problación de *Porcellidium rubrum* Pallares 1966, (Copepoda, Harpacticoida) en Cerro Verdo, Bahai de Concepción. *Boletin Soc. Biol. Concepción*, **48**, 445–462.

Leslie, P.H. (1945) On the use of matrices in certain population mathematics. *Biometrika*, **33**, 183–212.

Leslie, P.H. (1966) The intrinsic rate of increase and the overlap of successive generations in a population of guillemots (*Uria aalge* Pont.). *J. Anim. Ecol.*, **35**, 291–301.

Levin, L.A. (1983) Drift tube studies of bay-ocean water exchange and implications for larval dispersal. *Estuaries*, **6**, 364–371.

Levin, S.A. (1976) Population dynamic models in heterogeneous environments. *Annu. Rev. Ecol. Syst.*, **7**, 287–311.

Levin, S.A. and Paine, R.T. (1974) Disturbance, patch formation and community structure. *Proc. Natn. Acad. Sci. U.S.A.*, **71**, 2744–2747.

Levin, S.A. and Paine, R.T. (1975) The role of disturbance in models of community structure. In, *Ecosystem Analysis and Prediction*, Society for Industrial and Applied Mathematics, Philadelphia, Penn., pp. 56–67.

Levings, S.C. and Garrity, S.D. (1983) Diel and tidal movement of two co-occurring neritid snails: differences in grazing patterns on a tropical shore. *J. Exp. Mar. Biol. Ecol.*, **67**, 261–278.

Levings, S.C. and Garrity, S.D. (1984) Grazing patterns in *Siphonaria gigas* (Mollusca, Pulmonata) on the rocky Pacific coast of Panama. *Oecologia (Berlin)*, **64**, 152–159.

Levins, R. and Culver, D. (1971) Regional coexistence of species and competition between rare species. *Proc. Natn. Acad. Sci. U.S.A.*, **68**, 1246–1248.

Levinton, J.S. and Suchanek, T.H. (1978) Geographic variation, niche breadth and genetic differentiation at different geographic scales in the mussels *Mytilus californianus* and *M. edulis. Mar. Biol.*, **49**, 363–375.

Lewbel, G.S. (1978) Sexual dimorphism and intraspecific aggression and their relationship to sex ratios in *Caprella gorgonia* Laubitz & Lewbel (Crustacea: Amphipoda: Caprellidae). *J. Exp. Mar. Biol. Ecol.*, **33**, 133–151.

Lewis, C.A. (1975) Development of the gooseneck barnacle *Pollicipes polymerus* (Cirripedia: Lepadomorpha): fertilization through settlement. *Mar. Biol.*, **32**, 141–153.

Lewis, J.B. (1963) Environmental and tissue temperatures of some tropical intertidal marine animals. *Biol. Bull. Mar. Biol. Lab., Woods Hole*, **124**, 277–284.

Lewis, J.R. (1954) Observations on a high-level population of limpets. *J. Anim. Ecol.*, **23**, 85–100.

Lewis, J.R. (1955) The mode of occurrence of the universal intertidal zones in Great Britain: with a comment by T.A. and Anne Stephenson. *J. Ecol.*, **43**, 270–290.

Lewis, J.R. (1961) The littoral zone on rocky shores – a biological or physical entity? *Oikos*, **12**, 280–301.

Lewis, J.R. (1964) *The Ecology of Rocky Shores*. English Universities Press, London, 323 pp.

Lewis, J.R. (1968) Water movements and their role in rocky shore ecology. *Sarsia*, **34**, 13–36.

Lewis, J.R. (1975) Laboratory charges. *Nature, Lond.*, **257**, p. 640 only.

Lewis, J.R. (1976) Long-term ecological surveillance: practical realities in the rocky littoral. *Oceanogr. Mar. Biol. Ann. Rev.*, **14**, 371–390.

Lewis, J.R. (1977a) Ch. 8. Rocky foreshores. In, *The Coastline*, ed. R.S.K. Barnes, John Wiley & Sons, London, pp. 147–158.

Lewis, J.R. (1977b) The role of physical and biological factors in the distribution and stability of rocky shore communities. In, *Biology of Benthic Organisms*, ed. B.F. Keegan, P.ÓCéidigh & P.J.S. Boaden, Pergamon Press, Oxford, pp. 417–424.

Lewis, J.R. (1978a) The implications of community structure for benthic monitoring studies. *Mar. Poll. Bull.*, **9**, 64–67.

Lewis, J.R. (1978b) Benthic baselines – a case for international collaboration. *Mar. Poll. Bull.*, **9**, 317–320.

Lewis, J.R. (1980a) Ch. 1. Objectives in littoral ecology – a personal viewpoint. In, *The Shore Environment*, Vol. 1, *Methods.*, ed. J.H. Price, D.E.G. Irvine & W.F. Farnham (Syst. Ass. Spec. Vol. **17**a), Academic Press, London, pp. 1–18.

Lewis, J.R. (1980b) Options and problems in environmental management and evaluation. *Helgoländer Wiss. Meeresunters.*, **33**, 452–466.

Lewis, J.R. (1982) Composition and functioning of benthic ecosystems in relation to the assessment of long-term effects of oil pollution. *Phil. Trans. R. Soc. Lond. B.*, **297**, 257–267.

Lewis, J.R. and Bowman, R.S. (1975) Local habitat-induced variations in the population dynamics of *Patella vulgata* L. *J. Exp. Mar. Biol. Ecol.*, **17**, 165–203.

Lewis, J.R., Bowman, R.S., Kendall, M.A. and Williamson, P. (1982) Some geographical components in population dynamics: possibilities and realities in some littoral species. *Neth. J. Sea Res.*, **16**, 18–28.

Lewis, J.R. and Powell, H.T. (1960) Aspects of the intertidal ecology of rocky shores in Argyll, Scotland. I. General description of the area. *Trans. R. Soc. Edinb.*, **64**, 45–74.

Lewis, J.R. and Seed, R. (1969) Morphological variations in *Mytilus* from South-West England in relation to the occurrence of *M. galloprovincialis* Lamarck. *Cah. Biol. Mar.*, **10**, 231–253.

Lincoln, R.J. (1979) *British Marine Amphipoda: Gammaridea*. Brit. Mus. (Nat. Hist.), London, 658 pp.

Lindberg, D.R. and Chu, E.W. (1983) Western gull predation on owl limpets: different methods at different localities. *Veliger*, **25**, 347–348.

Lindberg, D.R. and Dwyer, K.R. (1983) The topography, formation and role of the home depression of *Collisella scabra* (Gould). *Veliger*, **25**, 229–234.

Ling, S.W. (1973) A review of the status and problems of coastal aquaculture in the Indo-Pacific region. In, *Coastal Aquaculture in the Indo-Pacific Region*, ed. T.V.R. Pillay, Fishing News (Books) Ltd., London, pp. 2–25.

Linley, E.A.S. and Newell, R.C. (1981) Microheterotrophic communities associated with the degradation of kelp debris. *Kieler Meeresforsch.*, **5**, 345–355.

Lodge, S.M. (1948) Algal growth in the absence of *Patella* on an experimental strip of foreshore, Port St Mary, Isle of Man. *Proc. Trans. Lpool Biol. Soc.*, **56**, 78–83.

Logan, A., Page, F.H. and Thomas, M.L.H. (1984) Depth zonation of epibenthos on sublittoral hard substrates off Deer Island, Bay of Fundy, Canada. *Estuarine Coastal Shelf Sci.*, **18**, 571–592.

Loosanoff, V.L. and Davis, H.C. (1963) Rearing of bivalve molluscs. *Adv. Mar. Biol.*, **1**, 1–136.

Lopez, G., Riemann, F. and Schrage, M. (1979) Feeding biology of the brackish-water oncholaimid nematode *Adoncholaimus thalassophygas*. *Mar. Biol.*, **54**, 311–318.

Lowe, D.M., Moore, M.N. and Bayne, B.L. (1982) Aspects of gametogenesis in the marine mussel *Mytilus edulis* L. *J. Mar. Biol. Ass. U.K.*, **62**, 133–145.

Lowell, R.B. (1984) Desiccation of intertidal limpets: effects of shell size, fit to substratum, and shape. *J. Exp. Mar. Biol. Ecol.*, **77**, 197–207.

Lozada, E. (1968) Contribucion al estudio de la cholga *Aulacomya ater* en Putemun (Mollusca, Bivalvia, Mytilidae). *Biol. Pesq., Chile*, **3**, 3–39.

Lozada, E., Hernandez, J.M., Aracena, O. and Lopez, M.T. (1974) Cultivo de la cholga (*Aulacomya ater*), en Isletilla, Estero de Castro (Moll., Bivalvia, Mytilidae). *Boln Soc. Biol. Concepción*, **48**, 331–346.

Lozada, E. and Reyes, P. (1981) Reproductive biology of a population of *Perumytilus purpuratus* at El Tabo, Chile. *Veliger*, **24**, 147–154.

Lozada, E., Rolleri, J. and Yañez, R. (1971) Consideraciones biologicas de *Choromytilus chorus* en dos sustratos differentes. *Biol. Pesq., Chile*, **5**, 61–108.

Lubchenco, J. (1978) Plant species diversity in a marine intertidal community: importance of herbivore food preference and algal competitive abilities. *Am. Nat.*, **112**, 23–39.

Lubchenco, J. (1979) Consumer terms and concepts. *Am. Nat.*, **113**, 315–317.

Lubchenco, J. (1980) Algal zonation in the New England rocky intertidal community: an experimental analysis. *Ecology*, **61**, 333–344.

Lubchenco, J. (1982) Effects of grazers and algal competitors on fucoid colonization in tide pools. *J. Phycol.*, **18**, 544–550.

Lubchenco, J. (1983) *Littorina* and *Fucus*: effects of herbivores, substratum heterogeneity and plant escapes during succession. *Ecology*, **64**, 1116–1123.

Lubchenco, J. and Cubit, J. (1980) Heteromorphic life histories of certain marine algae as adaptations to variations in herbivory. *Ecology*, **61**, 676–687.

Lubchenco, J. and Gaines, S.D. (1981) A unified approach to marine plant-herbivore interactions. I. Populations and communities. *Annu. Rev. Ecol. Syst.*, **12**, 405–437.

Lubchenco, J.L. and Menge, B.A. (1978) Community development and persistence in a low rocky intertidal zone. *Ecol. Monogr.*, **59**, 67–94.

Lubet, P. (1959) Recherches sur le cycle sexuel et l'émission des gamètes chez les Mytilidae et les Pectinidae (Moll. Bivalves). *Revue Trav. Inst. (Scient. Tech.) Pêch. Marit.*, **23**, 387–548.

Lubet, P., Prunus, G., Masson, M. and Bucaille, D. (1984) Recherches expérimentales sur l'hybridation de *Mytilus edulis* L. et *M. galloprovincialis* Lmk. (Mollusques Lamellibranches). *Bull. Soc. Zool. Fr.*, **109**, 87–98.

Lucas, M.I., Walker, G., Holland, D.L. and Crisp, D.J. (1979) An energy budget for the free-swimming and metamorphosing larvae of *Balanus balanoides* (Crustacea: Cirripedia). *Mar. Biol.*, **55**, 221–229.

Luckens, P.A. (1970) Breeding, settlement and survival of barnacles at artificially modified shore levels at Leigh, New Zealand. *N. Z. Jl Mar. Freshwat. Res.*, **4**, 497–514.

Luckens, P.A. (1976) Settlement and succession on rocky shores at Auckland, North Island, New Zealand. *N. Z. Oceanogr. Inst. Mem.*, **70**, 1–64.

Lundälv, T. (1971) Quantitative studies on rocky-bottom biocoenoses by underwater photogrammetry. A methodological study. *Thalassia Jugosl.*, **7**, 201–208.

Lundälv, T. (1974) Underwater photogrammetry – a new device for biodynamical studies in the marine environment. In, *Yearbook of the Swedish Natural Science Research Council, 1974*, ed. B. Afzelius, Allmänna Förlaget, Stockholm, pp. 222–229.

Lunetta, J.E. (1969) Reproductive physiology of the mussel *Mytilus perna*. *Boln Fac. Filos., Ciênc. Letr., Univ. São Paulo (Zool. Biol. Mar.)*, **26**, 33–111.

Lüning, K. and Dring, M.H. (1979) Continuous underwater light measurement near Helgoland (North Sea) and its significance for characteristic light limits in the sublittoral region. *Helgoländer Wiss. Meeresunters.*, **32**, 403–424.

Lutz, R.A. (1976) Annual growth patterns in the inner shell layer of *Mytilus edulis* L. *J. Mar. Biol. Ass. U.K.*, **56**, 723–731.

Lutz, R.A. (1977) A comprehensive review of the commercial mussel industries in the United States. *U.S. Dept of Commerce, Natn Oceanic Atmos. Admin., Natn Mar. Fish. Serv.*, 134 pp.

Lutz, R.A. (ed.) (1980) *Mussel Culture and Harvest: a North American perspective*. Developments in Aquaculture and Fisheries Science, Vol. 7, Elsevier Scientific Publishing Co., Amsterdam, 350 pp.

Lutz, R.A. and Castagna, M. (1980) Age composition and growth rate of a mussel (*Geukensia demissa*) population in a Virginia salt marsh. *J. Moll. Stud.*, **46**, 106–115.

Lynch, M. (1979) Predation, competition and zooplankton structure: an experimental study. *Limnol. Oceanogr.*, **24**, 253–272.

MacArthur, R.H. (1964) Environmental factors affecting bird species diversity. *Am. Nat.*, **98**, 387–398.

MacArthur, R.H. and Levins, R. (1964) Competition, habitat selection and character displacement in a patchy environment. *Proc. Natn. Acad. Sci. U.S.A.*, **51**, 1207–1210.

MacArthur, R.H. and Pianka, E.R. (1966) On optimal use of a patchy environment. *Am. Nat.*, **100**, 603–609.

MacArthur, R.H. and Wilson, E.O. (1967) *The Theory of Island Biogeography*. Princeton University Press, Princeton, U.S.A., 216 pp.

MacDonald, M.A., Fensom, D.S. and Taylor, A.R.A. (1974) Electrical impedance in *Ascophyllum nodosum* and *Fucus vesiculosus* in relation to cooling, freezing and desiccation. *J. Phycol.*, **10**, 462–469.

MacGinitie, G.E. and MacGinitie, N. (1968) *Natural History of Marine Animals*. McGraw-Hill Book Co., New York, 523 pp.

MacKay, D.A. and Underwood, A.J. (1977) Experimental studies on homing in the intertidal patellid limpet *Cellana tramoserica* (Sowerby). *Oecologia (Berlin)*, **30**, 215–237.

MacKay, T.F.C. and Doyle, R.W. (1978) An ecological genetic analysis of the settlement behaviour of a marine polychaete. 1. Probability of settlement and gregarious behaviour. *Heredity*, **40**, 1–12.

Macleod, P. and Valiela, I. (1975) The effect of density and mutual interference by a predator: a laboratory study of predation by the nudibranch *Coryphella rufibranchialis* on the hydroid *Tubularia larynx*. *Hydrobiologia*, **47**, 339–346.

Manahan, D.T. (1983a) Nutritional implications of dissolved organic material for laboratory culture of pelagic larvae. In, *Culture of Marine Invertebrates*, ed. C.J. Berg, Hutchinson Ross Publishing Co., Stroudsburg, Pa, U.S.A., pp. 171–191.

Manahan, D.T. (1983b) The uptake and metabolism of dissolved amino acids by bivalve larvae. *Biol. Bull. Mar. Biol. Lab., Woods Hole*, **164**, 236–250.

Manahan, D.T. and Crisp, D.J. (1982) The role of dissolved organic material in the nutrition of pelagic larvae: amino acid uptake by bivalve veligers. *Am. Zool.*, **22**, 635–646.

Manahan, D.T. and Crisp, D.J. (1983) Autoradiographic studies on the uptake of dissolved amino acids from sea water by bivalve larvae. *J. Mar. Biol. Ass. U.K.*, **63**, 673–682.

Mann, K.H. (1973) Seaweeds, their productivity and strategy for growth. *Science*, **182**, 978–981.

Mann, K.H. (1977) Destruction of kelp beds by sea urchins: a cyclical phenomenon or irreversible degradation? *Helgoländer Wiss. Meeresunters.*, **30**, 455–467.

Mann, K.H. (1982) *Ecology of Coastal Waters: a systems approach*. Studies in Ecology, **8**, Blackwell Scientific Publications, Oxford, 322 pp.

Mann, K.H. and Breen, P.A. (1972) Relations between lobsters, sea urchins and kelp beds. *J. Fish. Res. Bd Can.*, **29**, 603–609.

Mapstone, B.D., Underwood, A.J. and Creese, R.G. (1984) Experimental analyses of the commensal relationship between intertidal gastropods *Patelloida mufria* and the trochid *Austrocochlea constricta*. *Mar. Ecol. Prog. Ser.*, **17**, 85–100.

Marcus, A. (1973) L'écologie des copépodes du substrat rocheuse. *Trav. Mus. Hist. Nat. Gr. Antipa*, No. 13, 89–100.

Margolin, A.S. (1964a) A running response of *Acmaea* to sea stars. *Ecology*, **45**, 191–193.

Margolin, A.S. (1964b) The mantle response of *Diodora aspera. Anim. Behav.*, **12**, 187–194.

Marincovich, L. (1973) Intertidal mollusks of Iquique, Chile. *Sci. Bull., Nat. Hist. Mus. Los Angeles Cnty*, No. 16, 49 pp.

Mason, J. (1976) Ch. 10. Cultivation. In, *Marine Mussels: their ecology and physiology*, ed. B.L. Bayne, Cambridge University Press, Cambridge, pp. 385–410.

Mateeva, T.A. (1948) The biology of *Mytilus edulis* L. in eastern Murman. *Trudȳ Murmansk. Biol. Inst.*, **1**, 215–241.

Mathieson, A.C. and Hehre, E.J. (1982) The composition, seasonal occurrence, and reproductive periodicity of the Phaeophyceae (brown algae) in New Hampshire. *Rhodora*, **85**, 275–299.

Matveeva, T.A. (1974) [Ecology and the life cycles of mass species of gastropods in the Barents and White Seas.] *Phenomena in the Life of the White and Barents Seas, Acad. Sci. U.S.S.R., Zool. Inst.*, **13** (21), 65–190, [In Russian].

Mayzaud, P., Taguchi, S. and Laval, P. (1984) Seasonal patterns of seston characteristics in Bedford Basin, Nova Scotia, relative to zooplankton feeding: a multivariate approach. *Limnol. Oceanogr.*, **29**, 745–762.

McAlister, R.O. and Fisher, F.M. (1968) Responses of the false limpet, *Siphonaria pectinata* Linnaeus (Gastropoda, Pulmonata) to osmotic stress. *Biol. Bull. Mar. Biol. Lab., Woods Hole*, **134**, 96–117.

McDougall, K.D. (1943) Sessile marine invertebrates of Beaufort, North Carolina. *Ecol. Monogr.*, **13**, 321–374.

McIntyre, A.D. (1969) Ecology of marine meiobenthos. *Biol. Rev.*, **44**, 245–290.

McKee, J. (1982) The winter feeding of Turnstones and Purple Sandpipers in Strathclyde. *Bird Study*, **29**, 213–216.

McKenzie, J.D. and Moore, P.G. (1981) The microdistribution of animals associated with the bulbous holdfasts of *Saccorhiza polyschides* (Phaeophyta). *Ophelia*, **20**, 201–213.

McLachlan, G.R. and Liversidge, R. (eds.) (1970) *Roberts' Birds of South Africa*. (3rd edn), Cape and Transvaal Printers, Cape Town, 643 pp.

McLachlan, J., Chen, L.C.-M. and Edelstein, T. (1971) The culture of four species of *Fucus* under laboratory conditions. *Can. J. Bot.*, **49**, 1463–1469.

McNair, J.N. (1979) A generalized model of optimal diets. *Theor. Populat. Biol.*, **15**, 159–170.

McQuaid, C.D. and Branch, G.M. (1984) The influence of sea temperature, substratum and wave action on rocky intertidal communities: an analysis of faunal and floral biomass. *Mar. Ecol. Prog. Ser.*, **19**, 145–151.

Meadows, P.S. and Campbell, J.I. (1972) Habitat selection by aquatic invertebrates. *Adv. Mar. Biol.*, **10**, 271–382.

Medawar, P.B. (1945) Size, shape and age. In, *Essays on Growth and Form presented to D'Arcy Wentworth Thompson*, ed. E. Le Gros Clark & P.B. Medawar, Clarendon Press Oxford, pp. 157–187.

Menge, B.A. (1974) Effect of wave action and competition on brooding and reproductive effort in the sea star *Leptasterias hexactis. Ecology*, **55**, 84–93.

Menge, B.A. (1975) Brood or broadcast? The adaptive significance of different reproductive strategies in the two intertidal sea stars *Leptasterias hexactis* and *Pisaster ochraceus. Mar. Biol.*, **31**, 87–100.

Menge, B.A. (1976) Organization of the New England rocky intertidal community: role of predation, competition and environmental heterogeneity. *Ecol. Monogr.*, **46**, 355–393.

Menge, B.A. (1978a) Predation intensity in a rocky intertidal community. Relation between predator foraging activity and environmental harshness. *Oecologia (Berlin)*, **34**, 1–16.

Menge, B.A. (1978b) Predation intensity in a rocky intertidal community: effect of an algal canopy, wave action and desiccation on predator feeding rates. *Oecologia (Berlin)*, **34**, 17–35.

Menge, B.A. (1979) Coexistence between the seastars *Asterias vulgaris* and *A. forbesi* in a heterogeneous environment: a non-equilibrium explanation. *Oecologia (Berlin)*, **41**, 245–272.

Menge, B.A. (1982a) Ch. 25. Effects of feeding on the environment: Asteroidea. In, *Echinoderm Nutrition*, ed. M. Jangoux & J.M. Lawrence, A.A. Balkema, Rotterdam, pp. 521–551.

Menge, B.A. (1982b) Reply to a comment by Edwards, Conover, and Sutter. *Ecology*, **63**, 1180–1184.

Menge, B.A. (1983) Components of predation intensity in the low zone of the New England rocky intertidal region. *Oecologia (Berlin)*, **58**, 141–155.

Menge, B.A. and Lubchenco, J. (1981) Community organization in temperate and tropical rocky intertidal habitats: prey refuges in relation to consumer pressure gradients. *Ecol. Monogr.*, **51**, 429–450.

Menge, B.A. and Sutherland, J.P. (1976) Species diversity gradients: synthesis of the roles of predation, competition, and temporal heterogeneity. *Am. Nat.*, **110**, 351–369.

Menge, J.L. (1974) Prey selection and foraging period of the predaceous rocky intertidal snail, *Acanthina punctulata*. *Oecologia (Berlin)*, **17**, 293–316.

Menge, J.L. (1975) Effects of herbivores on community structure of the New England rocky intertidal region: distribution and diversity of algae. Ph. D. Thesis, Harvard University, 165 pp.

Metcalfe, N.B. (1984a) The effects of habitat on the vigilance of shorebirds: is visibility important? *Anim. Behav.*, **32**, 981–985.

Metcalfe, N.B. (1984b) The effects of mixed species flocking on the vigilance of shorebirds: who do they trust? *Anim. Behav.*, **32**, 986–993.

Metcalfe, N.B. and Furness, R.W. (1984) Changing priorities: the effect of pre-migration fattening on the trade-off between foraging and vigilance. *Behav. Ecol. Sociobiol.*, **15**, 203–206.

Micallef, H. (1969) The zonation of certain trochids under an artificial tidal regime. *Neth. J. Sea Res.*, **4**, 380–393.

Mihn, J.W., Banta, W.C. and Loeb, G.L. (1981) Effects of adsorbed organic and primary fouling films on bryozoan settlement. *J. Exp. Mar. Biol. Ecol.*, **54**, 167–179.

Mileikovsky, S.A. (1971) Types of larval development in marine bottom invertebrates, their distribution and ecological significance: a re-evaluation. *Mar. Biol.*, **10**, 193–213.

Mileikovsky, S.A. (1974) On predation of pelagic larvae and early juveniles of marine bottom invertebrates and their passing alive through their predators. *Mar. Biol.*, **26**, 303–311.

Millar, R.H. (1971) The biology of ascidians. *Adv. Mar. Biol.*, **9**, 1–100.

Miller, B.A. (1980) Historical review of U.S. mussel culture and harvest. In, *Mussel Culture and Harvest: a North American perspective*, ed. R.A. Lutz, Elsevier Scientific Publishing Co., Amsterdam, pp. 18–37.

Miller, R.J. and Mann, K.H. (1973) Ecological energetics of the seaweed zone in a marine bay on the Atlantic Coast of Canada. III. Energy transformations by sea urchins. *Mar. Biol.*, **18**, 99–114.

Miller, S.L. and Vadas, R.L. (1984) The population biology of *Ascophyllum nodosum*: biological and physical factors affecting survivorship of germlings. *Br. Phycol. J.*, **19**, p. 198 only.

Minot, C.S. (1908) *The Problem of Age, Growth and Death*. John Murray, London, 272 pp.

Miranda, O. and Acuna, E. (1979) *Mytilus edulis chilensis* (Hupe, 1854) en Cabo Negro (provincia de Magallanes) (Mollusca. Bivalvia, Mytilidae). *Rev. Biol. Mar. Dep. Oceanol. Univ. Chile*, **16**, 331–353.

Mitchell, J.M. (1977) The changing climate. In, *Energy and Climate*, ed. Geophysics Study Committee, Natn. Acad. Sci. U.S.A., Studies in Geophysics, Washington, D.C., pp. 51–58.

Mladenov, P.V. and Emson, R.H. (1984) Divide and broadcast: sexual reproduction in the West Indian brittle star *Ophiocomella ophiactoides* and its relationship to fissiparity. *Mar. Biol.*, **81**, 273–282.

Montague, J.R., Morgan, R.L. and Starmer, W.T. (1981) Reproductive allocation in the Hawaiian Drosophilidae: egg size and number. *Am. Nat.*, **118**, 865–871.

Montfort, C. (1937) Die Trockenresistenz der Gezeitenpflanzen und die Frage der Ükereinstimmung von Standort und Vegetation. *Ber. Dt. Bot. Ges.*, **55**, (85)–(95).

Moore, D.R. and Reish, D.J. (1969) Studies on the *Mytilus edulis* community in Alamitos Bay, California. 4. Seasonal variation in gametes from different regions of the bay. *Veliger*, **11**, 250–255.

Moore, H.B. (1936a) The biology of *Balanus balanoides*. V. Distribution in the Plymouth area. *J. Mar. Biol. Ass. U.K.*, **20**, 701–716.

Moore, H.B. (1936b) The biology of *Purpura lapillus*. I. Shell variation in relation to environment. *J. Mar. Biol. Ass. U.K.*, **21**, 61–89.

Moore, H.B. (1938a) The biology of *Purpura lapillus*. Part II. Growth. *J. Mar. Biol. Ass. U.K.*, **23**, 57–66.

Moore, H.B. (1938b) The biology of *Purpura lapillus*. Part III. Life history and relation to environmental factors. *J. Mar. Biol. Ass. U.K.*, **23**, 67–74.

Moore, H.B. (1939) The colonization of a new rocky shore at Plymouth. *J. Anim. Ecol.*, **8**, 29–38.

Moore, H.B. and Kitching, J.A. (1939) The biology of *Chthamalus stellatus* (Poli). *J. Mar. Biol. Ass. U.K.*, **23**, 521–541.

Moore, H.B. and Sproston, N.G. (1940) Further observations on the colonization of a new rocky shore at Plymouth. *J. Anim. Ecol.*, **9**, 319–327.

Moore, P.G. (1971) The nematode fauna associated with holdfasts of kelp (*Laminaria hyperborea*) in North East Britain. *J. Mar. Biol. Ass. U.K.*, **51**, 589–604.

Moore, P.G. (1972) Particulate matter in the sublittoral zone of an exposed coast and its ecological significance with special reference to the fauna inhabiting kelp holdfasts. *J. Exp. Mar. Biol. Ecol.*, **10**, 59–80.

Moore, P.G. (1973a) The kelp fauna of Northeast Britain. I. Introduction and the physical environment. *J. Exp. Mar. Biol. Ecol.*, **13**, 97–125.

Moore, P.G. (1973b) The kelp fauna of Northeast Britain. II. Multivariate classification: turbidity as an ecological factor. *J. Exp. Mar. Biol. Ecol.*, **13**, 127–163.

Moore, P.G. (1973c) The larger Crustacea associated with holdfasts of kelp (*Laminaria hyperborea*) in North East Britain. *Cah. Biol. Mar.*, **14**, 493–518.

Moore, P.G. (1973d) *Campyloderes macquariae* Johnston 1938 (Kinorhyncha, Cyclorhagida) from the northern hemisphere. *J. Nat. Hist.*, **7**, 341–354.

Moore, P.G. (1974) The kelp fauna of Northeast Britain. III. Qualitative and quantitative ordinations, and the utility of a multivariate approach. *J. Exp. Mar. Biol. Ecol.*, **16**, 257–300.

Moore, P.G. (1975) The role of habitat selection in determining the local distribution of animals in the sea. *Mar. Behav. Physiol.*, **3**, 97–100.

Moore, P.G. (1977a) Inorganic particulate suspensions in the sea and their effects on marine animals. *Oceanogr. Mar. Biol. Ann. Rev.*, **15**, 225–363.

Moore, P.G. (1977b) Additions to the littoral fauna of Rockall, with a description of *Araeolaimus penelope* sp. nov. (Nematoda: Axonolaimidae). *J. Mar. Biol. Ass. U.K.*, **57**, 191–200.

Moore, P.G. (1977c) Organization in simple communities: observations on the natural history of *Hyale nilssoni* (Amphipoda) in high littoral seaweeds. In, *Biology of Benthic Organisms*, ed. B.F. Keegan, P. ÓCéidigh & P.J.S. Boaden, Pergamon Press, Oxford, pp. 443–451.

Moore, P.G. (1978) Turbidity and kelp holdfast Amphipoda. I. Wales and S.W. England. *J. Exp. Mar. Biol. Ecol.*, **32**, 53–96.

Moore, P.G. (1981) The life histories of the amphipods *Lembos websteri* Bate and *Corophium bonnellii* Milne Edwards in kelp holdfasts. *J. Exp. Mar. Biol. Ecol.*, **49**, 1–50.

Moore, P.G. (1983a) Ch. 5. Biological interactions. In, *Sublittoral Ecology: the ecology of the shallow sublittoral benthos*, ed. R. Earll & D.G. Erwin, Clarendon Press, Oxford, pp. 125–143.

Moore, P.G. (1983b) The apparent role of temperature in breeding initiation and winter population structure in *Hyale nilssoni* Rathke (Amphipoda): field observations 1972–83. *J. Exp. Mar. Biol. Ecol.*, **71**, 237–248.

Moran, M.J. (1980) Ecology and effects on its prey of the intertidal predatory whelk *Morula marginalba* Blainville. Ph. D. Thesis, University of Sydney, 194 pp.

Moran, M.J., Fairweather, P.G. and Underwood, A.J. (1984) Growth and mortality of the predatory intertidal whelk *Morula marginalba* Blainville (Muricidae): the effects of different species of prey. *J. Exp. Mar. Biol. Ecol.*, **75**, 1–17.

Moreno, C.A., Sutherland, J.P. and Jara, H.F. (1984) Man as a predator in the intertidal zone of southern Chile. *Oikos*, **42**, 155–160.

Moreno, de A., Moreno, V.J. and Malaspina, A.M. (1971) Estudios sobre el mejillón (*Mytilus platensis* d'Orb) en explotación comercial del sector bonaerense Mar Argentino. 2. Ciclo anual en los principales componentes bioquimicos. *Contr. Inst. Mar. Biol., Mar de Plata*, **156**, 1–15.

Morgan, C.L. (1894) The homing of limpets. *Nature, Lond.*, **51**, p. 127 only.

Morris, R.H., Abbott, D.P. and Haderlie, E.C. (1980) *Intertidal Invertebrates of California*. Stanford University Press, Stanford, Calif., 690 pp.

Morris, S. and Taylor, A.C. (1983) Diurnal and seasonal variation in physico-chemical conditions within intertidal rock pools. *Estuar. Coastal Shelf Sci.*, **17**, 339–355.

Morrison, R.I.G. (1976) Moult of the Purple Sandpiper, *Calidris maritima*, in Iceland. *Ibis*, **118**, 237–246.

Morrison, R.I.G. and Wilson, J.R. (1972) *Cambridge Iceland Expedition*. 1971 Report, University of Cambridge, 89 pp.

Morse, M.P. (1969) On the feeding of the nudibranch, *Coryphella verrucosa rufibranchialis*, with a discussion of its taxonomy. *Nautilus*, **83**, 37–40.

Morton, B. (1980) Selective site segregation in *Patelloida (Chiazacmea) pygmaea* (Dunker) and *P. (C.) lampanicola* Habe (Gastropoda: Patellacea) on a Hong Kong shore. *J. Exp. Mar. Biol. Ecol.*, **47**, 149–171.

Morton, J.E. and Miller, M.C. (1973) *The New Zealand Sea Shore*. (2nd edn), Collins, Glasgow, 653 pp.

Moss, B. (1974) Attachment and germination of the zygotes of *Pelvetia canaliculata* (L.) Dcne. et Thur. (Phaeophyceae, Fucales). *Phycologia*, **13**, 317–322.

Mountford, M.D. (1962) An index of similarity and its application to classificatory problems. In, *Progress in Soil Zoology*, ed. P.W. Murphy, Butterworths, London, pp. 43–50.

Mountford, M.D. (1968) The significance of litter-size. *J. Anim. Ecol.*, **37**, 363–367.

Muenscher, W.L.G. (1915) Ability of seaweeds to withstand desiccation. *Publs Puget Sd Biol. Stn, Univ. Washington*, **1**, 19–23.

Mukai, H. (1971) The phytal animals on the thalli of *Sargassum serratifolium* in the *Sargassum* region, with reference to their seasonal fluctuations. *Mar. Biol.*, **8**, 170–182.

Murdoch, W.W. (1969) Switching in general predators: experiments on predator specifity and stability of prey populations. *Ecol. Monogr.*, **39**, 335–354.

Murdoch, W.W. (1979) Predation and the dynamics of prey populations. *Fortschr. Zool.*, **25**, 295–310.

Murdoch, W.W. and Oaten, A. (1975) Predation and population stability. *Adv. Ecol. Res.*, **9**, 1–131.

Murphy, G.I. (1968) Pattern in life-history and environment. *Am. Nat.*, **102**, 391–403.

Murphy, P.G. (1976) Electrophoretic evidence that selection reduces ecological overlap in marine limpets. *Nature, Lond.*, **261**, 228–230.

Muus, B.J. (1967) The fauna of Danish estuaries and lagoons. Distribution and ecology of dominating species in the shallow reaches of the mesohaline zone. *Meddr. Danm. Fisk.-og Havunders.*, (n.s.), **5**, 1–316.

Mwaiseje, B. (1977) Biological communities and colonization in tidepools. Ph. D. Thesis, University of Wales, 93 pp.

Myers, A.A. (1969) A revision of the amphipod genus *Microdeutopus* Costa (Gammaridea: Aoridae). *Bull. Br. Mus. Nat. Hist. (Zool.)*, **17**, 93–148.

Myers, J.P., Connors, P.G. and Pitelka, F.A. (1979) Territoriality in non-breeding shorebirds. *Stud. Avian Biol.*, No. 2, 231–246.

Nagabhushanam, R. and Mane, U.H. (1978) Seasonal variation in the biochemical composition of *Mytilus viridis* at Ratnagiri on the West coast of India. *Hydrobiologia*, **57**, 69–72.

Navrot, J., Amiel, A.J. and Kronfeld, J. (1974) *Patella vulgata*: a biological monitor of coastal metal pollution – a preliminary study. *Environ. Pollut.*, **7**, 303–308.

Naylor, R. and Begon, M. (1982) Variation within and between populations of *Littorina nigrolineata* Gray, on Holy Island, Anglesey. *J. Conch., Lond.*, **31**, 17–30.

Nelson, T.C. (1928a) Relation of spawning of the oyster to temperature. *Ecology*, **9**, 145–154.

Nelson, T.C. (1928b) Pelagic dissoconchs of the common mussel, *Mytilus edulis*, with observations on the behavior of the larvae of allied genera. *Biol. Bull. Mar. Biol. Lab, Woods Hole*, **55**, 180–192.

Nelson-Smith, A. (1965) Marine biology of Milford Haven: the physical environment. *Fld Stud.*, **2**, 155–188.

Nelson-Smith, A. (1968) Biological consequences of oil pollution and shore cleansing. *Fld Stud.*, **2** (suppl.), 73–80.

Newcombe, C.L. (1935a) Growth of *Mya arenaria* (L.) in the Bay of Fundy region. *Can. J. Res.*, (D) **13**, 97–137.

Newcombe, C.L. (1935b) A study of the community relationships of the sea mussel, *Mytilus edulis* L. *Ecology*, **16**, 234–243.

Newell, R.C. and Lucas, M.I. (1981) The quantitative significance of dissolved and particulate organic matter released during fragmentation of kelp in coastal waters. *Kieler Meeresforsch.*, **5**, 356–369.

Newell, R.I.E., Hilbish, T.J., Koehn, R.K. and Newell, C.J. (1982) Temporal variation in the reproductive cycle of *Mytilus edulis* L. (Bivalvia, Mytilidae) from localities on the East coast of the United States. *Biol. Bull. Mar. Biol. Lab, Woods Hole*, **162**, 299–310.

Newkirk, G.F. and Doyle, R.W. (1975) Genetic analysis of shell-shape variation in *Littorina saxatilis* on an environmental cline. *Mar. Biol.*, **30**, 227–237.

Newman, W.A. and Ross, A. (1976) Revision of the balanomorph barnacles: including a catalog of the species. *Mem. S. Diego Soc. Nat. Hist.*, **9**, 1–108.

Nichols, D. and Barker, M.F. (1984) Growth of juvenile *Asterias rubens* L. (Echinodermata: Asteroidea) on an intertidal reef in southwestern Britain. *J. Exp. Mar. Biol. Ecol.*, **78**, 157–165.

Nicotri, M.E. (1977) Grazing effects of four marine intertidal herbivores on the microflora. *Ecology*, **58**, 1020–1032.

Niell, F.X. (1977) Método de recolección y área mínima de muestreo en estudios estructurales del macrofitobentos rocoso intermareal de la Ría de Vigo. *Investigación Pesq.* **41**, 509–521.

Nielsen, C. (1975) Observations on *Buccinum undatum* L. attacking bivalves and on prey responses, with a short review on attack methods of other prosobranchs. *Ophelia*, **13**, 87–108.

Nishihira, M. (1968) Brief experiments on the effects of algal extracts in promoting the settlement of the larvae of *Coryne uchidai* Stechow (Hydrozoa). *Bull. Biol. Stn. Asamushi*, **13**, 91–101.

Nixon, S.W., Oviatt, C.A., Rogers, C. and Taylor, K. (1971) Mass and metabolism of a mussel bed. *Oecologia (Berlin)*, **8**, 21–30.

Noble, J.P.A., Logan, A. and Webb, G.R. (1976) The recent *Terebratulina* community in the rocky subtidal zone of the Bay of Fundy, Canada. *Lethaia*, **9**, 1–17.

Noodt, W. (1957) Zur Ökologie der Harpacticoidea (Crust. Cop.) des Eulitorals der deutschen Meeresküste und der angrenzenden Brackgewässer *Z. Morph. Ökol. Tiere.*, **46**, 149–242.

Noodt, W. (1970) Zur Ökologie der Copepoda Harpacticoidea des Küstengebietes von Tvärminne (Finnland). *Acta Zool. Fenn.*, No. 128, 3–35.

Noodt, W. (1971) Ecology of the Copepoda. In, *Proceedings of the First International Conference on Meiofauna*, ed. N.C. Hulings, *Smithson. Contr. Zool.*, **76**, 97–102.

Norton, T.A. (1973) Orientated growth of *Membranipora membranacea* (L.) on the thallus of *Saccorhiza polyschides* (Lightf.) Batt. *J. Exp. Mar. Biol. Ecol.*, **13**, 91–95.

Norton, T.A. (1976) Why is *Sargassum muticum* so invasive? *Br. Phycol. J.*, **11**, 197–198.

Norton, T.A. and Fetter, R. (1981) The settlement of *Sargassum muticum* propagules in stationary and flowing water. *J. Mar. Biol. Ass. U.K.*, **61**, 929–940.

Norton, T.A., Hiscock, K. and Kitching, J.A. (1977) The ecology of Lough Ine. XX. The *Laminaria* forest at Carrigathorna. *J. Ecol.*, **65**, 919–941.

Norton, T.A., Mathieson, A.C. and Neushul, M. (1981) Ch. 12. Morphology and Environment. In, *The Biology of Seaweeds*, ed. C.S. Lobban & M.J. Wynne, Blackwell Scientific Publications, Oxford, pp. 421–451.

Norton, T.A., Mathieson, A.C. and Neushul, M. (1982) A review of some aspects of form and function in seaweeds. *Botanica Mar.*, **25**, 501–510.

Nuwayhid, M.A., Davies, P.S. and Elder, H.Y. (1978) Gill structure in the common limpet *Patella vulgata*. *J. Mar. Biol. Ass. U.K.*, **58**, 817–823.

Nuwayhid, M.A., Davies, P.S. and Elder, H.Y. (1980) Changes in the ultrastructure of the gill epithelium of *Patella vulgata* after exposure to North Sea crude oil and dispersants. *J. Mar. Biol. Ass. U.K.*, **60**, 439–448.

Obrebski, S. (1979) Larval colonizing strategies in marine benthic invertebrates. *Mar. Ecol. Prog. Ser.*, **1**, 293–300.

Obusan, R.A. and Urbano, E.E. (1968) Tahong – food for the millions. *Tech. Pap. Indo-Pacif. Fish. Counc.*, No. 29, 25 pp. (mimeo)

Ockelmann, K.W. (1965) Developmental types in marine bivalves and their distribution along the Atlantic coast of Europe. *Proc. 1st Europ. Malac. Congr.*, *1962*, ed. L.R. Cox & J.F. Peake, Conch. Soc. Great Britain and Ireland, and Malac. Soc. Lond., pp. 25–35.

Ockelmann, K.W. and Nielsen, C. (1981) On the biology of the prosobranch *Lacuna parva* in the Oresund. *Ophelia*, **20**, 1–16.

O'Connor, R.J., Boaden, P.J.S. and Seed, R. (1975) Niche breadth in Bryozoa as a test of competition theory. *Nature, Lond.*, **256**, 307–309.

O'Connor, R.J. and Brown, R.A. (1977) Prey depletion and foraging strategy in the Oystercatcher *Haematopus ostralegus*. *Oecologia (Berlin)*, **27**, 75–92.

O'Connor, R.J. and Lamont, P. (1978) The spatial organization of an intertidal *Spirorbis* community. *J. Exp. Mar. Biol. Ecol.*, **32**, 143–169.

O'Connor, R.J., Seed, R. and Boaden, P.J.S. (1979) Effects of environment and plant characteristics on the distribution of Bryozoa in a *Fucus serratus* L. community. *J. Exp. Mar. Biol. Ecol.*, **38**, 151–178.

O'Connor, R.J., Seed, R. and Boaden, P.J.S. (1980) Resource space partitioning by the Bryozoa of a *Fucus serratus* L. community. *J. Exp. Mar. Biol. Ecol.*, **45**, 117–137.

Ohm, G. (1964) Die Besiedlung der *Fucus*-Zone der Kieler Bucht und der westlichen Ostsee unter besonderer Berucksichtigung der Mikrofauna. *Kieler Meeresforsch.*, **20**, 30–64.

Olson, R.R. (1983) Ascidian-*Prochloron* symbiosis: the role of larval photoadaptations in midday larvae release and settlement. *Biol. Bull. Mar. Biol. Lab., Woods Hole*, **165**, 221–240.

Olsson, A. (1961) *Mollusks of the tropical eastern Pacific.* Paleontol. Res. Inst., Ithaca, New York, 574 pp.

Orton, J.H. (1928) Observations on *Patella vulgata*. Part I. Sex-phenomena, breeding and shell-growth. *J. Mar. Biol. Ass. U.K.*, **15**, 851–862.

Orton, J.H. (1929) Observations on *Patella vulgata*. Part III. Habitat and habits. *J. Mar. Biol. Ass. U.K.*, **16**, 277–288.

Orton, J.H. and Southward, A.J. (1961) Studies on the biology of limpets. IV. The breeding of *Patella depressa* Pennant on the North Cornish coast. *J. Mar. Biol. Ass. U.K.*, **41**, 653–662.

Orton, J.H., Southward, A.J. and Dodd, J.M. (1956) Studies on the biology of limpets. II. The breeding of *Patella vulgata* L. in Britain. *J. Mar. Biol. Ass. U.K.*, **35**, 149–176.

Osman, R.W. (1977) The establishment and development of a marine epifaunal community. *Ecol. Monogr.*, **47**, 37–63.

Osman, R.W. (1978) The influence of seasonality and stability on the species equilibrium. *Ecology*, **59**, 383–399.

Osman, R.W. and Haugsness, J.A. (1981) Mutualism among sessile invertebrates: a mediator of competition and predation. *Science*, **211**, 846–847.

Ostarello, J. (1976) Larval dispersal in the subtidal hydrocoral *Allopora californica* Verrill (1866). In, *Coelenterate Ecology and Behavior*, ed. G.O. Mackie, Plenum Press, New York, pp. 331–337.

Oswald, R.C., Telford, N., Seed, R. and Happey-Wood, C.M. (1984) The effect of encrusting bryozoans on the photosynthetic activity of *Fucus serratus* L. *Estuarine Coastal Shelf Sci.*, **19**, 697–702.

Ott, J. (1967) Vertikalverteilung von Nematoden in Bestanden nordadriatischer Sargassaceen. *Helgoländer Wiss. Meeresunters.*, **15**, 412–428.

Otto, G. (1936) Die Fauna der *Enteromorpha*-zone der Kieler Bucht. *Kieler Meeresforsch.*, **1**, 1–48.

Ottway, S. (1972) The toxicity of oil to animals subjected to salinity stress. *Fld Stud. Council U.K., Oil Poll. Res. Unit, 1972, Ann. Rept*, pp. 24–30.

Padilla, D.K. (1984) The importance of form: differences in competitive ability, resistance to consumers and environmental stress in an assemblage of coralline algae. *J. Exp. Mar. Biol. Ecol.*, **79**, 105–127.

Padilla, M. (1973) Observaciones biologicas relacionadas con el cultivo de *Mytilus edulis chilensis* en Aysen. *Inst. de Fomento Pesq., Santiago, Chile, Publ.* No. 54, 21 pp.

Page, G. and Whiteacre, D.F. (1975) Raptor predation on wintering shorebirds. *Condor*, **77**, 73–83.

Paine, R.T. (1966) Food web complexity and species diversity. *Am. Nat.*, **100**, 65–75.

Paine, R.T. (1969a) A note on trophic complexity and community stability. *Am. Nat.*, **103**, 91–93.

Paine, R.T. (1969b) The *Pisaster-Tegula* interaction: prey patches, predator food preferences, and intertidal community structure. *Ecology*, **50**, 950–962.

Paine, R.T. (1971) A short-term experimental investigation of resource partitioning in a New Zealand rocky intertidal habitat. *Ecology*, **52**, 1096–1106.

Paine, R.T. (1974) Intertidal community structure: experimental studies on the relationship between a dominant competitor and its principal predator. *Oecologia (Berlin)*, **15**, 93–120.

Paine, R.T. (1976a) Size-limited predation: an observational and experimental approach with the *Mytilus: Pisaster* interaction. *Ecology*, **57**, 858–873.

Paine, R.T. (1976b) Biological observations on a subtidal *Mytilus californianus* bed. *Veliger*, **19**, 125–130.

Paine, R.T. (1977) Controlled manipulations in the marine intertidal zone and their contributions to ecological theory. In, *The Changing Scenes in Natural Sciences, 1776-1976*, ed. C.E. Goulden, Natn. Acad. Sci. U.S.A., Spec. Publ. No. 12, pp. 245–270.

Paine, R.T. (1979) Disaster, catastrophe, and local persistence of the sea palm *Postelsia palmaeformis*. *Science*, **205**, 685–687.

Paine, R.T. (1980) Food webs: linkage, interaction strength and community infrastructure. *J. Anim. Ecol.*, **49**, 667–685.

Paine, R.T. (1981) Barnacle ecology: is competition important? Disturbance and predation: proxy for competition. *Paleobiology*, **7**, 553–560.

Paine, R.T. (1984) Ecological determinism in the competition for space. *Ecology*, **65**, 1339–1348.

Paine, R.T., Castilla, J.C. and Cancino, J. (1985) Perturbation and recovery patterns of starfish dominated intertidal assemblages in Chile, New Zealand and Washington State. *Am. Nat.*, (IN PRESS).

Paine, R.T. and Levin, S.A. (1981) Intertidal landscapes: disturbance and the dynamics of pattern. *Ecol. Monogr.*, **51**, 145–178.

Paine, R.T. and Palmer, A.R. (1978) *Sicyases sanguineus*: a unique trophic generalist from the Chilean intertidal zone. *Copeia*, 1978, 75–81.

Paine, R.T. and Suchanek, T.H. (1983) Convergence of ecological processes between independently evolved competitive dominants: a tunicate-mussel comparison. *Evolution, Lancaster, Pa.*, **37**, 821–831.

Paine, R.T. and Vadas, R.L. (1969) The effects of grazing by sea urchins, *Strongylocentrotus* spp., on benthic algal populations. *Limnol. Oceanogr.*, **14**, 710–719.

Palichenko, Z.G. (1948) On the biology of *Mytilus edulis* in the White Sea. *Zool. Zh.*, **27**, 411–420. [In Russian]

Pallares, R.E. and Hall, M.A. (1974a) Analisis bioestadistico-ecologico de la fauna de copepodos asociados a los bosques de *Macrocystis pyrifera*. *Physis (Buenos Aires)* (A), **33**, 275–319.

Pallares, R.E. and Hall, M.A. (1974b) Analisis bioestadistico-ecologico de la fauna de copepodos asociados a los bosques de *Macrocystis pyrifera*. (Conclusión). *Physis (Buenos Aires)* (A), **33**, 409–432.

Palmer, A.R. (1979) Fish predation and the evolution of gastropod shell sculpture: experimental and geographic evidence. *Evolution, Lancaster, Pa.*, **33**, 697–713.

Palmer, A.R. (1983a) Growth rate as a measure of food value in thaidid gastropods: assumptions and implications for prey morphology and distribution. *J. Exp. Mar. Biol. Ecol.*, **73**, 95–124.

Palmer, A.R. (1983b) Relative cost of producing skeletal organic matrix versus calcification: evidence from marine gastropods. *Mar. Biol.*, **75**, 287–292.

Palmer, A.R. (1984) Prey selection by thaidid gastropods: some observational and experimental field tests of foraging models. *Oecologia (Berlin)*, **62**, 162–172.

Palmer, A.R. and Strathmann, R.R. (1981) Scale of dispersal in varying environments and its implications for life histories of marine invertebrates. *Oecologia (Berlin)*, **48**, 308–318.

Palmer, J.B. and Frank, P.W. (1974) Estimates of growth of *Cryptochiton stelleri* (Middendorff, 1846) in Oregon. *Veliger*, **16**, 301–304.

Paris, O.H. (1960) Some quantitative aspects of predation by muricid snails on mussels in Washington Sound. *Veliger*, **2**, 41–47.

Parke, M.[W.] (1948) Studies on British Laminariaceae. I. Growth in *Laminaria saccharina* (L.) Lamour. *J. Mar. Biol. Ass. U.K.*, **27**, 651–709.

Parry, G.D. (1982a) The evolution of the life histories of four species of intertidal limpets. *Ecol. Monogr.*, **52**, 65–91.

Parry, G.D. (1982b) Reproductive effort in four species of intertidal limpets. *Mar. Biol.*, **67**, 267–282.

Parsons, R. (1972) Some sub-lethal effects of refinery effluent upon the winkle *Littorina saxatilis*. *Fld Stud. Council (U.K.), Oil Poll. Res. Unit., 1972 Ann. Rept.*, pp. 21–23.

Parulekar, A.H., Dalal, S.F., Ansari, Z.A. and Harkantra, S.N. (1982) Environmental physiology of raft grown mussels *Perna viridis* in Goa, India. *Aquaculture*, **29**, 83–94.

Patterson, M.R. (1985) Patterns of whole colony prey capture in the octocoral *Alcyonium siderium*. *Biol. Bull. Mar. Biol. Lab., Woods Hole*, **167**, 613–629.

Paynter, R.A. (1971) Nasal glands in *Cinclodes nigrofumosus*, a maritime passerine. *Bull. Br. Orn. Club*, **91**, 11–12.

Pearse, J.S. and Hines, A.H. (1979) Expansion of a central California kelp forest following the mass mortality of sea urchins. *Mar. Biol.*, **51**, 83–91.

Peattie, M.E. and Hoare, R. (1981) The sublittoral ecology of the Menai Strait. II. The sponge *Halichondria panicea* (Pallas) and its associated fauna. *Estuarine Coastal Shelf Sci.*, **13**, 621–635.

Pechenik, J.A. (1979) Role of encapsulation in invertebrate life histories. *Am. Nat.*, **114**, 859–870.

Pechenik, J.A. (1980) Growth and energy balance during the larval lives of three prosobranch gastropods. *J. Exp. Mar. Biol. Ecol.*, **44**, 1–28.

Pechenik, J.A. (1984) The relationship between temperature, growth rate, and duration of planktonic life for larvae of the gastropod *Crepidula fornicata* (L.). *J. Exp. Mar. Biol. Ecol.*, **74**, 241–257.

Pechenik, J.A., Chang, S.C. and Lord, A. (1984) Encapsulated development of the marine prosobranch gastropod *Nucella lapillus*. *Mar. Biol.*, **78**, 223–229.

Pechenik, J.A., Perron, F.E. and Turner, R.D. (1979) The role of phytoplankton in the diets of adult and larval shipworms, *Lyrodus pedicellatus* (Bivalvia: Teredinidae). *Estuaries*, **2**, 58–60.

Penchaszadeh, P.E. (1971) Estudios sobre el mejillón (*Mytilus platensis* d'Orb.) en exploitacion commercial del sector Bona erense Mar Argentino. 1. Reproducción, crecimiento y estructura de la problación. *Contr. Inst. Mar. Biol., Mar del Plata*, **153**, 1–15.

Penchaszadeh, P.E. (1973) Ecologia de la comunidad del mejillin (*Brachidontes rodriguezi* d'Orb.) en el mediolitoral rocoso de Mar del Plata (Argentina): el proceso de recolonizacion. *Physis (Buenos Aires)*, **32**, 51–64.

Penney, A.J. and Griffiths, C.L. (1984) Prey selection and the impact of the starfish *Marthasterias glacialis* (L.) and other predators on the mussel *Choromytilus meridionalis* (Krauss). *J. Exp. Mar. Biol. Ecol.*, **75**, 19–36.

Pérès, J.M. and Molinier, R. (1957) Compte rendu du colloque tenue à Gênes par la comité du benthos de la Commission Internationale pour l'Exploration scientifique de la Mer Mediterranée. *Recl Trav. Stn Mar. Endoume*, **22**, 5–15.

Perron, F.E. (1981a) Larval biology of six species of the genus *Conus* (Gastropoda: Toxoglossa) in Hawaii, U.S.A. *Mar. Biol.*, **61**, 215–220.

Perron, F.E. (1981b) The partitioning of reproductive energy between ova and protective capsules in marine gastropods of the genus *Conus*. *Am. Nat.*, **118**, 110–118.

Perron, F.E. (1982) Inter- and intraspecific patterns of reproductive effort in four species of cone shells (*Conus* spp.). *Mar. Biol.*, **68**, 161–167.

Perron, F.E. and Carrier, R.H. (1981) Egg size distributions among closely related marine invertebrate species: are they bimodal or unimodal? *Am. Nat.*, **118**, 749–755.

Petersen, J.H. (1984a) Establishment of mussel beds: attachment behavior and distribution of recently settled mussels (*Mytilus californianus*). *Veliger*, **27**, 7–13.

Petersen, J.H. (1984b) Larval settlement behavior in competing species: *Mytilus californianus* Conrad and *M. edulis* L. *J. Exp. Mar. Biol. Ecol.*, **82**, 147–159.

Peterson, C.H. (1979) The importance of predation and competition in organizing the intertidal epifaunal communities of Barnegat Inlet, New Jersey. *Oecologia (Berlin)*, **39**, 1–24.

Peterson, R.T. (1961) *A Field Guide to Western Birds*. Houghton Mifflin Company, Boston, 366 pp.

Petraitis, P.S. (1978) Distributional patterns of juvenile *Mytilus edulis* and *Mytilus californianus*. *Veliger*, **21**, 288–292.

Pettitt, C.[W.] (1973a) An examination of the distribution of shell pattern in *Littorina saxatilis* (Olivi) with particular regard to the possibility of visual selection in this species. *Malacologia*, **14**, 339–343.

Pettitt, C.[W.] (1973b) A proposed new method of scoring the colour morphs of *Littorina saxatilis* (Olivi, 1792) (Gastropoda: Prosobranchia). *Proc. Malac. Soc. Lond.*, **40**, 531–538.

Pettitt, C.[W.] (1975) A review of the predators of *Littorina*, especially those of *L. saxatilis* (Olivi) (Gastropoda: Prosobranchia). *J. Conch., Lond.*, **28**, 343–357.

Phillips, B.F. (1969) The population ecology of the whelk *Dicathais aegrota* in Western Australia. *Aust. J. Mar. Freshwat. Res.*, **20**, 225–265.

Phillips, B.F. and Campbell, N.A. (1974) Mortality and longevity in the whelk *Dicathais orbita* (Gmelin). *Aust. J. Mar. Freshwat. Res.*, **25**, 25–33.

Phillips, B.F., Campbell, N.A. and Wilson, B.R. (1973) A multivariate study of geographic variation in the whelk *Dicathais*. *J. Exp. Mar. Biol. Ecol.*, **11**, 27–69.

Phillips, D.W. (1975) Distance chemoreception-triggered avoidance behaviour of the limpets *Acmaea (Collisella) limatula* and *Acmaea (Notoacmea) scutum* to the predatory starfish *Pisaster ochraceus. J. Exp. Zool.,* **191**, 199–210.

Phillips, D.W. (1976) The effect of species-specific avoidance response to predatory starfish on the intertidal distribution of two gastropods. *Oecologia (Berlin),* **23**, 83–94.

Pianka, E.R. (1970) On *r-* and *K*-selection. *Am. Nat.,* **100**, 592–597.

Pianka, E.R. (1976) Natural selection of optimal reproductive tactics. *Am. Zool.,* **16**, 775–784.

Picken, G.B. (1980) The distribution, growth and reproduction of the Antarctic limpet *Nacella (Patinigera) concinna* (Strebel 1908). *J. Exp. Mar. Biol. Ecol.,* **42**, 71–85.

Picken, G.B. and Allen, D. (1983) Unique spawning behaviour by the Antarctic limpet *Nacella (= Patinigera) concinna* (Strebel 1908). *J. Exp. Mar. Biol. Ecol.,* **71**, 283–287.

Pielou, E.C. (1974) Competition on an environmental gradient. In, *Mathematical Problems in Biology,* ed. P. van den Driessch, Springer-Verlag, Berlin, pp. 184–204.

Pienkowski, M.W. (1981) How foraging plovers cope with environmental effects on invertebrate behaviour and availability. In, *Feeding and Survival Strategies of Estuarine Organisms,* ed. N.V. Jones & W.J. Wolff, Plenum Press, New York, pp. 179–192.

Pienkowski, M.W. (1983a) The effects of environmental conditions on feeding rates and prey-selection of shore plovers. *Ornis Scandinavica,* **14**, 227–238.

Pienkowski, M.W. (1983b) Surface activity of some intertidal invertebrates in relation to temperatures and the foraging behaviour of their shorebird predators. *Mar. Ecol. Prog. Ser.,* **11**, 114–150.

Pienkowski, M.W., Lloyd, C.S. and Minton, C.D.T. (1979) Seasonal and migrational weight changes in Dunlin. *Bird Study,* **26**, 134–148.

Pierce, S.K. (1970) The water balance of *Modiolus* (Mollusca: Bivalvia: Mytilidae): osmotic concentrations in changing salinities. *Comp. Biochem. Physiol.,* **36**, 521–533.

Pike, R.B. (1971) Report on mussel farming and mussel biology for the fishing industry board. *N. Z. Fish. Ind. Bd Tech. Rep.,* No. 71, 1–7.

Pipe, A.R. (1982) Epizoites on marine invertebrates: with particular reference to those associated with the pycnogonid *Phoxichilidium tubulariae* Lebour, the amphipod *Caprella linearis* (L.) and the decapod *Corystes cassivelaunus* (Pennant). *Chem. Ecol.,* **1**, 61–74.

Platt, H.M. and Warwick, R.M. (1980) Ch. 10. The significance of free-living nematodes to the littoral ecosystem. In, *The Shore Environment,* Vol. 2, *Ecosystems,* ed. J.H. Price, D.E.G. Irvine & W.F. Farnham (Syst. Ass. Spec. Vol. **17**a), Academic Press, London, pp. 729–759.

Plough, H.H. (1978) *Sea squirts of the Atlantic Continental Shelf from Maine to Texas.* Johns Hopkins University Press, Baltimore, Maryland, 118 pp.

Pollock, D.E. (1979) Predator-prey relationships between the rock lobster *Jasus lalandii* and the mussel *Aulacomya ater* at Robben Island on the Cape West coast of Africa. *Mar. Biol.,* **52**, 347–356.

Pollock, D.E., Griffiths, C.L. and Seiderer, L.J. (1979) Predation of rock lobsters on mussels. *S. Afr. J. Sci.,* **75**, p. 562 only.

Popper, K.R. (1963) *Conjecture and Refutations: the growth of scientific knowledge.* Harper and Row, New York, 417 pp.

Porter, J.W. (1974) Community structure of coral reefs on opposite sides of the Isthmus of Panama. *Science,* **186**, 543–545.

Powell, A.W.B. (1979) *New Zealand Mollusca.* Collins, Auckland, 500 pp.

Prater, A.J. (1981) *Estuary Birds of Britain and Ireland.* Poyser, Berkhamstead, 440 pp.

Primack, R.B. and Antonovics, J. (1982) Experimental ecological genetics in *Plantago plantago*: 7. Reproductive effort in populations of *Plantago lanceolata. Evolution, Lancaster, Pa,* **36**, 742–752.

Pringle, J.S. and Cooper, J. (1977) Wader populations (Charadrii) on the marine littoral of the Cape Peninsula, South Africa. *Ostrich,* **48**, 98–105.

Pulliam, H.R. (1974) On the theory of optimal diets. *Am. Nat.,* **108**, 59–74.

Purcell, J.E. (1977) Aggressive function and induced development of catch tentacles in the sea anemone *Metridium senile* (Coelenterata, Actiniaria). *Biol. Bull. Mar. Biol. Lab., Woods Hole,* **153**, 355–368.

Pyefinch, K.A. (1948) Notes on the biology of cirripedes. *J. Mar. Biol. Ass. U.K.,* **27**, 464–503.

Pyke, G.H., Pulliam, H.R. and Charnov, E.L. (1977) Optimal foraging: a selective review of theory and tests. *Q. Rev. Biol.*, **52**, 137–154.

Quasim, S.Z. (1957) The biology of *Blennius pholis* L. (Teleostei). *Proc. Zool. Soc. Lond.*, **128**, 161–208.

Quayle, D.B. (1951) The rate of growth of *Venerupis pullastra* (Montagu) at Millport, Scotland. *Proc. R. Soc. Edinb.*, B, **64**, 384–406.

Quinn, J.F. (1979) Disturbance, predation and diversity in the rocky intertidal zone. Ph. D. Thesis, University of Washington, Seattle, 225 pp.

Quinn, J.F. (1982) Competitive hierarchies in marine benthic communities. *Oecologia (Berlin)*, **54**, 129–135.

Raffaelli, D.G. (1976) The determinants of zonation patterns of *Littorina neritoides* and the *Littorina saxatilis* species-complex. Ph. D. Thesis, University of Wales, 206 pp.

Raffaelli, D.G. (1978a) The relationship between shell injuries and habitat characteristics of the intertidal snail *Littorina rudis* Maton. *J. Moll. Stud.*, **44**, 166–170.

Raffaelli, D.G. (1978b) Factors affecting the population structure of *Littorina neglecta* (Bean). *J. Moll. Stud.*, **44**, 223–230.

Raffaelli, D.[G.] (1979a) The taxonomy of the *Littorina saxatilis* species-complex, with particular reference to the systematic status of *Littorina patula* Jeffr[e]ys. *Zool. J. Linn. Soc.*, **65**, 219–232.

Raffaelli, D.[G.] (1979b) Colour polymorphism in the intertidal snail *Littorina rudis* Maton. *Zool. J. Linn. Soc.*, **67**, 65–73.

Raffaelli, D.G. (1979c) The grazer-algae interaction in the intertidal zone on New Zealand rocky shores. *J. Exp. Mar. Biol. Ecol.*, **38**, 81–100.

Raffaelli, D.[G.] (1982) Recent ecological research on some European species of *Littorina*. *J. Moll. Stud.*, **48**, 342–354.

Raffaelli, D.G. and Hughes, R.N. (1978) The effects of crevice size and availability on populations of *Littorina rudis* and *Littorina neritoides*. *J. Anim. Ecol.*, **47**, 71–83.

Ragan, M.A. and Jensen, A. (1977) Quantitative studies on brown algal phenols. I. Estimation of absolute polyphenol content of *Ascophyllum nodosum* (L.) Le Jol. and *Fucus vesiculosus* (L.) *J. Exp. Mar. Biol. Ecol.*, **30**, 209–221.

Ramirez, G.V. (1965) Observaciones sobre la población de *Perumytilus purpuratus* (Lamarck) en Antofagasta, 1962–63. *Mem. Pru. Opt. Titul. Prof. Biol. Quim., Univ. de Chile*, 17 pp.

Rasmussen, E. (1973) Systematics and ecology of the Isefjord marine fauna (Denmark). *Ophelia*, **11**, 1–495.

Rau, G.H. and Hedges, J.I. (1979) Carbon-13 depletion in a hydrothermal vent mussel: suggestion of a chemosynthetic food source. *Science*, **203**, 648–649.

Raup, D.M. (1966) Geometric analysis of shell coiling: general problems. *J. Paleont.*, **40**, 1178–1190.

Read, K.R.H. and Cumming, K.B. (1967) Thermal tolerance of the bivalve molluscs, *Modiolus modiolus* L., *Mytilus edulis* L. and *Brachidontes demissus* Dillwyn. *Comp. Biochem. Physiol.*, **22**, 149–155.

Recher, H.F. (1972) Territorial and agonistic behaviour of the Reef Heron. *Emu*, **72**, 126–130.

Recher, H.F. and Recher, J.A. (1972) The foraging behaviour of the Reef Heron. *Emu*, **72**, 85–90.

Reid, P. (1974) Estudios preliminares sobre la biologia de *Mytilus chilensis* Hupe, 1854 (Moll. Biv. Mytilidae). Tesis de Grado, Universidad de Concepción, Chile, 85 pp.

Reimchen, T.E. (1974) Studies on the biology and colour polymorphism of two sibling species of a marine gastropod (*Littorina*). Ph. D. Thesis, University of Liverpool, 389 pp.

Reimchen, T.E. (1981) Microgeographical variation in *Littorina mariae* Sacchi & Rastelli and a taxonomic consideration. *J. Conch., Lond.*, **30**, 341–350.

Remane, A. (1933) Verteilung und Organisation der benthonischen Mikrofauna in der Kieler Bucht. *Wiss. Meeresunters., Pr. Komm. Abt. Kiel*, **21**, 163–221.

Remane, A. (1940) Einfuhrung in die zoologische Ökologie der Nord-und Ostsee. *Tierwelt der Nord-und Ostsee*, **I**a, 1–238.

Reynolds, W.W. and Reynolds, L.J. (1977) Zoogeography and the predator-prey 'arms race', a comparison of *Eriphia* and *Nerita* species from three faunal regions. *Hydrobiologia*, **56**, 63–67.

Ricketts, E.F. and Calvin, J. (1939) *Between Pacific Tides*. Stanford University Press, Stanford, Calif., 320 pp.

Ricketts, E.F., Calvin, J. and Hedgpeth, J.W. (1968) *Between Pacific Tides*. (4th edn), Stanford University Press, Stanford, Calif. 614 pp.

Rigg, G.R. and Miller, R.C. (1949) Intertidal plant and animal zonation in the vicinity of Neah Bay, Washington. *Proc. Calif. Acad. Sci.*, **26**, 323–357.

Risbec, J. (1937) Les irrégularités et les anomalies du développement embryonnaire chez *Murex erinaceus* L. et chez *Purpura lapillus* L. *Bull. Lab. Marit. Dinard*, **17**, 25–38.

Rivest, B.R. (1983) Development and the influence of nurse egg allotment on hatching size in *Searlesia dira* (Reeve, 1846) (Prosobranchia: Buccinidae). *J. Exp. Mar. Biol. Ecol.*, **69**, 217–241.

Roberts, C.D. (1975) Investigations into a *Modiolus modiolus* (L.) (Mollusca Bivalvia) community in Strangford Lough, N. Ireland. *Rep. Underwat. Ass.*, **1**, 27–49.

Roberts, D.J. and Hughes, R.N. (1980) Growth and reproductive rates of *Littorina rudis* from three contrasted shores in North Wales, U.K. *Mar. Biol.*, **58**, 47–54.

Robertson, A.I. and Mann, K.H. (1982) Population dynamics and life history adaptations of *Littorina neglecta* Bean in an eelgrass meadow (*Zostera marina* L.) in Nova Scotia. *J. Exp. Mar. Biol. Ecol.*, **63**, 151–171.

Robertson, D. (1888) A contribution towards a catalogue of the Amphipoda and Isopoda of the Firth of Clyde. *Proc. Nat. Hist. Soc. Glasg.*, **2**, 9–99.

Robertson, D. (1894) *Amphithoe podoceroides* Rathke and *Podocerus pulchellus* Milne Edwards. *Trans. Nat. Hist. Soc. Glasg.*, **4**, 80–81.

Roff, D.A. (1975) Population stability and the evolution of dispersal in a heterogeneous environment. *Oecologia (Berlin)*, **19**, 217–237.

Roff, D.A. (1980) A motion for the retirement of the von Bertalanffy function. *Can. J. Fish. Aquat. Sci.*, **37**, 127–129.

Roland, W. (1978) Feeding behaviour of the kelp clingfish *Rimicola muscarum* residing on the kelp *Macrocystis integrifolia*. *Can. J. Zool.*, **56**, 711–712.

Root, R.B. (1967) The niche exploitation pattern of the blue-gray gnatcatcher. *Ecol. Monogr.*, **37**, 317–350.

Rosenzweig, M.L. and MacArthur, R.H. (1963) Graphical representation and stability conditions of predator-prey interactions. *Am. Nat.*, **97**, 209–223.

Rostron, D.M. and Hiscock, K. (in prep.) A quantitative study of a hard substratum community and an assessment of sampling problems.

Round, F.E., Sloane, J.F., Ebling, F.J. and Kitching, J.A. (1961) The ecology of Lough Ine. X. The hydroid *Sertularia operculata* (L.) and its associated flora and fauna: effects of transference to sheltered water. *J. Ecol.*, **49**, 617–629.

Rowell, T.W. (1967) Some aspects of the ecology, growth and reproduction of the horse mussel *Modiolus modiolus*. M. Sc. Thesis, Queen's University, Ontario, Canada, 138 pp.

Rubin, J.A. (1980) Spatial interaction in a sublittoral benthic community. In, *Progress in Underwater Science*, ed. H.M. Platt, Rep. Underwater Ass., **5**(n.s.), 137–146.

Rusanowski, P.C. and Vadas, R.L. (1973) A tide-simulating apparatus for the study of intertidal marine algae. *Bull. Ecol. Soc. Am.*, **54**, p. 35 only.

Russ, R.G. (1980) Effects of predation by fishes, competition and structural complexity of the substratum on the establishment of a marine epifaunal community. *J. Exp. Mar. Biol. Ecol.*, **42**, 55–69.

Russ, R.G. (1982) Overgrowth in a marine epifaunal community: competitive hierarchies and competitive networks. *Oecologia (Berlin)*, **53**, 12–19.

Russell, G. and Fielding, A.H. (1981) Individuals, populations and communities. In, *The Biology of Seaweeds*, ed. C.S. Lobban & M.J. Wynne, Blackwell Scientific Publications, Oxford, pp. 393–420.

Russell-Hunter, W.D. (1983) Ch. 1. Overview: planetary distribution of and ecological constraints upon the Mollusca. In, *The Mollusca*, Vol. 6, *Ecology*, ed. W.D. Russell-Hunter, Academic Press, London, pp. 1–27.

Russell-Hunter, W.D. and McMahon, R.F. (1975) An anomalous sex-ratio in the sublittoral marine snail, *Lacuna vincta* Turton, from near Woods Hole. *Nautilus*, **89**, 14–16.

Rützler, K. (1970) Spatial competition among Porifera: solution by epizoism. *Oecologia (Berlin)*, **5**, 85–95.

Ryland, J.S. (1959) Experiments on the selection of algal substrates by polyzoan larvae. *J. Exp. Biol.*, **36**, 613–631.

Ryland, J.S. (1962) The association between Polyzoa and algal substrates. *J. Anim. Ecol.*, **31**, 331–338.

Ryland, J.S. (1974a) Observations on some epibionts of gulf-weed *Sargassum natans* (L.) Meyen. *J. Exp. Mar. Biol. Ecol.*, **14**, 17–25.

Ryland, J.S. (1974b) Behaviour, settlement and metamorphosis of bryozoan larvae: a review. *Thalassia Jugosl.*, **10**, 263–296.

Ryland, J.S. (1976) Physiology and ecology of marine bryozoans. *Adv. Mar. Biol.*, **14**, 285–443.

Ryland, J.S. (1979) Taxes and tropisms of bryozoans. In, *Biology of Bryozoans*, ed. R.M. Woollacott & R.L. Zimmer, Academic Press, London, pp. 411–436.

Sacchi, C.F. and Rastelli, M. (1966) *Littorina mariae* nov. sp.: les différences morphologiques et écologiques entre 'nains' et 'normaux' chez l''espèce' *L. obtusata* (L.) (Gastr. Prosobr.) et leur signification adaptive et évolutive. *Atti. Soc. Ital. Sci. Nat.*, **105**, 351–369.

Sadykhova, I.A. (1967) Some data on the biology and growth of *Mytilus grayanus* Dunker in experimental cages in Peter the Great Bay. *Proc. Symp. Mollusca*, **2**, 431–435.

Sadykhova, I.A. (1970a) On the determination of the duration of life in *Crenomytilus grayanus*. In, *Osnovi biologicheskoy productivnosti okeana e eë ispolsovanie, Nauka, Moscva*, pp. 263–276. [In Russian]

Sadykhova, I.A. (1970b) A contribution to the biology of *Crenomytilus grayanus* (Dysodonta, Mytilidae). *Zool. Zh.*, **49**, 1408–1410.

Sadykhova, I.A. (1970c) On the allometry of growth of *Crenomytilus grayanus* (Dunker) from the Gulf of Peter the Great. *Trudȳ Molodykh Uchēnykj V.N.I.R.O.*, **3**, 108–115. [In Russian]

Saito, S. and Sakamoto, E. (1951) On the reproduction of *Mytilus grayanus* Dunker. *Bull. Jap. Soc. Scient. Fish.*, **17**, 23–26.

Sale, P.K. (1977) Maintenance of high diversity in coral reef fish communities. *Am. Nat.*, **111**, 337–359.

Sammarco, P.W. (1980) *Diadema* and its relationship to coral spat mortality: grazing, competition and biological disturbance. *J. Exp. Mar. Biol. Ecol.*, **45**, 245–272.

Sandison, E.E. (1966) The effect of salinity fluctuations on the life cycle of *Balanus pallidus stutsburi* Darwin in Lagos Harbour, Nigeria. *J. Anim. Ecol.*, **35**, 363–378.

Sandison, E.E. (1967) Respiratory response to temperature and temperature tolerance of some intertidal gastropods. *J. Exp. Mar. Biol. Ecol.*, **1**, 271–281.

Santelices, B., Montalva, S. and Oliger, P. (1981) Competitive algal community organization in exposed intertidal habitats from central Chile. *Mar. Ecol. Prog. Ser.*, **6**, 267–276.

Sarà, M. (1970) Competition and cooperation in sponge populations. *Symp. Zool. Soc. Lond.*, No. 25, 273–284.

Sarma, A.L.N. (1974) Phytal fauna of *Caulerpa taxifolia* and *C. racemosa* off Visakhapatnam coast. *Indian J. Mar. Sci.*, **3**, 155–164.

Sarma, A.L.N. and Ganapati, P.N. (1972) Faunal associations of algae in the intertidal region of Visakhapatnam. *Proc. Indian Acad. Sci.*, **38**, 380–396.

Sarma, A.L.N. and Ganapati, P.N. (1975) Phytal fauna of the Visakhapatnam harbour buoys. *Bull. Dept Mar. Sci., Univ. Cochin*, **7**, 243–255.

Sastry, A.N. (1968) The relationships among food, temperature, and gonad development of the bay scallop *Aequipecten irradians* Lamarck. *Physiol. Zool.*, **41**, 44–53.

Savilov, I.A. (1953) The growth and variations in growth of the White Sea invertebrates *Mytilus edulis*, *Mya arenaria* and *Balanus balanoides*. *Trudȳ Inst. Okeanol.*, **7**, 198–259. [In Russian]

Scarratt, D.J. (1961) The fauna of *Laminaria* holdfasts. Ph. D. Thesis, University of Wales, 200 pp.

Scattergood, L.W. and Taylor, C.C. (1950) The mussel resources of the North Atlantic region. *U.S. Dept Int., Fish Wildl. Serv., Fishery Leaflet* No. 364, 34 pp.

Schaffer, W.M. (1974) Optimal reproductive effort in fluctuating environments. *Am. Nat.*, **108**, 783–790.

Schaffer, W.M. and Gadgil, M.D. (1975) Selection for optimal life histories in plants. In, *Ecology and Evolution of Communities*, ed. M.L. Cody & J. M. Diamond, Belknap Press, Cambridge, Mass., pp. 142–157.

Scheibling, R.E. and Stephenson, R.L. (1984) Mass mortality of *Strongylocentrotus droebachiensis* (Echinodermata: Echinoidea) off Nova Scotia, Canada. *Mar. Biol.*, **78**, 153–164.

Scheltema, R.S. (1974) Biological interactions determining larval settlement of marine invertebrates. *Thalassia Jugosl.*, **10**, 263–296.

Scheltema, R.S. (1978) On the relationship between dispersal of pelagic veliger larvae and the evolution of marine prosobranch gastropods. In, *Marine Organisms: genetics, ecology and evolution*, ed. B. Battaglia & J.A. Beardmore, Plenum Press, New York, pp. 303–322.

Schoener, T.W. (1971) Theory of feeding strategies. *Annu. Rev. Ecol. Syst.*, **2**, 369–404.

Schoener, T.W. (1983) Field experiments on interspecific competition. *Am. Nat.*, **122**, 240–285.

Schonbeck, M.W. and Norton, T.A. (1978) Factors controlling the upper limits of fucoid algae on the shore. *J. Exp. Mar. Biol. Ecol.*, **31**, 303–313.

Schonbeck, M.W. and Norton, T.A. (1979a) The effects of brief periodic submergence on intertidal fucoid algae. *Estuarine Coastal Mar. Sci.*, **8**, 205–211.

Schonbeck, M.W. and Norton, T.A. (1979b) An investigation of drought avoidance in intertidal fucoid algae. *Botanica Mar.*, **22**, 133–144.

Schonbeck, M.W. and Norton, T.A. (1979c) Drought-hardening in the upper-shore seaweeds *Fucus spiralis* and *Pelvetia canaliculata*. *J. Ecol.*, **67**, 687–696.

Schonbeck, M.W. and Norton, T.A. (1980a) The effects on intertidal fucoid algae of exposure to air under various conditions. *Botanica Mar.*, **23**, 141–147.

Schonbeck, M.W. and Norton, T.A. (1980b) Factors controlling the lower limits of fucoid algae on the shore. *J. Exp. Mar. Biol. Ecol.*, **43**, 131–150.

Schroeter, S.C. (1978) Experimental studies of competition as a factor affecting the distribution and abundance of purple sea urchins, *Strongylocentrotus purpuratus* (Stimpson). Ph. D. Thesis, University of California, Santa Barbara, 184 pp.

Seapy, R.R. and Hoppe, W.J. (1973) Morphological and behavioural adaptations to desiccation in the intertidal limpet *Acmaea (Collisella) strigatella*. *Veliger*, **16**, 181–188.

Sebens, K.P. (1976) The ecology of Caribbean sea anemones in Panama: utilization of space on a coral reef. In, *Coelenterate Ecology and Behavior*, ed. G. Mackie, Plenum, New York, pp. 67–77.

Sebens, K.P. (1981a) Recruitment in a sea anemone population: juvenile substrate becomes adult prey. *Science*, **213**, 785–787.

Sebens, K.P. (1981b) Reproductive ecology of the intertidal sea anemones *Anthopleura xanthogrammica* (Brandt) and *A. elegantissima* (Brandt): body size, habitat, and sexual reproduction. *J. Exp. Mar. Biol. Ecol.*, **54**, 225–250.

Sebens, K.P. (1982a) Recruitment and habitat selection in the intertidal sea anemones *Anthopleura elegantissima* (Brandt) and *A. xanthogrammica* (Brandt). *J. Exp. Mar. Biol. Ecol.*, **59**, 103–124.

Sebens, K.P. (1982b) Competition for space: growth rate, reproduction and escape in size. *Am. Nat.*, **120**, 189–197.

Sebens, K.P. (1983a) Settlement and metamorphosis of a temperate soft-coral larva (*Alcyonium siderium* Verrill): induction by crustose algae. *Biol. Bull. Mar. Biol. Lab., Woods Hole*, **165**, 286–304.

Sebens, K.P. (1983b) The larval and juvenile ecology of the temperate octocoral *Alcyonium siderium* Verrill. I: Substrate selection by benthic larvae. *J. Exp. Mar. Biol. Ecol.*, **71**, 73–89.

Sebens, K.P. (1983c) Larval and juvenile ecology of the temperate octocoral *Alcyonium siderium* Verrill. II. Fecundity, survivorship, and juvenile growth. *J. Exp. Mar. Biol. Ecol.*, **72**, 263–285.

Sebens, K.P. (1984) Agonistic behavior in the intertidal sea anemone *Anthopleura xanthogrammica*. *Biol. Bull. Mar. Biol. Lab., Woods Hole*, **166**, 457–472.

Sebens, K.P. (in press a) Spatial relationships among encrusting marine organisms in the New England subtidal. *Ecology*.

Sebens, K.P. (in press b) Water flow and coral colony size: interhabitat comparisons of the octocoral *Alcyonium siderium*. *Proc. Natn. Acad. Sci. U.S.A.*

Sebens, K.P. (in review) Alternate states of the New England rocky subtidal community: predator effects and topography. *Ecol. Monogr.*

Sebens, K.P. and Koehl, M.A.R. (1984) Predation on zooplankton by the benthic anthozoans *Alcyonium siderium* (Alcyonacea) and *Metridium senile* (Actiniaria) in the New England subtidal. *Mar. Biol.*, **81**, 255–271.

Sebens, K.P. and Lewis, J.R. (1985) Rare events and population structure of the barnacle *Semibalanus cariosus* (Pallas 1788). *J. Exp. Mar. Biol. Ecol.*, **87**, (IN PRESS).

Seed, R. (1968) Factors influencing shell shape in the mussel *Mytilus edulis*. *J. Mar. Biol. Ass. U.K.*, **48**, 561–584.

Seed, R. (1969a) The ecology of *Mytilus edulis* L. (Lamellibranchiata) on exposed rocky shores. I. Breeding and settlement. *Oecologia (Berlin)*, **3**, 277–316.

Seed, R. (1969b) The ecology of *Mytilus edulis* L. (Lamellibranchiata) on exposed rocky shores. II. Growth and mortality. *Oecologia (Berlin)*, **3**, 317–350.

Seed, R. (1971) A physiological and biochemical approach to the taxonomy of *Mytilus edulis* L. and *M. galloprovincialis* Lmk, from S.W. England. *Cah. Biol. Mar.*, **12**, 291–322.

Seed, R. (1972) Morphological variations in *Mytilus* from the French coast in relation to the occurrence and distribution of *M. galloprovincialis* Lamarck. *Cah. Biol. Mar.*, **12**, 357–384.

Seed, R. (1974) Morphological variations in *Mytilus* from the Irish coasts in relation to the occurrence and distribution of *M. galloprovincialis* Lmk. *Cah. Biol. Mar.*, **15**, 1–25.

Seed, R. (1975) Reproduction in *Mytilus* (Mollusca: Bivalvia) in European waters. *Pubbl. Staz. Zool. Napoli*, **39** (Suppl), 317–334.

Seed, R. (1976a) Observations on the ecology of *Membranipora* (Bryozoa) and a major predator *Doridella steinbergae* (Nudibranchiata) along the fronds of *Laminaria saccharina* at Friday Harbor, Washington. *J. Exp. Mar. Biol. Ecol.*, **24**, 1–17.

Seed, R. (1976b) Ch. 2. Ecology. In, *Marine Mussels: their ecology and physiology*, ed. B.L. Bayne, Cambridge University Press, Cambridge, pp. 13–65.

Seed, R. (1978a) Observations on the adaptive significance of shell shape and body form in dogwhelks (*Nucella lapillus* (L.)) from N. Wales. *Nature Wales*, **16**, 111–122.

Seed, R. (1978b) The systematics and evolution of *Mytilus galloprovincialis* Lmk. In, *Marine Organisms: genetics, ecology and evolution*, ed. B. Battaglia & J.A. Beardmore, Plenum Press, New York, pp. 447–468.

Seed, R. (1980a) Predator-prey relationships between the mud crab *Panopeus herbstii*, the blue crab, *Callinectes sapidus* and the Atlantic ribbed mussel *Geukensia (= Modiolus) demissa*. *Estuarine Coastal Mar. Sci.*, **11**, 445–458.

Seed, R. (1980b) A note on the relationship between shell shape and life habits in *Geukensia demissa* and *Brachidontes exustus* (Mollusca: Bivalvia). *J. Moll. Stud.*, **46**, 293–299.

Seed, R. and Boaden, P.J.S. (1977) Epifaunal ecology of intertidal algae. In, *Biology of Benthic Organisms*, ed. B.F. Keegan, P. ÓCéidigh & P.J.S. Boaden, Pergamon Press, Oxford, pp. 541–548.

Seed, R. and Brown, R.A. (1975) The influence of reproductive cycle, growth, and mortality on population structure in *Modiolus modiolus* (L.), *Cerastoderma edule* (L.), and *Mytilus edulis* L. (Mollusca: Bivalvia). *Proc. 9th Europ. Mar. Biol. Symp.*, ed. H. Barnes, Aberdeen University Press, Aberdeen, pp. 257–274.

Seed, R. and Brown, R.A. (1977) The reproductive cycles of *Cerastoderma edule*, *Modiolus modiolus* and *Mytilus edulis* in Strangford Lough, N. Ireland. *Oecologia (Berlin)*, **30**, 173–188.

Seed, R. and Brown, R.A. (1978) Growth as a strategy for survival in two marine bivalves, *Cerastoderma edule* and *Modiolus modiolus*. *J. Anim. Ecol.*, **47**, 283–292.

Seed, R., Elliott, M.N., Boaden, P.J.S. and O'Connor, R.J. (1981) The composition and seasonal changes amongst the epifauna associated with *Fucus serratus* L. in Strangford Lough, Northern Ireland. *Cah. Biol. Mar.*, **22**, 243–266.

Seed, R. and Harris, S. (1980) The epifauna of the fronds of *Laminaria digitata* Lamour in Strangford Lough, Northern Ireland. *Proc. R. Ir. Acad.* B, **80**, 91–106.

Seed, R. and O'Connor, R.J. (1981a) Community organization in marine algal epifaunas. *Annu. Rev. Ecol. Syst.*, **12**, 49–74.

Seed, R. and O'Connor, R.J. (1981b) A study of the epifaunal associates of *Fucus serratus* L. at Dale in South-west Wales. *Holarct. Ecol.*, **4**, 1–11.

Seed, R. and O'Connor, R.J. (in press) The occurrence and distribution of the major epifaunal associates of *Fucus serratus* L. in Argyll, Western Scotland. *Scott. Nat.*

Seed, R., O'Connor, R.J. and Boaden, P.J.S. (1983) The spatial niche of *Dynamena pumila* (L.) and *Gonothyraea loveni* (Allman) (Hydrozoa) within a *Fucus serratus* L. community. *Cah. Biol. Mar.*, **24**, 391–419.

Segal, E. (1956) Microgeographic variation as thermal acclimation in an intertidal mollusc. *Biol. Bull. Mar. Biol. Lab., Woods Hole*, **111**, 129–152.

Segal, E., Rao, K.P. and James, T.W. (1953) Rate of activity as a function of intertidal height within populations of some littoral molluscs. *Nature, Lond.*, **172**, 1108–1109.

Seiderer, L.J., Hahn, B.D. and Lawrence, I. (1982) Rock-lobsters, mussels and man: a mathematical model. *Ecol. Modelling*, **17**, 225–241.

Seip, K.L. (1983) Mathematical models of the rocky shore ecosystem. In, *Application of Ecological Modelling in Environmental Management*, Part B, ed. S.E. Jorgensen & W.J. Mitsch, Elsevier, Amsterdam, pp. 341–433.

Sharrock, J.T.R. (1976) *The Atlas of Breeding Birds in Britain and Ireland*. British Trust for Ornithology/Irish Wildlife Conservancy, Tring, 477 pp.

Sheader, M. (1978) Distribution and reproductive biology of *Corophium insidiosum* (Amphipoda) on the North-East coast of England. *J. Mar. Biol. Ass. U.K.*, **58**, 585–596.

Sheppard, P.M. (1951) Fluctuations in the selective value of certain phenotypes in the polymorphic land snail *Cepaea nemoralis* (L.). Heredity, **5**, 125–134.

Shetty, S.D. (1981) Induction of spawning in 4 species of bivalves of the Indian coastal waters. *Aquaculture*, **25**, 153–160.

Shick, J.M. and Hoffman, R.J. (1980) Effects of the trophic and physical environments on asexual reproduction and body size in the sea anemone *Metridium senile*. In, *Developmental and Cellular Biology of Coelenterates*, ed. P. Tardent & R. Tardent, Elsevier/North Holland Biomedical Press, Amsterdam, pp. 211–216.

Shillaker, R.O. and Moore, P.G. (1978) Tube building by the amphipods *Lembos websteri* Bate and *Corophium bonnellii* Milne Edwards. *J. Exp. Mar. Biol. Ecol.*, **33**, 169–185.

Shin, P.K.S. (1981) The development of sessile epifaunal communities in Kylesalia, Kilkieran Bay (West coast of Ireland). *J. Exp. Mar. Biol. Ecol.*, **54**, 97–111.

Shoemaker, V.H. (1972) Osmoregulation and excretion in birds. In, *Avian Biology*, Vol. III, ed. D.S. Farner & J.R. King, Academic Press, London, pp. 527–574.

Sieburth, J. McN. (1968) The influence of algal antibiosis on the ecology of marine microorganisms. *Adv. Microbiol. Sea*, **1**, 63–94.

Sieburth, J. McN. and Conover, J.T. (1965) *Sargassum* tannin, an antibiotic which retards fouling. *Nature, Lond.*, **208**, 52–53.

Sieburth, J. McN. and Conover, J.T. (1966) Antifouling in *Sargassum natans*: re-recognition of tannin activity. *Proc. Vth Int. Seaweed Symp., Halifax, Nova Scotia*, Pergamon Press, Oxford, p. 207 only.

Siegel, S. (1956) *Nonparametric Statistics for the Behavioral Sciences*. McGraw Hill Book Co., New York, 312 pp.

Simberloff, D.S. (1983) Competition theory, hypothesis testing, and other community ecological buzzwords. *Am. Nat.*, **122**, 626–635.

Simpson, R.D. (1976) Physical and biotic factors limiting the distribution and abundance of littoral molluscs on Macquarie Island (Sub-Antarctic). *J. Exp. Mar. Biol. Ecol.*, **21**, 11–49.

Simpson, R.D. (1982) Reproduction and lipids in the sub-Antarctic limpet *Nacella (Patinigera) macquariensis* (Finlay 1927). *J. Exp. Mar. Biol. Ecol.*, **56**, 33–48.

Skibinski, D.O.F., Ahmad, M. and Beardmore, J.A. (1978) Genetic evidence for naturally occurring hybrids between *Mytilus edulis* and *Mytilus galloprovincialis*. *Evolution, Lancaster, Pa.*, **32**, 354–364.

Skibinski, D.O.F. and Beardmore, J.A. (1979) A genetic study of intergradation between *Mytilus edulis* and *M. galloprovincialis*. *Experientia*, **35**, 1442–1444.

Skibinski, D.O.F., Beardmore, J.A. and Cross, T.F. (1983) Aspects of the population genetics of *Mytilus* (Mytilidae Mollusca) in the British Isles. *Biol. J. Linn. Soc.*, **19**, 137–183.

Skibinski, D.O.F., Cross, T.F. and Ahmad, M. (1980) Electrophoretic investigation of systematic relationships in the marine mussels *Modiolus modiolus* L., *Mytilus edulis* L. and *Mytilus galloprovincialis* Lmk. (Mytilidae; Mollusca). *Biol. J. Linn. Soc.*, **13**, 65–73.

Slatkin, M. (1974) Competition and regional coexistence. *Ecology*, **55**, 128–134.

Sloane, J.F., Bassindale, R., Davenport, E., Ebling, F.J. and Kitching, J.A. (1961) The ecology of Lough Ine. IX. The flora and fauna associated with undergrowth-forming algae in the rapids area. *J. Ecol.*, **49**, 353–368.

Slobodkin, L.B. (1961) *Growth and Regulation of Animal Populations*. Holt, Rinehart and Winston, Inc., New York, 184 pp.

Slocum, C.J. (1980) Differential susceptibility to grazers in two phases of an intertidal alga: advantages of hetero-morphic generations. *J. Exp. Mar. Biol. Ecol.*, **46**, 99–110.

Smith, C.G. and Fretwell, S.D. (1974) The optimal balance between size and number of offspring. *Am. Nat.*, **104**, 1–24.

Smith, D.A.S. (1973) The population biology of *Lacuna pallidula* (da Costa) and *Lacuna vincta* (Montagu) in North-East England. *J. Mar. Biol. Ass. U.K.*, **53**, 493–520.

Smith, D.A.S. (1976) Disruptive selection and morph-ratio clines in the polymorphic snail *Littorina obtusata* (L.) (Gastropoda: Prosobranchia). *J. Moll. Stud.*, **42**, 114–135.

Smith, D.A.S. and Sebens, K.P. (1983) The physiological ecology of growth and reproduction in *Onchidoris aspera* (Alder & Hancock) (Gastropoda: Nudibranchia). *J. Exp. Mar. Biol. Ecol.*, **72**, 287–304.

Smith, F.E. (1972) Spatial heterogeneity, stability and diversity in ecosystems. *Trans. Conn. Acad. Arts Sci.*, **44**, 309–335.

Smith, F.G.W. (1935) The development of *Patella vulgata*. *Phil. Trans. R. Soc. Lond.* B, **225**, 95–125.

Smith, J.E. (ed.) (1968) *'Torrey Canyon' Pollution and Marine Life*. Cambridge University Press, London, 196 pp.

Smith, J.E. (1981) The natural history and taxonomy of shell variation in the periwinkles *Littorina saxatilis* and *Littorina rudis*. *J. Mar. Biol. Ass. U.K.*, **61**, 215–241.

Smith, J.E. and Newell, G.E. (1955) The dynamics of the zonation of the common periwinkle (*Littorina littorea* (L.)) on a stony beach. *J. Anim. Ecol.*, **24**, 35–56.

Smith, P.C. and Bleakney, J.S. (1969) Observations on oil pollution and wintering Purple Sandpipers *Erolia maritima* (Brunnich), in Nova Scotia. *Can. Fld Nat.*, **83**, 19–22.

Smith, S.M. (1982) A review of the genus *Littorina* in British and Atlantic waters (Gastropoda: Prosobranchia). *Malacologia*, **22**, 535–539.

Smith, W.C.T. (1984) The feeding ecology of the Grey Heron (*Ardea cinerea*) on the rocky shore in east Fife, October to February (1982–1984). B. Sc. Thesis, University of St. Andrews, 40 pp.

Snow, B.K. (1974) The Plumbeous Heron of the Galapagos. *The Living Bird*, **13**, 15–72.

Soot-Ryen, T. (1955) A report on the family Mytilidae (Pelecypoda). *Allan Hancock Pacif. Exped.*, University of Southern California Press, Los Angeles, **20**, 1–174.

Soot-Ryen, T. (1959) Pelecypoda. *Rep. Lund Univ. Chile Exped. (1948–49)*, No. 35, 1–86.

Sousa, W.P. (1979a) Experimental investigations of disturbance and ecological succession in a rocky intertidal algal community. *Ecol. Monogr.*, **49**, 227–254.

Sousa, W.P. (1979b) Disturbance in marine intertidal boulder fields: the nonequilibrium maintenance of species diversity. *Ecology*, **60**, 1225–1239.

Sousa, W.P. (1980) The responses of a community to disturbance: the importance of successional age and species' life histories. *Oecologia (Berlin)*, **45**, 72–81.

Sousa, W.P. (1985) Disturbance and patch dynamics on rocky intertidal shores. In, *Natural Disturbance: the patch dynamics perspective*, ed. S.T.A. Pickett & P.S. White, Academic Press, New York, pp. 101–124.

Southgate, T. (1982) A comparative study of *Lacuna vincta* and *Lacuna pallidula* (Gastropoda: Prosobranchia) in littoral algal turfs. *J. Moll. Stud.*, **48**, 302–309.

Southward, A.J. (1953) The ecology of some rocky shores in the south of the Isle of Man. *Proc. Trans. Lpool. Biol. Soc.*, **59**, 1–50.

Southward, A.J. (1956) The population balance between limpets and seaweeds on wave-beaten rocky shores. *Rep. Mar. Biol. Stn Port Erin*, **68**, 20–29.

Southward, A.J. (1958) Note on the temperature tolerances of some intertidal animals in relation to environmental temperatures and geographical distribution. *J. Mar. Biol. Ass. U.K.*, **37**, 49–66.

Southward, A.J. (1964) Limpet grazing and the control of vegetation on rocky shores. In, *Grazing in Terrestrial and Marine Environments*, ed. D.J. Crisp, Blackwell Scientific Publications, Oxford, pp. 265–273.

Southward, A.J. (1976) On the taxonomic status and distribution of *Chthamalus stellatus* (Cirripedia) in the North-East Atlantic region: with a key to the common intertidal barnacles of Britain. *J. Mar. Biol. Ass. U.K.*, **56**, 1007–1028.

Southward, A.J. and Crisp, D.J. (1954) Recent changes in the distribution of the intertidal barnacles *Chthamalus stellatus* Poli and *Balanus balanoides* L. in the British Isles. *J. Anim. Ecol.*, **23**, 163–177.

Southward, A.J. and Southward, E.C. (1978) Recolonisation of rocky shores in Cornwall after use of toxic dispersants to clean up the Torrey Canyon spill. *J. Fish. Res. Bd Can.*, **35**, 682–706.

Spight, T.M. (1973) Ontogeny, environment, and shape of a marine snail *Thais lamellosa* Gmelin. *J. Exp. Mar. Biol. Ecol.*, **13**, 215–228.

Spight, T.M. (1974) Sizes of populations of a marine snail. *Ecology*, **55**, 712–729.

Spight, T.M. (1975) Factors extending gastropod embryonic development and their selective cost. *Oecologia (Berlin)*, **21**, 1–16.

Spight, T.M. (1976a) Hatching size and the distribution of nurse eggs among prosobranch embryos. *Biol. Bull. Mar. Biol. Lab., Woods Hole*, **150**, 491–499.

Spight, T.M. (1976b) Colors and patterns of an intertidal snail, *Thais lamellosa*. *Researches Popul. Ecol., Kyoto Univ.*, **17**, 176–190.

Spight, T.M. (1976c) Ecology of hatching size for marine snails. *Oecologia (Berlin)*, **24**, 283–294.

Spight, T.M. (1977a) Latitude, habitat and hatching type for muricacean gastropods. *Nautilus*, **91**, 67–71.

Spight, T.M. (1977b) Do intertidal snails spawn in the right places? *Evolution, Lancaster, Pa*, **31**, 682–691.

Spight, T.M. (1979) Environment and life history: the case of two marine snails. In, *Reproductive Ecology of Marine Invertebrates*, ed. S.E. Stancyk, University of South Carolina Press, Columbia, South Carolina, pp. 135–143.

Spight, T.M. (1982a) Risk, reward and the duration of feeding excursions by a marine snail. *Veliger*, **24**, 302–308.

Spight, T.M. (1982b) Population sizes of two marine snails with a changing food supply. *J. Exp. Mar. Biol. Ecol.*, **57**, 195–217.

Spight, T.M. and Emlen, J.M. (1976) Clutch sizes of two marine snails with a changing food supply. *Ecology*, **57**, 1162–1178.

Sribhibhadh, A. (1973) Status and problems of coastal aquaculture in Thailand. In, *Coastal Aquaculture in the Indo-Pacific Region*, ed. T.V.R. Pillay, Fishing News (Books) Ltd, London, pp. 74–83.

Staiger, H. (1954) Der Chromosomendimorphismus beim Prosobranchier *Purpura lapillus* in Beziehung zur Ökologie der Art. *Chromosoma*, **6**, 419–478.

Standing, J.D. (1976) Fouling community structure: effects of the hydroid, *Obelia dichotoma*, on larval recruitment. In, *Coelenterate Ecology and Behavior*, ed. G.O. Mackie, Plenum Press, New York and London, pp. 155–165.

Stanley, S.M. (1968) Post-Paleozoic adaptive radiation of infaunal bivalve molluscs – a consequence of mantle fusion and siphon formation. *J. Paleont.*, **42**, 214–229.

Stanley, S.M. (1972) Functional morphology and evolution of byssally attached bivalve mollusks. *J. Paleont.*, **46**, 165–213.

Stearns, S.C. (1976) Life history tactics: a review of the ideas. *Q. Rev. Biol.*, **51**, 3–47.

Stearns, S.C. (1977) The evolution of life history traits: a critique of the theory and a review of the data. *Annu. Rev. Ecol. Syst.*, **8**, 145–171.

Stearns, S.C. (1980) A new view of life-history evolution. *Oikos*, **35**, 266–281.

Stebbing, A.R.D. (1971) The epizoic fauna of *Flustra foliacea* (Bryozoa). *J. Mar. Biol. Ass. U.K.*, **51**, 283–300.

Stebbing, A.R.D. (1972) Preferential settlement of a bryozoan and serpulid larvae on the younger parts of *Laminaria* fronds. *J. Mar. Biol. Ass. U.K.*, **52**, 765–772.

Stebbing, A.R.D. (1973a) Competition for space between the epiphytes of *Fucus serratus* L. *J. Mar. Biol. Ass. U.K.*, **53**, 247–261.

Stebbing, A.R.D. (1973b) Ch. 3. Observations on colony overgrowth and spatial competition. In, *Living and Fossil Bryozoa*, ed. G.P. Larwood, Academic Press, New York, pp. 173–183.

Steele, D.H. (1977) Correlation between egg size and developmental period. *Am. Nat.*, **111**, 371–372.

Steen, E. (1951) Ecological observations on some *Gammarus* and *Marinogammarus* species on the Scandinavian west coast. *Oikos*, **3**, 232–242.

Steneck, R.S. (1978) Factors influencing the distribution of crustose coralline algae (Rhodophyta, Corallinaceae) in the Damariscotta River estuary, Maine. M.S. Thesis, University of Maine, Orono, 58 pp.

Steneck, R.S. (1981) Adaptive trends in the ecology and evolution of crustose coralline algae (Rhodophyta, Corallinaceae). Ph. D. Thesis, Johns Hopkins University, Baltimore, 240 pp.

Steneck, R.S. (1982) A limpet-coralline alga association: adaptations and defenses between a selective herbivore and its prey. *Ecology*, **63**, 507–522.

Steneck, R.S. (1983) Escalating herbivory and resulting adaptive trends in calcareous algal crusts. *Paleobiology*, **9**, 44–61.

Steneck, R.S. and Watling, L. (1982) Feeding capabilities and limitation of herbivorous molluscs: a functional group approach. *Mar. Biol.*, **68**, 299–319.

Stephen, A.C. (1928) Notes on the biology of *Tellina tenuis* da Costa. *J. Mar. Biol. Ass. U.K.*, **15**, 683–702.

Stephenson, T.A. (1936) The marine ecology of the South African coasts, with special reference to the habits of limpets. *Proc. Linn. Soc. Lond.*, **148**, 74–79.

Stephenson, T.A. (1939) The constitution of the intertidal fauna and flora of South Africa. Part I. *J. Linn. Soc. (Zool.)*, **40**, 487–536.

Stephenson, T.A. (1943) The causes of the vertical and horizontal distribution of organisms between tide-marks in South Africa. *Proc. Linn. Soc. Lond.*, **154**, 219–232.

Stephenson, T.A. (1947) The colours of marine animals. *Endeavour*, **6**, No. 24, 152–159.

Stephenson, T.A. and Stephenson, Anne (1949) The universal features of zonation between tide-marks on rocky coasts. *J. Ecol.*, **37**, 289–305.

Stephenson, T.A. and Stephenson, Anne (1972) *Life Between Tidemarks on Rocky Shores*. W.H. Freeman and Co., San Francisco, 425 pp.

Stickle, W.B. (1973) The reproductive physiology of the intertidal prosobranch *Thais lamellosa* (Gmelin). I. Seasonal changes in the rate of oxygen consumption and body component indexes. *Biol. Bull. Mar. Biol. Lab., Woods Hole*, **144**, 511–524.

Stimson, J.[S.] (1970) Territorial behavior of the owl limpet, *Lottia gigantea*. *Ecology*, **51**, 113–118.

Stimson, J.[S.] (1973) The role of the territory in the ecology of the intertidal limpet *Lottia gigantea* (Gray). *Ecology*, **54**, 1020–1030.

Stiven, A.E. and Kuenzler, E.J. (1979) The response of two salt marsh molluscs, *Littorina irrorata* and *Geukensia demissa*, to field manipulations of density and *Spartina* litter. *Ecol. Monogr.*, **49**, 151–171.

Stobbs, R.E. (1980) Feeding habits of the giant clingfish *Chorisochismus dentex* (Pisces: Gobiesocidae). *S. Afr. J. Zool.*, **15**, 146–149.

Stocker, O. and Holdheide, W. (1937) Die Assimilation Helgoländer Gezeitenalgen während der Ebbezeit. *Z. Bot.*, **32**, 1–59.

Stoecker, D. (1980) Relationships between chemical defense and ecology in benthic ascidians. *Mar. Ecol. Prog. Ser.*, **3**, 257–265.

Stoner, A.W. (1982) The influence of benthic macrophytes on the foraging behavior of pinfish, *Lagodon rhomboides* (Linnaeus). *J. Exp. Mar. Biol. Ecol.*, **58**, 271–284.

Strathmann, R.R. (1974) The spread of sibling larvae of sedentary marine invertebrates. *Am. Nat.*, **108**, 29–44.

Strathmann, R.R. (1977) Egg size, larval development, and juvenile size in benthic marine invertebrates. *Am. Nat.*, **111**, 373–376.

Strathmann, R.R. (1978a) Larval settlement in echinoderms. In, *Settlement and Metamorphosis of Marine Invertebrate Larvae*, ed. F.-S. Chia & M.E. Rice, Elsevier/North-Holland Biomedical Press, New York, pp. 235–246.

Strathmann, R.R. (1978b) The evolution and loss of feeding larval stages of marine invertebrates. *Evolution, Lancaster, Pa*, **32**, 894–906.

Strathmann, R.R. and Branscombe, E.S. (1979) Adequacy of cues to favourable sites used by settling larvae of two intertidal barnacles. In, *Reproductive Ecology of Marine Invertebrates*, ed. S.E. Stancyk, University of South Carolina Press, Columbia, pp. 77–89.

Strathmann, R.R., Branscombe, E.S. and Vedder, K. (1981) Fatal errors in set as a cost of dispersal and the influence of intertidal flora on set of barnacles. *Oecologia (Berlin)*, **48**, 13–18.

Strathmann, R.R. and Strathmann, M.F. (1981) The relationship between adult size and brooding in marine invertebrates. *Am. Nat.*, **119**, 91–101.

Strathmann, R.R., Strathmann, M.F. and Emson, R.H. (1984) Does limited brood capacity link adult size, brooding and simultaneous hermaphroditism? A test with the starfish *Asterina phylactica*. *Am. Nat.*, **123**, 796–818.

Strömgren, T. (1977) Apical length growth of five intertidal species of Fucales in relation to irradiance. *Sarsia*, **63**, 39–47.

Struhsaker, J.W. (1968) Selection mechanisms associated with intraspecific shell variation in *Littorina picta* (Prosobranchia: Mesogastropoda). *Evolution, Lancaster, Pa.*, **22**, 459–480.

Stuardo, J. (1960) Notas sobre ecologia y distribucion de *Choromytilus chorus* en dos sustratos diferentes. *Biol. Pesq., Chile*, **5**, 61–108.

Stuart, V., Field, J.G. and Newell, R.C. (1982) Evidence for adsorption of kelp detritus by the ribbed mussel *Aulacomya ater* using a new ^{51}Cr-labelled microsphere technique. *Mar. Ecol. Prog. Ser.*, **9**, 263–271.

Stuart, V., Lucas, M.I. and Newell, R.C. (1981) Heterotrophic utilisation of particulate matter from the kelp *Laminaria pallida*. *Mar. Ecol. Prog. Ser.*, **4**, 337–348.

Stuart, V., Newell, R.C. and Lucas, M.I. (1982) Conversion of kelp debris and faecal material from the mussel *Aulacomya ater* by marine micro-organisms. *Mar. Ecol. Prog. Ser.*, **7**, 47–57.

Suchanek, T.H. (1978) The ecology of *Mytilus edulis* L. in exposed rocky intertidal communities. *J. Exp. Mar. Biol. Ecol.*, **31**, 105–120.

Suchanek, T.H. (1979) The *Mytilus californianus* community: studies on the composition, structure, organization, and dynamics of a mussel bed. Ph. D. Thesis, University of Washington, Seattle, 285 pp.

Suchanek, T.H. (1980) Diversity in natural and artificial mussel bed communities of *Mytilus californianus*. *Am. Zool.*, **20**, p. 807 only.

Suchanek, T.H. (1981) The role of disturbance in the evolution of life history strategies in the intertidal mussels *Mytilus edulis* and *Mytilus californianus*. *Oecologia (Berlin)*, **50**, 143–152.

Suchanek, T.H. (in prep.) Diversity and dynamics of the species-rich community associated with the intertidal mussel *Mytilus californianus*.

Suchanek, T.H. and Duggins, D.O. (in prep.) Slow recovery from disturbance in the rocky intertidal zone of an Alaskan fjord, Torch Bay.

Suchanek, T.H. and Levinton, J.S. (1974) Articulate brachiopod food. *J. Paleont.*, **48**, 1–5.

Sugiura, Y. (1959) Seasonal change in sexual maturity and sexuality of *Mytilus edulis*. *Bull. Jap. Soc. Scient. Fish.*, **25**, 1–6.

Summers, R.W., Atkinson, N.K. and Nicoll, M. (1975a) Wintering wader populations on the rocky shores of eastern Scotland. *Scott. Birds*, **8**, 299–308.

Summers, R.W., Atkinson, N.K. and Nicoll, M. (1975b) Aspects of Turnstone ecology in Scotland. *Tay Ringing Group Report 1974*, 3–10.

Summers, R.W. and Buxton, N.E. (1983) Winter wader populations on the open shores of northern Scotland. *Scott. Birds*, **12**, 206–211.

Summers, R.W., Cooper, J. and Pringle, J.S. (1977) Distribution and numbers of coastal waders (Charadrii) in the south-western Cape, South Africa, summer 1975–76. *Ostrich*, **48**, 85–97.

Summers, R.W., Corse, C., Meek, E., Moore, P. and Nicoll, M. (1984) The value of single counts of waders on rocky shores. *Wader Study Group Bulletin*, **41**, 7–9.

Summers, R.W. and Smith, S.M. (1983) The diet of the Knot (*Calidris canutus*) on rocky shores of eastern Scotland in winter. *Ardea*, **71**, 151–153.

Summers, R.W. and Waltner, M. (1979) Seasonal variations in the mass of waders in southern Africa, with special reference to migration. *Ostrich*, **50**, 21–37.

Sutherland, J.P. (1970) Dynamics of high and low populations of the limpet *Acmaea scabra* (Gould). *Ecol. Monogr.*, **40**, 169–188.

Sutherland, J.P. (1974) Multiple stable points in natural communities. *Am. Nat.*, **108**, 859–873.

Sutherland, J.P. (1975) Effects of *Schizoporella* removal on the fouling community at Beaufort, N.C. In, *Ecology of Marine Benthos*, ed. B.C. Coull, University of South Carolina Press, Columbia, South Carolina, pp. 155–189.

Sutherland, J.P. (1978) Functional roles of *Schizoporella* and *Styela* in the fouling community at Beaufort, North Carolina. *Ecology*, **59**, 257–264.

Sutherland, J.P. (1980) Dynamics of the epibenthic community on roots of the mangrove, *Rhizophora mangle*, at Bahia de Buche, Venezuela. *Mar. Biol.*, **58**, 75–84.

Sutherland, J.P. and Karlson, R.H. (1977) Development and stability of the fouling community at Beaufort, North Carolina. *Ecol. Monogr.*, **47**, 425–446.

Svane, I. (1983) Ascidian reproductive patterns related to long-term population dynamics. *Sarsia*, **68**, 249–255.

Svane, I. (1985) Observations on the long-term population dynamics of the perennial ascidian, *Ascidia mentula* O.F. Müller, on the Swedish West coast. *Biol. Bull. Mar. Biol. Lab., Woods Hole*, **167**, 630–646.

Svane, I. and Lundälv, T. (1981) Reproductive patterns and population dynamics of *Ascidia mentula* O.F. Müller on the Swedish West coast. *J. Exp. Mar. Biol. Ecol.*, **50**, 163–182.

Svane, I. and Lundälv, T. (1982a) Population dynamics and reproductive patterns of *Boltenia echinata* (Ascidiacea) on the Swedish West coast. *Neth. J. Sea Res.*, **16**, 105–118.

Svane, I. and Lundälv, T. (1982b) Persistence stability in ascidian populations: long-term population dynamics and reproductive pattern of *Pyura tessellata* (Forbes) in Gullmarfjorden on the Swedish West coast. *Sarsia*, **67**, 249–257.

Swinbanks, D.D. (1982) Intertidal exposure zones: a way to subdivide the shore. *J. Exp. Mar. Biol. Ecol.*, **62**, 69–86.

Sze, P. (1980) Aspects of the ecology of macrophytic algae in high-shore rockpools at the Isle of Shoals, U.S.A. *Botanica Mar.*, **23**, 313–318.

Tan, E.L. (1971) Nutritive value of *Mytilus viridis* as a potential protein source for animal feeds. *J. Singapore Natn Acad. Sci.*, **1**, 82–84.

Tan, W.H. (1975a) The effects of exposure and crawling behavior on the survival of recently settled green mussels (*Mytilus viridis* L.). *Aquaculture*, **6**, 357–368.

Tan, W.H. (1975b) Egg and larval development in the green mussel *Mytilus viridis*. *Veliger*, **18**, 151–155.

Tay and Orkney Ringing Groups (1984) The Shore-birds of the Orkney Islands. *Tay Ringing Group, Perth, Scotland*, 78pp.

Tegner, M.J. and Dayton, P.K. (1981) Population structure, recruitment and mortality of two sea urchins (*Strongylocentrotus franciscanus* and *S. purpuratus*) in a kelp forest. *Mar. Ecol. Prog. Ser.*, **5**, 255–268.

Tham, A.K., Yang, S.W. and Tan, W.H. (1973) Experiments in coastal aquaculture in Singapore. In, *Coastal Aquaculture in the Indo-Pacific Region*, ed. T.V.R. Pillay, Fishing News (Books) Ltd, London, pp. 375–383.

Theisen, B.F. (1972) Shell cleaning and deposit feeding in *Mytilus edulis* L. (Bivalvia). *Ophelia*, **10**, 49–55.

Thom, R.M. and Widdowson, T.B. (1978) A resurvey of E. Yale Dawson's 42 intertidal algal transects on the southern California mainland after 15 years. *Bull. Sth. Calif. Acad. Sci.*, **77**, 1–13.

Thompson, D'A.W. (1917) *On Growth and Form*. Cambridge University Press, Cambridge, 794 pp.

Thompson, G.B. (1979) Distribution and population dynamics of the limpet *Patella aspera* (Lamarck) in Bantry Bay. *J. Exp. Mar. Biol. Ecol.*, **40**, 115–135.

Thompson, G.B. (1980) Distribution and population dynamics of the limpet *Patella vulgata* L. in Bantry Bay. *J. Exp. Mar. Biol. Ecol.*, **45**, 173–217.

Thorson, G. (1941) Marine Gastropoda Prosobranchiata. *The Zoology of Iceland*, **4**, 1–150.

Thorson, G. (1944) Zoology of East Greenland. Marine Gastropoda Prosobranchiata. *Meddr Grønland*, **121**, 1–181.

Thorson, G. (1946) Reproduction and larval development of Danish marine bottom invertebrates, with special reference to the planktonic larvae in the Sound (Øresund). *Meddr Kommn Danm. Fisk. -og Havunders., Serie: Plankton*, **4**, 1–523.

Thorson, G. (1950) Reproductive and larval ecology of marine bottom invertebrates. *Biol. Rev.*, **25**, 1–45.

Thorson, G. (1957) Bottom communities (sublittoral or shallow shelf). In, *Treatise on Marine Ecology and Paleoecology*, ed. J.W. Hedgpeth, Vol. 1, Geol. Soc. Am., Mem., **67**, pp. 461–534.

Thorson, G. (1966) Some factors influencing the recruitment and establishment of marine benthic communities. *Neth. J. Sea Res.*, **3**, 267–293.

Tiemann, H. (1975) Zur Eidonomie, Anatomie, Systematik und Biologie der Gattung *Porcellidium* Claus, 1860 (Copepoda, Harpacticoida). Ph. D. Thesis, Universitat Hamburg, 103 pp.

Tietjen, J.H. and Lee, J.J. (1977) Feeding behavior of marine nematodes. In, *Ecology of Marine Benthos*, ed. B.C. Coull, University of South Carolina Press, Columbia, pp. 21–35.

Tinkle, D.W. and Hadley, N.F. (1975) Lizard reproductive effort: caloric estimates and comments on its evolution. *Ecology*, **56**, 427–434.

Tittley, I., Irvine, D.E.G. and Jephson, N.A. (1976) The infralittoral marine algae of Sullom Voe, Shetland. *Trans. Bot. Soc. Edinb.*, **42**, 397–419.

Todd, C.D. (1979a) The population ecology of *Onchidoris bilamellata* (L.) (Gastropoda: Nudibranchia). *J. Exp. Mar. Biol. Ecol*, **41**, 213–255.

Todd, C.D. (1979b) Reproductive energetics of two species of dorid nudibranchs with planktotrophic and lecithotrophic larval strategies. *Mar. Biol.*, **53**, 57–68.

Todd, C.D. and Doyle, R.W. (1981) Reproductive strategies of marine benthic invertebrates: a settlement-timing hypothesis. *Mar. Ecol. Prog. Ser.*, **4**, 75–83.

Todd, C.D. and Lewis, J.R. (1984) Effects of low air temperature on *Laminaria digitata* in south-western Scotland. *Mar. Ecol. Prog. Ser.*, **16**, 199–201.

Tomicic, J. (1966) Contribución al estudio de la cholga *Aulacomya ater* (Molina) en la Bahia de Mejillónes. Tesis de Grado, Universidad de Chile, 20 pp.

Tomicic, J. (1968) La cholga de los bancos de Mejillónes. *Ap. Oceanol.*, **4**, 14–15.

Torlegård, A.K.I. and Lundälv, T.L. (1974) Under-water analytical system. *Photogramm. Engng.*, **40**, 287–293.

Townsend, C.R. and Hughes, R.N. (1981) Maximizing net energy returns from foraging. In, *Physiological Ecology: an evolutionary approach to resource use*, ed. C.R. Townsend & P. Calow, Blackwell Scientific Publications, Oxford, pp. 86–108.

Trevelyan, G.A. and Chang, E.S. (1983) Experiments on larval rearing of the California mussel (*Mytilus californianus*). *J. World Maricult. Soc.*, **14**, 137–148.

Trotter, D. and Webster, J.M. (1983) Distribution and abundance of marine nematodes on the kelp *Macrocystis integrifolia*. *Mar. Biol.*, **78**, 39–43.

Trotter, D.B. and Webster, J.M. (1984) Feeding preferences and seasonality of free-living marine nematodes inhabiting the kelp *Macrocystis integrifolia*. *Mar. Ecol. Prog. Ser.*, **14**, 151–157.

Truchot, J.-P. (1963) Étude faunistique et écologique des amphipodes des facies rocheux intertidaux de Roscoff. *Cah. Biol. Mar.*, **4**, 121–176.

Truchot, J.-P. and Duhamel-Jouve, A. (1980) Oxygen and carbon dioxide in the marine intertidal environment: diurnal and tidal changes in rockpools. *Resp. Physiol.*, **39**, 241–254.

Tsuchiya, M. (1979) Quantitative survey of intertidal organisms on rocky shores in Mutsu Bay, with special reference to the influence of wave action. *Bull. Biol. Stn Asamushi*, **16**, 69–86.

Tsuchiya, M. (1980) Biodeposit production by the mussel *Mytilus edulis* L. on rocky shores. *J. Exp. Mar. Biol. Ecol.*, **47**, 203–222.

Tsuchiya, M. (1982) Catching of organic matter by the mussel *Mytilus edulis* L. on rocky shores. *Bull. Biol. Stn Asamushi*, **17**, 99–107.

Tsuchiya, M. (1983) Mass mortality in a population of the mussel *Mytilus edulis* L. caused by high temperature on rocky shores. *J. Exp. Mar. Biol. Ecol.*, **66**, 101–111.

Tsuchiya, M. and Nishihira, M. (in prep. a) *Mytilus* island as a habitat for small intertidal animals: effect of island size on community structure.

Tsuchiya, M. and Nishihira, M. (in prep. b) *Mytilus* island as a habitat for small intertidal animals: effect of age structure of *Mytilus edulis* population on the species composition of the associated fauna and community organization.

Turner, R.L. and Lawrence, J.M. (1979) Volume and composition of echinoderm eggs: implications for the use of egg size in life history models. In, *Reproductive Ecology of Marine Invertebrates*, ed. S.E. Stancyk, University of South Carolina Press, Columbia, pp. 25–40.

Turner, T. (1983) Facilitation as a successional mechanism in a rocky intertidal community. *Am. Nat.*, **121**, 729–738.

Underwood, A.J. (1972a) Observations on the reproductive cycles of *Monodonta lineata* (da Costa), *Gibbula umbilicalis* (da Costa) and *Gibbula cineraria* (L.). *Mar. Biol.*, **17**, 333–340.

Underwood, A.J. (1972b) Spawning, larval development and settlement behaviour of *Gibbula cineraria* (Gastropoda: Prosobranchia) with a reappraisal of torsion in gastropods. *Mar. Biol.*, **17**, 341–349.

Underwood, A.J. (1974) On models for reproductive strategy in marine benthic invertebrates. *Am. Nat.*, **108**, 874–878.

Underwood, A.J. (1976) Food competition between age-classes in the intertidal neritacean *Nerita atramentosa* Reeve (Gastropoda: Prosobranchia). *J. Exp. Mar. Biol. Ecol.*, **23**, 145–154.

Underwood, A.J. (1978a) The refutation of critical tidal levels as determinants of the structure of intertidal communities on British shores. *J. Exp. Mar. Biol. Ecol.*, **33**, 261–276.

Underwood, A.J. (1978b) An experimental evaluation of competition between three species of intertidal prosobranch gastropods. *Oecologia (Berlin)*, **33**, 185–202.

Underwood, A.J. (1979) The ecology of intertidal gastropods. *Adv. Mar. Biol.*, **16**, 111–210.

Underwood, A.J. (1980) The effects of grazing by gastropods and physical factors on the upper limits of distributions of intertidal macroalgae. *Oecologia (Berlin)*, **46**, 201–213.

Underwood, A.J. (1981a) Structure of a rocky intertidal community in New South Wales: patterns of vertical distribution and seasonal changes. *J. Exp. Mar. Biol. Ecol.*, **51**, 57–85.

Underwood, A.J. (1981b) Techniques of analysis of variance in experimental marine biology and ecology. *Oceanogr. Mar. Biol. Ann. Rev.*, **19**, 513–605.

Underwood, A.J. (1984a) The vertical distribution and seasonal abundance of intertidal microalgae on a rocky shore in New South Wales. *J. Exp. Mar. Biol. Ecol.*, **78**, 199–220.

Underwood, A.J. (1984b) Microalgal food and the growth of the intertidal gastropods *Nerita atramentosa* Reeve and *Bembicium nanum* (Lamarck) at four heights on a shore. *J. Exp. Mar. Biol. Ecol.*, **79**, 277–291.

Underwood, A.J. (1984c) Vertical and seasonal patterns in competition for microalgae between intertidal gastropods. *Oecologia (Berlin)*, **64**, 211–222.

Underwood, A.J. (1985) The analysis of competition by field experiments. In, *Community Ecology: pattern and process*, ed. D.J. Anderson & J. Kikkawa, Blackwell Scientific Publications, Oxford.

Underwood, A.J. and Denley, E.J. (1984) Paradigms, explanations and generalizations in models for the structure of intertidal communities on rocky shores. In, *Ecological Communities: conceptual issues and the evidence*, ed. D.R. Strong jr., D. Simberloff, L.G. Abele & A.B. Thistle, Princeton University Press, New Jersey, U.S.A., pp. 151–180.

Underwood, A.J., Denley, E.J. and Moran, M.J. (1983) Experimental analyses of the structure and dynamics of mid-shore rocky intertidal communities in New South Wales. *Oecologia (Berlin)*, **56**, 202–219.

Underwood, A.J. and Jernakoff, P. (1981) Effects of interactions between algae and grazing gastropods on the structure of a low-shore intertidal algal community. *Oecologia (Berlin)*, **48**, 221–233.

Underwood, A.J. and Jernakoff, P. (1984) The effects of tidal height, wave-exposure, seasonality and rock-pools on grazing and the distribution of intertidal macroalgae in New South Wales. *J. Exp. Mar. Biol. Ecol.*, **75**, 71–96.

Underwood, A.J. and McFadyen, K.E. (1983) Ecology of the intertidal snail *Littorina acutispira* Smith. *J. Exp. Mar. Biol. Ecol.*, **66**, 169–197.

Vadas, R.L. (1972) Ecological implications of culture studies on *Nereocystis luetkeana*. *J. Phycol.*, **8**, 196–203.

Valentine, J.W. (1973) *Evolutionary Paleoecology of the Marine Biosphere*. Prentice Hall, Englewood Cliffs, New Jersey, 511 pp.

Van Marion, P. (1981) Intra-population variation of the shell of *Littorina rudis* (Maton) (Mollusca: Prosobranchia). *J. Moll. Stud.*, **47**, 99–107.

Vance, R.R. (1973a) On reproductive strategies in marine benthic invertebrates. *Am. Nat.*, **107**, 339–352.

Vance, R.R. (1973b) More on reproductive strategies in marine benthic invertebrates. *Am. Nat.*, **107**, 353–361.

Vance, R.R. (1974) Reply to Underwood. *Am. Nat.*, **108**, 879–880.

Vance, R.R. (1978) A mutualistic interaction between a sessile marine clam and its epibionts. *Ecology*, **59**, 679–685.

Vance, R.R. (1979) Effects of grazing by the sea urchin, *Centrostephanus coronatus*, on prey community composition. *Ecology*, **60**, 537–546.

Vance, R.R. (1980) The effect of dispersal on population size in a temporally varying environment. *Theor. Popul. Biol.*, **18**, 343–362.

Vance, R.R. (1984) The effect of dispersal on population stability in one-species, discrete-space population growth models. *Am. Nat.*, **123**, 230–254.

Vance, R.R. (in review) Ecological succession and the climax community on a marine subtidal rock wall. *Ecology*.

Velez, A. and Epifanio, C.E. (1981) Effect of temperature and ration on gametogenesis and growth in the tropical mussel *Perna perna*. *Aquaculture*, **22**, 21–26.

Velimirov, B., Field, J.G., Griffiths, C.L. and Zoutendyk, P. (1977) The ecology of kelp bed communities in the Benguela upwelling system. Analysis of biomass and spatial distribution. *Helgoländer Wiss. Meeresunters.*, **30**, 495–518.

Velleman, P.F. and Hoaglin, D.C. (1981) *Applications, Basics and Computing of Exploratory Data Analysis*. Duxberry Press, Boston, 354 pp.

Verderber, G.W., Cook, S.B. and Cook, C.B. (1983) The role of the home scar in reducing water loss during aerial exposure of the pulmonate limpet *Siphonaria alternata* (Say). *Veliger*, **25**, 235–243.

Vermeij, G.J. (1971) Gastropod evolution and morphological diversity in relation to shell geometry. *J. Zool., Lond.*, **163**, 15–23.

Vermeij, G.J. (1972) Intraspecific shore-level size gradients in intertidal molluscs. *Ecology*, **53**, 693–700.

Vermeij, G.J. (1973) Morphological patterns in high-intertidal gastropods: adaptive strategies and their limitations. *Mar. Biol.*, **20**, 319–346.

Vermeij, G.J. (1974) Regional variations in tropical high intertidal gastropod assemblages. *J. Mar. Res.*, **32**, 343–357.

Vermeij, G.J. (1975) Marine faunal dominance and molluscan shell form. *Evolution, Lancaster, Pa.*, **28**, 656–664.

Vermeij, G.J. (1976) Interoceanic differences in vulnerability of shelled prey to crab predation. *Nature, Lond.*, **260**, 135–136.

Vermeij, G.J. (1977) Patterns in crab claw size: the geography of crushing. *Syst. Zool.*, **26**, 138–151.

Vermeij, G.J. (1978) *Biogeography and Adaptation: patterns of marine life*. Harvard University Press, Cambridge, 332 pp.

Vermeij, G.J. (1982a) Phenotypic evolution in a poorly dispersing snail after arrival of a predator. *Nature, Lond.*, **299**, 349–350.

Vermeij, G.J. (1982b) Environmental change and the evolutionary history of the periwinkle (*Littorina littorea*) in North America. *Evolution, Lancaster, Pa.*, **36**, 561–580.

Vermeij, G.J. and Currey, J.D. (1980) Geographical variation in the strength of thaidid snail shells. *Biol. Bull. Mar. Biol. Lab., Woods Hole*, **158**, 383–389.

Vernberg, W.B. and Coull, B.C. (1981) Ch. 5. Meiofauna. In, *Functional Adaptations of Marine Organisms*, ed. F.J. Vernberg & W.B. Vernberg, Academic Press, New York, pp. 147–177.

Viviani, C.A. (1975) Las communidades marinas litorales en el norte grande de Chile. *Occ. Publ. Lab. Ecol. Mar., Iquique, Chile*, 196 pp.

Walker, A.J.M. (1972) Introduction to the ecology of the Antarctic limpet *Patinigera polaris* (Hombron and Jacquinot) at Signy Island, South Orkney Islands. *Br. Antarct. Surv. Bull.*, **28**, 49–69.

Walne, P.R. (1979) *Culture of Bivalve Molluscs: 50 years experience at Conwy*. (2nd edn), Fishing News (Books) Ltd, London, 189pp.

Walsby, J.R. (1979) Whelks, Family Thaisidae. *Pamphlet No. 14 for Cape Rodney to Okari Point Marine Reserve, University of Auckland Marine Laboratory, Leigh, N. Z.*, 7 pp.

Warburton, K. (1976) Shell form, behaviour and tolerance to water movement in the limpet *Patina pellucida* (L.) (Gastropoda: Prosobranchia). *J. Exp. Mar. Biol. Ecol.*, **23**, 307–325.

Warwick, R.M. (1977) The structure and seasonal fluctuations of phytal marine nematode associations on the Isles of Scilly. In, *Biology of Benthic Organisms*, ed. B.F. Keegan, P. ÓCéidigh & P.J.S. Boaden, Pergamon Press, Oxford, pp. 577–585.

Warwick, R.M. (1981) Survival strategies of meiofauna. In, *Feeding and Survival Strategies of Estuarine Organisms*, ed. N.V. Jones & W.J. Wolff, Plenum Press, New York, pp. 39–52.

Waters, E. (1966) Purple Sandpipers feeding above the littoral zone. *Br. Birds*, **59**, 345–346.

Watkin, E.E. (1941) Observations on the night tidal migrant Crustacea of Kames Bay. *J. Mar. Biol. Ass. U.K.*, **25**, 81–96.

Watson, D.C. and Norton, T.A. (1985) Dietary preferences of the common periwinkle *Littorina littorea*. *J. Exp. Mar. Biol. Ecol.*, (IN PRESS).

Waugh, D.L. (1972) Upper lethal temperatures of the pelecypod *Modiolus demissus* in relation to declining environmental temperatures. *Canad. J. Zool.*, **50**, 523–527.

Weinberg, S. (1978) The minimal area problem in invertebrate communities of Mediterranean rocky substrata. *Mar. Biol.*, **49**, 33–40.

Weins, J.A. (1977) On competition in variable environments. *Am. Scient.*, **65**, 590–597.

Weldon, W.F.R. (1901) A first study of natural selection in *Clausilia laminata* (Montagu). *Biometrika*, **1**, 109–124.

Wellington, G.M. (1980) Reversal of digestive interactions between Pacific reef corals: mediation by sweeper tentacles. *Oecologia (Berlin)*, **47**, 340–343.

Wells, H.W. and Gray, I.E. (1960) The seasonal occurrence of *Mytilus edulis* on the Carolina coast as a result of transport around Cape Hatteras. *Biol. Bull. Mar. Biol. Lab., Woods Hole*, **119**, 550–559.

Wells, R.A. (1980) Activity pattern as a mechanism of predator avoidance in two species of acmaeid limpet. *J. Exp. Mar. Biol. Ecol.*, **48**, 151–168.

West, D.A. (1976) Aposematic coloration and mutualism in sponge-dwelling tropical zoanthids. In, *Coelenterate Ecology and Behavior*, ed. G.O. Mackie, Plenum Press, New York, pp. 443–452.

Wethey, D.S. (1979) Demographic variation in intertidal barnacles. Ph. D. Thesis, University of Michigan, U.S.A., 260 pp.

Wethey, D.S. (1983) Geographic limits and local zonation: the barnacles *Semibalanus (Balanus)* and *Chthamalus* in New England. *Biol. Bull. Mar. Biol. Lab., Woods Hole*, **165**, 330–341.

Wethey, D.S. (1984) Spatial pattern in barnacle settlement: day to day changes during the settlement season. *J. Mar. Biol. Ass. U.K.*, **64**, 687–698.

Wethey, D.S. (1985) Catastrophe, extinction and species diversity: a rocky intertidal example. *Ecology*, **66**, 445–456.

Weymouth, F.W., McMillin, H.C. and Rich, W.H. (1931) Latitude and relative growth in the razor clam *Siliqua patula*. *J. Exp. Biol.*, **8**, 228–249.

Wharton, W.G. and Mann, K.H. (1981) Relationships between destructive grazing by the sea urchin *Strongylocentrotus droebachiensis*, and abundance of American lobster, *Homarus americanus* on the Atlantic coast of Nova Scotia. *Can. J. Fish. Aquat. Sci.*, **38**, 1339–1349.

Whatley, R.C. and Wall, D.R. (1975) The relationship between Ostracoda and algae in littoral and sublittoral marine environments. *Bull. Am. Paleont.*, **65**, 173–203.

Whittaker, R.H. (1975) *Communities and Ecosystems*. (2nd edn), Macmillan Publishing Co., New York, 385 pp.

Whittaker, R.H. and Levin, S.A. (1977) The role of mosaic phenomena in natural communities. *Theor. Populat. Biol.*, **12**, 117–139.

Wiborg, K.F. (1946) Undersokelser over oskjellet (*Modiola modiolus* (L.)). *Rep. Norw. Fishery Mar. Invest.*, **8**, 1–85.

Wickens, P.A. and Griffiths, C.L. (in press) Predation by *Nucella cingulata* (Linnaeus, 1771) on mussels, particularly *Aulacomya ater* (Molina, 1782). *Veliger*.

Wieser, W. (1951a) Untersuchungen über die algenbewohnende Mikrofauna mariner Hartböden. I. Zur Oekologie und Systematik der Nematodenfauna von Plymouth. *Öst. Zool. Z.*, **3**, 425–480.

Wieser, W. (1951b) Über die quantitative Bestimmung der algenbewohnenden Mikrofauna felsiger Meeresküsten. *Oikos*, **3**, 124–131.

Wieser, W. (1952) Investigations on the microfauna inhabiting seaweeds on rocky coasts. IV. Studies on the vertical distribution of the fauna inhabiting seaweeds below the Plymouth Laboratory. *J. Mar. Biol. Ass. U.K.*, **31**, 145–174.

Wieser, W. (1953a) Die Beziehung zwischen Mundhöhlengestalt, Ernährungsweise und Vorkommen bei freilebenden marinen Nematoden: Eine ökologisch-morphologische Studie. *Ark. Zool.*, **4**, 439–484.

Wieser, W. (1953b) Free-living marine nematodes. I. Enoploidea. *Reports of Lund University Chile Expedition, 1948-1949, No. 10. Lunds Univ. Årsskr., N.F. Avd. 2*, **49**, 1–155.

Wieser, W. (1954) Untersuchungen über die algenbewohnende Mikrofauna mariner Hartböden. III. Zur Systematik der freilebenden Nematoden des Mittelmeeres mit einer Ökologische Untersuchung über die beziehung zwischen Nematodenbesiedlung und sedimentreichtum des Habitats. *Hydrobiologia*, **6**, 144–217.

Wieser, W. (1959) Zur Ökologie der Fauna mariner Algen mit besonderer Berücksichtigung des Mittelmeeres. *Int. Revue Ges. Hydrobiol.*, **44**, 137–180.

Wieser, W. and Kanwisher, J. (1959) Respiration and anaerobic survival in some sea weed-inhabiting invertebrates. *Biol. Bull. Mar. Biol. Lab., Woods Hole*, **117**, 594–600.

Wigham, G.D. (1975) The biology and ecology of *Rissoa parva* (da Costa) (Gastropoda: Prosobranchia). *J. Mar. Biol. Ass. U.K.*, **55**, 45–67.

Wilbur, H.M. (1977) Propagule size, number, and dispersion patterns in *Ambystoma* and *Asclepias. Am. Nat.*, **111**, 43–68.

Wilbur, K.M. and Owen, G. (1964) Ch. 7. Growth. In, *Physiology of the Mollusca*, Vol. I, ed. K.M. Wilbur & C.M. Yonge, Academic Press, London, pp. 211–242.

Williams, E.E. (1964) The growth and distribution of *Littorina littorea* (L.) on a rocky shore in Wales. *J. Anim. Ecol.*, **33**, 413–432.

Williams, G.B. (1964) The effect of extracts of *Fucus serratus* in promoting the settlement of larvae of *Spirorbis borealis* (Polychaeta). *J. Mar. Biol. Ass. U.K.*, **44**, 397–414.

Williams, G.C. (1966a) Natural selection, the costs of reproduction, and a refinement of Lack's principle. *Am. Nat.*, **100**, 687–692.

Williams, G.C. (1966b) *Adaptation and Natural Selection: a critique of some current evolutionary thought.* Princeton University Press, Princeton, New Jersey, 307 pp.

Williams, R. (1969) Ecology of the Ostracoda from selected marine intertidal localities on the coast of Anglesey. In, *The Taxonomy, Morphology and Ecology of Recent Ostracoda*, ed. J.W. Neale, Oliver and Boyd, Edinburgh, pp. 299–329.

Williamson, P., Cameron, R.A.D. and Carter, M.A. (1976) Population density affecting adult shell size of snail *Cepaea nemoralis* L. *Nature, Lond.*, **263**, 496–497.

Williamson, P. and Kendall, M.A. (1981) Population age structure and growth of the trochid *Monodonta lineata* determined from shell rings. *J. Mar. Biol. Ass. U.K.*, **61**, 1011–1026.

Wilson, B.R. and Hodgkin, E.P. (1967) A comprehensive account of the reproductive cycles of five species of marine mussels (Bivalvia: Mytilidae) in the vicinity of Fremantle, Western Australia. *Aust. J. Mar. Freshwat. Res.*, **18**, 175–203.

Wilson, S.R. (1982) Horizontal and vertical density distribution of polychaete and cirripede larvae over an inshore rock platform off Northumberland. *J. Mar. Biol. Ass. U.K.*, **62**, 907–917.

Winer, B.J. (1971) *Statistical Principles in Experimental Design.* (2nd edn), McGraw-Hill Kogakusha, Tokyo, 907 pp.

Winterhalder, B. (1983) Opportunity-cost foraging models for stationary and mobile predators. *Am. Nat.*, **122**, 73–84.

Wisely, B. (1960) Observations on the settling behaviour of larvae of the tube worm *Spirorbis borealis* Daudin (Polychaeta). *Aust. J. Mar. Freshwat. Res.*, **11**, 55–72.

Wisely, B. (1964) Aspects of reproduction, settling and growth in the mussel *Mytilus edulis planatus* Lamarck. *J. Malac. Soc. Aust.*, **8**, 25–30.

Witman, J.D. (1980) Community structure of subtidal *Modiolus modiolus* (L.) beds. *Am. Zool.*, **20**, p. 807 only.

Witman, J.D. (1983) The importance of competition, physical disturbance, and mutualism in maintaining the depth zonation of kelp and mussels. *Am. Zool.*, **23**, p. 1001 only.

Witman, J.D. (1984) Ecology of rocky subtidal communities: the role of *Modiolus modiolus* (L.) and the influence of disturbance, competition, and mutualism. Ph. D. Thesis, University of New Hampshire, Durham, 199 pp.

Witman, J.D. and Cooper, R.A. (1983) Disturbance and contrasting patterns of population structure in the brachiopod *Terebratulina septentrionalis* (Couthouy) from two subtidal habitats. *J. Exp. Mar. Biol. Ecol.*, **73.**, 57–79.

Witman, J.D. and Suchanek, T.H. (1984) Mussels in flow: drag and dislodgement by epizoans. *Mar. Ecol. Prog. Ser.*, **16**, 259–268.

Wolcott, T.G. (1973) Physiological ecology and intertidal zonation in limpets (*Acmaea*): a critical look at 'limiting factors'. *Biol. Bull. Mar. Biol. Lab., Woods Hole*, **145**, 389–422.

Wood, L.H. (1968) Physiological and ecological aspects of prey selection by the marine gastropod *Urosalpinx cinerea* (Prosobranchia: Muricidae). *Malacologia*, **6**, 267–320.

Wood, V. (1983) A population study of the major sedentary faunal associates of *Fucus serratus* L. Ph. D. Thesis, University of Wales, 238 pp.

Wood, V. and Seed, R. (1980) The effects of shore level on the epifaunal communities associated with *Fucus serratus* (L.) in the Menai Strait, North Wales. *Cah. Biol. Mar.*, **21**, 135–154.

Woodin, S.A. and Jackson, J.B.C. (1979) Interphyletic competition among marine benthos. *Am. Zool.*, **19**, 1029–1043.

Woods, R. (1975) *The Birds of the Falkland Islands*. Nelson, Oswestry, Shropshire, 240 pp.

Woollacott, R.M. and North, W.J. (1971) Bryozoans of California and North Mexico kelp beds. *Beih. Nova Hedwigia*, **32**, 455–479.

Workman, C. (1983) Comparisons of energy partitioning in contrasting age-structure populations of the limpet *Patella vulgata* L. *J. Exp. Mar. Biol. Ecol.*, **68**, 81–103.

Wright, J.R. and Hartnoll, R.G. (1981) An energy budget for a population of the limpet *Patella vulgata*. *J. Mar. Biol. Ass. U.K.*, **61**, 627–646.

Wright, W.G. (1977) Avoidance and escape: two responses of intertidal limpets to the presence of the territorial owl limpet *Lottia gigantea*. *West. Soc. Naturalists*, 1977, p. 50 only.

Wright, W.G. (1982) Ritualized behavior in a territorial limpet. *J. Exp. Mar. Biol. Ecol.*, **60**, 245–251.

Yamaguchi, M. (1975) Estimating growth parameters from growth rate data: problems with marine sedentary invertebrates. *Oecologia (Berlin)*, **20**, 321–332.

Yamaguchi, M. (1977) Shell growth and mortality rates in the coral reef gastropod *Cerithium nodulosum* in Pago Bay, Guam, Mariana Islands. *Mar. Biol.*, **44**, 249–263.

Yañez, R. (1974) El cultivo experimental de choros y choritos en Putemun y Talcan, Chiloe. *Boln Soc. Biol. Concepción*, **48**, 315–330.

Yonge, C.M. (1962) On the primitive significance of the byssus in the Bivalvia and its effects in evolution. *J. Mar. Biol. Ass. U.K.*, **42**, 113–125.

Yonge, C.M. (1976) Ch. 1. The 'mussel' form and habit. In, *Marine Mussels: their ecology and physiology*, ed. B.L. Bayne, Cambridge University Press, Cambridge, pp. 1–12.

Yoshioka, P.M. (1982) Predator-induced polymorphism in the bryozoan *Membranipora membranacea* (L.). *J. Exp. Mar. Biol. Ecol.*, **61**, 233–242.

Young, C.M. and Chia, F.-S. (1981) Laboratory evidence for delay of larval settlement in response to a dominant competitor. *Int. J. Invertebr. Reprod.*, **3**, 221–226.

Young, R.T. (1942) Spawning season of the California mussel *Mytilus californianus*. *Ecology*, **23**, 490–492.

Young, R.T. (1945) Stimulation of spawning in the mussel (*Mytilus californianus*). *Ecology*, **26**, 58–69.

Young, R.T. (1946) Spawning and setting season of the mussel, *Mytilus californianus*. *Ecology*, **27**, 354–363.

Young, T.P. (1981) A general model of comparative fecundity for semelparous and iteroparous life histories. *Am. Nat.*, **118**, 27–36.

Zander, C.D. and Heymer, A. (1977) Analysis of ecological equivalents among littoral fish. In, *Biology of Benthic Organisms*, ed. B.F. Keegan, P. ÓCéidigh & P.J.S. Boaden, Pergamon Press, Oxford, pp. 621–630.

Zaneveld, J.S. (1937) The littoral zonation of some Fucaceae in relation to desiccation. *J. Ecol.*, **25**, 431–468.

Zipser, E. and Vermeij, G.J. (1978) Crushing behavior of tropical and temperate crabs. *J. Exp. Mar. Biol. Ecol.*, **31**, 155–172.

INDEX

'. . . *Then on the shore*
Of the wide world I stand alone, and think . .'

Keats, *Sonnets*